SOCIAL WORK LAW IN SCOTLAND

AUSTRALIA
Law Book Co.
Sydney

CANADA and USA
Carswell
Toronto

HONG KONG
Sweet & Maxwell Asia

NEW ZEALAND
Brookers
Wellington

SINGAPORE and MALAYSIA
Sweet & Maxwell Asia
Singapore and Kuala Lumpur

SOCIAL WORK LAW IN SCOTLAND

2nd Edition

Craig Anderson, LL.B. (Hons)
Lecturer in Law, The Robert Gordon University

Lisa Gibbons-Wood, BA (Hons)
Lecturer in Law, The Robert Gordon University

Diego Quiroz-Onate, LL.B., LL.M.
Lecturer in Law, The Robert Gordon University

Jennifer Richmond, LL.B., Dip. L.P., NP, LL.M.
Lecturer in Law, The Robert Gordon University

Laura Sharp, LL.B (Hons), Dip. L.P., MA (Hons), LL.M.
Lecturer in Law, The Robert Gordon University

Alison Stuart, LL.B., Dip. L.P., LL.M.
Lecturer in Law, The Robert Gordon University

Linda J. Taylor, MA, LL.B., Dip. L.P., NP
Senior Solicitor, North Ayrshire Council and former Lecturer in Law,
The Robert Gordon University

Published in 2008 by
W. Green & Son Ltd
21 Alva Street
Edinburgh EH2 4PS

www.wgreen.thomson.com

Typeset by YHT Ltd, London.
Printed and bound in Great Britain by Ashford Colour Press, Gosport, Hants.

No natural forests were destroyed to make this product;
only farmed timber was used and replanted

A CIP catalogue record for this book is available from
the British Library.

ISBN 978-0-414-01448-0

CONTENTS

PREFACE TO THE SECOND EDITION

The last edition of this book was published some nine years ago. It proved to be extremely popular and we are proud to have been able to complete the second edition. We are a new team, contributing in our specialist areas and aim to present the law in an easy to read format.

There are so few Scottish texts dedicated to social work law, and our aim is to offer a book with current and relevant practice information. Due to the scope of social work, we have tried to focus our attention on what we believe are the main issues. Coverage has been given to key Acts and cases and some reference is made to practice documents. The new edition updates the existing material, makes provision for new legislation, and includes two new topical chapters: Antisocial Behaviour and Immigration and Asylum. The first edition proved to be popular amongst social work students and professionals, and we hope that this second edition proves to be as useful as the first.

As always, there are many people to thank. We must pay tribute to the hard work and dedication of Richard Mays, Veronica Strachan and Vikki Smith (now Cuthbert) in producing the first edition of this book. We would also like to acknowledge the tremendous support we received from Jill Hyslop, who continuously encouraged us and drove us on. Our thanks goes to the rest of the publishing team at W. Greens, including Mel Alexander and Lauren Brown, who have helped to produce this second edition to the same high standard as the original book. Also, special thanks goes to Dr Karen Fullerton, who gave us the opportunity to write the book. Finally, of course, we thank our families and friends for being there for us.

We attempt to update the law to December 1, 2007, however, given the broad issues surrounding social work law, it is inevitable that the law will move on quite soon after publication and so we remind the reader that amendments may have been made to the legal provisions cited. Any errors and omissions in the new edition remain our responsibility.

Lisa Gibbons-Wood
Laura Sharp
Jennifer Richmond
Linda Taylor
Craig Anderson
Alison Stuart
Diego Quiroz-Onate

Table of Cases

Table of Statutes

TABLE OF SCOTTISH STATUTES

TABLE OF STATUTORY INSTRUMENTS

Table of Scottish Statutory Instruments

Table of European Legislation

Directives

Regulations

Chapter 1

Social Work Law in Scotland

Background

1.01 "Social work law" constitutes an amalgam of several disparate areas of law forged together in a new and emerging identity. Not only is the recognition of this congregation of legal topics as a subject in its own right relatively recent, but also much of the law itself is new. There are few other areas of law that can be viewed as more dynamic and the pace of this development shows no sign of abating. The emergence over the past 40 years of modern welfare services in large monolithic social work departments substantially explains why the collection of law is only now beginning to be considered a subject in its own right.

What Is "Social Work"?

1.02 There are varying definitions of the concept of "social work". All emphasise the personalised nature of the concept and the idea of enablement rather than resolving problems for those in need of assistance. Bowers, for example, asserts that:

> "social casework is an art in which knowledge of the science of human relations and skills in relationships are used to mobilise capacities in the individual and resources in the community appropriate to better adjustment between the client and all or any part of his total environment."[1]

Similarly, the British Association of Social Workers describes the nature of the occupation of social work as extending:

> "its interest beyond the immediate issue to understanding the client's background, social situations, motivation, attitudes, values, personality and behaviour and attempts to encourage development and change by a wide variety of methods which amongst many others may well include the development of strong relationships with clients, insight giving techniques, behaviour modification and practical help."[2]

Often social work is best understood by reference to the client groups it seeks to serve. Problems relating to old age, handicap, mental illness, low income, family relationships and children tend

---

[1] S. Bowers, "The Nature and Definition of Social Casework" (1949) 30 *Journal of Social Casework*, 412–417, quoted in Younghusband, *Social Work in Britain 1950–1975: A Follow Up Study* (1978), p.26.

[2] British Association of Social Workers, "The Future of Probation Officers in Borstals and Prisons" (1975) 6 *Social Work Today*, 317–319, quoted in Younghusband, *Social Work in Britain*.

to be prominent in social work activities.[3] Cooper describes the subject by reference to the broad areas of involvement, defining social services as:

> "the assortment of provisions common to modern industrialised societies and usually include up to six main services: education, employment and training, health, housing, income maintenance, and the sixth conglomerate of welfare provisions for those whose age, status or condition gives rise to the need for special social care and sometimes control."[4]

1.03 Social work services are both expansive and expanding.[5] The correlation between poverty and the provision of social services has been noted by many commentators. It has been said by one writer that "social work operates in conditions of material distress which often render its therapeutic orientations irrelevant".[6] However, while there is a strong connection, "social work is not only about the alleviation of poverty or struggles against inequality, but these issues remain fundamental to it".[7]

Parry et al. suggest that the tasks of social work can be categorised in four ways:

> "(a) the provision of routine caring and supportive services of a non-expert kind, for example supportive visiting, a range of domiciliary services, caring and supportive services for those in residential establishments;
> (b) specialist skills, for example, different types of social work expertise (such as family counselling), occupational therapy, an expert service for the blind and deaf;
> (c) the mobilisation of community activity, including participation in decision making, in the running of welfare services, and involvement in voluntary and paid capacities, in the provision of caring services;
> (d) engaging in pressure for policy changes at local and national levels, backed by research, analysis and experiment undertaken by members of social services departments."[8]

Many of the social work texts refer to "personal social services" to describe social work provision. For example, Parker suggests that:

> "the personal social services are usually considered to be those, lying outside the general fields of health and education, which are adjusted in some special way to the particular social needs of individuals, families or groups and which require personal contact between the provider and recipient. The skill involved in the provision of those services is often labelled 'social work'."[9]

"Personal" implies a service tailored to individual or human needs, as distinct from technical and environmental services, which tend to be more standardised.[10] It has been said that "personal social services directly affect only a minority of the population. It is a minority made up largely of people with the lowest incomes and the worst living conditions in our society."[11] Ironically, though demand does not diminish, as in many public services there are periods of relative austerity, which often lead to crisis for the recipients of those services.

---

[3] Young, *Mastering Social Welfare*, 2nd edn (1989), p.177.
[4] Cooper, *The Creation of the British Personal Social Services 1962–74* (1983), p.8.
[5] See Bryne and Padfield, *Social Services Made Simple* (1990), pp.2–3.
[6] Parry, Rusdtin and Satyamurti (eds), *Social Work Welfare and the State* (1979), p.162.
[7] Parry et al., *Social Work Welfare and the State*, p.166.
[8] Parry et al., *Social Work Welfare and the State*, p.172.
[9] Parker in Robson and Crick (eds), *The Future of Social Services* (1970), p.105.
[10] Cooper, *The Creation of the British Personal Social Services*, p.8.
[11] English (ed.), *Social Services in Scotland* (1988), p.136.

A HISTORICAL PERSPECTIVE

1.04 Welfare provision and care and concern for others in the community are not modern phenomena. There is a long history of voluntary provision by private individuals, charitable organisations and religious orders.[12] The trade guilds and Friendly Societies (the forebears of modern trade unionism) were very active in providing for members and their families.[13] State mechanisms for such provision have an altogether shorter history. The public provision that originally existed was directed to poor law relief, which carried considerable social stigma for the recipients. The transition has been a rapid one from "mere provision of material benefits by the state to a wide range of individually focused services which attempt to meet varied personal needs".[14] Whatever the case may be, there can be little doubt that social service provision has expanded beyond the very poor and now spans a much broader community.[15]

When reflecting on the historical development of social work law in Scotland undoubtedly two statutory developments will stand out. The Social Work (Scotland) Act 1968 represents essentially the founding statute of modern social work departments; it was instrumental in welding together disparate welfare agencies into modern unitary services. The second landmark statute is the Children (Scotland) Act 1995, which has substantially reformed the framework law relating to the care and protection of children and introduced other significant reforms. However, to focus exclusively on these two statutory enactments would be to neglect a large number of other statutory developments, principally since the Second World War, which have influenced and propelled the dramatic process of change, from relative disparity and obscurity, to cohesion and recognition.[16]

Historically, welfare provision throughout the United Kingdom was based on the poor law and its associated poorhouses. The Scottish poor law required recipients to be disabled as well as destitute.[17] Historical developments—population expansion, war and the industrial revolution—combined to exacerbate poverty and escalated the problem of the poor to one of national importance. As a consequence, a Royal Commission on the poor laws was established in 1832 and was the impetus for the Poor Law Amendment Act 1834—the "new" poor law.

1.05 The revised system introduced by the Poor Law Amendment Act reflected many of the recommendations of the Commission. The general concept was that work was valuable and that all effort should be made to get the impoverished from poor law relief into work by providing disincentives to remain in receipt of poor law provision. The new poor law also sought to ensure that the sick and children should be housed separately from the able-bodied poor.

Whatever deficiencies there were in other fields of what is now known as social work law, there was a considerable amount of legislation designed to protect the interests of children in the nineteenth century. Naturally, it did not have the benevolence and scope of the legislation that was to follow. The nineteenth-century developments in this field were prompted by the fact that "[t]he public conscience was ... more easily stirred on behalf of children than any other group".[18] Concern about children was considerable at the turn of the century and the advent of a new Liberal Government provided impetus for reform. The Children Act 1908 provided that children being neglected could be removed to a place of safety. Various other prohibitions relating to children were introduced by the statute on such matters as smoking, consumption of alcohol, allowing children in brothels, or causing them to beg.

The philanthropy and paternalism that existed at the turn of the century focused primarily on children. The elderly and the chronically sick received limited attention. In 1909, the *Report of*

[12] *Stair Memorial Encyclopaedia*, Vol.22, *Social Work*, p.1.
[13] Ferguson, *Scottish Social Welfare, 1864–1914* (1958), p.4.
[14] *Stair Memorial Encyclopaedia*, Vol.22, *Social Work*, p.1.
[15] *Stair Memorial Encyclopaedia*, Vol.22, *Social Work*, p.2.
[16] Ferguson, *Scottish Social Welfare*, p.10.
[17] Ferguson, *Scottish Social Welfare*, p.2.
[18] Watkin, *Documents on Health and Social Services 1834 to the Present Day* (1975), p.414.

the Royal Commission on the poor laws and the relief of distress[19] had noted that the vast majority of the elderly poor in institutions were in substandard large establishments, described by one commentator as "human warehouses".[20] Under the Local Government Act 1929 administration of the poor law had transferred to county councils, city councils and large burgh councils. The service was restyled as public assistance. The restructuring provided limited improvements to the way in which the elderly and chronically sick were treated in institutions.

Post-war reform

1.06 In the historical analysis of social work provision, the catalytic events of the Second World War were of signal importance. The adversity of conflict had produced a collective consciousness of community and a desire for change. Importantly, "the state planning furnace, stoked by experience ideals and new social values, stood fired and ready to forge new systems".[21] The advent of a Labour Government committed to a programme of welfare reform ensured that the immediate post-war period was one of considerable development and transition for social services. The poor law was finally abolished in 1948 by the National Assistance Act 1948. The new approach to the provision of welfare represented a departure from past practice.[22]

Under the newly created welfare state,

> "a formula for basing social welfare on the promotion of individual need without recourse to guilt or shame had been elaborated. The Government had struck a balance between promoting the rights of individuals within a more advanced industrial society, guaranteeing working-class interests and ensuring the maintenance of order."[23]

In the immediate aftermath of the Second World War the social work profession could be characterised by three constituent sources: the social workers in local authorities who dealt with the welfare provision under the National Assistance Act 1948; the various groups of specialist workers who owed their jobs to specialist legislation responding to an identified need; and finally the semi-professional voluntary sector located ostensibly in charitable organisations.[24]

The post-war welfare consciousness was also evident in a number of Commissions and committees set up to look at particular aspects of social need. In 1945 in England the Care of Children Committee was set up under the chairmanship of Myra Curtis:

> "[t]o enquire into existing methods of providing for children, who from loss of parents or any cause whatever, are deprived from a normal home life with their own parents or relatives; and to consider what further measures should be taken to ensure that these children are brought up under conditions best calculated to compensate them for lack of parental care."[25]

The Curtis Report gave the findings of the first major inquiry into children deprived of a normal home life. The inquiry was restricted to looking at children who were already in need of care by someone other than their parents. Later the emphasis of legislation was to consider the plight of the child in the context of the family and to seek to provide assistance before a need for care arose. Curtis was of the view that the response to a child in need of care was a home or a good substitute home. This home would be one where the child would receive affection and personal interest, respect for his personality, a sense of belonging and security, stability, opportunity, and a share in the common life of a small group of people in a homely environment.[26] The Curtis

---

[19] Cd.4499.
[20] Murphy, *British Social Services—The Scottish Dimension* (1992), p.35.
[21] Murphy, *British Social Services*, p.17.
[22] Levitt, *Poverty and Welfare in Scotland 1890–1948* (1990), p.199.
[23] Levitt, *Poverty and Welfare in Scotland*, p.205.
[24] English, *Social Services in Scotland*, p.106.
[25] *Report of the Care of Children Committee*, Cmd.6922 (HMSO, 1946).
[26] Watkin, *Documents on Health and Social Services, 1834 to the Present Day* (1975), p.421.

Report was particularly favourable to the concept of adoption or alternatively fostering if it was sufficiently supervised. The Children Act 1948, which followed the Curtis Report, set up an Advisory Council in Child Care in England and Wales and in Scotland. The 1948 Act (in language subsequently replicated in s.15 of the Social Work (Scotland) Act 1968) placed a duty on local authorities to receive a child into care where there was no parent or guardian, the child was abandoned or lost, or where the parent or guardian was temporarily or permanently by reason of incapacity unable to look after the child. The local authority could in certain circumstances assume all parental rights over the child. Unlike the later provisions in the Social Work (Scotland) Act 1968, the provisions of the 1948 Act did not give local authorities any powers to work with families to resolve difficulties and prevent the receipt into care of children. Their responsive approach was to rescue and place in a substitute home as Curtis had recommended.

1.07 In a spirit of equality, Scotland was granted its own Committee for Homeless Children under the chairmanship of Lord Clyde, though the Clyde Report[27] was somewhat overshadowed by the Curtis Report.[28] In Scotland at that time there were four main childcare agencies: the Public Assistance Committees, the Education Committees, the Voluntary Homes and the Royal Society for the Prevention of Cruelty to Children. The poor law (Scotland) Act 1934 had conferred the obligation on local authorities to make arrangements for the lodging, boarding and maintenance otherwise than in a poorhouse, of children under 16 who were orphans, separated from their parents or had been deserted. It was estimated that this covered some 7,000 children.[29] Throughout Scotland education authorities had duties under the Children and Young Persons (Scotland) Act 1937 which required them to bring children in need of care and protection before the juvenile court, and in addition to deal with children who were the subject of approved school orders. Childcare in this era took place either in voluntary sector children's homes or by boarding out. There were few public children's homes run by local authorities or foster homes. The Clyde Report was essentially supportive of rural boarding out (which had been a feature of wartime arrangements). The Report was critical of sending children to the poorhouse.

A further dimension of both Curtis and Clyde Reports was that they recommended the setting up of a unitary government department with the transference of existing responsibilities to it from separate government departments and a corresponding creation of single committees to exercise functions at local level. The response to the Clyde Report was to consolidate matters under the Home Department of the Scottish Office. Local authorities were required to set up Children's Committees and to appoint a children's officer who would supervise children separated from their parents.

The Second World War dramatically changed perceptions of the elderly. Titmuss notes that:

> "The problem of the aged and the chronic sick had been serious enough in peacetime; in war it threatened to be come unmanageable. Thousands who had formerly been nursed at home were clamouring for admission to hospitals, when families were split up, when houses were damaged or destroyed."[30]

The all-round displacement and alienation occasioned by the war had dramatic effects on the plight of the elderly and provoked a considerable social problem. The demand for beds during wartime prompted the discharge of tens of thousands of patients into the community, exacerbating an already growing problem.[31] The post-war response to this burgeoning problem was the Beveridge-inspired National Assistance Act 1948. That Act not only abolished the poor law, but enacted that there should be local government provision for the aged and the needy. The

---

27 *Report of the Committee on Homeless Children*, Cmd.6911 (HMSO, 1946).
28 See Murphy, *British Social Services*, pp.25–26.
29 Murphy, *British Social Services*, p.26.
30 Titmuss, *Problems of Social Policy* (HMSO, 1950), p.559.
31 Murphy, *British Social Services*, pp.40–42.

National Assistance Act 1948 was later to be accredited as a "launch pad for further legislative advance" in relation to the chronically sick and disabled.[32]

Mental health services

1.08 Prior to the war, the provision of mental health services was delivered via health departments rather than local government. In 1948 new localised health authorities were set up. The law however continued to be of some antiquity. The principal statutes were the Lunacy Acts 1857–1913 and the Mental Deficiency (Scotland) Acts 1913 and 1940. The Mental Health (Scotland) Act 1960 heralded dramatic change. The emphasis no longer revolved round hospitalised treatment but rather was directed towards community treatment.

Criminal justice

1.09 Historical analysis also reveals that there has been social care provision for offenders in Scotland for some considerable time. Probation was first established in Britain by the Probation of First Offenders Act 1887 and later extended in the Probation of Offenders Act 1907. Concern at the increased numbers of criminals prompted calls for reform, which arrived in the form of the Criminal Justice (Scotland) Act 1949. The 1949 Act required the constitution of ad hoc local authority committees. These committees included magistrates, justices of the peace, sheriffs and sheriff-substitutes. In addition, the probation officer's role was expanded to include assisting, advising and befriending the probationer. Until 1949 the probation services that had existed were limited in scope and size; from 1950 and especially in the 1960s the service was to expand immeasurably.[33] Probation as a service came under further scrutiny under the Morrison Committee set up in 1959. This Committee was to conclude that probation had not developed as it should have because it was viewed as an inconsequential local authority function. The Committee formed the view that, in Scotland, probation should be provided by local committees with reduced local authority representation. In effect this meant only half the committee members were to be local authority appointees.

Childcare

1.10 In the period immediately prior to the Kilbrandon Report[34], a further influential committee reported: the McBoyle Committee[35]—a Committee of the Scottish Advisory Council on Childcare—was requested by the Secretary of State to report on whether local authorities should be given new powers and duties to forestall the suffering of children through neglect in their own homes. Not surprisingly, the Committee recommended that local authorities should indeed be given powers to provide a comprehensive service designed to prevent neglect. The recommendation included the giving of cash or practical help in kind. The Committee identified the need to put greater emphasis on a service designed to provide assistance *in situ* of the family rather than bring children into care.

The move towards unification

1.11 In the years after the Second World War through to the passage of the Social Work (Scotland) Act 1968, social work services were provided by four agencies: welfare, health, probation and children's departments.[36] Welfare, health and children's departments were all local authority

---

[32] Murphy, *British Social Services*, p.47.
[33] Murphy, *British Social Services*, p.74.
[34] Cmnd.2306 (HMSO, 1964) found at *http://www.scotland.gov.uk/Publications/2003/10/18259/26877* [Accessed July 8, 2008].
[35] Cmnd.1966 (1963).
[36] Murphy, *British Social Services*, p.49.

provided. Most Scottish local authorities established a welfare committee to oversee the provision of welfare generally. The duty to provide welfare emanated from ss.21 and 29 of Pt III of the National Assistance Act 1948. These welfare provisions offered scope for assistance to be given to the physically handicapped and, through innovative interpretation, problem families.[37]

While there were reports on specific social care issues and areas of concern, there was until the mid-1950s little or no emphasis on the role of the social worker and the organisation of social work services. In 1955 the Younghusband Committee was established to consider the issue of staffing in local authorities and health services, and in particular to consider if there was a place for a general purpose social worker as a basic grade. The Report in 1959 was to conclude that there was such a need. In this context, the Younghusband Committee Report[38] constituted a significant development in the process of viewing social work as a coherent and cohesive discipline and a profession in its own right.

Relatively small as the profession was at that time, there was increased interest in the 1960s among social workers in identifying the common elements of their profession and practice.[39] Indeed, it subsequently came to be recognised that one of the driving thrusts for unification was the fact that social workers themselves began to see the importance of recognising and dealing with the common elements behind the range of problems brought to them by their clientele. The Working Party set up to examine the operation of the Social Work (Scotland) Act 1968 subsequently noted that:

> "[t]hose with experience in social work were not happy with the administrative structure of the social services. In spite of the real achievements of co-ordinating committees, the administrative structure worked against attempts to give social help to individuals within the context of the family and community, and left gaps in provision that were not always recognised."[40]

1.12 By the mid-1960s the process of unification in Scotland was well ahead of that in England. By now there appeared to be a better understanding of the nature of the problem of diversification and how it had come about. According to one commentator,

> "the defects in the prevailing organisation of local authority social work and welfare services were seen in the White Paper as arising from their piecemeal development in response to the identification at different times of certain groups of people who needed social help."[41]

Kilbrandon's proposals had included the unification of social work under education (Kilbrandon called these "social education departments"). Although the location of this unified service was not ultimately education, the notion of unification was, nonetheless, universally accepted. Until this point social workers had been variously employed as childcare officers, probation officers, welfare officers, mental health officers, psychiatric social workers and medical social workers.[42] Following Kilbrandon's Report, it became apparent that these and other services would need to be included in new "social work departments". To this end, a Joint Working Group was set up by the Government to consider the integration of social services into a coherent service. The Working Group was charged with seeking the views of all the relevant professions on the proposal to amalgamate. In 1966 a White Paper entitled *Social work and the community*[43] expounded the Government's view of the desirability for a one-door approach to social work services. The nature of these new departments was described in the White Paper in the following terms:

---

[37] Murphy, *British Social Services*, p.53.
[38] *Report of the working party on social workers in local authority health and welfare services* (HMSO, 1959).
[39] Ford, in English, *Social Services in Scotland*, p.119.
[40] Mackenzie Report (also known as Rowntree Report): *Report of a Working Party on the Social Work (Scotland) Act 1968* (Dept of Social Study, Edinburgh University, 1969), p.8.
[41] English, *Social Services in Scotland*, p.120.
[42] See Murphy, *British Social Services*, p.140.
[43] Cmnd.3065 (1966).

> "the existing powers of local authorities to provide advice and assistance, and to promote welfare, are set out mainly in the National Health Service (Scotland) Act 1947, the National Assistance Act 1948, the Children Act 1948, the Mental Health (Scotland) Act 1960, the Education (Scotland) Act 1962 and the Children and Young Persons Act 1963. These powers will be continued, with the adjustments necessary to fit the new organisation. They are already very wide, and only two substantial groups of people appear not to be fully covered. Services for old people under the National Assistance Act are limited to the provision of accommodation, meals and recreation. For adults who are not aged, handicapped, ill or parents of young children, there is at present no express power by which a local authority may at its own hand provide personal advice and guidance. It is proposed that the local authority should in the future have power to provide all citizens, of whatever age or circumstances, with advice and guidance in the solution of personal and social difficulties and problems."[44]

1.13 Finally, the Social Work (Scotland) Act 1968 brought together into a comprehensive service existing provision for children, offenders and people who were elderly, physically handicapped and mentally handicapped.[45] The amalgamated function represented more than simply a combination of local authority services—several health authority functions were transferred as well. Most of the Act came into force in November 1969. Part III of the Act relating to children's hearings was delayed until April 15, 1971. The 1968 Act has significance attached to its title in the respect that it is deemed to create professional recognition and to be "characterising the nature of the service to be provided to the community".[46] The new legal structure required local authorities (principally the county councils) to set up social work committees and to appoint Directors of Social Work.

Certainly the 1968 Act represented a break with the past, rectifying poorly conceived welfare services as well as building a professional staffing structure.[47]

The underpinning philosophy of Kilbrandon's Report is also largely credited with creating a distinctly Scottish pattern of social work services and approaches.[48] The particular proposals for children drew most acclaim. Cooper for example describes the Kilbrandon proposals as opening up a "fair, humane and holistic approach to children in need".[49] Though it is the childcare provisions which perhaps are most renowned, the developments of the 1960s were much wider in their significance. As one writer has explained, it is difficult to grasp the:

> "sense of release and pioneering which the two reports, the White Paper and the Act generated in Scotland. For years the personal social services in Scotland had been static, sparse and old fashioned, but now they were given the potential to become among the most advanced in the world."[50]

1.14 Importantly, while the general pattern of development of social services has been similar throughout the United Kingdom as has the diagnosis of problems, the 1968 Act represented a divergence between Scotland and the rest of the United Kingdom. Viewing the newly created structures, one writer has argued that Scotland was the first country in the United Kingdom to develop a comprehensive system of personal social services.[51]

In the period immediately following Kilbrandon there were several further drivers for change. Most importantly, there was a coincidence of "political and professional evangelism".[52] One illustration of the unity of purpose in practice was in the constitution of a Working Party on the

---

44 Cmnd.3065 (1966), para.7.
45 Murphy, *British Social Services*, p.165.
46 Cooper, *The Creation of the British Personal Social Services*, p.50.
47 Moore and Wood, *Social Work and the Criminal Law in Scotland*, 2nd edn (1992), p.287.
48 Moore and Wood, *Social Work and the Criminal Law in Scotland*, p.1.
49 Cooper, *The Creation of the British Personal Social Services*, p.36.
50 Younghusband, *Social Work in Britain*, p.253.
51 Cooper, *The Creation of the British Personal Social Services*, p.33.
52 Cooper, *The Creation of the British Personal Social Services*, p.42.

Social Work (Scotland) Act 1968, set up in 1968 just before Royal Assent was given to the 1968 Act. The Working Party sought to outline the tasks of the newly constituted social work departments and identified the need for policy statements.

The consensual nature of the developments throughout the 1960s undoubtedly helped to smooth the transition towards a unified coherent service. Moreover, that embryonic consensus can largely assume credit for cementing fairly solid foundations of the modern Scottish social work system.

Kilbrandon and the 1968 Act are not the final words in the development of either social work or social work law. Since Kilbrandon there has been considerable political change. First, there was, as noted above, local government reorganisation in 1975. In little over a five-year period from 1971 50 social work departments were reduced to 12 (albeit much larger) departments. Then, in 1979, a Conservative Government was elected with a radically different agenda, one hostile to state provision and the allegedly suffocating and mollycoddling effect of state welfare provision. Throughout the 1980s and most of the 1990s the Conservative Government pursued a policy away from welfarism.[53]

Modern social work services

1.15 Recently, there have been further changes, which have substantially altered the shape of social work practice in Scotland. A second significant reorganisation of Scotland into unitary council authorities has again transformed the structural environment for the provision of social work services. Not surprisingly, this reform engendered some concern among social work professionals.[54] A number of particular areas stand out for special mention: namely the development of care in the community, the radical restructuring of childcare law in Scotland and the laws relating to vulnerable adults. The legislative enactments in these areas have substantially redefined the provision of certain key social work services.

Furthermore, the consultation paper entitled *Modernising Social Work Services* led to the enactment of the Regulation of Care (Scotland) Act 2001. This Act brought about the new regulatory body, the Scottish Commission for the Regulation of Care ("Care Commission"), which has the responsibility for the registration and discipline of social workers, the regulation of professional and vocational education and the publication of codes of practice.[55] What is clear is that there was pressure for enhancement of the professional status of the social worker and greater cohesion in the profession itself.

---

[53] Moore and Whyte, *Social Work and the Criminal Law in Scotland*, 3rd edn (1998), pp.3–20.

[54] See Davidson, Fairley and Stafford, *Local Government Restructuring and the Management of the Child Protection System* (1997).

[55] *Modernising Social Work Services—A Consultation Paper on Workforce Regulation and Education* (SWSG, 1998), paras 11 and 12.

Chapter 2

The Scottish Legal Framework

Introduction

2.01 Some knowledge of the legal context in which social work law operates is central to any understanding of the subject. Knowledge of the sources of Scots law, the court system, the rules of evidence in those courts, and the personnel involved in the operation of the legal system is important for the social worker. At some point in their career, they will have some interaction with the courts, the police, lawyers, or some other aspects of the legal system.

Sources of Scots Law

Legislation

2.02 A large volume of the law one now calls "social work law" is made up of legislation.[1] Legislation comprises Acts of Parliament, Acts of the Scottish Parliament and subordinate, or delegated, legislation, as well as legislation of the European Union.[2] Between 1707 and 1999 Great Britain had a united Parliament. That Parliament and the legislation it has enacted continues to be of significance to social work.[3] Since 1999 and the creation of the Scottish Parliament, a considerable body of legislation that has been passed on devolved matters has had, and will continue to have an impact in the area of social work in Scotland.

Acts of (the Westminster) Parliament are legislative enactments ordinarily passed by both chambers of the House of Parliament (the House of Commons and the House of Lords) and given Royal Assent on behalf of her Majesty the Queen. In certain circumstances it is possible to dispense with the approval of the House of Lords. The vast majority of legislative enactments that emanate from Parliament are government sponsored. In conformity with its election manifesto (and sometimes not) the Government will present Bills to Parliament for approval. After various parliamentary stages including an intensive committee stage scrutiny of the detailed proposals, the Bill passes from one chamber to the other. Finally on approval by both (or if appropriate the House of Commons alone) it is presented for Royal Assent. This is done on behalf of the Queen by Royal Commissioners. The Act itself will state when the law is to come into force.

It is possible for an individual Member of Parliament to present a Bill for approval under the

---

[1] See R. Mays (ed.), *Scottish Social Work Legislation* (Edinburgh: W. Green).

[2] A discussion of European legislation is not included here. The reader is referred to specialist texts, e.g. P. Beaumont and S. Weatherill, *EU Law*, 3rd edn (London: Penguin, 1999), Ch.5.

[3] For example, the Social Work (Scotland) Act 1968 and the Children (Scotland) Act 1995.

Private Member's Bill procedure, but the prospects of success are extremely restricted. Social reform can be a fertile area for Private Member activity but without cross-party support, or government support, it is almost impossible to see a proposal through to legislative enactment. However, the real role of backbench Bills is often to attract, or maintain, publicity for a particular issue, or to put pressure on the Government to introduce a Bill of its own on the subject.

As a general position, it is the case that legislative provisions of the United Kingdom Parliament will be given supremacy over any other domestic law. Only in situations where it conflicts with legislation of the European Union does that rule not hold good.[4]

2.03 Judges must interpret statutory provisions. In so doing, they hold considerable sway over how the law is understood and applied. There are certain approaches to interpreting statutes.[5] Some judges will apply words and phrases literally while others may adopt a more liberal approach.[6] To the student, or practitioner, the understanding of the language of a statutory provision may be difficult. One may need to resort to judicial pronouncements to gain further insight. Within the statute there will always be an interpretation section, which will offer definitions of words and phrases used within that statute. The preamble to the statute may also offer guidance on the purpose and philosophy of the statute. Likewise, it is a feature of modern academic writing that law publishers are engaging academic writers to annotate provisions of legislation to offer guidance to those having to resort to legal materials. As useful as these are, it must be borne in mind that they are simply one person's view and advice.

The advent and impact of the Scottish Parliament

2.04 The Scottish Parliament has altered both the way in which Scotland is governed and the making of law relating to Scotland. Members of the Scottish Parliament ("MSPs") have legislative capacity over a number of very important issues including social work and related domestic matters. The Scottish Parliament makes laws known as Acts of the Scottish Parliament.[7] The power of the Westminster Parliament to make laws pertaining to Scotland remains in force.[8]

When a legislative measure is introduced in the Scottish Parliament by the governing party, a member of the ruling Scottish Executive (the equivalent of the Cabinet) will make a statement that the Bill is within the legislative competence of the Parliament. The Presiding Officer of the Parliament has the power to rule that a Bill is outwith the legislative competence of the Parliament. There is also scope for Scottish Law Officers (the Lord Advocate, the Advocate General, or the Attorney General) to refer the matter to the Judicial Committee of the Parliament for a ruling of whether a legislative provision is within the competence of the Scottish Parliament. In addition the Secretary of State has the power to intervene where he believes a Bill (a) is incompatible with international obligations, or interests in defence and security; or (b) modifies law relating to reserved matters. This intervention will be in the form of passing an order that prevents the legislative measure receiving Royal Assent.[9]

In the normal course of events the legislative process will entail having a general debate on the Bill with the opportunity to vote on general principles. Thereafter there is an opportunity for MSPs to consider the details of the proposal followed by a final stage at which the Bill can be accepted or rejected. Bills may be reconsidered once they have been passed if the Judicial

---

[4] See A. Bradley and K. Ewing, *Constitutional and Administrative Law*, 14th edn (England: Pearson/Longman, 2007), pp.139–149. *R. v Secretary of State for Transport Ex p. Factortame (No.1)* [1990] 2 A.C. 85; *(No.2)* [1991] 1 A.C. 603; [C221/89] [1992] QB 680. Beaumont and Weatherill, *EU Law* (1999), pp.433–453.

[5] See D. Walker, *The Scottish Legal System*, 8th edn (Edinburgh: W. Green, 2001) pp.415–428.

[6] See Walker, *The Scottish Legal System* (2001), pp.415–418; Walker, "Discovering the Intention of Parliament", 1993 S.L.T. (News) 121; G. Maher, "Statutory Interpretation: The Wilsonian Analysis" in H. MacQueen (ed.), *Scots Law into the 21st Century* (Edinburgh: W. Green, 1996); D.M. Walker, "The Crumbling Pillars of Statutory Interpretation" in MacQueen, *Scots Law into the 21st Century* (1996).

[7] Scotland Act 1998 s.28(1).

[8] Scotland Act 1998 s.28(7).

[9] Scotland Act 1998 ss.31, 33 and 35.

Committee decides that the Bill is outwith the legislative competence of the Scottish Parliament, or the Secretary of State makes an order prohibiting the Royal Assent.[10]

Schedule 4 to the Scotland Act 1998 prohibits the Scottish Parliament from attempting to alter the Human Rights Act 1998, certain provisions of the European Communities Act 1972, and the Acts of Union 1706 and 1707. Nor can an Act of the Scottish Parliament modify, or confer power by subordinate legislation to modify, certain parts of the Scotland Act 1998 dealing with its constitution and legislative capacity. Furthermore, there are a number of matters reserved to the Westminster Parliament of the United Kingdom. Irrespective of these reservations, the Scottish Parliament legislates for large areas of domestic law.

Delegated legislation

2.05 Delegated legislation is produced where Parliament delegates its law-making capacity to some other subordinate body or persons. Bodies or persons ordinarily entrusted with the framing of delegated legislation are government ministers, local authorities, courts and other public bodies. One finds a considerable amount of delegated legislation promulgated under the Children (Scotland) Act 1995 and other principal social work statutes. For example, detailed rules of procedure for the children's hearing system have been promulgated under delegated legislation.[11] Most delegated legislation comes into force once it is published, or shortly thereafter.

If properly made in accordance with the procedure set down for it, delegated legislation becomes a powerful part of the general body of law called legislation. Because those persons to whom legislative capacity has been delegated have limited powers, individuals may challenge the validity of delegated legislation, either on the basis that the powers of the person or body have been exceeded (known as ultra vires), or that the correct procedure has not been followed. In contrast to the courts' approach to Acts of Parliament, there are numerous judicial decisions where the validity of delegated legislation has been challenged.[12] Scottish Ministers also have the power to make regulations under Acts of the Scottish Parliament.

Judicial precedent

2.06 All major legal systems operate a system of judicial precedent whereby cases that have been decided in the past guide decisions in cases before the courts today. Judicial precedents are prior decisions that contain important principles of law. On a practical level, previously decided case law represents an extremely important source of Scots law. Even where legislation exists (as it does in much of social work law) legal practitioners and social work practitioners will look to judicial precedent to offer guidance on principles of law, or illumination of statutory provisions. Although not always the case,[13] it is accepted in modern Scots law that in certain circumstances previous decisions are not only helpful, but may be binding on a court hearing a legal case. It is the legal principle and not the factual circumstances that are applied to the case in hand. Essential to the application of judicial precedent is an effective system of reporting of judicial principles and reasons. Scotland, like other countries, now has several journals and books reporting significant cases of legal importance. In Scotland the main series of reports are the *Scots Law Times* (S.L.T.), *Session Cases* (S.C.) and *Justiciary Cases* (J.C.), the *Scottish Civil Law Reports* (S.C.L.R.) and the *Scottish Criminal Case Reports* (S.C.C.R.). Many of these law reports are now being presented on computer databases or in CD ROM version. New judgments in civil and criminal cases are posted on a daily basis on the Scottish Courts website.[14]

The doctrine of stare decisis (standing by one's previous decisions) operates in such a way that

---

[10] Scotland Act 1998 ss.35 and 36.

[11] Act of Sederunt, Children's Hearings (Scotland) Rules 1996 (SI 1996/3261).

[12] See Bradley and Ewing, *Constitutional and Administrative Law* (2007), pp.674–692; for an example see *Secretary of State for Defence v Percy* [1999] 1 All E.R. 732.

[13] See Walker, *The Scottish Legal System* (2001), p.422.

[14] See *http://www.scotcourts.gov.uk* [Accessed July 2, 2008].

where two golden rules are applicable to a case, this case must be followed by the court considering it. Those two rules are that: first the precedent is a decision of a court superior in the Scottish legal hierarchy to the court of the current case, and secondly that the precedent had the same legal principle in dispute as the current case before the court. Where the court decides that the principle of law in dispute is the same, the precedent is said to be "in point". Essentially, this means that decisions of the House of Lords in Scottish cases are binding on all other courts in the Scottish civil court hierarchy where the principle of law is the same. The Inner House of the Court of Session binds the Outer House and the sheriff courts. Judicial precedents of the Outer House of the Court of Session are binding in the sheriff courts. Decisions of the sheriff principal only bind a sheriff in his own sheriffdom. Given that all sheriff courts are supposedly of equal standing, one sheriff court can never bind another. In criminal cases decisions of the Scottish Court of Criminal Appeal bind all other courts in the criminal hierarchy. Precedent plays a somewhat lesser role in the criminal courts. Much of their work revolves round an assessment of the facts in determining guilt. However, precedent is still important in many cases not only on points of law but also in determining sentences.

2.07 Where a precedent is "in point" and is from a court higher in the hierarchy, the judge must apply it—failure to do so will only result in an appeal and severe criticism of the judge. In many situations judges will attempt to evade application of a precedent by arguing that it is not in point and as such can be distinguished from the case in hand. Even where cases do not satisfy the two golden rules they may still have major significance. Precedents of courts of equal standing or from a senior court of another jurisdiction (e.g. England) may well be termed "persuasive" so that judges may follow them if they wish.

Not all cases that go to court are reported in the law reports. Those reports that do find their way into the law reports might mention only an aspect of a particular case that is considered important by those reporting it. In other instances a very fulsome report may be given of the judges' opinions. Usually when a case is reported the form it will take is that there will be a section of catchwords of legal headings. It is then followed by a summary known as the "rubric". There will then follow a brief summary of the facts and a statement of the point of law decided by the court. The statement of law will usually occur after the word "held". If one or more of the judges has not agreed with the majority opinion of the court there will almost certainly be an indication of this. In most law reports there will then follow a list of the sources of law to which the court was referred or did refer to determine the case. After these preliminaries one can expect to find the substantive body of the report, which will detail the steps in the litigation, sometimes summarise arguments, perhaps include extracts from earlier court hearings of the same case, and will conclude with the text of the judges' opinions. Sometimes only one opinion will be delivered as the unanimous opinion of the court.

Other sources of Scots law

2.08 Such has been the development of Scots law over the past 300 years that it is rare when neither European law, nor legislation, nor precedent can be applied to the matter in hand. Occasionally though that is the case, and one needs to go further back to find a source of law to provide guidance on a subject. One such repository of law is the institutional writings.[15] These are writings of historic scholars given an exalted status in Scots law[16] and are frequently referred to even in cases where there are other sources of law.

In addition, courts and legal practitioners will often refer to other legal textbooks not afforded the status of institutional writings but important nonetheless. Custom and equity may be other sources of law and increasingly the laws of foreign jurisdictions are offering guidance on a number of legal issues.[17]

---

[15] Walker, *The Scottish Legal System* (2001), pp.475–477.
[16] For a full list of the institutional writings see Walker, *The Scottish Legal System* (2001), p.506.
[17] For a discussion of these sources see Walker, *The Scottish Legal System* (2001), pp.477–486.

Codes, guidance and circulars

2.09 In addition to the formal sources of law outlined above, the professional social worker must have regard to a number of codes of practice, guidance notes and circulars. These may be issued by government, or other public bodies, such as the Equal Opportunities Commission or the Commission for Racial Equality.[18] In Scotland, guidance and circulars on aspects of social work practice are regularly issued by the Scottish Government.[19] While not given the same weight as law, codes and guidance are nevertheless extremely important as evidence of best practice and the expected standard. Some of the codes of practice may be in the form of National Standards (for example those in respect of dealing with criminal offenders).[20]

THE COURT SYSTEM

2.10 Civil law courts can be broadly viewed as existing for the resolution of disputes between two or more parties whether those parties be individuals, corporate entities, the state or state bodies. In the social work context, it is more likely that disputes will arise between individuals, or between individuals and the state or voluntary organisations as providers of social work related services. The sort of civil law disputes that may affect the social work client are debt, housing matters, family law disputes such as contact or residence, or disputes involving childcare law, or indeed any disputes pertaining to most of the areas of law covered in this book.

Criminal law can be distinguished on the basis that it is a body of rules designed for the harmonious coexistence of society which the state on behalf of society enforces. Central to an understanding of the criminal law and the criminal prosecution system is the fact that transgression of the law is an offence against society as a whole and not principally the specific "victim" of the crime. The criminal law courts provide a mechanism for the state to prosecute those accused of crimes, and where a conviction ensues to impose appropriate punishment.[21] The distinction between criminal law and civil law gives rise to two separate court structures.

The criminal courts

The district court

2.11 The lowest court in the criminal court structure is the district court. There are 56 district courts located in towns and cities throughout Scotland. The only exceptions were the sheriff court districts of Lochmaddy, Orkney and Shetland. The courts were administered by the unitary local authorities.[22] The geographic jurisdiction of the court only extended to the area of the local authority district, and accordingly, only crimes committed within the district could competently be brought before the court. However with effect from the beginning of 2008, a new system of JP (justice of the peace) courts will be introduced, which will eventually replace the existing district courts. The JP courts will be administered by the Scottish Court Service ("SCS") to create a unified system of summary criminal courts in Scotland. The JP courts will match the territorial jurisdiction of the existing sheriff court districts and will be able to try an offence committed within the sheriff court district in which it is situated or in any other sheriff court district in the sheriffdom.[23] It is anticipated that there will be at least one JP court for each sheriff court

[18] See paras 10.11 and 10.17 respectively.

[19] See generally *http://www.scotland.gov.uk/Topics/justice/jdcirculars/listjdcirculars* [Accessed July 3, 2008].

[20] See *http://www.scotland.gov.uk/Publications* [Accessed July 2, 2008] for the full range of National Objectives and Standards.

[21] Further discussion of social workers and the criminal justice system is to be found in Ch.8.

[22] The current structure of local government was established by the Local Government etc. (Scotland) Act 1994 and came into effect on April 7, 1995. The structure consists of 29 single tier councils, replacing the 53 district and 9 regional councils established in 1975.

[23] Criminal Proceedings etc. (Reform) (Scotland) Act 2007 s.62(1) and (2).

district although there appear to be no plans to introduce them in Orkney, Shetland or Lochmaddy.[24] JP courts will be introduced during 2008, first in the sheriffdom of Lothian and Borders and then in Grampian Highland and Islands. The other sheriffdoms will follow at dates to be announced.

As the lowest court in the country, the district court has jurisdiction over the less serious offences. For example, such crimes as breach of the peace, minor assault and theft, and minor statutory offences are tried in the district court and will continue to be tried in the JP court. Uniquely among the Scottish criminal courts, the district court and JP courts are presided over by a person or persons who are not legally qualified. These lay persons are known as justices of the peace (JP). In some district courts a JP will sit alone; in others there may be a panel of justices. JPs are appointed by Scottish Ministers on behalf of the Queen to a sheriffdom for a period of five years at a time and must retire at the age of 70.[25] JPs are eligible for reappointment at the expiry of the five-year period.[26]

The procedure in the district court is summary criminal procedure (see Ch.8) and as such there is no jury present. The JP determines the guilt of the accused and imposes sentence. The JP is assisted in court by a legally qualified clerk. Clerks of the new JP courts will be solicitors or advocates employed by the Scottish Court Service. In the district courts the clerk is a full-time employee of the local authority. The clerk offers legal advice and guidance where that is necessary.

The longest prison sentence that can be imposed in the district court is 60 days, and the maximum fine up to level 4 on the standard scale, at present £2,500.[27] There is a range of other punishments that the court may impose (see Ch.8). Because of the volume of criminal court work, there is a special arrangement in Glasgow where a legally qualified stipendiary magistrate sits in the district court. The stipendiary magistrate has the same powers as a sheriff sitting in the summary criminal court (see below).

The sheriff court (summary procedure)

2.12 Second lowest in the hierarchy of Scottish criminal courts is the sheriff court (summary). Scotland is divided into six sheriffdoms divided into sheriff court districts.[28] Sheriff courts are located in 49 towns and cities across Scotland. A number of legally qualified judges known as sheriffs are appointed to each sheriffdom. As the name implies the court operates summary criminal procedure, and as such the sheriff acts as judge and jury in each case. In a similar fashion to the district court, the sheriff court has a geographic jurisdiction over summary crimes committed in its area. An accused can expect to be brought before the sheriff court for the area in which the offence took place. Offences tried in this court are more serious than those taken to the district court or JP court. Typically, cases such as assault, breach of the peace, less serious drugs offences, road traffic offences, and theft and theft by housebreaking will be prosecuted before the sheriff court sitting as a summary court. The sheriff has the power to impose a sentence of up to 12 months' imprisonment or detention.[29] The sheriff may also impose a fine

---

[24] Criminal Proceedings etc. (Reform) (Scotland) Act 2007 Explanatory Note para.350.

[25] Criminal Proceedings etc. (Reform) (Scotland) Act 2007 s.67.

[26] Criminal Proceedings etc. (Reform) (Scotland) Act 2007 s.70.

[27] Criminal Procedure (Scotland) Act 1995 s.7(6).

[28] Grampian, Highland and Islands; Tayside, Central and Fife; Lothian and Borders; Glasgow and Strathkelvin; North Strathclyde; South Strathclyde, Dumfries and Galloway.

[29] This applies to cases that called for the first time or where a warrant to commence proceedings was granted on or after December 10, 2007. See the Criminal Proceedings etc. (Reform) (Scotland) Act 2007 (Commencement No.2 and Transitional Provisions and Savings) Order 2007 (SSI 2007/479) art.12. In proceedings that were under way before that date, the sheriff may impose a period of imprisonment or detention not exceeding three months, or six months if the offender was being sentenced for a second or subsequent offence inferring violence or dishonesty: Criminal Procedure (Scotland) Act 1995 s.5(3).

not exceeding £10,000 for an offence that may be tried either summarily or on indictment.[30] See Ch.8 for the range of sentences available to the sheriff.

The sheriff court (solemn procedure)

2.13 More serious offences may also come before the sheriff court. These will be tried under solemn procedure, a feature of which is the involvement of a jury to determine guilt where guilt is denied. A sheriff will preside, sum up for the jury, and will pass sentence if there is a finding of "guilty". The sort of cases one can typically find being tried under solemn procedure include fraud, embezzlement, serious road traffic offences, serious health and safety offences, robbery, and aggravated assaults and less serious drug trafficking offences. Again the sheriff court has geographic jurisdiction over offences of this type in the locality of the area it covers. In keeping with the gravity of the crimes tried, the sentencing powers of the sheriff are somewhat more severe. In solemn procedure cases the sheriff can, among other things, impose a sentence of up to five years' imprisonment, or an unlimited fine.

The High Court of Justiciary

2.14 The highest criminal trial court in Scotland is the High Court of Justiciary. The High Court of Justiciary is a "circuit court". Scotland is divided into four circuits—Home, North, West and South. Without a permanent home, the High Court of Justiciary sits at various times in different places throughout Scotland. The volume of business in places such as Glasgow and Edinburgh ensures that the Home and the West circuits are in permanent session. In keeping with its status as the highest criminal court in the land, it hears the most serious cases. Murder, rape, treason, incest and offences under the Official Secrets Act must be tried in the High Court of Justiciary. However, one can also expect to see other serious offences tried there. Armed robbery, culpable homicide, serious drugs offences, sexual abuse cases and cases alleging causing death by dangerous driving or while under the influence of drink or drugs are typical examples of the type of case tried in Scotland's most senior trial court. The court operates solemn procedure[31] and as such a jury of 15 persons will determine the issue of guilt where that is in dispute. The judge, a Lord Commissioner of Justiciary will preside over the proceedings and impose sentence. The powers of sentence in this court are unlimited although where there is a mandatory penalty (such as life imprisonment for the crime of murder) the judge has no discretion.

Criminal appeals and the Scottish Court of Criminal Appeal

2.15 All appeals from decisions of the Scottish criminal courts are heard in Edinburgh before the High Court of Justiciary sitting as the Scottish Court of Criminal Appeal. Three senior judges of the High Court of Justiciary will hear appeals against conviction on points of law and against sentence.

A miscarriage of justice in solemn cases may be based on (a) the existence and significance of evidence that was not heard at the original proceedings; and (b) the jury's having returned a verdict that no reasonable jury properly directed could have returned.[32] The fresh evidence need not come from a new witness.[33] However, the court must be convinced that there is a reasonable

[30] Where proceedings commenced on or after December 10, 2007: Criminal Proceedings etc. (Reform) (Scotland) Act 2007 s.48 and Criminal Proceedings etc. (Reform) (Scotland) Act 2007 (Commencement No.2 and Transitional Provisions and Savings) Order 2007 art.12.

[31] See para.8.15.

[32] Criminal Procedure (Scotland) Act 1995 s.106(3), as amended by the Crime and Punishment (Scotland) Act 1997.

[33] See P. Ferguson, "Fresh Evidence Appeals" (1995) 40 J.L.S.S. 264; P. Ferguson, "Miscarriages of Justice and the Criminal Appeal Court" (1998) 43 J.L.S.S. 100; M. Scott, "New Criminal Appeal Provisions—Back to the Future", 1997 S.L.T. (News) 249.

explanation as to why the evidence was not led at the original trial.[34] The appeal court will hear the explanation before it will hear the evidence. In summary cases the only basis for a miscarriage of justice is fresh evidence.[35] There has been criticism of the restrictive basis of establishing a miscarriage of justice.[36]

There are several ways an accused can subsequently challenge his conviction.[37] One which is complex and unlikely is a referral under the appeal court's *nobile officium*.[38] Another option is a Royal Pardon which has occurred only twice in recent Scottish legal history.

Since April 1999 it has been possible to refer cases to the Scottish Criminal Cases Review Commission which has the power to investigate and refer cases to the High Court.[39] The Commission was established as an independent body to review possible miscarriages of justice. If it thinks fit, the Commission may refer to the High Court of Justiciary any conviction and/or sentence passed, at any time, on a person who has been convicted of an offence on indictment or complaint whether or not an appeal has already been heard and determined upon by the High Court of Justiciary or the person is deceased. The grounds for reference are that it believes that a miscarriage of justice has occurred and that it is on the interests of justice that the reference should be made. The Commission has the power to undertake enquiries, precognosce witnesses, obtain documents and statements or may request the Lord Advocate or others to do so. Since its establishment, the Commission has received 887 cases and as at March 31, 2007 had completed the review of 841 cases of which 67 had been referred to the High Court.[40]

The Judicial Committee of the Privy Council

2.16 There is no right of appeal against conviction or sentence to the House of Lords in Scottish criminal cases.

However, appeals may be brought before the Judicial Committee of the Privy Council in criminal cases in which a devolution issue has been raised. The devolution issues set out in Sch.6 to the Scotland Act 1998 are as follows:

- whether an Act of the Scottish Parliament or any of its provisions is within the legislative competence of the Parliament;
- whether any function is a function of the Scottish Ministers, the First Minister or the Lord Advocate;
- whether a purported or proposed exercise of a function by a member of the Scottish Executive is or would be within devolved competence;
- whether a purported or proposed exercise of a function by a member of the Scottish Executive is, or would be, incompatible with any Convention rights or European Community law;
- whether a failure to act by a member of the Scottish Executive is incompatible with any Convention rights or Community Law;
- any other question about whether a function is exercisable within devolved competence

[34] Criminal Procedure (Scotland) Act 1995 s.106(3C), as amended by the Crime and Punishment (Scotland) Act 1997 s.17.

[35] Criminal Procedure (Scotland) Act 1995 s.175, as amended by the Crime and Punishment (Scotland) Act 1997 s.17(2).

[36] See Ferguson, "Miscarriages of Justice" (1998) 43 J.L.S.S. 100, 101.

[37] See A. Poole, "Remedies in Miscarriages of Justice Cases", 1998 S.L.T. (News) 65.

[38] See Poole, "Remedies in Miscarriages of Justice Cases", 1998 S.L.T. (News) 65; P. Ferguson, "The Scope of the Nobile Officium to Review Appeal Court Decisions" (1993) 38 J.L.S.S. 439.

[39] See generally *http://www.sccrc.org.uk* [Accessed July 7, 2008] and the Criminal Procedure (Scotland) Act 1995 ss.194A–194L and Sch.9A.

[40] Scottish Criminal Cases Review Commission Annual Report and Accounts 2006–07 (2007), p.6. The first case to be referred was *Boncza-Tomaszewski v HM Advocate*, 2001 S.L.T. 336. The first to be determined was *Crombie v Clark*, 2001 S.L.T. 635. See also R. Anthony, "The Scottish Criminal Cases Review Commission: An End to Miscarriages of Justice?" (2001) 69(2) S.L.G. 41; P. Ferguson, "Case Comment *Crombie v Clark*", 2001 S.L.T. 155.

or in or as regards Scotland and any other question arising by virtue of the Act about reserved matters.

This power has been exercised in a number of criminal cases since the enactment of the Scotland Act 1998. Principally these have concerned a person's right, under art.6 of the European Convention on Human Rights, to a fair trial before an independent tribunal within a reasonable time.[41]

The civil courts

The sheriff court

2.17 The lowest court in the hierarchy of civil courts is the sheriff court. Its geographic jurisdiction is similar to that of the sheriff court in criminal matters. Disputes may result in legal action being initiated in this court. Common types of disputes include matrimonial disputes, disputes relating to children, debt, land and property disputes, personal injury cases and contract disputes. Although there is no upper financial limit as to the value of any case taken in the sheriff court, the sheriff court's privative jurisdiction dictates that any disputes involving cash sums up to £1,500 must be initiated in the sheriff court.

Operating in the sheriff court there are three distinct forms of procedure—small claims, summary cause and ordinary procedure. The least formal and cheapest procedure is the small claim. It was destined to be litigant-friendly and accessible to persons without legal representation. The pecuniary limit of a small claim for actions raised on or after January 14, 2008 is £3,000.[42] Claims with a financial value above £3,000 up to and including £5,000 ordinarily proceed by way of summary cause procedure.[43] It is also the case that actions for recovery of possession of heritable property by councils, housing associations or private landlords ordinarily proceed by way of this procedure. Though more formal than small claims, it is still intended to be relatively speedy and inexpensive. Finally, ordinary procedure applies to all claims with a value over £5,000 and applies to the vast bulk of the case load before the sheriff court.[44]

The sheriff principal

2.18 Each sheriffdom has a sheriff principal who acts as a senior judge in each sheriffdom. His role is largely one of hearing appeals from decisions of the sheriffs in his own sheriffdom. Appeals may be taken from a final judgment of the sheriff principal to the Inner House of the Court of Session on any point of law.

Outer House of the Court of Session

2.19 The highest court of "first instance" (where a case may start) in Scotland is the Outer House of the Court of Session. The Court of Session is located in Edinburgh and is divided into an Outer House and an Inner House. The Outer House is presided over by a Lord Ordinary, a judge appointed by the Sovereign. Judges at this level, as Senators of the College of Justice, are the most senior judicial appointments in Scotland. There is seniority within the College of Justice and it will be the case that more junior Lords Ordinary will preside in the Outer House of the Court of Session while the more senior judges will decide upon appeals in the Inner House. The

---

[41] *HM Advocate v R* [2004] 1 A.C. 462 and *Dyer v Watson*, 2002 S.C. (P.C.) 89 (unreasonable delay); *Sinclair v HM Advocate*, 2005 1 S.C. (P.C) 28 and *Holland v HM Advocate*, 2005 1 S.C. (P.C) 3 (the right to disclosure of the prosecution case); *Brown v Stott* 2001 S.C. (P.C) 43 (the right to silence); *Kearney v HM Advocate*, 2006 S.C. (P.C.) 1; 2006 S.L.T. 499 and *Robertson v Frame*, 2006 S.C. (P.C.) 22 (the right to a fair and impartial tribunal).

[42] Small Claims (Scotland) Amendment) Order 2007 (SSI 2007/496).

[43] Sheriffs Court (Scotland) Act 1971 (Privative Jurisdiction and Summary Cause) Order 2007 (SSI 2007/507).

[44] For a brief discussion of the various procedures see paras 9.70–9.78.

Outer House of the Court of Session has national jurisdiction and accordingly will hear cases of some complexity or importance from all over Scotland or cases having a national significance. Some actions must start there, for instance actions for declarator of marriage, and actions of judicial review.[45] By and large though there is no difference in the types of cases heard in the sheriff court and the Outer House and indeed often there is little difference in value. One would ordinarily expect very large value actions to be taken in the Outer House.

Inner House of the Court of Session

2.20 The Inner House of the Court of Session is almost exclusively an appeal court. For the purposes of convenience and workload, the court is divided into two courts—the First Division and the Second Division. The two courts have equal standing. The First Division is presided over by Scotland's most senior judge, the Lord President, while the second court is presided over by the second most senior judge, the Lord Justice-Clerk. Usually, they will sit with two other of the more senior Lords Ordinary to determine an appeal. Each court comprises four judges in all but usually only three sit. One cannot elect which division to take one's case to, nor is there any appeal from one division to the other. From time to time, the First Division and the Second Division are conjoined in a court of five or seven judges where the court considers the matter to be important enough to warrant such a step. All appeals in the Inner House will be on a point or points of law only.

The House of Lords

2.21 In civil law matters, unlike in criminal law, there is the possibility of an appeal being taken to the House of Lords located in London. Appeals are heard by legally qualified members of the House of Lords who are appointed to the Judicial Committee of the House of Lords to fulfil a judicial function. The most senior judge in the House of Lords is the Lord Chancellor. The other judges are known as the Lords of Appeal in Ordinary. Although the quorum is three, cases are usually heard by five judges. It is also usually the case that at least two of the judges operating in the House of Lords are of Scottish jurisdiction origin. However, there is no rule that in cases originating from Scotland a Scottish judge must be part of the court. In the normal course of things, a case will be heard by five judges, a majority of whom will be English. The scope for Anglicisation of Scots law is obvious, and has been severely criticised.[46] Decisions of the court are by a majority. It is not uncommon for cases of social importance to have been decided on three to two verdicts. Decisions in Scottish cases in the House of Lords are binding on inferior courts in Scotland.

The European Court of Justice

2.22 Although not part of the domestic court structure, the European Court of Justice is of crucial importance. It operates to deliberate upon matters of EU law brought to it under the Treaties applicable to the Community. A case brought before it may be an action against a Member State, or may be a referral by a court of a Member State for a preliminary ruling on a matter of EU law. The court comprises judges nominated by the Governments of the Member States. The president of the court is appointed by the judges themselves from among them. The judges of the court are assisted by six Advocates General who are appointed for a six-year renewable term. The role of Advocate General is of considerable importance. He considers the case and reaches his own personal conclusion as to what the law is and how the case should be resolved. The Advocate General does not represent the institutions of the community, the Member States or the public. He will propose to the court a solution to any case brought before the court, relate the proposed solution to existing case law, and in some circumstances outline the probable

---

[45] Discussed below at para.2.46.

[46] See for example, Walker, *The Scottish Legal System* (2001), p.297.

development of case law on this issue. Once the court has heard the views of the Advocate General, its judges will retire to deliberate upon their verdict. In most cases, the court will follow the views of the Advocate General. Very few, if any, cases of relevance in the social work context are likely to be decided by this court. Social work tends to be a matter of domestic law and rarely raises issues of European significance, although it is possible. Decisions of the court are binding and must be applied by domestic courts.[47]

The European Court of Human Rights

2.23 Quite distinct and unconnected to the European Union and its institutions is the European Court of Human Rights, set up under the auspices of the Council of Europe. The court was established originally in 1959 and ceased in 1998 when it was replaced with a full-time European Court of Human Rights, which though maintaining the same name has a new composition, functions and powers. The recognition of the European Convention on Human Rights did not confer rights on ordinary citizens enforceable in their own national courts. Aggrieved persons had to take their case to the European Court of Human Rights ("ECtHR"). Cases can now only be taken to ECtHR once domestic remedies have been exhausted. Participating states may also refer matters to the court.

The Human Rights Act 1998

2.24 The preamble to the Human Rights Act 1998 ("1998 Act") said that it was intended to give further effect to rights and freedoms guaranteed under the European Convention on Human Rights. In this respect, it does not go nearly far enough for many of those who had sought the full enactment of a Bill of Rights into United Kingdom law. The 1998 Act did not enact the entire European Convention on Human Rights directly into United Kingdom law. Instead it sought to enact certain core values into legal interpretation. In s.2(1) a duty is placed upon courts and tribunals to take account of (a) any judgment, decision, declaration, or advice of the European Court of Human Rights; (b) any opinion of the Commission given in a report adopted under art.31 of the Convention; (c) decisions of the Commission; and (d) decisions of the Committee of Ministers. It is further enacted under s.3(1) that "So far as it is possible to do so, primary legislation and subordinate legislation must be read and given effect in a way which is compatible with the Convention rights". However, in assessing compatibility no power is given in the legislation to alter the validity or continuing operational enforcement of incompatible legislation.[48] All that a British court can do is to issue a declaration that legislation in the United Kingdom is incompatible with the core values adopted.[49] Only the highest courts, namely the House of Lords and the Scottish Court of Criminal Appeal may make declarations of incompatibility.[50] A further dimension to the legislation is that it is enacted that public authorities must act in a way which is compatible with Convention rights and in the Act.[51] Individuals have the right to bring proceedings against public authorities where they believe that the public authority has acted in a way not compatible with an enacted Convention right.[52] Courts have the power to grant relief, or remedy, or to make any order within their power to address any unlawful act by a public authority. Specifically, the civil court has the power to award damages or compensation. In awarding damages, the court will need to take account of

---

[47] For a full discussion on the workings of the European Court of Justice see Beaumont and Weatherill, *EU Law* (1999), pp.173–211.

[48] See the Human Rights Act 1998 s.3(1)(b) and (c).

[49] Human Rights Act 1998 s.4(2).

[50] Human Rights Act 1998 s.4(5).

[51] Human Rights Act 1998 s.6(1).

[52] Human Rights Act 1998 s.7.

any other relief or remedy granted, and be satisfied that the award is necessary to afford just satisfaction to the person to whom it is made.[53]

There are provisions in the 1998 Act under s.10 whereby a statute or other legislation that has been declared incompatible may be amended by Order of the Minister of the Crown as he considers necessary to remove the incompatibility.[54] This represents a remarkable innovation in United Kingdom law and clearly impacts upon the concept of parliamentary supremacy.

The Human Rights Act 1998 has a considerable impact upon social work law and practice as an area of law dominated by the issue of rights, particularly, but not exclusively, in areas involving children, mental health and criminal justice.

TRIBUNALS

2.25 It is a feature of the modern legal system that the operation and influence of tribunals is on the increase. There are tribunals for employment disputes, social security, disability, child support and medical matters, as well as a range of other matters. Indeed it is believed that there are around 2,000 different tribunals operating in the United Kingdom.[55]

Tribunals exist to relieve the pressure on courts to resolve disputes, to provide a relatively informal arena for the resolution of some disputes, to allow the involvement of experts in settling particular disputes, to provide a relatively cheap mechanism for resolution of disputes, to infuse the system of adjudication with social policy considerations, and to deal with matters too trifling for the courts.[56] The extent to which any of these points is true is arguable. Certainly, tribunals are popular with government and the public. They play an increasingly pervasive part of modern life and social work professionals, or at least members of their client group, can expect to encounter some of these tribunals at some point in their career.

EVIDENCE IN COURT PROCEEDINGS

2.26 All material facts that are in dispute in a court case must be established by evidence. Evidence is the information that tends to prove or disprove any fact. Evidence may come in several forms—the oral or written testimony of a witness, documentary evidence, and other productions such as physical evidence (e.g. stolen goods, drugs, or a weapon).

In civil cases the person or body bringing the case to court is responsible for proving the facts upon which their case relies, and is known as the "pursuer". If he does not prove those facts, his case will fail. The task of the opposing party is simpler. To defend the case, he need only attack the evidence of the pursuer so that it fails to satisfy the court. He may of course lead his own evidence. In civil cases, a material fact, and the case as a whole, may be established on the balance of probabilities. As a consequence of provisions in the Civil Evidence (Scotland) Act 1988 the rules of evidence in civil cases are also less strict.

In the criminal court, a person is presumed innocent until proven guilty. The court must be satisfied beyond reasonable doubt that the accused is guilty by evidence led by the prosecution. There are strict rules of evidence, and corroboration (proof of material facts from more than one source) is required. The two material facts of paramount importance in a criminal case are that the acts set out in the complaint or indictment took place and that the accused committed them. Questions of fact in criminal cases are to be determined by the jury (or by the judge if there is no jury), while questions of law are to be determined by the judge. A question of fact concerns the truth or otherwise of something that can be appreciated by one of the five senses:

---

[53] Human Rights Act 1998 s.8.
[54] Human Rights Act 1998 s.10(2) and (3).
[55] See C. Ashton and V. Finch, *Administrative Law in Scotland* (Edinburgh: W. Green, 1997), p.185.
[56] Ashton and Finch, *Administrative Law in Scotland* (1997), p.185.

sight, sound, smell, taste, touch, i.e. what someone said or did, where and when. Evidence will be heard to decide questions of fact. A question of law concerns the rule of law, for instance what interpretation should be given to a particular Act of Parliament or what weight or interpretation is to be given to a judicial precedent.

Rules of evidence

2.27 Evidence in any proceedings must be relevant, admissible and credible. Relevance and admissibility are matters for the judge. To be relevant, evidence must bear upon the issues of the case. Not all relevant evidence is admissible. There are a number of exclusionary rules that render relevant evidence inadmissible.

Under the "best evidence" rule, a party should present the best available evidence to the court, although in civil proceedings a copy document can now be produced subject to certain conditions and treated as if it was the document itself.[57] However one does not present hearsay evidence where one can present the evidence of an actual observer.[58]

The "rule against hearsay" is a controversial feature of the law[59] which provides that a fact may not be established by calling A, who did not see an event or hear a statement, to tell the court that he heard B who did. For example, if a child tells a social worker that he has been sexually abused by his father, the rule prevents the social worker giving evidence of what the child said to prove that the abuse took place. The social worker's evidence is hearsay; the child must tell the court himself. As a basic premise hearsay is excluded in criminal proceedings because it is unreliable.[60] The rule against hearsay in civil proceedings was abolished by s.2 of the Civil Evidence (Scotland) Act 1988 and therefore hearsay is allowed. However, even in many criminal cases hearsay statements are admissible. There are now so many exceptions to the hearsay rule that it has been claimed that the rule has been "comprehensively circumscribed by the courts and statutory intervention".[61] Hearsay evidence that forms part of the whole circumstances immediately connected with the occurrence that is part of the facts at issue may be admissible.[62] The utterances are spontaneously related to the event and as such are an indication of what happened.[63] It follows that there must be proximity in time to the event and the hearsay.[64]

Section 259 of the Criminal Procedure (Scotland) Act 1995 also provides further statutory exceptions to the hearsay rule in criminal cases. It provides that evidence other than oral testimony may be admitted where:

- the witness is now deceased or by reason of bodily or mental condition unfit or unable to give evidence in any competent manner[65];
- the witness is outwith the United Kingdom and it is not reasonably practicable to obtain evidence by alternative means or secure his attendance;

---

[57] Civil Evidence (Scotland) Act 1988 s.6.

[58] See generally F. Raitt, *Evidence*, 3rd edn (Edinburgh: W. Green, 2001), Ch.9; D. Nicol, "Best Evidence in Criminal Cases", 1990 S.L.T. (News) 149; although note that the best evidence rule can be overcome with the admission of hearsay in civil cases: see *F v Kennedy*, 1993 S.L.T. 1284.

[59] See Raitt, *Evidence* (2001), Ch.8, p.197; Wilkinson, "The Hearsay Rule in Scotland", 1982 Jur. Rev. 213; *Report on Hearsay Evidence in Criminal Proceedings*, Scot. Law Com. No.149 (Edinburgh: HMSO, 1995).

[60] See rationale for hearsay rule in Raitt, *Evidence* (2001), para.8.03 and D. Auchie, *Evidence*, 2nd edn (Edinburgh: W. Green, 2005), p.39.

[61] Raitt, *Evidence* (2001), paras 8.09–8.16; see also D. Sheldon, "The Hearsay Rule Devoured", 1995 Jur. Rev. 504.

[62] Known as the res gestae; Raitt, *Evidence* (2001), paras 8.05–8.06.

[63] Raitt, *Evidence* (2001), para.8.05.

[64] *Teper v R.* [1952] A.C. 480; cf. *HM Advocate v Murray* (1866) 5 Irv. 232.

[65] This provision was used in an unusual way in Aberdeen High Court where the main witness for the Crown was so profoundly deaf that he was unable to be examined or cross-examined. His evidence following agreement of the prosecution and the defence was taken from a statement from a policeman's notebook which he had signed: *HM Advocate v Patterson*, 2000 J.C. 137; *HM Advocate v Nulty*, 2000 S.L.T 528; *McKenna v HM Advocate*, 2000 S.L.T. 508.

- the witness has been sufficiently identified but cannot be found and all reasonable steps have been taken to trace him;
- the witness refuses to give evidence having been advised that it might be incriminating to him; and
- the witness refuses to give evidence or to take the oath.[66]

Prior to 1996, where a witness gave oral evidence, any prior statement was inadmissible as evidence of the truth of its contents, but evidence that a prior inconsistent statement had been made was admissible as a means of challenging the credibility of the witness. However, by virtue of the Criminal Procedure (Scotland) Act 1995 s.260, prior statements of witnesses may be admissible where the statement is contained in a document, where the witness in the course of giving evidence indicates that the prior statement was made by him and he adopts it as evidence, and also at the time of making the statement the witness was a competent witness in the proceedings.[67] Although these rules do not apply to an accused in his own trial, the prior statements of that accused may be admissible at the instance of a co-accused.[68]

2.28 Corroboration is another rule of admissibility and is required in criminal proceedings. Corroboration requires that an item of evidence from an independent source supports another item of evidence.[69] Therefore in criminal cases the testimony of one witness alone cannot prove a fact.[70] Corroboration may be in the form of another witness testimony, documentary or other evidence. Although s.1 of the Civil Evidence (Scotland) Act 1988 abolished the requirement for corroboration in civil proceedings, corroborated evidence will always carry more weight.[71] The rules of corroboration and hearsay are not strictly applied in children's hearings.

In criminal cases a series of similar alleged acts may corroborate each other. The leading Scottish case, *Moorov v HM Advocate*,[72] concerned a number of charges of indecent assault of different women. The only direct evidence in each charge was the testimony of the woman assaulted. It was held that there was sufficient interrelation between the assaults in time, place and circumstances to amount to corroboration.[73] It is also the case that in respect of particular sexual offences, evidence of the victim's distress may corroborate her statement that she did not consent to the actions of the accused. It will not corroborate evidence of exactly what the accused did.[74]

The final rule for admissibility is privilege. This exonerates witnesses from answering particular questions.[75] For example, communications between a husband and wife are privileged,[76] as are most communications between solicitors and their clients.[77] However, the same is not true of

---

[66] *MacDonald v HM Advocate*, 1999 S.L.T. 533: a child became distressed in the witness box and refused to answer any more questions about abuse. The prosecutor successfully moved the court to admit the child's prior statement to a police officer but on appeal it was held that as the witness had not been directed by the court to answer questions, this precluded the use of s.259. It was suggested that s.259 is directed more at the issue of refusal rather than difficulty or inability to give evidence.

[67] See the Criminal Procedure (Scotland) Act 1995 s.260; *Jamieson v HM Advocate*, 1995 S.L.T. 666.

[68] Criminal Procedure (Scotland) Act 1995 s.261.

[69] Raitt, *Evidence* (2001), paras 7.03–7.04.

[70] See *Morton v HM Advocate*, 1938 J.C. 50, per Lord Justice-Clerk Aitchison at 55.

[71] *L v L*, 1996 S.L.T. 767.

[72] 1930 J.C. 68.

[73] See Raitt, *Evidence* (2001), paras 7.10–7.12.

[74] *Smith v Lees*, 1997 S.C.C.R. 139; F. Davidson, "Corroboration in Distress", 1997 S.L.P.Q. 30; Shiels, "Distress as Corroboration" (1994) 39 J.L.S.S. 293; Raitt, *Evidence* (2001), para.7.13; *Moore v HM Advocate*, 1991 S.L.T. 278; *Meek v HM Advocate*, 1983 S.L.T. 280; *Gracey v HM Advocate*, 1987 S.L.T. 749; *McLellan v HM Advocate*, 1992 S.L.T. 991; *Cannon v HM Advocate*, 1992 S.L.T. 709; *Stobo v HM Advocate*, 1994 S.L.T. 28; J. Chalmers, "Distress as Corroboration of Mens Rea", 2004 S.L.T. 141.

[75] Raitt, *Evidence* (2001), Ch.12.

[76] Evidence (Scotland) Act 1853 s.3 (in civil cases); Criminal Procedure (Scotland) Act 1995 s.264(2)(b) (in criminal cases).

[77] Raitt, *Evidence* (2001), paras 12.11–12.13.

doctors or social workers.[78] Privilege does not extend to a child when that child is asked to give evidence against a parent or relative. Courts will allow witnesses to refuse to answer questions, where it is deemed that the greater public good requires it (public interest immunity).[79] For example, in the case of *D v NSPCC*,[80] the NSPCC could refuse to disclose the name of the person who had told them of their suspicions that a child was being abused because he was a police informer. Where there is no privilege, refusal to answer a question is punishable as the criminal offence of contempt of court.

Important distinctions have to be drawn between fact and opinion, and evidence and argument. Witnesses as to fact tell the court what they have perceived with their senses, but only an expert witness may express an opinion in court. It is for the judge to decide if he thinks the witness has sufficient knowledge to give expert evidence. He need not have formal qualifications. Expertise may be based on experience. Social workers may be in a good position to give expert evidence by reason of their qualifications and experience. The function of the expert is not to present ready-made conclusions, but to provide the court with evidence on which it can reach its own conclusions.

Credibility of evidence is a matter for the jury or the judge where there is no jury. It is their task to decide whether to believe the witnesses. The court will take into account any motive the witness may have for putting matters in a particular light. In cases of assaults and sexual offences, evidence of a victim's statement is admissible to support his credibility, where the statement was made shortly after the event and no later than the first opportunity that the victim had to make a disclosure to a natural confidant.[81]

Child and adult vulnerable witnesses

2.29 The general principle is that all witnesses who are capable of giving intelligible evidence are competent as witnesses, and that all who are competent are compellable. Children and adults with learning difficulties or who suffer from mental disorders can be the victims of, or bystander witnesses to crimes. There is no minimum age below which a child will be prohibited from testifying although the party citing children in civil or criminal proceedings should satisfy him or herself that they will be able to give a comprehensible account of the events witnessed before putting them through the potentially distressing experience of giving evidence to a court. Children as young as three have been permitted to testify; however, this should be viewed as unusual.[82] When giving evidence, children over the age of 14 are sworn in. Children under 12 give evidence unsworn, but are warned to tell the truth. Children between 12 and 14 give sworn or unsworn evidence, depending on their level of understanding.[83] Whether a child gives evidence on oath, or not, is at the judge's discretion.[84]

Since April 2005, it has not been necessary for any witness in criminal or civil proceedings to undergo an examination of his or her competency to give evidence before being permitted to do so. The court must not, at any time before the witness gives evidence, take any step intended to establish whether the witness understands the duty to give truthful evidence or the difference between the truth and lies. The evidence of a witness is not inadmissible solely because the witness does not understand either of these issues.[85]

The rules of the court require a child to be served with the papers relating to the case in which he or she is the subject unless the court dispenses with service on the child. The court may

---

[78] Raitt, *Evidence* (2001), para.12.17.
[79] Raitt, *Evidence* (2001), paras 12.20–12.21.
[80] [1978] A.C. 171.
[81] *Morton v HM Advocate*, 1938 J.C. 50; *Andersons v McFarlane* (1899) 1 F. (J.) 36; *Begg v Tudhope*, 1983 S.C.C.R. 32.
[82] Raitt, *Evidence* (2001), para.11.05.
[83] Raitt, *Evidence* (2001), para.11.05.
[84] cf. the English decision of *R. v Smith* [1994] Crim. L.R. 458; also *R. v Norbury* (1992) 95 Cr.App.R. 256.
[85] Vulnerable Witnesses (Scotland) Act 2004 s.24.

appoint a curator *ad litem* to represent the child's interests.[86] In family actions where the interests of the child are involved, there has been since 1996 a system of child welfare hearings to address issues relating to the child which are held before the first major procedural hearing of the main family action.[87] The child may attend such hearings.

In other civil proceedings, a child cannot insist on giving evidence and can only give evidence if called to do so by one of the parties to the action. If a child wants to enter legal proceedings as a party, a solicitor must lodge a minute to this effect. It is then up to the judge to decide whether it is allowed. If a child wants to make sure his views are heard in court, he needs to instruct a solicitor who will act on his instructions. A child has the legal capacity to instruct a solicitor regarding any civil matter where the child has a general understanding of what it means to do so (a person of 12 years or more is presumed to have such understanding).[88] The child can also apply for legal aid.[89]

The evidence of vulnerable persons in criminal and civil cases

2.30 The increasing number of child abuse cases going to court in the late 1970s and early 1980s focused public attention on the unsatisfactory way in which the legal system then treated the evidence of children.[90,91] A number of important changes were made through the Law Reform (Miscellaneous Provisions) (Scotland) Act 1990, Prisoners and Criminal Proceedings (Scotland) Act 1993, and by the reworking of these provisions in the Crime and Punishment (Scotland) Act 1997 which amended the Criminal Procedure (Scotland) Act 1995. They permitted the use, at the court's discretion, in criminal cases in the High Court and sheriff court only of what have come to be known as "special measures" at first by child witnesses and latterly also by a very limited category of adult witnesses. The Vulnerable Witnesses (Scotland) Act 2004 now provides inter alia for the use of special measures for the purposes of the taking of evidence from children and adult vulnerable witnesses in criminal and, for the first time, in civil proceedings in the ordinary courts of law.[92] The Act came into force in stages between April 2005 and April 2008.[93]

Measures in the Vulnerable Witnesses (Scotland) Act 2004 make provision for the giving of evidence by vulnerable persons. A vulnerable person is a person who is giving or is to give evidence at or for the purposes of a trial in criminal proceedings or in any civil proceedings if he or she is under the age of 16 on the date of commencement of the proceedings in which the trial is being held, or where the person is aged 16 or over, there is a significant risk that as a result of mental disorder as defined by the Mental Health (Care and Treatment) (Scotland) Act 2003, or

---

[86] A curator *ad litem* is appointed when the parents or guardians are for some valid reason unable to act on the child's behalf, for instance if the parents are dead and no guardian has been appointed, if the child is subject to a ground of referral as a result of an alleged abuse or neglect by the parent, or if the child and parent are involved in an action against one another (see A. Wilkinson and K. Norrie, *The Law Relating to Parent and Child in Scotland*, 2nd edn (Edinburgh: W. Green, 1999) pp.403–404.). The curator *ad litem* is responsible for managing the affairs of the child and safeguarding his interests in all legal matters.

[87] See Cleland, "The New Ordinary Cause Rules for Family Actions", 1997 SCOLAG 100.

[88] Age of Legal Capacity (Scotland) Act 1991 s.2(4A).

[89] See *Journal of the Law Society of Scotland*, Feb. 1996, pp.83–85.

[90] See generally the Vulnerable Witnesses (Scotland) Act 2004, the Criminal Procedure (Scotland) Act 1995 ss.271–271M, and *http://www.scotland.gov.uk/Topics/Justice/Criminal* [Accessed July 2, 2008] for the Scottish Government's Victims and Witnesses web pages, the Guidance Pack and other information materials available.

[91] *Evidence of Children and Potentially Vulnerable Witnesses*, Scot. Law Com. No.125 (Edinburgh: HMSO, 1990); J. Spencer and R. Flin, *The Evidence of Children, the Law and the Psychology*, 2nd edn (1993).

[92] The taking of a child's evidence by live television link had been permitted since 1997 in a limited range of proceedings in court relating to child protection to which the Act of Sederunt (Child Care and Maintenance) Rules 1997 (SI 1997/291) as amended applied.

[93] The phased implementation of the Vulnerable Witnesses (Scotland) Act 2004 took place as follows: child witnesses in solemn proceedings, April 2004; adult vulnerable witnesses in solemn proceedings, April 2006; child witnesses in summary proceedings, April 2007; vulnerable witnesses in civil cases, November 2007; adult witnesses in summary criminal proceedings, April 2008.

fear and distress in connection with giving evidence at the trial or proceedings, there will be a diminution of the quality of the evidence given by the person.[94] Mental disorder includes learning disability. In deciding whether an adult witness is vulnerable by reason of fear and distress in connection with giving evidence, the court will take into account the nature and circumstances of the offence, the nature of the evidence that the witness is likely to give, the relationship if any that exists between the witness and the accused, the age and maturity of the witness, whether there is any evidence of intimidation or threats of intimidation on the part of the accused or any of his associates or family members, and other matters including the social and cultural background and ethnic origins of the witness, his or her sexual orientation, domestic and employment circumstances, religious beliefs or political opinions and any physical disability or impairment which the person has.[95]

Under the provisions of the Vulnerable Witnesses (Scotland) Act 2004, child witnesses now have an automatic entitlement to use one or more of range of special measures. Adult witnesses continue to have a discretionary entitlement to their use only.

The special measures are:

- the taking of evidence by a commissioner;
- the use of a live television link;
- the use of a screen;
- the use of a supporter; and
- in criminal cases only, the giving of evidence in chief in the form of a prior statement.[96]

In criminal cases, the live television link or a screen used alone or in combination with the use of a supporter are known as standard special measures and, where the party citing the witness intimates to the court in a child witness notice that one of the standard special measures is considered to be the most appropriate to assist the child to give his other evidence, the court must authorise the use of that measure.[97] In civil cases, there is no class of standard special measures but the provisions presume that a child will make use of one or more special measures unless cause can be shown why he or she should not. If use of the live television link, screens or a supporter is applied for, they are deemed to be the appropriate measure and their use will be authorised.

2.31 The child can choose to give evidence without the assistance of special measures but in such cases the court must be satisfied on the basis of the notice that it is appropriate for him or her to do so before it may make an order authorising the giving of evidence without the benefit of any special measure. If the party citing the witness seeks authorisation for the use of any other special measure, this will be granted if the court is satisfied on the basis of the child witness notice that it is appropriate to do so.

In criminal cases in which a child witness of less than 12 years of age is to give evidence in a trial in respect of murder, culpable homicide, a sexual offence, an offence that involves an assault on or injury or threat of injury to another person, abduction or plagium the court must not make an order that requires the child witness to be in the courtroom or any part of the court building in which the courtroom is situated, unless the child wishes to be so present and the court is satisfied that it is appropriate for the child to be present, or the taking of the evidence without the child being present would give rise to a significant risk of fairness to the trial or otherwise to the interests of justice and that risk significantly outweighs any risk of prejudice to the interests of the child if the order is made.[98] In such cases the child is expected to give evidence by means of a live television link from a remote location or to a commissioner in advance of the trial. When evidence is given to a commissioner, the child gives evidence in chief to the pro-

[94] Vulnerable Witnesses (Scotland) Act 2004 ss.1 and 11; s.1 of the Vulnerable Witnesses (Scotland) Act 2004 amends s.271 of the Criminal Procedure (Scotland) Act 1995 by substituting new ss.271–271M for the previous version of s.271.
[95] Criminal Procedure (Scotland) Act 1995 s.271(2)(a)–(f).
[96] Criminal Procedure (Scotland) Act 1995 s.271 and Vulnerable Witnesses (Scotland) Act 2004 s.18.
[97] Criminal Procedure (Scotland) Act 1995 s.271A(5)(a)(i).
[98] Criminal Procedure (Scotland) Act 1995 s.271B.

secutor and cross-examined by the accused's defence agent. The testimony is video recorded and admitted as evidence at a suitable point in the trial. There are, as yet, very few remote sites across Scotland from which vulnerable witnesses can give evidence and by no means will every sheriff court district be equipped with such equipment.

The special measures

Standard special measures

Live television link

2.32 The witness gives evidence in real time during the trial from a different room within the court building by means of a live television link.[99] The witness sits in front of a television set equipped with cameras and microphones. The witness can usually see and hear the person who is speaking to him or her from the courtroom only. The witness cannot see the jury or the accused but all the parties in court can see and hear the witness. The person examining the witness can see the head of the witness on the television screen. The judge or sheriff has an additional view of the witness room and the supporter if one is present and controls all the television equipment.[100]

Screens

2.33 A screen is used to conceal the accused from the view of the witness while he or she gives evidence in open court in the course of the trial. The accused is able to see and hear the witness by means of a television camera, which relays the image of the witness while he or she testifies to a monitor situated in the dock. The screen is placed so as not to prevent the parties conducting or trying the case from seeing the accused and witness.[101]

Supporter

2.34 The role of the supporter is to provide a reassuring and supportive presence for a witness when giving evidence. The supporter may offer verbal support before and after the witness testifies, be a physical support by sitting close to the witness in the courtroom or in the live television link room, keep the witness company during adjournments. However, the supporter must not say or do anything that would influence the witness's evidence in any way.[102]

Other special measures

Taking evidence by a commissioner

2.35 A commissioner is appointed by the court. He or she presides over proceedings and decides on questions of admissibility of evidence. The vulnerable witness gives evidence in advance of the trial. The evidence is taken in chief and in cross, with any re-examination as required by the parties to the action. The evidence of the witness is video recorded and the recording is received in evidence at the subsequent trial. The accused or party to proceedings is not ordinarily permitted to be present in the room in which proceedings are taking place but he or she is entitled to see and hear what is taking place usually by means of a live television link.[103] Although a form of this measure had been available to child witnesses and adult vulnerable

---

[99] See *http://www.scotcourts.gov.uk/resources/courtroomtech* [Accessed July 7, 2008] for the list of courtrooms equipped with vulnerable witness technology and its extent.

[100] Scottish Executive, *Special Measures for Vulnerable Adult and Child Witnesses: A Guidance Pack* (2005), Ch.6.

[101] Scottish Executive, *Special Measures* (2005), Ch.5.

[102] Scottish Executive, *Special Measures* (2005), Ch.7.

[103] Scottish Executive, *Special Measures* (2005), Ch.9.

witnesses in solemn criminal proceedings since 1994 and 1997 respectively, it was never used.[104] While the reasons for this have never officially been made explicit, it was a measure that found little favour with judges and practitioners on grounds of its impracticability.[105]

A prior statement as evidence in chief

2.36 This measure applies in criminal cases only. As a general rule a prior statement could already be used as evidence in civil cases. A prior statement is one that is made, usually to the police, before the case is heard in court. The statement may be contained in a police officer's notebook, or may be a written statement taken by a police officer or the transcript of an interview conducted by the police and social workers. A prior statement may also be contained in a map, plan or drawing, photograph or soundtrack and can also be contained in a film. Where the contents of the statement are agreed the witness does not need to appear in court to give evidence. If it has not been agreed, the witness appears and is either placed on oath or admonished to tell the truth. The statement will then be introduced as evidence.[106] Thereafter the witness will be cross-examined. In many cases the witness will be entitled to the use of special measures while being cross-examined.

The High Court of Justiciary Practice Note (No.2 of 2005: Child witnesses: Discretionary powers) offers guidance to judges on the exercise of their discretionary powers in cases where children are to give evidence in criminal cases in open court without the use of any special measures, "to ensure, so far as is reasonably practicable, that the experience of giving evidence by all children under the age of 16 causes as little anxiety and distress to the child as possible in the circumstances".[107] It makes the following recommendations: removal of gowns and wigs by judges, counsel and solicitors; seating the child at a table in the well of the court, along with judge and lawyers, rather than in the witness box; and clearing the courtroom of all people who are not involved in the proceedings.[108] There is thus far, no such guidance where a child is a witness in civil proceedings.

The Scottish Government has made concerted efforts to provide vulnerable witnesses and their carers with information about the range of special measures available and how they operate. Illustrated booklets are available in age-appropriate language and are produced in translations into several languages. The Scottish Government's Victims and Witnesses Unit produces a quarterly newsletter entitled *Vital Voices* and has produced an information guide for practitioners explaining the key changes contained in the Vulnerable Witnesses (Scotland) Act 2004. It is intended to be a statement of good practice to enable a consistent approach to be taken to the use of special measures throughout Scotland.

Witnesses in criminal cases

2.37 A party may examine or cross-examine any witness.[109] While a spouse is always a competent witness for or against their spouse, he or she is never compellable.[110] It is not possible to object to any witness on the grounds of (a) conviction of or punishment for an offence; (b) interest; (c) agency or partial counsel; (d) the absence of due citation to attend the court; or (e) that the witness has been precognosced subsequent to the citation to attend.[111] An accused is always a

---

[104] Scottish Executive, *Towards a Just Conclusion Action Plan* (2000), para.5.3.2.

[105] K. Murray, *Live Television Link: An Evaluation of its Use by Child Witnesses in Scottish Criminal Trials* (Edinburgh: Scottish Office, 1995), para.11.10.

[106] Scottish Executive, *Special Measures* (2005), Ch.8.

[107] See *http://www.scotcourts.gov.uk/justiciary/practicenotes/pn02_2005.pdf* [Accessed July 7, 2008].

[108] *http://www.scotcourts.gov.uk/justiciary/practicenotes/pn02_2005.pdf* [Accessed July 7, 2008].

[109] Criminal Procedure (Scotland) Act 1995 s.263(1).

[110] Criminal Procedure (Scotland) Act 1995 s.264. The refusal to give evidence by a spouse cannot be commented upon by the prosecution: see subs.(3).

[111] Criminal Procedure (Scotland) Act 1995 s.265(1).

competent witness for the defence at any stage of the case.[112] Only the defence can call the accused as a witness.[113] While an accused can be asked questions that might incriminate him of the charges before the court,[114] he cannot be asked questions designed to show that he has been convicted of, or charged with, a prior offence unless:

- the proof that he has committed or been convicted of a prior offence is admissible evidence to show that he is guilty of the offence with which he is currently charged;
- the accused or his counsel or solicitor has asked questions of the witnesses for the prosecution with a view to establishing the accused's good character or impugning the character of the complainer, or the accused has given evidence of his own good character, or the nature of conduct of the defence is such as to involve imputations on the character of the complainer or of the witnesses for the prosecution or complainer; or
- the accused has given evidence against any other person charged in the same proceedings.[115]

A court shall not admit questioning or evidence which shows a complainer in sexual offences is not of good character in relation to sexual matters, or that she is a prostitute or an associate of prostitutes or has engaged in sexual behaviour which is not the subject matter of the charge.[116]

Witnesses are not usually permitted to sit in the court prior to the giving of their evidence though an application for permission to do so may be made to the court. Even where the witness has been present in court without the permission of the court and the consent of the parties, he may still give evidence provided the court is satisfied that it was not the result of criminal negligence or criminal intent, and that the witness has not been unduly instructed or influenced by what took place during his presence, or that injustice will not be done by his giving evidence.[117] Certified transcripts of police interviews with the accused may be received into evidence. Transcripts must be served on the accused who has the right to challenge the transcript or its accuracy.[118]

THE PERSONNEL OF SCOTS LAW

Solicitors and advocates

2.38 Lawyers in Scotland are grouped into two distinct branches of the legal profession. The largest grouping is solicitors. The other much smaller grouping is court specialists called "advocates". Solicitors are regulated by the Law Society of Scotland, while the governing body for advocates is the Faculty of Advocates.

Some solicitors who specialise in court matters train to become solicitor-advocates. These solicitors have extended rights of audience in the supreme courts of Scotland. Hitherto only advocates had the right to speak in the Court of Session, the House of Lords, the High Court of Justiciary and the Scottish Court of Criminal Appeal. Solicitors who have not less than five years' continuous experience of court work may apply to practise in the superior civil or criminal courts or both. They must first undergo an induction course, observe cases in appropriate court(s), attend (subject to certain exemptions) a training course in the work of the courts, and pass examinations on subjects related to practice in the superior courts.[119]

---

[112] Criminal Procedure (Scotland) Act 1995 s.266(1).
[113] Criminal Procedure (Scotland) Act 1995 s.266(2).
[114] Criminal Procedure (Scotland) Act 1995 s.266(3).
[115] Criminal Procedure (Scotland) Act 1995 s.266(4).
[116] Criminal Procedure (Scotland) Act 1995 s.274; although note there are some exceptions to this rule in s.275.
[117] Criminal Procedure (Scotland) Act 1995 s.267(1)–(2).
[118] Criminal Procedure (Scotland) Act 1995 s.277(1)–(2).
[119] See the Admission as a Solicitor with Extended Rights (Scotland) Rules 1992.

Advocates (sometimes known as counsel) are specialist court practitioners who may further specialise in particular areas of law. Advocates have access to the superior courts of Scotland, most importantly the Court of Session, High Court of Justiciary, the House of Lords and Judicial Committee of the Privy Council in London, and, in Luxembourg, to the Court of Justice of the European Communities. After about 10 to 15 years of successful practice they may apply through the Lord President to be appointed by the Queen to the Roll of the Queen's Counsel in Scotland. As a Q.C. or senior counsel, the advocate is entitled to require that he be accompanied by a junior to assist him in the conduct of a case. Solicitors, or more properly solicitors' practices, often provide a more generalist and complete service than the sole practitioner advocate. They attend to negotiations and business matters and tender advice. However it is increasingly the case that solicitors in the larger towns and cities are also specialising in particular areas of the law.

Judges

2.39 In the foregoing discussion on the Scottish court system several different judges were identified as acting in those courts. These were: the justice of the peace sitting in the district court; the sheriff sitting in civil and criminal matters; the Senators of the College of Justice sitting in the superior Scottish courts; and the Lords of Appeal in Ordinary sitting in the House of Lords in civil matters. All judicial appointments in Scotland are now made under the auspices of the Judicial Appointments Board, which was set up in 2002 to provide the First Minister with a list of candidates recommended for judicial appointment. All vacancies are now publicly advertised and all eligible applicants must be considered for the post against objective criteria.[120]

As indicated previously, the JP is not a legal practitioner but a lay person drawn from the community in which he serves. Solicitors or advocates of at least 10 years' standing are eligible to be appointed as sheriffs. As well as the numerous full-time appointments, there are a considerable number of part-time appointments to help ensure the operation of the many sheriff court activities. Sheriffs may hold office until they are 72 years of age.

Senior judicial appointments in Scotland are made by the Queen on the recommendation of the First Minister (usually after consultation with the Lord Advocate and the Secretary of State for Scotland). There are currently 32 Senators of the College of Justice. Those eligible for appointment are sheriffs, sheriffs principal who have held office for five years, and advocates and solicitor-advocates who have had extended rights of audience in the superior courts of Scotland for a period of five years. In reality all appointments to senior judicial office have been lawyers who have practised as advocates at a very senior level. It is often the case that judges have previously been Dean, or vice-Dean, of the Faculty of Advocates, Lord Advocate or a senior Advocate Depute. Judges at this level are granted the honorary title of "Lord" although they have no entitlement to sit in the House of Lords. All judges have the same rank; promotion to the Inner House is by way of selection from among the body of judges. The two most senior judicial appointments may be appointed direct to their office. Scottish appointees to the post of Lord of Appeal in Ordinary sitting in the House of Lords are invariably judges promoted from the Court of Session.

The Law Officers

2.40 There are two Law Officers for Scotland: the Lord Advocate and the Solicitor General for Scotland. The post of Advocate General for Scotland who is the Law Officer for Scotland in the UK Government and advises the UK Government on Scots law was created by the Scotland Act 1998. Since the establishment of the Scottish Parliament in 1999, the Lord Advocate and Solicitor General have been members of the Scottish Government.[121] The Lord Advocate

[120] See generally *http://www.judicialappointmentsscotland.gov.uk* [Accessed July 2, 2008].

[121] Scotland Act 1998 s.44(1)(c).

advises the Scottish Executive on all legal matters that affect the Executive and its actings and intended actings. He may also refer a Bill of the Scottish Parliament to the Judicial Committee of the Privy Council if there is concern that the Bill may not be within the legislative competence of the Scottish Parliament.[122] The principal duty of the Solicitor General is to assist the Lord Advocate who is head of the systems of prosecution and of the investigation of sudden, accidental and unexplained deaths in Scotland. Although the Lord Advocate has traditionally been a political appointee, he adopts a politically neutral approach in the exercise of his prosecutorial function.[123] The Law Officers may appear for the Crown in particularly important cases, but day-to-day business in the High Court both at first instance and at appeal is conducted by a team of Advocates Depute appointed for a fixed term from the ranks of senior or junior counsel or experienced Procurators Fiscal to act for the Crown as prosecutors.

The Procurator Fiscal

2.41 The Procurator Fiscal is a legally qualified civil servant and a member of Crown Office and the Procurator Fiscal Service ("COPFS"), which became a department of the Scottish Executive by virtue of the Scotland Act 1998.[124] COPFS is headed by the Lord Advocate and is the sole public authority that has responsibility for the investigation and prosecution of crime and the investigation of sudden deaths in Scotland. On appointment, the Procurator Fiscal is commissioned by the Lord Advocate to investigate and prosecute on his behalf those crimes committed in areas corresponding to the sheriff court district for which he or she is appointed. COPFS divides Scotland into 11 areas each of which has an Area Procurator Fiscal. The areas generally coincide with the boundaries of the eight Scottish police forces. However four areas, namely Argyll and Clyde, Ayrshire, Glasgow and Lanarkshire match the Strathclyde police force area. Within each area, there is a Procurator Fiscal for each of the 48 sheriff court districts in Scotland—although some Procurators Fiscal are appointed to cover more than one district. This is particularly so in rural areas. In larger offices the Procurator Fiscal is assisted by legally qualified staff civil servants known as Assistant Procurators Fiscal, Principal Deputes and Procurators Fiscal Deputes who also hold commissions from the Lord Advocate authorising them to carry out his work.

Public Defence Solicitor's Office ("PDSO")

2.42 The office of the Public Defence Solicitor was set up in 1998 covering the summary courts in Edinburgh.[125] Public defence solicitors are employed directly by the Legal Aid Board to provide criminal legal advice and assistance. There are now offices in Edinburgh, Glasgow, Inverness, Ayr, Dundee Falkirk and Kirkwall. Public defence solicitors now defend clients in all the criminal courts in Scotland.

Ombudsmen

Parliamentary Ombudsman

2.43 The first Ombudsman in the United Kingdom was the Parliamentary Commissioner for Administration ("PCA") set up in 1967. The PCA (also known as the Parliamentary Ombudsman[126]) deals with allegations of maladministration on the part of the Westminster Government in the exercise of its functions and to that extent the post continues to be of

---

[122] Scotland Act 1998 s.33.

[123] Although the Lord Advocate will be referred to here as "he", since 2006 the office has been held by Elish Angiolini Q.C., a solicitor and former senior prosecutor who held the post of Solicitor General between 2001 and 2006.

[124] For further information about the role of the Procurator Fiscal see *http://www.copfs.gov.uk* [Accessed July 2, 2008].

[125] See generally *http://www.pdso.org.uk/history.html* [Accessed July 2, 2008].

[126] See Ashton and Finch, *Administrative Law in Scotland* (1997), Ch.7.

significance in post-devolution Scotland. Complaints of maladministration in respect of devolved matters are now the responsibility of the Scottish Public Services Ombudsman. Maladministration includes bias, neglect, inattention, delay, incompetence, ineptitude, perversity, turpitude and arbitrariness.[127] The definition is intended to be wide. It does not allow challenge to a decision that the complainant believes to be wrong on its merits, but rather is more concerned in how that decision was reached and the procedural methodology.

The Scottish Public Services Ombudsman

2.44 The office of Scottish Public Services Ombudsman ("SPSO")[128] was created by the Scottish Public Services Ombudsman Act 2002 ("SPSOA 2002"). The office replaced the previous posts of Scottish Parliamentary Commissioner for Administration (a role held by the PCA), Health Service Commissioner for Scotland, Local Government Ombudsman for Scotland and the Housing Association Ombudsman for Scotland. The Ombudsman also took over the investigation of complaints relating to mental health previously conducted by the Mental Welfare Commission and against Scottish Enterprise and Highlands and Islands Enterprise. The SPSO is appointed by the Queen on the recommendation of the Scottish Parliament. SPSOA 2002 sets out a uniform set of procedures for the investigation of complaints. Those organisations that the Ombudsman is empowered to investigate are set out in detail in Pts 1 and 2 of Sch.2 to SPSOA 2002. These include most organisations providing public services in Scotland including local authorities, the National Health Service, registered landlords, police boards, colleges and universities. The SPSO has the power to investigate complaints from members of the public or where requested to do so by a listed authority.[129] The SPSO may accept complaints direct from members of the public. The aggrieved person may make the complaint him or herself or may instruct another to do so for him. If a deceased person suffered maladministration before his or her death, the legal representatives of the person may make a complaint. The Ombudsman may investigate if a member of the public claims to have suffered injustice or hardship in consequence of maladministration.[130] "Service failures" may also be investigated but not where they are attributed to a family health service provider or a registered social landlord.[131] Complaints are usually only considered once the complaints procedure for the organisation in question has been exhausted. In most cases, complaints must be made within 12 months of the aggrieved person first having notice of the maladministration.[132]

2.45 The SPSO is not permitted to investigate, inter alia, complaints arising from actions taken in the investigation or prevention of crime by the police or a member of the Scottish Government (usually the Crown Office and Procurator Fiscal Service), the commencement or conduct of proceedings before a court or tribunal, contractual and commercial transactions of listed authorities, issues relating to terms and conditions of employment or issues relating to rent or service charges.[133] The Ombudsman may decline to investigate a complaint and cannot be compelled to investigate.[134] The most common reasons for declining to investigate are that the complaint concerns a matter or an organisation that the Ombudsman cannot investigate or where the aggrieved person has not exhausted the complaints procedures of the organisation complained of. In such circumstances, a statement of the decision and the reasons for it must be sent to the aggrieved person and the authority allegedly responsible for the maladministration.[135] The Ombudsman must give the organisation complained of the opportunity to comment

---

[127] See Ashton and Finch, *Administrative Law in Scotland* (1997), pp.173–175.
[128] See generally the Scottish Public Services Ombudsman Act 2002 and *http://www.spso.gov.uk* [Accessed July 2, 2008].
[129] SPSOA 2002 s.2.
[130] SPSOA 2002 s.5.
[131] SPSOA 2002 s.5(2).
[132] SPSOA 2002 s.10(1).
[133] SPSOA 2002 s.8 and Sch.4 for a complete list of excluded matters.
[134] SPSOA 2002 s.11.
[135] SPSOA 2002 s.11(2).

on the substance of the complaint.[136] Where an investigation takes place, SPSOA 2002 s.13 gives the SPSO the power to require any member, officer or member of staff of an authority or any other person who in her opinion is able to do so, to supply information or produce documents pertaining to the investigation. The section grants the Ombudsman the same powers of the Court of Session to require attendance and examination of witnesses and the production of documents. She cannot insist on the production of Scottish and UK Cabinet documents. Investigations are held in private.[137] At the conclusion of the investigation, the draft or "proposed" report is submitted to the aggrieved person and the organisation complained of for comments. Copies of the final "investigation report" are sent to the parties to the complaint and laid before the Scottish Parliament.[138] Where it appears to the Ombudsman that the aggrieved person has suffered injustice or hardship that has not been and is unlikely to be remedied, she may make a special report which is laid before the Scottish Parliament and copied to those who were sent the investigation report.[139] Special reports are intended to persuade the authority complained of to act upon the recommendations in the investigation report. The Ombudsman must also lay an annual general report on the performance of the functions of the Office before the Scottish Parliament.[140]

JUDICIAL REVIEW

2.46 The growth in the power and influence of government in the everyday lives of citizens has given rise to broadening concern. The court procedure by which citizens can legally challenge decisions of government or other public bodies is known as judicial review. Judicial review in Scotland is only possible in the Court of Session. Judicial review exists not to challenge the merits of government decisions, but rather to ensure that such decisions are made fairly, in conformity with the law, and within the powers of the authority making them.

Decisions of public authorities can be challenged on the basis that the authority has exceeded the power granted to it. This is known as acting ultra vires (outwith its powers). There are of course many instances where a public authority is entrusted with a duty. Many of the social work statutes confer such duties. The failure to fulfil a duty may result in a legal challenge to the authority, and it is possible that a court order compelling compliance with that duty may be sought. Under the Court of Session Act 1988, the Court of Session may order the specific performance of a statutory duty on such conditions and penalties as seem fit where the duty is not complied with.[141] The duty must be specific and unequivocal.[142] It is a remedy of last resort after other avenues have been exhausted.[143] Moreover, the exercise of powers and duties often requires the exercise of discretion. Judicial review can be used to legally challenge the exercise of discretion on the basis that it has exceeded the legal power of the person or body exercising that legal discretion. In addition there will often be challenges on the basis of procedural impropriety.

Under the common law, there is a right to seek judicial review of a decision of a public authority. This right exists whether a statute confers a right of appeal or not. Judicial review

---

[136] SPSOA 2002 s.11(2).
[137] SPSOA 2002 s.12.
[138] SPSOA 2002 s.15.
[139] SPSOA 2002 s.16.
[140] SPSOA 2002 s.17.
[141] Court of Session Act 1988 s.45(b).
[142] Ashton and Finch, *Administrative Law in Scotland* (1997), pp.220–221
[143] Ashton and Finch, *Administrative Law in Scotland* (1997), p.224; *O'Neill v Scottish Joint Negotiating Committee for Teaching Staff*, 1987 S.L.T. 648; *Strathclyde Buses Ltd v Strathclyde RC*, 1994 S.L.T. 724.

may be used to review the decisions of public authorities, voluntary organisations and some private bodies.[144] All decisions, acts and omissions of public authorities are potentially reviewable.[145]

2.47 Social work and housing services are likely subjects of judicial review cases where the member of the public is generally dissatisfied with his treatment at the hands of the public authority. The importance of judicial review in this regard cannot be overstated. The difficulty of accessing delictual remedies for a breach of statutory duty by a local authority (discussed in Ch.10) make judicial review often the major avenue of judicial redress for those dissatisfied with the way in which the local authority has carried out its functions.

The remedies available to a person or body seeking judicial review are relatively limited.[146] One can obtain a declarator[147] setting out one's rights or the duties of the authority; an order of reduction[148] cancelling the authority's decision; an interdict[149]; an order of specific performance[150]; damages[151]; and any other specific statutory remedy. Often the main remedy of reduction simply puts the person seeking judicial review back in the position he was in before the authority made the decision. So, for example, someone successfully winning a case against the allocation decision of a housing authority may not be allocated a house, but simply have the council's original decision not to allocate reduced. The local authority may subsequently reconsider the applicant's case, follow a correct procedure, and still not allocate. Furthermore, the court has discretion as to whether to grant a reduction. Therefore, even if the applicant proves the case against the authority, the court may refuse to grant a remedy if it is of the opinion that it would not lead to a change in the decision.[152]

NON-LEGAL AND NON-FORMAL REMEDIES/ADVICE

2.48 As an adviser, advocate or facilitator for the social work client, the social work professional will often need to enlist the advice and assistance of others for the benefit of their client. It is a fact that first resort to legal remedies may be neither appropriate nor particularly helpful. This is not to minimise the importance of the law, or the mechanisms that exist for enforcing legal rights. These can be powerful in the correct situation, and indeed may be the only resort in many cases. There exist, however, many agencies and avenues of advice and support that stop some way short of lawyers and the courts. In many instances these agencies can be more expert, more helpful and less expensive than enlisting the services of a lawyer and pursuing litigation. For example, there are a number of voluntary organisations that exist in a range of social work fields which provide valuable services and which can be the source of helpful advice and information. Consumer organisations such as Citizen's Advice Bureaux, Welfare Rights Organisations, and other groups for particular specialist client groups, may be the source of much help to the client and the professional alike. There are likewise a number of organisations that seek to assist the resolving of disputes by "alternative" means other than through the courts.[153]

---

[144] See J. Clyde, "The Nature of the Supervisory Jurisdiction and the Public/Private Distinction in Scots Administrative Law" in W. Finnie, C. Himsworth and D. Walker (eds), *Essays in Scots Law* (1991).

[145] V. Smith, "The Scope of Judicial Review Determined", 1997 Jur. Rev. 122; V. Smith, "Contract or Tripartite Arrangement—Rooney v. Chief Constable of Strathclyde Police", 1998 Jur. Rev. 193; Ashton and Finch, *Administrative Law in Scotland* (1997), p.243.

[146] See Ashton and Finch, *Administrative Law in Scotland* (1997), Ch.14.

[147] e.g. *Rossi v Edinburgh Magistrates* (1904) 7 F. (H.L.) 85; *Stirling CC v Falkirk Magistrates*, 1911 S.C. 1282; *Ayr Magistrates v Lord Advocate*, 1950 S.C. 102.

[148] e.g. *Smith v HM Advocate*, 1994 S.L.T. 1161 (partial reduction).

[149] e.g. *Deane v Lothian RC*, 1986 S.L.T. 22; *McColl v Strathclyde RC*, 1983 S.L.T. 616.

[150] *T Docherty Ltd v Monifieth Burgh Council*, 1970 S.C. 200.

[151] Only available in limited situations: see *Kelly v Monklands DC*, 1986 S.L.T. 169; *Ministry of Housing and Local Government v Sharp* [1970] 2 Q.B. 223.

[152] *King v East Ayrshire Council*, 1998 S.C. 182.

[153] See R. Mays and B. Clark, *Alternative Dispute Resolution in Scotland* (Scottish Office, 1996), Ch.2; B. Clark and R. Mays, "'Its Good to Talk': Community Mediation in Scotland", 1998 *The Police Journal* 4.

2.49 As many of the social and welfare services are provided by local and central government, the assistance of a councillor, MSP or MP may be of great importance. The elected representative holds considerable influence with officialdom and in any situation involving an exercise of discretion it is he more than any other person or agency who may have the capacity to influence matters to the benefit of the individual. Informal routes in general often yield better results than formal ones. The involvement of lawyers and ombudsmen can often instil rigidity in the exercise of discretion and in that way work against the interests of the client. It is difficult in a book of this nature to offer anything other than general advice. It will be a question of being aware of all the relevant avenues and making a value judgment as to the best course of action in the given circumstances but, as a basic premise, formality of complaint and formality of process does not necessarily secure the most expeditious and beneficial resolution to the problem at hand.

Chapter 3

Parents, Children, Family Relationships and the Law

3.01 As an integral feature of social work, practitioners must deal with people from a variety of backgrounds. Family history and family setting are often important issues in meeting a client's social work needs. Inevitably, a sound knowledge of the law relating to family life becomes a necessary supplement to the core knowledge of social work practice. Among the principal issues addressed in this Chapter are those that are deemed central to the functions of social workers on a daily basis—the formation of family relationships and the legal significance of those relationships, the key relationship between parent and child, and the obligations that arise from it.

Society has undergone major transformation in the past few years. Divorce is commonplace, single parentage has increased, cohabitation is widespread, civil partnership is now possible and there is remarriage and reconstitution of family in ever-increasing numbers. The law has also undergone substantial transformation to respond in part to the changing social circumstances. More than ever, the law is important to families and as a consequence the law that regulates, fashions and underpins family relationships is important to those who work with families in a social work capacity.

Marriage

3.02 The formation of the relationship of marriage in Scotland is primarily regulated by the Marriage (Scotland) Act 1977. All forms of irregular marriage are now abolished. Although marriage by cohabitation with habit and repute has been abolished[1] it may still be relevant if the parties started to cohabit prior to the coming into force of the Family Law (Scotland) Act 2006.[2] There are various restrictions on marriage. First, no one under 16 years of age may get married in Scotland.[3] Parental consent to marry is not necessary for young persons between 16 and 18.[4] Where either, or both, the parties to a marriage is/are under 16 the marriage is automatically void.[5] Certain parties stand in forbidden degrees of relationship to one another with the effect that any marriage between these parties is also void.[6] These relationships are all based upon consanguinity (blood relationship), affinity (through marriage) or adoption.

[1] Family Law (Scotland) Act 2006 s.3(1).

[2] See J. Thomson, *Family Law in Scotland*, 5th edn (Tottel, 2006), pp.20–25.

[3] Marriage (Scotland) Act 1977 ("1977 Act") s.1.

[4] See also Clive, "Parental Consent to Marry", 1968 S.L.T. (News) 129 for the pre-1977 position.

[5] 1977 Act s.1(2).

[6] 1977 Act s.2(1); see Sch.1 for a full list of the prohibited relationships; Ross, "Forbidden Degrees of Matrimony" (1987) 32 J.L.S.S. 20.

Relationships by consanguinity are relationships based on blood ties. A person cannot therefore marry family members closely related to them, e.g. their parents, grandparents, children, brothers and sisters. Relationships of the half blood are treated as relationships of the full blood.[7] Therefore a half sister and brother are prohibited from marrying in the same way as a full sister and brother could not marry. Anomalies exist as a result of the Human Fertilisation and Embryology Act 1990.[8]

Some relaxations were introduced by the Marriage (Prohibited Degrees of Relationship) Act 1986 so that certain parties who were once related by affinity can now marry provided they have:

- both attained the age of 21 at the time of the marriage; and
- the younger party has not at any time before attaining the age of 18 lived in the same house as the other party and has not been treated by the other party as a child of the family.[9]

Thus, for example, this relaxation might allow a woman to marry the former husband of her mother provided they satisfy the conditions laid down in the statute.

There is no congruity between the relationships of incest, for which there is criminal liability, and the forbidden degrees of marriage.[10] In some situations it is lawful to have sexual intercourse with a person who nevertheless one is forbidden to marry. Moreover, as forbidden relationships of affinity arise through marriage, no restrictions apply to partners of former cohabitees. It is not altogether certain why particular relations are prohibited from marrying each other. Principally, theories centre around two themes—genetic issues, and social and policy considerations. The latter must now be considered the predominant theme.

The prohibitions by adoption mean that a person cannot marry their adoptive parent, former adoptive parent, adoptive child or former adoptive child. Although an adopted child terminates his relationship with his genetic parents once adopted, this does not apply to determining the forbidden degrees of consanguinity and affinity by marriage.[11]

3.03 Scots law does not recognise same sex marriage[12] although same sex couples may enter into a civil partnership, which gives the parties rights similar to those acquired by marriage.[13] The Gender Recognition Act 2004 has allowed parties who have undergone gender realignment surgery to legally change their sex. So someone born a man who successfully undergoes a sex change operation can apply for a gender recognition certificate and, if the certificate is granted, would be able legally to marry as a woman. A person must be 18[14] or over, living in the other gender[15] and application is to the Gender Recognition Panel.[16] The Panel must grant the application if satisfied the applicant has or had gender dysporia; has lived in the acquired gender for two years; intends to live in the acquired gender until death and the necessary medical reports confirms this.[17] If the applicant is married an interim gender certificate will be issued.[18] Once such an applicant is divorced then a full certificate will be issued.[19]

Another major impediment to marriage is that persons who are already married may not

---

[7] 1977 Act s.2(2)(a).

[8] By ss.27 and 29 of the Human Fertilisation and Embryology Act 1990, where an egg or embryo is placed in a woman, she is treated as the child's mother and the genetic mother is not. So a child is prohibited from marrying his birth mother by s.2(1) of the 1977 Act yet is free to marry his genetic mother.

[9] 1977 Act s.2(1A), as inserted by the Marriage (Prohibited Degrees of Relationship) Act 1986 Sch.2 para.2(b).

[10] See Norrie, "Incest and Forbidden Degrees of Marriage in Scots Law" (1992) 37 J.L.S.S. 216.

[11] Adoption (Scotland) Act 1978 ss.39 and 41.

[12] 1977 Act s.5(4); *Corbett v Corbett* [1971] P. 83.

[13] See para.3.25 below.

[14] Gender Recognition Act 2004 s.1(1).

[15] Gender Recognition Act 2004 s.1(1)(a).

[16] Gender Recognition Act 2004 s.1(3).

[17] Gender Recognition Act 2004 s.2(1).

[18] Gender Recognition Act 2004 s.4(3).

[19] Gender Recognition Act 2004 s.5(1)(b).

enter into marriage until the prior subsisting marriage is dissolved.[20] Further, as marriage is a consensual agreement, it is the case that a number of matters which may indicate that consent was not truly given may impact on the validity of the marriage. These grounds can be variously stated as mental incapacity, intoxication, error or fraud, force and fear, or that the marriage is a sham. Mentally incapacitated people can marry but it is essential that they are capable of understanding the relationship of marriage and are capable of freely giving their consent.[21] If the party cannot understand the nature of the marriage and cannot consent to the marriage because of mental incapacity, then the marriage is void.[22] Attempts to have marriage dissolved on the basis that one or other of the parties was intoxicated so as to affect their consent must have a highly improbable prospect of success in the modern era.[23] The formal preliminaries to marriage will point towards an intention to be married, and with it there will be implicit consent notwithstanding the intoxication of one or both of the parties at the time of the ceremony. Similarly, error will only succeed as a basis of dissolution in the most unlikely of circumstances in respect of either the identity of the party to be married, or the nature of the ceremony.[24] One cannot seek to annul a marriage on the basis of error as to quality of the spouse.[25]

3.04 Altogether a more fertile ground of nullity is where the marriage is entered into under force and fear or where the marriage is a sham marriage. In respect of force and fear it must be shown that the consent of the party was genuinely overcome by the application of pressure inducing fear in that person.[26] A marriage entered into under duress is a void marriage.[27] In recent years in Scotland, there has been legal controversy over arranged marriages common in certain ethnic groups. It had been thought that simple parental pressure and disapproval might not be sufficient force and fear to invalidate the marriage. However, it now seems clear following the cases of *Mahmood*[28] and *Mahmud*[29] that the courts are prepared to consider whether the consent of the party was genuinely overcome by the force and fear induced by parental pressure and opprobrium. Arranged marriages per se are not invalid—they will only be so when the court considers that parental pressure has been forceful enough to overcome the party's true consent to be married.

Section 20A(4) of the Marriage (Scotland) Act 1977 effectively abolishes sham marriages.

Where a marriage is declared void the law presupposes that it was void from the beginning and treats it as though it did not take place at all. The normal route for a party wishing to annul their marriage would be to raise an action for declarator of nullity in the Court of Session or the sheriff court. Any party with an interest in having the marriage declared void may bring proceedings at any time. Where a marriage is declared null and void, the courts have the power to order financial settlement using a process similar to that which applies in divorce proceedings.[30] Fathers retain parental rights and responsibilities in respect of children born into the dissolved marriage (mothers automatically have them).[31] The status of children affected by a void marriage is unaffected, as the doctrine of illegitimacy is now abolished.[32]

There is one ground upon which a marriage is voidable as opposed to void, in other words legally valid until such times as it is challenged and subsequently declared void. This takes effect from the start of the marriage notwithstanding any delay in seeking a challenge. Where one of

[20] *Burke v Burke*, 1983 S.L.T. 331.
[21] *Long v Long*, 1950 S.L.T. (Notes) 32.
[22] 1977 Act s.20A(1) and (3).
[23] Contrast this with the dated case of *Johnston v Browne* (1823) 2 S. 495.
[24] 1977 Act s.20A(1), (4) and (5).
[25] *Lang v Lang*, 1921 S.C. 44.
[26] See *Buckland v Buckland* [1968] P. 296; *Mahmood v Mahmood*, 1993 S.L.T. 589; *Mahmud v Mahmud*, 1994 S.L.T. 599.
[27] 1977 Act s.20A(1).
[28] 1993 S.L.T. 589.
[29] 1994 S.L.T. 599.
[30] Family Law (Scotland) Act 1985 ("1985 Act") s.17(1).
[31] Children (Scotland) Act 1995 s.3(2).
[32] Law Reform (Parent and Child) (Scotland) 1986 s.1, as amended by the Family Law (Scotland) Act 2006.

the parties is incurably impotent a declarator can be sought to dissolve the marriage. Incurable impotency exists where one party is unable to have full and complete sexual intercourse with the other party and that incapacity is incurable.[33] The incurable impotency must have existed at the commencement of the marriage. A refusal to engage in sexual relations or the absence of procreative capacity will not be enough to make a marriage voidable, just as supervening impotency does not constitute a ground of nullity. A person may be personally barred from seeking a reduction in the marriage if he or she knew of their condition before the marriage and accepted it,[34] or where his or her actions were such that it would be inequitable to allow them to seek nullity. In situations where the party has acquiesced in artificial insemination of his wife, or adopted a child, there will be no prospect of the court granting a declarator of nullity.[35] It is possible for a party to found on their own incurable impotency.[36]

The legal consequences of marriage

3.05 While the social and legal significance of marriage is arguably diminishing there are nevertheless a number of important legal consequences that ensue from the relationship. Some consequences simply arise from cohabitation[37] but there are several consequences that are directly related to marriage. There is no longer a direct duty for a wife to reside with her husband where he chooses.[38] The obligation to stay impliedly arises from the law of divorce where irretrievable breakdown of marriage may be established by one year's non-cohabitation with consent of both parties, or two years' non-cohabitation without consent. There is also an implicit duty to be faithful to your spouse otherwise they may raise divorce proceedings on the grounds of adultery.[39]

An important legal consequences of marriage is a spouse's obligation to aliment the other during the subsistence of the marriage. Both husbands and wives owe the obligation of aliment to each other, i.e. to provide such support as is reasonable in the circumstances having regard to (a) the needs and resources of the parties; (b) the earning capacity of the parties; and (c) generally all the circumstances of the case.[40] No account should be taken of the conduct of the parties unless it is manifestly inequitable to leave it out.[41] Although unusual, it is possible for one spouse to raise an action for aliment against the other while living in the same house.[42] It will be a defence to a claim for aliment to prove that the obligation is already being fulfilled while the spouse is in the house and that this will continue in the future.[43] Indeed as a general defence, it might be proved that the defender has offered to maintain the claiming spouse in the defender's home in circumstances that it is reasonable to expect the spouse seeking aliment to accept.[44] It is possible to have awards of interim aliment and for variations of interim aliment where there is a material change in circumstances.[45] Parties may also by agreement reach a voluntary arrangement on the level of aliment.[46]

3.06 Another of the major legal consequences of marriage relates to rights in succession following the death of a spouse. Spouses have prior rights and legal rights. Under the Succession (Scot-

---

[33] *J v J*, 1978 S.L.T. 128; *M v M*, 1966 S.L.T. 152.
[34] *L v L*, 1931 S.C. 477.
[35] *AB v CB*, 1961 S.C. 347.
[36] *F v F*, 1945 S.C. 202.
[37] See para.3.22.
[38] Law Reform (Husband and Wife) (Scotland) Act 1984 ss.2 and 4; cf. *Stewart v Stewart*, 1959 S.L.T. (Notes) 70.
[39] See para.3.08 on divorce.
[40] 1985 Act s.4(1).
[41] 1985 Act s.4(3)(6).
[42] 1985 Act s.2(b).
[43] 1985 Act s.4(3)(b).
[44] 1985 Act s.2(6).
[45] See *Ritchie v Ritchie*, 1987 S.L.T. (Sh Ct) 7; *Neill v Neill*, 1987 (Sh Ct) 143; *Harper v Harper*, 1990 G.W.D. 40–2322; *Stenhouse v Stenhouse*, 1990 G.W.D. 28–1609; *Bisset v Bisset*, 1993 S.C.L.R. 284.
[46] 1985 Act s.7.

land) Act 1964 a spouse has "legal rights" over his or her spouse's estate irrespective of whether that spouse leaves a will. If there are children of the deceased a spouse is entitled to a third share of the moveable estate (basically everything that is not heritage). If there are no children then the surviving spouse is entitled to legal rights amounting to half of the moveable estate. In testate succession cases the provisions of the will are implemented insofar as they can be after the payment of legal rights to the spouse. Legal rights may be discharged by acceptance of the will's provisions or by agreeing to waive them during the lifetime of the deceased. Obviously, legal rights can be defeated by ensuring that one's estate comprises heritage alone or at least principally heritage.[47]

Where the deceased spouse leaves no will the surviving spouse may first claim prior rights.[48] This entitles the spouse to claim the dwelling house in which they were ordinarily resident prior to death up to a value of £300,000. Where the spouse leaves more than one house the surviving spouse may elect which home they will receive. In addition to the dwelling house the surviving spouse may claim furnishings and plenishings up to a value of £24,000 and money up to the value of £42,000 if the deceased has children, or £75,000 if there are no children.[49] Following the claiming of prior rights, the surviving spouse may then claim legal rights as discussed above. The remainder of the estate will then be distributed in line with the normal rules of succession.

There are specific legal provisions surrounding the ownership of property that pertains to married persons. Generally speaking property, other than matrimonial property, owned by a married person is separately owned.[50] Accordingly, property acquired before marriage or in some instances during it will belong to a particular spouse. Savings from housekeeping are shared equally between spouses, as is anything purchased from those savings.[51]

There are special rules on competence and compellability of witnesses where one spouse is a witness against the other in criminal proceedings.[52] Husbands and wives are always competent but never compellable. One spouse may sue the other in a civil action.[53] Other than matrimonial proceedings, there are a number of possible matters where a dispute might ensue. A delictual claim is most likely. A spouse also has the right to sue a third party in circumstances where the injury or death of their spouse is caused by that person or persons.[54] The spouse may sue where appropriate for loss of society, loss of support, funeral expenses and medical expenses. A spouse may also sue for recovery in respect of loss of services.[55]

SEPARATION AND DIVORCE

3.07 It is an accepted fact that some relationships may come to an end. Where once marriage was viewed as a relationship for life, it has come to pass that frequently marriage like other relationships terminates. The modern era is one characterised by high divorce rates.[56] In consequence the law has had to respond not only to regulate the termination of the relationship of marriage but also to regulate the various affairs of the separating spouses. As a prelude to divorce, it is common for separating spouses to regulate their various affairs by way of a separation agreement. It will often be the case that in reaching agreement the spouses ensure a relatively straightforward passage when they come to seek divorce. Others will wish to press for divorce almost immediately the relationship has failed.

---

[47] The Scottish Law Commission has called for legal rights to apply to heritable property as well as moveable. See *Report on Succession*, Scot. Law Com. No.124 (1990).

[48] Succession (Scotland) Act 1964 s.8.

[49] For current levels of prior rights see the Prior Rights of Surviving Spouse (Scotland) Order 2005 (SI 2005/252).

[50] 1985 Act s.24; *Maclure v Maclure*, 1911 S.C. 200; *Millar v Millar*, 1940 S.C. 56; see also 1985 Act s.25.

[51] 1985 Act s.26; *Pyatt v Pyatt*, 1966 S.L.T. (Notes) 73.

[52] Criminal Procedure (Scotland) Act 1995 s.264.

[53] Law Reform (Husband and Wife) Act 1962 s.2.

[54] Damages (Scotland) Act 1976 s.1.

[55] Administration of Justice Act 1982 ss.7–9.

[56] See Scottish Office Report, *Untying the Knot—Characteristics of Divorce in Scotland* (1993).

Divorce

3.08 Divorce will be granted in Scotland if (a) the marriage has broken down irretrievably; or (b) an interim gender recognition certificate under the Gender Recognition Act 2004 has, after the date of the marriage, been issued to either party to the marriage.[57]

Whether or not the marriage has broken down irretrievably will be determined by reference to four grounds[58]—adultery, behaviour, one year's non-cohabitation with both parties consenting to the divorce, or two years' non-cohabitation without consent. The courts do not insist on attempts to conciliate to prove that the marriage has irretrievably broken down and there is no obligation on the parties to attempt to salvage the marriage. All they must do is establish one of the "fault grounds" to ascertain that the marriage has irretrievably broken down.

Adultery is voluntary sexual intercourse by a married person with a person of the opposite sex where that person is not their spouse. A single act of sexual intercourse is sufficient to constitute adultery. Pre-marital sexual relations cannot constitute adultery, nor can involuntary sexual relations amount to adultery.[59] For adultery to take place there must be penetration of the female sexual organ by the male sexual organ. Accordingly, other forms of sexual relations—e.g. oral sex or anal sex—do not amount to adultery. Artificial insemination is likewise not adultery.[60]

A party may invoke two defences to an action for adultery although they are rarely pled. Condonation is applied where the spouse argues that the other forgave the adultery and resumed marital relations in the full knowledge of that indiscretion.[61] Equally, it will be a defence to show that the spouse seeking a divorce on the grounds of adultery actually encouraged or induced the defender to commit adultery.[62] This is known as *lenocinium*.[63]

3.09 A person may obtain a divorce on the basis that their spouse's behaviour since the marriage has been so bad that they cannot reasonably be expected to remain with them. Nearly a quarter of all divorce actions proceed on this basis.[64] The behaviour may be active or passive and may or may not be a result of mental abnormality.[65] Only behaviour since the date of marriage is relevant. One solitary instance of behaviour may be sufficient depending on its nature.[66] Behaviour is very widely construed and embraces a whole range of scenarios.[67] Each case will turn on its own merits. Obviously violence, abuse or cruelty are examples of unreasonable behaviour, as are certain sexual improprieties stopping short of adultery.

The third basis of establishing irretrievable breakdown of marriage is that the parties have not cohabited for one year and both consent to the divorce.[68] It is not important why the parties are not living together.[69] It is possible that parties may coexist in close proximity (even in the same house) and not be cohabiting as man and wife.[70] However, the mere absence of sexual relations does not amount to non-cohabitation. The non-cohabitation must be for a continuous period of one year. In recognition of the fact that parties may attempt to reconcile, the law determines that resumption of cohabitation for periods not exceeding six months do not break the con-

---

[57] Divorce (Scotland) Act 1976 s.1(1), as amended.
[58] Divorce (Scotland) Act 1976 s.1(2).
[59] *Stewart v Stewart*, 1914 2 S.L.T. 310 (rape); see also *Hunter v Hunter* (1900) 2 F. 771.
[60] *MacLennan v MacLennan*, 1958 S.C. 105.
[61] Divorce (Scotland) Act 1976 s.1(3). This subsection must be read with s.2(2) which stipulates a minimum period of cohabitation.
[62] *Gallacher v Gallacher*, 1928 S.C. 586; cf. *Thomson v Thomson*, 1908 S.C. 179. See Divorce (Scotland) Act 1976 s.1(3).
[63] See Thomson, *Family Law in Scotland* (2006), pp.132–134.
[64] See Scottish Office Report, *Untying the Knot* (1993).
[65] Divorce (Scotland) Act 1976 s.1(2)(b).
[66] See *Gray v Gray*, 1991 G.W.D. 8–477.
[67] See *Knox v Knox*, 1993 S.C.L.R. 381; *Findlay v Findlay*, 1991 S.L.T. 457; *White v White*, 1966 S.L.T. 288; *Stewart v Stewart*, 1987 S.L.T. (Sh Ct) 48.
[68] Divorce (Scotland) Act 1976 s.1(2)(d), as amended by the Family Law (Scotland) Act 2006.
[69] There is a suggestion in England that the parties must have the intention to be apart. See *Santos v Santos* [1972] 2 All E.R. 246.
[70] Divorce (Scotland) Act 1976 s.13(2).

tinuity of the one-year period but also do not count as part of it.[71] The spouse being divorced must consent to the granting of decree. They may withhold their consent for any reason or no reason[72] Indeed, consent to divorce may be withdrawn at any time.

The final avenue for a party seeking to establish irretrievable breakdown is that the parties have not cohabited for a continuous period of two years after the date of the marriage and immediately prior to bringing the action for divorce.[73] The consent of the spouse being divorced is not required. Again the parties are allowed a six-month trial reconciliation period.

If the parties are to divorce under either of the non-cohabitation grounds they may use the simplified divorce procedure if certain criteria are met.[74] Among other factors, this procedure may only be used if there are no children under 16 and neither party is seeking financial awards.

Judicial separation

3.10 As an alternative to divorce, judicial separation remains an option for parties whose marriage is at an end. The grounds for obtaining a judicial separation are exactly the same as those for obtaining a divorce.[75] A party may obtain a judicial separation order and thereafter proceed to obtain a divorce. Parties judicially separating still have an obligation to aliment each other and cannot remarry. There remains the obligation of fidelity and behaviour.[76] A further consequence is that a husband loses any rights in succession to his wife's property acquired after the parties separated if she dies leaving no will.[77] There have been calls for judicial separation to be abolished on the basis that it is no longer necessary.[78]

Financial provision on divorce

3.11 Scots law contains some far-reaching provisions designed to regulate the redistribution of financial assets following divorce. The philosophy inherent in these provisions is that so far as possible when the parties divorce there should be a "clean break" settlement of the financial matters. Section 8(2) of the Family Law (Scotland) Act 1985 ("1985 Act") provides that the court shall make an order justified by the principles set out in s.9 of the 1985 Act and one that is "reasonable" having regard to the resources of the parties.[79]

Orders under the Family Law (Scotland) Act 1985

3.12 Section 8(1) of the 1985 Act permits a court to make various orders in respect of financial provision on divorce. Given the clean break philosophy of the legislation, the most common orders are for payment of a capital sum or for the transfer of property. Notwithstanding this, the court can order that a capital sum be paid in instalments. Moreover a capital transfer may be appropriate in addition, and not just as an alternative, to a property transfer order. Either order may be made at the date of divorce or at some other time specified by the court. It may also come into effect at a specified future date.[80]

In the event that the court is satisfied that it is not possible to cater for financial provision by way of a capital transfer order and/or a property transfer order, it may order the payment of a

---

[71] Divorce (Scotland) Act 1976 s.2(4).
[72] *Boyle v Boyle*, 1977 S.L.T. (Notes) 69; *Donnelly v Donnelly*, 1991 S.L.T. (Sh Ct) 9.
[73] Divorce (Scotland) Act 1976 s.1(2)(e), as amended by the Family Law (Scotland) Act 2006.
[74] Divorce Jurisdiction, Court Fees and Legal Aid (Scotland) Act 1983 s.2.
[75] Divorce (Scotland) Act 1976 s.4.
[76] See Clive, *Husband and Wife*, 3rd edn (1992), p.363.
[77] Conjugal Rights (Scotland) Amendment Act 1861 s.6.
[78] *Report on Family Law*, Scot. Law Com. No.135 (1992), para.12–19; Edwards and Griffiths, *Family Law*, 2nd edn (2006), p.511.
[79] *Crockett v Crockett*, 1992 S.C.L.R. 591.
[80] See generally 1985 Act s.12; *Little v Little*, 1990 S.L.T. 785.

periodical allowance.[81] As the name implies this is a regular payment. It may be for a definite period, an indefinite period or until a specified event.[82] A periodical allowance ends with the death of the person to whom it is being paid but not necessarily upon the death of the payer.[83]

In addition to these main orders there are a number of incidental orders at the disposal of the court.[84] These incidental orders operate in conjunction with an order for financial provision.[85] They may order the sale of the property, the valuation of property or a declarator of ownership of any property.[86] A court may also grant an order that regulates occupancy of the matrimonial home and the usage of furniture and plenishings within it.[87] Beside these powers there are a number of others specific to certain situations including an order that security be given for any financial provision.[88] It is fair to claim that the courts have a broad array of powers which ensure ultimate flexibility in dealing with the issue of financial provision on divorce.

Principles of financial provision on divorce

3.13 The key to determining financial provision on divorce lies in the s.9 principles. The first of those states that the net value of the matrimonial property should be shared fairly among the parties to the marriage.[89] Fair sharing is to be viewed as equal sharing unless special circumstances justify another approach.[90] Matrimonial property is defined as,

> "all the property belonging to the parties or either of them at the relevant date which was acquired by them or him (otherwise than by gift or succession from a third party)—
>
> (a) before the marriage for use by them as a family home or as furniture or plenishings for such a home; or
>
> (b) during the marriage but before the relevant date."[91]

The relevant date is the earlier of either the date the parties ceased to cohabit, or the date when a summons for divorce is served.[92] Some financial property acquired after the relevant date may nevertheless form part of the matrimonial property, for example, damages received after the relevant date but relating to an accident before that date.[93] Pensions and life policies are considered matrimonial property.[94] Similarly, a tax rebate received after the relevant date but relating to the period when the parties were together may also be matrimonial property.[95] Redundancy payments may in some circumstances also be considered matrimonial property.[96]

Many things are excluded from the calculation of matrimonial property. Property acquired before marriage and not intended for use as matrimonial property is not included. Something bought prior to the marriage but which subsequently becomes shared in the marriage may still be considered matrimonial property.[97] The real test appears to be whether the property has been bought for family use.[98] Some problems arise in respect of homes purchased prior to marriage

---

[81] 1985 Act s.13(2); *Mackin v Mackin*, 1991 S.L.T. (Sh Ct) 22 at 24, per Sh. Pr. Ireland.
[82] 1985 Act s.13(3); *Mitchell v Mitchell*, 1993 S.L.T. 426.
[83] 1985 Act s.13(7)(b).
[84] 1985 Act s.14.
[85] *MacClue v MacClue*, 1994 S.C.L.R. 933.
[86] 1985 Act s.14(2).
[87] 1985 Act s.14(2)(d); *Little v Little*, 1990 S.L.T. 785.
[88] 1985 Act s.14(2)(d); *Murley v Murley*, 1995 S.C.L.R. 1138.
[89] 1985 Act s.9(1)(a).
[90] 1985 Act s.10(1).
[91] 1985 Act s.10(4).
[92] 1985 Act s.10(3).
[93] *Skarpaas v Skarpaas*, 1991 S.L.T. (Sh Ct) 15; cf. *Petrie v Petrie*, 1988 S.C.L.R. 390.
[94] 1985 Act s.10(5) as amended by the Welfare Reform and Pensions Act 1999 s.34 and Sch.12 para.8(2). See discussion in Edwards and Griffiths, *Family Law* (2006), pp.461–467 regarding calculation of pensions apportionment.
[95] *MacRitchie v MacRitchie*, 1994 S.L.T. (Sh Ct) 72.
[96] *Tyrrell v Tyrrell*, 1990 S.C.L.R. 244; *Smith v Smith*, 1989 S.L.T. 668.
[97] See *Mitchell v Mitchell*, 1995 S.L.T. 426 at 426; *Buczynska v Buczynski*, 1989 S.L.T. 558.
[98] *Maclellan v Maclellan*, 1988 S.C.L.R. 399; cf. *Jacques v Jacques*, 1997 S.L.T. 459.

where the parties reside in that home during their marriage. If it can be shown that the original intention was not for use as a family home or indeed as that marriage's family home then the property will not be considered matrimonial property.[99] Section (9)(1)(a) specifically excludes property acquired during the marriage which has been inherited by or donated to one of the spouses. Gifts between spouses are not excluded. Where a gift prior to marriage is utilised to purchase a house in which the parties reside then it may be that the house will not be matrimonial property.[100] Where a gift or inheritance is sold and the proceeds used to purchase an asset then that asset can become matrimonial property.[101]

3.14 It is the net value of matrimonial property that must be divided fairly. Accordingly, any mortgage over heritable property must be deducted from the value. Outstanding debts as at the relevant date must be deducted.[102] Although the relevant date is normally considered to be the date of separation or the date of service of the summons in a divorce action, for the purposes of a property transfer order[103] the relevant date is the appropriate valuation date.[104] The appropriate valuation date is a date agreed on by the parties[105]; or if no such agreement is reached the date of making the order[106]; or such date as the court may determine.[107]

Deviation from the basic rule that there should be fair sharing is permitted under s.10(1), which provides that "special circumstances" may allow such deviation. Section 10(6) goes on to suggest several circumstances where deviation might be appropriate:

- the source of the funds or assets used to acquire any of the matrimonial property were not derived from the income or efforts of the parties during the marriage[108];
- where it seems appropriate, having regard to the nature of the matrimonial property, the use made of it (including use for business purposes or as a matrimonial home) and the extent to which it is reasonable to expect it to be realised or divided or used as security[109];
- where there has been any destruction, dissipation or alienation of property by either party[110];
- where there is any agreement between the parties on the ownership or division of the matrimonial property[111]; and
- where there is actual or prospective liability for any expenses of valuation or transfer of property in connection with the divorce.[112]

The matters specifically mentioned in s.10(6) are not designed to be exclusive. Other reasons can be entertained for a deviation from the fair sharing principle. However, one factor that may not be taken into account is the conduct of the parties unless it has had an impact on the financial assets.[113]

---

[99] See Edwards and Griffiths, *Family Law* (2006), pp.454–456; Meston, "Matrimonial Property and the Family Home", 1993 S.L.T. (News) 62; Kinloch, "Wife's Claims where Home not Matrimonial Property", 1996 Fam. L.B. 20–24.

[100] *Latter v Latter*, 1990 S.L.T. 805.

[101] *Jacques v Jacques*, 1995 S.L.T. 963.

[102] 1985 Act s.10(2)(a) and (b); *Jesner v Jesner*, 1992 S.L.T. 999; *Mackin v Mackin*, 1991 S.L.T. (Sh Ct) 22; cf. *McCormick v McCormick*, 1994 G.W.D. 35–2078.

[103] 1985 Act s.8(1)(aa).

[104] 1985 Act s.10(3A), as amended by the Family Law (Scotland) Act 2006.

[105] 1985 Act s.10(2A)(a), as amended by the Family Law (Scotland) Act 2006.

[106] 1985 Act s.10(2A)(b), as amended by the Family Law (Scotland) Act 2006.

[107] 1985 Act s.10(2B), as amended by the Family Law (Scotland) Act 2006.

[108] *Cordiner v Cordiner*, 2003 Fam. L.R. 39; *Kerrigan v Kerrigan*, 1988 S.C.L.R. 603; *Mukhtar v Mukhtar*, 2002 Fam. L.R. 607.

[109] *Skarpaas v Skarpaas*, 1993 S.L.T. 343; *Peacock v Peacock*, 1994 S.L.T. 40; *Geddes v Geddes*, 1993 S.L.T. 494; *Stephen v Stephen*, 1995 S.C.L.R. 175; *Bannon v Bannon*, 1993 S.L.T. 999.

[110] *Short v Short*, 1994 G.W.D. 21–1300; *Goldie v Goldie*, 1992 G.W.D. 21–1225; *Fraser v Fraser*, 1994 Fam. L.B. 10–3.

[111] See Thomson, *Family Law in Scotland* (2006), p.174.

[112] See e.g. *Farrell v Farrell*, 1990 S.C.L.R. 717; cf. *Adams v Adams (No.1)*, 1997 S.L.T. 144.

[113] 1985 Act s.11(7)(a).

3.15 The second of the s.9 principles states that,

> "fair account should be taken of any economic advantage derived by either party from contributions of the other, and of any economic disadvantage suffered by either party in the interests of the other party or of the family;"[114]

This provision is intended to ensure that where one spouse has stayed at home perhaps to look after children, they are not financially disadvantaged in the long term. In applying s.9(1)(b) the courts must take account of circumstances where:

> "(a) the economic advantages or disadvantages sustained by either party have been balanced by the economic advantages or disadvantages sustained by the other party, and
> (b) any resulting imbalance has been or will be corrected by a sharing of the matrimonial property or otherwise."

In other words if it can be shown that the fair sharing of the matrimonial assets will correct the imbalance no award will be made under this section.[115]

Section 9(1)(c) states that "any economic burden of caring, after divorce, for a child of the marriage under the age of 16 should be shared fairly between the parties". The court must consider the age and health of the child, the educational, financial and other circumstances of the child and the needs and resources of the parties.[116] In addition to this, account may be taken of any support provided by the defendant spouse to dependants.[117] Awards may be in the form of periodical payments and/or a lump sum or property transfer orders.[118] Awards under this section are somewhat less important following the advent of the Child Support Act 1991. That Act and the Agency it created, the Child Support Agency ("CSA"), are central to the award of financial support for children.[119] Their involvement in a case may operate to bar a financial award under s.9(1)(c).

Under s.9(1)(d) a spouse who is financially dependent on the other spouse to a substantial degree may be awarded such financial provision as is reasonable to allow him or her to adjust over a period not exceeding three years from the date of divorce. Under s.11(4) the court in considering an award must take into account the duration and extent of the dependency. It has been suggested that where a spouse is able to survive without support in the period from separation to divorce, this may prejudice an award under s.9(1)(d) on the basis that the spouse has shown themselves to be not substantially dependent on the other.[120] Payment under this heading is usually by way of a periodical allowance although a capital sum or property transfer are also competent.[121] The three-year period is designed to allow time for the dependent spouse to adjust perhaps by retraining. It is often the case that payments are for a much shorter duration than three years.[122]

3.16 Finally, s.9(1)(e) provides that a party who, at the time of divorce, seems likely to suffer serious financial hardship as a result of the divorce should be awarded such financial support as is reasonable to relieve his or her hardship over a reasonable period. This principle is likely to become effective only when the others are inappropriate. It is likely to be applicable where at the

---

[114] 1985 Act s.9(1)(b).

[115] See *Welsh v Welsh*, 1994 S.L.T. 828; *Petrie v Petrie*, 1988 S.C.L.R. 390; *De Winton v De Winton*, 1996 Fam. L.B. 23–6; cf. *Clokie v Clokie*, 1994 G.W.D. 3–149; *McCormick v McCormick*, 1994 G.W.D. 35–2078; *Coyle v Coyle*, 2004 Fam. L.R. 67; *Adams v Adams (No.1)*, 1997 S.L.T. 144; *Buchan v Buchan*, 2001 Fam. L.R. 48.

[116] 1985 Act s.11(3).

[117] 1985 Act s.11(6).

[118] 1985 Act s.13(2); *Morrison v Morrison*, 1989 S.C.L.R. 574; *Macdonald v Macdonald*, 1994 G.W.D. 7–404.

[119] See para.3.42 below.

[120] See Edwards and Griffiths, *Family Law* (2006), p.485; *Dever v Dever*, 1988 S.C.L.R. 352; *Millar v Millar*, 1990 S.C.L.R. 666.

[121] 1985 Act s.13(2)(a).

[122] *Muir v Muir*, 1989 S.L.T. (Sh Ct) 20; *Sheret v Sheret*, 1990 S.C.L.R. 799; *Sweeney v Sweeney*, 1993 S.L.T. (Sh Ct) 892.

time of divorce the spouse is old or so ill that he or she is unable to work.[123] Payment can be made by way of a periodical allowance if the court considers that a capital sum or property transfer order is inappropriate or insufficient. In making an order under this section again the courts must have regard to the age, health and earning capacity of the applicant, the duration of the marriage, the standard of living of the parties during the marriage, and the needs and resources of the parties, as well as all other circumstances of the case.[124] Account may be taken of any support a spouse is giving to another person. Conduct will only be taken into account where it affects the financial resources of the parties or when it is manifestly inequitable to leave it out. As Professor Thomson notes, resort to s.9(1)(e) should be very rare. It is likely that in a marriage of considerable duration the parties will have accumulated sufficient assets to enable an award under one or more of the other principles.[125] In some circumstances the conferment of an award under s.9(1)(e) may result in the diminution of benefits from other sources, for instance those received from the state, and as such there could not be said to be hardship from the divorce.[126]

THE MATRIMONIAL HOME AND DOMESTIC VIOLENCE

3.17 The significance of the "matrimonial" home cannot be overstated in family law matters. Not only is it likely to be the principal matrimonial asset, it is also the seat of most domestic matters. Nowhere is the importance of the home more vividly illustrated than in situations where the relationship is dysfunctional, and a feature or cause of that dysfunctionalism is violence by one spouse towards the other. The spouse who is the victim of such behaviour often has two stark choices—to leave and find alternative accommodation, or to have the violent spouse leave.[127] To leave may appear to be the simpler solution, but if there are children and no alternative accommodation, matters become extremely difficult. Moreover, it seems somewhat unjust for the violent spouse to remain in the family home while the victim is compelled to leave. It is with these thoughts in mind that, in the 1980s, the Matrimonial Homes (Family Protection) (Scotland) Act 1981 was introduced which had as its principal object the desire to regulate occupancy of the matrimonial home and to offer additional protection to those victims of domestic violence. It is a law that conflicts at several points with the ordinary law of property.

Matrimonial homes are either rented or owned. The modern trend is away from rental towards ownership.[128] Although the incidence is decreasing, it is not uncommon to find that title to the matrimonial home, or the tenancy agreement, is in the sole name of one spouse (usually the man). It is a basic tenet of property law that those with title have all the possessory rights of such property. Left unchallenged as a basic premise, it would mean that a spouse without title either in the title deeds or in the tenancy agreement would face severe hardship were a relationship to break up or become dysfunctional. He or she could simply be asked to leave the home. Alternatively, if they have nowhere to go, they may be compelled to remain in a violent environment. The Matrimonial Homes (Family Protection) (Scotland) Act 1981 ("1981 Act") among other things seeks to address these types of problems and dilemmas.

3.18 Under s.1(1) of the 1981 Act, where there is an entitled spouse, namely one who is the owner or tenant of the matrimonial home, and a non-entitled spouse (someone whose name is not on the title or tenancy agreement), the non-entitled spouse has the statutory right:

---

[123] *Johnstone v Johnstone*, 1990 S.C.L.R. 358; *Galloway v Galloway*, 2003 Fam. L.R. 10; *Haugan v Haugan*, 1996 S.L.T. 321; *MacKenzie v MacKenzie*, 1991 S.L.T. 461.

[124] See generally 1985 Act s.11.

[125] Thomson, *Family Law in Scotland* (2006), p.190; cf. *Bell v Bell*, 1988 S.C.L.R. 457.

[126] See *Barclay v Barclay*, 1991 S.C.L.R. 205.

[127] Arguably there is a third way of mediation but this is fraught with problems: see F. Raitt, "Ethics of Mediation in Abusive Relationships", 1997 Jur. Rev. 76.

[128] *Report on Matrimonial Property*, Scot. Law Com. No.86 (1984); see also Manners and Rauta, *Family Property in Scotland* (1981).

- if in occupation, to continue to occupy the matrimonial home;
- if not in occupation, to enter into and occupy the matrimonial home.[129]

These rights are exercisable with any child of the family.[130] It would clearly be nonsensical to have the right to occupy if it could in practice be defeated by denying any child the right to occupy with you.

"Matrimonial home" includes any house, caravan, houseboat or other structure that has been provided as or has become a family residence.[131] It is enough that it is intended to be used as a family home.[132] The rights of a non-entitled spouse commence as soon as the parties are married and a matrimonial home is acquired. Again, to facilitate the proper exercise of these statutory rights, a non-entitled spouse is authorised without needing the permission of the entitled spouse to pay any rent or mortgage, to carry out essential repairs and non-essential repairs approved by the court, or any other necessary step with a view to reasonable enjoyment of occupancy of the matrimonial home.[133]

Exclusion orders

3.19 An order may be sought under s.3 of the 1981 Act regulating the occupancy rights. However, of altogether more significance is the ability to have a spouse excluded from the matrimonial home under s.4 of the 1981 Act. An exclusion order can be sought by an entitled spouse[134] or a non-entitled spouse. Section 4(2) of the Act provides that the court,

> "shall make an exclusion order if it appears to the court that the making of the order is necessary for the protection of the applicant or any child of the family from any conduct or threatened or reasonably apprehended conduct of the non-applicant spouse which is or would be injurious to the physical or mental health of the applicant or child."

Section 4(3) goes on to state that notwithstanding the provisions of s.4(2), the court shall not make an order if it would be "unjustified or unreasonable" to do so having regard to all the circumstances of the case including the conduct of the spouses in relation to each other, the respective needs and financial resources of the spouses, the needs of any child of the family and the extent to which the matrimonial home is used in connection with a trade, business or profession, and whether the non-applicant spouse has made any suitable alternative offer of accommodation.[135] Exclusion, as one will have noted from the terminology of the statute, may be ordered even in circumstances where there is no physical violence, although in practice it will be easier to satisfy sheriffs of the necessity of the order where physical violence is evident.[136]

Although many exclusion order cases turn upon the concept of "necessity", it is clear that such a test does not require the spouse to be in the matrimonial home at the time of seeking an order.[137] It is also equally apparent that the test of "necessity" can be satisfied without first resorting to other remedies such as matrimonial interdicts to see if they work.[138] Nevertheless, a judge in determining a case must decide if a lesser remedy would be sufficient to protect the applicant or the children, and if it would not, the judge must establish his reasons why it would not.[139] The necessity test is a difficult one to satisfy. It is not simply a balance of convenience test

[129] Matrimonial Homes (Family Protection) (Scotland) Act 1981 ("1981 Act") s.1(1), as amended by the Law Reform (Miscellaneous Provisions) (Scotland) Act 1985 s.13(2).
[130] 1981 Act s.1(1A), added by the Law Reform (Miscellaneous Provisions) (Scotland) Act 1985 s.13(3).
[131] 1981 Act s.22.
[132] *O'Neill v O'Neill*, 1987 S.L.T. (Sh Ct) 26.
[133] 1981 Act s.2(1).
[134] See e.g. *Brown v Brown*, 1985 S.L.T. 376; *Millar v Millar*, 1991 S.C.L.R. 649.
[135] 1981 Act s.3(3) for details of the factors to be considered.
[136] *Anderson v Anderson*, 1993 Fam. L.B. 6–4.
[137] See *Colagiacomo v Colagiacomo*, 1983 S.L.T. 559; *Armour v Anderson*, 1994 S.L.T. (Sh Ct) 14; cf. *Bell v Bell*, 1983 S.L.T. 224; *Smith v Smith*, 1983 S.L.T. 275; *Ward v Ward*, 1983 S.L.T. 472.
[138] *Roberton v Roberton*, 1999 S.L.T. 38; *Brown v Brown*, 1985 S.L.T. 376.
[139] *McCafferty v McCafferty*, 1986 S.L.T. 650.

in the same way that interdicts are.[140] It is possible to obtain an exclusion order on the basis that the non-applicant's conduct is injurious to the mental health of the applicant or child, but not simply that the applicant is distressed about the breakdown of the marriage.[141] In *Roberton v Roberton*[142] it was held that the sheriff was entitled to take a particular view of the applicant's mental health and to reject that it related solely to the breakdown of the marriage. Although the twofold test is slightly confused, it is hard to imagine there will be many situations where the exclusion is thought necessary for the protection of the spouse or child, and it is then refused on the ground that it is unreasonable or unjustified.[143]

Rather helpfully, Lord Dunpark offered a four-question test in the case of *McCafferty v McCafferty*, which he said should be applied in all exclusion order applications.[144] He claimed one should ask the following questions:

(1) What is the nature and the quality of the alleged conduct?
(2) Is the court satisfied that the conduct is likely to be repeated if cohabitation continues?
(3) Has the conduct been or, if repeated, would it be injurious to the physical or mental health of the applicant or to any child of the family?
(4) If so, is the order sought necessary for the future protection of the physical or mental health of the applicant or spouse?

Matrimonial interdicts

3.20 A further avenue of protection for the victim of domestic violence is the matrimonial interdict. Such interdicts are available even where the spouses are living together. Interdicts may be sought from the sheriff court or the Court of Session. A matrimonial interdict (including an interim interdict):

"(a) restrains or prohibits any conduct of one spouse towards the other spouse or a child of the family; or
(b) subject to subsection (3), prohibits a spouse from entering or remaining in—

(i) a matrimonial home;
(ii) any other residence occupied by the applicant spouse;
(iii) any place of work of the applicant spouse;
(iv) any school attended by a child in the permanent or temporary care of the applicant spouse."[145]

It is important in framing interdict writs that the conduct to be restrained is not too widely defined.[146] It is not possible for a non-entitled spouse to seek to use a matrimonial interdict to exclude the entitled spouse from the matrimonial home.[147] It is however possible for an entitled spouse to use it as a remedy against a non-entitled spouse, but this may be countered with an application to have occupancy rights declared and enforced.

Matrimonial interdicts seek to regulate the conduct of one spouse towards the other. If a matrimonial interdict is made ancillary to an exclusion order the court must attach a power of arrest if the applicant requests this.[148] If a matrimonial interdict is not ancillary to an exclusion order, i.e. a non-molestation interdict, the court must attach a power of arrest if it believes it is necessary to do so to prevent the interdict being breached.[149]

---

[140] *Smith v Smith*, 1983 S.L.T. 275; *Hampsey v Hampsey*, 1988 G.W.D. 24–1035; *Millar v Millar*, 1991 S.C.L.R. 649.
[141] *Matheson v Matheson*, 1986 S.L.T. (Sh Ct) 2.
[142] 1999 S.L.T. 38.
[143] *Brown v Brown*, 1985 S.L.T. 376, per Lord Dunpark at 378; *Millar v Millar*, 1991 S.C.L.R. 649 at 651.
[144] *McCafferty v McCafferty*, 1986 S.L.T. 650.
[145] 1981 Act s.14(2), as amended by the Family Law (Scotland) Act 2006 s.10.
[146] *Murdoch v Murdoch*, 1973 S.L.T. (Notes) 13.
[147] *Tattersall v Tattersall*, 1983 S.L.T. 506; the proper route is to seek occupancy rights and an exclusion order.
[148] Protection from Abuse (Scotland) Act 2001 s.1(1A).
[149] Protection from Abuse (Scotland) Act 2001 s.1(2).

The interdict with power of arrest must be served on the person to be effective,[150] and the police must be notified of the power of arrest.[151]The police have a discretionary power to arrest and detain the person believed to have breached the interdict.[152] The police can arrest someone without warrant if they have reasonable cause to suspect that a breach of interdict has occurred and that if the person is not arrested he will continue to abuse.[153] If a person is arrested they must be informed immediately of the reason for the arrest and taken to a police station.[154] At the police station the person may be charged with an offence or brought before a court.[155] Once a person appears in court, he may be detained for a further period of up to two days.[156]

Anyone subject to violence or harassment may ask the court for a non-harassment order[157] under the Protection from Harassment Act 1997. It is possible to obtain an interdict and interim interdict[158] under this Act and the court may award damages.[159] Sanctions will be imposed for breach of the non-harassment order.

Other protection

3.21 The other protections contained in the 1981 Act concern provisions designed to ensure that the intention of the Act is not defeated by the non-applicant spouse "dealing" in the property. The occupancy rights of a non-entitled spouse are not defeated by the entitled spouse dealing in the matrimonial property.[160] Dealings include the sale or lease of the property, or the grant of a security over it. This is not to say that an entitled spouse cannot deal in the property, only that if they do, the non-entitled spouse still has occupancy rights. A purchaser is not entitled to occupy the property while the spouse is in the matrimonial home with occupancy rights over it, or part of it. A non-entitled spouse may renounce their occupancy rights in writing as long as the renunciation is before a notary public and is done freely without any coercion whatsoever.[161] As an alternative, the non-entitled spouse may consent to the dealing and this will have the effect of ending occupancy rights.[162] Where the court believes that the non-entitled spouse is refusing unreasonably to consent it may dispense with that consent.[163] The 1981 Act recognises two situations where consent is unreasonably being withheld. First, where the entitled spouse has been led to believe that the consent would be forthcoming and there has been no change of circumstances which would prejudice the non-entitled spouse. Secondly, where the entitled spouse has taken all reasonable steps to obtain the consent but has been unable to obtain an answer to a request for consent.[164]

If the parties do not cohabit for a continuous period of two years during which the non-entitled spouse does not occupy the matrimonial home, then the statutory rights come to an end.[165] In practice though, the most common exemptions are to be found in s.6(3)(e), which states that occupancy rights are not enforceable against a third party where:

> "the dealing comprises a transfer for value to a third party who has acted in good faith if there is produced to the third party by the transferor—

---

[150] Protection from Abuse (Scotland) Act 2001 s.2.
[151] Protection from Abuse (Scotland) Act 2001 s.3.
[152] Protection from Abuse (Scotland) Act 2001 s.4.
[153] Protection from Abuse (Scotland) Act 2001 s.4(1)(a).
[154] Protection from Abuse (Scotland) Act 2001 s.4(2).
[155] Protection from Abuse (Scotland) Act 2001 s.4(2).
[156] Protection from Abuse (Scotland) Act 2001 s.5(4).
[157] Protection from Harassment Act 1997 ("1997 Act") s.8(5)(b)(ii).
[158] 1997 Act s.8(5)(b)(i).
[159] 1997 Act s.8(5)(a).
[160] 1981 Act s.6(1).
[161] 1981 Act s.1(5) and (6).
[162] 1981 Act s.6(3)(a)(i).
[163] 1981 Act s.7.
[164] 1981 Act s.7(2).
[165] 1981 Act s.1(7) as inserted by the Family Law (Scotland) Act 2006 s.5.

(i) a written declaration signed by the transferor, or a person acting on behalf of the transferor under a power of attorney or as a guardian (within the meaning of the Adults with Incapacity (Scotland) Act 2000), that the subjects of the transfer are not, or were not at the time of the dealing a matrimonial home in relation to which a spouse of the transferor has or had occupancy rights; or

(ii) a renunciation of occupancy rights or consent to the dealing which bears to have been properly made or given by the non-entitled spouse or a person acting on behalf of the non-entitled spouse under a power of attorney or as a guardian (within the meaning of the Adults with Incapacity (Scotland) Act 2000)."[166]

If the affidavit declaration turns out to be false the non-entitled spouse's only remedy is a court action against the entitled spouse.[167]

If the property is owned in common by the spouses, either may bring an action for division and sale of the property. Section 19 allows the court discretion in granting decree if the property is a matrimonial home. After considering all the factors in s.3(3) and considering whether the applicant has offered to make available to the defender suitable alternative accommodation, the court may refuse decree[168]; postpone decree[169] or grant decree subject to conditions.

Where the spouses occupy their matrimonial home by virtue of a tenancy agreement it is possible for a non-entitled spouse, or an entitled spouse holding the tenancy in common with the other spouse, to seek a court order transferring the tenancy to their sole name paying just and reasonable compensation.[170] The landlord must be notified and may be conjoined in the legal proceedings. Even in situations where an entitled spouse ceases to occupy a tenanted property, the non-entitled spouse who remains in the home still enjoys the protection of the Rent (Scotland) Act 1984 (which among other things prevents harassment by a landlord and permits eviction only if authorised by a court order).[171]

COHABITATION

3.22 The Family Law (Scotland) Act 2006 ("2006 Act") gives cohabitees limited legal rights. For the purposes of the 2006 Act, a cohabitant means different sex couples[172] and same sex cohabitants living together as if they were civil partners.[173] In deciding if a couple are indeed cohabitants, the court will look at:

- the length of period they have been together;
- the nature of their relationship during that period; and
- the nature and extent of any financial arrangements during that period.[174]

Whether or not they are indeed to be considered a cohabiting couple is a question of fact for the court. The court will consider the couple's lifestyle and indeed all material factors when considering if they are cohabitants. Cohabitants are under no obligation to aliment each other. There is a presumption that each cohabitant has a right to an equal share in household goods acquired during the period of cohabitation although this presumption is rebuttable.[175] Household goods are defined as goods kept or used at any time during the cohabitation in any

---

166 1981 Act s.6(3)(e).
167 1981 Act s.3(7).
168 *Hall v Hall*, 1987 S.L.T. (Sh Ct) 15.
169 *Crow v Crow*, 1986 S.L.T. 270.
170 1981 Act s.13(1) and (9).
171 1981 Act s.2(8).
172 Family Law (Scotland) Act 2006 s.25(1)(a).
173 2006 Act s.25(1)(b).
174 2006 Act s.25(2).
175 2006 Act s.26(1) and (2).

residence in which the cohabitants are (or were) cohabiting for their joint domestic purposes.[176] Money, securities, motor cars, caravans, other road vehicles or any domestic animal are excluded.[177] Any savings or property acquired from joint household expenses shall belong equally to the cohabitants.[178]

If the relationship breaks down either cohabitant can apply to the court for financial provision.[179] The court can—

(a) make an order requiring the other cohabitant to pay a capital sum of an amount specified in the order to the applicant[180];
(b) make an order requiring the defender to pay such amount as may be specified in the order in respect of any economic burden of caring, after the end of the cohabitation, for a child of whom the cohabitants are the parents[181];
(c) make such interim order as it thinks fit.[182]

The application needs to be submitted to the court one year after cohabitation ceases.[183]

3.23 For orders under s.28(2)(b) it would seem that a periodical allowance is possible under this section as well as a capital sum. In making awards under this section the court will specify what sum is to be paid and when[184] and this sum can be paid in instalments.[185] In considering an application for financial provision the court has to consider (a) whether (and if so to what extent) the defender has derived economic advantage from the contributions made by the applicant; and (b) whether (and if so, to what extent) the applicant has suffered economic disadvantage in the interests of the defender or any relevant child.[186] If the court wishes to make an award of a capital sum under s.28(2)(a) it further needs to consider the matters in s.28(5) and (6). This enables the court to carry out a balancing process before making any award, similar to the principle in s.9(1)(b) of the 1985 Act relating to the financial provisions on divorce. Outwith the provisions of the 2006 Act, the normal property law rules prevail. If there is a property dispute and a cohabitant does not have a remedy under the 2006 Act they may do so under the law of unjust enrichment.[187]

A surviving partner has some statutory rights if their partner dies intestate. For the provisions to apply the deceased must have died without leaving a will, and immediately before his death he was domiciled in Scotland and cohabiting with the cohabitant. The surviving cohabitant needs to apply to the court[188] within six months of the death[189] for:

- payment to the survivor out of the deceased's net intestate estate of a capital sum of such amount as may be specified in the order[190];
- transfer to the survivor of such property (whether heritable or moveable) from that estate as may be so specified[191];
- such interim order that the court thinks fit.[192]

---

176 2006 Act s.26(4).
177 2006 Act s.26(4).
178 2006 Act s.27(1) and (2). Property does not include a residence used by the cohabitants as the sole residence in which they live together: s.27(3).
179 2006 Act s.28.
180 2006 Act s.28(2)(a).
181 2006 Act s.28(2)(b).
182 2006 Act s.28(2)(c).
183 2006 Act s.28(8).
184 2006 Act s.28(7)(a).
185 2006 Act s.28(7)(b).
186 2006 Act s.28(3). Contributions, economic advantage and disadvantage are defined in s.28(9).
187 *Shilliday v Smith*, 1998 S.C. 725; *Scanlon v Scanlon*, 1990 G.W.D. 12–598.
188 Either the Court of Session or the sheriff court: 2006 Act s.29(5).
189 2006 Act s.29(6).
190 2006 Act s.29 (2)(a)(i).
191 2006 Act s.29(2)(a)(ii).
192 2006 Act s.29(2)(b).

Before making such an order the court has to consider:

(a) the size and nature of the deceased's net intestate estate[193];
(b) any benefit received, or to be received, by the survivor: (i) on, or in consequence of, the deceased's death [194]; and (ii) from somewhere other than the deceased's net intestate estate[195] (e.g. life policy, an annuity);
(c) the nature and extent of any other rights against, or claims on, the deceased's net intestate estate[196] (e.g. whether children may be claiming legitim); and
(d) any other matter the court considers appropriate.[197]

The net estate is the estate remaining after deduction of inheritance tax, other liabilities and the legal rights and prior rights of a spouse or civil partner.[198] How much a cohabitant would get is a matter for the court, but they are not entitled to get more than if they had been a spouse or civil partner.[199] Any capital sum awarded can be paid at a future date or in instalments [200] and the transfer of property can take effect on a date specified by the court.[201]

3.24 Cohabiting couples who experience violence or abuse in their relationship need protection. The provisions of the Matrimonial Homes (Family Protection) (Scotland) Act 1981 Act apply to cohabiting same sex and different sex couples.[202] In deciding if they are a cohabiting couple the court will look at how long they have been living together and whether there are children.[203] A non-entitled partner may apply for occupancy rights of the family home for up to six months[204] and this period may be extended.[205] If occupancy rights are granted then many other provisions of the Act are available to cohabitants. These include subsidiary and consequential rights, regulatory orders and exclusion orders.[206]

An interdict may be necessary to protect the cohabitant or child from an abusive partner[207] and a power of arrest may be attached for a period of up to three years.[208]

The provisions of the Protection from Harassment Act 1997 are also available to cohabitees who find themselves in an aggressive relationship. A cohabitant is considered a relative for the purposes of the Administration of Justice Act 1982[209] and for the purposes of the Damages (Scotland) Act 1976[210] is a member of the deceased's immediate family. This enables a cohabitee to raise a court action for damages if their partner dies as a result of personal injury.

Some cohabiting couples may wish to regulate matters between them with a cohabitation agreement. Such an agreement will specify all relevant matters between the couple and will deal with financial and property issues.[211]

---

193 2006 Act s.29(3)(a)
194 2006 Act s.29(3)(b)(i).
195 2006 Act s.29(3)(b)(ii).
196 2006 Act s.29(3)(c).
197 2006 Act s.29(3)(d).
198 2006 Act s.29(10).
199 2006 Act s.29(4).
200 2006 Act s.29(7).
201 2006 Act s.29(8).
202 Matrimonial Homes (Family Protection) (Scotland) Act 1981 s.18.
203 1981 Act s.18(2).
204 1981 Act s.18(1).
205 1981 Act s.18(1).
206 1981 Act s.18(3).
207 1981 Act ss.18A and 18B.
208 Protection from Abuse (Scotland) Act 2001 s.1.
209 As amended by the Law Reform (Miscellaneous Provisions) (Scotland) Act 1990 s.69 and the Family Law (Scotland) Act 2006 s.30.
210 As amended by the 2006 Act s.35 and Sch.2 para.2.
211 See Fiona Gavin, Sheena Inness and Kirsty Malcolm, *Cohabitation* (Edinburgh: W. Green, 2005), pp.46–49.

CIVIL PARTNERSHIP

3.25 The Civil Partnership Act 2004 came into force on December 5, 2005. Same sex couples may now enter into civil partnerships, which in effect give them the same rights as married couples.[212] As at June 22, 2006, 343 civil partnerships had been recorded in Scotland.[213] A civil partnership is defined as a relationship between two people of the same sex which is formed when they register as civil partners.[214] The partnership must be registered in the presence of both parties, two witnesses over 16 and the registrar at a registration office or some other agreed place.[215] To be eligible both parties must be of the same sex; must not be related in the forbidden degree[216]; must be 16 or over; cannot be married or in a civil partnership and must be capable of understanding the nature of the civil partnership or of validly consenting to its formation.[217] District registrars are appointed to carry out the registration of civil partnerships.[218] To enter into a civil partnership each civil partner has to submit a notice of intention to enter a civil partnership.[219] This notice must be accompanied by the birth certificates; divorce certificates or death certificates if appropriate; and a signed declaration that states the parties are eligible to enter a civil partnership.[220] The particulars are entered into the civil partnership book.[221] The details are then publicised and the parties have to wait 14 days[222] during which time anyone may object to the registration. The registration may take place at the registration office or at another agreed place[223] but religious premises are expressly excluded.[224] Once the registrar is satisfied there are no legal impediments and the 14 days have expired he can complete the civil partnership schedule.[225] At the ceremony the schedule is checked and then signed by the couple in the presence of the witnesses and registrar.[226] Thereafter the particulars are entered into the civil partnership register.[227] An accelerated procedure is available if the parties were married and one party has been issued with a full gender recognition certificate.[228]

Once the civil partnership is formed the civil partners have rights and responsibilities similar to those arising from marriage. Civil partners have a duty to aliment each other,[229] rights in succession[230] and delict.[231]

---

[212] For differences between marriage and civil partnership see K. McNorrie, "What the Civil Partnership Act 2004 Does Not Do", 2005 S.L.T. 35.
[213] *http://www.scotland.gov.uk* [Accessed July 2, 2008]. News release dated June 22, 2006.
[214] Civil Partnership Act 2004 ss.1 and 85.
[215] Civil Partnership Act 2004 s.85.
[216] Civil Partnership Act 2004 s.86 and Sch.10.
[217] Civil Partnership Act 2004 s.86(1).
[218] Civil Partnership Act 2004 s.87.
[219] Civil Partnership Act 2004 s.88(1).
[220] Civil Partnership Act 2004 s.88(2), (5) and (6).
[221] Civil Partnership Act 2004 s.89.
[222] This period of time may be shortened in certain circumstances: s.91.
[223] Civil Partnership Act 2004 s.93(1).
[224] Civil Partnership Act 2004 s.93(3).
[225] Civil Partnership Act 2004 s.94.
[226] Civil Partnership Act 2004 ss.95 and 85.
[227] Civil Partnership Act 2004 s.95(2).
[228] Civil Partnership Act 2004 s.96.
[229] Family Law (Scotland) Act 1985 as amended by the Civil Partnership Act 2004 Sch.28.
[230] Succession (Scotland) Act 1964 as amended by the Civil Partnership Act 2004 Sch.28.
[231] Damages (Scotland) Act 1976 as amended by the Civil Partnership Act 2004 Sch.28.

THE FAMILY HOME AND DOMESTIC VIOLENCE

3.26 Civil partners have rights similar to those of spouses regarding occupancy of the family home.[232] This does not affect property rights in the home, only the right of occupancy. The non-entitled partner[233] is entitled to occupy the family home[234] or if not in occupation, the right to enter and occupy the home,[235] with a child of the family.[236] The non-entitled partner can without the consent of the entitled partner make loan payments, etc. on the family home.[237] The court can regulate the occupancy rights of the partners,[238] by enforcing or restricting the occupancy rights. Before doing so the court needs to consider the factors in s.103(3) of the Civil Partnership Act 2004. Either partner may ask for an exclusion order suspending the occupancy rights of the other partner[239] and the court can grant this if necessary to protect the applicant or child of the family.[240] However, the court will not grant the exclusion order if it appears to the court that to do so is unjustified or unreasonable[241] having regard to the criteria in s.103(3). If the court grants the exclusion order, it must also grant the orders in s.104(4) and may grant the orders in s.104(5). Additionally if an interdict[242] is requested by one partner, it would "restrain or prohibit any conduct of one civil partner towards the other civil partner or a child of the family"[243] and a partner would be prohibited from entering or remaining in (i) a family home; (ii) any other residence occupied by the partner; (iii) any place of work; (iv) any school attended by the child.[244] A power of arrest may be attached to the interdict.[245]

The court may transfer the tenancy of the family home to one partner.[246] A non-entitled partner's right to occupy the family home is not defeated by any dealing[247] by the entitled partner. Therefore it is necessary from a conveyancing point of view to ensure that the correct consent[248] or renunciation[249] from the non-entitled partner is in place. The court can dispense with the consent of a non-entitled partner if such consent is unreasonably withheld.[250] In an action for division and sale the court may postpone granting decree, after considering the matters in s.103(3).[251]

DISSOLUTION OF CIVIL PARTNERSHIP

3.27 If civil partners separate they may enter into a separation agreement or may raise an action of separation[252] and the obligation to aliment continues. If the parties decide to end the relationship they will need to dissolve the civil partnership. An action for dissolution needs to be

---

232 See para.3.17 for further details.
233 Defined in s.101(1) of the Civil Partnership Act 2004.
234 Civil Partnership Act 2004 s.101(1)(a).
235 Civil Partnership Act 2004 s.101(1)(b).
236 Civil Partnership Act 2004 s.101(2). Child of the family is defined in s.101(7).
237 Civil Partnership Act 2004 s.102.
238 Civil Partnership Act 2004 s.103.
239 Civil Partnership Act 2004 s.104(1).
240 Civil Partnership Act 2004 s.104(2).
241 Civil Partnership Act 2004 s.104(3).
242 Civil Partnership Act 2004 s.113.
243 Civil Partnership Act 2004 s.113(2)(a).
244 Civil Partnership Act 2004 s.113(2)(b).
245 By the Protection of Abuse (Scotland) Act 2001 s.1.
246 Civil Partnership Act 2004 s.112.
247 Civil Partnership Act 2004 s.106(2).
248 Civil Partnership Act 2004 s.106(3)(a)(i).
249 Civil Partnership Act 2004 s.106(3)(a)(ii).
250 Civil Partnership Act 2004 s.107(1).
251 Civil Partnership Act 2004 s.110.
252 Civil Partnership Act 2004 s.120.

brought in the Court of Session or sheriff court.[253] The only grounds for dissolution are that the civil partnership has irretrievably broken down or an interim gender recognition certificate has been issued.[254] Irretrievable breakdown can be established if unreasonable behaviour (both active and passive) has existed since the date of registration[255]; there has been no cohabitation for a period of one year and the other party consents to the dissolution[256]; or there has been no cohabitation for a period of two years and the other party does not consent to the dissolution.[257] A civil partnership cannot be dissolved on the ground of adultery. The civil partners are allowed a period of up to six months for a trial reconciliation and the courts are to grant any continuation to encourage reconciliation.[258] A dissolution is entered in the Register of Dissolutions of Civil Partnerships.[259] Financial provision on dissolution is the same as financial provision on divorce.[260] A simplified form of dissolution is available if certain criteria are met.[261]

THE RELATIONSHIP OF PARENT AND CHILD

Parental rights and responsibilities

3.28 The Children (Scotland) Act 1995 ("1995 Act") attempts to make the first comprehensive statutory statement of the rights and responsibilities of parents in respect of their children. A parent has responsibility:

- to safeguard and promote the child's health, development and welfare;
- to provide direction and guidance to the child in a manner appropriate to the stage of the child's development;
- if the child is not living with the parent, to maintain personal relations and direct contact with the child on a regular basis; and
- to act as the child's legal representative.[262]

As a corollary to those responsibilities the 1995 Act also confers the following rights upon parents:

- to have the child living with the parent or otherwise to regulate the child's residence;
- to control, direct or guide the child's upbringing in a manner appropriate to the child's stage of development;
- if the child does not live with the parent, to maintain personal relations and direct contact with the child on a regular basis;
- to act as the child's legal representative.[263]

Other Acts contain specific parental rights and these are not affected by the provisions of the 1995 Act.[264] Parental rights are only exercisable in the interests of the child.[265] The responsibility to provide guidance endures until the child is 18, but in all other respects parental responsibilities end when the child is 16.[266] The parent must so far as is reasonably practicable have

253 Civil Partnership Act 2004 s.117(1).
254 Civil Partnership Act 2004 s.117(2).
255 Civil Partnership Act 2004 s.117(3)(a).
256 Civil Partnership Act 2004 s.117(3)(c).
257 Civil Partnership Act 2004 s.117(3)(d).
258 Civil Partnership Act 2004 ss.118 and 119.
259 Civil Partnership Act 2004 s.122.
260 See paras 3.11–3.16 on financial provision on divorce.
261 Act of Sederunt (Ordinary Cause Rules) Amendment (Civil Partnership Act 2004) 2005 (SSI 2005/638).
262 Children (Scotland) Act 1995 (1995 Act) s.1(1).
263 1995 Act s.2(1).
264 1995 Act s.2(5). Note, however, the 1995 Act does supersede many common law rights.
265 1995 Act ss.1(1) and 2(7).
266 1995 Act s.1(2)(a).

regard to the views of the child in reaching any decision affecting that child if the child wishes to express any view.[267] The 1995 Act provides that a child of 12 years of age and over will be of sufficient age and maturity to express a view although younger children may be consulted if they are deemed to be of sufficient age and maturity.

3.29 A mother automatically has parental rights and responsibilities ("PRRs") in respect of her child. The child's natural father also automatically has rights and responsibilities if he is or was married to the child's mother at the date of the child's conception, or at any time thereafter.[268] This includes any voidable marriage, or any marriage that was in fact void but that both parties believed to be valid.[269] Where the child was registered on/after May 4, 2006, and the father's name is on the birth certificate, he will also acquire these PRRs automatically.[270]

In circumstances where the father is not, or was not, married to the mother he may acquire parental rights and responsibilities in two alternative ways. If the mother retains parental rights and responsibilities, she may enter into a voluntary agreement that confers parental rights and responsibilities on the child's father.[271] Such an agreement may be entered into even where the parents are under the age of 16. This type of agreement (known as a s.4 agreement) to be effective must be registered in the Books of Council and Session.[272] A registered agreement is irrevocable except by court order.[273]

Alternatively, a father may make an application to the court under s.11 of the 1995 Act for an order conferring parental rights and responsibilities.[274] In determining any application, the welfare of the child is the paramount consideration for the court.[275] The father will only acquire parental rights and responsibilities if it is thought to be in the interests of the child.[276] It is possible for others who have an interest (genetic or otherwise) to seek a parental rights and responsibilities order under s.11(3)(a)(i). Where two or more persons have parental rights they may exercise them independently of the other.[277]

The law also recognises that a person over 16 may have responsibility for the care of a child under 16 without having parental rights and responsibilities. Section 5 of the 1995 Act imposes a duty on such persons to do all that is reasonable in the circumstances to safeguard the child's health, development and welfare. Specifically, they may give consent to any surgical, medical or dental treatment or procedure where the child is unable to give their own consent, and it is not in the carer's knowledge that the parent would refuse to consent. In exercising this power, the carer must consult the child. Nothing in s.5 confers a right on anyone who has care and control of a child at school.

A parent may appoint a person to be their child's guardian in the event of the parent's death.[278] Appointments must be in writing and signed by the parent. For the appointment to be effective the parent must have been entitled to act as the child's legal representative. Any parental rights and responsibilities that a surviving spouse has continue to coexist with those of the appointed guardian.

3.30 Undoubtedly, the principal responsibilities and rights of a parent are to have residence or

---

[267] 1995 Act s.6(1).
[268] See 1995 Act s.3(1).
[269] 1995 Act s.3(2)(a).
[270] 1995 Act s.3(2)(b), as inserted by the Family Law (Scotland) Act 2006 s.23(2)(b).
[271] 1995 Act s.4(1).
[272] 1995 Act s.4(2).
[273] 1995 Act ss.4(4) and 11(11).
[274] An application may be made under s.11 even where an applicant is under 16: *E v E*, 2004 G.W.D. 26–548.
[275] 1995 Act s.11(7)(a).
[276] *Porchetta v Porchetta*, 1986 S.L.T. 105; *Russell v Russell*, 1991 S.C.L.R. 429, per Sheriff Gordon at 430; *Sanderson v McManus*, 1996 S.L.T. 750.
[277] 1995 Act s.2(3), although a child cannot be removed from the UK without the consent of anyone who has parental rights relating to the child's residence or contact.
[278] 1995 Act s.7(1).

contact with their child. The 1995 Act makes specific statutory provision for this. It is the right of a parent to have their child live with them or to regulate where they do live.[279] This right, like all parental rights, must be exercised in the child's interests. There are clear instances where it is not in the child's interest to be resident with their parent and as such the parental right of residence is one that can be lost.[280] Integral to the right of residence is the parent's right to determine residence of a temporary nature and accordingly the parent can control the child's temporary absence from home—perhaps to stay with friends or other relatives. Where a non-custodial parent wants a court order for their child to reside with him, or her, for particular periods such as holidays or weekends, the appropriate order is a contact order not a residence order.[281]

One of the innovations of the 1995 Act is the requirement that a non-resident parent maintain direct contact and personal relations with the child on a regular basis.[282] It is both a "right" and a "requirement". Insofar as it is a right, it must be exercised in accordance with the welfare principle. Naturally, given the statutory requirements of taking the child's own views into account, the child may well have a substantial say in whether a parent is denied contact with his child.

An area of considerable controversy has been a parent's right to discipline their child. The 1995 Act confers on the parent the right to control their child in accordance with the welfare principle. Ironically, that right includes the right to physically chastise the child. Many will consider being physically punished as inconsistent with the welfare principle and not in the child's interests. Notwithstanding this, the law permits justifiable assaults.[283] Where the parent uses excessive force they may face a common law charge of assault or criminal neglect.[284] The Criminal Justice (Scotland) Act 2003 provides guidance as to the evaluation of justifiable assaults. Prior to this Act taking effect, the parent's motivation in chastisement was largely irrelevant; the real test related to the severity of the force used.[285] However, this led to a series of discrepancies.[286] The Criminal Justice (Scotland) Act 2003 lists the factors that are to be used in assessing whether an action was justifiable. These are: the nature of what was done; its duration and frequency; any effect (physical and mental); the child's age and personal characteristics. Section 51(3) also states that the action will never be justifiable where it included or consisted of a blow to the head, shaking or use of an implement. Where there is excessive force used, there is likely to be a referral to a children's hearing of the child in question. The right to physically punish a child ends when the child reaches 16 years of age.[287]

3.31 One of the other areas where parents have corresponding rights and responsibilities is in the field of education. These rights and responsibilities are more fully discussed in Ch.5. Suffice to say a parent has the obligation to ensure that their child is educated under education legislation[288] and also as part of their duty under s.2 of the 1995 Act to promote the development of their child.

An area of potential conflict, given its dynamic in the Scottish nation, is that of religion.

---

[279] 1995 Act s.2(1)(a); Professor Thomson suggests that this is integral to the promotion of the child's development: see *Family Law in Scotland* (2006), pp.267–268.

[280] See *J v C* [1970] A.C. 668 (HL); *Cheetham v Glasgow Corporation*, 1972 S.L.T. (Notes) 50; *M v Dumfries and Galloway RC*, 1991 S.C.L.R. 481.

[281] *McBain v McIntyre*, 1997 S.C.L.R. 181.

[282] 1995 Act s.1(1)(c).

[283] Criminal Justice (Scotland) Act 2003 s.51.

[284] Children and Young Persons (Scotland) Act 1937 s.12(1); *G v Templeton*, 1998 S.C.L.R. 180; *A v UK*, 1998 E.C.H.R. 23; see also on neglect Mays, "Home Alone Left Alone—Criminal Neglect of Children" (1996) 64 S.L.G. 94.

[285] *B v Harris*, 1990 S.L.T. 208.

[286] See Scot. Law Com., "Report on Family Law; *Kennedy v A*", 1993 S.L.T. 1134; Ross, "Reasonable Parenting—Borders of Acceptability", 1994 Fam. L.B. 7; and for the international human rights dimension see Smith, "To Smack or Not to Smack—A review of *A v United Kingdom* in an International and European Context", 1999 *Web Journal of CLI* 1.

[287] See *Stewart v Thain*, 1981 S.L.T. (Notes) 2.

[288] See generally Education (Scotland) Act 1980, discussed in Ch.6.

Acting in accordance with the welfare principle, parents have a right to choose their child's religion from the outset. Although the Scottish courts have shown a preference for having some religion in a child's life, they have not shown any bias towards one particular religion or another.[289] Parental choice of religion should not conflict with the interests of the child. In circumstances where adherence to a particular religious persuasion is damaging to the child's health, it is likely that the courts will override the parents' wishes.[290] As children mature, they may wish to choose their own religion. The current position is that a child on attaining the age of 16 has the right to choose his or her own religion. Below that age there is a suggestion that a child can choose an alternative religion and that a parent's responsibility is only breached if it were against the welfare of the child to change it.[291]

3.32 The statutory statement of parental responsibilities specifically includes the requirement to promote the child's health and in that context, as a basic premise, parents have a right to consent to medical treatment or procedures as the child's legal representative.[292] The past two decades have seen much academic and judicial comment on this topic.[293] Like all decisions in respect of the child it is one governed by the welfare principle.[294] There will be circumstances where the refusal to consent will be overridden by the courts as not in the interests of the child's welfare.[295] Similarly, there will be situations where the parent's desire for a medical procedure or operation, for instance the sterilisation of a handicapped child, may not be in the child's interest.[296] In the normal course of events parents will give consent where the medical treatment is likely to benefit the child and that will be viewed as a proper exercise of parental rights and responsibilities. It is also the case that parents can consent to medical procedures and treatment in respect of their child even where that treatment or procedure is not positively in the interests of the child (for example, blood tests for paternity purposes).[297]

A person over 16 has the right to consent to medical treatment or procedures of his own accord.[298] In certain circumstances a child under 16 may also receive medical treatment or undergo a medical procedure in the absence of parental consent.[299] Indeed the child's desire to undergo medical treatment or procedure may overrule the parent's objection.[300] Professor Thomson canvasses a dilemma which the law has so far not resolved. Is a parent able to overrule a child where that child is competent but refuses medical treatment, and the parent considers the refusal of medical treatment not to be in their interest or to be against the welfare of the child?[301] One view is that the empowerment of the child excludes the parent's rights and responsibilities. Another is that the parent retains the right to direct the child presupposing that he knows about the proposed medical procedure.[302] It seems likely that the courts' own view of what is in the interests of the child will be the determinant of such controversial cases.[303]

3.33 In line with the duty to promote the health, development and welfare of the child it is incumbent on parents to attend to the safety of their child and to ensure that adequate care

---

[289] *McNaught v McNaught*, 1955 S.L.T. (Sh Ct) 9; *McClements v McClements*, 1958 S.C. 286; *MacKay v MacKay*, 1957 S.L.T. (Notes) 17.

[290] Professor Thomson advises that it is likely that a child protection order will be sought with a direction that medical treatment be obtained under s.58(5).

[291] See Thomson, *Family Law in Scotland* (2006), p.272.

[292] See Mason and McCall-Smith, *Law and Medical Ethics*, 6th edn (2005) pp.354–359.

[293] See Norrie and Wilkinson, *Parent and Child* (1993), pp.182–189.

[294] Edwards and Griffiths, *Family Law* (1997), pp.125–128.

[295] *Re B (A Minor)* [1981] 1 W.L.R. 1421 (CA); cf. *Re C (A Minor)* [1990] Fam. 26; *Finlayson (Applicant)*, 1989 S.C.L.R. 601.

[296] *Re B (A Minor)* [1976] 1 All E.R. 326; cf. *Re B (A Minor)* [1988] A.C. 199.

[297] See Thomson, *Family Law in Scotland* (2006), p.274; *Docherty v McGlynn*, 1983 S.L.T. 645.

[298] See para.3.35 below.

[299] See the Age of Legal Capacity (Scotland) Act 1991 s.2(4).

[300] See para.3.35 below.

[301] Thomson, *Family Law in Scotland* (2006), p.275.

[302] See Professor Thomson's interesting discussion, *Family Law in Scotland* (2006), pp.275–278; see also Norrie, "Medical Treatment: Overriding the Wishes of Children and Young Persons in Scotland", 1992 Fam. L.B. 1–3.

[303] See discussion in Edwards and Griffiths, *Family Law* (2006), pp.51–55.

arrangements are made for the child in the parents' absence. In circumstances where the child is abandoned, neglected or simply left alone parents may face criminal prosecution.[304] Interestingly, merely leaving a child alone unattended is not criminal neglect. Neglect is determined by looking at all the circumstances of the case—the age of the child, the arrangements for care, reasons for leaving the child alone and the duration for which the child is left with inadequate care as well as the surrounding dangers.[305]

It is customary in Scotland for children of married couples to take the name of the father. It is not a legal requirement. Certainly parents have the right to name their child in respect of both the Christian name (or forename) and the surname. Children born out of marriage may take either the father's or the mother's surname. Problems arise in practice in situations where the natural parents divorce and in particular if a custodial mother decides to remarry. It is not uncommon for such parents to seek to change the child's name to that of the step-parent. Here again the right of the parent is governed by the welfare principle.[306] An assessment of two competing claims must be taken—is it in the child's interest to have the same surname as the new family name or to retain the important link with the natural birth name? It will always be a matter of assessment of all the circumstances as to what is in the child's best interests. Courts have jurisdiction in such matters under s.11(1) as it is clearly a matter relating to the exercise of parental rights and responsibilities.

Children's rights

3.34 One of the emerging issues of the late twentieth century is the increasing recognition of the important status of children in society. It is a fact that their rights have been expanded at a time when the rights of parents have arguably been diminished. This realignment in the parent–child relationship is hardly surprising given that children's rights and parental responsibilities and rights are essentially two sides of the same coin. The debate on this highly important area of law has been fuelled in part by the UN Convention on the Rights of the Child and a series of Law Commission and Scottish Office White Papers on the subject, *Scotland's children*.[307] In addition there have been two major Acts of Parliament with important statutory provision—the Age of Legal Capacity (Scotland) Act 1991 and the Children (Scotland) Act 1995.

Contract

3.35 The Age of Legal Capacity (Scotland) Act 1991 realigned and rationalised the age at which children attain full contractual capacity. As a basic premise a person has full contractual capacity when they attain 16 years of age.[308] Equally, as a basic principle children under 16 years of age have no contractual capacity. However, the simplicity of these statutory provisions is dislodged somewhat by a range of caveats to these general rules. Those under 16 require their legal representative (usually their parent) to act in their stead. Where a child under 16 purports to enter into a contract by themselves then the contract is null and void. Where a parent enters into a contract on behalf of a child the contract will be valid even if not in the interests of the child; the child though will have a right of action against the errant parent for failing to fulfil their parental responsibilities properly.[309]

A child under the age of 16 may enter into a contract of a kind commonly entered into by a child of that child's age and circumstances on terms not unreasonable to the child.[310] There is

---

[304] Children and Young Persons (Scotland) Act 1937 s.12; Mays, "Home Alone Left Alone" (1996) 64 S.L.G. 94.

[305] See *M v Orr*, 1995 S.L.T. 26; *H v Lees*, 1994 S.L.T. 908; *D v Orr*, 1994 S.L.T. 908.

[306] See *Cosh v Cosh*, 1979 S.L.T. (Notes) 72; *Flett v Flett*, 1995 S.C.L.R. 189; cf. *Dawson v Wearmouth* [1998] 1 All E.R. 271.

[307] Cm.2286 (Edinburgh: HMSO, 1993); Tisdall, *The Children (Scotland) Act 1995: Developing Policy and Law for Scotland's Children* (1998).

[308] Age of Legal Capacity (Scotland) Act 1991 s.1(1).

[309] 1995 Act s.10(1).

[310] Age of Legal Capacity (Scotland) Act 1991 s.2(1)(a) and (b).

some dubiety as to the meaning of "commonly"—does it mean "frequently" or "not unusually"? [311] One anticipates that this section permits children to enter into basic contracts such as suitable purchases at a local shop or school tuckshop. It is also the case that the Age of Legal Capacity (Scotland) Act 1991 does not affect the ability of a child aged 12 and over to make a will.[312] Moreover, a child over 12 has the right to consent or otherwise to the making of an adoption order or a freeing for adoption order.[313] Where a medical or dental practitioner is of the view that the child is of sufficient age and maturity to understand the nature and possible consequences of medical procedure or treatment the child may enter into a transaction for such medical procedure without parental consent.[314] Although this is viewed as a right of the child it is nevertheless one where a medical practitioner acts as gatekeeper. It appears from the statutory provisions (although they are not explicit on this question) that a child may refuse medical treatment.[315] It appears also to be the case that a child may consent to medical procedures ostensibly not in their own interest, for instance the donation of an organ tissue or blood to another.[316]

Children under 16 have the right to instruct a solicitor in any civil matter. Indeed the thrust of the 1995 Act is to engage children in family actions and it seems a prerequisite that legal advice is available to the child. A child aged 12 or above is presumed to have sufficient age, maturity and understanding to justify the engagement of a solicitor. There is nothing to stop a child under 12 engaging a solicitor where he too has such understanding of the enterprise in which he is engaged.[317] It is also possible for a child to obtain legal aid for the advice and instruction of a solicitor.[318]

Although the basic rule is that children who attain the age of 16 have full contractual capacity, the Age of Legal Capacity (Scotland) Act 1991 makes provisions for children aged 16–18 to challenge certain contracts entered into by them if such contracts are unfairly prejudicial to them. The court has the power to set aside contracts deemed unfairly prejudicial until the person attains the age of 21.[319] There are exemptions and ways round any attack on a transaction with a child but discussion is outwith the scope of this book.

Delict

3.36 Where a child under 16 is injured by the actions of another they may have a remedy in delict. Ordinarily, if the person is under 16 this will be pursued on their behalf by their legal representative (probably their parent). A child may sue his parent for any wrongful action that results in damage to him or her.[320] Actions of this type are commonplace in respect of road traffic accidents where the child sustains damage as a result of a parent's negligence. They are also thought to be possibilities where the child is damaged as a result of the parent's negligent or deliberate infliction of harm while the child is *in utero* (in the womb). Drinking, smoking and drug addiction might provide interesting possibilities for such an action.

Children can be liable for their own delicts. In most circumstances they will have very few assets and as such will be considered "men of straw" and unable to meet any award of damages or legal expenses. Given that a court decree can subsist for a considerable time an action against a child may be more productive where the child is nearing working age and court-awarded damages can be derived from their future earnings. Only in circumstances where the parent has

---

[311] See Norrie, "The Age of Legal Capacity (Scotland) Act 1991" (1991) 36 J.L.S.S. 434.
[312] Age of Legal Capacity (Scotland) Act 1991 s.2(2).
[313] Age of Legal Capacity (Scotland) Act 1991 s.2(3) and Adoption (Scotland) Act 1978 ss.12(8) and 18(8).
[314] Age of Legal Capacity (Scotland) Act 1991 s.2(4).
[315] See Thomson, *Family Law in Scotland*, 5th edn (2006), p.190; 1995 Act s.90; Age of Legal Capacity (Scotland) Act 1991 s.2(4).
[316] See though Norrie, "Medical Treatment", 1992 Fam. L.B. 1–3.
[317] Age of Legal Capacity (Scotland) Act 1991 s.2(4A), inserted by the 1995 Act Sch.4 para.53(3).
[318] See para.3.35 above.
[319] Age of Legal Capacity (Scotland) Act 1991 s.3(1).
[320] *Young v Rankin*, 1934 S.C. 499; *Wood v Wood*, 1935 S.L.T. 431 (where the mother sued her son).

instructed or authorised the child to perpetrate the delictual wrong can a parent be vicariously liable for the delict of their child. Actions that it is hoped will access the parent's wealth for the wrongs of their child are largely ineffectual. So, for example, where a youth deliberately assaults another, there will be no right of action against the parent unless the child was acting as an agent of the parent. It is possible that a parent may be personally liable where they have inadequately supervised a child who perpetrates a civil wrong.[321]

The third facet of a child's rights in delict is that a child has title to sue a third party where that third party wrongfully, or negligently, injures or kills their parent or parents.[322] A child can sue a third party for damage or injury to his or her father even where the father is not married to his mother. The child can seek loss of support and "non-patrimonial" benefits.[323]

Miscellaneous statutory rights, responsibilities and protections

3.37 Many of a child's rights are enforceable against their parents but there are a number of rights, responsibilities and protections pertaining to the child that are conferred or imposed by society as a whole. For example, a child has the right to marry at the age of 16 without requiring parental consent.[324] In addition there are statutory rights to make a will, consent to or refuse adoption[325] and also a right to seek a child maintenance assessment order.[326] Likewise, there are a number of statutory age limits restricting the rights of young persons that are not affected by the operation of the Age of Legal Capacity (Scotland) Act 1991. Some restrictions are well known, such as being able to hold a driving licence at the age of only 17,[327] while to buy or attempt to buy alcohol one must be 18 or over,[328] to place a bet in a betting office one must be 18,[329] and to have a tattoo inscribed on one's body a person must be 21. A child has criminal responsibility in Scots law at the age of eight.[330]

Sexual offences

3.38 The law also intervenes to proscribe certain sexual activities. There is a defence to the common law offence of sodomy or shameless indecency where homosexual partners are over 18 and the consensual sexual act takes place in a private place.[331] It is an offence for a man to have sex with a girl under the age of 16.[332] If the girl is below the age of 12 it is an offence of rape to have sexual intercourse with her even in circumstances where she consents.[333] Where the girl is under the age 13, the man will be charged with an offence under s.5(1) of the Criminal Law (Consolidation) (Scotland) Act 1995, which carries a penalty of life imprisonment. Consent will not constitute an adequate defence. Where the girl is aged between 13 and 16 it is still a statutory offence but the law does countenance a defence whereby a man under the age of 24 who has not previously been charged with a like offence can satisfy the court that he had reasonable cause for believing that the girl was 16 or over.[334] Where the girl is under 16 years of age and the boy is over 16 years of age and there is close proximity in the ages of both, a prosecution is unlikely. In

---

321 See *Hastie v Magistrates of Edinburgh*, 1907 S.C. 1102; *Hardie v Sneddon*, 1917 S.C. 1.

322 Damages (Scotland) Act 1976; it is possible for a child born after the parent has died to sue: see *Cohen v Shaw*, 1992 S.L.T. 1022.

323 See Thomson, *Family Law in Scotland* (2006), p.235.

324 Marriage (Scotland) Act 1977 s.1.

325 Age of Legal Capacity (Scotland) Act 1991 s.2.

326 Child Support Act 1991 s.7.

327 Road Traffic Act 1988 s.101.

328 Licensing (Scotland) Act 1976 s.68(2).

329 Betting, Gaming and Lotteries Act 1963 s.222.

330 Criminal Procedure (Scotland) Act 1995 s.41; see para.4.45.

331 Criminal Law (Consolidation) (Scotland) Act 1995 s.13(5); see Gane and Stoddart, *Scottish Criminal Law*, 3rd edn (2001), p.362 for a discussion of sexual offences against under-age boys.

332 Criminal Law (Consolidation) (Scotland) Act 1995 s.5.

333 This is a common law offence: *C v HM Advocate*, 1987 S.C.C.R. 104.

334 Criminal Law (Consolidation) (Scotland) Act 1995 s.5(5)(b).

addition a girl below the age of 16 who consents to sexual intercourse with a man commits no offence but may nevertheless be referred to the children's hearing.

There are also statutory offences that prohibit sexual intercourse with a child in breach of trust,[335] procuring a girl for unlawful sexual intercourse,[336] intercourse with a step-child,[337] incest,[338] indecent behaviour towards a girl aged between 12 and 16,[339] detention of a girl with the intention of having unlawful intercourse,[340] as well as a range of prostitution offences designed to prevent the involvement of children.[341] The Sexual Offences (Amendment) Act 2000 created the new offence, "abuse of a position of trust".

Criminal neglect

3.39 In addition to the number of offences that restrict sexual abuse of children there is an offence in s.12 of the Children and Young Persons (Scotland) Act 1937. Anyone aged 16 or over, having custody, charge or care of a child or young person under 16 years of age, who wilfully assaults, ill-treats, neglects, abandons or exposes the child in a manner likely to cause unnecessary suffering or injury to health, including loss of sight, hearing, limb, organ or body, or any mental derangement, commits an offence. What amounts to neglect is open to some question. Certainly the wilful failure to provide food, clothing, medical aid or accommodation will be viewed as neglect.[342]

Aliment

3.40 Arguably, the principal right a child has against his or her parents is the right to financial support. Prior to 1991, the main financial assistance took the form of aliment. However, after 1991 the main form of financial assistance is child support (discussed below). Court actions for aliment remain for particular categories of young persons.[343] Aliment is the right to support from the parent and is governed by the Family Law (Scotland) Act 1985. The obligation to aliment falls upon both a father and a mother. There is no need for the parents to have been married for the obligation to financially support the child.[344] The obligation also extends to persons who have accepted the child as part of their household.[345] The obligation to aliment extends ordinarily to age 18 (even in respect of mentally handicapped children)[346] but may be applicable to children aged 18–25 who are reasonably and appropriately undergoing instruction at an educational establishment or training for employment, or for a trade, vocation or profession.[347]

Parents must provide such support as is reasonable in the circumstances having regard to the needs and resources of the parties, their earning capacities and all other circumstances.[348] It is possible to obtain an interim award of aliment. The child himself may bring the action against the parent or other person for aliment.[349] Where the child is under 16 the action may be brought

---

[335] Criminal Law (Consolidation) (Scotland) Act 1995 s.3(1).

[336] Criminal Law (Consolidation) (Scotland) Act 1995 s.7(1).

[337] Criminal Law (Consolidation) (Scotland) Act 1995 s.2.

[338] Criminal Law (Consolidation) (Scotland) Act 1995 s.1.

[339] Criminal Law (Consolidation) (Scotland) Act 1995 s.6.

[340] Criminal Law (Consolidation) (Scotland) Act 1995 s.8(1).

[341] Criminal Law (Consolidation) (Scotland) Act 1995 ss.9–12.

[342] See *Stair Memorial Encyclopaedia*, Vol.3, pp.604–605, para.1246.

[343] See Edwards, "Aliment Actions in the Courts after April 1993", 1993 Fam. L.B. 2–6.

[344] Law Reform (Parent and Child) (Scotland) Act 1986 Sch.1 para.21.

[345] 1985 Act s.1(1)(d); note this does not apply to foster parents boarded out by a local authority or voluntary organisations: *Watson v Watson*, 1994 Fam. L.B. 13–7.

[346] *McBride v McBride*, 1995 S.C.L.R. 1021.

[347] 1985 Act s.1(5)(a) and (b); *Jowett v Jowett*, 1990 S.C.L.R. 348.

[348] 1985 Act ss.1(2) and 4(1); *Winter v Thornton*, 1993 S.C.L.R. 389; *Walker v Walker*, 1991 S.L.T. 649; *Bell v McCurdie*, 1981 S.C. 64.

[349] 1985 Act s.2(4)(a).

by the child's parent, guardian or anyone seeking a residence order in respect of the child.[350] An action may be brought even where the child is still living with a person who has an obligation to aliment.[351] Obviously in those circumstances, it is possible for that person to defend an action by proving to the court that they are alimenting the child and will continue to do so.[352] An absent father cannot defend an action brought against him on the basis that he is willing to aliment the child if that child resides with him.[353]

Aliment will be paid in the form of periodical payments, usually weekly or monthly. An order may subsist for a definite period, indefinitely or until the occurrence of a specified event.[354] It is possible to have an award of aliment backdated.[355] It also possible to have an award varied or recalled where there is a material change of circumstances.[356] A variation may similarly be backdated and repayment ordered.[357]

Child support

3.41 Increasingly, resort is made to the provisions of the Child Support Act 1991 to obtain financial provision for the support of children under 16 years of age. The system of aliment which operated alone prior to the child support provisions was criticised on the basis that awards were difficult to predict and inconsistent and on the ground that often aliment was simply not paid.[358] Promoted as a measure to ensure that absent fathers started to pay for their children rather than having the state pay through the benefit system, child support has engendered a fair measure of controversy. On the one hand it has been criticised as a cynical measure to reduce public expenditure on state benefits[359] and on the other it has been seen as an attack on second families.

Under the new statutory arrangements most cases of child maintenance are now assessed by the Child Support Agency ("CSA") rather than the courts and in addition the assessment is carried out by way of a formula. The initial criticisms which both the CSA and the law attracted resulted in modifications to the law in 1995.[360]

A person who has care of a child or who is the non-resident parent of a qualifying child may apply for a child maintenance assessment.[361] A qualifying child 12 years old or over may apply for an assessment in their own right as long as the parent with care or the non-resident parent has not applied for an assessment.[362] A person seeking an assessment authorises the collection and enforcement of the maintenance by the CSA. Where the parent who has residence of the child is in receipt of income support, family credit or disability working allowance that parent must authorise a compulsory assessment.[363] The parent will not need to give authorisation for

---

[350] 1985 Act s.2(4)(c)(i) and (iii), as amended by the Age of Legal Capacity (Scotland) Act 1991 Sch.1 para.40 and Children (Scotland) Act 1995 Sch.4 para.36(b).

[351] 1985 Act s.2(6).

[352] 1985 Act s.2(7).

[353] 1985 Act s.2(8); unless of course the child is over 16, in which case it may be a defence: s.2(9); see also *McKay v McKay*, 1980 S.L.T. (Sh Ct) 111.

[354] 1985 Act s.3(2); it is also possible for one-off special payments to be made for specific occurrences, e.g. hospital bills or school fees; in respect of the latter see *Macdonald v Macdonald*, 1995 S.L.T. 72.

[355] 1985 Act s.3(1)(c).

[356] 1985 Act s.5(1).

[357] 1985 Act s.5(4); a variation of interim aliment cannot be backdated: *McColl v McColl*, 1993 S.L.T. 617.

[358] See White Paper, *Children come first*, Cm.1264 (London: HMSO, 1990).

[359] Graham and Knights, *Putting the Treasury First: The Truth About Child Support* (1994).

[360] *Improving child support*, Cm.2745 (London: HMSO, 1995); Abbot, "The Price of Private Parental Responsibility", 1994 N.L.J. 681; Jones, "Child's Pay Not Child's Play", 1993 *Law Gazette* 90/23, 28; McLean, "The Making of the Child Support Act of 1991: Policy Making at the Intersection of Law and Social Policy" (1994) 21 J. Law and Soc. 505; Diduck, "The Unmodified Family: The Child Support Act and the Construction of Legal Subjects" (1995) 22 J. Law and Soc. 527; Ross and McKenzie, "Financial Support for the Child in Disputed Parentage Cases", 1995 Jur. Rev. 166; see continuing criticism of legislative amendments in Cavanagh, "An Unworkable Act", 1996 SCOLAG 10; Mears, "Paper over the Cracks", 1995 *Law Gazette* 92/06, 16.

[361] Child Support Act 1991 ("1991 Act") s.4.

[362] 1991 Act s.7.

[363] 1991 Act s.6.

an assessment where there are reasonable grounds for believing that there would be a risk to the parent of suffering undue harm or distress as a result of having to give the authorisation. In most circumstances the parent must provide information to trace the absent parent, to allow the assessment to be made. At inception this proved controversial; many single parents who had their children residing with them simply did not wish to have the absent parent in their lives in any shape or form. They had perhaps dissociated themselves from violent partners, or indeed the child had been the product of a casual relationship and they had no wish to resume contact with the natural father. Those on state benefits faced a 20 per cent reduction in their benefit if they refused to co-operate with the authorities.

3.42 Once the CSA has made an assessment, maintenance becomes a legal obligation. Where the assessment has been at the instance of the Secretary of State or where the person seeking the assessment has so authorised, collection and enforcement can be arranged by the Secretary of State. The major power open to the Secretary of State is an earnings order[364] which is an instruction to an employer to deduct the sums due from earnings and remit them to the Secretary of State. This order may be used to collect arrears and/or current maintenance due. A liability order[365] allows the recovery of arrears, and when this is made an earnings order would be inappropriate or ineffective. The liability order can be enforced by means of diligence such as poindings, warrant sales and inhibitions, but not an earnings assessment.

In assessing child maintenance the CSA utilises a formula to calculate the amount payable. The maintenance requirement is the amount required to meet the needs of the child but will not necessarily be the amount payable, which will reflect other factors. Where a non-resident parent's income is over £200 per week, they will pay the basic rate,[366] thus an income assessment is necessary. Assessable income is the element of the non-resident parent's or carer's income that is available for child maintenance. Some of the income of the non-resident parent or carer will be exempt and deducted. The basic rate is a percentage calculation of their weekly assessable income.[367] The rates are as follows: 15 per cent for one qualifying child; 20 per cent for two qualifying children; and 25 per cent for three or more qualifying children. Once this figure has been calculated, deductions are made to take into account children within a new family and of any residency with the non-resident parent. The non-resident parent and child's carer may appeal to the appeals tribunal.[368] On points of law there is further appeal to the Child Support Commissioners and Inner House of the Court of Session.[369]

ADOPTION

3.43 Adoption is the legal process whereby the legal relationship between a child and his natural parents is severed and a new legal relationship between the child and his adoptive parents is created.[370] An adoption order can only be made in respect of a child who is under 18 years of age.[371] A child who is married or has been married cannot be adopted.[372] However, it is possible for a child to be re-adopted.[373] Although the process severs and recreates a family relationship, it is one heavily overseen and regulated by the state, with the involvement of both the court and also the local authority.

[364] 1991 Act ss.31–32.
[365] 1991 Act s.33.
[366] The two other rates are the flat rate and the nil rate. For a fuller discussion of child support, see Edwards and Griffiths, *Family Law* (2006), pp.190–203.
[367] 1991 Act Sch.1 as substituted by the Child Support, Pensions and Social Security Act 2000 Sch.1.
[368] 1991 Act s.20, as substituted by the Child Support, Pensions and Social Security Act 2000 s.10.
[369] 1991 Act ss.24 and 25.
[370] For a brief discussion of the changing nature of adoption see Edwards and Griffiths, *Family Law* (1997), pp.166–168; for more detail, see McNeil, *Adoption of Children in Scotland*, 3rd edn (1998).
[371] Adoption (Scotland) Act 1978 s.12(1), as amended by the Children (Scotland) 1995 Act Sch.2 para.7.
[372] Adoption (Scotland) Act 1978 ("1978 Act"), s.12(5).
[373] 1978 Act s.12(7).

All local authorities are required to provide an adoption service for their area.[374] Integral to the process of adoption is the adoption agency. The law recognises two types of adoption agency—the local authority and other registered adoption services.[375] Non-local authority adoption services are required to be approved by the Commission for the Regulation of Care, and may provide the full range of adoption services or only some of those services.[376] The local authority will have a full range of services including post-placement support for anyone with problems about adoption.[377] The work of adoption agencies has undergone a subtle transformation in modern times. Where once they acted as a service to place healthy babies, they now face the considerable problem of placing many highly disadvantaged children. Such children may have a long association with the social work department of the local authority. For example, the children may already be in care under other provisions (discussed in Ch.4). The adoption agency, once it has decided that adoption is the best course of action for the child, must decide the best route to that objective whether it be placing the child for adoption or obtaining a freeing order for adoption which prepares the child for prospective adoption. Only local authorities can seek a freeing order.[378] The purposes of freeing is to sever the connection with the birth parents and remove the complication, at an early stage, of obtaining their consent to adoption. It is necessary before a freeing order will be granted to satisfy the court that a child has been placed for adoption or is likely to be placed.[379]

3.44 Obviously before proceeding to placing or any other adoption process, the local authority has to carefully assess the child's needs, taking advice where appropriate from current carers and other professionals acquainted with the child. In preparing for placement a considerable amount of work must be undergone with the child. There will also need to be a great deal of work to link the child and the prospective adopters.[380] This matching process is extremely delicate and sensitive and can often result in failure. Once a link is established attempts will be made to introduce the child to the prospective adopters. Again this is a delicate process, which calls for a great deal of professional skill.[381]

Once the child is placed the adoption agency must visit the prospective adopters within one week of the placement.[382] A written report will be made of the visit. Initially at least, the child will have his own separate social worker who will maintain contact on a regular basis. If the placement is not working a decision to withdraw the child may be made but only after careful consideration. Where the placement is successful a decision is likely to be made for the prospective adopters to lodge an adoption petition in court.

In placing children, and particularly disadvantaged children, the adoption agency faces a considerable task. To ensure selection of the most appropriate adopter, the agency will prepare information for prospective adopters including a written statement of the criteria that are applied to those wishing to be assessed as prospective adopters.[383] Applicants will complete a questionnaire, which will be a prelude to assessment as prospective adopters.[384] The assessment will include medical and police checks.[385]

Adoption agencies are required to have adoption panels whose functions include considering: whether it is in the best interests of a particular child to be adopted; alternatives to adoption; the

---

[374] 1978 Act s.1.
[375] Regulation of Care (Scotland) Act 2001 s.2(11)(a) and (b).
[376] Regulation of Care (Scotland) Act 2001 ss.7 and 2(11)(b).
[377] See *Scotland's children*, Cm.2286 (1993), Vol.3, "Adoption and PROs", para.4.
[378] 1978 Act s.18(1), as amended by the Children (Scotland) Act 1995.
[379] 1978 Act s.18(3).
[380] See *Scotland's children*, Cm.2286 (1993), Vol.3, paras 17–19.
[381] *Scotland's children*, Cm.2286 (1993), Vol.3, paras 20–24.
[382] Adoption Agencies (Scotland) Regulations 1996 (SI 1996/3266) reg.19(2).
[383] Adoption Agencies (Scotland) Regulations 1996 reg.10(1).
[384] Adoption Agencies (Scotland) Regulations 1996 reg.10(3).
[385] See *Scotland's children*, Cm.2286 (1993), Vol.3, paras 76–88.

suitability of prospective adopters, and whether prospective adopters would be suitable adoptive parents for a particular child.[386]

3.45 In 2003, roughly one-third of all adoptions were step-parent adoptions where one of the birth parents had entered a new relationship and both that person and their new partner wished to formalise the relationship between the child and the step-parent.[387] It is also the case that other family members may wish to adopt a child.[388] Naturally, these children are not placed by the adoption agency but are already in situ with the prospective adopters. Nevertheless there is a key role for the adoption agency and it must be notified of the intention to lodge an adoption petition in court.[389]

Irrespective of the mode of adoption there are general rules as to who can adopt. In adoptions where the child is placed with an adoption agency or the adoption is by a step-parent, parent or relatives, the child must be at least 19 weeks old by the time the order is made and must have lived with the prospective adopter for the preceding 13 weeks.[390] Currently single persons or married couples can adopt. Adopters must have been domiciled or habitually resident in the United Kingdom for one year prior to the application for adoption. Where the application is from a married couple they must be at least 21 years of age unless one of them is the natural parent of the child in which case that person need only be 18.[391] Where the applicant is single the court requires to be satisfied that the applicant's spouse cannot be found, or that he or she is not married, or that the party's spouse is incapable of making an application through mental or physical ill health, or that the parties are separated and living apart and that separation is likely to be permanent.[392] Cohabitees cannot make a joint application to adopt, albeit the Adoption and Children (Scotland) Act 2007 will change this upon commencement. A single gay person in a stable relationship can adopt.[393] As noted earlier adoption agencies operate criteria for prospective adopters, which are made available to those seeking to adopt.[394] The panel of men and women receive information about the child to be adopted and the prospective adopters as well as a case history and a home study report prepared by a social worker on the prospective adopters.

3.46 Following the amendments to the law introduced by the Children (Scotland) 1995 Act it is now possible for a step-parent alone to make an application for adoption. There is no longer any need for them to be conjoined in the application by the natural birth parent with whom they are now in a relationship.[395] Commentators have regularly lamented the fact that when a step-parent adoption takes place it often severs the legal ties with a natural birth parent, usually the natural father. The child and the birth parent inevitably lose rights vis-à-vis each other. Under the minimalist intervention strategy of the 1995 Act the courts are implored to make an order only where they consider it better for the child's welfare to do so than not to do so.[396] The duty on the court is to take a decision on the basis that the welfare of the child throughout his life is paramount.[397] Birth parents have the right to withhold consent to an adoption order. One exception to this is that natural fathers who have never been married to the mother do not have

[386] Adoption Agencies (Scotland) Regulations 1996 reg.11; on the composition and role of the adoption panel see *Scotland's children*, Cm.2286 (1993), Vol.3, paras 93–137.

[387] *Adoption Applications 2003* (Scottish Executive National Statistics Publication, 16 March 2004), Table 5.

[388] *Adoption Applications 2003* (2004), Table 6.

[389] 1978 Act s.22.

[390] 1978 Act s.13.

[391] 1978 Act s.14(1A), substituted by the Children Act 1989 Sch.10 para.33.

[392] 1978 Act s.15.

[393] *T, Petr*, 1997 S.L.T. 724.

[394] Adoption Agencies (Scotland) Regulations 1996 reg.17A.

[395] See Margaret Ross, "Adoption and the Children (Scotland) Act 1995" (1995) J.L.S.S. 395.

[396] 1978 Act s.24(3), as amended by the 1995 Act Sch.2 para.16; Ross, "Adoption and the Children (Scotland) Act 1995" (1995) J.L.S.S. 395.

[397] 1978 Act s.6A, as inserted by the 1995 Act s.96.

such rights. Even in situations where the birth parent is withholding consent it is possible for the court to dispense with it on the basis that it is being withheld unreasonably.[398]

In all adoptions not involving an adoption agency (step-parent or other relative) at least three months' notice must be given to the local authority of the proposed adoption to allow suitable investigations to take place.[399] The local authority must be given access to the child in the home environment even where the child is living with parents, step-parents or relatives.[400]

Private arrangement of adoption other than in conformity with s.11(1) of the Adoption (Scotland) Act 1978 is a criminal offence.[401] The payment of money to procure an adoption or consent to adoption is also an offence,[402] although it may not bar the eventual adoption.[403] It is nevertheless possible for foster parents who adopt "hard to place" children in certain circumstances to continue to receive payments following adoption.[404]

As indicated earlier, in adoptions where the adoption agency has placed the child it is a requirement of law that the child must have been so placed for 13 weeks prior to the court granting the order. The agency must have sufficient time to observe the child in the home environment. During the placement, if informal consent has been given by the natural parents to the placement of the child with prospective adopters, the child cannot be removed by the parents without the consent of the adoption agency or the courts.[405] In all other respects, natural parents retain rights and responsibilities over their child until the adoption order is made unless the child is the subject of a supervision order or a parental rights and responsibilities order or freeing for adoption order.

The key test for adoption orders

3.47 Section 6(1) of the Adoption (Scotland) Act 1978 ("1978 Act") states that:

> "in reaching any decision relating to the adoption of a child, a court or adoption agency shall have regard to all the circumstances but—
>
> (a) shall regard the need to safeguard and promote the welfare of the child concerned throughout his life as the paramount consideration; and
>
> (b) shall have regard so far as practicable—
>
> (i) to his views (if he wishes to express them) taking account of his age and maturity; and
>
> (ii) to his religious persuasion, racial origin and cultural and linguistic background."

A child aged 12 or more is to be presumed to be of sufficient age and maturity to form and express a view.[406] In all adoption applications where the child is 12 years of age or over an order cannot be made without the child's consent.[407] Even if the child is under 12 years of age his view should be given due consideration. In placing a child for adoption the adoption agency must have regard so far as is practicable to the religious views of the parents or guardians of the child as to the religious upbringing of the child. The child's religious persuasion is to be considered as a part of the welfare principle. Regardless of all this it is not a fast rule that children cannot be adopted by persons of a religious persuasion different from that of the parents, guardians or the child.

---

[398] 1978 Act s.16(2); see also *A v B*, 1987 S.L.T. (Sh Ct) 121.
[399] 1978 Act s.22.
[400] 1978 Act s.13.
[401] 1978 Act s.11(3).
[402] 1978 Act s.51.
[403] 1978 Act s.24, as amended by the 1995 Act Sch.2 para.16.
[404] 1978 Act s.51A, as inserted by the 1995 Act Sch.2 para.25.
[405] 1978 Act s.27.
[406] 1978 Act s.6(2); see *H v M*, 1995 S.C.L.R. 401, where child of six was held to be too young to form a view.
[407] 1978 Act s.12(8).

Application can be made to the Court of Session but it is more usual for the application to be made to the sheriff court for an adoption order.[408] All hearings on adoption will take place in private.[409] The court must appoint a curator *ad litem* to safeguard the interests of the child. The curator will also provide the court with a report on the child's interests.[410] In addition to this a court reporter is required to witness the necessary consents to the adoption. It will often be the case that the reporter will also be the curator *ad litem*. The adoption agency or the local authority is required to submit a report on the suitability of the prospective adopters and the welfare of the child. These reports are of vital importance in assisting the court in its determination.[411]

Where the court has reservations about making an adoption order but does not wish to simply refuse it, it may postpone a decision for up to two years with or without a parental rights and responsibilities order being made instead of the adoption order.[412] Where a child is already the subject of a supervision requirement and it is proposed that they be adopted, the hearing must be asked to review the case and provide advice to the court on the adoption application.[413] In making the adoption order the court may discharge the supervision requirement if it sees fit to do so.[414] It is also the case that the courts can, in granting an adoption order, make an order for contact with the birth parents but this is exercised rarely.[415]

Parental consent

3.48 It is essential that a parent or guardian of the child must freely and with full understanding of what is involved, agree unconditionally to the making of an adoption order.[416] A "parent" means the mother or father of the child where they both have (or one has) parental rights and responsibilities.[417] A father who has never been married to the mother or is not registered on a child's birth certificate from May 4, 2008 will not automatically have parental rights and responsibilities. He may acquire parental rights and responsibilities under the Children (Scotland) Act 1995 by means of a s.4 agreement with the mother or a s.11 court order. A guardian in the context of adoption is someone appointed by deed or court order.[418] A mother cannot give agreement until six weeks after the birth of the child.[419] Unless they are guardians, grandparents have limited scope for involvement in adoption proceedings.[420]

If a child has been freed for adoption there will be no need for a parent or guardian to consent. In the event that consent is required and is refused it is possible that the court may dispense with it. The grounds for dispensation are as follows:

- the parent or guardian is not known, cannot be found or is incapable of giving agreement;
- the parent or guardian is withholding agreement unreasonably;
- the parent or guardian has persistently failed, without reasonable cause, to fulfil one or other of his or her parental responsibilities in relation to the child;
- the parent or guardian has seriously ill-treated the child, whose reintegration into the

[408] 1978 Act s.56.
[409] 1978 Act s.57.
[410] 1978 Act s.58.
[411] See e.g. *Central RC v M*, 1991 S.C.L.R. 300.
[412] 1978 Act s.25, as amended by the 1995 Act Sch.2 para.17.
[413] 1978 Act s.22A, as inserted by the 1995 Act Sch.2 para.15.
[414] 1978 Act ss.12(9) and 18(9), inserted by the 1995 Act Sch.2 paras 7(d) and 11(d).
[415] *FB and AB, Petrs*, 1998 Fam. L.B. 35–6, *B v C*, 1996 S.L.T. 1370; see Sutherland, "D v Grampian Regional Council: Parental Rights and Adoption", 1996 S.L.P.Q. 159.
[416] 1978 Act s.16(1)(b).
[417] 1978 Act s.65(1), as amended by the 1995 Act Sch.2.
[418] 1978 Act s.65(1), as amended by the 1995 Act Sch.2 para.9.
[419] 1978 Act s.16(4).
[420] See Sutherland, "Grandparents and the Law", 1994 Fam. L.B. 7–3.

same household as the parent or guardian is, because of the serious ill-treatment, or for other reasons, unlikely.[421]

Where the assertion is that the parent or guardian cannot be found or is not known the court will require to be satisfied by the report of the curator *ad litem* and any other available information of the steps taken to establish who the parents are or their whereabouts. If the basis of the dispensation of the agreement is that the parent is incapable of giving consent then medical evidence in the form of a medical report to that effect will be necessary. Establishment of the situation does not necessarily mean that the court will dispense with the agreement. In situations where the incapability is likely to be temporary the court will be reluctant to do so.

3.49 The persistent failure "without reasonable cause" to safeguard and promote the child's welfare will be exhibited by a pattern of conduct. The failure to pay aliment is likely to be viewed as an example of such conduct. Conversely, simply being absent from the house when one's marriage is disintegrating will not.[422] In *Angus Council Petitioners*[423] it was held that a mother's personality disorder did not constitute "reasonable cause" for her failure to safeguard and promote her child's welfare. Failure to pay aliment because of unemployment can amount to reasonable cause.[424] Again even if neglect is established the court must proceed to assess whether agreement should be dispensed with. There may be situations in which the prognosis of the parent's behaviour is favourable, which leads the court to determine, in giving paramount consideration to the welfare of the child, that agreement should not be dispensed with.

In conformity with one of the themes of the 1995 Act of maintaining family contact, persistent failure of contact with a child without reasonable cause may result in parental agreement to adoption being dispensed with. Imprisonment and voluntarily not contacting the child over a period of time are examples likely to meet the objective assessment of without "reasonable cause".

In contrast, serious ill-treatment can be established by a solitary instance of sufficient gravity if it is the case that the child cannot be reintegrated back into the family home. Where reintegration is possible parental agreement will not be dispensed with. The operation of the twofold test is such that where the ground is established the welfare principle will operate in such a way that the court will invariably dispense with parental agreement.

Somewhat more controversial are the cases where the court has to decide that the parent is withholding their agreement unreasonably. It is not the case that, simply because the adoption order (having regard to the paramount interest of the child's welfare) would be better than no order, any refusal of the parent(s) will be rendered unreasonable.[425] The test is "would a reasonable parent have withheld consent?".[426] There need be no culpability on the part of the parent or guardian.[427] Where a child has been with the prospective adopters for a considerable period of time it is likely that a reasonable parent would see the likely disruption in removal and agree to the adoption.[428]

3.50 Once the order is made it is registered in the Adopted Children Register. When the adopted person reaches the age of 16, he is entitled to obtain information in respect of his birth. The adopted person may be allowed access to court processes relating to the adoption[429] and also to

---

[421] 1978 Act s.16(2), as amended by the 1995 Act Sch.2 para.10.

[422] *Re D (Minors)* [1973] 3 All E.R. 1001; cf. *H and H, Petrs*, 1976 S.L.T. 80; see also *A and B v C*, 1977 S.L.T. (Sh Ct) 55. See also Thomson, *Family Law in Scotland*, 3rd edn (1996), p.248.

[423] Reported in 1998 Fam. L.B. 35–5.

[424] *A v B*, 1987 S.L.T. (Sh Ct) 121.

[425] See Thomson, *Family Law in Scotland*, 3rd edn (1999), p.250; *Re W (An Infant)* [1971] A.C. 682 (HL), per Lord Hodson at 718.

[426] *P v Lothian RC*, 1989 S.L.T. 739, per Lord Justice-Clerk Ross at 741; see also *Lothian RC v A*, 1992 S.L.T. 858.

[427] See *Re D (Infant)* [1977] A.C. 602 (HL).

[428] *O v Central RC*, 1987 G.W.D. 22–813; *Lothian RC v R*, 1988 G.W.D. 28–1172. Ross, "Adoption and the Children (Scotland) Act 1995" (1995) J.L.S.S. 395.

[429] Act of Sederunt (Child Care and Maintenance Rules) 1997 (SI 1997/291) Sheriff Court r.2.33(2)(a) and Court of Session r.67.32(2)(a). These papers will have been transferred to the Scottish Record Office in Edinburgh.

see his original birth certificate.[430] In addition the adopted person may seek information from the adoption agency. Adopted persons seeking such information often do so as a prelude to searching for their birth parents. At the time of receiving the information they will also be entitled to receive counselling services to help them cope emotionally with their situation. Such counselling is not obligatory nor is it a prelude to the release of information. The adoption agency is restricted in its role in assisting a search for the birth parent. The desire to locate must come from the adopted person. However, it is suggested that initial contact with a located birth parent be made by a social worker.[431] Adopted persons under 16 years of age have no right of access to information but guidance suggests that it is important to explore the reasons why the young person has approached the adoption agency for information and with the adopted child's consent it is thought appropriate to inform the adoptive parents.[432]

Adoption and Children (Scotland) Act 2007

3.51 In April 2001, the Scottish Executive established the independent Adoption Policy Review Group to "address questions surrounding the place of adoption in securing permanence for 'looked after children'".[433] Phase I of the review focused upon the everyday practice of adoption and long-term care, while Phase II considered the legal framework. The ensuing Reports made 107 far-reaching recommendations, which helped to form the basis of the Adoption and Children (Scotland) Act 2007.[434] This Act received Royal Assent on January 15, 2007, but is unlikely to come into force until 2008 or 2009. It will repeal the Adoption (Scotland) Act 1978 other than Pt IV—status of adopted children, although much of the current law will subsist in the new Act. Fundamental changes relate to the following.

Adoption services

3.52 Local authorities will have a new duty to prepare and publish Adoption Service Plans. Such services will be available to the extended class of persons identified under s.1(3) of the Adoption and Children (Scotland) Act 2007. Furthermore, ss.9–12 include new changes in relation to the duty to assess the need for, and provision of, adoption support services. Support services are defined under s.1(5) to include counselling, guidance and other assistance appropriate in the circumstances.

Who can adopt

3.53 Section 29 provides for adoption by an unmarried couple. The new provisions refer to a relevant couple which is satisfied by means of marriage, civil partnership, or living together as a man and wife/civil partners in an enduring family relationship.

Parental consent

3.54 The grounds for dispensing with parental consent have been replaced under s.31 of the Adoption and Children (Scotland) Act 2007. The new grounds allow for this where:

- the parent or guardian is dead; or
- the parent or guardian cannot be found or is incapable of giving consent; or
- a parent or guardian with parental rights and responsibilities is, in the court's opinion, unable to discharge or exercise them and likely to continue to do so; or
- the welfare of the child requires the consent to be dispensed with.

---

[430] 1978 Act s.45(5), as amended by the Children Act 1989 and the Children (Scotland) Act 1995.
[431] See *Scotland's children*, Cm.2286 (1993), Vol.3, para.234.
[432] *Scotland's children*, Cm.2286 (1993), Vol.3, para.236.
[433] Adoption Policy Review Group—Report Phase I (2002), p.1.
[434] Adoption Policy Review Group—Report Phase I (2002) and Adoption: Better Choices for Our Children (2005).

Permanence orders

3.55 Permanence orders are court orders providing for the long-term care of children when adoption is not the best option. They are intended to provide stability, based on the individual child's need, and repeal the freeing for adoption order and the parental responsibility order since it subsumes many of these powers. Sections 80–104 prescribe the new rules (see Ch.4 for a full discussion).

Chapter 4

Care and Protection of Children

Introduction

4.01 Law and policy formulation relating to the care and protection of children operates on several key principles, namely that:

- each child has a right to be treated as an individual;
- each child who can form a view on matters affecting him or her has the right to express those views if he or she so wishes;
- parents should normally be responsible for the upbringing of their children and should share that responsibility;
- each child has the right to protection from all forms of abuse, neglect or exploitation;
- so far as is consistent with safeguarding and promoting the child's welfare, the public authority should promote the upbringing of children by their families; and
- any intervention by a public authority in the life of a child must be properly justified and should be supported by services from all relevant agencies working in collaboration.[1]

Although the law is becoming more prescriptive in the parent–child relationship (see Ch.2), for the most part family autonomy is respected and in recent times there has been a political rhetoric of support for the family, to provide a stable, loving and ultimately caring environment for the nurturing of children to adulthood and self-sufficiency. The need to have respect for family ties is more present since the Human Rights Act 1998. Inevitability, there arise occasions where nurturing within the child's own family is impossible, impracticable or ultimately detrimental to that child's health, welfare or development. Where such situations arise, there is clearly a need for intervention whether in the form of assistance or some other more direct action. In a civilised society, one should expect no less. The proper consideration given to children in our society ensures that a large segment of the collective services we call social work are dedicated to the care and protection of children.

Childcare Reform

4.02 The Children (Scotland) Act 1995 is the primary Act in relation to childcare and protection. Most of its provisions came into effect in 1997 and the following decade has highlighted many

[1] *Scotland's children, regulation and guidance*, Cm.2286 (1993), Vol.1, "Support and Protection for Children and their Families", p.vii.

deficiencies in the legal framework. In November 2002, an audit of child services reported its findings in "It's Everyone's Job to Make Sure I'm Alright" and recommended:

- that agencies renewed their procedures and processes so that all agencies are familiar with their duties;
- the remit of Child Protection Committees be expanded and the structure changed;
- strengthening the arrangements for disseminating knowledge between agencies;
- an Integrated Child Service Plan;
- a review of children's hearings, in particular the grounds of referral.[2]

In the same month, the Scottish Executive responded to these recommendations and announced a three-year programme of child protection reform. The first response[3] was to review the children's hearings system and child services around it. The finding[4] was that most parties, as a whole, were confident in the hearings process; however, there were key issues. These were that children did not get the help when it was required and were being drawn into the hearings process unnecessarily; the system was inadequate to deal with more persistent or serious offenders; and panel members were often poorly supported and frustrated when their decisions were not always acted upon. *Getting It Right for Every Child: Proposals for Action*[5] set out to consult on proposed changes for all children's services. Key areas of change focused on encouraging joint working; introducing co-ordinated assessments and child service plans; rewriting the grounds of referral and addressing panel members concerns. The Scottish Executive announced a three-pronged approach to implement these changes. The first addressed a practice change whereby systems are developed to allow people to do their job better, e.g. single assessment records. Secondly, barriers that prevent joint working should be removed. Finally, there will be legislative change to impose new duties on agencies to share information and ways of being alerted to the needs of children and remedying key difficulties in the children's hearings system.

To date, as a consequence of the reform programme, a Children's Services Steering group has been established to oversee child services issues; implementation of an Integrated Child or Young Person's Service Plan; and legal reform via Protection of Children (Scotland) Act 2003, Protection of Vulnerable Groups (Scotland) Act 2007 and the draft Children's Service (Scotland) Bill. Part 1 of the draft Bill compels agencies to help children access appropriate and timely services. It is envisaged that this will be achieved through new duties covering arrangements for co-ordinated joint working, considering the views of appropriate children and persons, detailed assessing of the child's well-being and taking appropriate action. A second element is change for the hearings, a discussion of this is provided at para.4.78.

LOCAL AUTHORITY POWERS AND DUTIES

4.03 Local authorities have a number of legal responsibilities and powers in relation to childcare provision. Those responsibilities and powers emanate from several important statutory duties. Understanding these duties provides a useful starting point in the understanding of the broader body of law relating to the care and protection of children.

[2] "It's Everyone's Job to Make Sure I'm Alright", Report of the Child Protection Audit and Review (November 25, 2002). *http://www.scotland.gov.uk/Publications/2002/11/15820/14009.*

[3] *Getting It Right for Every Child*: Phase I of the Review of the Children's Hearings System (Scottish Executive, 2004).

[4] Report on the Responses to Phase One Consultation (2004).

[5] *http://www.scotland.gov.uk/Publications/2005/06/20135608/56173* [Accessed July 2, 2008].

Children looked after by the local authority

4.04 In seeking to alter the tone of childcare legislation, children previously said to be in local authority care are now referred to as children "looked after" by the local authority.[6] Children are looked after by local authorities when they are provided with accommodation under s.25 of the Children (Scotland) Act 1995, or are the subject of a supervision requirement of a children's hearing, or are subject to any order, authorisation or warrant under which the local authority has responsibilities in respect of the child, or the child is living in Scotland but in respect of whom local authorities have responsibilities under the Children (Reciprocal Enforcement of Prescribed Orders etc. (England and Wales and Northern Ireland)) (Scotland) Regulations 1996.[7]

Local authorities have certain duties towards children looked after by them. These are:

- to safeguard and promote the child's welfare, taking the child's welfare as the paramount consideration;
- to make use of services that would be available for children were they cared for by their parents;
- to take steps to promote regular and direct contact between the child and any person with parental responsibilities, so far as is practicable, appropriate and consistent with the duty to safeguard the child's welfare;
- to provide advice and assistance with a view to the time when the child is no longer looked after by them;
- to find out and have regard to the views of the child, the child's parents and any other relevant person, so far as is practicable when making decisions about the child; and
- to take account as far as is practicable of the child's religious persuasion, racial origin, and cultural and linguistic background.[8]

The local authority may deviate from these obligations where necessary to protect members of the public from serious harm.

Devising a care plan

4.05 In practice the local authority is expected to develop a care plan for any child looked after by it. The care plan will be based on gathered information which will allow the short- and long-term assessment of the child's needs.[9] The arrangements put in place for the child should be committed to writing, and where possible agreed with the child's parents, or a person having parental responsibility for him/her. Discussion is encouraged even in circumstances where the child must be looked after by the local authority, such as with a supervision requirement by a children's hearing. The care plan is designed to ensure that those involved know their obligations under it.

Local authorities are expected to act as "good parents" to children looked after by them.[10] Care plans should reflect healthcare needs, health promotion, general assessment, surveillance and assessment of developmental progress, as well as treatment of illness and accidents, in order to promote the physical, social, and emotional health and development of the child.[11] The local authority is also expected to encourage and facilitate the child's educational development.[12] Where the child is placed with foster carers and the parents have signed a consent form, those

---

[6] Children (Scotland) Act 1995 (1995 Act) s.17(6).

[7] SI 1996/3267.

[8] See the 1995 Act s.17.

[9] See reg.3(2)(a) of the Arrangements to Look After Children (Scotland) Regulations 1996 (SI 1996/3262) ("1996 Regs"): the information required to be obtained is detailed in Sch.1.

[10] 1996 Regs reg.13.

[11] *Scotland's children*, Cm.2286 (1993), Vol.2, "Children Looked after by Local Authorities", p.12.

[12] 1996 Regs reg.5(2)(c).

carers may authorise consent for medical, surgical and dental treatment where the child is not of sufficient age and maturity to give his or her own consent.

Reviewing the care plan

4.06 Local authorities must review the cases of all children looked after by them. Regulations set out how those reviews should be carried out.[13] The objectives of care review will be:

- to provide an opportunity to take stock of the child's needs and circumstances at regular prescribed time intervals;
- to consult formally with parents and children;
- to assess the effectiveness of current care plans as a means of securing the best interests of the child;
- to provide an opportunity to oversee and make accountable the work of professional staff involved; and
- to formulate future care plans.[14]

Where the child is looked after by the local authority and placed away from his or her own home, the first review must take place within six weeks. A subsequent review will take place within three months of the first review, and thereafter at intervals of six months. Where the child is being looked after as a result of a children's hearing, a review meeting should take place prior to any further consideration by the children's hearing under s.73(4) and (5) of the Children (Scotland) Act 1995 where the local authority believes the supervision requirement should be ended or varied or is considering an application for a parental responsibilities order, a freeing for adoption order or a placing for adoption.[15] The outcome of the review meeting will be communicated to the hearing.

There is a legal requirement on authorities to insist that any persons with whom the child is placed must notify them forthwith of any accident, injury or illness, disability, unauthorised absence, or the death of the child.[16] In respect of the death of the child, the local authority is required to notify the Secretary of State and as far as practicable the child's parents and other persons who have parental responsibilities for the child.[17] The Secretary of State will be notified via the Social Work Services Group who must be notified within one day of the death of the child.[18]

Home supervision

4.07 One of the means by which a child will be looked after by a local authority is under a supervision requirement of a children's hearing. Home supervision has the followings objectives:

- to provide effective measures for the care, protection, support, guidance, treatment or control of children living at home with their families;
- to enable children and their families to recognise and tackle successfully the difficulties and problems that led to the child being referred to a children's hearing;
- to reduce offending behaviour;
- to provide protective measures for a child from others or from himself or herself, where this is an issue;
- to ensure school attendance where this is an issue;
- to provide programmes of supervision that will maintain the confidence of panel

[13] *Scotland's children*, Cm.2286 (1993), Vol.2, pp.18–24; see also Annex 2, p.35, for suggested format of reviews and issues to be discussed.

[14] *Scotland's children*, Cm.2286 (1993), Vol.2, p.18.

[15] 1996 Regs reg.9.

[16] 1996 Regs reg.14.

[17] 1996 Regs reg.15; see *Scotland's children*, Cm.2286 (1993), Vol.2, Annex 4, p.38.

[18] *Scotland's children*, Cm.2286 (1993), Vol.2, p.29.

members and the public in the effectiveness of home supervision as a decision of the hearing; and
- to provide programmes of supervision that aim to integrate the child in the community and maintain the confidence of the community.[19]

In ensuring achievement of any of these objectives, the social worker has a key role in maintaining contact as agreed in the care plan and in working directly with the child and his or her family.[20]

Residential supervision

4.08 In some cases children will be looked after by the local authority in residential care establishments. In this regard, there are key provisions in the Residential Establishments—Child Care (Scotland) Regulations 1996.[21] The Regulations lay down rules for the operation of such establishments. Before a child is placed in a residential establishment the person in charge should be provided with a report on the child.[22] The managers of residential care establishments in conjunction with the person in charge are required to prepare a statement of functions and objectives of the establishment.[23] In addition the Regulations attempt to address the issue of staff, the number of children to be accommodated and the quality of care. Within a residential care establishment there may be secure accommodation for those children who require it and from which the child cannot leave. These units are inspected by the Scottish Care Commission for the Regulation of Care and are governed by the Regulation of Care (Scotland) Act 2001.

Foster care

4.09 One of the most common ways in which a child is looked after by a local authority is by foster care. Fostering is principally governed by the Fostering of Children (Scotland) Regulations 1996,[24] but also by the Arrangements to Look After Children (Scotland) Regulations 1996. The concept of fostering is that the child is looked after for a limited period of time before being returned to their own family. On a practical basis, foster care forms part of the local authorities' children's services plans. Those plans will identify particular need for fostering, and it is anticipated that the local authority will supplement volunteers with recruited foster parents.[25]

Each local authority is required to form a fostering panel.[26] The fostering panel considers all those wishing to become foster parents and makes recommendations as to their suitability for a particular child, any child or certain categories of child.[27] A child may be fostered by a man and a woman living and acting jointly together, or a man or a woman living and acting alone.[28] Where the household contains other persons, a person can still be approved provided those persons are relatives of the prospective foster carers. If a foster carer dies, or leaves the household, it may not be necessary for the child to be removed if the local authority is satisfied that another member of the household can act as a foster parent.[29]

Those applying to become foster parents will have to be assessed by the local authority. They will be interviewed by or on behalf of the local authority and a report will be passed to the

---

[19] *Scotland's children*, Cm.2286 (1993), Vol.2, p.40.

[20] *Scotland's children*, Cm.2286 (1993), Vol.2, pp.43–45.

[21] SI 1996/3256.

[22] Residential Establishments—Child Care (Scotland) Regulations 1996 (SI 1996/3256) reg.17.

[23] Residential Establishments—Child Care (Scotland) Regulations 1996 reg.5; see also, A. Skinner, *Another Kind of Home* (Edinburgh: HMSO, 1992).

[24] SI 1996/3263.

[25] *Scotland's children*, Cm.2286 (1993), Vol.2, pp.46–48.

[26] Fostering of Children (Scotland) Regulations 1996 reg.4(1).

[27] Fostering of Children (Scotland) Regulations 1996 reg.6(1).

[28] Fostering of Children (Scotland) Regulations 1996 reg.12(4).

[29] Fostering of Children (Scotland) Regulations 1996 reg.12(5).

fostering panel.[30] The interviewing process may take place over a series of visits, and will involve the inspection of documents such as birth and marriage certificates. It may also involve what might be perceived as intrusive questioning as to the nature and extent of relationships within the household, lifestyle and standard of living, religion, views on discipline, and other analogous matters.[31] An assessment should take place as to amenities and schools available in the locality of the prospective foster carers. On receipt of a report by the fostering panel, if the local authority considers that a prospective foster carer is a suitable person with whom to place a child, they will approve that person as a foster carer.[32] Prospective foster carers may be invited to meet with the foster panel. Once approved, a written agreement is entered into between the foster carer and the local authority.[33] There are allowances payable to foster carers.[34] The local authority is charged with keeping under review foster carers and at intervals of not more than one year it must decide whether the foster carer continues to be a suitable person with whom to place children. Following review, the local authority may revise the terms of the agreement or revoke it in entirety. A foster carer may intimate that they no longer wish to be considered as a foster parent and the local authority will simply terminate the agreement.[35]

4.10 Where a local authority is looking after a child under s.17(6)(a), (b) and (d) of the Children (Scotland) Act 1995 (essentially those provided with accommodation), they must not place a child with foster parents unless those foster carers have been approved as foster carers in advance and the authority has satisfied itself that placement with that particular foster carer is in the child's best interests. Special agreements must be entered into by the local authority and the foster carers.[36]

In emergency situations the local authority may place a child for up to 72 hours with any approved foster carer. Before doing this, the local authority is required to satisfy itself that foster placement is the most suitable way of meeting the child's needs.[37] Where a local authority is satisfied that the immediate placement of a child is necessary it may for a period not exceeding six weeks place the child with a person who is not an approved foster carer, after interviewing the person, inspecting the accommodation, and obtaining information about the person and others living in the household, provided that:

- the person is a relative or friend of the child;
- the person has entered into a written agreement to carry out specified duties in respect of the child; and
- the authority is satisfied that a foster placement is the most suitable way of meeting the child's needs.[38]

4.11 Kinship care is a key policy of the Scottish Government since it allows a flexible, child-centred approach to care. In 2006 the National Kinship and Foster Care Strategy stated that:

> "If children and young people need to live away from their parents, for however short a time and for whatever reasons, given the choice, most children want to live with a member of their family or a friend, or with a foster carer. However, for some young people, residential care may be the preferred option to foster care. For those children and young people whose needs *are* best served by foster or kinship care, this option can provide them

---

[30] The particulars to be considered are listed in Sch.1 to the Fostering of Children (Scotland) Regulations 1996.

[31] See *Scotland's children*, Cm.2286 (1993), Vol.2, pp.48–51.

[32] See generally the Fostering of Children (Scotland) Regulations 1996 reg.7.

[33] Fostering of Children (Scotland) Regulations 1996 reg.8 and Sch.2 for the matters to be covered in foster carer agreements.

[34] Fostering of Children (Scotland) Regulations 1996 reg.9; see also for a full discussion on this issue *Scotland's children*, Cm.2286 (1993), Vol.2, pp.59–61.

[35] Fostering of Children (Scotland) Regulations 1996 reg.10.

[36] Fostering of Children (Scotland) Regulations 1996 reg.12.

[37] Fostering of Children (Scotland) Regulations 1996 reg.13.

[38] Fostering of Children (Scotland) Regulations 1996 reg.14(1).

with the best chance of overcoming the disruption and damage that they have faced and to develop happily and confidently."[39]

At March 31, 2007 2,094 children were looked after and living with a kinship carer, being defined as care by a relative or close friend who cares for a child or young person. [40] The Scottish Government and local government want to build on this potential, and future reform is intended to support this policy, including providing allowances equivalent to those provided for foster carers. This will help to remove financial barriers that might prevent a child being sustained within the family network, where that is the best option for the child.[41]

A local authority may enter into arrangements with voluntary organisations to discharge duties in relation to foster care on its behalf.[42] Case records will be compiled and maintained for each foster carer and also each person who is not an approved foster carer with whom the local authority places a child, as well as a file for each prospective foster carer.[43] These records are to be maintained for at least 10 years, and the local authority is charged with their safekeeping and to ensure that the information which it contains is kept confidential.[44]

Under the Social Work (Representations Procedure) (Scotland) Directions 1996, foster carers have the right to make representations including complaints concerning the authority's discharge of, or failure to discharge, any of its legal functions in relation to a child, although prospective foster carers may not make representations about the failure to approve them as foster carers, nor can foster carers complain about termination of approval.[45]

The costs of care

4.12 Local authorities are entitled to recover financial contributions towards the costs of looking after children. If the child is under 16, recovery will be from anyone who has parental responsibilities over the child. Where the young person is over 16 and in paid employment, he or she will have liability. In most authorities, there will be a sliding scale of charges based on the means of the person liable. Parents who are on state benefits will not normally be expected to make a contribution.[46] It is possible to enforce payment of a contribution by means of a contribution order obtained from the court.[47] Natural fathers who do not have parental rights may nevertheless be liable for a contribution to the costs of care of the child.

Duties of local authorities in respect of children

4.13 It is the duty of a local authority to make available general advice, guidance and assistance to "persons in need" living in the area covered by the jurisdiction of the local authority.[48] This is written into the Social Work (Scotland) Act 1968 at s.12. However, children are no longer included within these general welfare provisions and are now covered by the more specific terms of the Children (Scotland) Act 1995.[49] The 1995 Act introduced a broad duty to provide services to "children in need" and a number of additional duties complement this key obligation. Of course, children who have been receiving services under the 1995 legislation may become "persons in need" once they reach the age of 18.

---

[39] Scottish Executive (2006). *http://www.scotland.gov.uk/Publications/2007/04/25144002/0*, p.4 [Accessed July 3, 2008].

[40] "Getting it Right for Every Child in Foster Care and Kinship Care—a National Strategy" (Scottish Executive, 2007). *http://www.scotland.gov.uk/Publications/2007/12/03143704/8*.

[41] "Getting it Right for Every Child" (2007). *http://www.scotland.gov.uk/Publications/2007/12/03143704/8*.

[42] Fostering of Children (Scotland) Regulations 1996 reg.16.

[43] Fostering of Children (Scotland) Regulations 1996 reg.18.

[44] Fostering of Children (Scotland) Regulations 1996 reg.19.

[45] *Scotland's children*, Cm.2286 (1993), Vol.2, p.59.

[46] Social Work (Scotland) Act 1968 s.78A, inserted by the Health and Social Services and Social Security Adjudications Act 1983 s.19(6)(b).

[47] Social Work (Scotland) Act 1968 ss.80–83.

[48] Social Work (Scotland) Act 1968 s.12, as amended by the 1995 Act Sch.4 para.15(11).

[49] 1995 Act s.105(4) and Sch.4 para.15(11).

Most fundamentally perhaps, a local authority is under a duty to (a) safeguard and promote the welfare of children in its area who are in need; and (b) so far as is consistent with that duty, promote the upbringing of such children by their families. There is an implicit presumption that the maintenance of children at home is to be preferred. However, the local authority's duty to safeguard and promote the welfare of the child must be given greater weight. In fulfilling its obligations, it will be incumbent on the local authority to have regard, so far as is reasonably practicable, to each child's religious persuasion, racial origin, and cultural and linguistic background.[50]

Information needs

4.14 Each local authority must prepare and publish a plan for the provision of relevant services for and in respect of children in their area. It must keep that plan under review and modify it where appropriate. In preparing the plan, each local authority must consult every health board and NHS trust, such voluntary organisations as appear to the authority to represent the interests of persons who use, or are likely to use, the services in that area or who provide such services, the chairman of the children's panel for the area, and the housing associations and voluntary housing associations in the area.[51] Guidance indicates that plans should have five strategic aims:

(1) to ensure the welfare of children;
(2) to clarify strategic objectives in relation to services;
(3) to promote integrated provision of services and effective use of available resources;
(4) to ensure a consistent approach to planning by local authorities; and
(5) to establish a high standard of co-ordination, co-operation and collaboration between service departments within local authorities and with other agencies and organisations that have a contribution to make to effective local services.[52]

Many local authorities now publish the standards of service that the public can expect to receive. Information should be made available in doctors' surgeries, children's hearing centres, hospital outpatient departments, clinics, schools, libraries, community centres, nurseries, CABs, law centres, benefit agencies and churches.[53]

As well as drawing up a plan the local authority has a duty to prepare and publish information:

- about relevant services that are provided by it for and in respect of children (including services for and in respect of disabled children or children otherwise affected by disability) in its area or by any other local authority for those children; and
- where it considers it appropriate, about services that are provided by voluntary organisations and by other persons for those children, being services that the authority has power to provide, and that, were it to do so, it would provide as relevant services.[54]

Assessment and service provision

4.15 The assessment of a child's needs is crucial in identifying need and providing service. A child is in need of care and attention if he satisfies one of the following conditions:

(1) he is unlikely to achieve or maintain, or to have an opportunity of achieving or maintaining, a reasonable standard of health or development unless the local authority provides services for him;

---

[50] 1995 Act s.22(2); see *Valuing Diversity* (Scottish Office, 1998).
[51] 1995 Act s.19.
[52] *Scotland's children*, Cm.2286 (1993), Vol.1, p.9. See generally Ch.2 of Vol.1.
[53] *Scotland's children*, Cm.2286 (1993), Vol.1, p.22.
[54] 1995 Act s.20(1).

(2) his health or development is likely significantly to be impaired unless such services are provided;
(3) he is disabled; or
(4) he is affected adversely by the disability of any other person in his family.[55]

Local authorities are required to screen referrals and in appropriate instances provide advice and assistance, refer to another agency, undertake an assessment, make enquiries under local child protection procedures, or undertake joint investigation into the child's welfare or safety.[56]

Services may be provided for a particular child, or for his family, or any other member of the child's family, if provided with a view to safeguarding or promoting the child's welfare. It seems probable that assistance other than to children will be to the child's parent or guardian to enable them to care for the child. As with the general social work duty under s.12 of the 1968 Act,[57] assistance may be given in kind or in exceptional circumstances in cash.[58] Examples of goods in kind include household furniture or cooking equipment. Any cash may be given unconditionally, or may be subject to full or part repayment. The local authority must have regard to the means of the child and the means of his or her parent(s) before imposing such a condition, and in any event no repayment condition can be imposed on persons on income support or family credit or jobseeker's allowance. There is clearly a considerable discretion given to the local authority as to whether it gives a cash payment or not and the terms on which it gives such payments. One must however be cautious: the law does not delineate the resources available to the local authority for the many services it provides, and financial pressures may have a direct bearing on a local authority's attitude to cash assistance.

4.16 The services provided by the local authority in respect of any disabled child within its area shall be designed to minimise the effect of his disability, and also to minimise the effect on any child within their area who is adversely affected by the disability of any other person in his family. The services should be designed to give children the opportunity to lead lives that are as normal as possible. A person is to be treated as disabled if he is chronically sick or disabled or suffers from mental disorder. Where requested to do so the local authority must carry out an assessment of a child, or any member of his family, to determine the needs of the child insofar as they are attributable to his disability or to that of the other person.[59] A child may be entitled to more than one assessment depending on his particular needs, though the guidance suggests a streamlined, aggregate approach whereby one comprehensive assessment takes account of both special educational needs in terms of the Education (Scotland) Act 1980, and disability needs under the Chronically Sick and Disabled Persons Act 1970 and the Disabled Persons (Services, Consultation and Representation) Act 1986.

Where a child is found to be adversely affected by the disability of any other person in his family, of that other person's disability; the local authority will, where requested, undertake an assessment of the child and/or family members.[60]

Local authorities are under a duty to provide services plans for their area.[61] These detail services that are available for a child in need within an authority's area. Any child requiring these services is given an Integrated Child Service Plan.[62]

---

[55] 1995 Act s.93(4).

[56] *Scotland's children*, Cm.2286 (1993), Vol.1, para.14, p.3; Fuller and Brown, *Joint Police and Social Work Investigations in Child Protection* (Stirling: SWRC, 1991).

[57] See para.7.25.

[58] 1995 Act s.22.

[59] See generally the 1995 Act s.23.

[60] Legal provisions relating to children and adults who are chronically sick and disabled are given fuller treatment elsewhere in this book: see Ch.7.

[61] 1995 Act ss.19–21.

[62] See "Guidance for Integrated Children's Services Plans" (Scottish Executive, 2005). *http://www.scotland.gov.uk/Topics/People/Young-People/childrensservices/22341.*

Providing accommodation

4.17 A local authority may provide accommodation for any child in its area if it considers that to do so would safeguard or promote the child's welfare. In certain circumstances the provision of accommodation becomes a duty. Section 25(1) of the Children (Scotland) Act 1995 states:

> "A local authority shall provide accommodation for any child who, residing or having been found in their area, appears to them to require such provision because—
>
> (a) no-one has parental responsibility for him;
> (b) he is lost or abandoned; or
> (c) the person who has been caring for him is prevented, whether or not permanently and for whatever reason, from providing him with suitable accommodation or care."

In the context of s.25, the accommodation provided is for a continuous period of 24 hours including, by implication, a place to sleep. A child is someone under the age of 18 although it is open to a local authority to provide accommodation for any person within the area who is at least 18 but not yet 21, if it considers that to do so would safeguard or promote welfare. Local authorities do not have a mandatory legal obligation to accommodate persons aged over 18 years in the same way that they must do if the child is under 18 and appears to require such assistance. Given the wording of the section, if a child has no local connection with the area but simply arrives in a locality the authority will nevertheless have a duty towards that person certainly in the first instance. That authority may look to the local authority applicable to the child's normal place of residence or origin to assume the duty to provide accommodation. Where the accommodation is being provided under the mandatory duty and the child happens to be ordinarily resident in another local authority area, it is incumbent on the local authority to contact the other authority in writing to advise that such provision is being made. The notified authority may subsequently take over the provision of accommodation for the child.

4.18 Before providing a child with accommodation under s.25, the local authority must have regard to his or her views (if he or she wishes to express them). A child 12 years of age or over will generally be considered to be of sufficient age and maturity to form a view. Notwithstanding this, children under 12 where they are of sufficient age and maturity should also have their views taken into account. The local authority cannot provide accommodation for a child where there is someone who has parental rights and responsibilities for him or her and that person is willing and able either to provide, or to arrange to have provided, accommodation for him or her and they object to the local authority providing accommodation. Moreover, a parent with subsisting responsibilities and rights has the right to remove their child from accommodation provided by the local authority. Parental rights and responsibilities will not be affected by the mere placing of a child in accommodation.

The power to object to the provision of accommodation does not apply to children aged over 16 who agree to be provided with accommodation, or when a person who has a residence order in their favour agrees that the child should be provided with accommodation. The power to remove a child from accommodation provided by the local authority is qualified with a condition that where the child has been in the said accommodation for a continuous period of six months or more, the person removing the child must give the local authority 14 days' written notice of their intention to remove the child.[63] This effectively offers the local authority a window of time in which to decide if it should seek an order that would thwart the parent's desire to remove the child or put in place some protective order.

In satisfying its obligations under the statute, the local authority may place a child with one of his relatives, with an alternative foster family, or with any other suitable person "on such terms as to payment, by the authority or otherwise, as the authority may determine". Alternatively, it may place him in a residential establishment or make such other arrangements as appear

---

[63] For an illustration of parental attempt at recovery under the Social Work (Scotland) Act 1968 s.15, see *M v Dumfries and Galloway RC*, 1991 S.C.L.R. 481.

appropriate, which may include placing the child with a person or local authority accommodation elsewhere in the United Kingdom.[64]

While providing accommodation for the child, and in making any decisions with respect to that child, the local authority must fulfil its statutory obligations under s.17 of the 1995 Act, set out at the beginning of the Chapter. It is open to the local authority to depart from the obligations on the basis that it is necessary to do so to protect the public from serious harm whether or not that is physical harm. Under s.31(1) of the 1995 Act, there is a duty placed upon the local authority that is looking after a child to review the child's case at regular intervals.[65]

Young persons

4.19 There is a further duty on the local authority, unless it is satisfied that a child's welfare does not require it, to advise, guide and assist any person in the area who is over school age but not yet 19 years old and who has previously been looked after by the local authority.[66] This is qualified to the extent that children who ceased to be looked after before they ceased to be of school age need not be given help by the local authority. These important statutory innovations are designed to help young persons make the transition from local authority care into the wider community. An attempt to compensate for the absence of parental guidance at this formative stage of their lives is made by placing certain duties and powers on the local authority in whose care they have previously been. A young person who has been looked after by the local authority until he or she ceased to be of school age may, if over 19 but under 21, apply to the local authority to request advice, guidance and assistance. Although not compelled to do so, the local authority may grant such an application. The assistance to young persons in both situations may be in cash or in kind. It is also open to the local authority to make grants to any person in its area who ceased to be looked after by the local authority at the time he or she ceased to be of school age or subsequently, to enable him or her to meet expenses in connection with education or training, or to make contributions to accommodation and maintenance costs to enable him or her to be near a place of employment or education and training. This support can go on beyond the young person attaining the age of 21 until he completes the education or training. Although a broad enabling power, there must be some doubt as to its practicable application.

Recent measures in the Regulation of Care (Scotland) Act 2001 have been implemented to strengthen existing duties on Scottish local authorities to provide a needs assessment to all young people leaving care. The details of these are found in subsequent Regulations, the Support and Assistance of Young People Leaving Care (Scotland) Regulations.[67] The first provision relates to the assessments of a young person's need: when they leave care over school age but under 19, or if they apply for support after the age of 19 or if they are being prepared for leaving care but are still formally looked after. The second part concerns the manner in which cash support can be given. Finally, the third section details a new user-friendly method for complaints.

Short-term refuges for children at risk of harm

4.20 Where it appears to a local authority that a child may be at risk of harm, it may at a child's request provide the child with refuge in a residential establishment controlled, managed and designated by it.[68] Alternatively, it may arrange for refuge with a person whose house has been approved and designated by the authority. Short-term refuge ordinarily lasts for seven days but may in exceptional circumstances be for 14 days. The limitation of this section is that it is only

---

[64] 1995 Act s.26.
[65] See also the Arrangements to Look After Children (Scotland) Regulations 1996 (SI 1996/3262).
[66] See the 1995 Act ss.29 and 30.
[67] SSI 2003/608.
[68] 1995 Act s.38.

applicable to children old enough to request refuge themselves.[69] Obviously, the short duration of the refuge is ameliorated by the local authority's duty to safeguard and promote the welfare of the child and it may take further steps under the extensive powers of the 1995 Act. A child who is in refuge is not "looked after" and may not, based on their location in a residential establishment, enforce the numerous obligations of the local authority to provide children and their families with support.

In related provisions, the 1995 Act states that where a child is in residential accommodation in hospitals or nursing homes, and it appears that there has been no parental contact for a continuous period of three months, or it is likely that the child will have no parental contact for a period of three months, the hospital or home must notify the local authority. The local authority must on notification take steps to safeguard and promote the child's welfare and consider whether to exercise its statutory powers.[70]

CARE AND PROTECTION COURT ORDERS

4.21 The Children (Scotland) Act 1995 empowers local authorities to intervene to provide care and protection where it is necessary to do so. The Act provides for several court orders that the local authority can seek in furtherance of its statutory obligations. These orders are relatively novel and in many respects practical experience of them is limited.

Child assessment orders

4.22 One of the interesting new orders introduced by the 1995 Act is the child assessment order ("CAO"). It is intended to allow local authorities, and local authorities alone, to undertake preliminary investigation and assessment where they have suspicions of neglect or abuse. It is not intended for cases where the child is thought to be at immediate risk.[71] The information provided by the assessment may allow the activation of other local authority measures under the Act for which direct evidence is necessary, or it may simply reassure the local authority that its initial fears are unfounded. Clearly an important new power, the Act and the guidance issued to accompany it attempt to address some of the sensitivities of an order that has civil liberty implications. It is intended that there should be the minimum possible disruption to the child and the family's routine.

A sheriff, on application by the local authority, may grant a CAO for an assessment of the state of the child's health or development.[72] He may only do so if he is satisfied that:

- the local authority has reasonable cause to suspect that the child in respect of whom the order is sought is being so treated (or neglected) that he is suffering or is likely to suffer significant harm;
- such an assessment is required in order to establish whether or not there is reasonable cause to believe that the child is so treated (or neglected); and
- such assessment is unlikely to be carried out, or carried out satisfactorily, unless the order is granted.

Significant harm in this context is harm that is serious and not of a minor or transient nature. It may be physical or emotional.[73] It is believed that the level of "reasonable cause" may be low given that the order is an investigatory order. A simple allegation of abuse may be sufficient to allow the authority to assert "reasonable cause". It is likely that a sheriff will allow an authority some latitude and as long as the authority has some basis for seeking the order there should be

---

[69] See Norrie, Annotations in Mays (ed.), *Scottish Social Work Legislation* (Edinburgh: W. Green), C.191.2.
[70] 1995 Act s.36.
[71] *Scotland's children*, Cm.2286 (1993), Vol.1, p.54.
[72] 1995 Act s.55.
[73] Norrie, Annotations in Mays (ed.), *Scottish Social Work Legislation*, C.208.3.

no impediment to it being obtained. The sheriff is not compelled to grant the order if the grounds exist: he still has discretion to refuse but this will be highly unlikely. He will focus on his obligation under s.16 of the 1995 Act to make the child's welfare throughout the child's life his paramount consideration. In any situation where abuse is alleged, it will be hard to dislodge a presumption that the child's welfare is better served by investigation and detection.

4.23 Before applying for a CAO the local authority should discuss its statutory duty to "cause inquiries to be made"[74] and offer the parents an opportunity to comment. The purpose of the initial discussions is to allow the parents an opportunity to give access to the child so that an assessment can be carried out voluntarily. It will also help establish, if such be the case that the parents "unreasonably" refused access. The local authority must serve notice and a copy of the application for a CAO on the persons named in the order. The child must also receive a copy unless the sheriff dispenses with service on the child as inappropriate. At least 48 hours' notice must be given. Those served with the application and notice have the right to appear or be represented at the child assessment hearing.

Where the sheriff considers that the conditions for the making of another of the new statutory orders, for instance a child protection order ("CPO"), are satisfied he must proceed to make such an order rather than simply a CAO.[75] It may well prove to be the case in Scotland that local authorities will be inclined to seek CPOs rather than CAOs primarily because if there are reasonable grounds for suspicion that the child is at risk it is better to move to protect the child than carry out further investigation.[76]

Child assessment orders[77] must specify both the date on which the assessment is to begin and the dates for commencement and duration of the assessment, which must be not longer than seven days. They must also require any person to produce the child to an authorised person and to permit that person or another authorised person to carry out the assessment in accordance with the order. The CAO will be carried out by an authorised person in accordance with the order. It is the local authority that authorises any person to carry out the assessment. It is expected that the order should not normally entail the physical separation of the child from his family. However, where it is necessary, the CAO may permit the taking of the child to a place of safety for the purposes of the assessment and authorise the detention of the child for such period as may be specified in the order. Where the sheriff does authorise removal to, or detention in, a place of safety or other place, he may in granting the CAO make such directions as he considers appropriate as to the contact which the child will be allowed to have with any other person while there.

4.24 The appeal procedure against a sheriff's decision to grant a CAO is thought to be through the normal appeal process of decisions of a sheriff, that is, to the sheriff principal. However, constraints of time dictate that this is an unlikely occurrence unless the assessment is not to commence for some weeks and that fact itself would appear to be unlikely given the grounds for obtaining a CAO.

A child who has capacity under the Age of Legal Capacity (Scotland) Act 1991 s.2(4) may refuse to consent to any assessment that involves medical treatment or examination and thus defeat the object of the order.[78]

The local authority is expected to discuss with the family how the assessment is to be carried out. Professionals familiar with the family should be consulted on the best way to carry it out.[79] Once the assessment has been carried out the local authority will be in a position to determine what further action, if any, it should now take. This may involve referral to the children's hearing or recourse to further orders available under the 1995 Act.

---

[74] 1995 Act s.53.
[75] 1995 Act s.55(2). See paras 4.36–4.42 below.
[76] Norrie, Annotations in Mays (ed.), *Scottish Social Work Legislation*, C.208.2.
[77] See generally the 1995 Act s.55.
[78] 1995 Act s.90.
[79] *Scotland's children*, Cm.2286 (1993), Vol.1, p.57.

Exclusion orders

4.25 Another major innovation of the 1995 Act is the exclusion order, which bears striking similarity to exclusion orders in domestic violence situations.[80] These orders, which represent a major aspect of the Government's anti-child abuse strategy, were originally mooted by Lord Clyde in his Report of the Inquiry into the Removal of Children from Orkney in 1992.[81] They operate in a simple way to exclude an alleged abuser from the home rather than have the child displaced. As Professor Thomson argues, they are "consonant with the aim of the 1995 Act that, so far as is consistent with the local authorities' duty to safeguard and promote the child's welfare, a child should be brought up by his or her own family".[82] Nevertheless an exclusion order is a short-term protective mechanism designed to offer respite and protection and the opportunity to search for a longer-term solution. An order is thought to be appropriate where there is an acknowledgement from the alleged abuser that abuse has occurred, and there is no apparent reduction in risk to the child or other children; where the child has made a clear disclosure implicating the alleged abuser and the child's account is believed by the non-abusing parent, but denied or minimised by the alleged abuser; where the child or non-abusing parent is afraid to remain in the household with the alleged abuser; or where fear, distress or a conflict of loyalties caused by the alleged abuser's presence in the household prevent the non-abusing parent from meeting the child's needs and protecting the child from further harm.[83] There may be an absence of, or in any event limited, corroboration of the alleged abuse but nevertheless an exclusion order may be appropriate. There must be evidence of abuse and of continuing risk before an exclusion order can be granted. Before applying for an exclusion order it is thought that the local authority will consider other alternatives. It may be that exclusion can be obtained on a voluntary basis but such voluntary arrangements will have no force of law and may easily be reneged upon. Other options open to the local authority include applying for a CPO, or assisting the child and the non-abusing parent to leave the house. There will undoubtedly be circumstances where the child is better protected by removal. While the exclusion order adds to the "weaponry" of the local authority in its efforts to protect the child, the fact that the whereabouts of the child and other members of the family are known may make the very people whom the authority seeks to protect a sitting target.

A local authority may apply to the sheriff seeking an exclusion order with the effect that a named person is excluded from the child's family home.[84] A named person need not be the child's parent or someone who is living with the child. The sheriff must be satisfied that the following conditions pertain:

(a) that the child has suffered, is suffering, or is likely to suffer, significant harm, as a result of any conduct, or any threatened or reasonably apprehended conduct, of the named person;

(b) that the making of an exclusion order against a named person—

  (i) is necessary for the protection of the child, irrespective of whether the child is for the time being residing in the family home[85]; and

  (ii) would be better to safeguard the child's welfare than the removal of the child from the family home; and

(c) that, if an order is made, there will be a person specified in the application who is

---

[80] 1995 Act s.76 and para.3.20 above.

[81] E. Sutherland, "Clyde and Beyond", 1993 Jur. Rev. 178 (Case and Comment).

[82] Thomson, *Family Law in Scotland*, 5th edn (2006), p.348.

[83] *Scotland's children*, Cm.2286 (1993), Vol.1, p.66.

[84] See generally the 1995 Act s.76.

[85] A family home is defined as "any house, caravan, houseboat or other structure which is used as a family residence and in which the child ordinarily resides" with a person who has parental responsibilities in relation to him or who ordinarily has charge of or control over him. It includes any garden or other ground and any building attached to or usually occupied with the house, caravan, houseboat or other structure: 1995 Act s.76(12), (13) and (14).

capable of taking responsibility for the provision of appropriate care for the child and any other member of the family who requires such care and who is or will be residing in the family home.

It is interesting to note that the remedy is not available to the non-abusing parent directly; he must involve and enlist the assistance of the local authority, which has sole right to bring exclusion order proceedings. In contrast, exclusion orders under the Matrimonial Homes (Family Protection) (Scotland) Act 1981 may be sought directly by either party to a marriage or cohabitation and may have the effect of protecting a child at risk of abuse. Furthermore, it follows from paragraph (c) above that exclusion orders will not be appropriate where the alleged abuse is by a lone parent who is the sole carer of the child or where both carers are thought to be abusing the child.

Making the order

4.26 In an application for an exclusion order under the 1995 Act, the welfare of the child is the paramount consideration.[86] This must be seen to qualify what would ordinarily be a considerable hurdle, that the exclusion order be "necessary". Where the order is thought to be in the paramount interests of the child it is going to take an unconscionable impediment for the sheriff to then decide that it is not "necessary". More than this though, the sheriff has a duty to consult the child before making an order. The sheriff must be satisfied that making an order is better than not making one at all. "Necessary" is not to be interpreted in such a way that an exclusion order is always refused where another order is available, such as a CPO.[87]

Like other exclusion orders, no order seeking to exclude an alleged abuser can be granted on the basis of ex parte statements—the person to be excluded must be given the opportunity of being heard or represented before the sheriff.[88] Exclusion orders are only applicable in situations where the child is under 16 years of age, or under 18 where the child is already the subject of a supervision requirement of the children's hearing system.[89] Where the sheriff is satisfied that the conditions exist for the grant of an exclusion order but has not heard the named person or any other person who has been served notice of the proceedings, he may nevertheless grant an interim exclusion order.[90] Interim orders can usually be obtained within 48 hours of the initial application. An interim order has the same effect as a full order but will require the sheriff to hold a further hearing to afford the opportunity to those parties who are entitled to be heard but have not been. At that further hearing, the sheriff may confirm or vary the interim order until final determination of the proceedings. In any event, the sheriff may pronounce an interim order if he is satisfied that the grounds exist until such times as a final determination of the case takes place. Where the sheriff is satisfied that the conditions for making a child protection order under s.57 of the 1995 Act exist, he may make such an order.

The sheriff shall not make an exclusion order if it appears to him that to do so would be unjustifiable or unreasonable having regard to all the circumstances of the case.[91] In assessing those circumstances he may take into account (a) the conduct of the members of the child's family (whether in relation to each other or otherwise); (b) the respective needs and financial resources of the members of that family; and (c) the extent (if any) to which the family home and any relevant item in that home is used in connection with a trade, business or profession by any member of that family. In seeking to balance these considerations with the welfare of the child the court may face a difficult task. The legislation does not seek to address this anomaly. The

---

[86] See generally the 1995 Act s.16.

[87] Norrie, Annotations in Mays (ed.), *Scottish Social Work Legislation*, C.229.4. Professor Norrie goes on to suggest that an order will be necessary when it is the most appropriate of the available means of protecting the child from significant harm.

[88] 1995 Act s.76(3).

[89] 1995 Act s.93(2)(b).

[90] 1995 Act s.76.

[91] 1995 Act s.76.

sheriff must also have regard to the fact that the named person may be required to reside in the family home because it is a tenancy under the Agricultural Holdings (Scotland) Act 1991, or is let to the person by his employer as incidental to his employment.

The effect of an exclusion order

4.27 An exclusion order has the effect of suspending the named person's occupancy rights in the home of the child.[92] It prevents the named person from entering the home without the express permission of the local authority who sought the order. Incidental to the exclusion order, the sheriff may grant ancillary orders:

- a warrant for the summary ejection of the named person from the home;
- an interdict prohibiting the named person from entering the home without the express permission of the local authority;
- an interdict prohibiting the removal by the named person of any relevant item specified in the interdict except with the written consent of the local authority or of an appropriate person or by order of the sheriff;
- an interdict prohibiting the named person from entering or remaining in a specified area in the vicinity of the home;
- an interdict preventing the named person from taking any step in relation to the child; and
- an order regulating the contact between the child and the named person.[93]

In fact, the 1995 Act grants the power to the sheriff to make any order incidental to the exclusion order that he considers necessary. The named person may defend these ancillary orders on the basis that they are unnecessary. Where the sheriff grants warrant for summary ejection, he may make an order for preservation of the named person's goods and effects that remain in the family home.

Power of arrest

4.28 As with the interdicts in the Matrimonial Homes (Family Protection) (Scotland) Act 1981, there is scope for attachment of the power of arrest both to the final order or any interim order.[94] The sheriff may attach a power of arrest to any interdict granted under s.77 of the 1995 Act whether or not an application is made. A local authority may, at any time while an exclusion order has effect, apply for the attachment of a power of arrest. Only once the named person has been served with the interdict with the attached power of arrest will it become effective. When a power of arrest is attached to any interdict granted under s.77, it is incumbent on the local authority "as soon as possible" after the interdict with the power of arrest has been served on the named person to ensure that it, and the court order granting it, are delivered to the chief constable of the police area in which the family home is situated. Where the power of arrest relates to the taking of any step in respect of the child, the documents must be passed to the chief constable in the area where the step or conduct was prevented. Variations or recall of the interdict with the attached power of arrest must also be advised to the chief constable.

The power of arrest allows a constable to arrest without warrant the named person if he has reasonable cause for suspecting the person to be in breach of the interdict. Where a named person has been arrested, the officer in charge of the police station may liberate him if satisfied that that there is no likelihood of that person further breaching the interdict to which the power of arrest has been attached. Alternatively he may refuse to liberate him. Even where the police officer releases the named person he must notify the Procurator Fiscal forthwith of the facts and

---

[92] 1995 Act s.77.
[93] The sheriff can make an order regulating contact whether applied for or not: see s.77(6).
[94] 1995 Act s.78.

circumstances that led to the arrest. A person arrested and not released must be brought before a sheriff sitting as a court of summary jurisdiction in the area in which he was arrested on the first working day after the arrest. The Procurator Fiscal will present a petition containing a statement of the particulars of the person, the facts and circumstances that gave rise to the arrest, and a request that the person be detained for a period not exceeding two days. If it appears to the sheriff that the Procurator Fiscal's statement discloses a prima facie case of breach of interdict, that breach of interdict proceedings will be taken, and that there is a substantial risk of violence by the arrested person against any member of the family, or an appropriate person, resident in the family home, he may order that the named person be detained for a period not exceeding two working days.

Where a person is liberated by the police or is brought before a sheriff, it is the duty of the Procurator Fiscal at the earliest opportunity (and in respect of the latter situation before the person is brought before the sheriff) to intimate to the local authority that brought the application for an exclusion order or an appropriate person who will reside, or who remains in residence, in the family home (or the solicitor who acted for them or who acts for them now), that he has decided that no criminal proceedings should be taken in respect of the arrest of the named person.

4.29 Exclusion orders if granted exist for up to a maximum of six months after being made.[95] They may cease to have effect on that appointed date or cease earlier where (a) the order contains a direction by the sheriff that it shall; (b) the sheriff recalls the exclusion order; or (c) permission given by a third party to the spouse or partner of the named person, or to an appropriate person, to occupy the home to which the order relates is withdrawn. On application by the local authority, the named person or the spouse or heterosexual partner of the named person (if that person is not also excluded and is not also an appropriate person) may recall or vary the exclusion order as well as any ancillary or incidental order such as interdicts, warrants or directions. An exclusion order cannot be renewed. However, the safety net it hopefully provides allows the local authority to intervene with other measures if it considers it appropriate, and allows the family the opportunity to consider how best to secure the welfare of the child.

In response to the exclusion, local authorities are expected to discuss with the excluded person where they should go and the impact of the order on him. The excluded person is likely to be viewed as intentionally homeless and as such will be refused housing by the local authority under the homeless persons legislation. Nor is it likely that an excluded person will be in priority need.[96] The local authority may nevertheless provide other assistance to the excluded person. The local authority should discuss with both parents arrangements for contact between the excluded person and the child and any siblings. It is expected that the local authority will regularly review the need for an exclusion order to continue. The excluded person should nevertheless be enabled to fulfil parental responsibilities in respect of the child where that is practicable and in the interests of the child.[97]

Parental responsibility orders

4.30 There will be many situations where the local authority's duty to reinvigorate and reinforce the family unit under s.22 of the 1995 Act is simply not appropriate. In fact, there will be situations where re-establishing the child in his own family is wholly detrimental to that child's interests. Referral to a children's hearing might be one solution to the child's need for compulsory measures of supervision. However, there is another alternative and that is for the local authority to seek a parental responsibility order ("PRO"), which has the effect of vesting parental rights and responsibilities in relation to the child in the local authority and removing the same from

[95] 1995 Act s.79.
[96] See paras 9.22–9.24.
[97] *Scotland's children*, Cm.2286 (1993), Vol.1, pp.70–71.

the child's parents.[98] An application for a PRO can be made whether or not a child is looked after by the local authority although the former situation is likely to be the norm. Once the local authority has been granted a PRO, it must undertake full parental responsibilities in respect of the child.

Only a local authority may apply to the sheriff for an order transferring (but only during the subsistence of the order) the appropriate parental rights and responsibilities.[99] However this order will be replaced when permanence orders come into force under the Adoption and Children (Scotland) Act 2007 (see below).

Permanence orders

4.31 Permanence orders arose from the wide-ranging review of adoption and fostering by the Adoption and Policy Review Group[100] and were formally introduced by the Adoption and Children (Scotland) Act 2007. Only the local authority may apply to the court for a permanence order ("PO"), in effect transferring parental responsibilities and rights, although all of these may not be removed from a parent or guardian. Each PO, if granted by the court, will consist of mandatory provisions, and may include other appropriate conditions, and consent for adoption.[101]

Mandatory provisions stipulate that the local authority will be responsible for guiding the child appropriate to their stage of development and for the regulation of the child's residency[102]; these end when the child is 18 and 16 respectively. Other (ancillary) conditions[103] attached to the PO may include:

- the local authority having all other parental responsibilities and rights, other than contact, vested in them[104];
- allowing another person to acquire parental responsibilities and rights[105];
- extinguishing any of the parent or guardian's parental responsibilities and rights over the child, providing these will vest in another[106];
- arrangements for contact between the child and a third party providing it is in the child's best interests[107];
- determining other questions apropos parental responsibilities and rights and welfare of the child.[108]

The third type of condition relates to adoption.[109] Where a local authority requests for adoption to be granted in the PO the court must be satisfied that the child is, or is likely to be, placed for adoption and ultimately, adoption must be better for the child than not to adopt.[110] Furthermore, every parent and guardian of the child must understand the effects of the order and

---

[98] See generally the 1995 Act s.86.
[99] 1995 Act s.86(1).
[100] See para.3.51.
[101] The Adoption and Children (Scotland) Act 2007 s.80(3) states that upon the making of a permanence order the court must ensure that someone has parental responsibility and rights over the child.
[102] Adoption and Children (Scotland) Act 2007 s.81.
[103] The responsibility to guide ends when the child is 18, but all other ancillary conditions cease when the child is 16.
[104] Adoption and Children (Scotland) Act 2007 s.82(1)(a).
[105] Adoption and Children (Scotland) Act 2007 s.82(1)(b).
[106] Adoption and Children (Scotland) Act 2007 s.82(1)(c) and (d).
[107] Adoption and Children (Scotland) Act 2007 s.82(1)(e).
[108] Adoption and Children (Scotland) Act 2007 s.82(1)(f).
[109] Under s.93, the PO may be amended at a later date to include a condition for adoption.
[110] Adoption and Children (Scotland) Act 2007 s.83(1)(b) and (d).

consent to it, although in certain circumstances the court may dispense with their consent.[111] A local authority must, upon requesting the adoption condition, notify any person whose consent is required or, if no such person can be found, a relative; and any father of the child without parental responsibilities and rights.[112]

4.32 Before a permanence order is granted,[113] there are a number of conditions and considerations to which the court shall have regard. First, as per freeing for adoption, no PO shall be granted where a child aged 12 or over does not consent, unless they are incapable of consenting. Furthermore, taking the child's age and maturity into account,[114] and where reasonably practicable, the child will be allowed to express their views. Further regard is given to the child's religious persuasion, racial origin, cultural and linguistic background, and any effect on the child should the order be made. In fact, the PO shall not be made where it is not appropriate for the child, and in deciding this, consideration is given to the need to safeguard and promote the welfare of the child throughout their childhood. Two final considerations are whether there is a person able to regulate the child's residence and whether the person with whom the child is living is likely to be seriously detrimental to the child.

Those with parental responsibilities and rights before the making of the order may make representations to the court—it right extends to local authorities, the child or their representative, and any other person claiming an interest.[115] Such persons, along with other affected persons,[116] will be permitted to apply for a variation or revocation of any PO granted.[117] A local authority must apply for a variation or revocation where there has been a material change in the child's circumstances, otherwise POs automatically terminate when a child is adopted or aged 16 in respect of rights and 18 in relation to the responsibility to guide the child.[118]

Effect of a permanence order

4.33 The PO extinguishes a person's parental right to determine their child's residence and any parental responsibilities and rights granted under a prior PO or s.11 of the Children (Scotland) Act 1995.[119] However, the new PO must ensure full parental responsibilities and rights vest in a person, or persons, not necessarily the local authority in respect of the child. In the instance of two or more persons holding such rights, they may exercise them without the consent of the other.

Hierarchy of orders

4.34 Given the extensive nature of the PO, provision has been made in the Adoption and Children (Scotland) Act 2007 to deal with its linkage with other legislation—most notably supervision requirements. Where the child is subject to a supervision requirement the court may revoke it, subject to its necessity. Conversely, supervision requirements may not be made or modified while a PO is being determined, unless the court makes a referral to the Children's Reporter. In the latter instance a court report must be made by the hearings. Notwithstanding that a PO has

---

[111] Adoption and Children (Scotland) Act 2007 s.83(1)(c). A court may dispense with consent where the parent or guardian with parental responsibilities and rights ("PRRs") is dead; or incapable of giving consent; or where they are unable to satisfactorily discharge or exercise the PRRs and likely to continue to be unable to do so; or where the parent and guardian will lose these PRRs by virtue of the PO, and it is unlikely that they will regain them; or where the welfare of the child requires dispensation.

[112] Adoption and Children (Scotland) Act 2007 s.104.

[113] Throughout the proceedings a curator *ad litem* and reporting office will be appointed: s.108.

[114] A child aged 12 or over is presumed to have the maturity: s.84(6).

[115] Adoption and Children (Scotland) Act 2007 s.86(2).

[116] These include those with parental responsibilities and rights and any person with a duty under the order: Adoption and Children (Scotland) Act 2007 s.94(3).

[117] However, they must first be granted leave by the court which is founded on the criteria under s.94(5) and (6) for a variation and s.98 for revocations.

[118] Adoption and Children (Scotland) Act 2007 ss.99 and 102.

[119] Adoption and Children (Scotland) Act 2007 ss.87–91.

been made, where the local authority has full parental responsibilities and rights, it must not act incompatibly with any other court order or supervision requirement.

Another area of possible conflict lies in the provisions under s.11 of the 1995 Act. Hence, to prevent confusion and conflict s.103 of the Adoption and Children (Scotland) Act 2007 states that no decision shall be made under the aforementioned section of the 1995 Act.[120]

EMERGENCY PROTECTION OF CHILDREN

4.35 In many instances it becomes necessary to intervene in the child's interests through the provision of compulsory measures of supervision, primarily through the work of the children's hearing system operating in Scotland. In addition to this there are often situations where intervention is undertaken on an emergency basis to protect the child. It is a fact that child protection has been given greater prominence in the 1990s, primarily because of increased recognition of the incidence of child sex abuse and increasing emphasis on the rights of the child. Local authorities have a crucial role to play in prevention, support, detection, intervention and sanction. As child abuse and neglect have implications for child welfare, criminal justice and other agencies' responsibilities, there is clearly a need for inter-agency co-operation. In an effort to promote local co-operation there are in operation Child Protection Committees.[121] These local authority committees develop guidance as to the circumstances likely to be appropriate to initiate child protection procedures, the information required, and the recording of information and procedures for joint investigation with the police. Training is clearly central to properly discharged functions in relation to child protection.[122] It is also the case that a Child Protection Register is maintained by each local authority, either alone or in conjunction with others. These registers will contain details of children considered to be at risk.

The child protection order

4.36 Yet a further innovation of the Children (Scotland) Act 1995 is the child protection order ("CPO"),[123] which replaces the old "place of safety orders" previously available under s.37 of the Social Work (Scotland) Act 1968.[124] The CPO is to be regarded as a serious step and not a routine response to allegations of child abuse. In contrast to other orders under the 1995 Act, which only a local authority can seek, an application may be made to the sheriff court for a CPO by "any person". Where the applicant is someone other than the local authority that person must notify the local authority and the Principal Reporter to the children's hearing that the order has been made. Where the sheriff is satisfied that there are reasonable grounds for believing that the child is being so treated or neglected that he is suffering significant harm or that he will suffer such harm if he is not removed to a place of safety then, he may make an order to protect the child from the significant harm.

Notwithstanding that others may make an application under the foregoing provisions, it is envisaged that in most instances the applicant will be the local authority acting under slightly different provisions designed to permit the local authority to act in particular circumstances. A sheriff may make a CPO if first, the local authority has reasonable grounds for believing that the child is suffering or will suffer significant harm as a result of the way the child is being treated or neglected; secondly, the local authority is making enquiries to allow it to decide if it should act to safeguard the welfare of the child; and thirdly, those enquiries are being frustrated by access

[120] Except in relation to interdicts, appointing judicial factors and removing guardians,

[121] See SWSG Circular 14/97.

[122] See Davies, Marshall and Robertson, *Child Abuse; Training Investigating Officers*, Police Research Series, Paper 94 (Home Office, 1998).

[123] See the 1995 Act s.57.

[124] As discussed in E. Sutherland, "The Orkney Case", 1992 Jur. Rev. 93.

to the child being unreasonably denied and the authority has reasonable cause to believe that access is required as a matter of some urgency.

Unreasonable denial of access

4.37 It is difficult to offer definitive guidance on what a court will consider to be an unreasonable denial of access. Guidance to the new order suggests that it might be unreasonable if the parent has had explained to him the reason for the enquiries and fails to respond positively to a reasonable request for access, perhaps by having the child seen by a medical practitioner. Of course the child himself may be in a position to refuse medical examination or treatment.[125] Such a voluntary response may make a refusal of access reasonable but only in circumstances where a prior voluntary agreement has not been reneged on.[126] Sheriffs will doubtless have their own views as to the question of the reasonableness of any refusal and each case will inevitably rest on its own circumstances. The imminence of the risk to the child is likely to diminish regard for the parents' rights to deny access but it should not be taken that any refusal must in consequence be deemed "unreasonable". The significant harm test assesses the current situation but also looks to the future. Moreover, where the applicant for the CPO is the local authority, the test under s.57(2) of the 1995 Act is that the applicant has reasonable cause to believe, whereas where the application is made by any person under s.57(1) it is the court that must have reasonable cause to believe that the child is suffering or will suffer significant harm. There is doubtless a difficult balance to be struck between the rights of parents and the need to protect children.[127] Professionals face considerable problems in this regard, aptly alluded to in a speech by Lord Nicholls in *Re H (Minors)*[128] where he said,

> "I am very conscious of the difficulties confronting social workers and others in obtaining hard evidence, which will stand up when challenged in court, of the maltreatment meted out to children behind closed doors. Cruelty and physical abuse are notoriously difficult to prove".

Lord Nicholls recognised that the law could be made unworkable by demanding unreasonable expectations as to proof. In Scotland the phraseology of the law errs on the side of the need to protect the child at the expense of the parental right to family autonomy.

Making an application for a CPO

4.38 In practice the arrangements for CPOs are that they are usually dealt with on the same day that the application is made. There is out of normal hours provision in Glasgow and Edinburgh where duty sheriffs will make themselves available to hear cases. In other areas it is possible for persons to attend at the sheriff's house where the emergency situation dictates. Sheriffs will consider evidence including hearsay in CPO applications. Anecdotal evidence suggests that hearings may take around an hour. Social workers may be put on oath though this is not

---

[125] Age of Legal (Capacity) Scotland Act 1991 s.2(4).

[126] *Scotland's Children—The Children (Scotland) Act 1995 Regulations and Guidance: Volume 1 Support and Protection for Children and Their Families* (Scottish Government, 2004) para.20.

[127] See Hayes, "Reconciling Protection of Children with Justice for Parents in Cases of Alleged Child Abuse" (1997) 17 *Legal Studies* 1.

[128] [1996] 1 All E.R. 1 at 22; on the difficulty of proof see also Muram, "Child Sexual Abuse: Relationship Between Sexual Acts and Genital Findings" (1989) 13 *Child Abuse and Neglect* 211; Bays and Chadwick, "Medical Diagnosis of the Sexually Abused Child" (1993) 17 *Child Abuse and Neglect* 91; *Re G* [1987] 1 F.L.R. 310; *Re M (A Minor) (No.2) (Appeal)* [1994] 1 F.L.R. 59; *Physical Signs of Sexual Abuse: Report of a working party of the Royal College of Physicians* (Royal College of Surgeons, 1991); *Diagnosis of Child Sexual Abuse: Guidance for Doctors* (DHSS Standing Medical Advisory Committee, 1988); W. Stainton Rogers, *Child Abuse and Neglect: Facing the Challenge* (Open University, 1989); Waterhouse, Dobash and Carnie, *Child Sexual Abusers* (Scottish Office, 1994).

necessary. Sheriffs may ask if the views of the children have been ascertained and, if so, what they are.[129]

Before making an application for a CPO a local authority will wish to assess alternative courses of action. It will also require to ascertain the wishes and feelings of the child having regard to his age and understanding. In addition to this there will need to be some consideration of what will happen to the child if the order is made. In practical terms there will be much to consider and plan for. Prior preparation not only may help determine whether to seek an order but also will ensure that the local authority is ready to fulfil its obligations following the granting of the CPO. Much of the preparatory work may arise from child protection case conferences where there is inter-agency consideration of children believed to be at risk. The case conference seeks to ensure that all information about the child is shared, to assess the degree of existing and likely future risk to the child, to identify the child's needs and to review any child protection plan. In the child protection case conference, professionals from a broad array of disciplines are brought together to discuss a child's case. The parents and the child will be fully involved in the process. A case conference may decide to put a child on the Child Protection Register, following which there will require to be periodic review conferences.[130]

4.39 The application for a CPO must identify the applicant and where practicable the child. It must also state the grounds on which the application is made and must be accompanied by supporting evidence.[131] In determining whether to make a CPO the sheriff must make the welfare of the child his paramount consideration.[132] The CPO may require any person in a position to do so to produce the child and to authorise the child's removal to a place of safety. It may also prevent the child being removed from the place he or she is currently accommodated in. In addition it may order that the place at which the child is being kept should not be disclosed to any person or persons.[133] In taking any action required by the CPO the applicant must only act in a way that he reasonably believes is necessary to safeguard or promote the welfare of the child.[134] Where it removes a child to a place of safety the local authority will have a duty to safeguard and promote the child's welfare and to take such steps to promote on a regular basis personal relations and direct contact between the child and any person with parental responsibilities towards the child.[135] Notwithstanding the local authority's obligations, s.58 makes specific provision for the sheriff to make a direction as to contact with the child. He may prohibit contact or allow it on certain conditions as he sees fit. Applicants for a CPO may at the same time seek a direction if they believe it is necessary to safeguard and promote the child's welfare on the issue of exercise or fulfilment of parental rights and responsibilities in relation to the child. It is suggested for example that a sheriff may direct a limit to the number of examinations a child may undergo.[136] A CPO may direct the authorisation of an examination of the child's physical and mental state, or some other assessment or interview and related treatment.[137] In implementing the order, local authorities are counselled to ensure that where siblings are removed from home they are kept together unless there are compelling reasons for not so doing. If siblings are separated they should be kept under regular review and permitted contact with each other. Children should be allowed to retain such personal possessions as they reasonably wish or require. Access to the child in the place of safety should be allowed by parents,

---

[129] Kearney, "Children's Hearings, Child Protection and the Children (Scotland) Act 1995", 1996 SCOLAG 102, 106.
[130] See *Protecting Children—A Shared Responsibility* (Scottish Office, 1998), pp.31–39.
[131] 1995 Act s.57.
[132] 1995 Act s.16(1).
[133] On the scope of CPOs see the 1995 Act s.57(4).
[134] 1995 Act s.57(6).
[135] 1995 Act s.57(7).
[136] *Scotland's Children—The Children (Scotland) Act 1995 Regulations and Guidance: Volume 1 Support and Protection for Children and Their Families* (Scottish Government, 2004) para.8.
[137] Subject to the proviso that a child with capacity under the Age of Legal Capacity (Scotland) Act 1991 may refuse to consent to medical treatment or examination: 1995 Act s.90.

friends and relatives, albeit on such restrictions as are necessary. In addition there should be attempts to secure the continued education of the child.[138]

Given the emergency nature of the order, the speed which is inherent in the legal process, and the fact that the initial application will be heard by the sheriff in private with only the applicant represented, the order will be served by the applicant on the child, any relevant person (usually parent or guardian) and, where the applicant is not the local authority, on it and the Principal Reporter for the area in which the child is resident. The order will be accompanied by a notice, which will also inform of the right to seek a variation or discharge of the CPO.

The Reporter to the children's hearing has the power to discharge a CPO where, having regard to the welfare of the child and the change in circumstances of the case, or further information, he concludes that the conditions for making the CPO no longer exist.[139] He may likewise discharge a condition or direction of a CPO. CPOs are designed to last as short a time as possible. It is an emergency procedure to offer immediate protection of the child. The system of CPOs has a number of checks and balances as well as mechanisms for speedy recall. Professor Thomson has said of CPOs that they are "paradigmatic of the tension inherent in any system of child protection law between the autonomy of the family and the obligation of the state to intervene in order to protect a child".[140]

The initial hearing

4.40 Unless he discharges the referral or receives notification of an application to the sheriff to vary or discharge a CPO, the Reporter must arrange a reference to a children's hearing to determine whether or not, in the interests of the child, the CPO should continue.[141] This hearing, known as the "initial hearing", must take place on the second working day after the order has been implemented. Where the initial hearing is satisfied that the conditions for making a CPO exist it may continue it, with or without variation, until a second children's hearing is arranged to decide whether compulsory measures of supervision are required.

If no attempt is made to implement the CPO within 24 hours of the order being made by the sheriff, it will cease to have effect. In circumstances where the Reporter has exercised his powers under the 1995 Act to discharge the CPO or vary the conditions attached to it, he must notify the sheriff.

Variation or discharge of a CPO

4.41 There is no formal right of appeal to the sheriff principal in respect of a decision of a sheriff to grant a CPO or a children's hearing to continue it.[142] However, as noted earlier there is a right to seek to have a CPO discharged or varied.[143] An application for variation or discharge is again made to a sheriff and may be made immediately on receipt of the order. Such an application must be made before the initial children's hearing organised by the Reporter. Applications may be made by the child, a person having parental rights over the child, a relevant person, anyone to whom notice of the application was given under the rules, or the person who made the original application. The applicant must give notice of the application to discharge or vary to the Reporter forthwith. The Reporter for his part may convene a children's hearing for the purposes of giving the sheriff appropriate advice to assist in the determination of the application. Where the application is for variation of the decision of the initial hearing to continue the CPO, it must be heard by the sheriff within two days of the hearing. The sheriff, after hearing the parties to the application and the Reporter (if he wishes to make representations), will

---

[138] *Scotland's children*, Cm.2286 (1993), Vol.1, p.63.
[139] 1995 Act s.60(3)(c).
[140] Thomson, *Family Law in Scotland* (1996), p.278.
[141] See the 1995 Act ss.59–60.
[142] 1995 Act s.51(15).
[143] See generally the 1995 Act s.60.

determine whether the conditions for making a CPO are satisfied or whether any direction or condition should be varied or cancelled. He may thereafter vary any term or condition, confirm or vary any direction, and continue the order. He may, of course, decide to recall the order and cancel any direction.

The second hearing

4.42 Where no application to vary or discharge is made to the sheriff, a second children's hearing shall be convened to take place on the eighth working day after the order was implemented.[144] This hearing will have the same powers as a children's hearing convened to deal with a child thought to be in need of compulsory measures of care under s.52.[145] There may well be the need to issue a warrant to detain the child in a place of safety where the hearing is unable to dispose of the case and it believes that it is necessary to safeguard and promote the child's welfare.[146] Warrants last for 22 days and thereafter they lapse. There is scope for a warrant to be extended during that period, on cause shown by the Reporter, for further periods of 22 days but for no more than 66 days from the day the child was first taken into the place of safety. However, the Reporter can apply to the sheriff to keep the child in the place of safety after any warrant by a children's hearing has expired and he may grant it on cause shown.[147] Any warrant granted by the sheriff to detain the child in a place of safety must specify the date on which it expires. Further applications can be made to the sheriff for a warrant at any time before the expiry of a warrant and there is no limit specified on the maximum duration that a child can be detained by a sheriff granting warrants. It is thought that a right of appeal against the sheriff's decision will be subject to the normal sheriff court orders appeals procedure.[148] Children must be consulted in warrant proceedings.[149]

Other emergency measures

4.43 There is scope under the legislation for any person to make an application to a justice of the peace to remove a child to a place of safety or to prevent a child's removal from a place of safety in circumstances where it is not practical to make an application to the sheriff for a CPO.[150] The justice of the peace must be satisfied that the conditions in s.57(1) of the 1995 Act for the making of a CPO exist and it is likely that there would be a direction to remove the child to a place of safety, before giving the authorisation. Where the application is made by the local authority the justice of the peace must be satisfied that the grounds in s.57(2) are met and that an authorisation to remove to a place of safety would be granted, before giving authorisation. The authorisation of the justice of the peace operates in similar fashion to that of the sheriff in that it requires any person to produce the child to the applicant; prevents anyone from removing the child from a place of safety; and authorises the removal of the child to the place of safety. This authorisation lasts for 12 hours if arrangements have been made to remove the child to, or to prevent the child's removal from, a place of safety. Where arrangements have been made the authorisation ceases after 24 hours or, if earlier, when an application for a CPO has been disposed of.

The Act also confers a power on the police to intervene and remove a child to a place of safety where a constable has cause to believe that the conditions for a CPO exist, it is not practicable to make an application to the sheriff and it is in order to protect the child from significant harm. Children can only be detained in a place of safety for up to 24 hours where removed to such a

[144] 1995 Act s.65(2).
[145] See para.4.47.
[146] 1995 Act s.66.
[147] 1995 Act s.67.
[148] See Thomson, *Family Law in Scotland* (2006), p.375.
[149] 1995 Act s.16(2) and (4).
[150] 1995 Act s.61.

place by the police. One can anticipate in such cases an application for a CPO being made to the sheriff within the 24 hours. The Principal Reporter, if he considers that the conditions for granting authorisation are not satisfied or that it is no longer in the best interests of the child, can authorise the release of the child from a place of safety.

THE CHILDREN'S HEARING SYSTEM

4.44 Part III of the Social Work (Scotland) Act 1968 introduced a system of children's hearings to Scotland. Both the scheme itself and the principles underpinning it were of huge significance.[151] The original scheme has undergone a process of modernisation and the new provisions are to be found in Pt II of the Children (Scotland) Act 1995. These in turn have undergone modernisation; most notably by the significant Scottish case *S v Miller*[152] and the drive to tackle young offenders.

S v Miller addressed a legal challenge that the hearings were incompatible with human rights. A number of grounds for non-compliance were raised and consequently children over 12 now have access to their reports and legal representatives have been introduced.[153] Other changes include fast track hearings; forms of restorative justice[154] and provisions under the Antisocial Behaviour etc. (Scotland) Act 2004.[155]

Criminal responsibility of children

4.45 Before the children's hearing system was introduced, children who offended were prosecuted before the ordinary criminal courts albeit that there were some specialist juvenile courts. Although the courts were charged with dealing with juvenile offenders in their best interests, there was clearly dissatisfaction with the way in which children who offended were being dealt with. The Kilbrandon Committee recognised that children who offended were just as likely to need support as those children who were offended against. Accordingly, the children's hearing system is imbued with a welfare-orientated approach. The scheme operates to divert into the hearing system most child offenders, victims of abuse and those threatened with abuse. It is of course the case that some children who offend are still dealt with in the criminal courts. Section 42(1) of the Criminal Procedure (Scotland) Act 1995 provides that:

> "No child under the age of 16 shall be prosecuted for any offence except on the instructions of the Lord Advocate, or at his instance; and no court other than the High Court and the sheriff court shall have jurisdiction over a child under the age of 16 years for an offence."

Such prosecutions are rare and will proceed only if it is absolutely necessary. If the prosecuting authorities consider an offence serious enough to proceed by solemn procedure, it is likely they will ensure that the case is not diverted into the hearing system.[156] Moreover, where a child commits an offence in conjunction with an adult and the prosecuting authorities believe that it will be prejudicial to separate the accused, the child may stand trial with his co-accused. It is not uncommon for young offenders jointly involved in the commission of an offence to fall either

---

[151] *Report of the Committee on Children and Young Persons, Scotland*, Cmnd.2306 (HMSO, 1964), para.1.

[152] 2001 S.L.T. 531.

[153] See L. Edwards, "S v Miller: The End of the Children's Hearings System as We Know It?", 2001 S.L.T 187 where Lilian Edwards considers that possible future challenges to the hearings system may consider the panel's independence and supervision requirements restricting contact and residence.

[154] In June 2005, the then Education Minister Peter Peacock identified key measures to deal with persistent young offenders including "making some young offenders face up to the victims" and diversion schemes: Scottish Executive News Release, October 21, 2005; *Guide on the Use of Restorative Justice Services in the Children's Hearings System* (Edinburgh: Scottish Executive, July 11, 2005).

[155] These are discussed at paras 4.73–4.75.

[156] See paras 8.12 et seq.

side of the dividing line of "childhood".[157] In addition, as the children's hearings have no power to confiscate weapons or disqualify from driving,[158] it may be that the prosecuting authorities will proceed in the criminal courts in order to facilitate confiscation or disqualification.

4.46 In Scots law children under eight years of age have no criminal responsibility whatsoever and will accordingly never be prosecuted in the court.[159] Such children who commit what would otherwise be a criminal offence will be referred into the hearing system. Because it only deals with very minor offences, no child will be prosecuted in the district court. If the matter is of such limited consequence, it is clearly inappropriate for the child to face prosecution. Where a child has committed an offence or is accused of an offence, or there is some other ground of referral, that matter will ordinarily be referred to the Reporter to the children's hearing in the first instance. In 2005–06, 53,883 children in Scotland were referred to the Children's Reporter.[160] Of these 40,931 were referred on non-offence (care and protection) grounds and 17,624 on offence grounds. Of the boys, 76 per cent were referred for offence-related grounds compared to 24 per cent of girls.[161]

A review of the age of criminal responsibility was embarked upon in October 2000 when the Scottish Law Commission was asked by Scottish Ministers to consider the rules determining the age of criminal responsibility. After a process of consultation the Commission published the *Report on Age of Criminal Responsibility*.[162] In the report there were three main recommendations: (1) abolish the rule that a child under eight years of age cannot be guilty of an offence; (2) amend the law to provide that a child under 12 years of age cannot be prosecuted; and (3) allow any child to be referred to a children's hearing on the ground of having committed an offence. There are no current plans to implement these recommendations.

Compulsory measures of supervision

4.47 Any person who has reasonable cause to believe that a child requires compulsory measures of supervision may make a referral to the Reporter.[163] Those most likely to make a referral are social workers, school authorities, the police, a relative or neighbour.[164] The police will notify the Reporter to the children's hearing as well as the Procurator Fiscal whenever an offence has been committed by a child. The law compels the police to give the Reporter such information as they have been able to discover and enables other persons to do so.[165] In circumstances where information is received by the social work department of the local authority that a child may be in need of compulsory measures of care, the local authority is under a statutory duty to "cause enquiries to be made into the case unless they are satisfied that such enquiries are unnecessary".[166] If after an investigation the authority believes that the child may be in need of such care then it is under a duty to pass to the Reporter such information as it has been able to discover. Additionally, under s.54(2) of the 1995 Act a court may refer a case to the Reporter if during "relevant proceedings" it is satisfied that one or more of the grounds of referral (except the ground that the child has committed an offence) are established. "Relevant proceedings" are defined as actions for divorce or separation, declarations of marriage, nullity, parentage or non-parentage, actions relating to parental rights and responsibilities, adoption proceedings or freeing for adoption proceedings, and proceedings against a parent for failing to secure regular

---

[157] In *X v Sweeney*, 1982 J.C. 70 one finds an illustration of young offenders being prosecuted together.

[158] Disqualification is possible even for those who have not legally held a licence because they are too young.

[159] Criminal Procedure (Scotland) Act 1995 s.41.

[160] Scottish Children's Reporter Administration Annual Report, 2005–06, p.20.

[161] Scottish Children's Reporter Administration Annual Report, 2005–06, p.20.

[162] Scot. Law Com. No.185 (2001).

[163] 1995 Act s.53(2)(b).

[164] The police are thought to be the main source of referrals to the Reporter. See Hallet and Murray, *The Evaluation of Children's Hearings in Scotland: Deciding in Children's Interests* (Edinburgh: Scottish Office Central Research Unit, 1998), Vol.1, p.iv.

[165] 1995 Act s.53(2) and (3).

[166] 1995 Act s.53(1).

attendance at school.[167] Given the strict construction of statutory provisions it is only in these cases that referrals from court may occur, although in other cases anyone including a judge is at liberty to pass information to the Reporter.[168] There are other ways in which a child or consideration of a child may come before a children's hearing. For example, there are referrals by the criminal courts for guidance and disposal in sentencing of children prosecuted before the criminal courts.[169] Moreover, children detained in a place of safety where prosecution does not follow will be the subject of a referral to a children's hearing by the Principal Reporter, unless he considers that compulsory measures of care are not required.[170] Any hearing organised under this latter provision must be held no later than the third day after the Principal Reporter receives the information.[171]

The Reporter to the children's hearing

4.48 The person who stands at the very centre of the children's hearing system from an administrative point of view is the Reporter. The Reporter is an officer of the Scottish Children's Reporter Administration and cannot without the Secretary of State's permission be employed by a local authority.[172] Many Reporters will be legally qualified but that is not an essential prerequisite of the post-holder. The 1995 Act empowers Reporters to conduct proceedings in the sheriff court where that proves necessary irrespective of whether they are legally qualified or not.[173]

The Reporter has a varied role.[174] On the one hand he or she is responsible for gathering information and arranging the hearing. In that sense they act as the administrator of the hearing. However, the Reporters also have a major decision-making role in that they will decide, following receipt of a referral, whether the matter should be referred to a hearing. In conjunction with the Procurator Fiscal they will have to determine whether a child offender should be dealt with by the hearing system or prosecuted in the criminal courts. Finally, the Reporter has the responsibility of arguing matters before the sheriff, particularly where the grounds of referral to the children's hearing are disputed.

On receipt of information that suggests that a child may be in need of compulsory measures of care the Reporter is required to undertake an initial investigation. In his capacity of gatherer of information, the Reporter may request a report from the local authority on any issue he thinks relevant. The local authority is obliged to supply this report. This report may be wide-ranging and far more extensive than any report made by the authority in originally referring the matter to the Reporter, if the authority is the source of the original reference. Reports are likely to come from social workers and/or the child's school.[175] A report at this stage is designed to assist the Reporter in his initial investigation. Once the Reporter has conducted his initial investigation and gathered any reports he requires, he may decide that a hearing does not need to be arranged. Research has disclosed that the main factors taken into account by Reporters in their initial decision-making role include families' co-operation (or lack of it), school-related issues, current social work input, evidential issues, the seriousness of any offence, any prior record of the child or young person offending, the attitude of the family, the age of the child or young person, risk to the child or young person, and aspects of family functioning (for example attitudes, relationships, presence of addiction, aggression).[176] The majority of decisions are

---

[167] 1995 Act s.54(2)(a)–(d).

[168] Norrie, Annotations in Mays (ed.), *Scottish Social Work Legislation*, C.207.3.

[169] Discussed at para.4.45.

[170] 1995 Act s.63(1), as amended by Criminal Procedure (Consequential Provisions) (Scotland) Act 1995.

[171] 1995 Act s.63(2).

[172] 1995 Act s.40(2).

[173] 1995 Act s.40(4)(a).

[174] 1995 Act s.56.

[175] Examples of pro forma reports are to be found in the now dated Moore, *Guide to the Children's Hearing System in Scotland* (1989).

[176] See Hallet and Murray, *The Evaluation of Children's Hearings in Scotland* (1998), p.i.

relatively straightforward. A substantial proportion of decisions are taken within a month of receipt of notification. Reporters' decision-making has been described as:

> "characterised by an individual and non-formulaic approach, the exercise of independent judgement, a wide amount of discretion, principles of diversion and minimal intervention, a degree of cultural relativism and, at times, the operation of form of a tariff".[177]

The decision to convene a hearing

4.49 Where the Reporter decides that a hearing should not be convened, he must inform the child, any "relevant person", and the person who brought the case to his notice, and anyone else he considers should be informed.[178] A relevant person is a parent or other person with parental rights or responsibilities, or someone who appears to be a person who ordinarily has charge of, or control over, the child in question.[179] The Reporter can if he considers it appropriate refer the matter to the local authority with a view to the authority providing advice, guidance and assistance to the child and his family. Once the Reporter has decided that a hearing need not be arranged and he has advised the parties accordingly, in the absence of new circumstances, he cannot revoke his decision and arrange a hearing on the basis of the information he obtained in his initial investigation.

Where on the basis of the information he has, it appears to the Reporter that the child may be in need of compulsory measures of care, the Reporter must arrange a hearing to consider and determine the child's case. Basically, the Reporter must be convinced that one of the grounds of referral in s.52 of the 1995 Act exist before making the referral to the hearing. Where he has not already done so he must arrange for reports from the local authority. Equally he may seek an additional report where a preliminary report has been made referring the child.

Composition and procedure

4.50 For every local government area in Scotland there is a children's panel. These panels are constituted and operate under the guidance of a Children's Panel Advisory Committee ("CPAC"), which every local authority is required to form.[180] Local authorities may band together and form joint Advisory Committees. It is the duty of the CPAC to submit names of possible panel members to the Secretary of State for Scotland and to advise on their suitability and on general matters of administration. The composition of the CPAC is 60 per cent nominated by the Secretary of State and 40 per cent nominated by the local authority. Each CPAC will seek to compile a panel of members for the children's hearings from among the locality. There is no gender bias nor need panel members be parents or be married. Once appointed the list of names and addresses of the members of the children's panel is published in each locality. It is from this list that the members of the actual hearing are drawn. Each hearing of a child's case will be constituted by three members of the panel. Hearings cannot consist solely of males or female members.[181] One of three will act as chairman of the hearing[182] but that person's voice carries no more authority than other panel members. In most cases the hearing members reach a unanimous decision.[183]

---

[177] See Hallet and Murray, *The Evaluation of Children's Hearings in Scotland* (1998), p.ii.
[178] 1995 Act s.56.
[179] 1995 Act s.93(2)(b).
[180] 1995 Act Sch.1.
[181] 1995 Act s.39(5).
[182] 1995 Act s.39(5).
[183] See Hallet and Murray, *The Evaluation of Children's Hearings in Scotland* (1998), p.ii.

Informality of proceedings

4.51 Children's hearings are designed to be as informal as possible.[184] With this in mind they are conducted in private. No other person than those whose presence is necessary for the proper consideration of the case or whom the chairman allows shall be present.[185] As if to reinforce this point s.43(2) of the 1995 Act insists that the chairman should take all reasonable steps to ensure that the numbers are kept to a minimum. Research has shown that between seven and nine persons usually attend the hearing with between five and seven non-family members.[186] In the ordinary course of events one may find the panel members, the Reporter, the child, relevant persons and a social worker present, occasionally with other professionals in attendance. Parties are not normally legally represented, except in two special circumstances a child will be appointed a legal representative.[187] However, any child who comes before a hearing and any relevant person who attends may each be accompanied by one person for the purpose of assisting the child, or as the case may be the relevant person, at the hearing. The same person may represent both the child and the relevant person though if they are a lawyer no legal aid will be made available.[188] Given the limitations on attendance it is impossible for even small groups of students to attend as observers but from time to time solitary students are allowed to attend. Bona fide members of a newspaper or news agency may attend the hearing although they may be excluded from the hearing or parts of it where the hearing is satisfied that such exclusion is necessary in the interests of the child, to obtain the child's view of the case, or their presence is causing, or likely to cause, the child "significant distress".[189] In such situations where exclusion has taken place, the chairman may subsequently explain to the person excluded the substance of what has taken place in his absence.[190] In reporting the children's hearing the press are prohibited from publishing information that is intended or likely to identify any child[191] concerned in the proceedings, the child's address or school.[192] The Secretary of State has the power to lift such a ban in the case of a children's hearing where he considers it to be in the interest of justice.[193] Despite attempts to make the proceedings relatively informal, there is often an inescapable degree of formality in the hearings associated with ensuring their proper conduct and protecting the rights of families. Families have described feeling nervous and apprehensive about hearings. The majority of hearings last less than an hour.[194]

Attendance and notification

4.52 Attendance at the hearing by the child and relevant persons prior to the 1995 Act was something of a controversial legal area.[195] The provisions in the 1995 Act now clarify the matter.[196] As a general proposition of law a child has the right to attend all stages of the hearing and is obliged to do so. The child may be excused attendance where the hearing is satisfied in a Sch.1 offence case (case of bodily injury or sexual abuse)[197] that the attendance of the child is not necessary for a just hearing or in any type of case where it would be detrimental to the interests of the child to be in attendance. The Reporter is responsible for notifying the child of the hearing and ensuring

---

[184] See J. Rose, "Procedure in Children's Hearings", 1994 S.L.T. (News) 137.
[185] 1995 Act s.43(1).
[186] See Hallet and Murray, *The Evaluation of Children's Hearings in Scotland* (1998), p.ii.
[187] Children's Hearings (Legal Representation) (Scotland) Rules 2002 (SSI 2002/63). See para.4.55.
[188] See the Children's Hearings (Scotland) Rules 1996 (SI 1996/3261), constituted under the 1995 Act s.42(2)(i).
[189] 1995 Act s.43(4).
[190] 1995 Act s.43(5).
[191] See *McArdle v Orr*, 1994 S.L.T. 463.
[192] 1995 Act s.44.
[193] 1995 Act s.44(5).
[194] See Hallet and Murray, *The Evaluation of Children's Hearings in Scotland* (1998), pp.ii and iii.
[195] See Norrie, "Excluding Children from Children's Hearings", 1993 S.L.T. (News) 67; Wilkinson and Norrie, *Parent and Child* (1993), p.464; *Sloan v B*, 1991 S.L.T. 530.
[196] 1995 Act ss.45 and 46.
[197] See para.4.62.

their attendance. In the normal course of events the child will come along with his or her parents. In circumstances where the Reporter thinks it unlikely that the child will attend voluntarily he may apply to a children's hearing for a warrant to have the child detained in a place of safety and brought before a children's hearing.

Similarly, a "relevant person" has the right to attend all stages of the hearing and is obliged to attend.[198] If the hearing is satisfied that it would be unreasonable to require their attendance or their attendance is unnecessary for the proper consideration of the case they will not be compelled to attend. In fact, the hearing may exclude the relevant person (or his representative) if it is satisfied that in the interests of the child the presence of the person is causing or is likely to cause the child significant distress, or that it is necessary in order to obtain the views of the child. As Professor Norrie explains:

> "It may frequently happen that a child is likely to speak more openly in the absence of the parent. This may be because there is a conflict of interest between the parent and the child, or because the child is embarrassed to talk about certain personal things in front of a parent".[199]

4.53 It is also thought that parents disrupting the hearing by continually interrupting or answering on behalf of the child may be properly excluded under this ground. Exclusion may be particularly relevant where the child has been the victim of parental abuse. Where a relevant person is excluded the chairman must explain the substance of what has taken place in the person's absence; however, provisions under the Adoption and Children (Scotland) Act 2007 will allow the Reporter not to disclose such information where necessary to protect the child's interests.

A major criticism aimed at the hearing process until quite recently was the inability of the parents or the child to be served with the reports before the hearing took place. In *McMichael v United Kingdom*[200] the European Court of Human Rights held that the failure to give a parent full access to medical and social enquiry reports placed before the tribunal was an infringement of human rights. The position is now regulated by the Children's Hearings (Scotland) Rules 1996, which require relevant persons to receive identified documents that the chairman and members of the hearing themselves receive from the Principal Reporter.[201] The child will not be entitled to receive the documents, though he or she must be made familiar with the substance of relevant reports unless, in the opinion of the chairman, such a disclosure would be detrimental to the child.[202]

Appointing a safeguarder

4.54 A safeguarder may be appointed by the hearing to protect and represent the interests of the child. He or she is entitled to the papers of the case and thereafter makes appropriate enquiries. He or she may decide to become a party to the action. If the safeguarder decides to do so he must lodge a report before the sheriff on the extent and findings of his enquiry and conclusions on the interests of the child. If the safeguarder is a legal practitioner he or she may appear before the sheriff for the child but not as the child's solicitor or advocate. Safeguarders are not very well remunerated and accordingly their appointments are not as extensive as they might be. In contrast curators *ad litem* can be funded from legal aid and as a consequence there is often dual appointment of safeguarder and curator *ad litem*.

---

198 cf. *L v H*, 1996 S.L.T. 612.
199 Norrie, Annotations in Mays (ed.), *Scottish Social Work Legislation*, C.199.3.
200 [1995] Fam. Law 478.
201 Children's Hearings (Scotland) Rules 1996 r.5(3).
202 Children's Hearings (Scotland) Rules 1996 rr.20(4) and 22(4).

Appointing a legal representative

4.55 Legal representatives are a product of the Scottish case, *S v Miller*[203] after the hearings were challenged on the basis that, since a child never had access to legal aid during a hearing, the system was not compliant with the right to a fair trial. Subsequently, the Scottish Government took legislative action to bring the hearings into line with art.6.

The Children's Hearings (Legal Representation) (Scotland) Rules 2002[204] took effect from February 23, 2002 and provide for an independent legal representative to be assigned to a child where it will allow the child to effectively participate in the proceedings, or where the child may be placed in secure accommodation. If either of these conditions is satisfied the decision to appoint a legal representative will be taken at either a business meeting or at the hearing itself. Legal representatives are solicitors employed by the local authority holding a practising certificate, and must be a safeguarder or curator *ad litem*. This appointment will not preclude a child from appointing their own legal counsel.

The obvious note of caution is that allowing a solicitor into the system may legalise the informal process that is at the heart of Kilbrandon. Another aspect of concern is whether it is the best way to allow children to effectively communicate.[205]

Child's age

4.56 It is the duty of the hearing at the commencement of the proceedings to enquire as to the child's age. Only on being satisfied that the person is a child over whom it has jurisdiction may the hearing proceed.[206] Any declaration or finding as to the child's age will be deemed to be the true age of the child and any decision of the hearing will not be invalidated by subsequent evidence that the person was not a child over whom it had jurisdiction.[207] The hearing only has jurisdiction over persons under 16 years of age or a person under 18 who is already the subject of a supervision requirement of the children's hearing.

Stating the grounds of referral

4.57 Having asked the child or his parent to state his age, the chairman of the hearing will explain the ground of referral stated by the Principal Reporter as the reason for the referral.[208] The hearing can only proceed if the ground of referral is accepted. All relevant persons must accept the grounds of referral though if they are not present at the hearing this will not be necessary. If the ground of referral is accepted the role of the hearing will be to decide how the case should be disposed of. However, where the ground of referral is rejected by either, or both, the child or the relevant persons the hearing must direct the Principal Reporter to make an application to the sheriff for a finding as to whether such grounds of referral are established. Alternatively, the hearing may discharge the referral completely. These two options are also available where either the child or the relevant persons reject part of the ground of referral and the hearing does not consider it appropriate to continue with the hearing. Where there is part acceptance of the grounds of referral the hearing may proceed in respect of those grounds that are accepted. It will often be the case that there are numerous grounds of referral. In some circumstances only one or some of those grounds are accepted while others are rejected. It may also be the case that a ground of referral is broadly accepted. For example, the child may have committed an offence but deny the extent or magnitude of the offence. The hearing may proceed in these circumstances.

---

[203] 2001 S.L.T. 531. See para.4.44.
[204] SSI 2002/63.
[205] L. Edwards, "Legal Representation Arrives at the Children's Hearing—But at What Cost?" (2002) 57 Fam. L.B. 2.
[206] 1995 Act s.47(1).
[207] 1995 Act s.47(2) and (3).
[208] 1995 Act ss.65 and 66.

In situations where the child is incapable of understanding the ground of referral or any explanation by the chairman, the hearing may direct the Reporter to make an application to the sheriff to determine if the grounds of referral are established or it may discharge the hearing. The chairman is under a duty to explain to the child and the relevant persons the purpose of the application and to advise them that they must attend the hearing before the sheriff. Where the hearing is not able to dispose of a case because the matter has been referred to the sheriff, it may nevertheless grant a warrant to detain the child in a place of safety if it has reason to believe that the child is unlikely to attend any subsequent hearing or that it is necessary in order to safeguard or promote the child's welfare.

REFERRING CHILDREN TO THE CHILDREN'S HEARING SYSTEM

4.58 The grounds of referral of a child to a children's hearing have remained substantially the same throughout the past 30 years.[209] There have been moderate amendments to cater for recognition of contemporary social problems as well as changes to update and refine the law in the light of experience. These grounds are of crucial importance in the hearing process, though it was held in *O v Rae*[210] that hearings may take into account matters that are not contained within these specific grounds, including "disputed facts". That case involved an allegation of sexual abuse by the father of four children against one of those children, which he emphatically denied. On the basis of this assertion and another ground that had been accepted by the father, the four children were retained in local authority care while arrangements for foster care were made. The court overruled a previous decision that a hearing could only proceed where grounds were accepted or established.[211] In the light of this decision Professor Norrie explains that:

> "[T]he existence of the grounds of referral founds the jurisdiction of the children's hearing. When the children's hearing are deciding whether to impose compulsory measures of care a consideration of the grounds of referral is central, but it is open to them to take account of any other factor (including a disputed factor) that touches upon the child's welfare."[212]

Taking account of information other than that relating to the ground of referral has been criticised by Sheriff Mitchell.[213] Notwithstanding, the ground or grounds of referral will set in context the extent of the child's need for compulsory care and for the most part will guide the solution to the child's need. Identification and acceptance of the problem will by definition tailor the solution in nearly all cases. The grounds of referral, previously set in out in the Social Work (Scotland) Act 1968, are now to be found in s.52 of the Children (Scotland) Act 1995.[214]

The grounds of referral

Section 52(2)(a): "is beyond the control of any relevant person"

4.59 A "relevant person" is described as any parent enjoying parental responsibilities or parental rights, or anyone in whom parental rights and responsibilities are vested or any person who appears to be someone who ordinarily has charge of or control over the child.[215] Professor

---

[209] See Statistical Bulletin: *Referrals of Children to Reporters and Children's Hearings* (Scottish Office, 1994), referred to in Breustedt et al., "The Evolution of the Children's Hearings System over the Last Twenty-Five Years", 1997 S.L.P.Q. 73, 81.

[210] 1993 S.L.T. 570.

[211] *K v Finlayson*, 1974 S.L.T. (Sh Ct) 51.

[212] Norrie, "In Defence of *O v Rae*", 1995 S.L.T. 353, 355.

[213] 1997 SCOLAG 13.

[214] In 1996, 27,000 children were referred to Reporters, 23 per cent more than 10 years previously. Source: Scottish Abstract of Statistics No.26 (1998).

[215] 1995 Act s.93(2)(b).

Norrie[216] suggests that "control" must be viewed as subjective to the particular child and there will be a diminution of parental control as the child matures. One may of course read too much into this view. On a purely factual assessment generally "control" of a child weakens as that child matures and formulates his or her own independent thinking. Professor Norrie appears to suggest that a Reporter considering the circumstances of a particular child may reflect on the expectations of control over a child by a "relevant person".[217] While it is difficult to hypothesise one may also imagine that the Reporter will dwell not just on the nature or quality of the lack of control, but rather more on the consequences of the failure to control. In so doing one of the other grounds of referral may come into consideration as a more suitable alternative basis for referral.

Section 52(2)(b): "is falling into bad associations or is exposed to moral danger"

4.60 This ground also previously existed in the 1968 Act. The continuing failure to define concepts such as "bad association" and "moral danger" leave a great deal of subjectivity to the assessment of the child's circumstances. The lack of definition ensures some linkage to varying standards of public decency and morality. Wilkinson and Norrie argue that "Moral danger is commonly equiperated with the risk of sexual corruption, but there is no warrant for restricting it to such cases." Some illustrations of the matters that will constitute evidence of falling into bad associations or exposure to moral danger may by their very nature offer the opportunity of pursuing a referral under a "better" and more precise ground. Solvent or drug abuse might for example offer considerable evidence of falling into bad associations as might a pattern of criminal conduct. In seeking to define the parameters of the aforementioned concepts there is much merit in Wilkinson and Norrie's view that "there are obvious hazards and difficulties in going beyond recognised categories such as sexual corruption and criminality".[218] Notwithstanding this in *Constanda v M*[219] one finds an illustration of a Reporter utilising the "exposure to moral danger" based on the commission of a criminal act. The Court of Session took the view that exposure to moral danger should be approached in a "practical fashion" referring to the whole circumstances, but in this particular case where only criminal behaviour was alleged, it would need to be established before the sheriff using the criminal standard of proof and not the usual civil standard of proof ordinarily used when assessing whether a child has been exposed to moral danger. Professor Norrie has suggested that a child at threat from a visiting absent father may be referred under this ground[220] but with respect this must only be in the most unusual of circumstances.

Section 52(2)(c): "is likely (i) to suffer unnecessarily; or (ii) be impaired seriously in his health or development, due to a lack of parental care"

4.61 The concept of parental care and parenting continues to be further defined in academic writings,[221] case law[222] and indeed the 1995 Act itself.[223] In exploring the terminology of the paragraph certain matters require further explanation. First, the reason for the absence of parental care is of little importance[224] and emphasis is on the likelihood[225] that there will be unnecessary suffering or serious impairment to the health or development of the child rather

[216] Norrie, Annotations in Mays (ed.), *Scottish Social Work Legislation*, C.205.5.
[217] Norrie, Annotations in Mays (ed.), *Scottish Social Work Legislation*, C.205.5.
[218] Wilkinson and Norrie, *Parent and Child* (1993), p.450.
[219] 1997 S.L.T. 1396.
[220] Norrie, "The Meaning of Household in Referrals to Children's Hearings", 1993 S.L.T. 192.
[221] See e.g. Ross, "Reasonable Parenting—Borders of Acceptability", 1994 Fam. L.B. 7, 10–12.
[222] See e.g. *Kennedy v S*, 1986 S.L.T. 679 at 682.
[223] 1995 Act s.2.
[224] See the obiter comment in *D v Kelly*, 1995 S.L.T. 1220 at 1224.
[225] *H v Lees; D v Orr*, 1994 S.L.T. 908; Mays, "Home Alone, Left Alone", 1996 64(2) S.L.G. 94.

than any attempt to attribute culpability to the parental conduct. On the face of things this ground might be established not just by reference to the nebulous concept of "normal" parenting but more properly by considering medical, psychological and other professional reports, which might narrate the damage or impairment to the child in less emotive and more precise terms, particularly given that parental culpability is not an essential component of this ground. Sheriffs may of course discount professional advice. In *Kennedy v M*[226] the child allegedly sustained bruising to his forehead after becoming involved in an altercation between the respondent and his estranged wife. A few days later the child's hand was burned after touching an iron. No medical help was sought and in a subsequent medical examination bruising was noticed to the boy's buttocks and his penis. The doctor's evidence was that these were not accidental injuries. After hearing a court-appointed safeguarder's report the sheriff was unable to support a finding that there was sufficient lack of parental care, and that many of the events simply reflected the "difficulties of looking after a lively toddler and no parent can be 100 per cent vigilant". In *D v Kelly*[227] the sheriff held that the development of two adopted girls was being impaired by the overly protective regime imposed by their parents. The parents had sought professional help and according to the sheriff were acting responsibly. Nevertheless he found that the ground of referral was established in that the children's development was being impaired. This view was rejected by the Court of Session, which contended that there had to be a lack of parental care in the first instance leading to the impairment of development.

Sheriffs must not simply decide that the child would be better off elsewhere but must apply the statutory test. In *H v Harkness*,[228] a case considered under the analogous provisions of the 1968 Act, two children of an incestuous relationship were taken into care because of the lack of parental care. There was a supervision requirement in respect of the children which had been allowed to lapse owing to an administrative error and the Reporter made a further referral. The mother successfully appealed to the Court of Session arguing that in the fresh application the statutory test must still be applied and that the sheriff should not simply reflect upon whether it would be better for the children to remain with the foster parents with whom they were now placed. The Court of Session also expressed the view that the lack of parental care must be such as is likely to cause serious harm or impairment to health and development of the child even where it might not be possible to be specific about what that harm might be. For an illustration where this ground of referral was upheld see *Finlayson, Applicant*[229] where the parents of a haemophiliac child refused to consent to conventional treatment. A recent decision has also highlighted the fact that on this ground, as indeed in all others, one cannot appeal further from the sheriff court to the Inner House and seek to have new reports placed before the court.[230]

Section 52(2)(d): "is a child in respect of whom any of the offences mentioned in Schedule 1 of the Criminal Procedure (Scotland) Act 1995 (offences against children to which special provisions apply) has been committed"

4.62 The offences referred to by Sch.1 to the Criminal Procedure (Scotland) Act 1995 are as follows[231]:

(1) Incest.
(2) Intercourse with a step-child.
(3) Intercourse of person in position of trust with child under 16.
(4) Intercourse with girl under 16.

---

226 1989 S.L.T. 687; see also *Kennedy v S*, 1986 S.L.T. 679.
227 1995 S.L.T. 1220.
228 1998 S.L.T. 1431.
229 1989 S.C.L.R. 601 (Sh Ct).
230 *Stirling v R*, 1996 S.C.L.R. 191.
231 See the Criminal Law (Consolidation) (Scotland) Act 1995 ss.1–13; Children and Young Persons (Scotland) Act 1937 ss.12, 15, 22 and 23.

(5) Indecent behaviour towards girl between 12 and 16.
(6) Procuring.
(7) Abduction and unlawful detention.
(8) Permitting girl to use premises for intercourse.
(9) Seduction, prostitution, etc. of girl under 16.
(10) Trading in prostitution and brothel-keeping.
(11) Allowing child to be in brothel.
(12) Homosexual offences.
(13) Cruelty to persons under 16.
(14) Causing or allowing persons under 16 to be used for begging.
(15) Exposing children under seven to risk of burning.
(16) Failing to provide for safety of children at entertainments.
(17) Any other offence involving bodily injury to a child under the age of 17 years.[232]
(18) Any offence involving the use of lewd, indecent and libidinous practice or behaviour towards children under the age of 17 years.[233]

Evidence suggests that 99 per cent of child sex abusers are male. Frequently they are fathers or stepfathers of the children concerned, or friends of the family. There is also evidence that around three-quarters of abused children are female and the majority of children were under 12 when abuse begins.[234] The standard of proof in establishing whether the child has been a victim of some form of physical or sexual abuse is the balance of probabilities[235] despite the allegation being a criminal offence. The Reporter is not concerned with proving guilt, rather that the child is in need of protection. In *M v Kennedy* one finds a reported illustration of a sheriff rejecting this ground of referral on the balance of probabilities.[236] The case is also authority for the proposition that a sheriff can hold the ground of referral not established on the basis that he cannot decide which particular offence had been committed. The original allegation was that the child had been the subject of penile penetration by a member of her own household. Medical evidence established that sexual penetration could have taken place at any time between 12 and 15 years of age. Sex with a child under 13 is a different offence from that of sex with a female child over 13 years of age. Emphasis must be placed on the word "any" in the ground of referral.

4.63 There may be a referral where there has been no criminal conviction.[237] Where there has been a criminal complaint this will in no way inhibit the right of the Reporter to place evidence before the sheriff if the ground of referral is contested.[238] The conduct complained of need not have occurred in Scotland and the alleged offence need not be capable of being tried in Scotland.[239] The identity of the offender need not be established,[240] nor need the time and the place of the offence.[241] In establishing the ground of referral hearsay evidence is allowable[242] and corroboration is not necessary.[243] In assessing whether the ground of referral is established it can be argued that the interests of the child take primacy over the interests of natural justice.

[232] e.g. *B v Harris*, 1990 S.L.T. 208; *Kennedy v A*, 1993 S.L.T. 1134.
[233] e.g. *Harris v E*, 1989 S.L.T. (Sh Ct) 42.
[234] See Waterhouse, Dobash and Carnie, "Child Sex Abusers" (1994) 3 *Social Work and Research Findings* 1.
[235] *B v Kennedy*, 1987 S.L.T. 765; *Harris v F*, 1991 S.L.T. 242.
[236] 1996 S.L.T. 434. Note however he upheld an alternative ground of referral.
[237] See *M v Kennedy*, 1987 S.L.T. 765; it may also arise that in subsequent criminal proceedings the alleged abuser is found not guilty and this will not necessarily interfere with the referral, which proceeds on the lesser standard of proof: see *Kennedy v DB*, 1992 S.C.L.R. 55 (IH).
[238] *P v Kennedy*, 1995 S.L.T. 476.
[239] *S v Kennedy*, 1996 S.L.T. 1087.
[240] *McGregor v K*, 1982 S.L.T. 293; *Kennedy v F*, 1985 S.L.T. 22; *S v Kennedy*, 1987 S.L.T. 667.
[241] See *W v Kennedy*, 1988 S.L.T. 563; *S v Kennedy*, 1996 S.L.T. 1087.
[242] *W v Kennedy*, 1988 S.L.T. 583.
[243] *Harris v F*, 1991 S.L.T. 242.

The liberal and indeed purposive approach to construction of this ground of referral can be found in the statement of Lord Justice-Clerk Ross in *S v Kennedy*[244] where he contended that:

> "Parliament has not stated expressly that the offences referred to must be offences which can be prosecuted in Scotland. In my opinion, it is doing no violence to the language used to construe 'offence' in its context as including conduct amounting to such an offence."[245]

Section 52(2)(e): "is, or is likely to become, a member of the same household as a child in respect of whom any of the offences referred to in paragraph (d) above has been committed"

4.64 Clearly it would be anomalous if only children who were the victims of Sch.1 offences rather than those who are at risk of exposure to them were referred to the hearing system. The whole purpose of the hearing system is to provide for children in need of compulsory measures of care. The welfare concept of the system dictates that agencies and the system should be proactive as well as reactive. The fact that a child has not yet been a victim of the abusive conduct set out in Sch.1 should not in any way detract from the obvious potential peril they face where they reside with someone who has already been the victim of such abuse. For the victim the system may act in the form of rescue from a hideous ordeal and, for the sibling or other child resident with the victim, the hearing system offers the prospect of prevention and safety. It seems almost trite that where one child has been the subject of abuse by a source of danger, that source is likely to pose a continuing threat to children that he or she has access to.[246]

An illustration of this type of referral is to be found in *Ferguson v P*.[247] A referral of two children whose father was charged with the culpable homicide of a two-year-old child whom he had allegedly wilfully neglected by leaving her in a bath of water without adequate supervision, as a result of which she suffered injury leading to her death. In this case the father rejected the grounds of referral, and additionally sought (and was granted) an adjournment before the sheriff. The Inner House overturned the adjournment reaffirming that the primary concern was the welfare of the child and that the referrals would ordinarily be disposed of before criminal proceedings were concluded or, in some instances, commenced. The potential prejudice to the parent in pursuant criminal proceedings was of secondary importance. In *Templeton v E*[248] the court distinguished between the continuing existence of family ties and continuing membership of the same household when the father of three children was alleged to have committed an offence under Sch.1 during overnight contact. The fact that a contact order might be imminent did not suggest that the children were likely to become part of the same household as their father and this did not thereby constitute a ground of referral.

Section 52(2)(f): "is, or is likely to become, a member of the same household as a person who has committed any of the offences referred to in paragraph (d) above"

4.65 Unlike the preceding ground of referral there is, it is submitted, a requirement to identify the offender who is part of the household or is to become part of the household. There is no requirement that the Sch.1 offence has been committed against a child.[249] The term "household" in this (as well as the preceding and the following) ground of referral is of some interest. In the normal scheme of things one would imagine that it relates to a group of individuals living

[244] 1996 S.L.T. 1087; cf. *Merrin v S*, 1987 S.L.T. 193 and Professor Thomson's comments in *Family Law in Scotland* (1996), p.284.

[245] 1996 S.L.T. 1087 at 1090.

[246] Norrie, Annotations in Mays (ed.), *Scottish Social Work Legislation*, C.205.6.

[247] 1989 S.L.T. 681.

[248] 1998 S.C.L.R. 672.

[249] Professor Thomson in *Family Law in Scotland* (1996), p.283 offers the illustration of non-consensual homosexual intercourse against an adult.

together. However in the context of the various grounds of referral its meaning is something more expansive than this. In *McGregor v H*[250] Lord Emslie said:

> "The word 'household' is plainly intended to connote a family unit or something akin to a family unit—a group of persons, held together with a particular kind of tie who normally live together, even if individual members of the group may be temporarily separated from it".

In *Kennedy v R's Curator ad Litem*[251] Lord Hope argues that "the important question ... is whether the ties of affection and regular contact which hold the parties together as a group of persons will continue". Persons can be considered part of the same household even where they live apart. In Professor Norrie's view the requirement is that there has to be some living together either in the present or at some time in the past. This point is important in the context where a child is born into a "household" that has changed in composition. An illustration of such a case is to be found in *A v Kennedy*[252] where a child was born some eight and a half years after the death of another child of the mother following that child's wilful ill-treatment. The mother objected to the referral on the basis that the household was immeasurably changed from that in which the dead child existed. The court disagreed pointing out that household membership may change but still continue. The question remains one of degree. In certain circumstances a child born into a household that has previously had a child referred may be referred irrespective of the lapse in time between the original referral and the birth of the new child.[253] Moreover, a household may still be said to exist despite the fact that the original perpetrator of the offence has left that household. One would imagine that the hearing would simply dismiss the referral on the basis that the child no longer needed protection.

Section 52(2)(g): "is, or is likely to become, a member of the same household as a person in respect of whom an offence under sections 1 to 3 of the Criminal Law (Consolidation) (Scotland) Act 1995 (incest and intercourse with a child by step-parent or person in position of trust) has been committed by a member of that household"

4.66 Incest and related offences are now consolidated in the Criminal Law (Consolidation) (Scotland) Act 1995. The analogous provision in s.32 of the Social Work (Scotland) Act 1968 only provided for the referral of female children whereas the current provision creates parity between the sexes. There is a suggestion that this ground of referral is superfluous in that the offences to which it refers are all Sch.1 offences and may be thought to be covered elsewhere.[254] Notwithstanding this there have been a few referrals on this specific ground.[255]

Section 52(2)(h): "has failed to attend school regularly without reasonable excuse"

4.67 The ground of referral in s.52(2)(h) on the face of things represents one of the clearer grounds of referral. The current provision is a complete re-enactment of the earlier provision in the 1968 Act. Despite its evident clarity Wilkinson and Norrie[256] point to several uncertainties. First, they contend that the ground of referral can only be open to a parent who has chosen to have his

---

[250] 1983 S.L.T. 626 at 628.
[251] 1993 S.L.T. 295 at 300.
[252] 1993 S.C.L.R. 107.
[253] The writer has dealt in practice with one such referral where the lapse was 18 months.
[254] Norrie, Annotations in Mays (ed.), *Scottish Social Work Legislation*, C.205.6.
[255] Thirteen out of 13,395 females in 1993: Statistical Bulletin, Scottish Office.
[256] Wilkinson and Norrie, *Parent and Child* (1993), p.454.

child educated at school. Exclusion from school for an allegation of misconduct that is not admitted may amount to reasonable excuse.[257] The onus of establishing reasonable excuse undoubtedly rests with the parent.[258] Under the Education (Scotland) Act 1980 where a parent is charged with an offence in respect of the child not attending school regularly and the court is satisfied that the child has not attended school regularly, the court may direct that the ground of referral is established for the purposes of a referral to the children's hearing.[259]

Section 52(2)(i): "has committed an offence"

4.68 Despite the fact that the majority of grounds of referral are welfare-orientated, this particular provision remains of great importance especially in relation to male children where statistics point to over two-thirds of all referrals to be for offence-related matters.[260] In respect of female children the percentage drops to almost one-quarter.[261] Given the number of referrals in respect of both sexes, there must by definition be a high incidence of referrals for offending behaviour. Where the matter comes before a sheriff for a finding on this ground of referral the standard of proof, unlike other grounds, is the criminal standard of proof. No child under the age of eight may be referred under this ground.[262]

Section 52(2)(j): "has misused alcohol or any drug, whether or not a controlled drug within the meaning of the Misuse of Drugs Act 1971"

4.69 Growing concern surrounding the misuse of drugs by children undoubtedly influenced the inclusion of this new ground of referral.[263] The inclusion was primarily to bring Scots law into line with art.33 of the United Nations Convention on the Rights of the Child.[264] A provision such as this may well have found intellectual merit with legislators irrespective of the Convention. While drug or alcohol abuse are not new phenomena, there is growing public and governmental concern on these issues. In the past the manifestations of the problem would undoubtedly have led to the child being referred under some other heading. It is the nature of social and welfare problems that many of the issues addressed by the grounds of referral are not always found in isolation. For example truancy may be accompanied by offending behaviour. The absence of parental control may similarly be accompanied by drug or alcohol abuse. The permutations are manifold. Fortunately the issue of referral need not be overly concerned with the primary causative or dominant factor. That may of course be of great importance at the disposal stage. The inclusion of this new ground of referral, given its clarity, may offer a more

---

[257] cf. *D v Kennedy*, 1988 S.L.T. 55.

[258] The writer has represented one such parent who was able to satisfy the sheriff that the lack of attendance of her child at school was due to neither the child's unwillingness to attend nor the parent's lack of desire to send the child but rather circumstances related to the parent's peripatetic lifestyle and administrative procedures in enrolling the child in school.

[259] Education (Scotland) Act 1980 s.44(1).

[260] Breustedt et al., "The Evolution of The Children's Hearings System", 1997 S.L.P.Q. 73.

[261] Breustedt et al., "The Evolution of The Children's Hearings System", 1997 S.L.P.Q. 73, 82.

[262] *Merrin v S*, 1987 S.L.T. 193.

[263] See C. Henderson, J. Hardin and E. McCaig, *Use of Controlled Drugs in Scotland: Findings from the 1993 Scottish Crime Survey* (The Scottish Office, 1993), pp. 6–25; McKeagney, "Pre-teen Drug Users in Scotland", Univ. of Glasgow, Unpublished; Miller and Plant, "Drinking, Smoking and Illicit Drug Use Among 15 and 16 Year Olds in the United Kingdom" (1996) 31 B.M.J. 394; Parker, Bury and Egginton, "New Heroin Outbreaks Amongst Young People in England and Wales", Police Research Group, Home Office Paper 92 (1998); Haw, *Drug Problems in Greater Glasgow*, (SCODA, 1985); Russell, *Adolescent Drug Dependency and Its Treatments* (1998); Scottish Health Education Group, *Drugs and Young People in Scotland* (1988); Perri, *The Substance of Youth: The Place of Drugs in Young People's Lives Today* (1997); O'Connor, *Glue Sniffing and Solvent Abuse* (1986); Watson, *Solvent Abuse: The Adolescent Epidemic?* (1986); O'Connor, *Profiles of Glue Sniffing and Volatile Substance Abuse in Children and Adolescents* (1983); Ives (ed.), *Solvent Misuse in Context* (National Children's Bureau, 1986).

[264] Norrie, Annotations in Mays (ed.), *Scottish Social Work Legislation*, C.205.7.

simplistic route into the hearing system where the child can receive appropriate welfare-predicated measures.

Section 52(2)(k): "has misused a volatile substance by deliberately inhaling its vapour, other than for medicinal purposes"

4.70 This particular ground of referral was introduced in 1983 by the Solvent Abuse (Scotland) Act 1983 s.1, in response to a perceived social problem. Despite being supplanted in the public consciousness by the arguable greater evil of "hard" drug abuse it remains a problem within Scottish society and as such the provision remains relevant.

Section 52(2)(l): "is being provided with accommodation by a local authority under section 25, or is the subject of a parental responsibilities order obtained under section 86, of this Act and, in either case, his behaviour is such that special measures are necessary for his adequate supervision in his interest or the interest of others"

4.71 This ground of referral permits a referral to a children's hearing where a child subject to one of the aforementioned orders is behaving in such a way that special measures are required for his "adequate supervision". One slight modification to the analogous ground of referral in the 1968 Act is the inclusion of the words "or the interest of others". One can only speculate that those legislating perceived a situation where other persons in care, or perhaps even those looking after such children, may need the help of the children's hearing in identifying adequate measures of supervision.

Section 52(2)(m): "(a) a requirement is made of the Principal Reporter under section 12(1) of the Antisocial Behaviour etc. (Scotland) Act 2004 (power of sheriff to require Principal Reporter to refer case to children's hearing) in respect of the child's case; and (b) the child is not subject to a supervision requirement"

4.72 The introduction of the Antisocial Behaviour etc. (Scotland) Act 2004 brought about this new ground of referral whereby the court instructs the Principal Reporter to call a hearing, thus removing a Reporter's usual power of discretion. Antisocial behaviour orders are fully discussed in Ch.12.

Reference to the sheriff

4.73 Where the ground of referral is rejected or not accepted either in full or in part, the Reporter may refer the matter to the sheriff court for a ruling as to whether the ground of referral is established.[265] Referrals to the sheriff for proof have increased markedly, particularly in respect of cases referred on care and protection grounds.[266] Any application by a Reporter must be heard by the sheriff within 28 days of the referral being lodged. Reference will be made to the sheriff court which would have jurisdiction if the child had committed a criminal offence. The child has a right and a duty to attend. Notwithstanding this, the sheriff can release the child from the duty to attend if he is satisfied that in cases involving the grounds in s.52(2)(d), (e), (f) or (g) above, the child's attendance is not necessary for the just hearing of the case or, on any ground of referral, that it would be detrimental to the interests of the child to be present.[267] If the

[265] See generally the 1995 Act s.68.

[266] See Hallet and Murray, *The Evaluation of Children's Hearings in Scotland* (1998), p.iv.

[267] Thomson, *Family Law in Scotland* (1996), p.286, suggests that a child can be released from the obligation to attend even although it would not be detrimental to his interests to be present.

child fails to attend the sheriff can make an order to have the child brought before him and for the child to be detained in a place of safety. The child and any relevant person have the right to be represented.[268] In all probability they will have legal representation; legal aid is available for this purpose where applicants qualify.

The Reporter must establish the ground or grounds or referral. If during the hearing the child and the relevant persons accept the grounds of referral the sheriff may dispense with evidence and refer the case back to the children's hearing. Similarly, evidence may be dispensed with if the referral arises because the child was incapable of understanding the ground of the referral and the sheriff becomes satisfied that he or she now understands. The standard of proof in cases other than that the child has committed an offence is the balance of probabilities.[269] As in analogous civil proceedings there is no need for corroboration.[270] Where the ground of referral alleges that the child has committed an offence the standard of proof is beyond a reasonable doubt and corroboration is required.

Section 68(9) of the 1995 Act provides that:

> "Where a sheriff decides that none of the grounds of referral in respect of which the application has been made are established, he shall dismiss the application, discharge the referral to the children's hearing in respect of those grounds and recall, discharge or cancel any order or warrant or direction under [the Act] which relates to the child in respect of those grounds."

Occasionally, it will not be necessary for an evidential hearing to reach this point. It may be that in the intervening time between the original child's hearing and the referral to the sheriff new information has come to the Reporter's attention that obviates the need for evidence and allows the sheriff to pronounce such an order.[271]

In cases where the sheriff decides that the grounds of referral or any part of them are established, he will remit the case to the Reporter to arrange for a children's hearing to determine the child's case. If he thinks it necessary in the child's interests, he may make an order either keeping a child in a place of safety or, if he thinks it likely that the child may abscond before the hearing, he may issue an order directing that the child be kept in a place of safety until the sitting of the children's hearing. Any such order of the sheriff will only be valid for either three days or until consideration of the child's case by the children's hearing. The hearing may of course grant a fresh warrant to keep the child in a place of safety.[272]

4.74 The 1995 Act permits a procedure whereby a sheriff's finding that the grounds of referral are established can be reviewed in the light of new evidence.[273] This will only be possible where the applicant claims to have new evidence not considered by the sheriff on the original application, which might have materially affected the determination of the original application. In addition to this, the evidence must be likely to be credible and reliable as well as admissible in relation to the ground of referral that was established at the original referral. Moreover, there must be a reasonable explanation for the failure to lead such evidence at the original application. On satisfaction of these criteria the sheriff may proceed to consider the new evidence brought before him, failing which the application must be dismissed. On consideration of the new evidence, if the sheriff is satisfied that none of the grounds of referral are established he may proceed to discharge the referral, possibly terminating any supervision requirement immediately, or at some future date. Alternatively, he may find that the ground of referral is still established and remit the case to the Reporter. Appeals can be taken from any review decision to the sheriff principal or the Court of Session.[274] The deficiency in this new appeal procedure is that it does

---

[268] See *S v Lynch*, 1997 S.L.T. 1377.
[269] See *S v Kennedy*, 1987 S.L.T. 667; *Harris v F*, 1991 S.L.T. 242.
[270] Civil Evidence (Scotland) Act 1988 s.1.
[271] The writer dealt with one such case where information came to hand that a child had been attending school.
[272] 1995 Act s.69(7).
[273] 1995 Act s.85.
[274] 1995 Act s.51(11)(a)(iii) and (b).

not allow review on the basis of the quality of evidence but only on the basis of new evidence.[275] It is also the case that the number of appeals is reasonably small.[276]

Where a ground of referral is established before a sheriff and evidence that assisted the sheriff is later retracted, it is for the children's hearing to consider the matter in the review process.[277]

DISPOSAL AND POWERS OF THE CHILDREN'S HEARING

4.75 Where the grounds of referral are accepted by the child and the relevant persons or where the grounds have been established before the sheriff, the children's hearing may proceed to dispose of the case.[278] The hearing will have before it reports and other relevant information.[279] However, if it requires further information the hearing may continue a case to a subsequent hearing to allow further investigation. Where the hearing continues the case, it may require a child to attend or reside in any clinic, hospital or other establishment for a period not exceeding 22 days for the purposes of investigation. If the child fails to fulfil such a requirement the hearing may grant a warrant to find the child and to remove that child to a place of safety and possibly to take the child from the place of safety to a clinic or hospital or other such establishment. These warrants also expire after 22 days. As an alternative, the hearing may decide that it is in the child's interests to be detained in a place of safety and in such cases it may grant a warrant for such detention. These warrants allow detention for a maximum of 22 days and may contain conditions as to contact with the child as well as requiring the child to submit to a medical or other examination or treatment. Under s.2(4) of the Age of Legal Capacity (Scotland) Act 1991 children, in the opinion of the medical practitioner of sufficient knowledge and understanding, may refuse to consent to such treatment.[280] Section 16 requires the hearing to consult the child in making a warrant and to decide to grant a warrant only if it thinks to grant such an order is better than to grant no such order at all.[281]

Supervision requirement

4.76 In proceeding with the child's case, the children's hearing must act in the child's best interest. In so doing it may simply discharge the referral after consideration of the child's case.[282] This course of action is likely if the hearing believes that the child's problem is being tackled at source. For example, a child not attending school is to be henceforth the subject of monitoring by parents and the school. Alternatively, the hearing may be convinced that the original problem that led to the referral has been resolved. However, in circumstances where the hearing is of a mind that the child needs a compulsory measure of supervision it can make a "supervision requirement".[283] Before making a supervision requirement the hearing must consult the child and be convinced that in making such an order it is better for the child than not making any order at all.[284] There is evidence that the contributions of children and young people to discussion at the hearings is limited.[285] In the majority of cases the decision of the hearing usually

---

[275] See Thomson, *Family Law in Scotland* (1996), pp.292–293; *K v Kennedy*, 1993 S.L.T. 1281.

[276] See Hallet, and Murray, *The Evaluation of Children's Hearings in Scotland* (1998), p.iv.

[277] *H, Petrs*, 1997 S.L.T. 3.

[278] See generally the 1995 Act s.69.

[279] *O v Rae*, 1993 S.L.T. 570 (allegations against a relevant person not previously used in the ground of referral accepted or established); Norrie, "In Defence of *O v Rae*", 1995 S.L.T. News 353; cf. *M v Kennedy*, 1993 S.L.T. 431 (allegations rejected by the sheriff).

[280] 1995 Act s.90.

[281] 1995 Act s.16(4)(a)(ii).

[282] 1995 Act s.69(1)(b).

[283] 1995 Act s.69(1)(c).

[284] 1995 Act s.16(2), (3), (4)(a)(i).

[285] See Hallet and Murray, *The Evaluation of Children's Hearings in Scotland* (1998), p.ii.

conforms with the social worker's recommendation.[286] Accordingly, the extent of consultation and its genuineness must be left open to question.

A supervision requirement may require a child to reside at a particular place or places.[287] The supervision requirement will constitute authority for the person in charge of any place where the child is required to reside to restrict the child's liberty.[288] Moreover, the hearing may impose any condition to the supervision requirement it sees fit.[289] It may be, for example, that a condition will require a child to attend for a medical or some other examination or treatment.[290] In addition, the children's hearing may regulate contact with any other person or persons.[291] It is thought incompetent for a court to regulate contact during the existence of a supervision requirement.[292] In conjunction with this, it may be a part of the supervision requirement that the place where the child is required to reside should not be disclosed to certain persons.[293] Given the various grounds of referral, it is obvious that there may be circumstances where concealment of the child's whereabouts will be an essential prerequisite to the protection of the child. Where the hearing is satisfied that it is necessary for the child to be supervised in secure accommodation, it may order this on the basis that the child has previously absconded, is likely to abscond again, or it is likely that his physical, mental or moral welfare will be at risk.[294] Secure accommodation may also be ordered where the child is likely to injure himself or someone else unless he is detained in such accommodation.[295] Under s.71 of the 1995 Act, a local authority is under a duty to provide a place in any specified residential establishment, and where the child is the subject of a supervision requirement staying with a parent, relatives or associated person or in any accommodation not provided by the local authority, that authority will nonetheless have a duty from time to time to check that the child is resident there and that the conditions of the supervision requirement are being observed.[296]

4.77 Some children who are subject to a supervision requirement may be required to live in accommodation provided by the local authority and this will impose further obligation on that authority.[297] However, the supervision requirement conditions must still be complied with. Where the local authority finds any requirement unduly burdensome and unnecessary, it may seek a variation of the supervision requirement by referring the matter back to the children's hearing.[298] Following the imposition of a supervision requirement parents do not lose parental rights and responsibilities, but to all intents and purposes the supervision requirement operates to limit severely the exercise of those rights, especially if the child is required to reside in a residential establishment. Thus, for example, the parent will have the right to give medical consent where that right is consistent with the rights of the child but the parent is unlikely to be able to exercise discipline or dictate particular aspects of education.[299] In situations where the child remains with their family or relatives, parental rights and responsibilities will have more potency. It is obviously far easier to guide and direct from a custodial position than not.

More recent expansion of powers under a supervision requirement has arisen from the Scottish Executive's focus to target antisocial behaviour, particularly that committed by young

---

[286] See Hallet and Murray, *The Evaluation of Children's Hearings in Scotland* (1998), p.ii.
[287] 1995 Act s.70(3)(a); that place may be in England and Wales: see s.70(4).
[288] 1995 Act s.70(4).
[289] 1995 Act s.70(3)(b).
[290] 1995 Act s.70(5)(a); again any child who has capacity under the Age of Legal Capacity (Scotland) Act 1991 s.2(4) may refuse to consent to medical treatment.
[291] 1995 Act s.70(5)(b).
[292] *A v G*, 1996 S.C.L.R. 787.
[293] 1995 Act s.70(6).
[294] 1995 Act s.70(10)(a).
[295] 1995 Act s.70(10)(b).
[296] 1995 Act s.71(2)(b): see also *Re J (Accommodation By a Local Authority)* [1995] 1 F.L.R. 159.
[297] The principles in s.17 will apply, including the duty to safeguard and promote the child's welfare which shall be their paramount concern.
[298] See para.4.80 below.
[299] See paras 3.31–3.35 above.

offenders. It is envisaged that, among other things, the option to impose a movement restriction condition will tackle offending behaviour since it may restrict the child to a specified place. This condition was inserted into the 1995 Act by virtue of the Antisocial Behaviour etc. (Scotland) Act 2004. Subsequent Regulations[300] elucidate the arrangements of the condition. Such arrangements oversee monitoring the compliance of the condition; designing a care plan; and stating relevant personnel's functions. Electronic monitoring, or tagging, is permitted where the hearing believes it is necessary,[301] and it may only impose this in one or two instances: the child has previously absconded, or is likely to abscond, and if he absconds it is likely that his physical, mental or moral welfare will be at risk and he is likely to injure himself or others.[302]

It is now the case that the hearing may request the Principal Reporter to apply to the court challenging a local authority for not complying with any obligation to oversee the conditions of a supervision requirement.[303]

Parenting orders

4.78 Section 75A of the 1995 Act[304] permits the children's hearing to require the Principal Reporter to apply to the court for a parenting order in respect of the parent of a child. The court may make the order if it is satisfied that the child has engaged in antisocial behaviour, or that the child has engaged in criminal conduct and that the making of the order is desirable in the interests of preventing the child from engaging in such behaviour, or that the making of the order is desirable in the interests of improving the welfare of the child.

As the Guidance on Parenting Orders[305] states:

> "A parenting order is designed to provide the help and support a parent needs to change their behaviour. It is not designed to punish the parent. An order will be appropriate where the behaviour of the parent is such that they are not prepared to take steps to address serious concerns about their child's welfare or behaviour and where voluntary help and support offered to them has not been taken up."[306]

A full discussion of these orders is given in Ch.12.

Fast track hearings

4.79 One initiative aimed to tackle persistent young offenders and reduce re-offending is fast track hearings. A pilot scheme, run between February 2003 and September 2005, was trialled in six local authority areas.[307] Children and young people falling within the test of persistent offender, or chosen at the discretion of the Reporter, were referred to the pilot. "Persistent offender" is defined as a person who has offended five or more times in the previous six months. Findings from the pilot found a reduction in the number of offences being referred to hearings compared with the previous six months, albeit the period was felt to be too short to suggest any real significance; and cases were dealt with speedily. The Scottish Executive concluded "The verdict from the evaluation of Fast Track is definitely positive with regard to timescales ... , but not proven with regard to impact on offending."[308]

---

[300] Intensive Support and Monitoring (Scotland) Regulations 2006 (SSI 2006/15).
[301] 1995 Act s.70(9), inserted by the Antisocial Behaviour etc. (Scotland) Act 2004.
[302] 1995 Act s.70(10).
[303] 1995 Act s.70(7A) and (7B).
[304] Inserted by s.116 of the Antisocial Behaviour etc. (Scotland) Act 2004.
[305] See Scottish Executive, "Guidance on Parenting Orders" (2005). *http://www.scotland.gov.uk/Resource/Doc/37432/0011355.pdf* [Accessed July 2, 2008].
[306] Scottish Executive, "Guidance on Parenting Orders" (2005), para.40. *http://www.scotland.gov.uk/Resource/Doc/37432/0011355.pdf* [Accessed July 2, 2008].
[307] Dundee, Scottish Borders, East Lothian and North, East and North Ayrshire: Fast Track Children's Hearings Pilot—Final Update (Scottish Children's Reporter Administration, 2005), p.3.
[308] Fast Track Children's Hearings Pilot—Final Update (2005), p.15.

Appeal and review

4.80 Supervision requirements will endure for a period no longer than is necessary in the interests of promoting or safeguarding the welfare of the child.[309] Unless reviewed or varied, a supervision requirement will not last longer than a year.[310] If nothing is done to continue it, the requirement automatically ceases. A supervision requirement will cease on the child attaining 18 years of age. The local authority through its social work department has the power to refer a case to the Reporter where it believes the requirement in respect of a child ought to cease to have effect or be varied. Authorities may also refer a case to the Reporter if they apprehend that a condition of the requirement is not being complied with or they are of the opinion that it is right to seek a parental responsibilities order, or freeing for adoption order or where they are placing the child for adoption and intend to apply for such an order.[311] Likewise if the local authority is aware that an application for an adoption order has been made or is pending it must as soon as practicable notify the Reporter.

In addition to the right of the local authority to refer a case back to the children's hearing the child, or any relevant person, may also seek a review not less than three months after the supervision requirement has been made or at least three months after the most recent continuation or variance of the supervision requirement. Where it is proposed that the child be removed from Scotland other than as a condition of the supervision order, the person proposing to do so must report the matter to the Reporter and the children's hearing.

Once the matter has been referred to the Reporter for review it is his role to arrange for a children's hearing to review the child's case. The hearing for its part may order a further investigation into the child's situation, terminate the requirement, vary the requirement, impose further conditions, or simply continue the order without variation.

4.81 Referral back to the children's hearing via the Reporter is not the only means of redress that a child or relevant person has against the original decision of the children's hearing or for that matter any subsequent review decision. There is scope under the legislation for judicial redress. A child or a relevant person may, within three weeks of the children's hearing decision, appeal to the sheriff court against that decision.[312] It is the duty of the Reporter to ensure that all information and reports before the hearing are lodged with the sheriff clerk along with a report of the hearing's proceedings and decision.[313] It is competent to appeal not only against the decision but also any condition imposed by the hearing.[314] The sheriff may decide to hear evidence from or on behalf of the parties. He may also question the Reporter, the persons who wrote or compiled the reports or, alternatively, he may call for further reports.[315]

It is also the case that the sheriff may appoint a safeguarder to look after the child's interests.[316] If he rejects the appeal, the sheriff simply confirms the decision of the hearing.[317] Moreover, if the sheriff determines that the appeal was frivolous he may also decree that no further appeal against the decision of the hearing to continue a supervision requirement may be taken within 12 months of that decision.[318] On the other hand he may uphold the appeal and direct that any condition of the supervision requirement cease to have effect or he may remit the case, discharge the child from the referral or substitute a decision that the hearing itself would

---

309 See generally the 1995 Act s.73.
310 *Stirling v D*, 1995 S.L.T. 1089.
311 See para.3.43 for discussion on adoption.
312 1995 Act s.51(1); *S, Appellants*, 1979 S.L.T. (Sh Ct) 37.
313 1995 Act s.51(2).
314 *Kennedy v A*, 1986 S.L.T. 358.
315 1995 Act s.51(3).
316 See the 1995 Act s.41(1); *Catto v Pearson*, 1990 S.L.T. (Sh Ct) 77; *Kennedy v M*, 1989 S.L.T. 687.
317 1995 Act s.51(4).
318 1995 Act s.51(7).

have imposed.[319] If the child or a relevant person lodges an appeal with the sheriff against supervision requirement they may also request that the hearing itself suspend the supervision requirement pending the outcome of the appeal.[320]

Further appeal from any decision of the sheriff can be taken by stated case to the sheriff principal[321] and to the Court of Session with leave of the sheriff principal.[322] It is open to the Reporter as well as the child and relevant persons to appeal.[323] There is no scope for appeal beyond the Court of Session.[324] Successful appeals to the sheriff principal or the Court of Session will result in the case being remitted back to the sheriff with or without guidance on disposal.[325]

CHILDREN'S HEARING AND THE CRIMINAL COURTS

4.82 Where a child who is not the subject of a supervision requirement of a children's hearing pleads guilty to an offence, the court:

(a) instead of making an order on that plea or finding, may remit the case to the Principal Reporter to arrange for the disposal of the case by a children's hearing; or
(b) on that plea or finding may request the Principal Reporter to arrange a children's hearing for the purposes of obtaining their advice as to the treatment of the child.[326]

Having sought the advice under (b) above the court may proceed to dispose of the case or remit the case back to the children's hearing for disposal.

In cases where the child who is the subject of a supervision requirement pleads guilty or is found guilty of an offence, the High Court *may* and the sheriff court *shall* request the Principal Reporter to arrange a children's hearing for the purpose of obtaining their advice as to the treatment of the child, and on consideration of that advice they may dispose of or remit the case back to the children's hearing for disposal. Once the case is remitted for disposal to the children's hearing it stands as a referral and the jurisdiction of the court in respect of the child ceases. There can be no remit to the children's hearing where the penalty is fixed by law. It is also the case that a court of summary jurisdiction can remit a person who is not subject to a supervision requirement, over 16 but not yet 17 years and six months old, where that person has pled guilty or been found guilty, for advice as to how the case should be disposed. Following receipt of that advice the matter may be remitted to the hearing for disposal.

A certificate that the child has pled, or has been found, guilty acts as conclusive proof that the ground of referral is established in all such referrals to the children's hearing. The hearing will have before it social enquiry reports prepared by the local authority.

Draft Children's Services (Scotland) Bill and the children's hearings

4.83 As discussed at the beginning of the Chapter, one of the results of *Getting It Right for Every Child* is the draft Children's Services (Scotland) Bill consultation.[327] As the title suggests, the Bill

[319] 1995 Act s.51(5); Professor Norrie is hostile to the idea that the sheriff should "trespass" into what should properly be the role of the children's hearing: see Norrie, *Children's Hearings in Scotland* (2006), p.219.

[320] 1995 Act s.51(9); the Reporter must arrange a hearing as soon as practicable: see s.51(10).

[321] Sheriff Mitchell criticises the right of appeal to the sheriff principal on the basis that the appeal should go to a tribunal and not a solitary judge: see 1997 SCOLAG 16.

[322] 1995 Act s.51(11); see e.g. *G v Templeton*, 1998 S.C.L.R. 180; Act of Sederunt (Child Care and Maintenance Rules) 1997 (SI 1997/291) rr.3.59–3.61.

[323] See e.g. *Sloan v B*, 1991 S.L.T. 53, where the Reporter took an appeal but on a point of principle only.

[324] 1995 Act s.51(11)(b).

[325] 1995 Act s.51(14).

[326] 1995 Act s.49.

[327] *Getting It Right For Every Child*, found at *http://www.scotland.gov.uk/Publications/2005/06/20135608/56173* [Accessed July 2, 2008].

is not currently in the legal process but merely suggested legal reform, proposed by the former Labour administration.

Among other things, the Bill advocates changes to the current grounds of referral. If implemented, the new approach would separate the tests for referral into three separate conditions. These are: the child has unmet need with respect to well-being (needs condition); a relevant situation applies (situational condition); and compulsory measures of supervision are necessary to meet the child's needs (supervision condition).

The needs condition requires a clear and consistent approach to be taken towards the child, whereas the situational condition replaces the current grounds of referral, albeit replicating or clarifying many. These new factors aim to improve on existing grounds and to address possible gaps such as self-harm and exposure to domestic abuse.[328] Other factors of attention are upon situations where the child is subject to abuse, harm, ill-treatment or inappropriate care.

Further amendments to the hearings system include introducing interim supervision requirements and amending warrants; removing the restriction upon panel members so that they are no longer restricted to a stated area; detailing the appointment of legal representatives; removing the role of the Principal Reporter from the Scottish Children's Reporters Administration; amending rules on disclosure to allow restriction of information where it would be against the child's interests—the new s.46A would directly specify persons excluded from the proceedings; impose duties on agencies; and introducing rules allowing the manager of a secure home or the chief social workers to have the discretion to remove a child from secure accommodation. New rules on procedure are also set out to permit the aforementioned changes. One should remember that these are only draft provisions and are likely to change should the new Scottish administration give them its support.

CHILDMINDING AND DAY CARE FOR YOUNG CHILDREN

4.84 The Regulation of Care (Scotland) Act 2001 contains the relevant provisions in respect of care services including childcare.[329] Under this Act, childminders shall register their services with the Care Commission. A person is a childminder if he or she looks after one or more children on domestic premises for reward for a period exceeding two hours. Parents, relatives, foster parents or anyone with parental responsibility for the child are not childminders for the purposes of the legislation. Likewise there are exemptions for schools. Nannies who look after children wholly or mainly in the child's own home are not required to be registered as childminders even where their care includes other parents' children. Organisations such as nurseries providing day care services are also required to register with the Commission.

The local authority may refuse to register an applicant for registration on the basis that the service is not fit for purpose. Alternatively, the local authority may grant registration subject to conditions.[330] Following registration, the local authority must issue a certificate of registration. Premises must be inspected once per year for which the Commission can charge a fee.[331] Care services are inspected to measure the services against the National Standards of Care. A registration may be cancelled by the Commission after the expiry of an improvement notice where any person has been convicted of a relevant offence; where the service is being carried out inappropriately; or for some other prescribed reason.[332] There is a right of appeal against cancellation to the sheriff court.

---

[328] Draft Children's Services (Scotland) Bill Consultation, Explanatory Notes, p.62 (Scottish Executive).

[329] See ss.18–25. See also generally the Children Act 1989 s.71.

[330] Regulation of Care (Scotland) Act 2001 s.9.

[331] Regulation of Care (Scotland) Act 2001 s.25(5).

[332] Regulation of Care (Scotland) Act 2001 s.12.

DISQUALIFICATION FROM WORKING WITH CHILDREN

4.85 In a bid to strengthen child protection, the Scottish Executive announced plans to disqualify certain persons from working with children. To this effect, the Protection of Children (Scotland) Act 2003 requires Scottish Ministers to keep a list of individuals that they consider to be unsuitable to work with children and prohibit these persons and others from working with children.[333] Scottish Ministers can remove anyone from the list. Organisations are compelled to refer cases to Scottish Ministers where the organisation dismissed a person because that person harmed a child or placed a child at risk; or where an employee has resigned, retired, been made redundant or their fixed-term contract ended in circumstances such that the organisation would have dismissed or considered dismissing that individual, on the ground of risk to a child, if the individual had not resigned, retired or been made redundant.[334] Where these organisations fail to act upon their legal duties they are liable to imprisonment or a fine.

Section 4 obliges other agencies—Scottish Commission for Regulation of Care, Scottish Social Services Council, General Teaching Council for Scotland, to make referrals. A person will also be added to the list if named in a relevant inquiry or if they are convicted of an offence against the child.[335] Notifications of intention to include a person on the list must be provided to the named person and to the organisation where working with children. A person's name is to be removed from the list if no decision has been made within the "relevant period".[336] Effectively if a person is included in the list it is an offence for that person to work or apply to work with children but a person is granted a defence if they did not know they were so disqualified.[337] An application for removal from the list can be sought from the sheriff, who will remove a person from the list if considers the person is not unsuitable to work with children.

As a means of strengthening provisions under the 2003 Act, a further Act was introduced, the Protection of Vulnerable Groups (Scotland) Act 2007 to achieve advanced, flexible and efficient measures to protect children (and protected adults) from unsuitable people working with them. The main provisions include extending the current disqualified persons list; introduction of a system to continuously update; establishment of a central barring system; and establishment of duties and powers for agencies to share information.

SCOTLAND'S COMMISSIONER FOR CHILDREN AND YOUNG PEOPLE

4.86 The Commissioner for Children and Young People (Scotland) Act 2003 created the role of Scotland's Commissioner for Children and Young People ("SCCYP").[338] Principles underpinning this role are that there is an independent body to consider the best interests of the child and that children will be consulted in the promotion of children. The role of the SCCYP is to:

- promote awareness of rights of children, young persons and adults;
- keep under review the law;
- promote best practice;
- publish research;
- investigate;
- report to Parliament.[339]

---

[333] Protection of Children (Scotland) Act 2003 s.1.

[334] Protection of Children (Scotland) Act 2003 s.2.

[335] Protection of Children (Scotland) Act 2003 s.10. This section also has retrospective effect.

[336] Where organisations and bodies refer the case and the employee is subject to legal or disciplinary proceedings, the relevant period is six months from the date of determination of the findings, or from day provisionally on the list, or subject to extension by the sheriff of up to six months.

[337] 2003 Act s.11.

[338] Professor Kathleen Marshall, Scotland's first Commissioner.

[339] *http://www.sccyp.org.uk/.*

Chapter 5

Education Law

Introduction

5.01 Educational and social needs are often interlinked, and increasingly inter-professional liaison is being recognised as essential. This Chapter deals essentially with primary and secondary school education.

Within Scotland there are currently the following types of schools:

- Public schools—are managed by the education authority.[1] The duty of each education authority is to ensure there is adequate and efficient provision of school education in its relevant area.[2] Public education includes pre-school education[3]; primary education and secondary education. Denominational schools[4] are run by the education authority[5] with some extra provisions. Most special schools[6] are run by the education authority. Community schools were set up in 1998 as a new project and are also run as public schools.[7] New Community Schools were established in April 1998 to modernise schools, improve pupil attainment and promote social inclusion. The emphasis is on integrated services including education, social work, health education and promotion services.[8] The assessment of Phase 1 of the project showed positive findings.[9] The scheme is presently in phase 3 with over 400 schools in Scotland being involved in the scheme. These schools are public schools and subject to the same legislation as all public schools.
- Grant-aided schools—are run by Boards of Managers, mainly dealing with additional support for learning pupils. Funding is received from the Scottish Government. Jordanhill School in Glasgow is the only non-special school in this category.
- Independent schools—are independent of the education authority and receive their funding through school fees charged to parents.

---

[1] Education (Scotland) Act 1980 ("1980 Act") s.135(1).

[2] 1980 Act s.1(1).

[3] 1980 Act s.1(1A), (1B) and (1C).

[4] Denominational schools are schools with links to a religious body, e.g. Catholic schools.

[5] 1980 Act s.21(1) and (5).

[6] A special school is for children needing additional support for learning.

[7] Community schools are an attempt to modernise education and promote positive values by integrating services such as school education, family support and health services.

[8] Scottish Office, "New Community Schools Prospectus". *http://www.scotland.gov.uk* [Accessed July 2, 2008].

[9] Scottish Executive, "Key Findings from the National Evaluation of the New Community Schools Pilot Programme in Scotland". *http://www.scotland.gov.uk* [Accessed July 2, 2008].

Some parents choose to home school their child. In 2006, 706[10] children were educated at home out of a total of 702,737 pupils in public school[11]; 216 of these children had never attended school. Provided the parents ensure efficient education for the child, suitable to his age, ability and aptitude,[12] the local authority has no right to intervene.

In certain circumstances the education authority may have to make special arrangements for pupils to be educated elsewhere than an educational establishment.[13] Instances include if the child is ill,[14] has been granted an exemption from attending school,[15] or has been excluded from school.[16] In 2005–06, 877 children were educated at home or in hospital because of ill health and 213 children were educated at home for other extraordinary circumstances.[17]

In Scotland there is not a statutory national curriculum as there is in England and Wales. There are national guidelines for children aged 5–14 and it is assumed that public schools will comply with these guidelines. All public schools are subject to inspection by Her Majesty's Inspectorate of Education ("HMIE").[18] Notwithstanding the apparent degree of flexibility within Scottish education parents and local government have a clear duty to provide their children with appropriate education.

DUTY TO EDUCATE

Local education authorities

5.02 Education services are provided by the education authority, which is in reality the local authority.[19] Scotland has 32 education authorities each responsible for the provision of education in their particular area. Each education authority has a duty to provide adequate and efficient schooling and further education in its area.[20] They need to provide adequate facilities for social, cultural and recreational activities and for physical education and training.[21] School education means progressive education appropriate to the requirements of pupils, regard being had to the age, ability and aptitude of such pupils.[22] The education authority has also a duty to children under school age.[23] There is a responsibility to teach Gaelic in Gaelic speaking areas.[24] The education authority also needs to provide a psychological service[25] and may provide a library service[26] and hostels for pupils attending educational establishments in that area.[27]

Every child has the right to be provided with a school education[28] and it is the duty of the education authority to ensure it is directed to the development of the personality, talents and mental and physical abilities of the child.[29] The education authority needs to consider the views of the child as far as practicable in carrying out this duty.[30] There is a specific duty on the

[10] Scottish Executive, "High Level Summary of Statistics Trend". *http://www.scotland.gov.uk* [Accessed July 2, 2008].
[11] Scottish Executive, "High Level Summary of Statistics Trend". *http://www.scotland.gov.uk* [Accessed July 2, 2008].
[12] 1980 Act s.30.
[13] 1980 Act s.14.
[14] 1980 Act s.14(1)(b).
[15] 1980 Act s.14(2).
[16] 1980 Act s.14(3).
[17] Scottish Executive, "Statistics Publication Notice" (November 2006). *http://www.scotland.gov.uk*.
[18] 1980 Act s.66.
[19] 1980 Act s.135.
[20] 1980 Act s.1(1).
[21] 1980 Act s.1(3), s.6.
[22] 1980 Act s.1(5)(a).
[23] 1980 Act s.1(1A), s.1(5)(a).
[24] 1980 Act s.1(5)(a)(iii), s.1(5)(b)(iv).
[25] 1980 Act s.4.
[26] 1980 Act s.12.
[27] 1980 Act s.13.
[28] Standards in Scotland's Schools etc. Act 2000 ("SSSA 2000") s.1.
[29] SSSA 2000 s.2(1).
[30] SSSA 2000 s.2(2).

education authority to endeavour to secure improvement in the quality of school education provided by the authority and to raise standards of education.[31] This duty extends to children not educated at school.[32]

In fulfilling its duty to secure improvement in the quality of school education, the education authority annually has to prepare and publish a statement of improvement objectives.[33] This annual statement needs to include:

- how the local authority will involve parents to promote their children's education[34];
- how the local authority will encourage equal opportunities and the observance of the equal opportunity requirements[35];
- the way and circumstances in which the authority will provide a Gaelic medium education and if so provided how it will be developed.[36]

An annual report on the success or otherwise of the objectives of the annual statement is also published.[37]

5.03 Additionally each school managed by the education authority needs to have prepared a development plan that takes account of the objectives in the authority's annual statement.[38] Various bodies have first to be consulted.[39] The development plans will specify ways in which and the extent to which the headmaster will consult the pupils attending the school and seek to involve them when decisions need to be made about the daily running of the school.[40] A yearly report on the implementation of the plan is provided.[41] Parents receive copies of these items in summarised form.[42] The development plan is reviewed by education authorities and can be revised or reviewed as required.[43]

The education authority has to define and publish measures and standards of performance for each school, with different measures and standards applying for different categories of schools.[44]

These provisions place an onus on the education authorities and the school to improve standards in education. The Scottish Ministers[45] likewise have a duty to secure improvement in the quality of school education and should exercise their powers with a view to raising standards of education.[46] They have a duty to define priorities in educational objectives for school education.[47] The priorities are called "national priorities in education"[48] and are to be found in the Education (National Priorities) (Scotland) Order 2000.[49] The five national priorities are the high level outcomes that are expected of the education authority and the school.[50] Education authorities have to make yearly reports showing how they have progressed towards these national priorities.[51]

---

31 SSSA 2000 s.3(2).
32 SSSA 2000 s.3(3).
33 SSSA 2000 s.5(1).
34 SSSA 2000 s.5(2)(a).
35 SSSA 2000 s.5(2)(b).
36 SSSA 2000 s.5(2)(c).
37 SSSA 2000 s.5(6).
38 SSSA 2000 s.6(1).
39 SSSA 2000 s.6(2).
40 SSSA 2000 s.6(3).
41 SSSA 2000 s.6(4).
42 SSSA 2000 s.6(5).
43 SSSA 2000 s.6(6).
44 SSSA 2000 s.7(1).
45 The Scottish Ministers have had responsibility for education in Scotland since May 20, 1999 and their role is one of policy making, policy implementation and regulation.
46 SSSA 2000 s.3(1).
47 SSSA 2000 s.4.
48 SSSA 2000 s.4(1).
49 SSI 2000/443.
50 "National Priorities in Education Performance Report 2003". *http://www.scotland.gov.uk/Publications.*
51 "National Priorities in Education Performance Report 2003". *http://www.scotland.gov.uk/Publications.*

Scottish Ministers have power to hold an education authority or any other person with such a duty, to have failed to discharge their duty, and can make an order that they are in default and request them to discharge their duty.[52] If the duty is not discharged within the specified date, the Scottish Ministers can make arrangements as they see fit.[53]

A party can still opt for judicial review if they feel that the local authority has not fulfilled its statutory duties, although this has only occurred in a few cases and none have been successful.[54] If the education authority complies with all statutory requirements, then it is unlikely it will be held not to have fulfilled its duty.[55] The duty of the education authority to provide adequate and efficient school education[56] is met if it acts reasonably regarding this duty, even if there is a deficiency in the provision of education.[57]

Complaints against education authorities and the Scottish Government may be investigated by the Scottish Public Services Ombudsman.[58]

Parental duty to educate

5.04 The prime duty of a parent in relation to education is to ensure that their child receives appropriate education while they are of school age, which can be at a fee paying school, at a local authority school or indeed at home.[59] Although this duty may seem to form part of the general responsibilities of parents under s.1 of the Children (Scotland) Act 1995 ("1995 Act"), in practice education problems are dealt with under the Education (Scotland) Acts. The definition of parent for the purposes of education law means more than the natural parent or the parent with custody of the child:

> "'parent' includes guardian and any person who is liable to maintain or has parental responsibilities within the meaning of section 1(3) of the Children (Scotland) Act 1995 in relation to, or has care of, a child or young person."[60]

Therefore even after divorce both parents have duties and therefore rights in relation to the education of their child. Where the relationship between the parents is such that no agreement can be reached between them regarding education issues, a specific issue order under s.11 of the 1995 Act would be appropriate.

If the local authority has assumed the parental responsibilities for a child, in other words the child is a "looked after" child in terms of s.17(6) of the 1995 Act, the local authority must comply with the duties of parents in respect to education.

It is important to note that in general the Act imposes duties and rights on parents, and it is only once a child attains the age of 16 that they have an independent right of action in terms of the Education (Scotland) Act 1980. Of course, they have a general ability from the age of 12 onwards to instruct a solicitor in connection with any civil matter, which would include education issues such as exclusion.[61]

Where parents send their child to a local education authority school, the education authority has a general duty to educate the child in accordance with the parents' wishes.[62] As part of this, parents now have a right to choose which local education authority school they would prefer their child to attend through the placing request system.

---

[52] 1980 Act s.70(1).
[53] 1980 Act s.70(1)(a).
[54] *Walker v Strathclyde RC (No.2)*, 1987 S.L.T. 81.
[55] *Harvey v Strathclyde RC*, 1989 S.L.T. 612.
[56] 1980 Act s.1(1).
[57] *Walker v Strathclyde RC (No.2)*, 1987 S.L.T. 81.
[58] Scottish Public Services Ombudsman Act 2002. See Ch.2.
[59] 1980 Act s.30.
[60] 1980 Act s.135(1), as amended by the Children (Scotland) Act 1995 ("1995 Act") s.105(4) and Sch.4 para.28(5).
[61] Age of Legal Capacity (Scotland) Act 1991 s.4A, inserted by the 1995 Act Sch.4 para.53.
[62] 1980 Act s.28.

CHILDREN'S RIGHTS IN RELATION TO EDUCATION

5.05 Since the enactment of the Standards in Scotland's Schools etc. Act 2000, every child of school age has the right to a school education by virtue of arrangements made, or entered into by, an education authority.[63] The education has to develop the personality, talents and mental and physical abilities of the child[64] and the views of the child have to be considered.[65] This gives the child a right to education and the right to challenge any failure to be so provided. A child with legal capacity can oppose their exclusion from school.[66]

PARENTAL CHOICE IN LOCAL AUTHORITY EDUCATION

General issues

5.06 Parental choice as defined by the legislation refers to the obligation on education authorities to ensure that " ... so far as is compatible with the provision of suitable instruction ... and the avoidance of unreasonable public expenditure, pupils are to be educated in accordance with the wishes of their parents."[67]

This section gives to parents a general right to ensure that their child is educated in accordance with their wishes; however, it does not give parents an overriding say in all matters relating to their child's education.[68]

Although the principle of education in accordance with the parents' wishes may suggest that the parents should have an ongoing right to determine how their child's education should progress, the ability of parents to challenge local authority decisions on the running of schools has been strictly limited by the courts. In the case of *Walker v Strathclyde RC*[69] a parent challenged the decision of the local authority to temporarily close its schools due to strike action, but his challenge was not successful.

Furthermore, following the Scottish courts' approval[70] of the dictum of Lord Denning L.J. in *Watt v Kesteven CC*,[71] the courts have limited the scope of the principle of education in accordance with the wishes of parents. Denning L.J. held that the equivalent English law section applying to the County Council,

> "does not say that pupils must in all cases be educated in accordance with the wishes of their parents. It only lays down a general principle to which the County Council must have regard. This leaves it open to the County Council to have regard to other things as well, and also to make exceptions to the general principle if it thinks it fit to do so".

As a result of this approach by the court, it is clear that parental wishes cannot be treated as enforceable parental rights. This position was not greatly changed by the recognition of the right of parents to have their child educated in accordance with their religious or philosophical conviction under the Human Rights Act 1998.[72]

The education authority considers that matters other than the wishes of parents and parental choice are limited by financial restraints, the existence of catchment areas and denominational

[63] SSSA 2000 s.1. This brings the law into line with the United Nations Convention on the Rights of the Child 1989 art.28.
[64] SSSA 2000 s.2(1); United Nations Convention on the Rights of the Child 1989 art.29.
[65] SSSA 2000 s.2(2).
[66] SSSA 2000 s.41. See *S v Glasgow City Council*, 2004 S.L.T. (Sh Ct) 128.
[67] 1980 Act s.28.
[68] 1980 Act s.28A(3), as amended by the Education (Scotland) Act 1996 s.33.
[69] 1986 S.L.T. 523.
[70] *Keeney v Strathclyde RC*, 1986 S.L.T. 490.
[71] [1955] 1 Q.B. 408 at 424.
[72] First Protocol art.2; Human Rights Act 1998 ss.1, 6 and 7 and Sch.6.

matters. The limitations of the rights of parents are evident in the disappointment experienced by those who are unsuccessful in saving their local school from closure or in getting their child into the school of their choice under the placing request system.[73] Parents have a say on certain matters through their school council.[74]

Placing requests

5.07 Which school a child attends depends on where the child resides. The education authority is responsible for the child's education if he lives in an area where his parent is ordinarily resident.[75] Education authorities can make whatever arrangements they think appropriate for placing children in schools, but must publish or otherwise make available such information.[76] Parents must be advised of which school the child will be placed in[77] and of the right to make a placing request.[78] Simple guidance on choosing a school has been produced by the Scottish Government.[79]

A parent can place a request that their child be educated at school other than that provided by the education authority. This is in compliance with the right that the child be educated in accordance with the wishes of the parent.[80] This can lead to certain schools being too much in demand and therefore the education authority has to formulate guidelines to be followed when these circumstances arise.[81] A placing request can only be made if the child is at school or about to start school[82] and the education authority has to consider the views of the child if the child is already attending school.[83] If the pupil is over 16 he can make the placing request himself.[84]

The placing request is made in writing to the education authority and can be made at any time during a child's education. Most are made prior to the commencement of the child's primary or secondary education. The request must go to the authority that manages the school. Parents can make as many requests as they wish, but the authority need only consider the first mentioned school.[85]

When an education authority receives a placing request it makes a decision based on its guidelines. The education authority can refuse a placing request if certain statutory conditions are met.[86] These are:

(a) if placing the child in the specified school would:

(i) make it necessary for the authority to take an additional teacher into employment[87];

(ii) give rise to significant expenditure on extending or otherwise altering the accommodation at or facilities provided in connection with the school[88];

(iii) be seriously detrimental to the continuity of the child's education[89];

---

[73] e.g. in 1996–97 12.7 per cent of placing requests were unsuccessful: see *Statistical Bulletin—Education Series*, Scottish Office Edn/B6/1998/1 (February 1998).

[74] The Scottish Schools (Parental Involvement) Act 2006 abolished school boards and replaced them with school councils.

[75] 1980 Act s.23(3).

[76] 1980 Act s.28B(1)(a).

[77] 1980 Act s.28B(1)(b)(i).

[78] 1980 Act s.28B(1)(b)(ii).

[79] Scottish Executive, *Choosing a School, A Guide for Parents* (2006).

[80] 1980 Act s.28.

[81] 1980 Act s.28B(1)(c).

[82] 1980 Act s.28A(6).

[83] SSSA 2000 s.2(2).

[84] 1980 Act s.28G.

[85] 1980 Act s.28A(2).

[86] 1980 Act s.28A(3).

[87] 1980 Act s.28A(3)(a)(i).

[88] 1980 Act s.28A(3)(a)(ii).

[89] 1980 Act s.28A(3)(a)(iii).

(iv) be likely to be seriously detrimental to the order and discipline in the school[90];
(v) be likely to be seriously detrimental to the educational well-being of pupils attending the school[91];
(vi) assuming that pupil numbers remain constant, make it necessary, at the commencement of a future stage of the child's primary education, for the authority to elect either to create an additional class (or an additional composite class) in the specified school or to take an additional teacher into employment at that school[92]; or
(vii) though neither of the tests set out in sub-paragraphs (i) and (ii) above is satisfied, have the consequence that the capacity of the school would be exceeded in terms of pupil numbers[93];

(b) if the education normally provided at the specified school is not suited to the age, ability or aptitude of the child[94];
(c) if the education authority has already required the child to discontinue his attendance at the specified school[95];
(d) if, where the specified school is a special school, the child does not have additional support needs requiring the education or special facilities normally provided at that school[96];
(e) if the specified school is a single sex school (within the meaning given to that expression by s.26 of the Sex Discrimination Act 1975) and the child is not of the sex admitted or taken (under that section) to be admitted to the school, but an education authority may place a child in the specified school notwithstanding paragraphs (a) to (e) above[97];
(f) the acceptance of a placing request in respect of a child who is resident outwith the catchment area of the specified school would prevent the education authority from retaining reserved places at the specified school or in relation to any particular stage of education at the school[98];
(g) in respect of a child with additional support needs, if the school is not a public school and the authority is able to make provision for the additional support needs of the child in a school other than the specified school; and it is not reasonable to place the child in the specified school considering the suitability and cost of provision in comparison to the cost of the school the child would otherwise attend.[99]

5.08 In the period 2005–06 the total number of placing requests received was 30,240 of which 84 per cent were granted, with the main ground for lack of success being accommodation restraints.[100] Requests for early entry into primary school are not properly considered placing requests unless it is requested that the child attend an alternative school.[101]

The education authority must inform parents of the outcome of their placing request in writing, and if it is refusing the request must give reasons for the refusal. These reasons must

---

[90] 1980 Act s.28A(3)(a)(iv).
[91] 1980 Act s.28A(3)(a)(v).
[92] 1980 Act s.28A(3)(a)(vi).
[93] 1980 Act s.28A(3)(a)(vii).
[94] 1980 Act s.28A(3)(b).
[95] 1980 Act s.28A(3)(c).
[96] 1980 Act s.28A(3)(d).
[97] 1980 Act s.28A(3)(e).
[98] 1980 Act s.28A(3A); for meaning of reserved places see s.28A(3C) and for catchment area see s.28A(3D).
[99] Education (Additional Support for Learning) (Scotland) Act 2004 s.22 and Sch.2. See para.5.11 for further information on additional support for learning.
[100] Scottish Executive, "Statistics Publication Notice—Education Series", ISSN1479-7569. *http://www.scotland.gov.uk* [Accessed July 2, 2008].
[101] In the period 2005–06 there were 196 requests for early entry into primary school and 23 requests for early entry for alternative schools. Only the latter are considered as placing requests.

relate to one or more of those listed above. Any parent not satisfied with the reasons for refusal can refer the matter to an education appeal committee[102] within 28 days of the receipt by the parent of the education authority's decision, provided that they have not already referred a previous refusal to the committee within the last 12 months.[103] In dealing with the appeal the education appeal committee should take into account the matters detailed in the refusal, which requires the authority to satisfy the appeal committee of the reason for refusal by the authority.

The appeal committee is obliged to notify the parents of its decision in writing. If the committee refuses to confirm the decision of the authority to refuse the request, then the authority must immediately make the place requested available.[104] However, if the committee confirms the authority's refusal, then the parent has again 28 days to make a further appeal to the sheriff, although the sheriff can on cause shown hear an appeal made outwith the 28-day period.[105] The appeal hearing is in private and a complete rehearing of the case.[106]

Both the appeal committee and the sheriff need initially to consider whether one of the grounds of refusal exist.[107] This is a question of fact based on all the evidence. If a ground of refusal does exist then they need to consider if it is appropriate to confirm the decision of the education authority.[108] The appeal committee and the sheriff therefore can allow an appeal even if one of the grounds of refusal exist.

The sheriff's decision is final[109] unless the decision is incompetent[110] and can therefore be appealed to the sheriff principal. Judicial review is available if the sheriff has acted outwith his jurisdiction.[111]

RELIGIOUS AND DENOMINATIONAL EDUCATION

Religious education

5.09 Within Scottish education, there has always been a tradition of religious education,[112] and as such all public schools in Scotland will provide instruction in religion (now known as religious and moral education ("RME")) unless the withdrawal of such provision has been approved by the majority of electors in a ballot of electors in the area.[113] The Scottish Executive has issued guidance on religious education in schools[114] and the basis of the teaching should be Christianity but with all other religions being taught. All schools under education authority management must include in the school handbook a statement of school policy in relation to the development of pupils' spiritual, moral, social and cultural values.[115] Notwithstanding the importance attached to religious education, parents can elect to have their child withdrawn from any religious instruction or observance, and that child must not be placed at a disadvantage as a

[102] The Scottish Executive has run a consultation (February 2007) regarding improving education appeal committees, after concerns were voiced about their independence.

[103] 1980 Act s.28C, as amended by the Education (Scotland) Act 1981 s.1(1).

[104] 1980 Act s.28E(4), as amended by the Education (Scotland) Act 1981 s.1(1).

[105] 1980 Act s.28F(3), as amended by the Education (Scotland) Act 1981 s.1(1).

[106] *Coates v Lothian RC*, 1999 F.L.R. 8.

[107] 1980 Act ss.28E(1) and 28F(5)(a).

[108] 1980 Act ss.28E(1)(b) and 28F(5)(b).

[109] 1980 Act s.28F(9).

[110] *Lamont v Strathclyde RC*, 1988 S.L.T. (Sh Ct) 9.

[111] *Dundee City Council, Ptrs*, 1999 Fam. L.R. 13; *Aberdeen City Council v Wokoma*, 2002 S.L.T. 878.

[112] The Religious Observance Review Group was set up to review the religious observance in schools. Its report was published in 2004 and is available at *http://www.scotland.gov.uk/library5/education/rorg-00.asp*.

[113] 1980 Act s.8, as amended by the Self-Governing Schools etc. (Scotland) Act 1989 s.82 and Sch.10 para.8(3).

[114] The current guidance is *Provision of Religious Education and Religious Observance in Primary and Secondary Schools*, SOED Circular 6/91. See also SOED, *Religious and Moral Education 5-14 National Guidelines* (SOED, 1992).

[115] Education (School and Placing Information) (Scotland) Regulations 1982 (SI 1982/950) Pt II Sch.1 para.2(fff), inserted by the Education (School and Placing Information) (Scotland) Amendment etc. Regulations 1993 (SI 1993/1604) Sch. para.2.

result of their withdrawal from the religious education.[116] Although the rights of parents in regard to the religious education of their child are now further entrenched by virtue of the Human Rights Act 1998, it remains to be seen how far parents can enforce these rights.[117]

Denominational schools

5.10 Denominational schools are public schools having an association with a religious body. There are 430 faith schools in Scotland; 401 Catholic; 1 Jewish; 4 Episcopalian with others being special schools of various faiths.[118] A denominational school can be set up in two ways: by transfer of an existing school to the education authority[119] or the education authority can itself establish a new denominational school, if it is satisfied that such a school is required.[120] The law in relation to denominational schools is the same as for other public schools, with some modifications.[121] The education authority has the sole power to regulate the curriculum and appoint teachers.[122] Any teacher appointed needs to satisfy the denominational body associated with the school.[123] An unpaid supervisor of religious instruction is appointed by the education authority and this person can enter the school at all times set apart for religious instruction.[124] In addition the education authority shall provide facilities for holding religious exams.[125]

Such schools have their own programme of religious education, normally adapting government guidelines to their own faith.[126] The schools may cease to be a denominational school and become a non-denominational school if certain conditions are met.[127] Denominational schools are open to all children regardless of their faith, and it is the right of parents to choose that their child shall not take part in the religious observance of that school[128] provided the child is not placed at a disadvantage by so doing. Religious groups can set up independent schools.[129]

ADDITIONAL SUPPORT FOR LEARNING

5.11 The Education (Additional Support for Learning) Act 2004 ("EASLA 2004") came into effect on November 2005. It replaces in its entirety the previous system, based on special educational needs. The Scottish Ministers have published a code of practice and education authorities and appropriate agencies must have regard to this when exercising their functions under EASLA 2004.[130] The aim of the Act is to give additional help and support to all children with additional support needs and requirements.

In 2006, 36,148 pupils had additional support needs, 67 per cent of which were taught in a

[116] 1980 Act ss.8 and 9, as amended by the Self-Governing Schools etc. (Scotland) Act 1989 s. 82 and Sch.10 para.8(3) and (4).

[117] See discussion in D. Auchie, "An Oasis; Education, Placing Requests and Religion", 2002 (7) S.L.P.Q. 3 in relation to *Wokoma v Aberdeen City Council*, 2002 G.W.D. 2–72.

[118] Scottish Executive at *http://www.scotland.gov.uk* [Accessed July 2, 2008].

[119] 1980 Act s.16.

[120] 1980 Act s.17(2).

[121] 1980 Act s.21.

[122] 1980 Act s.21(2).

[123] 1980 Act s.21(2A).

[124] 1980 Act s.21(3).

[125] 1980 Act s.21(4).

[126] See for example, SOED, *Religious and Moral Education 5-14 Guidelines: Roman Catholic Schools* (SOED, 1994).

[127] 1980 Act s.22(4). Consultation is necessary first and the Scottish Executive has to consent: 1980 Act ss.22A–22D.

[128] 1980 Act ss.8(1) and 9.

[129] There are currently three independent Catholic schools and there have been independent Muslim schools in Glasgow and Dundee.

[130] Education (Additional Support for Learning) Act 2004 ("EASLA 2004") s.27(8).

mainstream school all of the time, with 19 per cent of pupils attending a special school.[131] Over 70 per cent of pupils with additional support needs are boys.[132]

A child or young person has additional support needs if they are likely to be unable without the provision of additional support to benefit from school education.[133] The concept of additional support is wider than that of special needs and covers any child who needs additional support in learning for any reason including social, emotional, cognitive, linguistic, through disability or family and care situations.[134] A child or young person will be entitled to a "co-ordinated support plan", if the education authority is responsible for their education[135]; and they have additional support needs arising from one or more complex factors[136] or multiple factors[137]; the needs are likely to continue for longer than one year[138]; and significant additional support is to be provided by the education authority[139] or by another appropriate agency[140] as well as the education authority. Therefore before a child is entitled to a co-ordinated support plan all the criteria in s.2 of EASLA 2004 must be met. Additional support must be provided by two or more providers or by one provider carrying out two different functions. The additional support required must be significant.[141]

Section 4 of EASLA 2004 specifies the duty of the education authority, which is to make adequate and efficient provision of additional support as required by the child or young person[142] and to make appropriate arrangements for keeping under consideration the additional support needs of[143] and the adequacy of the additional support so provided to the child or young person.[144] In so doing the education authority does not need to incur unreasonable public expenditure.[145] In addition when providing school education, the education authority needs to take account of the additional support needs of children and young persons having these needs.[146] If a child is under school age, and has a disability that has been brought to the authority's attention by a health board the education authority must provide additional support for that child.[147] An education authority may provide appropriate additional support for children for whose school education they are not responsible.[148]

5.12 The education authority has a duty to identify the children who have additional support needs[149] from the children and young persons for whose school education they are responsible, and which of those children needs a co-ordinated support plan.[150] A child's parent[151]; young

---

[131] Scottish Executive, "Schools Inclusion—Additional Support Needs—High Level Summary of Statistics", as at February 28, 2007. *http://www.scotland.gov.uk* [Accessed July 2, 2008].

[132] Scottish Executive, News Release, "Pupils in Scotland 2006". *http://www.scotland.gov.uk*.

[133] EASLA 2004 s.1(1).

[134] Scottish Executive, "Summary Handout on the Additional Support for Learning Act", 2nd edn. *http://www.scotland.gov.uk* [Accessed July 2, 2008].

[135] EASLA 2004 s.2(1)(a).

[136] EASLA 2004 s.2(1)(b)(i).

[137] EASLA 2004 s.2(1)(b)(ii).

[138] EASLA 2004 s.2(1)(c).

[139] EASLA 2004 s.2(1)(d)(i).

[140] EASLA 2004 s.2(1)(d)(ii).

[141] See the discussion of "significant" in the decision in the Outer House in *JT as Legal Guardian for KT v ASNT* [2007] CSOH 67, available at *http://www.scotscourts.gov.uk* [Accessed July 2, 2008].

[142] EASLA 2004 s.4(1)(a).

[143] EASLA 2004 s.4(1)(b)(i).

[144] EASLA 2004 s.4(1)(b)(ii).

[145] EASLA 2004 s.4(2)(b).

[146] EASLA 2004 s.5(1).

[147] EASLA 2004 s.5(2) and (3).

[148] EASLA 2004 s.5(4). This would cover children educated at home or at an independent school or under the age of three.

[149] EASLA 2004 s.6(1)(a)(i).

[150] EASLA 2004 s.6(1)(a)(ii).

[151] EASLA 2004 s.6(3)(a).

person[152] or young person's parent[153] can ask the education authority to establish whether the child or young person has additional support needs or requires a co-ordinated support plan.[154] If so requested the education authority must comply with their request[155] and then inform the person who made the request if the child or young person has additional support needs.[156] It is possible for children being educated outwith the remit of the education authority to be assessed as having additional support needs by the authority.[157]

If it is established that a co-ordinated support plan is required then the education authority must prepare one[158] within a period of 16 weeks[159] unless it is impractical to do so within that specified time limit.[160] The plan has to be in the form set out in the Schedule to the Regulations.[161]

The co-ordinated support plan must contain a statement of the education authority's conclusions as to:

- the factor or factors from which the additional support needs of the child or young person arise[162];
- the educational objectives sought to be achieved taking account of that factor[163];
- the additional support required by the child or young person to achieve those objectives[164];
- the persons by whom the support should be provided[165];
- details of the school attended by the child or young person[166];
- contact details of the officer responsible to discharge the authority's duty.[167]

A co-ordinator is appointed to discharge this duty and their job is to ensure that the services required in the co-ordinated support plan are delivered. The co-ordinator will work closely with the family and any other agency.

The plan must be reviewed at least once every 12 months and earlier if the authority thinks there has been a significant change in the child's circumstances.[168] At the review it will be considered whether the educational changes have been met. A review must also be carried out if requested by the child's parent,[169] the young person[170] or the young person's parent.[171] At the review the plan can be continued,[172] amended[173] or discontinued.[174] In preparing any plan or conducting a review the authority must before proceeding inform the parent or young person or

[152] EASLA 2004 s.6(3)(b)(i).
[153] EASLA 2004 s.6(3)(b)(ii).
[154] EASLA 2004 s.6(2)(a) and (b).
[155] EASLA 2004 s.6(2).
[156] EASLA 2004 s.6(4).
[157] EASLA 2004 s.7. If it is ascertained that the child has additional support needs the education authority must give information and advice to the child's parents: s.7(7) and (8).
[158] EASLA 2004 s.9(1).
[159] Additional Support for Learning (Co-ordinated Support Plan) (Scotland) Amendment Regulations 2005 (SSI 2005/518) ("2005 Regs") reg.4.
[160] 2005 Regs reg.7.
[161] 2005 Regs reg.3(1)(a).
[162] EASLA 2004 s.9(2)(a)(i).
[163] EASLA 2004 s.9(2)(a)(ii).
[164] EASLA 2004 s.9(2)(a)(iii).
[165] EASLA 2004 s.9(2)(a)(iv).
[166] EASLA 2004 s.9(2)(b).
[167] EASLA 2004 s.9(2)(c).
[168] EASLA 2004 s.10(3).
[169] EASLA 2004 s.10(5)(a).
[170] EASLA 2004 s.10(5)(b)(i).
[171] EASLA 2004 s.10(5)(b)(ii).
[172] EASLA 2004 s.10(6)(a).
[173] EASLA 2004 s.10(6)(a).
[174] EASLA 2004 s.10(6)(b).

young person's parent of its intention[175] and the outcome of the proceedings[176] and the rights of appeal to the Additional Support Needs Tribunal.[177]

When a plan is prepared or amended a copy of the plan is given to the child's parent[178] or young person or young person's parent.[179] The authority must ensure that the child receives the additional support in accordance with the plan.[180] This support can be provided by someone other than the education authority, such as another agency[181] and the education authority has a duty to inform these persons of the plan and to co-ordinate it.[182]

5.13 The authority has a duty to children about to leave school. At least 12 months prior to the young person about to leave school, it must contact appropriate agencies as it thinks fit and request information about their provision of services to the young person once they leave school.[183] The views of the child must be sought.[184] Agencies are entitled to receive relevant information about the young person six months prior to them leaving school[185] and decisions about provision of services once the young person leaves school need to be taken.[186]

A supporter can be present at any discussions with the parents or young person.[187] The purpose of the supporter is to provide support to the person. It is also possible to have another person known as an advocate to conduct discussions or make representations to the authority on behalf of the parents or young person.[188]

The authority must provide free and independent mediation services, which can resolve disagreements between the authority and the parents.[189] Although parents have the option of mediation to resolve disputes it is not compulsory and they can still refer the matter to the Additional Support Needs Tribunal.[190] A supporter or advocate may be present at mediation, but legal representation is not encouraged.[191]

A dispute between parents and the authority may be resolved by independent adjudication.[192] Dispute resolution is a formal process whereby an independent third party will consider the disagreement, make a decision on it and make a written report to the authority, with his recommendations attached as to how he believes the dispute will be resolved.[193] The procedure is free but parents cannot be compelled to use the procedure. They are encouraged to use mediation first. If the authority receives an application for referral it must request the Scottish Ministers to nominate an adjudicator within 10 days.[194] The Scottish Ministers will nominate a person from a panel and that person must be independent.[195] The authority must appoint the person so nominated and pay them a fee as appropriate.[196] The adjudicator must review the

---

175 EASLA 2004 s.11(2)(b).
176 EASLA 2004 s.11(2)(b)(i).
177 EASLA 2004 s.11(2)(b)(ii). See para.5.14.
178 EASLA 2004 s.11(5)(a)(i).
179 EASLA 2004 s.11(5)(a)(ii).
180 EASLA 2004 s.11(5)(b).
181 EASLA 2004 s.11(5)(c).
182 EASLA 2004 s.11(5)(d).
183 EASLA 2004 s.12(5)(a) and (b) and s.12(6)(a).
184 EASLA 2004 s.12(6)(b)(i) and (ii).
185 EASLA 2004 s.13(1).
186 EASLA 2004 s.13(2)(b)(i).
187 EASLA 2004 s.14(1)(a).
188 EASLA 2004 s.14(1)(b).
189 EASLA 2004 s.15(1).
190 EASLA 2004 s.15(3)(b).
191 Scottish Executive, Code of Practice, Ch.7 "Resolving Disagreements". *http://www.scotland.gov.uk*.
192 EASLA 2004 s.16 allows ministers to make regulations on this and the current regulations are the Additional Support for Learning Dispute Resolution (Scotland) Regulations 2005 (SSI 2005/501).
193 *Education (Additional Support for Learning) (Scotland) Act 2004—Dispute Resolution*, Guidance for Education Authorities (Scottish Executive, Additional Support Needs Division, 2005) available at *http://www.scotland.gov.uk* [Accessed July 3, 2008].
194 Additional Support for Learning Dispute Resolution (Scotland) Regulations 2005 regs 3 and 4.
195 Additional Support for Learning Dispute Resolution (Scotland) Regulations 2005 reg 5.
196 Additional Support for Learning Dispute Resolution (Scotland) Regulations 2005 reg.6.

matter and give a written report with recommendations within a specified time.[197] The authority within 10 days then has to give notice in writing to the applicant of the adjudicator's decision, stating whether or not it intends to follow the adjudicator's recommendations, and also must send the parents a copy of the report. It would be expected that the decision of the adjudicator would be accepted in all but exceptional circumstances.[198]

Additional Support Needs Tribunals

5.14 Additional Support Needs Tribunals[199] have been set up to hear references from the parent[200] or the young person.[201] The following can be referred to a tribunal:

- a decision of the education authority that the child requires a co-ordinated support plan[202];
- a decision of the education authority that after a review a plan is still necessary[203];
- a decision of the education authority that the child does not require a plan[204];
- a decision of the education authority that the child no longer needs a plan, after a review[205];
- failure by the education authority to prepare a plan timeously[206];
- the education authority's conclusions in the plan regarding the factors giving rise to the additional support needs; the educational objectives to be achieved; the additional support required and the persons who provide the support[207];
- failure by the education authority to carry out a review[208];
- failure by the education authority to complete the review timeously[209];
- a decision of the local authority not to review a plan on request by the parent[210];
- a decision of the local authority refusing a placing request.[211]

When considering a reference the tribunal may confirm the decision of the education authority or overturn it.[212] The tribunal can require the authority to rectify any failure on its part. In reaching a decision the tribunal must consider the code of practice.[213] A decision of the tribunal can be appealed to the Court of Session on a point of law,[214] by the person who made the reference or by the education authority.

Placing requests under EASLA 2004

5.15 If the parents of a child with additional support needs make a placing request to place their child in a specific school the authority has a duty to place the child in that school[215] provided certain

---

[197] Additional Support for Learning Dispute Resolution (Scotland) Regulations 2005 reg 9.
[198] Scottish Executive, Code of Practice, Ch.7 "Resolving Disagreements". *http://www.scotland.gov.uk* [Accessed July 2, 2008].
[199] EASLA 2004 s.17(1).
[200] EASLA 2004 s.18(2)(a) and (b)(ii).
[201] EASLA 2004 s.18(2)(b)(i).
[202] EASLA 2004 s.18(3)(a)(i).
[203] EASLA 2004 s.18(3)(a)(ii).
[204] EASLA 2004 s.18(3)(b)(i).
[205] EASLA 2004 s.18(3)(b)(ii).
[206] EASLA 2004 s.18(3)(c).
[207] EASLA 2004 s.18(3)(d)(i).
[208] EASLA 2004 s.18(3)(d)(ii).
[209] EASLA 2004 s.18(3)(d)(iii).
[210] EASLA 2004 s.18(3)(d)(iv).
[211] EASLA 2004 s.18(3)(e).
[212] EASLA 2004 s.19.
[213] EASLA 2004 s.19(7). See Scottish Executive, Code of Practice, Ch.7 "Resolving Disagreements". *http://www.scotland.gov.uk* [Accessed July 2, 2008].
[214] EASLA 2004 s.21(1).
[215] EASLA 2004 Sch.2 para.2(1) and (2).

criteria are met. The local authority does not have such a duty if certain circumstances exist.[216] There is a presumption that children will be educated in mainstream schools.[217] The parents must be informed in writing of the decision of the authority.[218] If unhappy with the decision, the parent can refer the matter to the appeal committee,[219] unless the circumstances in EASLA 2004 s.18 are fulfilled and the appeal goes to the tribunal.[220] A further appeal can be made to the sheriff from a decision of the appeal committee.[221] The sheriff's decision is final.[222]

DISABILITY DISCRIMINATION

5.16 In addition to the legislation on additional support for learning the pupil has the protection of the disability discrimination legislation, and the two are meant to work closely together. A child with a disability may require additional support for learning but will in any event be protected by the provisions of the disability discrimination legislation.

It is unlawful for the body responsible for a school to discriminate against a disabled person in its admissions policy, by the education or associated services provided by the school and by excluding the child from school.[223] Discrimination exists if:

- the responsible body treats a child less favourably than it would treat others and the treatment is unjustified[224]; or
- the responsible body fails, without justification, to take reasonable steps to ensure that disabled children are not at a substantial disadvantage compared to non-disabled children.[225]

Less favourable treatment of a pupil is justified if it is the result of a permitted form of selection.[226] The failure to take a reasonable step would not amount to discrimination if the responsible body did not know and could not reasonably be expected to know that the pupil was disabled.[227]

Proceedings against the education authority may be brought in the sheriff court within six months if the pupil is discriminated against.[228] The Disability Rights Commission can provide assistance in any dispute.[229]

PROVISION FOR SCHOOL CHILDREN

5.17 The duty of the education authority to provide appropriate education is supplemented by other duties towards children of school age.

Of these the five main duties are: the duty to provide guidance; the duty to provide transport; the duty to provide clothing; the duty to provide school meals; and the duty to provide medical and dental treatments.

---

[216] The circumstances are as detailed in EASLA 2004 Sch.2 para.3. If any of these circumstances exist there is no obligation on the local authority to place the child in the requested school.

[217] EASLA 2004 s.15.

[218] EASLA 2004 Sch.2 para.4(1).

[219] EASLA 2004 Sch.2 para.5(1).

[220] EASLA 2004 Sch.2 para.5(2). Difficulties have arisen as to the correct procedural appeal route. See *Gordon v ASNT* Unreported August, 2006 CSOH, available at *http://www.scotscourts.gov.uk* [Accessed July 2, 2008].

[221] EASLA 2004 Sch.2 para.7(1).

[222] EASLA 2004 Sch.2 para.7(2).

[223] Disability Discrimination Act 1995 s.28A(1)(2) and (4).

[224] Disability Discrimination Act 1995 s.28B(1).

[225] Disability Discrimination Act 1995 ss.28B(2) and 28C.

[226] Disability Discrimination Act 1995 s.28B(6).

[227] Disability Discrimination Act 1995 s.28B(3) and (4).

[228] See *A v East Ayrshire Council*, 2006 Fam. L.R. 112.

[229] Their website is at *http://www.drc-gb.org* [Accessed July 2, 2008].

Guidance

5.18 One of the most crucial services provided to school pupils is that of guidance. Guidance covers personal, curricular and vocational matters, and should not be confused with the careers service, which is operated under the Scottish Government and deals purely with careers advice.[230] The fundamental objective is to ensure guidance provision for all pupils and to provide a consistent relationship between the pupil and a teacher. Depending on the stage of school the focus of guidance changes, for example for those pupils newly entering secondary schools guidance will focus most likely on personal settling-in problems, whereas for those in fifth year the focus will be on careers assistance. As the guidance teacher has the first hand knowledge of the pupil, it is the guidance teacher who often updates the pupil progress records, and who would be most appropriate to attend children's hearings and other meetings. Therefore the guidance staff provide an important link to social work, although often this link is not established effectively enough.[231]

Transport

5.19 The power of the educational authority to provide transport is set out in s.51(1) of the Education (Scotland) Act 1980 as amended which gives the authority a broad discretion as to the form of the facilities it makes available, although the authority is obliged to have regard to the safety of pupils in so doing.[232]

The key duty of the authority is to make transportation facilities available to those pupils who attend the school nominated by the education authority, where that school is more than walking distance (defined as being "in the case of a child who has not attained the age of eight years, two miles and in the case of any other child, three miles"[233]) away from the pupils' home. If the authority has not made transportation available for a child to attend the nominated school (allocated by the authority) which is outwith walking distance, the parents will have a reasonable excuse for the non-attendance of their child at school,[234] although they would need to educate their child themselves.

Where a child lives within walking distance the onus is on the parents to make arrangements to ensure that the child attends school. Clearly the implication is that parents will supervise their children getting to and from school. In the older case of *Skeen v Tunnah*[235] the parents were successful in defending the prosecution of them under the similar provision of the Education (Scotland) Act 1962, on the ground that, while they lived just over a mile from the school, owing to the father's employment and the mother having to look after a younger child, the parents had a reasonable excuse for their child not attending school as such attendance would have required them to walk along a main road without pavements, unaccompanied. Therefore in certain circumstances such as the unavailability of public transport or a safe walking route, or indeed because of the medical condition of the pupil, the education authority may make transport available to such pupils regardless of the fact that they live within walking distance.[236]

Where the pupil attends a school other than that nominated by the authority, through a placing request for instance, the authority need not provide transport, even if the selected school

---

[230] For a discussion on the careers service see Marr and Marr, *Scots Education Law* (Edinburgh: W. Green, 2005), paras 04.16–04.17.

[231] C. Howieson and S. Semple, "Guidance in Secondary Schools", Interchange No.41 (SOEID, 1996).

[232] 1980 Act s.51(2C), as amended by the Education (Scotland) Act 1996 Sch.5 para.2.

[233] 1980 Act s.42(4).

[234] 1980 Act s.42(1), as amended by the Education (Scotland) Act 1981.

[235] 1970 S.L.T. (Sh Ct) 66.

[236] In the event of special circumstances the local education authority's policy should be consulted initially, e.g. in Aberdeen City the authority has produced a booklet *Notes for Parents*, which details their transport policy, pp.9–10.

is outwith walking distance.[237] Although in such cases the authority can choose to provide that pupil with transport, in practice few authorities exercise this discretion.[238] Furthermore, the authority is under no obligation to provide transport for a pupil who, although attending one of its schools, is a pupil who normally resides in another local authority area in Scotland, or indeed in England or Wales.[239] Where transport is provided the education authority is liable for the safety of the pupils.[240]

There is no duty to provide transport to nursery school[241] but again there is a discretion to do so.[242] The education authority has a discretion to pay travelling costs or provide transport if specific exceptional circumstances exist.[243]

Clothing grants

5.20 Education authorities can recommend that pupils attending their schools wear a school uniform, although they cannot legally enforce such a recommendation. The school policy on school uniform will be[244] in the school handbook. The requirement to wear school uniform is not a breach of the pupil's human rights[245] but it must not be discriminatory to the child.[246] The authority is legally required to provide suitable clothing for all children who would not be able to participate fully in their education because of a lack of adequate clothing. Therefore, the authority may have to provide clothing for daily wear and clothing for physical exercise, etc. Again, while authorities must provide such clothing for pupils attending schools under their management, they have no obligation to provide clothing for pupils attending other schools in their area, although they have a discretion to so do. In respect of a self-governing school the provision of special clothing may be made by the Board of Management and it may provide it free or at a charge[247] or it may come to an agreement with the local education authority for the authority to provide clothing in certain circumstances.[248]

It will always be open to schools to determine whether, in the individual circumstances of a particular pupil, the clothing worn is completely unacceptable, for which the ultimate sanction would be exclusion. It is generally acknowledged that some items of clothing could be prohibited on the grounds of safety.

School meals

5.21 An education authority may make arrangements to provide milk, meals and other refreshments for pupils.[249] When providing school meals the authority has a discretion as to charging, except where the pupil is entitled to free school meals. The authority must provide a school meal in the middle of the day free of charge for any pupil whose parents are in receipt of income support or income-based jobseeker's allowance, help under Pt VI of the Immigration and Asylum Act 1999 or receive child tax credit and earn less than £14,155 per annum, or for any pupil who is personally in receipt of either of those benefits.[250] However, it is the responsibility of the pupil or

[237] 1980 Act s.51(2A).

[238] See *GG, Petr* Unreported July 11, 2001 CSOH, available at *http://www.scotcourts.gov.uk* [Accessed July 2, 2008], for judicial review of decision by Glasgow City Council refusing to fund transport costs.

[239] 1980 Act s.51(2B).

[240] Marr and Marr, *Scots Education Law*, paras 07.11–07.14.

[241] 1980 Act s.51(4).

[242] SSSA 2000 s.37.

[243] 1980 Act s.50.

[244] Education (School and Placing Information) (Scotland) Regulations 1982 (SI 1982/950).

[245] See the House of Lords decision in the English case of *R. (on the application of SB) v Denbigh High School Governors* [2006] UKHL 15; [2007] 1 A.C. 100.

[246] Disability Discrimination Act 1995 as amended by the Disability Discrimination Act 2005.

[247] Self-Governing Schools etc. (Scotland) Act 1989 s.11(3)(b).

[248] 1980 Act s.55(b), as amended.

[249] 1980 Act s.53(1)(a), as amended.

[250] 1980 Act s.53(3), as amended.

parent to bring their entitlement to the attention of the authority, although most authorities do make provision for this. Fifty-three per cent of schools operate an anonymised system to preserve the identity of the pupils. As at June 2007, 16 per cent of pupils were registered for free school meals, although only 67.5 per cent actually took the free meals.[251] The quality of school meals has been improved dramatically owing to increased funding.[252] All schools should be health promoting schools.[253]

Medical and dental care

5.22 The Scottish Ministers are primarily responsible for ensuring, under s.39 of the National Health Service (Scotland) Act 1978,[254] the proper medical and dental inspection and treatment of children and young persons. In practice the Scottish Ministers have delegated this function to the local health boards. In consequence, arrangements are made for medical and dental inspections at school, to which parents are required to submit their child. If the pupil fails to attend the examination the parent or young person (if the pupil is over 16 years of age) will be guilty of an offence.

In this respect there appears to be an anomaly between education law and the capacity of children under the age of 16 to consent to medical treatment where in the opinion of the medical practitioner they understand the nature and consequence of the treatment.[255] Therefore, good practice requires their consent to be taken and indeed, even if the medical or dental practitioner does not believe that the child can consent, they should take into account the wishes of the child.[256] Note that the child retains this capacity to consent even where they are a "looked after" child by the local authority. If a pupil has the capacity to consent to the examination, it cannot proceed without their consent.[257]

In addition to such power to provide for medical and dental examination, the education authority has powers to authorise a medical officer to carry out examinations of the clothing and/or bodies of all or any pupil(s) where the medical officer considers such inspection necessary in the interests of cleanliness.[258] Moreover the schools have a general duty to promote good health by virtue of the Schools General (Scotland) Regulations 1975 (SI 1975/1135).

DISCIPLINARY ISSUES

5.23 Disciplinary issues involving pupils often focus on the tripartite relationship between parent, pupil and school. Certainly a child's poor performance or lack of attendance could be the result of problems at home. In this section the duty to ensure that a pupil attends school will be examined together with a review of the methods of punishment available to teaching staff, and of the procedures relating to the exclusion of pupils from school. All schools should have school

[251] Scottish Executive, News Release, "School Meals in Scotland", June 5, 2007. *http://www.scotland.gov.uk* [Accessed July 2, 2008].

[252] Scottish Executive, "Improving School Meals". *http://www.scotland.gov.uk* [Accessed July 2, 2008].

[253] The Schools (Health Promotion and Nutrition) (Scotland) Act 2007 will come into effect in 2008 and places an obligation on the education authority to ensure that schools and hostels are health promoting. A school is health promoting if it provides activities and an environment and facilities that promote the physical, social, mental and emotional health and well-being of pupils in attendance at the school (Schools (Health Promotion and Nutrition) (Scotland) Act 2007 s.1(5)).

[254] As amended by the Health and Medicines Act 1988 and Self-Governing Schools etc. (Scotland) Act 1989.

[255] Age of Legal Capacity (Scotland) Act 1991 s.2(4); see Edwards and Griffiths, *Family Law*, 2nd edn, (Edinburgh: W. Green, 2006) paras 2.29–2.37.

[256] *A Guide to Consent to Examination, Investigation, Treatment or Operation* (NHS in Scotland Management Executive, October 1992).

[257] 1980 Act s.131A, inserted by SSSA 2000 s.57.

[258] 1980 Act s.58.

behavioural policies which ought to encourage good behaviour, and which should include a range of sanctions of differing severity suited to different circumstances.[259]

Attendance

Enforcing attendance

5.24 The Education (Scotland) Act 1980 s.30, places a very clear duty upon parents:

> "It shall be the duty of the parent of every child of school age to provide efficient education for him suitable to his age, ability and aptitude either by causing him to attend a public school regularly or by other means."

The duty relates to parents of children who are of school age, which is defined as those children who have attained the age of five years but are under 16 years of age.[260] However, the education authority must discharge its duty of providing suitable education to those children who, although not five years of age at the school commencement date, will be of such an age by the "appropriate latest date" (normally by the end of February following the commencement date).[261]

For the year 2005–06, the overall rate of attendance was 93.1 per cent (95 per cent for primary schools; 93.1 per cent for secondary schools and 90.1 per cent for special schools).[262]

Obviously a parent may elect to educate their child at home, and hence they are not obliged to send their child to school. However once a child has attended an education authority school at least once, the parent will be in breach of their duty if that child does not, without reasonable excuse, regularly attend the school.[263] The parents will in fact be committing an offence for which they may be prosecuted, and could be fined or imprisoned for up to one month.[264] The fact parents can be prosecuted criminally for the actings of their child seems to be compatible with the Human Rights legislation.[265] In addition to the possibility of prosecution, the failure of a child to regularly attend school amounts to a ground of referral to the Reporter.[266]

The 1980 Act defines three categories of reasonable excuse for non-attendance, which comprise[267]:

(1) where there is no school within walking distance that is prepared to receive the child, and either no transport arrangements have been made by the authority, or the transport arrangements made by the authority would require the pupil to walk more than the walking distance in getting to school;
(2) where the child has been prevented by sickness from attending; or
(3) where the circumstances in the view of the education authority or court amount to a reasonable excuse.

In relation to a child whose attendance at a school was the result of a placing request, the lack of transport would not amount to a reasonable excuse, provided the authority had made an alternative school available either within the walking distance, or if outwith had made suitable

---

[259] *Guidance on Issues Concerning Exclusion from School*, SOEID Circular 2/98, s.1, para.2.

[260] 1980 Act s.31.

[261] 1980 Act s.32.

[262] Scottish Executive, "Attendance and Absence in Scottish Schools 2005–06". *http//www.scotland.gov.uk* [Accessed July 2, 2008].

[263] 1980 Act s.35.

[264] 1980 Act s.43.

[265] In *Hagan v Rea*, 2001 S.L.T. (Sh Ct) 30 a parent challenged the fact that she was potentially criminally liable under s.35 of the 1980 Act and yet the refusal to go to school were the actings of her child. She challenged s.35 of the 1980 Act as incompatible with art.6(1) and (2) of the European Convention on Human Rights. The sheriff held there was no breach of the human rights legislation provided the 1980 Act was given a wide enough meaning.

[266] Children (Scotland) Act 1995 s.52(2)(h).

[267] 1980 Act s.42(1).

transport arrangements.[268] Moreover in determining what either the court or the authority would deem a reasonable excuse, it is interesting to note that in *Skeen v Tunnah*[269] the sheriff accepted as a reasonable excuse the fact that the children would need to walk one mile along a main road with no pavement without supervision, as the father was prevented by his employment and the mother was prevented from other family commitments from accompanying the children. Even if a parent successfully defends a criminal prosecution for failing to ensure their child's attendance at school, they are still obliged to satisfy the courts that they are providing adequate education for their child. Where the pupil is absent because of illness, it should be noted that not all forms of illness will amount to a reasonable excuse. In *Kiely v Lunn*[270] the court decided that a pupil of 15 years of age whose absence was due to glue sniffing illnesses was not absent for a reasonable excuse, the illness being caused by the actions of the pupil. The mother of a 14-year-old girl who was the subject of bullying, but did not report it to the authorities, did not have a reasonable excuse.[271]

As well as providing reasonable excuses for non-attendance, the 1980 Act also creates a limited exemption from the obligation to attend school, which applies to children over 14 years of age where the authority is satisfied that in view of the home circumstances of the child, their attendance at school would cause an exceptional hardship.[272]

Enforcing attendance procedure

5.25 All education authorities will provide schools in their area with a detailed procedure on how to deal with non-attendance by a pupil. Usually the procedure will commence somewhat informally, such as by letter to the parents.[273] However if attendance does not improve the Home School Liaison Officer will become involved and eventually the statutory scheme will come into effect. Where a parent has failed to secure the regular attendance of their child at school the authority must issue a notice to the parent requiring them within a period of not less than 48 hours, but not more than seven days, to attend the authority and explain the reason for the absence. If the parents fail to satisfy the authority that the absence was due to a reasonable excuse, the authority will either move for prosecution of the parents or may warn the parent and defer the matter for a period of up to six weeks.[274] Should the parents be prosecuted, the court may also refer the matter to the Principal Reporter under s.54(1) of the 1995 Act. The Principal Reporter will carry out an investigation of the case, and if he or she thinks that compulsory measures of supervision are necessary, will arrange a children's hearing to consider the case. Where the decision to prosecute has been postponed, the authority may make an attendance order, which will require the child to attend a specified school.

Equally, attendance orders are used where a child has been withdrawn from school and the authority is not satisfied that the child is receiving adequate appropriate education.[275] The order specifies the school to be attended, and therefore the authority is bound to take account of the wishes of the parent in preparing the order, and in particular, the authority cannot specify a fee paying school except at the request of the parent. An attendance order can be made for a child for as long as they are of school age.[276] If a parent is aggrieved at the contents of an attendance order they have 14 days from their receipt of the copy order in which to appeal against it to the sheriff.[277]

Once made, an attendance order is served on the parent and thereafter the parent will be

---

[268] 1980 Act s.42(1A), as amended by the Education (Scotland) Act 1981 s.2(1).
[269] 1970 S.L.T. (Sh Ct) 66.
[270] 1983 S.L.T. 207 (High Ct).
[271] *Montgomery v Cumming*, 1999 S.C.L.R. 179.
[272] 1980 Act s.34(1).
[273] e.g. in Aberdeen City Council Circular PP/ASC/16/97.
[274] 1980 Act s.36.
[275] 1980 Act s.37.
[276] 1980 Act s.40, as amended by the Education (Scotland) Act 1981 Sch.2 Pt II para.6 and Sch.8.
[277] 1980 Act s.38(5).

guilty of an offence if the child fails to attend the specified school without reasonable excuse.[278] However, the attendance order may be amended to change the name of the specified school, either due to a decision of the education authority or by the parent, if for example the family has moved house.[279] Where the change is due to a decision of the authority, the parent has 14 days to raise objections with the authority, which objections must be considered by the authority.

Indeed, the parents may have the order revoked if they have made arrangements for the child to receive efficient education at a school other than that named in the order or elsewhere than at school.[280] The authority should grant the request by the parents unless satisfied that the change of school is not in the best interests of the child or that the arrangements made are not satisfactory. Where the authority does not reach a decision on the parental request within one month, or where the authority refuse the request, the parent has the right to appeal to the sheriff, who has the power to make any direction he thinks fit.

Discipline

5.26 In general, a school pupil may not be subjected to corporal punishment in school[281] but may be disciplined in other ways such as additional homework or a verbal reprimand. In the most serious cases a child may be excluded from school. If this happens the parent must be notified and they have the right to appeal.

Corporal punishment

5.27 Corporal punishment was abolished in 1986.[282] Now no teacher can use corporal punishment to punish any pupil, whichever school they attend.[283] Corporal punishment is for the purpose of punishing a pupil and constitutes a physical assault upon the pupil.[284] This applies to anyone who works as a teacher or other person who works at the school or provides services there and has lawful control or charge of the pupil.[285] If someone acts to avert an immediate danger of personal injury to any person or an immediate danger to property, it will not be corporal punishment.[286]

Other punishment

5.28 There is little statutory regulation on other forms of punishment, although it is generally accepted that punishment administered by teaching staff, such as writing lines, should have an educational value. Punishment must be compatible with the Human Rights Act 1998 and should not be discriminatory. It is thought unlikely that detention would be contrary to the human rights legislation but the matter has not come before the courts.

Within the ambit of punishment by staff, it is important to remember that dealing with classroom problems often involves overlap with other areas of law. For instance if a member of staff discovers a child with a drug problem, they may initially choose to deal with that as a school matter and should follow the local education authority's policy on dealing with a drugs-related incident. Such action will involve the police, the parents and the pupil's guidance tea-

---

[278] 1980 Act s.41.

[279] 1980 Act s.39.

[280] 1980 Act s.39(4).

[281] SSSA 2000 s.16.

[282] 1980 Act s.48A, inserted by the Education (No.2) Act 1986 as a result of the decision in *Campbell and Cosans v United Kingdom* (1982) 4 E.H.R.R. 293.

[283] SSSA 2000 s.16(1).

[284] SSSA 2000 s.16(3).

[285] SSSA 2000 s.16(6).

[286] SSSA 2000 s.16(4).

cher. However, in addition, there is the potential to refer the matter to the Reporter to the children's panel for appropriate advice.[287]

Exclusion

5.29 One of the priorities for the Scottish Executive is to promote positive behaviour in schools. A joint action plan is in force to improve school discipline in response to the Behaviour in Scottish Schools Survey 2004.[288] The action plan enables the Positive Behaviour Team to work with the schools, teachers and councils to promote positive behaviour using a range of approaches and measures. The ultimate disciplinary action that can be taken against a pupil is to exclude the pupil from the school. In the year 2005–06 there were 42,990 exclusions from public schools[289]; 31 per cent of exclusions were for persistent disobedience; 25 per cent for verbal abuse of staff and 15 per cent for insolent behaviour.[290]

Circular 8/03 gives Scottish Executive guidance to education authorities on exclusion from school.[291] Only an education authority has the power to exclude a pupil and each education authority should produce its own local guidelines on exclusion. The emphasis of the guidelines is to ensure safety and to provide a positive learning and teaching environment for the entire school; to recognise shared responsibilities of pupils and parents in maintaining positive behaviour and to support victims of antisocial behaviour and to reintegrate the excluded pupil back into the school.[292]

The exclusion of a pupil by the education authority is only allowed where:

- it is of the opinion that the parent of the pupil refuses or fails to comply, or to allow the pupil to comply, with the rules, regulations, or disciplinary requirements of the school; or
- it considers that in all the circumstances to allow the pupil to continue his attendance at the school would be likely to be seriously detrimental to order and discipline in the school or the educational well-being of the pupils there.[293]

As regards the distinction between the two grounds of exclusion, the case *Wyatt v Wilson*[294] well illustrates the point.

Exclusion can be either temporary exclusion or exclusion/removed from the register. The length of the period of exclusion should be proportional to the severity of the breach of discipline and the pupil's past school record. The term "temporary exclusion" is to be used where a pupil is excluded from the school but remains on the school register, as it is expected that the pupil will return to that school when the period of exclusion has ended. Exclusion/removed from the register is where the school does not anticipate the pupil returning to that school—the term "permanent exclusion", which may have been previously used in such circumstances, has been deemed inappropriate.[295] An education authority will usually allow a head teacher to make a temporary exclusion whereas a permanent exclusion is reserved to the Director of Education.

---

[287] 1995 Act s.52(2)(i).

[288] See Scottish Executive, News Release, "Improving School Discipline: Behaviour". *http://www.scotland.gov.uk* [Accessed July 2, 2008].

[289] Scottish Executive, News Release, "Exclusions from Schools 2005/06". *http://www.scotland.gov.uk* [Accessed July 2, 2008].

[290] Scottish Executive, News Release, "Exclusions from Schools 2005/06". *http://www.scotland.gov.uk* [Accessed July 2, 2008].

[291] *Exclusion from School*, Circular 8/03. *http://www.scotland.gov.uk* [Accessed July 2, 2008].

[292] *Exclusion from School*, Circular 8/03. *http://www.scotland.gov.uk* [Accessed July 2, 2008].

[293] Schools General (Scotland) Regulations 1975 (SI 1975/1135) reg.4, substituted by the Schools General (Scotland) (Amendment) Regulations 1982 (SI 1982/56) reg.3, and amended by the Schools General (Scotland) Amendment (No.2) Regulations 1982 (SI 1982/1735) reg.3. See *Wallace v City of Dundee Council*, 2000 S.L.T. (Sh Ct) 60; *S v Glasgow City Council*, 2004 S.L.T. (Sh Ct) 128.

[294] 1994 S.L.T. 1135.

[295] *Guidance on Issues Concerning Exclusion from School*, SOEID Circular 2/98, paras 14–16.

5.30 Where it has been decided to exclude a pupil, the school must advise, either orally or in writing, the parents of the pupil, or in the case of a young person aged over 16, the young person, on the day of that decision. The notice must also include a date and time, within seven days of the date of exclusion, where the parent or young person can meet with the head teacher, another teacher at the school or an official of the education authority to discuss the exclusion.[296] So although there is no right for the child to be heard prior to the decision to exclude, they have a right to be heard within seven days from the exclusion decision. If the child is looked after by the local authority, then the case social worker and the carer of the child will also need to be informed.

At the meeting the parent, or the young person, will have the opportunity to accept the decision to exclude. If the decision is accepted and the pupil re-admitted within the seven-day period no further action is necessary—although the education authority may provide the parent with any information that it considers appropriate. However, if the pupil is not re-admitted within seven days or if the parent or the pupil, being a young person, does not accept the decision to exclude and does not inform the head teacher of the school, either orally or in writing, whether they intend to take the matter to appeal or not, then the education authority must intimate to the parent or young person the reasons for exclusion, the grounds for re-admission, the right to refer the decision to an education appeal committee and any other information that the authority considers appropriate.[297] In the event of an appeal, the education appeal committee can either confirm or annul the decision to exclude, and moreover it may amend any conditions to be attached to re-admission. The decision of the appeal committee may be appealed by the parent or pupil to the sheriff.[298] The sheriff may confirm or annul the decision of the education authority.[299]

A child with additional support needs may be excluded,[300] but the education authority is still under a duty to provide alternative schooling for the child.

Human rights issues have not been raised in Scotland but have been considered by the House of Lords in an English appeal.[301]

ACCESS TO EDUCATIONAL RECORDS

5.31 Education authorities maintain and preserve individual educational records for all pupils, and pupils or their parents are entitled to access their educational records.[302] Educational records include any records of information that:

- are processed by or on behalf of the responsible body;
- relate to any person who is or has been a pupil at the school;
- relate to the school education of that person; and
- originated from or were supplied by a teacher, other employee of the responsible body, the pupil or parent of the pupil.[303]

Such records have to be kept for a period of five years after the pupil leaves school.[304] The responsible body has to make the records available within 15 school days[305] unless circum-

[296] See generally, the Schools General (Scotland) Regulations 1975 reg.4A, inserted by the Schools General (Scotland) Amendment (No.2) Regulations 1982 reg.4.
[297] 1980 Act s.28H.
[298] 1980 Act s.28H(6).
[299] 1980 Act s.28H(7).
[300] *F v Glasgow City Council*, 2004 S.L.T. (Sh Ct) 123.
[301] *A v Headteacher and Governors of Lord Grey School* [2006] UKHL 14.
[302] Pupils' Educational Records (Scotland) Regulations 2003 (SI 2003/581).
[303] Pupils' Educational Records (Scotland) Regulations 2003 reg.3.
[304] Pupils' Educational Records (Scotland) Regulations 2003 reg.4.
[305] Pupils' Educational Records (Scotland) Regulations 2003 reg.5

stances apply that disallow the disclosure.[306] The disclosure may be made in an alternative language if appropriate[307] and fees may be charged.[308] If the educational records are inaccurate the parents may request them to be rectified.[309]

Additionally pupils and their parents also have a right of disclosure of all records held by the education authorities under the Data Protection Act 1998. The Data Protection Act 1998 gives protection to pupils by prohibiting unauthorised processing of personal data.

The confidentiality of school records may in some limited circumstances be overridden by the courts. In the case *McLeod v British Railways Board*,[310] which was an action for damages resulting from the pupil falling on a power cable, a substantial change in the pupil's character resulting in behavioural problems and truancy was alleged. The court therefore allowed the school records to be disclosed to establish whether the behavioural problems and truancy predated the accident.

INJURY TO PUPILS WHILE AT SCHOOL

5.32 At common law, an education authority has a legal duty of care towards pupils in its charge. Therefore the authority can be sued for damages where a pupil suffers injury as a result of the failure to provide reasonable care for the safety of the pupil. By contrast, in the private independent school sector it is ultimately the school governors who are responsible, and many take out liability insurance.

The common law duty of care extends to pupils in the playground,[311] within the school building,[312] on school trips and possibly on school buses.[313] If an authority has failed to satisfy the duties placed upon it, the injured person would be entitled to damages for the authority's negligence. The duty of care requires the taking of reasonable measures to prevent foreseeable injury, so not every accident will mean that there has been a breach of the duty of care. For example, in the case *Taylor v Fife RC*[314] a sixth year schoolgirl was unsuccessful in claiming damages from the authority in respect of an acid burn received in school while working on her biology project, because in the circumstances the court was satisfied that the teacher had provided adequate supervision. A teacher has a duty of care to her pupils and traditionally the standard of care of a teacher was considered to be that of a "reasonable parent".[315] However it is now seen as unrealistic that this standard of care should be applied in every case regardless of circumstances.[316]

5.33 The general common law duty of care has been supplemented by specific statutory duties under the Occupiers' Liability (Scotland) Act 1960 and the Health and Safety at Work etc. Act 1974. In addition, there are regulations that impose specific duties with which the authority must comply.[317]

The Occupiers' Liability (Scotland) Act 1960 creates a duty to persons who are lawfully on the premises.[318] The importance of this Act is that the reasonableness of the care taken will be assessed by reference to the person injured, and in particular their right to be in the place where the injury took place. In schools, especially primary schools, the legal duty to take reasonable

---

[306] Pupils' Educational Records (Scotland) Regulations 2003 reg.6.

[307] Pupils' Educational Records (Scotland) Regulations 2003 reg.8.

[308] Pupils' Educational Records (Scotland) Regulations 2003 reg.9.

[309] Pupils' Educational Records (Scotland) Regulations 2003 reg.10.

[310] 1997 S.L.T. 434.

[311] *McPherson v Perth and Kinross Council* Unreported January 26, 2001 CSOH available at *http://www.scotscourts.gov.uk* [Accessed July 2, 2008].

[312] *Ahmed v Glasgow City Council*, 2000 S.L.T. (Sh Ct) 153.

[313] *Hunter v Perth and Kinross Council*, 2001 S.C.L.R. 856.

[314] 1991 S.L.T. 80.

[315] *Gow v Glasgow Education Authority*, 1922 S.C. 260.

[316] *Ahmed v Glasgow City Council*, 2000 S.L.T. (Sh Ct) 153.

[317] Schools (Safety and Supervision of Pupils) (Scotland) Regulations 1990 (SI 1990/295).

[318] Occupiers' Liability (Scotland) Act 1960 s.2.

care for the safety of the pupils will be rather higher, and certainly a warning notice or similar is less likely to excuse the school from liability.

The duty applies to any failure by the authority to ensure that the premises are safe, both inside and out, so where playground equipment is fitted, the authority is under a duty to ensure that the equipment is safe, otherwise they will have failed in their duty. In the unreported English case *J (A Minor) v Staffordshire CC*,[319] which involved a 13-year-old pupil pushing open a glass door in the corridor, missing the push plate and putting her hand through a pane of glass, the authority was found to be in breach of its duty under the equivalent English legislation[320] for failing to comply with the British Standards Institute Code of Practice regarding glass thickness and glass toughening.

The duty on the authority requires that it ensure the ongoing safety of pupils in response to events such as bad weather. The court in such circumstances will be considering the adequacy of the system used to combat the danger. In another English case *Murphy v Bradford MDC*[321] the court found the authority liable for injuries to a teacher who slipped on an icy path at 8.30am. The path had been cleared and salted at 6.30am; however, in view of the steepness of the path, and the fact that a handrail was installed after the incident, the authority was found to be in breach of its duty.

Where children have entered school premises out of hours then the duty owed to them will be lessened. In the case *Devlin v Strathclyde RC*[322] the parents of a 14-year-old boy who died when, on a Saturday, he fell through a skylight on the roof of his former primary school while playing tig, were unsuccessful in claiming damages. The court decided that in all the circumstances the actions of the boy were outwith the reasonable foresight of the authority.

5.34 The Health and Safety at Work etc. Act 1974 places employers under a duty to ensure the health and safety of employees and others, which means that for education purposes the local education authority (or the Board of Management in respect of fee paying schools) owes this duty to teachers.[323] Teachers have a duty to take reasonable care for their own safety and for that of others likely to be affected by their actions. There are very few prosecutions under the Health and Safety at Work etc. Act involving schools, and indeed there are no special provisions in the Act exclusively aimed at schools. Guidance for schools is supplemented by training and information from the Scottish Executive. In addition, minimum standards for premises have been set down by the Workplace (Health, Safety and Welfare) Regulations 1992, which apply to schools.[324] Fire safety is normally shared between the education authority and the head teacher of each school. The school has to comply with the health and safety legislation.[325]

The Scottish Executive may make regulations prescribing standards to premises and equipment of educational establishments.[326] Pupil safety is also covered by the Schools (Safety and Supervision of Pupils) (Scotland) Regulations 1990,[327] which provide that every education authority will take reasonable care for pupils under its charge, and in particular as regards playground supervision they require that in every primary school with 50 or more pupils, and in every special school, there must be at least one adult in the playground at break time. If an education authority fails to provide the minimum level of supervision then it will be liable in damages for any injury to pupils.

Just as the education authority has a duty to take reasonable care for the health and safety of pupils while at school, it also has a duty of care where the pupils are taken on school transport

---

[319] Unreported August 1, 1997 CC (Stafford).

[320] Occupiers' Liability Act 1957.

[321] [1992] P.I.Q.R. 68.

[322] 1993 S.L.T. 699.

[323] For a general discussion of this Act, see Craig and Miller, *Law of Health and Safety* (1995), Ch.5.

[324] SI 1992/3004. See Craig and Miller, *Law of Health and Safety* (1995), para.4.67.

[325] Fire Precautions (Workplace) Regulations 1997 (SI 1997/1840) as amended; Management of Health and Safety at Work Regulations 1999 (SI 1999/3242).

[326] 1980 Act s.19(1).

[327] SI 1990/295.

and also on school trips. In relation to pupils attending activity centres, by virtue of the Activity Centres (Young Persons' Safety) Act 1995, any centre providing adventure facilities and instruction for persons under 18 years of age must be licensed; failure to have a licence will result in criminal prosecution.

Bullying

5.35 Bullying has seen increased attention over the past few years and can indeed result in the child suffering psychiatric or psychological harm. There are few reported cases on bullying, although numerous claims have been submitted to education authorities in recent years.[328] In *Scott v Lothian RC* a young woman raised an action of damages against Lothian Regional Council for bullying she sustained while a pupil at one of its schools. She was unsuccessful in her action as she failed to prove the actions and decisions of the relevant guidance teachers were such that no guidance teacher of ordinary skill would have taken in the circumstances if acting with ordinary care.[329] The education authority may be liable for bullying outwith the school premises[330] but as yet no court has awarded damages for any bullying claim.

All schools have been issued with anti-bullying packs[331] and schools have a duty to deal with any reported bullying otherwise they may be in breach of the duty of care to the child. The Scottish Executive set up the Anti-Bullying Network as an initiative to eliminate bullying. Identifying and reporting the bullies is seen as the first step to eliminating the bullying.[332]

PARENTAL INVOLVEMENT

5.36 The Scottish Schools (Parental Involvement) Act 2006 came fully into force on August 1, 2007.[333] The Act abolishes school boards and replaces them with school councils. It is the duty of the Scottish Ministers[334] and the education authority[335] to promote the involvement of the parents of pupils in attendance at public schools. Each education authority has to prepare a "strategy for parental involvement", which includes their policy for implementing their duties under the Act.[336]

All parents of each school are automatically part of and known as the "parent forum"[337] and they can be represented by the "parent council".[338] The purpose of the parent forum is to encourage parents become more involved with the school and to express their views and wishes. The function of the parent council is to support the work of the school, encourage links between the school and the community and represent the views of the parents. It is an opportunity for all parents to be involved in their child's school.

The parent council has to be set up according to the Act[339] and its functions are as detailed in

---

[328] Jane Shields, "Bullying at School: A New Playground for Lawyers", 2003 SCOLAG 61.

[329] *Scott v Lothian RC*, 1999 Rep. L.R. 15. See further Andrew J. Bowen, "Teachers as Professionals: Hunter v Hanley Rides Again", 1999 S.L.T. 11.

[330] See the English case of *Bradford-Smart v West Sussex CC* [2002]1 F.C.R. 425, where a school pupil was unsuccessful in her action against the local authority for damages for bullying on the bus to and from school.

[331] SCRE, "Action Against Bullying" (1991) and SCRE, "Supporting Schools Against Bullying: The Second Anti-Bullying Pack"(1993).

[332] Lesley-Anne Barnes, "Fighting the Bullies", 2006 L.S.J.S. 2006. See also *Montgomery v Cumming* Unreported December 17, 1998 HCJ available at *http://www.scotscourts.gov.uk*, where unreported bullying could not be used as a reasonable excuse for failing to attend school.

[333] Scottish Schools (Parental Involvement) Act 2006 (Commencement No.1) Order 2006 (SSI 2006/454); Scottish Schools (Parental Involvement)Act 2006 (Commencement No.2) Order 2007 (SSI 2007/31).

[334] Scottish Schools (Parental Involvement) Act 2006 s.1(1).

[335] Scottish Schools (Parental Involvement) Act 2006 s.1(2).

[336] Scottish Schools (Parental Involvement) Act 2006 s.2.

[337] Scottish Schools (Parental Involvement) Act 2006 s.5(1).

[338] Scottish Schools (Parental Involvement) Act 2006 s.5(2).

[339] Scottish Schools (Parental Involvement) Act 2006 ss.6 and 7.

s.8. The council will hold meetings as arranged and the head teacher has the right and duty to attend any meeting of the council.[340] All meetings of the parent council are open to the public[341] and the education authority needs to support and advise the parent councils.[342] The head teacher must report to the parent council evaluating the performance of the school and stating what the head teacher's objectives and ambitions are.[343] An appointment of the head teacher or deputy must involve the parent council[344] and an education authority has to establish a complaints procedure for matters under the Act.[345] Two or more schools may decide to have a combined council.[346]

School closure

5.37 One of the principal questions that arises at the time of school closure is to what extent parents and indeed pupils have any rights to determine the range of educational facilities to be made available.

Even with the support of the majority of the parents, a parent may not be able to prevent the authority from closing a school. The leading Scottish case on this point is that of *Harvey v Strathclyde RC*.[347] The proposed closure of Stanley Green High School in Paisley along with John Neilson and Paisley Grammar sparked a great deal of public debate on school closure, resulting in the Education (Publication and Consultation etc.) (Scotland) Amendment Regulations 1988,[348] which prevented the closure of Paisley Grammar but not Stanley Green. Despite the strong parental campaign, the court action by the parents was unsuccessful, parental wishes being only one of the relevant factors to which the authority had to have regard.

Undeniably one of the most sensitive aspects of school closure is the closure of denominational schools, especially in rural communities. The sensitivity of such proposals is emphasised by the protection afforded to denominational schools by ss.22A–22D of the Education (Scotland) Act 1980,[349] which effectively require the Secretary of State's approval where the proposed school closure would result in the discontinuation of denominational education for the pupils of the school. The requirement to obtain approval was unsuccessfully challenged in *Scottish Hierarchy of the Roman Catholic Church v Highland Regional Council*.[350]

Before an authority may close a school, regardless of denomination, consultation is required.[351] In terms of the legislation the authority must consult with those who "would be affected by that implementation or by an implementation of any part of the proposal and such a reference shall include a school to which pupils may be transferred".[352] At first sight the duty appears to be capable of very wide interpretation. However in *Regan v Dundee City Council*[353] the court was reluctant to apply this duty too widely. As part of the consultation the neighbouring four non-denominational schools had been consulted but not the parents of those attending S.S. Peter and Paul Primary School, a denominational school with an overlapping catchment area. The court decided that the duty to consult was confined to those schools to

[340] Scottish Schools (Parental Involvement) Act 2006 s.9(1).
[341] Scottish Schools (Parental Involvement) Act 2006 s.9(2).
[342] Scottish Schools (Parental Involvement) Act 2006 ss.11 and 12.
[343] Scottish Schools (Parental Involvement) Act 2006 s.13.
[344] Scottish Schools (Parental Involvement) Act 2006 s.14(2).
[345] Scottish Schools (Parental Involvement) Act 2006 s.15.
[346] Scottish Schools (Parental Involvement) Act 2006 s.16.
[347] 1989 S.L.T. 25.
[348] SI 1988/107.
[349] Inserted into the Education (Scotland) Act 1980 by the Education (Scotland) Act 1981 Sch.9.
[350] 1987 S.L.T. 708.
[351] 1980 Act s.22, being supplemented by the Education (Publication and Consultation etc.) (Scotland) Regulations 1981 (SI 1981/1558) as amended.
[352] Education (Publication and Consultation etc.) (Scotland) Regulations 1981 reg.2(3).
[353] 1997 S.L.T. 139.

which the authority proposed to relocate the pupils, not those schools to which placing requests would be made as a result of the proposed closure.

The consultation process should be as full as possible with all those consulted feeling they have been listened to.[354]

Parents challenging closures cannot rely automatically on receiving the remedy sought against a closure decision solely because a procedural irregularity has been proved. The court reserves the right to consider the practical effect of granting the reduction. In *King v East Ayrshire Council*,[355] although the petitioner, an aggrieved parent, successfully proved that the authority had erred by not having regard to historic attendance figures in calculating whether the school it proposed closing exceeded a pupil capacity of 80 per cent (hence being a proposal requiring the approval of the Secretary of State), the court nonetheless refused to reduce the authority's decision because it was not satisfied that in any event the proposal would have had to go to the Secretary of State for approval.

WORK EXPERIENCE AND THE EMPLOYMENT OF SCHOOLCHILDREN

5.38 It is now a generally accepted part of secondary education that schoolchildren will participate in some work experience as part of their education. Pupils undergoing compulsory education may undergo work experience in their last year at school.[356] Where work placements are arranged by the school the normal statutory prohibitions regarding the employment of children in particular types of employment will not apply. However, pupils cannot be employed in any type of employment for which the employment of young persons is prohibited. Note that for the purpose of any enactment relating to the employment of children, child means a person under school-leaving age.[357]

As for the employment of schoolchildren in general, no child may be employed if they are under 14 years of age.[358] Children over 13 may only be employed for light work, if authorised by local authority byelaws.[359] In addition, the employment of a child is now prohibited unless it is for either light work or work for the purposes of performance in cultural, artistic, sports or advertising activities.[360] Light work is defined as being work which is unlikely to be harmful to either the health, safety or development of the child or the child's attendance at school. Employers are now under a duty to carry out a risk assessment of work being undertaken by young persons, and to inform the parent of the child of the potential risks to the child and the protective/preventive measures being taken.[361] Currently the child cannot be employed before 7am or after 7pm[362] and, moreover, a child can only be employed for a maximum of two hours on any school-day or Sunday. In addition, on a school-day, the child cannot be employed during school hours. As well as these general statutory restrictions, the local authority may pass byelaws relating to the general employment of schoolchildren in their area. After June 22, 2000 the working time of a child at school will be restricted to a maximum of two hours on a school-day and 12 hours per week for work performed outside hours fixed for school attendance.[363] Where the child is to be employed in performances the child will in many situation require a

[354] Scottish Executive, "School Closure Guidance". *http://www.scotland.gov.uk* [Accessed July 2, 2008]. See also *Buchan v West Lothian Council*, 2001 S.L.T. 1452.
[355] 1998 S.C. 182.
[356] 1980 Act s.123.
[357] 1980 Act s.125.
[358] Children and Young Persons (Scotland) Act 1937 s.28(1)(a).
[359] Children (Protection at Work) Regulations 1998 (SI 1998/276).
[360] Council Directive 94/33/EC on the protection of young people at work art.3.
[361] Health and Safety (Young Persons) Regulations 1997 (SI 1997/135) reg.5.
[362] Children and Young Persons (Scotland) Act 1937 s.28(1)(c), (e).
[363] Council Directive 94/33/EC on the protection of young people at work art.8(1)(b).

licence from the authority, and naturally the authority will refuse the licence if it is of the opinion that the child's education would suffer.[364]

5.39 There is now an increased recognition of the rights of parents in education of their child within the general legal framework applying to education. Nonetheless it is the education authority that retains the main control over educational decisions such as school closure or placing requests.

The link between education and other needs cannot be ignored. Especially in the area of additional support for learning there is expected to be co-operation between all the different professionals involved—medical, education and social work. Certainly, the development of the role of guidance teachers at schools as well as the new community schools signals an increasing acceptance of the need to bring social work and education into a closer relationship.

[364] Children and Young Persons Act 1963 s.37.

Chapter 6

Vulnerable Adults and the Law

Historical Overview of Scots Law Relating to Vulnerable Adults

6.01 Scots law provides for intervention in a whole range of ways in the lives of those who are mentally incapacitated or otherwise vulnerable members of society. The issues with which this Chapter is concerned include the compulsory detention of mentally disordered individuals in hospital, medical treatment of mentally disordered persons, protection of the property rights of mentally disordered patients and other vulnerable adults, guardianship and intervention orders, the role of the Mental Welfare Commission and Office of the Public Guardian, mental health, incapacity and criminal justice, and the role of the state in safeguarding the interests of vulnerable persons and society as a whole. It does not cover care in the community dimensions of mental health care, which are addressed in Ch.7. There are many mentally disordered and other vulnerable persons who with support and assistance from their families and agencies live relatively normal lives in the community. As for many able citizens, the law will play an unintrusive role in their lives. There are, however, many others for whom the law that follows will be of considerable importance whether they are liable to be compulsorily detained in hospital, an offender with a mental disability, or incapable of managing their own welfare or financial affairs.

One of the first pieces of civil legislation put in place to deal with people with a mental disorder was the Lunacy (Scotland) Act 1857. Of particular difficulty was the inability to distinguish between different types of need and intervention for any given individual—intervention always proceeded on an "all or nothing" basis. Prior to the Adults with Incapacity (Scotland) Act 2000, the law relating to those with incapacity was complex and subject to historical inconsistencies, as reported in the Scottish Law Commission report on incapable adults.[1]

In 1997 the Scottish Law Commission published a further report on vulnerable adults.[2] This report provided the basis for both the Mental Health (Care and Treatment) (Scotland) Act 2003 and the recent Adult Support and Protection (Scotland) Act 2007. Reform in England and Wales has been considerably slower than that in post-devolution Scotland, although for many years the absence of a fundamental overhaul has been a matter of some concern.[3]

The law relating to mental health is governed principally by the Mental Health (Care and Treatment) (Scotland) Act 2003 ("2003 Act") although for a complete picture of how the law

---

[1] Report No.151 (1995).

[2] Report No.158 (1997).

[3] See A. Ward, "A Review of Mental Health Law—At Last" (1999) 44(2) J.L.S.S. 20.

treats mentally disordered people in society one must travel beyond that Act to other areas of law such as criminal justice. The 2003 Act came into effect on a phased basis between October 2004 and May 2006.

6.02 The Adults with Incapacity (Scotland) Act 2000 ("2000 Act") provides a mechanism for in loco decision making in respect of adults who are incapable, through illness or other disability, to safeguard themselves or their property and financial interests. Although there is a steady growth in early intervention through the use of continuing powers of attorney (particularly given modern transient lifestyles), a large number of adults are brought to the attention of local authorities every year requiring some form of intervention. The 2000 Act was one of the first major pieces of legislation passed by the Scottish Parliament and came into effect on a phased basis between April 2001 and August 2004.

The Adult Support and Protection (Scotland) Act 2007, while not yet fully in force,[4] aims to provide protection and services to those vulnerable members of society who do not fall within the remit of either the 2000 or 2003 Acts, but require a level of intervention to ensure their safety within the community. Limited liability for breach of duty of care is afforded solely to those persons who act in good faith in accordance with the principles of any of these Acts. Together, the Adults with Incapacity (Scotland) Act 2000, the Mental Health (Care and Treatment) (Scotland) Act 2003 and the Adult Support and Protection (Scotland) Act 2007 provide the trinity of statutes created to protect the rights and affairs of all vulnerable adults in Scotland.

All three Acts share an underlying philosophy, namely that any intervention must:

- be in the best interests of the adult;
- be the least restrictive course of action;
- take into account the wishes and feelings of the adult past and present (and, if reasonably practicable, those of the nearest relatives, named person and/or primary carer);
- endeavour to maximise the adult's remaining skills and abilities.[5]

There are a number of regulations, statutory instruments and codes of practice associated with the 2000, 2003 and 2007 Acts, all of which can be found on the Scottish Executive website.[6]

THE MENTAL HEALTH (CARE AND TREATMENT) (SCOTLAND) ACT 2003

6.03 The Mental Health (Care and Treatment) (Scotland) Act 2003 received Royal Assent in April 2003 and provided a long-overdue replacement for the Mental Health (Scotland) Act 1984 ("1984 Act"). It was described[7] during the debate on stage 3 of the Bill as being:

> "a landmark Bill that places patients and their welfare at its heart ... a Bill that revolutionises mental health law in Scotland, that puts the patient at the centre of treatment and care decisions, and ensures that their well-being is, and will be, paramount."

The Act itself at 333 sections long is lengthy in comparison with its 1984 predecessor.

The 2003 Act provides a statutory basis for support, access to services and ultimately, measures of compulsion in mental health care. It also allows for the establishment of a Mental Health Tribunal for Scotland and outlines the roles and duties of the Mental Welfare Commission, local authorities and health boards (among other parties), including those who fall under the remit of the Act through the criminal justice system.

---

[4] All sections of the 2007 Act relating to amendments to the Adults with Incapacity (Scotland) Act 2000 will be in force by April 1, 2008. An implementation date has yet to be announced for several other sections of the 2007 Act.

[5] Adults with Incapacity (Scotland) Act 2000 ("2000 Act") s.1.

[6] *http://www.scotland.gov.uk* [Accessed July 1, 2008].

[7] Malcolm Chisholm, Minister for Health, Official Report, March 20, 2003, cols.19807 and 19809.

The Millan Committee

6.04 The radical reform of mental health law followed that of incapacity law, and was reflective of a growing trend towards community-based care. In 1999, the Millan Committee[8] was established to consider the current state of mental health law in Scotland and requirement to change. A report was published in 2001[9] with a number of recommendations later incorporated in the 2003 Act. One of the most significant proposals was the transfer of determination of rights under the new legislation from sheriff courts to a new Mental Health Tribunal acting in a judicial capacity. Legal representation and advocacy services in the new setting were to be positively encouraged.

The definition of "mental disorder" in particular was reworked to avoid the archaic distinctions contained within the 1984 Act, most importantly to include those with personality disorder. Compulsion in care and treatment was to be a matter solely at the discretion of the Tribunal. Treatment provided, whether under compulsion or on a voluntary basis, was to be the least restrictive or invasive necessary to achieve the desired end. Significantly, no changes were made to the periods of emergency detention (72 hours) or short-term detention (28 days) enshrined in the 1984 Act. Rights in respect of representation of an individual are now exercisable by a "named person" rather than "nearest relative" and consequently, less weight is given to ties of consanguinity which had on occasion previously resulted in abuse of patients.

6.05 The ethical principles underlying the 2003 Act were developed by the Millan Committee and reflect and extend those of both the Adults with Incapacity (Scotland) Act 2000 and emerging human rights jurisprudence. In particular, Millan recognised that persons may receive treatment on an *ex facie* informal or voluntary basis while under the threat of compulsion and the new legislation required to provide adequate protection in such circumstances.

The principles include:

- Non-discrimination. Patients should not be treated less favourably than a non-patient, unless on cause shown.
- Equality. Equal opportunity legislation should be considered.
- Respect for diversity. Care and treatment should be provided without regard to the patient's age, sex, sexual orientation, religious persuasion, racial origin, cultural or linguistic background.
- Reciprocity. Compulsory care should provide access to all facilities reasonably available and provision of services while a patient is being treated should be complemented by continuing care post-treatment.
- Informal care. Informal care should be used wherever possible.
- Participation. Patients should be encouraged to participate fully in the care process, with support from advocacy workers or solicitors as required. Past and present wishes of the patient should be taken into consideration unless it is unreasonable or impracticable to do so.
- Respect for carers. The views, needs and circumstances of a patient's named person or other carer, guardian or welfare attorney should be taken into account, except in limited circumstances.
- Least restrictive alternative. Treatment should involve the minimum restriction on the freedom of the patient necessary to achieve the desired end.
- Benefit. Intervention under the 2003 Act must always provide maximum benefit to the patient.
- Child welfare. The welfare of any mentally disordered person under 18 is paramount.[10]

---

[8] Chaired by the Rt Hon Bruce Millan, a former Secretary of State for Scotland.

[9] Scottish Executive, *New Directions*, Report on the Review of the Mental Health (Scotland) Act 1984 (Scottish Executive, 2001).

[10] Millan Report, 3.3.

Mental disorder and other key definitions

6.06 Central to any understanding of the application of the 2003 (and other) Acts is a working knowledge of some of the key definitions of the Acts. Mental disorder[11] is defined as any mental illness, personality disorder or learning disability however caused or manifested. This does not include persons who are sexually deviant, transsexual, transvestite, dependent on substances such as drugs or alcohol,[12] displaying antisocial behavioural tendencies or acting imprudently (although it should be noted that one judge has said that sexual deviancy is only to be discounted when unaccompanied by mental disorder).[13] Defining the person's status impacts upon the reception, care and treatment of persons who suffer, or appear to suffer, from mental disorder, and to the management of their property and affairs.

A carer[14] is a person who regularly provides care and support to a patient on a non-professional or remunerated basis.

A welfare attorney[15] is an individual named and authorised by another *capax*[16] individual to act on their behalf by virtue of a power of attorney granted under the 2000 Act. This may usefully be contrasted with a welfare guardian[17] who is appointed by the court to act on behalf of an *incapax* adult where no power of attorney exists and where the adult is unable to consent to such power of attorney being granted by reason of mental deficiency.

An approved medical practitioner[18] ("AMP") is a doctor with particular experience and training in the diagnosis and treatment of mental disorder. Only AMPs may utilise particular powers under the 2003 Act. Every health board in Scotland is obligated to compile and maintain a list of AMPs. The responsible medical officer[19] ("RMO") is the AMP designated by hospital managers to have particular responsibility for a named patient or patients.

A mental health officer[20] ("MHO") is a local authority officer, usually a social worker with particular training and experience in respect of people with a mental disorder. The MHO, while employed by the local authority, is expected to act as an independent professional. Previously, appointment as an MHO was for the duration of the practitioner's working life, but it is now time limited with reappointment being dependent on evidence of continuing professional competence.[21]

The Mental Welfare Commission for Scotland

6.07 Under the 1984 Act, the Commission had a general duty to exercise protective functions in respect of persons who may, by reason of mental disorder, be incapable of adequately protecting their person or their interests. The 2003 Act allows for the continuing existence of the Mental Welfare Commission following the repeal of the Mental Health (Scotland) Act 1984. Directions on the composition and proceedings of the Commission are laid out in Sch.1 to the 2003 Act. The role of the Commission is primarily to oversee the discharge of functions by local authorities, health bodies and other bodies (in respect of the 2000 and 2003 Acts[22]) in accordance with best practice, and to provide advice to any party who seeks it. It is further responsible for

---

[11] Mental Health (Care and Treatment) (Scotland) Act 2003 ("2003 Act") s.328.

[12] See e.g. *Carver v Fraser*, 1997 S.C.C.R. 653.

[13] *W v Secretary of State for Scotland*, 1998 S.L.T. 841.

[14] 2003 Act s.329.

[15] 2000 Act ss.16 and 19.

[16] A *capax* individual is a person with full cognitive capacity.

[17] 2000 Act s.64(1)(a) or (b).

[18] 2003 Act s.22.

[19] 2003 Act s.230.

[20] 2003 Act s.32. A detailed direction from the Secretary of State for Scotland on the precise qualifications expected of mental health officers (SWAG Circular 5/88) was superseded in March 2005, when the National Standards for Mental Health Officers were published.

[21] See generally, commentary by Franks and Cobb, *Mental Health (Care and Treatment) (Scotland) Act 2003* (Greens Annotated Acts).

[22] 2003 Act s.4 et seq.

visiting patients and inspecting premises where patients receive medical treatment or are otherwise resident. The Commission may investigate concerns relating to the care and treatment of those suffering from mental disorder[23] and ultimately revoke compulsory measures of treatment or refer the case to the Mental Health Tribunal for further consideration.[24] The Commission publishes an annual report, which is available for public inspection.

The Mental Health Tribunal for Scotland

6.08 The tribunal system has been in existence in England and Wales for some time, but was first introduced to Scotland under the 2003 Act.[25] The Tribunal aims to consider long-term detention and controlled community residence in a non-adversarial setting.[26] Under the 1984 Act, few patients attended court for detention proceedings and even fewer gave evidence, with the consequent effect on the patient's civil liberties. Concerns were raised in various quarters that this was due to the formal and intimidating nature of the court process. There was no right of appeal against the sheriff's decision, contrary to emerging human rights jurisprudence. Despite the well-intentioned reforms, in practice tribunal hearings remain protracted, non-conciliatory and legalistic and it is a matter for the Tribunal Chair to discourage this and proceed as envisaged by the reformers. A key improvement is the right of appeal to the sheriff principal and Court of Session,[27] with the exception of a limited number of cases. The composition, organisation and internal procedures of the Tribunal are set out in some detail in Sch.2 to the Act and associated regulations. Tribunals also play an important role in unlawful detention of voluntary patients.

Health board and local authority functions

6.09 Functions specific to these bodies are outlined in some detail in Pt 4 of the 2003 Act. Particular attention is given to the needs of children and young persons to have specialist facilities, distinct from adult psychiatric wards, and strengthened by the principle set out in s.2(4) which requires a function under the Act to be discharged in the manner which "best secures the welfare of the child".[28] Services and accommodation must also be provided for mothers and children of less than one year old, to allow for continuity of maternal care, where the mother has been admitted suffering from post-natal depression.[29] This service will not be provided where clinical judgment suggests that the mother is likely to endanger the health or welfare of the child.

Obligations are also placed on the local authority for the provision of care and support services for those with historical or subsisting mental health disorders living in the community.[30] The authority is under a duty to minimise the impact of the disorder on day-to-day living and promote well-being and social development. This may include social, cultural and recreational activities and assistance to find and sustain employment.[31] The local authority may also provide these services for persons detained in hospital. There is no indication within the 2003 Act as to how long the services should be provided for, which may lead to inconsistencies between local

[23] 2003 Act ss.11–16.
[24] 2003 Act, e.g. s.81, s.98.
[25] 2003 Act Pt 3.
[26] As a result of the Millan Report, see para 6.05 above.
[27] 2003 Act ss.320–322.
[28] 2003 Act s.23. Franks and Cobb note that in 2002, The Royal College of Psychiatrists suggested that the admission of any person under 16 to an adult ward should be treated as an "untoward critical incident and be considered a sign of inadequate resources". In March 2005, the Mental Welfare Commission issued "Guidance on the Admission of Young People to Adult Health Wards".
[29] 2003 Act s.24.
[30] 2003 Act ss.25–27. The local authority may alternatively arrange for them to be provided by the health board or other care provider under ss.30 and 31 of the 2003 Act.
[31] 2003 Act s.26.

authorities.[32] Local authorities may charge for services provided under ss.25–27 of the 2003 Act where the individual is of sufficient means to pay.[33]

Duties of local authorities

6.10 The local authority has a pivotal role in mental health services with several important duties placed upon it.

All local authorities in Scotland are under a duty to inquire[34] where a person over 16[35] with a mental disorder resides in the community in their area if the following circumstances exist:

- The person has, at any time, been ill-treated, neglected or suffered deficient care and treatment.
- The person has, at any time suffered or been at risk of suffering loss or damage to their property as the result of a mental disorder.
- The person is living alone or without sufficient care and is unable to look after his property or financial affairs.
- The person is a risk to others as a result of a mental disorder.

The local authority may call upon other statutory bodies to assist with these inquiries.[36] It is the responsibility of the MHO to assess the individual and his residence, consult with relevant professionals and ensure the establishment of, or continued protection and promotion of welfare. Further action may be required under the 2000 Act, 2003 Act or the Social Work (Scotland) Act 1968.[37] From time to time, an individual may thwart attempts to assess and assist, and in such circumstances, the MHO is obliged to seek a warrant to enable them to fulfil their duty.[38] This may be done by application to the local sheriff court or justice of the peace. The warrant may allow a named person to gain access to premises by force, permit detention of a named individual for up to three hours to allow a medical examination to be undertaken or allow a medical practitioner to obtain access to medical records where such consent is withheld. It may also cover any combination of these within the one application. Every application for a warrant must be justified on oath and a detailed history of events indicating a need to obtain the warrant must be provided. It would appear that only MHOs are entitled to apply for a warrant under the section. Unusually, and in contrast to the 2000 Act, there are no provisions under the 2003 Act for intimation to any party, including the individual affected by the warrant. If the warrant is refused, there is no right of appeal against the decision. There would appear to be nothing however to prevent a further application being made if additional information becomes available.

The local authority is also under a duty to carry out an assessment of needs relative to individuals identified by MHOs, their named person or primary carer.[39]

---

[32] See e.g. *Clunis v Camden and Islington HA* [1998] Q.B. 978, where the English courts decided that an individual did not have the right to enforce a duty to provide aftercare under s.117 of the Mental Health Act 1983.

[33] The 2003 Act s.28 makes consequential amendments to s.87 of the Social Work (Scotland) Act 1968 and ss.2 and 22(1) of the Community Care and Health (Scotland) Act 2002 to allow for such a charge to be levied.

[34] 2003 Act s.33. Section 33(1) uses the words "where it appears" indicating that the duty is incumbent upon the local authority in all situations where there are concerns or suspicions without certainty. Initial referrals may come from a variety of sources, and it is for each authority to develop its own protocol to assist in the inquiry process.

[35] Where a person is under 16 years of age the provisions of the Children (Scotland) Act 1995 will apply.

[36] 2003 Act s.34.

[37] Social Work (Scotland) Act 1968 s.12.

[38] 2003 Act s.35.

[39] 2003 Act ss.227 and 228.

Powers of detention and compulsion

Emergency detention

6.11 An emergency detention certificate ("EDC") permits the detention of any patient, including those under 16, for a maximum of 72 hours in order that their mental state may be assessed. This is the same period as authorised by emergency detention under the 1984 Act,[40] although under the 2003 Act, a relative cannot consent to an EDC. This certificate can be granted by any registered medical practitioner ("RMP", in practice often the patient's general practitioner), preferably but not necessarily with the consent of an MHO where this is possible. Before granting the EDC, the RMP must be satisfied that it is necessary as a matter of urgency to detain an individual in hospital for the purposes of determining what medical treatment may be necessary and to protect the health, safety and welfare of the individual concerned or the safety of any other person.[41] An EDC should only be sought where the delay required in seeking a short-term detention certificate would be potentially harmful. There is no right of appeal against an EDC, although perhaps surprisingly this has been found to be in line with the European Convention on Human Rights ("ECHR").[42] An EDC does not confer a general power to administer treatment.[43] Following grant of an EDC, hospital managers are under a duty to examine, review and possibly revoke the certificate where the grounds for detention are not met, as soon as practicable.[44]

The EDC can be used to admit community-based patients to hospital,[45] or to provide for a measure of compulsion in relation to patients who are attending hospital on a voluntary basis prior to deterioration in their mental health, as well as individuals previously unknown to mental health professionals. The authority to detain a patient in hospital under the EDC may be suspended for a particular purpose by the patient's RMO.[46] An EDC cannot be granted where the individual has been subject to certain orders immediately prior to the proposed grant of an EDC.[47]

Short-term detention

6.12 Under the 1984 Act, a patient could only be detained in hospital on short term detention following emergency detention. A short-term detention certificate[48] ("STDC") under the 2003 Act can be granted whether or not the individual is currently subject to compulsory measures, including an EDC.[49] The STDC is the preferred route to detention under the Act, where circumstances permit, and allows for the removal of a patient into hospital[50] within three days of

---

[40] Mental Health (Scotland) Act 1984 ss.24 and 25.

[41] 2003 Act s.36.

[42] *Winterwerp v Netherlands* A/33 (1979–80) 2 E.H.R.R. 387. The lack of appeal process is perhaps only tolerable as a result of the EDC's short-term nature.

[43] Although administration of treatment is permitted in an urgent situation by virtue of s.243 of the 2003 Act.

[44] 2003 Act ss.38 and 39.

[45] Where, for example, a patient subject to a community-based compulsory treatment order requires urgent hospital admission as a result of a sudden and unexpected deterioration in their condition and there is insufficient time to apply to the Tribunal for a variation of the CTO. In these circumstances, any measures authorised under the CTO will cease to have effect, with the exception of directions under s.66(1)(b) of the 2003 Act in relation to medical treatment (authorisation of the giving of medical treatment under Pt 16 of the 2003 Act).

[46] 2003 Act s.41. The suspension of detention was previously known as "leave of absence". Examples of where this may be used include for the purposes of rehabilitation, or for attendance at an event such as a wedding or funeral. There is no provision requiring the RMO to notify anyone of the suspension of detention, although good practice would dictate that at the very least, hospital managers are informed.

[47] 2003 Act ss.36(1), 44(1), 47(1), 68, 114(2) or 115(2).

[48] 2003 Act s.44.

[49] The STDC can be granted in respect of a community-based patient, a patient in hospital on a voluntary basis or as a result of an EDC. If the patient is on an EDC, the STDC can be granted at any time within the 72-hour emergency detention period of the EDC.

[50] Or from one hospital to another, if the patient is in a general hospital at the time of grant of the STDC and requires removal to a specialist psychiatric facility.

the granting of the certificate and thereafter detention for a period of up to 28 days[51] together with necessary medical treatment.[52]

An STDC can only be granted by an approved medical practitioner with the consent of an MHO. The grounds for granting a STDC are similar to those for granting an EDC.[53] The AMP should also have regard to the views of the patient's named person.[54] If, upon interviewing the patient (or for another reason) the MHO refuses to give consent to an STDC, it cannot be granted and it is not acceptable for the doctor to resort to either seeking an EDC or consulting another MHO as an alternative route to detention.[55] Unlike the 1984 Act, a relative cannot consent to an STDC. An STDC cannot be granted where the individual has been subject to certain orders immediately prior to the proposed grant of an STDC.[56] The authority to detain a patient in hospital under the STDC may be suspended for a particular purpose by the patient's RMO, in a similar way to the EDC.[57] It is incumbent upon hospital managers to notify certain persons of the granting of an STDC.[58] A STDC will of course not be necessary in circumstances where the individual consents to admission and treatment. In all cases, the patient should be informed of the availability of independent advocacy services[59] to assist them.

Difficulties may arise where a patient's mental health deteriorates unexpectedly towards the end of the 28-day detention period and in these limited circumstances, an extension certificate ("EC") may be sought by an AMP prior to the expiry of the STDC.[60] The purpose of the EC is to allow an application for a compulsory treatment order to be prepared. An AMP must consult with an MHO where possible, and if the MHO does not give consent to the EC, it cannot be granted. The extension certificate allows for detention for a further period of three working days[61] from the expiry of the STDC, together with necessary medical treatment. An EC can be revoked by the RMO[62] or Commission,[63] and the patient (or their named person) can also apply to the Tribunal for this purpose.[64] It is incumbent upon hospital managers to notify certain persons of the granting of an EC.[65] Where a patient is detained under a STDC, the patient's RMO must keep their condition under review, particularly in relation to whether the grounds for admission subsist[66] or whether it remains necessary for the patient to be treated on a compulsory basis. If the RMO is unsatisfied as to either matter, he is under a duty to revoke the certificate. Both the STDC and the EC can be extended[67] for five working days (beginning with the most recent certificate authorising detention) pending determination of an application for a compulsory treatment order by the Tribunal. During this period the Tribunal may either determine the application, or decide that an interim compulsory treatment order ("ICTO") should be made.

---

[51] 2003 Act s.44(5)(b).
[52] 2003 Act Pt 16.
[53] 2003 Act s.44(4).
[54] 2003 Act s.44(10) and (11).
[55] See Scottish Executive, *Mental Health (Care and Treatment) (Scotland) Act 2003 Code of Practice* ("2003 Act Code of Practice") (2005). The consent of the MHO is intended to act as a safeguard against capricious or whimsical detention by an AMP acting of his or her own volition.
[56] 2003 Act ss.44, 47, 68, 114(2) or 115(2). A patient who remains in hospital in the knowledge that an order for their detention has expired, may not competently object to the granting of a further detention certificate: *R v Lothian Health Board (No.2)*, 1993 S.L.T. 1021.
[57] 2003 Act s.53. See fn.46.
[58] 2003 Act s.46.
[59] 2003 Act s.259. This must be notified to the patient by the MHO, even where it is otherwise impracticable to interview the patient.
[60] The patient must be examined by the AMP and the extension certificate granted within 24 hours of the examination.
[61] Excludes Saturdays, Sundays and Bank Holidays.
[62] 2003 Act s.49.
[63] 2003 Act s.51.
[64] 2003 Act s.50.
[65] 2003 Act s.48.
[66] 2003 Act s.44(4)(a), (b) and (c).
[67] 2003 Act s.68.

Interim compulsory treatment order

6.13 An interim compulsory treatment order may be sought before a Mental Health Tribunal pending determination of a full CTO. The grounds for making an ICTO are similar to those for making an EDC.[68] An ICTO lasts for up to 28 days.[69] The Tribunal must allow for written or oral representations and the production or leading of evidence, similar to a hearing for a CTO. It is also considered good practice to prepare and implement a care plan where time permits. Similar measures to those included within a CTO may be specified by the Tribunal. As with the STDC, the patient's RMO must consider from time to time whether the grounds for admission subsist or whether it remains necessary for the patient to be treated on a compulsory basis. If the RMO is unsatisfied as to either matter, he is under a duty to revoke the certificate.[70] The RMO must inform a number of people when the ICTO is revoked, together with reasons for that decision.[71] An ICTO is automatically revoked on the grant of a CTO.

Compulsory treatment order

6.14 One of the major developments from the Mental Health (Scotland) Act 1984 is the inclusion of a new compulsory treatment order ("CTO"). It is designed to ensure an individualised, multi-agency care and treatment plan for all patients who require to be subject to compulsory measures[72] on a longer term basis, whether in the community or in hospital.

Originally, under the 1984 Act, long-term detention required to take place in a hospital, regardless of the patient's condition or personal circumstances. The earliest attempt at an individualised care plan was the community care order ("CCO"), introduced by the Mental Health (Patients in the Community) Act 1995. These proved unsuccessful, in that effective intervention was difficult where a patient refused to accept treatment. The Millan Committee recommended that these orders be abolished and thereafter with the introduction of the 2003 Act came the birth of the CTO, compatible with both the recommendations of the Millan Committee and the ECHR.

The care plan element of the CTO takes into account the support available from all relevant public sector and voluntary agencies and allows for more effective community-based orders. Compulsory treatment, whether in the hospital or the community, must be ratified by the Tribunal and will be reassessed regularly by it to ensure that detention occurs only in circumstances where there is no viable alternative and that compulsion remains necessary to ensure successful treatment.

An application for a CTO must be made by an MHO,[73] comprising two mental health reports[74] together with a report by the MHO[75] and a proposed care plan.[76] The grounds for

---

[68] 2003 Act s.57.

[69] An ICTO may last for a shorter period of time if, for example, a STDC and EC were granted prior to the ICTO bringing the continuous period of detention to more than 56 days. See the 2003 Act s.65.

[70] The Commission may revoke the ICTO for the same reasons. See the 2003 Act ss.72–73.

[71] Similarly, the Commission must notify relevant persons of revocation of an ICTO, including the patient's RMO. See the 2003 Act s.74.

[72] 2003 Act s.64.

[73] 2003 Act ss.57(1) and 63(1).

[74] 2003 Act s.58. One of the two reports may be carried out by the patient's GP, even where he is not an AMP. There are clear advantages to this, in that the GP is likely to be familiar with the patient and sensitive to any deterioration in his mental health. The reports must be carried out within five days of each other. For further information on mental health reports, see Franks and Cobb, *Mental Health (Care and Treatment) (Scotland) Act 2003* (Greens Annotated Acts), p.78.

[75] 2003 Act s.61. This should take the form of an interview (unless impracticable) followed by a written report from the MHO. The patient should be advised of their rights in relation to the application, including the availability of independent advocacy services.

[76] 2003 Act s.62. The care plan must be prepared in consultation with the authors of the two mental health reports and those likely to be providing the medical treatment, care or other services to the patient. "Medical treatment" is defined at s.329 of the 2003 Act. For further information on care plans, see Franks and Cobb, *Mental Health (Care and Treatment) (Scotland) Act 2003* (Greens Annotated Acts), p.85.

making a CTO are similar to those for making an EDC.[77] It may be made in respect of a patient who is in hospital as a voluntary patient or following on from a STDC. Before making the CTO, the Tribunal will consider the application and hear from a number of relevant parties.[78] It may grant an ICTO pending final determination of the application.[79] Where the CTO is granted, it will be for an initial period of up to six months, echoing the provisions for long-term detention[80] under the 1984 Act. The CTO may specify treatment, care or services to be administered to the patient.[81] Should these measures require to be changed, the RMO must apply to the Tribunal to vary the order.[82]

6.15 The RMO is under a duty to carry out a review of the CTO no earlier than two months before the order expires. This will involve an examination of the patient by the RMO or an AMP, in consultation with the MHO.[83] A CTO will expire after six months if it is not renewed. The RMO is entitled to renew the order (without variation) without recourse to the Tribunal.[84] Renewal is for a period of six months,[85] and thereafter for 12 months at a time. Where the renewal does not require referral to the Tribunal, it must nonetheless be reviewed by the Tribunal every two years. If both extension and variation of the CTO are sought, the matter must be referred back to the Tribunal.[86] The powers of the Tribunal on review are manifold.[87] As with the STDC, the patient's RMO must consider from time to time whether the grounds for admission subsist or whether it remains necessary for the patient to be treated on a compulsory basis. If the RMO is unsatisfied as to either matter, he is under a duty to revoke the certificate.[88] The RMO must inform a number of people when the CTO is revoked, together with reasons for that decision.[89] The Mental Welfare Commission[90] is entitled to refer the CTO to the Tribunal at any time for consideration. A CTO is unnecessary where the patient can be treated informally.

Community-based compulsory treatment order

6.16 Where the order is a community-based ICTO or CTO, it may include measures requiring the patient to attend at a specified place on specified dates for medical treatment. This is known as an "attendance requirement".[91] Should the patient fail to comply, the RMO[92] may have the patient taken into custody and detained for a maximum of six hours, for the purpose of providing medical treatment.[93] During this period a decision may be taken to detain the patient

[77] 2003 Act s.57.

[78] Including the named person, who should have been identified by the MHO at an early stage. See the 2003 Act ss.59, 60 and 64.

[79] 2003 Act s.65.

[80] Mental Health (Scotland) Act 1984 s.18.

[81] 2003 Act ss.64(4)(a)(ii) and 66. For further information on the conduct of the Tribunal, see Franks and Cobb, *Mental Health (Care and Treatment) (Scotland) Act 2003* (Greens Annotated Acts), pp.88–90. On grant of the CTO, the RMO is obliged to provide a care plan, similar to that of the MHO which is included as part of the application. See the 2003 Act s.76.

[82] The patient or their named person may also apply to the Tribunal to have the order varied. See the 2003 Act ss.99–100.

[83] 2003 Act s.77.

[84] 2003 Act ss.83–87.

[85] A further mandatory review must be carried out during this time: 2003 Act s.78.

[86] 2003 Act ss.88–95.

[87] 2003 Act ss.101–109.

[88] The Commission may also revoke the CTO for similar reasons: 2003 Act ss.80 and 81.

[89] Similarly, the Commission must notify relevant persons of revocation of a CTO, including the patient's RMO: 2003 Act s.82.

[90] 2003 Act s.98.

[91] 2003 Act s.66(1)(c).

[92] Together with the consent of the MHO, without which the power cannot be exercised. The patient may be taken to the hospital which they should have gone to under the attendance requirement, or to any other place. The RMO is likely to authorise the MHO or a police constable to remove the patient. Medical treatment can then be administered in terms of ss.66(1)(b), 241(4) and Pt 16 of the 2003 Act.

[93] 2003 Act s.112.

under an EDC, STDC or apply to the Tribunal for a variation of the CTO. Similar provisions apply in respect of non-compliance with any other part of a community-based CTO,[94] albeit in these circumstances the detention period is 72 hours. Where a patient on a CTO absconds, or a patient absconds from hospital while detained on another measure, they can be taken into custody.[95]

Removal order

6.17 A removal order[96] ("RO") may be made where a person over 16 years old has a mental disorder and is at risk of significant harm. The application must be made before a sheriff, following a hearing[97] at which a number of parties may make representations or lead or produce evidence. Where the RO is granted, it allows the MHO and any other person specified in the order (together with a police constable[98]) to enter the premises within 72 hours of the RO being granted. The person who is the subject of the RO may be removed to a place of safety[99] at any time prior to the expiry of the 72-hour period and detained there for the period specified in the RO.[100] This will allow for examination and observation of the patient, together with consideration of any further action that may require to be taken in terms of the 2000 or 2003 Acts. The RO may be recalled or varied.[101] There is no right of appeal against the sheriff for failure to grant the RO, or failure to make or refuse to make an order for variation or recall of the RO.[102] It is worth noting that a police constable who finds any person in a public place[103] and suspects that they may have a mental disorder that requires immediate care or treatment[104] may remove that person to a place of safety[105] and detain them there for up to 24 hours for examination, care or treatment. Notification must be made to relevant parties.[106] A psychiatric nurse, in the course of her normal duties, may also exercise a power to detain persons for up to two hours to allow a medical examination to be undertaken where they suspect that that person is likely to be suffering from a mental disorder.[107]

---

[94] 2003 Act s.113. This allows for detention of a patient in hospital for a period of up to 72 hours, providing that the CTO or ICTO does not otherwise provide for the patient's detention in hospital and the patient has failed to comply with a measure specified by the order. An RMO or AMP must examine the patient and decide if further action should be taken under ss.114 and 115 of the 2003 Act, including detention in hospital for a further period pending review of the CTO. Notification must thereafter be made to the relevant persons specified in s.116 of the 2003 Act. The RMO may later revoke the certificate authorising the continued detention of the patient in accordance with ss.117–119. The patient may also apply to the Tribunal to have the certificate revoked (s.120). Where this certificate is revoked, the original ICTO or CTO will remain in force up until the date on which it was originally due to expire. Authority to treat under Pt 16 of the 2003 Act will subsist throughout.

[95] 2003 Act ss.301 and 302. A warrant may require to be sought in order to enter premises to remove a patient. See s.292 of the 2003 Act (relating to warrants where an individual is already subject to the Act).

[96] 2003 Act s.293. The application may only be made by an MHO.

[97] The requirement for a hearing may be dispensed with in circumstances where the sheriff is satisfied that to do so would result in prejudice to the person who is the subject of the application. Where the application is particularly urgent, it may be made to a justice of the peace instead (s.294).

[98] Only the police constable is entitled to force entry.

[99] Defined at s.300 of the 2003 Act.

[100] The period may not exceed seven days: 2003 Act s.293(3)(c)(ii).

[101] 2003 Act s.295.

[102] 2003 Act s.296.

[103] 2003 Act s.297. "Public place" is defined at s.294(4).

[104] Removal to a place of safety must also be necessary to protect others, or be in the best interests of the individual.

[105] See fnn.95 and 99.

[106] 2003 Act s.298.

[107] Detention in hospital must also be necessary to protect others, or be in the best interests of the individual. The patient must not be subject to the provisions of the 2003 Act and a medical examination must be necessary to determine whether an EDC or STDC be granted. See the 2003 Act s.299.

Medical treatment under the 2003 Act

6.18 The designated medical practitioner ("DMP")[108] plays a vital role in protecting patients subject to the 2003 Act. The DMP provides an independent review/expert second opinion on the necessity or appropriateness of any proposed medical treatment[109] where a patient does not, or cannot, consent.

A patient who receives any surgical operation that destroys brain tissue, or the functioning thereof, must either consent in writing to the treatment, or where incapable of consenting, neither resist nor object to the treatment.[110] Similarly, electroconvulsive therapy (more commonly known as ECT) may only be given to a patient who consents in writing to the treatment, or where incapable of consenting, does not object to the treatment.[111] ECT cannot under any circumstances be given to a *capax* patient who refuses.

Any treatment given over a period of time, such as medicine administered for the purpose of suppressing libido or the provision[112] of nutrition by artificial means, must be subject to review two months after the patient first becomes subject to the provisions of the Act. Consent of the patient to continue with the treatment will be sought initially, and where this is not given, the DMP will be required to consider authorising the ongoing provision of treatment.[113] It is worthy of note that where the patient is community based, it does not authorise the giving of treatment by force.[114] Any other treatment is subject to the provisions of s.242 of the 2003 Act. Urgent medical treatment may be given where the patient is detained in hospital under the Criminal Procedure (Scotland) Act 1995 or the 2003 Act and does not consent or is incapable of consenting to treatment.[115] In these circumstances, the medical practitioner administering the treatment must have regard to any advance statement[116] made by the patient.

Offences under the 2003 Act

6.19 A number of offences have been created or extended under the 2003 Act[117] for both the protection of vulnerable persons subject to the Act and the punishment of those parties who

---

[108] 2003 Act s.233.

[109] The definition of medical treatment within the Act includes nursing care, psychological intervention, habilitation, rehabilitation, psychosurgery, ECT and medication. See the 2003 Act Pt 16.

[110] 2003 Act ss.234–236. The DMP must certify in writing that the patient is capable of consenting to the treatment (and does so in writing) and that it is in the patient's best interests that the treatment be given to alleviate or prevent further deterioration of their condition. Treatment must stop if the patient withdraws consent at any time before completion. Alternatively, the DMP may certify in writing that the patient is incapable of giving consent, but does not object to the treatment and that it is in the patient's best interests that the treatment be given to alleviate or prevent further deterioration of their condition. In either case, two lay persons appointed by the Commission must certify in writing whether the patient is capable or incapable of consenting to the treatment. Where the patient is incapable of consent, an order must be made by the Court of Session permitting treatment.

[111] See fn.110 above and the 2003 Act ss.237–239. In addition, the treatment must be authorised under the 2003 Act, or the Criminal Procedure (Scotland) Act 1995. Where a patient who is incapable of consent resists or objects to the ECT treatment, that treatment may only be continued where it is necessary to save the patient's life, prevent serious deterioration of the patient's condition or alleviate serious suffering.

[112] Without the consent of the patient.

[113] The DMP must certify in writing that the patient is either refusing to give consent, or is incapable of giving consent, and that it is in the patient's best interests that the treatment be given to alleviate or prevent further deterioration of their condition: 2003 Act s.241.

[114] The treatment may however be given by force where the patient is in hospital. See *M, Petr*, 2003 S.L.T. 219 where the court decided that giving compulsory treatment without consent to a patient detained in hospital was not a breach of arts 6, 8, or 14 of ECHR.

[115] 2003 Act s.243. These include for the purpose of saving the patient's life or preventing serious deterioration in their condition. This is the only section of the Act giving authority for the compulsory treatment of individuals subject to an EDC. ECT can only be given to patients under this section in very limited circumstances, namely where a patient is detained under an EDC and is incapable of consenting. If treatment is provided under the section, this must be notified to the Commission within seven days.

[116] 2003 Act ss.275–276.

[117] 2003 Act Pt 21.

deliberately try to obstruct the carrying out of provisions of the Act. The latter category is unlikely to be used in circumstances where a misguided carer or relative is trying to support a patient, or is coerced into assisting a party to abscond.

Sexual intercourse or other intimate act with an individual who does not consent or is incapable of consenting as a result of a mental disorder is a criminal offence. Consent cannot follow on from threats to, intimidation, deceit or inappropriate persuasion of the mentally disordered individual, nor can it be given where a party is unable to understand, form or communicate any opinion on what the act is. It is a valid defence to state that the accused could not reasonably have known that a party was mentally disordered or was incapable of giving the necessary consent.[118] Parties providing care services to a mentally disordered individual who engage in sexual activity with him are guilty of an offence.[119] Any party employed by a hospital or care services who ill-treats or neglects a patient is also guilty of an offence.[120]

Any party who knowingly induces or assists a person to abscond, or harbours a patient who they know to have absconded, is guilty of an offence.[121] It is also an offence to obstruct the carrying out of functions under the Act.[122] Any person who makes a false statement in an application under the Act, or relies on a statement made by another party knowing it to be false with intent to deceive, is guilty of an offence.[123]

In the event of any statutory offence, the Crown must normally raise summary proceedings within six months of the offence having been committed. However, given the particular difficulties of extracting evidence from mentally disordered persons, the six-month time bar will run from the time the Crown is in possession of sufficient evidence to commence proceedings.[124]

ADULTS WITH INCAPACITY (SCOTLAND) ACT 2000

6.20 Until the introduction of the 2000 Act, there was no comprehensive legal framework for protecting the affairs of incapacitated adults or of making decisions on their behalf. A curator *bonis* was appointed in the case of adults with substantial financial assets, but this proved a most

[118] 2003 Act s.311. The penalties for conviction under this section may result in life imprisonment (where the accused is tried on indictment) or any combination of up to three months' imprisonment and a £5,000 fine (where the accused is tried on summary complaint). A party convicted of assisting, procuring or inciting the commission of an offence under this section of the Act is likely to receive the same penalty as the principal accused at summary level and a sentence of up to two years' imprisonment, an unlimited fine or both on indictment.

[119] No regard is had to consent in these circumstances. It is a defence to the action where the accused did not know, and could not reasonably be expected to know that the victim had a mental disorder. Given the circumstances in which contact between the two parties occurred, it seems unlikely that this defence could be sustained. The only reasonable defence therefore available to the accused is that the mentally disordered individual is their spouse, or that there was a pre-existing sexual relationship. As well as the penalties relevant to a party convicted of assisting the commission of an offence noted in fn.118 above, a person convicted under s.313 of the 2003 Act may also be liable to be placed on the Sex Offenders Register: 2003 Act s.314.

[120] Volunteer services are excluded from this: 2003 Act s.315. There is a parallel offence set out in s.83 of the 2000 Act. The penalty for conviction under this section is any combination of imprisonment for up to six months and a fine of up to £5,000 (on summary conviction) and any combination of two years' imprisonment and an unlimited fine (when tried on indictment).

[121] 2003 Act s.316. It is a defence to the charge of harbouring a patient that it did not impede the carrying out of functions under the Act and it was merely intended to protect the patient. The onus however is on the accused to prove this. The penalty for conviction is the same as that for an offence under s.315 of the 2003 Act (see fn.118 above).

[122] 2003 Act s.317. Obstruction may occur where a party refuses access to premises or a mentally disordered person or fails to produce documents or records. The mentally disordered person cannot be convicted of an offence under this section. The penalty for conviction on summary complaint is any combination of imprisonment for up to three months and a fine of up to £1,000.

[123] 2003 Act s.318. The offence will not be committed in cases of innocent error and excludes the nomination of a named person, or an advance statement. The penalty for conviction under this section is any combination of imprisonment for up to six months and a fine of up to £5,000 (on summary conviction) and any combination of two years' imprisonment and an unlimited fine (when tried on indictment).

[124] 2003 Act s.319, which applies s.4 of the Criminal Law (Consolidation) (Scotland) Act 1995 to any offence committed under s.311 or s.313 of the 2003 Act.

expensive way of managing funds. It was possible for a *capax* adult to nominate in advance an adult with enduring powers of attorney to manage financial affairs *ad infinitum*[125] and this has been preserved under the 2000 Act. However, this did not extend to matters of an *incapax's* welfare. In this instance, a small number of people resorted to the common law for the appointment of tutors-dative by the Court of Session to act in *loco parentis* over an *incapax*. A tutor-in-law could also be appointed in limited circumstances[126] to manage both the welfare and financial aspects of an adult's estate. The 2000 Act then allowed for the replacement of piece-meal tutorship with a clear framework for intervention where necessary in the affairs of persons over 16.[127] The Act itself is short in comparison with the Mental Health (Care and Treatment) Scotland Act 2003 and consists of 89 sections, together with six Schedules and various associated regulations.

Guiding principles of the 2000 Act

6.21 Part 1 of the 2000 Act sets out its guiding principles: in effect the ethical context of decision making under the Act. Intervention must result in demonstrable benefit to the adult, which could not be achieved without such intervention.[128] The intervention must be the least restrictive option with regard to the freedom of the adult.[129] Past and present wishes[130] of the adult must be taken into consideration prior to any intervention, as well as those of nearest relatives and the primary carer.[131] The adult must also be encouraged to exercise any residual capacity[132] and to develop new skills where appropriate.

"Incapable" is defined at s.1(6) of the 2000 Act. This includes being incapable of:

- acting; or
- making decisions; or
- communicating decisions; or
- understanding decisions; or

---

[125] Without end, or requirement for renewal.

[126] Appointment of a tutor-dative was restricted to the nearest male relative by statute. Section 80 of the 2000 Act makes any appointment of a curator *bonis*, tutor-dative or tutor-at-law to a person aged 16 or over after the commencement of that Act incompetent. Oddly, it would appear to remain competent to appoint a curator *bonis* to a person under 16.

[127] This is in accordance with the Age of Legal Capacity (Scotland) Act 1991.

[128] There must be both incapacity and need, the latter of which the intervention must meet. Any act that would benefit a third party rather than the adult may be legally challengeable; but see, for example, *B's Curator Bonis*, 1995 S.C.L.R. 671 and *D's Curator Bonis*, 1998 S.L.T. 2 which allows for a curator *bonis* to make gifts or allow measured inheritance tax planning. There is nothing to suggest that the 2000 Act is attempting to curtail this trend and indeed s.66 contains provision for gifts from the estate of an adult subject to a guardianship order. In the commentary to the 2000 Act, Patrick and Ward, *Adults with Incapacity (Scotland) Act 2000* (Green's Annotated Acts) state that "neither this subsection nor any other provision of this Act sanctions the imposition *de facto* of intervention obtainable under this Act, without following this Act's procedures, upon an adult who appears to be compliant but cannot validly give consent. To impose *de facto* provisions, such as guardianship powers, without the appropriate procedure to obtain these powers, and thus without the resulting monitoring and safeguards, would contravene ECHR, Art 6." This standard has been somewhat relaxed by the recent Adult Support and Protection (Scotland) Act 2007.

[129] Notwithstanding the apparent hierarchy that a power of attorney is the least restrictive option (given that it is granted by the adult), and a guardianship order the most restrictive, each of these powers on an individual basis must be restricted to the minimum necessary to achieve the desired end. No cognisance may be taken of the financial implications in relation to this principle.

[130] The provisions relating to advance directives are among the most controversial aspects of this Act. Such directives must be taken into account but are not completely binding. Similarly, less formal statements of intent to friends and family members are important, but not binding.

[131] Statutory formalisation of what has always been considered good practice. The weight to be given to each of these elements is a matter for each individual case. It is of note that the obligation to take into account the adult's wishes and feelings is absolute.

[132] This would include such things as allowing an *incapax* adult to indicate a general preference regarding their diet.

- retaining the memory of decisions, as mentioned in any provision of the Act, by reason of mental disorder[133] or of inability to communicate because of physical disability.[134]

It is important to note that this is a legal, rather than medical, definition of incapacity and exists only for the particular purposes of the 2000 Act.[135] In nearly all provisions under the 2000 Act it is for a medical practitioner to undertake any assessment of capacity. A solicitor or advocate is permitted to assess capacity only in relation to the granting of powers of attorney.

Sections 2 to 5 of the 2000 Act make provision for applications under the Act to the sheriff court or Court of Session and the wide-ranging powers of the sheriff or Court of Session to dispose of any matter before them. Such disposals will be discussed in greater detail later in the Chapter.

Office of the Public Guardian

6.22 Section 6 of the 2000 Act creates a new official known as the Public Guardian. A similar post was previously held by the Accountant of Court[136] who was responsible for supervision and audit of all curator *bonis* cases. The Public Guardian is now a centralised body, based in Falkirk, although it remains part of the Scottish courts administration. The functions of the Public Guardian include[137]:

- supervision of any guardian or any other person who is authorised under an intervention order in the exercise of his functions relating to the property or financial affairs of the adult;
- the establishment and maintenance of registers of all documents relating to:
  - — continuing powers of attorney;
  - — welfare powers of attorney;
  - — authorisations to intromit funds;
  - — guardianship orders;
  - — intervention orders;
- investigation of complaints relating to the property or financial affairs of an *incapax* adult;
- investigation of any circumstances made known to him in which the property or financial affairs of an adult seem to be at risk;
- provision of advice to guardians, continuing attorneys and others relating to performance of functions granted to them under the Act;
- consultation with the Mental Welfare Commission and local authority where there is a common interest.

The 2000 Act extends the role of the Mental Welfare Commission to mirror the protective functions of the Public Guardian but in respect of personal welfare.[138] This maintains the historic distinction between personal welfare and finance. The Commission also has a particular role to play in relation to consent to treatment under Pt 5 of the 2000 Act. This will be discussed more fully later in the Chapter.

---

[133] "Mental disorder" is given the same meaning in this context as contained in the wider mental health legislation.

[134] Section 1(6)(e) of the 2000 Act goes on to say a "person shall not fall within this definition by reason only of a lack or deficiency in the faculty of communication if that lack or deficiency can be made good by human or mechanical aid (whether of an interpretative nature or otherwise)".

[135] It should not be considered an appropriate test in other matters, such as determining whether any act or transaction is void.

[136] It was thought that the term "Public Guardian" sounded more user friendly than "Accountant of Court".

[137] 2000 Act s.6(2)(a)–(f). These do not generally extend to matters of personal welfare, except in respect of subs.(2)(b) and (f).

[138] See, more particularly, the 2000 Act s.9.

Duties of local authorities

6.23 Section 10 of the 2000 Act creates a duty on local authorities to supervise guardians in the exercise of functions relating to the personal welfare of the *incapax* adult.[139] The local authority is bound to consult with the Public Guardian and Mental Welfare Commission on cases where there appears to be a common interest. Importantly, the local authority is under a duty to apply for intervention orders and guardianship orders in certain prescribed circumstances.[140]

Normal practice would allow for intimation of any application or other proceedings under the Act on the *incapax* adult. This is thought by some commentators to be a nonsense, for obvious reasons. Under s.11 of the 2000 Act however, such practice is waived in cases where notification would pose a serious risk to the health of the adult. Given recent developments in human rights legislation, the court will require robust evidence before exercising its discretion to dispense with intimation or notification, rather than simply as a matter of convenience for the applicant or to reduce the number of opposed applications. Section 14 allows for an appeal against a decision of incapacity to the sheriff court or Court of Session on the application of the adult, or any other person claiming an interest in their property, financial affairs or personal welfare.

Continuing and welfare powers of attorney

6.24 Part 2[141] of the 2000 Act is concerned with continuing powers of attorney and welfare powers of attorney. This allows for *capax* adults to create provision for the protection of their financial affairs and/or personal welfare in anticipation of later incapacity.[142] As the numbers of powers of attorney increase, so too the numbers of other applications under the Act will necessarily decrease, but, as with intestacy, not all adults have the foresight to plan in advance of their possible incapacity.

The power of attorney itself is a written document, and must be signed by the adult as granter.[143] It must also incorporate a certificate in the prescribed form (usually, but not necessarily) by a solicitor indicating that he has interviewed the granter immediately before he signed the document and is satisfied at that time that the granter understands both the nature and extent of the power of attorney and is not acting under undue influence.[144] Neither continuing nor welfare attorneys have the power to act until such time as the power of attorney is registered with the Office of the Public Guardian.[145] Sections 23 and 24 of the 2000 Act contain provisions for the resignation[146] or termination[147] of continuing or welfare attorneys.

---

[139] Where there is a significant dispute between the local authority and the guardian, the matter should properly be referred to the Mental Welfare Commission under the 2000 Act s.9(1) or to the sheriff for direction under the 2000 Act s.3(3).

[140] See s.53(3) intervention orders and s.57(2) guardianship orders. The local authority must apply where no application has been made or is likely to be made by another party, and the application is necessary to protect the property, financial affairs or personal welfare of the *incapax* adult.

[141] 2000 Act ss.15–24.

[142] Continuing attorneys are attorneys with financial powers which continue when an adult becomes incapable. Welfare attorneys have authority over personal welfare decisions. Such attorneys commence on the adult becoming *incapax*.

[143] It must incorporate a statement that the power is a continuing one: 2000 Act s.15(3)(b).

[144] The solicitor or any other proper person may not grant a certificate where he is the person to whom the power of attorney has been granted: 2000 Act ss.15(4) and 16(4).

[145] 2000 Act s.19(1).

[146] The attorney must write to the granter, the Public Guardian and any other applicable party to tender his resignation. The resignation will not take effect until the expiry of a period of 28 days commencing from the date of receipt of the notification by the Public Guardian. Where the resignation is of a welfare attorney, the Public Guardian will notify the local authority and (if applicable) the Mental Welfare Commission. See the 2000 Act s.23.

[147] Section 24 of the 2000 Act sets out the full circumstances in which a continuing or welfare power of attorney will terminate. This includes where the granter and attorney were married and subsequently divorce, unless otherwise provided for in the power of attorney.

Intromission with funds

6.25 As of April 1, 2008, Pt 3 of the 2000 Act relating to intromissions with funds will be repealed in its entirety[148] and replaced with a new simplified version known as "access to funds". The basic principle, that of allowing individuals to obtain authority to intromit with funds of an *incapax* adult where there is no existing guardianship or intervention order or power of attorney,[149] will remain the same. Intromission with funds may be for the purposes of payment of central or local government taxes, provision of sustenance, accommodation, fuel, clothing and related goods and services or any other service provided for the purpose of looking after or caring for the adult or the settlement of debts.[150]

A person or body[151] may apply to the Public Guardian for a certificate entitling them to receive whatever information they require from a fundholder[152] to establish where an account may be held in the name of the adult and what sum of money is available in it.[153] He may also wish to open an account on behalf of the adult for the purpose of intromitting with their funds.[154] A withdrawal certificate[155] may then be sought to allow, among other things, payment by direct debit or standing order from the adult's account to a creditor. Such applications must be submitted to the Public Guardian within 14 days of the date of countersignature.[156] A medical certificate will be required to accompany applications.[157] The application will thereafter be intimated upon the appropriate persons and time allowed for representations to be made to the Public Guardian.[158] Any funds released by the withdrawer must be used only for the benefit of the adult[159] and to this end, the withdrawer will be required to maintain full and accurate records of expenditure.

Management of residents' funds by nursing homes and hospitals

6.26 Part 4 of the 2000 Act provides a statutory, harmonised basis for the existing practice of management of residents' funds by managers of nursing homes and hospitals.[160] As with Pt 3, the provisions of Pt 4 of the 2000 Act do not apply where there is a superior order in force, such

[148] By s.58 of the Adult Support and Protection (Scotland) Act 2007.

[149] 2000 Act s.24B, inserted by the 2007 Act s.58. Where there is an existing financial guardianship, and access to funds would provide a less restrictive (but equally competent) method of managing the adult's monetary affairs, the guardianship should be recalled and an application granted under this section instead: 2000 Act s.31E, inserted by the 2007 Act s.58.

[150] 2000 Act s.24A(2), inserted by the 2007 Act s.58.

[151] 2000 Act s.25, inserted by the 2007 Act s.58.

[152] For example, a bank or building society.

[153] 2000 Act s.24C, inserted by the 2007 Act s.58.

[154] 2000 Act s.24D, inserted by the 2007 Act s.58.

[155] 2000 Act s.26A, inserted by the 2007 Act s.58. A withdrawal certificate is generally valid for three years from date of issue: 2000 Act s.31, inserted by the 2007 Act s.58. Should the account become overdrawn, the fundholder has a right of relief against the withdrawer, except where the withdrawer's authority has been terminated or suspended by the Public Guardian: 2000 Act ss.28, 28A and 29, inserted by the 2007 Act s.58. It is competent to apply to the Public Guardian as joint withdrawers; the joint withdrawers may act independently in the discharge of their functions: 2000 Act ss.26B and 26C, inserted by the 2007 Act s.58. A reserve withdrawer may also be appointed, to act as a withdrawer only where the main withdrawer is temporarily indisposed: 2000 Act ss.26D and 26E, inserted by the 2007 Act s.58. See also the 2000 Act s.26F, inserted by the 2007 Act s.58. The Public Guardian may withdraw or suspend the authority of a withdrawer under a withdrawal certificate at any time: 2000 Act s.31A, inserted by the 2007 Act s.58.

[156] 2000 Act ss.27 and 27A, inserted by the 2007 Act s.58.

[157] Applications under the 2000 Act ss.24C, 24D or 25 (inserted by the 2007 Act s.58) will require a medical certificate.

[158] 2000 Act ss.27C, 27D and 27E, inserted by the 2007 Act s.58. The applicant must be a "fit and proper" person. The Public Guardian may remit the matter to a sheriff for consideration: 2000 Act s.27F, inserted by the 2007 Act s.58.

[159] 2000 Act ss.30 and 30B, inserted by the 2007 Act s.58.

[160] 2000 Act ss.35 and 37.

as a financial guardianship.[161] It is intended that only small sums of money (including pensions and other moveable property) be administered under Pt 4, as may be prescribed from time to time by regulation.[162]

The managers of an authorised establishment must seek authority to manage the funds of a resident by making an application to their supervising body.[163] Before doing so, they must consider that their management of a resident's finances is the most appropriate course of action and would provide benefit to the adult. The adult must be examined by a medical practitioner, and where he is satisfied that the adult is *incapax* in relation to such matters, he should issue a certificate in prescribed form to that effect.[164] This certificate will expire three years after it was issued, or on earlier review of the adult as a result of a change in the adult's circumstances.[165] Section 41 of the 2000 Act provides further details of the duties and functions of managers of authorised establishments in relation to residents whose financial affairs they are managing.[166]

Where a resident ceases to live at a particular establishment which has the authority to manage his financial affairs, the managers of that establishment may continue to manage his affairs for a further period of three months or until alternative arrangements are made, thereby allowing for a more measured discharge from one care facility to another.[167] The power to manage residents' financial affairs may be revoked by a supervisory body. Any such revocation may be appealed to a sheriff, whose decision is final.[168]

Medical treatment and research—incapax adults

6.27 Until the 2000 Act, the legal right to medical treatment of *incapax* adults was shrouded in uncertainty.[169] In a limited number of cases, a tutor-dative could approach the Court of Session seeking powers to give consent by proxy.[170] More frequently, medical practitioners treated such patients under the common law of necessity.[171] Part 5 of the 2000 Act now allows a medical practitioner to provide medical treatment (which is reasonable in the circumstances) where it would safeguard or promote the physical or mental health of the adult.[172] To do so, the medical practitioner must have (1) examined the patient and found them to be *incapax* in relation to decisions about medical treatment; and (2) issued a certificate in the prescribed form to this effect.[173] This section does not apply where an application has been made to the sheriff for an intervention or guardianship order which contains provisions in relation to the medical treat-

---

[161] 2000 Act s.46.

[162] See the Adults with Incapacity (Management of Residents' Finances) (Scotland) Regulations 2003 (SSI 2003/155) and the Adults with Incapacity (Management of Residents' Finances) (No.2) (Scotland) Regulations 2003 (SSI 2003/266). Discretion is afforded where the current total assets are just above the prescribed limit and are expected to fall below the threshold within a short period of time. Assets may not include land or property. See the 2000 Act s.39 for further details.

[163] The appropriate supervisory bodies to which application should be made are listed at s.40 of the 2000 Act.

[164] 2000 Act s.37(2).

[165] 2000 Act s.37(7)(a) and (b).

[166] These include keeping the funds of residents separate from those of the establishment and keeping records of any transactions with funds held by them. See also the 2000 Act s.42.

[167] 2000 Act s.44.

[168] 2000 Act s.45.

[169] Scottish Law Commission, *Report on incapable adults*, No.151, Cm.2962 (1995) (cited in McManus and Thomson, below) "as far as authority to give medical treatment to incapable adults is concerned, the law in Scotland is uncertain."

[170] According to J.J. McManus and D.G. Thomson, *Mental Health and Scots Law in Practice* (Edinburgh: W. Green, 2005), p.111, between 1994 and 1998 only 42 such cases occurred.

[171] A concept more clearly established under English law. See McManus and Thomson, *Mental Health and Scots Law in Practice* (2005), para.4.33 for a fuller discussion on this topic.

[172] 2000 Act s.47(2). The definition of medical treatment is notably wide. Authority to treat extends to anyone acting on behalf of the medical practitioner (under his instructions) or with his approval or agreement. This would include both clinicians and family or carers.

[173] 2000 Act s.47(5). The duration of the certificate should not exceed one year from the date of the examination and may reasonably be shorter, depending on the medical condition or circumstances of the adult.

ment currently being proposed, even where that application has not yet been determined.[174] Where an interdict exists preventing treatment this cannot be overcome by either common law or statutory provision. The general authority to treat does not extend to treatment to which Pt 10 of the 2003 Act applies, nor to other controversial treatments.[175] It also does not extend to the use of detention or force unless immediately necessary. An *incapax* adult who does not dissent to admission to a psychiatric hospital should be treated in line with Pt 5 of the 2000 Act. Where an *incapax* adult does dissent to such admission, he should be detained in terms of the 2003 Act.[176] Section 52 of the 2000 Act deals with appeal against decisions in relation to medical treatment.

Research on an *incapax* adult may only be carried out where (1) it could not be carried out on a *capax* adult; (2) the purpose of the research is to obtain knowledge of the causes, diagnosis, treatment or care of the adult's incapacity or the effect of any treatment or care given during his incapacity relative to that condition; and (3) the research is likely to produce real and direct benefit to the adult,[177] and the adult has not indicated any unwillingness to participate in the research.[178]

Intervention and guardianship orders

6.28 Part 6 is one of the most important areas[179] of the 2000 Act and provides for a new scheme whereby sheriffs may grant intervention and guardianship orders in respect of *incapax* adults.[180] Intervention orders are dealt with under s.53 of the 2000 Act. Anyone claiming an interest in the property, financial affairs or personal welfare of an adult may apply for such an order, and the local authority is under a duty to do so where no application has been made or is likely to be made by another party. Such order is likely to be of short-term duration and is intended primarily for one-off decisions. Application should be made to the sheriff court, together with accompanying medical reports.[181] An intervention order[182] may direct the taking of a specific

[174] 2000 Act s.49. The only exception is where treatment is authorised by any other enactment or rule of law for the preservation of life or prevention of serious deterioration in a patient's condition. Section 50 of the 2000 Act applies where a guardian or other party has been appointed. This section was the subject of much debate by Parliament at Bill stage.

[175] Such as sterilisation, treatment for the purposes of reducing sex drive, electro-convulsive therapy or abortion. See Scottish Executive, *Adults with Incapacity (Scotland) Act 2000: Supplement to Code of Practice for Persons Authorised to Carry Out Medical Treatment or Research under Pt V of the Act* (2002) for further information.

[176] This follows the pre-2000 Act practice.

[177] Where the research is not likely to produce real and direct benefit to the adult it may nevertheless be carried out if it will contribute to the scientific understanding of the adult's incapacity to the attainment of real and direct benefit to the adult or others with that condition. See s.51(4) of the 2000 Act.

[178] 2000 Act s.51. The research must also be approved by the Ethics Committee and entail minimal risk or discomfort to the adult. Consent must be obtained from a guardian or welfare attorney who has power to consent to the adult's participation in research or where there is no such person, from the adult's nearest relative.

[179] Scottish Executive, *Adults with Incapacity (Scotland) Act 2000 Code of Practice: Persons Authorised under an Intervention Order and Guardians* (2002) provides much useful additional information on this subject.

[180] Replacing the curators *bonis* and guardianship provisions in the Mental Health (Scotland) Act 1984.

[181] Two medical reports are required as standard, one of which must be from a medical practitioner approved as having special experience in diagnosis and treatment of mental disorder. The second report is usually prepared by the adult's general practitioner. The reports must normally be based on an examination of the adult carried out not more than 30 days prior to the application, although this requirement has been relaxed in certain circumstances by the Adult Support and Protection (Scotland) Act 2007. In the case of welfare intervention, a third report is required from an MHO expressing an opinion as to the appropriateness of the order and the suitability of the nominee. For financial intervention orders, a third report should be submitted by a person with "sufficient knowledge" to report on the appropriateness of the order and the suitability of the nominee. Further guidance can be found in the Scottish Executive, *Adults with Incapacity (Scotland) Act 2000 Code of Practice: Persons Authorised under an Intervention Order and Guardians* (2002).

[182] While the scope of guardianship orders may be limited by regulations (2000 Act s.86) there is no similar provision in respect of intervention orders.

action narrated in the order or authorise a person[183] nominated in the application to take such action or make such a decision in relation to the property, financial affairs or personal welfare of the *incapax* adult.[184] It is possible that more than one intervention order may be in force at any one time, and an intervention order may be granted or in force concurrently with a guardianship order. The sheriff may, on application for a guardianship order, dispose of that application by way of an intervention order instead as the least restrictive and therefore preferred option.

Application for a guardianship order[185] can be made in the same way and by the same categories of person as an intervention order. Similar to intervention orders, the local authority is under a duty to make an application where no application has been made or is likely to be made by another party.[186] Sections 62 and 63 of the 2000 Act allow for the appointment of joint and substitute guardians. Where the sheriff is satisfied that the adult is incapable in relation to the matters specified in the guardianship application, and that no less restrictive provision under the 2000 Act would suffice to safeguard or promote the adult's property, financial affairs or personal welfare, he may grant the order.[187] Thereafter, the adult will be deemed to have no capacity in relation to any matter covered by the guardianship order, although the presumption of capacity otherwise remains.[188]

Guardianships are limited as to duration[189] but flexible in respect of powers granted.[190] Consequently, the applicant will have to show that the powers sought are appropriate and necessary, rather than competent. The sheriff may make an interim guardianship order pending full determination of the application in certain cases[191] where time is of the essence. An interim guardianship order will not be made where an intervention order would suffice. When the order is granted, the sheriff clerk will send a copy of the interlocutor to the Public Guardian for his register.[192]

6.29 It is competent for a guardian holding powers in relation to the property and financial affairs of an adult to make a gift out of the adult's estate if authorised to do so by the Public Guardian.[193] The guardian is also entitled to reimbursement for any outlays reasonably incurred by him in the exercise of his functions.[194]

Where an adult or any other person fails to comply with the welfare provisions of a guardianship order, the guardian may make application to a sheriff to ordain any person to

---

[183] There is no clear provision in the 2000 Act for the appointment of joint intervenors, although personal correspondence between the author and the Office of the Public Guardian (during early 2008) would suggest that such appointment has occurred on a limited number of occasions. It is likely that this would be "on cause shown".

[184] 2000 Act s.53(5). Where the intervention order specifies the acquisition or disposal of accommodation used for the time being as a dwelling house by the adult, the consent of the Public Guardian must be obtained in relation to the consideration. This is likely to include interests as tenant, lessee or owner. See also s.56 on the registration of an intervention order relating to heritable property.

[185] 2000 Act s.57. Section 59 of the 2000 Act details who may be appointed as a guardian.

[186] 2000 Act s.57(2).

[187] 2000 Act s.58(1). The sheriff will have regard to any intervention order or guardianship order previously made in relation to the adult. The sheriff may seek a bond of caution or other security to safeguard the administration of the adult's estate.

[188] 2000 Act s.67. Clearly, this will not endure beyond any relevant recall or termination of the order.

[189] 2000 Act s.58(4). A guardianship order may be granted for a period of up to three years, or longer on cause shown. A new simplified process for renewal is contained within the 2007 Act and will be in force from April 1, 2008.

[190] Section 64 of the 2000 Act outlines the functions and duties of a guardian. Section 61 of the 2000 Act provides separate procedures for the registration of a guardianship order relating to heritable property.

[191] In order to do this, there must be a crave for an interim order in the initial application. Any appointment of an interim guardian will currently cease either on the appointment of a full guardian or three months from the date of appointment, whichever is the earlier. See s.57(5) and (6) of the 2000 Act. The 2007 Act allows for appointment of an interim guardian for a period not exceeding six months.

[192] The Public Guardian will notify the relevant parties stipulated in Pt 1 of the 2000 Act.

[193] 2000 Act s.66.

[194] 2000 Act s.68. Reimbursement is from the adult's estate. This right is forfeited where the guardian is found to be in any breach of duty of care, or other duty or obligation imposed by the 2000 Act (see s.69). There is no corresponding provision for reimbursement for an adult appointed as an intervenor, although the author is aware that this has been successfully sought in an intervention order.

implement his decision.[195] Such application should be intimated on the adult and a period for objections allowed before considering grant of the application.

Sections 71 to 76 of the 2000 Act deal with recall[196] and variation[197] of guardianship orders, and the replacement, removal or resignation[198] of a guardian. Application may be made by the adult, or any person claiming an interest in the adult's property, financial affairs or personal welfare, including the Public Guardian or Mental Welfare Commission.[199] Any intervention or guardianship order granted under Pt 6 of the 2000 Act will cease to have effect on the death of the adult.[200]

Part 7 of the 2000 Act deals with miscellaneous matters, including repayment of funds by any person authorised to administer funds under any provision of the Act where such use of funds has been made outwith their authority or in breach of their fiduciary duty.[201] Section 82 of the 2000 Act states that no liability shall be incurred by any person appointed under the Act where he has acted reasonably and in good faith.[202] It is an offence, punishable by imprisonment, for any person exercising powers under the Act in relation to the personal welfare of the adult to ill-treat or wilfully neglect the adult.[203]

THE ADULT SUPPORT AND PROTECTION (SCOTLAND) ACT 2007

6.30 The Adult Support and Protection (Scotland) Act 2007 ("2007 Act") received Royal Assent on March 21, 2007 and completed the trilogy of Acts envisaged by the Scottish Parliament to ensure the adequate protection of vulnerable persons in society. The 2007 Act is divided into five parts, which can be broadly described as follows:

- Part 1: Protection of adults at risk of harm;
- Part 2: Adults with incapacity (provides for some amendments to the 2000 Act);
- Part 3: Adult support (provides for various amendments to the Social Work (Scotland) Act 1968 and the 2003 Act);
- Part 4: Mental health (provides for various amendments to the 2003 Act, the Mental Health Act 1983 (insofar as the provisions extend to Scotland) and the Criminal Procedure (Scotland) Act 1995);
- Part 5: Provides final provisions in relation to commencement and other similar matters.

Section 1 of the 2007 Act sets out the general principles on intervention in an adult's affairs. These principles echo those of the 2000 Act,[204] and state that intervention may only occur (or be authorised) where the intervention will provide benefit to the adult and is the least restrictive

---

[195] 2000 Act s.70. Where the non-compliance relates to place of residence of the adult, the sheriff may grant a warrant authorising a police constable to enter the premises and, using such force as is reasonable in the circumstances, remove the adult to a place directed by the guardian.

[196] 2000 Act s.73.

[197] 2000 Act s.74 allows for the sheriff, on application by any person, to vary an existing guardianship order.

[198] 2000 Act s.75. The guardian may only resign if there is continuity of guardianship (for example, if one of the joint guardians is left in post, or a substitute guardian has been appointed under s.63) or if it has been determined by a sheriff that a guardian is no longer necessary.

[199] The Public Guardian has specific powers under s.73 of the 2000 Act to recall the powers of a guardian in relation to the property and financial affairs of an adult. Similarly, the Mental Welfare Commission can recall the powers of a guardian in relation to the personal welfare of the adult.

[200] 2000 Act s.77. Section 78 is concerned with the effect of the adult's death or other termination or variation of the guardianship on any registration under s.61 of the 2000 Act.

[201] 2000 Act s.81.

[202] At common law, breach of such duty incurred by virtue of appointment under the Act would give rise to personal liability.

[203] 2000 Act s.83. Summary conviction may result in imprisonment for a term not exceeding six months or to a fine or both; conviction on indictment may result in imprisonment for a term not exceeding two years or to a fine or both.

[204] 2000 Act s.1.

option of any available that will meet the objective of the intervention. Section 2 continues in the same thread, and states that any public body or official must have regard to this general principle while carrying out any function under the Act. The adult should be encouraged to participate as fully as possible in the decision-making process through provision of appropriate information and support and due regard given to the adult's abilities, background and characteristics. Further consideration must be given to the feelings of the adult at risk and any other significant individuals with an interest.[205] An adult at risk[206] is defined as an adult (over 16 years old) who is (1) unable to safeguard their own well-being, property, rights or other interests; (2) at risk of harm[207]; and (3) because they are affected by disability, mental disorder, illness or physical and mental infirmity, are more vulnerable to being harmed than other adults who are not so affected.

6.31 Section 4 of the 2007 Act is reminiscent of the duties of the local authority prescribed by the 2003 Act in relation to a duty to inquire where an individual is thought to fall within the definition of an adult at risk and the authority knows or believes it may have to intervene to protect the adult's well-being, property or financial affairs. In doing so, the authority is entitled to seek the co-operation of a number of other public bodies.[208] When performing any intervention measure under the 2007 Act, the local authority must advise the adult of the availability of independent advocacy services.[209] Any visit carried out by an officer of the local authority must be at a reasonable time.[210] The officer must not use force to facilitate a visit, unless accompanied by a police constable with the relevant warrant.[211] A warrant or other order will usually be sought from the sheriff, except in extreme cases of urgency.[212]

An officer of the local authority is empowered to enter any place for the purpose of conducting inquiries under s.4 of the 2007 Act.[213] While in that place he is entitled to interview, in private, any adult found there.[214] Where it is impracticable for an interview to take place on those premises, an assessment order[215] must be sought to enable removal of the adult to a more suitable location. If, following interview, the adult is considered to be at risk then he may be examined by any health professional who accompanies the council officer for the purposes of s.7 of the 2007 Act.[216] The 2007 Act allows for disclosure of health, financial and other records relating to an adult at risk to an officer of the local authority or health professional.[217]

---

[205] Who are known to the party carrying out any function of the 2007 Act.

[206] Adult Support and Protection (Scotland) Act 2007 ("2007 Act") s.3.

[207] "Harm" is defined at s.53 of the 2007 Act. An adult is at risk of harm where either the adult or another person's conduct is causing (or is likely to cause) the adult to be harmed. See s.3(2) of the 2007 Act.

[208] 2007 Act s.5. Note that anybody who knows or believes that an adult is at risk is under a duty to report it to the relevant local authority.

[209] 2007 Act s.6. "Independent advocacy services" has the same meaning as in s.259(1) of the 2003 Act.

[210] 2007 Act s.36.

[211] 2007 Act ss.36(4) and 37. Only a police constable may use force and only where necessary to obtain entry. A warrant may be granted where the sheriff is satisfied on oath that a council officer has been or reasonably expects to be refused entry or is otherwise unable to enter or that any attempt to visit the place without a warrant would defeat the object of the visit: 2007 Act s.38(2)(a) and (b). Any warrant to enter expires 72 hours after it is granted, and does not allow for the continued presence in that place of a person who has entered in pursuance of the warrant beyond the stated period.

[212] 2007 Act s.40. Note that different timescales apply to orders and warrants granted by justices of the peace.

[213] 2007 Act s.7. Note that the right to enter any place also includes the right to enter an adjacent place for the same purposes.

[214] 2007 Act s.8. The adult must be informed that he is not required to answer any question prior to commencement of the interview. The power granted under s.8 of the 2007 Act is independent of any powers conferred under ss.11–13 of the same Act (assessment orders).

[215] See following paragraphs for further information, in particular para.6.32.

[216] 2007 Act s.9; "health professional" is defined in s.52(2) of the 2007 Act. The medical examination must take place on the premises where the adult is found unless an assessment order is granted that would permit the removal of the adult to more suitable accommodation.

[217] The records should be produced as soon as reasonably practicable. Note that medical records may only be examined in detail by a health professional: 2007 Act s.52(2).

Assessment orders

6.32 Three new orders may be made under the 2007 Act. The first of those is an assessment order ("AO"). A local authority officer may make an application to the sheriff for this order, which permits that officer or a health official to remove any person thought to be an "adult at risk" from any place to more suitable accommodation to complete an interview or private medical assessment. The AO is valid for seven days from the date of grant of the order.[218] The sheriff may only grant the AO where he is satisfied that (a) the officer has reasonable cause to suspect that the adult in question is "at risk"; (b) an assessment order is necessary to carry out the appropriate investigations to establish whether or not the adult is "at risk"; and (c) a suitable and available place has been located where the adult can be interviewed and assessed.[219] An AO will only be granted in circumstances where it is not possible to adequately interview or examine the adult at the initial contact location.[220]

Removal orders

6.33 The sheriff may also grant a removal order ("RO").[221] Again, it is for the local authority officer to make an application to the sheriff. The RO permits an officer of the authority or other nominated party[222] to move the adult to a specified place within 72 hours of the granting of the order and thereafter detain them there for a maximum of seven days, or such shorter period as may be specified in the RO. The sheriff may only grant the RO where he is satisfied that (a) the person in respect of whom the order is sought is an adult "at risk"; and (b) a suitable and available place has been located where the adult can be accommodated for the duration of the RO. The RO may contain directions as to who may have contact with the adult "at risk" and any conditions that may need to be attached to that contact. In considering this, the sheriff should have regard to representations by the officer seeking the RO, the adult "at risk", any person who wishes to have contact with the adult and any other party claiming an interest in the adult's well-being or property.[223] Where a RO is granted, an officer of the local authority may enter any premises in order to remove the adult to another place.[224] The sheriff is entitled to vary or recall a RO upon application by a relevant party[225] if satisfied that this is justified by a change in facts or circumstances from the original grant (or subsequent variation) of the order. The RO will not be varied where this would result in extending, for whatever reason, the duration of the detention of the adult or any other intervention by the local authority.[226] Where an order is recalled, the sheriff may direct the local authority to return the adult to the place from where they were initially removed, or he may specify an alternative venue (having due regard to the wishes of the adult).[227] While an adult is subject to a removal order, the local authority is under a duty to take reasonable steps to secure any property owned or controlled by that adult, and prevent loss or damage to same.[228] This allows an officer of the local authority to enter any place where they know or believe any such property exists and thereafter do anything which they consider reasonably necessary to prevent loss or damage of the property.[229] The local authority

[218] 2007 Act s.11. A sheriff who grants an AO must also grant a warrant for entry: 2007 Act s.38(1).
[219] 2007 Act s.12.
[220] 2007 Act s.13.
[221] 2007 Act s.14.
[222] This may be useful where the nominated party is more familiar to the adult.
[223] 2007 Act s.15.
[224] 2007 Act s.16. The sheriff must also grant a warrant for entry: 2007 Act s.39(1).
[225] Defined at s.17(4) as the adult "at risk", any person who has an interest in the adult's well-being or property or an officer of the local authority.
[226] 2007 Act s.17(2).
[227] 2007 Act s.17(3).
[228] 2007 Act s.18(1). Note that this duty only extends to property that the adult cannot protect or otherwise deal with by reason of their removal to another place and where no other suitable arrangements have been, or can be, put in place.
[229] 2007 Act s.18(2)–(4). This may necessitate removal of property to another place.

is not entitled to recover expenses incurred in discharge of this duty. The duty applies only for the duration of the removal order and any property that is removed by an officer must be returned to the adult as soon as reasonably practicable upon expiry of the RO.[230]

Banning orders

6.34 The final order that may be sought under the 2007 Act is a banning order ("BO"). This order is also granted by a sheriff and may (among other things) prevent the subject of the order from being in a specified place, being in the vicinity of that place, authorise summary ejection of a subject found in that place or in the vicinity or require or authorise the subject to do, or refrain from doing, anything that the sheriff thinks necessary for the proper enforcement of the order.[231] Where the subject is prevented from being in a particular place, this may be subject to further directions on time or circumstances where the subject may legitimately be found there.[232] Powers of arrest may also be attached to the BO and will become effective only after service of appropriate paperwork on the subject of the order.[233] A BO will expire six months after it is made.[234] The sheriff will grant the BO where he is satisfied that (a) an adult "at risk" is being, or is likely to be, seriously harmed by another person; and (b) that adult's well-being or property would be better safeguarded by banning the subject from the place where the adult is rather than removing the adult; and (c) that either the adult "at risk" is entitled or permitted by a third party or neither the adult "at risk" nor the subject is entitled or permitted by a third party to occupy the place from which the subject is to be banned.[235] The sheriff is also entitled to grant a temporary BO pending determination of an application for a BO.[236] The temporary BO may include any provision such as would be included in the full BO and will expire when the application for the full order has been determined by the sheriff, where the temporary BO is recalled or any specified expiry date, whichever is the earlier.[237] An application for a BO may be made by or on behalf of the adult at risk, any other person entitled to occupy the place concerned or the local authority[238] and may include an application for a temporary BO.[239] A sheriff may vary or recall a BO or temporary BO where he is satisfied that this is justified by a change in facts or circumstances since the grant of the original order. Any variation may not extend the duration of the BO beyond six months from the grant of the original order, nor, in the case of a temporary BO, extend the order beyond the date on which the sheriff is bound to determine the related application for a BO.[240] The variation or recall of the BO may be sought by those specified in s.24(3) of the 2007 Act. Should the variation or recall be sought by a person

---

[230] 2007 Act s.18(6)–(7).

[231] 2007 Act s.19(2)(a)–(f).

[232] 2007 Act s.19(3) and (4). Before a condition of this nature is included in the BO, regard will be had to representations from the adult "at risk", the applicant, any other person claiming an interest in the adult's well-being or property and the subject of the BO.

[233] 2007 Act s.25. The power of arrest must be notified to the chief constable for the relevant area. Any variation or recall of the BO should be similarly notified: 2007 Act s.27. The power of arrest expires at the same time as the order to which it is attached. Sections 28–34 detail the duties and responsibilities of both the police and the sheriff where a person is arrested under a power attached to the BO.

[234] Or on an earlier date specified in the BO or the date on which a BO is recalled: 2007 Act s.19(5).

[235] 2007 Act s.20. Note that the granting of a BO does not affect any right of the adult "at risk" under the Matrimonial Homes (Family Protection) (Scotland) Act 1981: 2007 Act s.23.

[236] 2007 Act s.21(1). The application for a full BO must thereafter be determined within the timescale set down within the Sheriff Court Rules.

[237] 2007 Act s.21(2)–(4).

[238] 2007 Act s.22. Note that the local authority may only apply where no one else is likely to apply and where no other proceedings to eject or ban the person concerned from the place concerned are currently before a court. In these circumstances the local authority is under a mandatory duty to make the application.

[239] 2007 Act s.22(3).

[240] 2007 Act s.24(2). The date on which the sheriff must have determined the application for a BO is prescribed by the Sheriff Court Rules.

other than the adult at risk, this must be intimated to the adult although curiously, a failure to do so does not invalidate the order, variation or recall.[241]

A sheriff may not make any of the orders noted above without the consent of the adult at risk except in limited circumstances.[242] The procedure for applications in respect of all three orders is covered in s.41 of the 2007 Act.

The Adult Protection Committee

6.35 As part of the 2007 Act, each local authority will be responsible for the establishment of an Adult Protection Committee ("APC"). Membership of the APC is defined by the Act.[243] The functions of the APC are listed at s.42 of the 2007 Act and include the provision of information and advice relating to the safeguarding of vulnerable adults to public bodies and other office-holders in the local authority area. This may include the drawing up of protocols to establish guidelines for multi-agency working and sharing of information. It is a key function of the APC to improve co-operation between all stakeholders.[244] A biennial report must be produced by the APC for each local authority area.[245] Each APC will be subject to guidance issued by the Scottish Ministers from time to time.[246] A code of practice will also be issued, following consultation with various bodies, and will be subject to review from time to time as determined by the Scottish Ministers.[247] The remaining provisions of the 2007 Act are, in the main, amendments to existing legislation and are dealt with elsewhere in this Chapter.

MENTAL HEALTH AND CRIMINAL JUSTICE

6.36 Millan made several controversial proposals concerning mentally disordered offenders within the criminal justice system, in particular recommending that the release of restricted patients be dealt with by the Parole Board[248] acting on the advice of a new Risk Management Authority.[249] Although many of the recommendations of the Millan Committee were accepted by the Scottish Ministers, those relating to mentally disordered offenders were, at best, modified considerably.[250]

Mens rea and Scots criminal law

6.37 There is a crucial relationship between mental health, capacity and criminal justice. Many of the offences known to Scots law require what is known as mens rea—effectively the criminal mind.[251] Mens rea is a strictly legal, rather than psychiatric concept. Where individuals with impaired mental functioning interact with the criminal justice system there inevitably requires to

---

[241] 2007 Act s.26.

[242] See 2007 Act s.35 generally, and s.35(3) in respect of grounds where a refusal to consent may be ignored by the sheriff.

[243] 2007 Act ss.43–45.

[244] 2007 Act s.42(2). "Stakeholders" include those listed in s.42(3) of the 2007 Act.

[245] 2007 Act s.46. A copy of the report must be sent to each of the bodies listed at s.46(b) of the 2007 Act.

[246] 2007 Act s.47.

[247] 2007 Act s.48.

[248] Sitting as a Restricted Patients Review Board.

[249] The creation of a Risk Management Authority was never approved.

[250] Scottish Executive, "Renewing Mental Health Law—Policy Statement", October 2001. In particular, the recommendation that the risk of self-harm should become one of the grounds for admission to the state hospital in Carstairs was not adopted on the basis that the state hospital should more usefully focus resources on those patients who presented a risk to others, rather than themselves.

[251] As noted in McManus and Thomson, *Mental Health and Scots Law in Practice* (2005), mens rea was not the term originally used in Scotland. Hume, in his 1844 writings *Commentaries on the Law of Scotland Respecting Crimes* (Edinburgh: Bell and Bradfute, 1844), makes reference to the term "dole" as "the corrupt and evil intention, which is essential ... to the guilt of any crime".

be a reappraisal of the status and position of that person, including whether they have the requisite mental capacity to commit the crime, sufficient understanding of the criminal justice process and ability to instruct a legal representative. An assessment of the nature and extent of the mental incapacity of each individual is therefore vitally important. Some individuals with impaired mental functioning will immediately be diverted from the criminal justice system into informal treatment or detention under the 2003 Act; others will continue to be dealt with by it or diverted at a later stage in the process. Similarly, an individual may be diverted back into the criminal justice system at any point in the process; transfer to a psychiatric hospital does not preclude concurrent or later action against an individual by the criminal justice system. For the sane, mental health might simply be a mitigating factor that affects sentence[252] and although the system generally attempts to preclude it, many individuals with impaired mental functioning will still find their way into prison.[253] Sadly, for many of those individuals, a court appearance may be the first time their needs become apparent.[254]

The pre-trial position

6.38 Upon charge, an individual is required to appear at a pre-trial hearing. The issue of fitness to plead may be raised by the prosecution, defence or trial judge. Determination will be made on the basis of evidence from two doctors.[255] Where the accused is found insane in bar of trial, the trial diet will be discharged and an Examination of Facts ("EOF")[256] ordered. Possible disposals at this hearing include being remanded on bail, in custody or in hospital.[257] At the EOF the court will determine beyond reasonable doubt whether the accused committed the acts as charged and on the lesser standard of proof of balance of probabilities whether or not there are grounds for acquittal. The accused need not be in attendance at this hearing.[258] Where the facts are not found, the accused must be acquitted and there are no further proceedings. Alternatively, where the facts are found, the court must then consider whether there are grounds for an acquittal by reason of insanity.[259] The various disposals are set out in s.57(2) of the Criminal Procedure (Scotland) Act 1995 and include a compulsion order, supervision and treatment order[260] and a guardianship order.[261] Appeals in relation to this matter may be made to the High Court.[262]

Psychiatric defences

6.39 There are a number of psychiatric defences that may be available to an accused if it can be shown that impaired mental functioning was present at the time the offence was committed. The two most well known are insanity and diminished responsibility.[263]

---

[252] See *Wilson v HM Advocate*, 1998 S.C.C.R. 437 where a first offender was sentenced to 12 months' imprisonment for producing cannabis, which was subsequently replaced by 18 months' probation.

[253] Fennell, "Diversion of Mentally Disordered Offenders from Custody" [1991] Crim. L.R. 333.

[254] Burney and Pearson, "Mentally Disordered Offenders: Finding a Focus for Diversion" (1995) 34(4) *Howard Journal of Criminal Justice* 291, 309.

[255] Criminal Procedure (Scotland) Act 1995 s.54. Evidence may be written or oral.

[256] Criminal Procedure (Scotland) Act 1995 s.55.

[257] Criminal Procedure (Scotland) Act 1995 s.54.

[258] Criminal Procedure (Scotland) Act 1995 s.55(5).

[259] Criminal Procedure (Scotland) Act 1995 s.55(4).

[260] Criminal Procedure (Scotland) Act 1995 s.57(2)(d). This disposal is only competent in insanity procedures. None of the measures can be enforced and consequently there is no sanction for failure to obtemper the conditions of the order.

[261] Note that the disposals available under s.57(2) are the same as those where the facts are found and the accused is not acquitted.

[262] By the accused or the Crown. The Crown may only appeal on points of law.

[263] Insanity has long been recognised in Scots law; diminished responsibility dates from the nineteenth century.

Insanity in bar of trial

6.40 Insanity in bar of trial is not strictly speaking a defence as it relates to an individual's capacity to participate in the judicial process rather than consideration of responsibility for their actions. Prior to the Criminal Procedure (Scotland) Act 1995, disposals in such cases were very limited.[264] Findings of "unfitness to plead" were more common in Scotland than elsewhere in the United Kingdom[265] until the 1980s. It was possible to raise proceedings against a person at a later date when they had regained sufficient fitness to plead; however, this proved rare in practice. The Criminal Procedure (Scotland) Act 1995 allowed for more flexibility in disposal of a person found unfit to plead.[266] There remains no statutory definition of insanity in bar of trial.[267]

Insanity at the time of the offence

6.41 Insanity at the time of the offence is a key psychiatric defence and provides a complete defence to a criminal charge as it negates the effect of the crucial mens rea aspect of most crimes.[268] Hume's definition[269] forms the original basis for the current Scottish criteria for insanity, which is thought to be:

> "An absolute alienation of reason ... such a disease as deprives the patient of the knowledge of the true aspect and position of things about him—hinders him from distinguishing friend from foe—and gives him up to the impulse of his own distempered fancy."[270]

Pre-1995, where a person was acquitted on the grounds of insanity he was automatically committed to the state hospital on a hospital order with restrictions on discharge. The disposals currently available are identical to those for persons found insane in bar of trial.[271]

Automatism

6.42 Automatism is a defence available where individuals commit offences while not conscious.[272] A distinction is drawn by the legal system in both Scotland and England and Wales between sane

---

[264] In solemn cases, disposal was by way of a mandatory hospital order with restrictions on discharge to the state hospital; in summary cases a mandatory hospital order with or without restrictions to any hospital.

[265] D. Chiswick, "Insanity in Bar of Trial in Scotland: A State Hospital Study" (1978) 132 *British Journal of Psychiatry* 598, cited in McManus and Thomson, *Mental Health and Scots Law in Practice* (2005).

[266] Criminal Procedure (Scotland) Act 1995, as amended by the Mental Health (Care and Treatment) (Scotland) Act 2003 and the Criminal Justice (Scotland) Act 2003.

[267] The leading case is *HM Advocate v Wilson*, 1942 J.C. 75. The relevant criteria were laid out more recently in *Stewart v HM Advocate (No.1)*, 1997 J.C. 183 as "The question for [the trial judge] was whether the appellant, by reason of his material mental handicap, would be unable to instruct his legal representatives as to his defence or to follow what went on at his trial."

[268] Usually intent or recklessness. Courts tend to view this objectively.

[269] Hume, *Commentaries on the Law of Scotland Respecting Crimes* (1844) cited in McManus and Thomson, *Mental Health and Scots Law in Practice* (2005). While Scotland traditionally favours the definition of insanity in these institutional writings, English law prefers the so-called M'Naghten Rules, based on the *M'Naghten* case (1843) 10 Cl & F 200.

[270] Lord Strachan's charge to the jury in *Lord Advocate v Kidd*, 1960 J.C. 61 is generally considered the leading modern judicial statement on insanity and is similar to that adopted by many American states.

[271] Criminal Procedure (Scotland) Act 1995 s.57. The most serious cases will result in a mandatory compulsion order with restrictions, in line with the Criminal Justice (Scotland) Act 2003. There is a flexible range of disposals dependent on the risk posed by the acquitted person due to their mental state. Similar rights of appeal are available as under insanity in bar of trial.

[272] For example, while asleep or as a result of hypoglycaemia. The earliest reported Scottish case is that of *Simon Fraser* (1878) 4 Couper 70. The most recent is that of *Sorley v HM Advocate*, 1992 S.C.C.R. 396.

and insane automatism, based entirely on whether the offending behaviour is of a recurring nature.[273] Flexibility of disposal exists in respect of either finding.

Diminished responsibility

6.43 Diminished responsibility was originally a defence peculiar to Scotland[274] and may be used in cases where the mental disorder of the accused has played a significant role in the commission of the criminal act, but is not severe enough to allow for acquittal on grounds of insanity. Most recently, the term has been redefined and widened in scope by the Court of Criminal Appeal,[275] to include where "there is an abnormality of mind which substantially impaired the ability of the accused ... to determine or control his acts". Where such a defence is upheld, there is flexibility for the court in its disposal. There are no appeal procedures specific to this defence.

The provisions relating to persons with mental health difficulties who come before the criminal courts are contained within a number of statutes relating to both mental health and criminal procedure. As a result, the law in this area can be difficult to follow for those ill-acquainted with the process.

A criminal court will make one of a number of possible mental health orders where an accused requires treatment for his or her disorder.[276] There is little difference between the treatment of offenders and any other person,[277] except where special restrictions are required to ensure public safety. The courts are not bound by the general principles of the Mental Health (Care and Treatment) (Scotland) Act 2003 as any order is made predominantly under the Criminal Procedure (Scotland) Act 1995 as amended.

Assessment and treatment orders

6.44 Where a person has been charged with an offence and appears before the court on an initial hearing he may be remanded in custody[278] or released on bail.[279] Alternatively, an accused person may be sent to hospital for assessment and/or treatment[280] by way of an assessment order or a treatment order. An assessment order authorises detention in hospital of a named person, together with treatment, for up to 28 days.[281] There is no right of appeal against the making of an assessment order. During the 28-day period a report will be drafted considering the accused's fitness to stand trial and/or mental state at the time of the offence. The responsible medical officer will also be required to state whether or not there are grounds for making the accused

---

[273] Where the behaviour is likely to reoccur as a result of a condition, such as epilepsy, it is said to be insane automatism, and will result in acquittal on the grounds of insanity. Likewise, where the behaviour is a one-off incident as a result of hypoglycaemia or concussion, the finding will be one of sane automatism and will result in a complete acquittal.

[274] See *HM Advocate v Dingwall* (1867) 5 Irv. 466 and in particular, the judgment of Lord Deas. The term "diminished responsibility" was first used in 1939, in the case of *Kirkwood v HM Advocate*, 1939 J.C. 36.

[275] See *Galbraith v HM Advocate (No.2)*, 2001 S.C.C.R. 551.

[276] Where a person with a mental disorder is charged with an offence that may result in a sentence of imprisonment from the district court, the case should be remitted to the sheriff court: Criminal Procedure (Scotland) Act 1995 s.52A, as amended by the 2003 Act.

[277] The exception occurs in relation to whether or not a person can make a decision about his medical treatment. As the order is made by the court as a direct alternative to other disposals, treatment decisions are considered irrelevant.

[278] An accused may also be remanded to a hospital for assessment: Criminal Procedure (Scotland) Act 1995 s.200.

[279] Bail may be granted with conditions attached and it is for the accused to prove that he can comply with such conditions to the satisfaction of the court. A number of courts operate bail supervision schemes and this may be of particular use to mentally disordered offenders. There is a right of appeal to the High Court in respect of bail conditions.

[280] The court is entitled to make such an order at any point during the criminal justice process.

[281] On the production of a medical report. This need not be from a psychiatrist. The prosecution may apply to the court for an assessment order, or the court may make such an order of its own volition. Criminal Procedure (Scotland) Act 1995 ss.52B–52E, as amended by the 2003 Act; Scottish Executive, *Mental Health (Care and Treatment) (Scotland) Act 2003 Code of Practice* ("2003 Act Code of Practice") (2005), Vol.3. Any party subject to an assessment order is subject to the general provisions of the 2003 Act, including those contained in Pt 16 (medical treatment). If the accused's condition changes, the court may vary or revoke the order accordingly.

subject to a treatment order.[282] If this is thought necessary a second medical report must be obtained. On receipt of the report, the court must revoke the assessment order[283] and make any other order it feels appropriate.[284]

A treatment order authorises detention of a person in hospital until a verdict is reached.[285] Application for such an order will generally be made by the prosecution or the court of its own volition.[286] When considering making an assessment order, a court must consider evidence from two doctors, one of whom must be an approved medical practitioner and the other a doctor from the hospital where the accused will be detained on the treatment order.[287] As with an assessment order, there is no right of appeal against the making of a treatment order. During the period of the treatment order, the responsible medical officer will consider the accused's fitness to stand trial and/or mental state at the time of the offence and prepare the appropriate report. He will also be required to consider what sentence or order might be made if the person is convicted.

Compulsion orders

6.45 An interim compulsion order may also be sought prior to sentencing to allow a full assessment as to whether a compulsion order would be a suitable disposal.[288] Such an order may authorise an accused's detention in hospital for up to 12 months.[289] Two medical reports are required to support the making of the order,[290] together with a further report from a mental health officer or criminal justice social worker.[291] Following assessment, the responsible medical officer must provide a report to the court confirming whether he considers a compulsion order or hospital direction an appropriate disposal.[292] A compulsion order mirrors the compulsory treatment order provided for under the 2003 Act and may be made by either the sheriff court or High Court. An accused may appeal against the making of a compulsion order as he would appeal against sentence.[293]

Where an accused is acquitted on grounds of insanity[294] the court may make one of the following orders:

- a supervision and treatment order;
- a compulsion order authorising detention in hospital[295];

[282] Criminal Procedure (Scotland) Act 1995 s.52G(1).

[283] In certain circumstances, the court can extend the assessment order for up to seven days after receipt of the report where necessary. See 2003 Act Code of Practice, Vol.3, para.2.114 for further information.

[284] The order will expire at the end of the statutory period, following the making of a treatment order or after sentence.

[285] Criminal Procedure (Scotland) Act 1995 s.52E(3). Detention and treatment includes the giving of medical treatment under Pt 16 of the 2003 Act. Where a person ceases to need psychiatric care, a court may discharge the order.

[286] Criminal Procedure (Scotland) Act 1995 ss.52K, 52L and 52N.

[287] Criminal Procedure (Scotland) Act 1995 ss.52M(3) and 61(1A). The grounds for making the order are contained within s.52M(3) and 61(1A) of the Criminal Procedure (Scotland) Act 1995.

[288] An interim order should be made unless there are compelling reasons for not doing so. See 2003 Act Code of Practice, Vol.3 for further information. An interim compulsion order cannot normally be made where an accused is convicted of murder as life sentence is mandatory.

[289] The initial order is made for a period of up to 12 weeks and is thereafter renewable for further periods of up to 12 weeks at a time, to a maximum of 12 months. Medical treatment may be given in accordance with Pt 16 of the 2003 Act.

[290] Criminal Procedure (Scotland) Act 1995 s.53.

[291] Criminal Procedure (Scotland) Act 1995 s.57C.

[292] Criminal Procedure (Scotland) Act 1995 ss.57A and 59A.

[293] Criminal Procedure (Scotland) Act 1995 s.60.

[294] Or alternatively, was unfit to plead and an Examination of Facts found the accused committed the offence.

[295] Criminal Procedure (Scotland) Act 1995 s.57A. This includes an interim compulsion order. The order may have restrictions attached. The compulsion order must include a restriction order where the accused would be of high risk to the public were he to remain at liberty. The accused may also appeal against a restriction order in the same way as an appeal against sentence. The grounds for making the order are set out in the Criminal Procedure (Scotland) Act 1995 s.57A(3).

- welfare intervention or guardianship orders under the 2000 Act[296];
- no order.[297]

A supervision and treatment order[298] requires the person who is subject to the order to follow directions from a social worker and comply with medical treatment. It is a less restrictive measure than a compulsion order; however, there are no sanctions where the person fails to comply and consequently it is of limited use.

Compulsion orders are discussed in some detail earlier in the Chapter. A hospital direction may be made where medical treatment is unlikely to reduce the risk that an accused poses to the public, or where the relationship between the offence and mental disorder is unclear.[299] This order combines a prison sentence with a hospital-based compulsion order.[300] The procedure for making the order is identical to that of the compulsion order, and similar rights of appeal exist.

A court may make an order for welfare intervention or guardianship under the Adults with Incapacity (Scotland) Act 2000.[301] The application for such an order may be made to the court in the normal way.[302]

Order for lifelong restriction

6.46 A court may impose a normal prison sentence or deferred sentence[303] even when a person has a mental disorder where this is considered the most appropriate disposal. Where a person is convicted of a serious violent or sexual offence, the court may make an order for lifelong restriction.[304] The order combines a prison sentence with a lifelong risk management plan, which will be revised and updated as necessary according to the changing circumstances of the offender. Prior to making such an order, the court will order a risk assessment, or impose an interim compulsion order to determine the suitability of the proposed disposal. The court may also make a probation order to allow a convicted person to seek treatment for his psychiatric or psychological condition.[305] The order may have conditions attached to it regulating residence or treatment. If a person subject to the order fails to comply with it, he may be brought back to court. The probation order may last for a maximum of three years.

Finally, a person with a mental disorder may be acquitted of a crime. Where there are residual concerns about risk to that person or another if the person was allowed to leave the court it is possible that the court may make an order to detain him for a medical examination. Two medical reports are required in support of the grant of such an order.[306] Detention may be for a maximum of six hours.[307] The order will lapse where an emergency or short-term detention certificate is signed.

---

[296] Financial guardianship or intervention order is not a competent disposal in this regard.
[297] Criminal Procedure (Scotland) Act 1995 s.57(3), as amended by the Criminal Justice (Scotland) Act 2003 s.2(b).
[298] Criminal Procedure (Scotland) Act 1995 s.57(2)(d) and Sch.4 para.1. Available only where a person is acquitted on grounds of insanity or is found unfit to plead and a subsequent examination of facts decides the person committed the offence.
[299] Criminal Procedure (Scotland) Act 1995 s.59A.
[300] When an offender no longer requires hospital care he carries out the remainder of his sentence in prison. See the Criminal Procedure (Scotland) Act 1995 s.59A.
[301] Criminal Procedure (Scotland) Act 1995 ss.58 and 60 (as amended by the 2000 Act).
[302] See paras 6.28–6.29 on intervention and guardianship orders for further details.
[303] Criminal Procedure (Scotland) Act 1995 s.202(1).
[304] Criminal Procedure (Scotland) Act 1995 s.210F(1), as amended by the Criminal Justice (Scotland) Act 2003.
[305] Criminal Procedure (Scotland) Act 1995 ss.58, 228, 230 and 232, as amended.
[306] Criminal Procedure (Scotland) Act 1995 s.60C(3).
[307] Criminal Procedure (Scotland) Act 1995 s.60C.

Chapter 7

COMMUNITY CARE

INTRODUCTION

Background

7.01 Community care exists to offer combined support and services to people with health and social care needs who are living in their own homes, with a view to preserving and sustaining their position within the community.[1] The legislation that was introduced to enforce this policy was accompanied by a transfer of earmarked resources from the NHS to local authorities.[2] Social work departments were to become the custodians of various client-care groups and were to ensure that social care could be effectively provided and managed in their area. The community care remit is generally understood to embrace people who are elderly, physically or mentally disabled, or suffering in some manner from a limiting illness.[3] It also includes people suffering from drug or alcohol dependence or release from any form of detention.[4]

The vision at the outset, which has subsisted until the present day, was of an enabling service whereby users could support themselves on a daily basis if an adequate range of services could be accessed by them. As a result, some people would be better off cared for in their own homes. Community care is essentially non-medical in nature as the object is principally one of social care. However, specific health needs are present in many of its users and where feasible they will receive medical treatment in the community setting, usually in their own homes.

Community care was extant for a number of years before legislative reform was undertaken on the basis of a formal set of objectives. Since the 1970s it has met with some mixed reactions

---

[1] For further reading on community care generally see J. Lewis and H. Glennerster, *Implementing the New Community Care* (Open University Press, 1996); Scottish Affairs Committee, *Implementation of Community Care in Scotland—a 2nd Report* (London: HMSO, 1996/97); Legg (ed.), *Care in the Community: Illusion or Reality?* (Chichester: John Wiley & Sons, 1997); S. Baldwin, *Needs Assessment and Community Care: Clinical Practice and Policy-Making* (Oxford: Butterworth-Heinemann, 1997); R. Smith and R. Means, *Community Care: Policy and Practice* (Basingstoke: Macmillan, 1998); M. Priestley, *Disability Politics and Community Care* (London: Jessica Kingsley Publishers, 1998); Scottish Office, *Modernising Community Care: An Action Plan* (Edinburgh: HMSO, 1998).

[2] By virtue of s.16A of the National Health Service (Scotland) Act 1978 health boards are empowered to transfer money to social work and housing departments, housing associations, Scottish Homes and independent voluntary non-profit making organisations providing housing or social care.

[3] The definition of "persons in need" under s.94 of the Social Work (Scotland) Act 1968 ("1968 Act") is generally used to determine who is entitled to community care services.

[4] 1968 Act s.12(6).

though has continued to provide a model for performance within social work practice.[5] In 1986 the Audit Commission Report *Making a Reality out of Community Care* stressed that the growing emphasis on residential and nursing home care was detracting severely from the development of services for people living in their own homes.[6] While there was confirmed support for care in the community, resources were conversely being directed at institutional care. The Report insisted that progress was only to be achieved by bringing services to people, not people to services.[7] It proved to be the impetus required for immediate action and in 1988 the Griffiths Report, *Community Care—An Agenda for Action*[8] and the Wagner Report, *Residential Care: A Positive Choice* together formed a response to the reproach of the Audit Commission.[9] Griffiths' recommendations were to become the rudiments of the prospective White Paper *Caring for people—community care in the next decade and beyond*,[10] which in turn formed the basis of the NHS and Community Care Bill published one week later. The substance of the Griffiths Report was that systems should be in place within social service and social work departments which could fully support community care and the assessment of community care needs. These components are now central to the present legislative provisions that regulate community care.

7.02 The objectives of the White Paper were laid down as follows[11]:

- To promote the development of domiciliary, day and respite services to enable people to live in their own homes wherever feasible and sensible.
- To ensure that service providers make practical support for carers a high priority.
- To make proper assessment of need and good case management the cornerstone of high quality care. Packages of care should then be designed in line with individual needs and preferences.
- To promote the development of a flourishing independent sector alongside good quality public services.
- To clarify the responsibilities of agencies and so make it easier to hold them to account for their performance.
- To secure better value for taxpayers' money by introducing a new funding structure for social care.

The NHS and Community Care Bill that followed aimed to transpose these objectives into a workable statutory framework.

Review of community care continued in December 1997 in the form of a Royal Commission. It was initiated by the Secretary of State for Health to examine the system of funding of long-term care for elderly people. The Commission's report on long-term care (the Sutherland

---

[5] One initial concern was that community care had not developed beyond a "catch-all phrase" and thus had little to give it the intended effect (see FICSS, *Community Care* (1985)) though much of the more recent criticism been based on the idea that community care is progressively becoming a "resource-led" exercise in the sense that arrangements are based around local authority budgets, often at the expense of prevailing individual needs. This is a point that the courts have sought to clarify but that continues to be much of an issue in social work generally.

[6] The Report promised that community care would improve the quality of life for the thousands of people located in residential care and for the millions of Britain's carers. Despite these aspirations it seemed that progress was slow and funds with which to bridge the transition of responsibility from NHS to local social work departments limited. The response to community care across Britain had been mixed, with copious examples of both good and bad practice among local social work and social services departments: Audit Commission for Local Authorities in England and Wales, *Making a Reality of Community Care* (London: HMSO, 1986), pp.2–3.

[7] Audit Commission, *Making a Reality of Community Care* (1986), p.10.

[8] *A Report to the Secretary of State for Social Services, Department of Health and Social Security* ("Griffiths Report") (London: HMSO, 1988).

[9] *The Report of the Independent Review of Residential Care* ("Wagner Report") (London: HMSO, 1988) was based principally on promoting good practice in residential care and was not concerned with promoting community care to the same extent as the report produced by Sir Roy Griffiths.

[10] Department of Health, Cm.849 (London: HMSO, 1989).

[11] Local authorities are told in guidance on community care to refine their arrangements in accordance with principles of the White Paper: SWSG Circular 11/91, para.22.2.

Report) made a number of far-reaching and innovative recommendations.[12] It advocated, among other things, free nursing care for the elderly and a National Commission overseeing minimum standards of care. The Sutherland Report focused the Scottish Executive's attention towards the need for change in these areas. The Report proved to be quite influential since two significant pieces of legislation, namely the Regulation of Care (Scotland) Act 2001 ("2001 Act") and the Community Care and Health (Scotland) Act 2002 ("2002 Act") followed addressing Sutherland's recommendations.

The legal structure that now forms the backbone of community care practice has emerged as the result of protracted and piecemeal efforts to realise a fairly tolerant set of objectives. Despite cries for statutory coherence the result has been a somewhat fragmented legal representation of community care rights. Alongside, an unrelenting string of government circulars have sought to translate the legal framework into more practical social work terms.

Statutory framework

7.03 The legislation ultimately regulates the operations of local government so as to ensure that community care clients can benefit from maximum levels of social welfare dispensed through their local authorities. Social work departments and often housing authorities are their primary source of assistance. Voluntary organisations are prompted by their own particular objectives and not by the law.

The activities of local government are governed by legislative duties and powers. Where a local authority is under a duty to discharge its functions, it is impelled to do so and is not granted the liberty of exercising discretion. A failure to observe such a term may render an authority in breach of its statutory obligations. A statutory empowerment, on the other hand, authorises or enables the local authority to act. It can exercise discretion in doing so, and will make a decision based on the individual circumstances of the case in hand. There is more limited recourse against an authority that is lawfully exercising discretion. The outcome of any legal action that is taken will rest upon the actual manner in which the decision was made and not its legality as such.[13]

The legal provisions that are currently of interest to us are contained within a range of social work statutes. There may be a number of valid reasons for this. First, "care" as we know it is multi-faceted and carries quite diverse objectives: support services seek to ensure that daily needs are met at home and in the wider community setting; housing services aim to meet physical disability and infirmity with the most suitable type of accommodation; residential and nursing care is designed for people with maximum care needs who cannot cope in their own homes, either alone or with domiciliary support. It would be impossible to confine these distinct elements of social work within an aggregate piece of legislation. Nevertheless, the need for one comprehensive Act has been highlighted by writers in the field.[14] Secondly, the area is a dynamic one which continually undergoes reform, often in the form of Private Members' Bills. Time and again the most critical of community care legislation has emerged from the parliamentary backbenches where the struggle for recognition can sometimes be most heartfelt.[15] And thirdly, the law has evolved in something of a piecemeal manner as new initiatives have come to fruition at irregular intervals. This alone makes a clear framework of the relevant provisions quite difficult to produce. It is for students simply to note that "community care law" is an umbrella term for an amalgam of social work statutes examined individually below.

7.04 The Social Work (Scotland) Act 1968 ("1968 Act") was largely responsible for the growth of a contemporary social work structure in Scotland. Section 12 placed an obligation for the

---

[12] *With respect to old age: long term care—rights and responsibilities*, Cm.4192 (London: HMSO, 1999).

[13] See Ch.2.

[14] See e.g. L. Clements, "Community Care—Towards a Workable Statute" (1997) 19(2) *Liverpool Law Review* 181.

[15] Chronically Sick and Disabled Persons Act 1970 ("1970 Act"), the Disabled Persons (Services, Consultation and Representation) Act 1986 ("1986 Act") and the Carers (Recognition and Services) Act 1995 were each Private Members Bills in turn.

organisation and provision of "welfare services" with social work departments throughout Scotland, and fundamentally defined a client base, namely "persons in need", upon which all future activity in this field would eventually turn. The Act has undergone a number of critical revisions in the years since its implementation with the result that its original content has been substantially modified.[16] It is largely the 1968 Act that regulates community care, incorporating the amendments of the National Health Service and Community Care Act 1990 ("1990 Act").[17]

Almost immediately following the 1968 Act, the Chronically Sick and Disabled Persons Act 1970 ("1970 Act") placed a further duty on local authorities to make arrangements for the provision of the welfare services which had been identified in s.12 of the 1968 Act, once it was satisfied that a need for them existed within a given individual.[18] This hinted at the need to undertake an assessment of needs but was not quite that specific. In addition, the 1970 Act produced a list of possible services which could be read alongside the more standard terms of s.12 and thus specifically guided service-users towards named facilities. Of course this was to apply in respect of people who were chronically sick or disabled.

The Disabled Persons (Services, Consultation and Representation) Act 1986 ("1986 Act") allowed disabled people, their carers or their representatives to actually request an assessment of need for the services outlined in s.2 of the 1970 Act.[19] As a result the local authority is bound to carry out an assessment, and to make the necessary arrangements thereafter. This Act was also the first evidence that carers of disabled people were valued in their role since local authorities were to undertake a carer's assessment where substantial amounts of care were being provided to a disabled person on a regular basis.[20]

7.05 Notwithstanding these fragmentary efforts to ensure comprehensive service provision, gaps in the law remained, as did the lack of co-ordinated planning. It was in the light of these difficulties that the 1990 Act was introduced, undertaking to supplement Pt II of the 1968 Act, which relates to welfare services. Among other things it placed a duty on local authorities to assess the need for "community care services". This enhanced the duty of local authorities to secure the provision of welfare services under s.12. Furthermore, it applied to people who were elderly, disabled, or suffering from mental or physical health problems, and thus improved the position for those who were omitted from the provisions of the 1970 Act. Its primary goal was to increase both the range and amount of services that were available to people in their own homes.

Further legislation has tried to extend this sort of recognition beyond the client to those directly and regularly involved with his or her welfare. The Carers (Recognition and Services) Act 1995 highlights the fundamental role that is played by carers and entitled them to an assessment of their own. It thereby amplifies the provisions of the 1986 Act that relate to carers. In addition, the provisions of the Community Care (Direct Payments) Act 1996 authorise local authorities to make cash payments in lieu of community care services. Individuals will then purchase the services and facilities that they require.

More recent legislation has focused on the regulation of Scotland's care system. The Regulation of Care (Scotland) Act 2001 provides a new framework for the monitoring of care services and the means to improve and standardise provision of care. To give effect to the aims of the Act the Scottish Commission for the Regulation of Care (Care Commission) was established. Alongside this Act, the Scottish Executive's attention was directed to elderly care

---

[16] For instance the National Health Service and Community Care Act 1990 ("1990 Act"), the Children (Scotland) Act 1995 which removed many of the provisions of the 1968 Act and placed them in a format specifically for children, the Local Government etc. (Scotland) Act 1994 which gave effect to local government reorganisation, the Health and Social Services and Social Security Adjudications Act 1983, the Carers (Recognition and Services) Act 1995 and the Community Care (Direct Payments) Act 1996.

[17] The 1968 Act repealed many of the provisions of the National Assistance Act 1948 which had represented first recognition of the need to make welfare provision for people who were disabled or of pensionable age. Some of it still operates in England and it continues to co-ordinate the funding arrangements for residential care in Scotland.

[18] Chronically Sick and Disabled Persons Act 1970 ("1970 Act") s.2.

[19] 1986 Act s.4.

[20] 1986 Act s.8.

which eventually led to the Community Care and Health (Scotland) Act 2002 ("2002 Act"). The 2002 Act implemented the recommendations of the Care Development Group[21] which was established by the Scottish Executive to "bring forward proposals to ensure that older people in Scotland have access to high quality and responsive long term care ... including proposals for the implementation of free personal care".[22] Adopting many of the Group's recommendations the 2002 Act made fundamental changes to the effect that specific social care services must now be provided free of charge. Other provisions in the Act include regulating certain deferred payments and direct payments, extending carers' rights to assessments and providing for joint working.

More recent legislation has sought to protect vulnerable adults at risk of harm. The Adult Support and Protection (Scotland) Act 2007 ("2007 Act") provides for, among other things, intervention and inquiries in such cases.

Guidance and direction

7.06 This piecemeal growth in legislation has compelled a catalogue of government guidance and direction stretching back for a number of years on the practical operation of social work, and more specifically community care law. In terms of their social work duties under the 1968 Act, local authorities are required to perform their duties in accordance with guidance issued by the Secretary of State.[23] To all intents and purposes this serves as a source of advice to local authorities on how to implement the rather vague terms of the legislation. Much of the guidance relating to community care is issued under s.5(1) of the 1968 Act.[24] However, while "policy" guidance issued under s.5(1) must be followed, "practice" guidance is an indication of good practice alone. Respectively, local authorities are told what to do and how to do it. It seems likely that a failure to observe guidance will render the body in question open to judicial review.

An oversight of practice guidance might constitute grounds for setting the decision of the local authority aside.[25] A breach of policy guidance would appear to carry more certain ramifications for the offending authority. In *R. v North Yorkshire CC Ex p. Hargreaves*[26] the applicant sought judicial review of a decision by his local authority to offer respite care to his sister on the grounds that the arrangements did not accord with her particular wishes. The court referred in its judgment to policy guidance that expressly stated the need to allow the user to participate actively in the assessment and in making any subsequent choices regarding the care package.[27] Failure to adhere to this policy guidance gave the court grounds to set the decision aside.[28]

In 1991 the Scottish Executive issued *Community Care in Scotland: Assessment and Care Management* to prepare local authorities for their new and emerging duties under the 1990 Act.[29] This provides essential practice guidance on the conduct of all bodies involved in com-

---

[21] The Care Development Group was established on the back on the Sutherland Report.

[22] Care Development Group, *Fair Care for Older People* (Scottish Executive, 2001) p.i. The full text of the report is available on the Scottish Executive website.

[23] This responsibility now falls on Scottish Ministers.

[24] Guidance is sometimes referred to as quasi-legislation in the sense that it is designed to have a regulatory effect on the appropriate bodies, supplementary to the legislative provisions that ultimately govern them. An instance of such guidance, often referred to as a government circular, is *Community Care in Scotland: Assessment and Care Management*, SWSG Circular 11/91, which is heavily relied upon in community care.

[25] In *R. v Islington LBC Ex p. Rixon* [1997] E.L.R. 66 it was the opinion of the court that Parliament had intended local authorities to follow the path charted by the Secretary of State's guidance, with liberty to deviate arising only with good reason judged on admissible grounds by the authority itself. However, this does not confer a general freedom to take a substantially different course from that contained in the guidance unless cogent reasons exist for doing so.

[26] (1997–98) 1 C.C.L. Rep. 104.

[27] Dept of Health, *Community Care in the Next Decade and Beyond: Policy Guidance* (London: HMSO, 1990), paras 3.9 and 3.25.

[28] Though this decision was based on policy guidance issued in England and Wales it is likely that Scottish courts would follow the reasoning.

[29] SWSG Circular 11/91.

munity care and stresses the lead role to be played by social work departments in deciding how assessment and care management are to operate. Some caution must be exercised when dealing with guidance.[30]

Quite distinctly, directions issued by Scottish Ministers place an obligation on the local authority to fulfil a legal duty supplementary to that defined in statutory provisions and carry more weight than the government circulars referred to above. For instance, the Social Work (Scotland) Act 1968 (Choice of Accommodation) Directions 1993 retain a resident's right to choose his or her residential accommodation. This carries the same force as the provisions of the 1968 Act itself. Directions are enforceable under s.5(1A).

COMMUNITY CARE SERVICES

7.07 At the core of community care is the provision of services that enable clients to remain in their own homes. The statutory provisions that govern this process are principally located within the 1968 Act.

Welfare services

7.08 Section 12 of the 1968 Act in a large sense forms the basis of social work operations in Scotland and seeks to specify the broad duty to provide social work services for adults.

Similar obligations towards children are contained in the Children (Scotland) Act 1995. The duty in respect of adults is to provide "advice, guidance and assistance" and in turn to secure the provision of facilities, including residential and other establishments. However, in avoiding a definition of what may or may not constitute a "welfare service", the Act seemed to recognise the potentially broad nature of care and assistance that was required. In this sense, it undertook to encourage needs-led service provision. It is for each local authority to specify the support services available in its area. However, the 1968 Act does expressly recognise the need that exists for a number of services.

Domiciliary services

7.09 Section 14 obliges local authorities to make arrangements for persons in need to receive domestic assistance in their own homes. This includes home help and laundry facilities. Before amendment by the 1990 Act this section referred to home help specifically but has been broadened to incorporate,

> "any services, being services provided in the home, which appear to the local authority to be necessary for the purpose of enabling a person to maintain as independent an existence as is practicable in his home."[31]

These provisions overlap with those contained in s.2 of the Chronically Sick and Disabled Persons Act 1970 to provide assistance in the home for chronically sick and disabled people.

Care and aftercare

7.10 Under s.13B of the 1968 Act local authorities are authorised to make arrangements for the prevention of illness, and for both the care and aftercare of those suffering from illness. This is essentially an NHS function under s.37 of the National Health Service (Scotland) Act 1978, which places an onus on Scottish Ministers to ensure that those arrangements are in place.

---

[30] Akin to legislation, guidance can be repealed, for example the guidance *Community Care and Health (Scotland) Act 2002. New Statutory Rights for Carers*, Circular CCD 2/2003 (providing advice on the new 2002 provisions in relation to carers) replaces SWSG Circular 11/96.

[31] 1990 Act s.66(1) and Sch.9.

However, local authorities are in a position to assist by virtue of this enabling section. The boundaries between NHS and social work responsibilities are quite often unclear, especially so in the region of community care where health and social care needs can easily seem to constitute the same thing. The Community Care and Health (Scotland) Act 2002 ensures that those receiving both NHS treatment and local authority care benefit from joint resourcing where payments can be made by one body to the other. Further, the Community Care (Joint Working etc.) (Scotland) Regulations 2002[32] expand upon the collaborative process.

Burial and cremation of the dead

7.11 Section 28 provides local authorities with a function towards people who have died while receiving their care or assistance, namely to bury or cremate the deceased in accordance with any religious persuasion. Local authorities are not responsible for subsidising the said arrangements though an application may be made to the social fund for assistance with funeral costs. However, where it appears that no suitable arrangements have been or are being made for the disposal of a body, the local authority is compelled to intervene and to bury or cremate the deceased whether or not the individual was in receipt of its services.[33]

Services under the 1970 Act

7.12 These are services provided specifically for people who are chronically sick or disabled. Section 2 of the 1970 Act is quite specific regarding the types of service that are to be available in meeting the needs of applicants, and in this sense serves to augment the more general content of s.12 of the 1968 Act. The services available are as follows:

- practical assistance in the home;
- radio, television, books or similar recreational facilities in the home;
- recreational facilities outside the home such as lectures, games and outings, and services that promote the use of educational facilities;
- assistance travelling to and from local authority services, or similar services run by other bodies;
- assistance arranging adaptation to the home in which a disabled person lives with a view to securing his greater safety, comfort or convenience;
- holidays;
- meals at home; and
- telephone and related equipment.

The scope for social work intervention is clearly quite broad. Nevertheless, guidance on the 1970 Act states that the local authority should look not only at the need for things expressly mentioned in s.2, but at all relevant needs. In other words, this is not intended to be an exhaustive list of options.[34]

Free personal care

7.13 Since July 1, 2002, the Community Care and Health (Scotland) Act 2002 has regulated provisions for free personal care ("FPC"). Consequently, local authorities are not permitted to charge for personal care, personal support, nursing care and other such care (not ordinarily charged for) that is provided or supplied by them.[35] "Personal care" relates to the everyday tasks and needs of the individual, for example eating and drinking, and to the "mental processes" of those tasks, for example remembering to eat and drink, while "personal support" refers to

---

[32] SSI 2002/533.

[33] National Assistance Act 1948 s.50.

[34] Dept of Health, *The Chronically Sick and Disabled Persons Act 1970*, Circular 12/70, para.7.

[35] Community Care and Health (Scotland) Act 2002 ("2002 Act") s.1.

programmed help, for example counselling.[36] There is no definition of "nursing care" other than it does not include care referred to above. Schedule 1 to the 2002 Act defines the broad categories of social care not ordinarily charged for. These are as follows:

- the personal hygiene of the person cared for, including shaving and cleaning teeth;
- the person's eating requirements including the preparation of food;
- dealing with an individual's immobility or substantial immobility;
- assisting with medical attention where required, for example applying creams;
- the person's general well-being including assisting with dressing.

Notably, Scottish Ministers reserve the right to amend the scope of free provision of social care and charges for other social care in future regulations.[37] Such regulations may also specify factors to be considered in charging, maximum charges and exemptions from payment.

With the exception of nursing care, a person must be over 65 years to be eligible for free social care.[38] Special rules apply to those living in residential accommodation or nursing homes prior to March 31, 2002. In these cases, an automatic payment of £149 will be given for personal care and where a person receives nursing care, a further £67 per week.[39]

7.14 Persons paying for a care or nursing home after March 31, 2002 must be assessed as requiring free personal services. In these instances, a flat rate payment of £145 is provided for assessed personal care needs to those aged 65 years and over and currently meeting their own costs; while flat rate payments of £67 for nursing care needs are available to all persons in nursing homes who meet their own costs.[40]

Different rules apply to persons aged 65 years and above who are living at home. In these instances, charges cannot be made for FPC services; however, the local authority may still charge for other domestic services.[41] The extent of local authorities' duty to provide for free personal care was tested in the Court of Session case *Argyll and Bute Council for Judicial Review*[42] In a landmark decision, Lord Macphail held that the 2002 Act cannot be interpreted to oblige local authorities to provide for social care which is not provided for by them.

Where FPC is subject to an assessment of needs, it is not to be affected by income, capital assets, marital status or care contribution of an unpaid carer.[43] Guidance provides further explanation of the implementation of free care.[44]

A report carried out by Age Concern Scotland found that despite the policy of free care being welcomed, a number of difficulties ensued.[45] In the summary of findings the report highlighted that local information strategies varied in quality and effectiveness; wide variations in access to services combined with waiting lists were experienced; there was a lack of clarity with regard to

---

[36] Regulation of Care (Scotland) Act 2001 ("2001 Act") s.2(28).

[37] This is particularly pertinent since it is speculated that the Scottish Executive is not providing sufficient funds to meet the demands of free social care: *Free Personal and Nursing Care—Some Concerns*, Age Concern Scotland Briefing Note (June 2002).

[38] Community Care (Personal Care and Nursing Care) (Scotland) Regulations 2002 (SSI 2002/303) reg.3. A person living in a care home and receiving FPC will lose their entitlement to attendance allowance or the care component of disability living allowance.

[39] Community Care (Assessment of Needs) (Scotland) Regulations 2002 (SSI 2002/304) regs 1 and 2.

[40] Community Care (Personal Care and Nursing Care) (Scotland) Regulations 2002 reg.2.

[41] 2002 Act s.1.

[42] Unreported October 17, 2007, Lord Macphail.

[43] 2002 Act s.2.

[44] *Implementation of Free Personal Care*, Circular CCD 4/2002 which has been consolidated in guidance, Circular CCD 5/2003.

[45] For a full discussion on the implementation of the Act, see Age Concern, "Free for All?" (February 2003) Age Concern Scotland's report into free personal and nursing care.

the extent and meaning of personal care[46] and a concern that certain services may be cut. These early concerns were found to still exist in a more recent study.[47]

In response to such concerns, the Scottish Government has announced a number of initiatives.[48] First, an independent review has been established, headed by Lord Sutherland, to investigate the availability of local authority resources. Secondly, FPC payments will finally increase. April 2008 saw the first increase in payments, along with a commitment to keep FPC payments in line with inflation. The final initiative responds to the vast criticism on the ambiguity of certain services definitions. The Scottish Executive has expressed its willingness to clarify the scope of terms/services, by the use of legislation where necessary.

Community care services

7.15 The 1968 Act expanded the network of support services available to persons in need. Supplementary provisions have since developed the range of services so as to facilitate the assessment process and subsequent care management. The 1990 Act appended to the social work provisions contained at s.12 of the 1968 Act a new s.12A requiring local authorities to assess the needs of anyone thought to be in need of a "community care service", defined as any service that a local authority has a duty or power to provide or secure the provision of under Pt II of the 1968 Act and ss.25, 26 and 27 of the Mental Health (Care and Treatment) (Scotland) Act 2003.[49] This essentially incorporates all of the services examined above with the effect that they can be classed as community care services.

It is now well established through case law in England and Wales that community care services incorporate the services listed under s.2 of the 1970 Act and that in inserting a duty to assess the need for community care services Parliament had intended that the obligation should apply equally to services under s.2.[50]

Voluntary and private bodies

7.16 When local authorities are obliged to make arrangements for service provision they are free to operate a tendering process whereby they purchase services and facilities from other bodies who may be in a better position to provide them. While the independent and voluntary sectors are encouraged to play an active role in service provision, contracting out by local authorities has yet to be developed to its full potential. It seems that the services offered by the private sector are presently complementing rather than substituting those provided by local authorities.[51]

Voluntary organisations, "the sole or primary object of which is to promote social welfare", are often funded by local authorities.[52] Scottish Ministers are further enabled by virtue of the same statutory discretion to make grants and loans to bodies or persons, including local and national charities, so that they can assist local authorities in exercising their social work functions under the 1968 Act. Supplementary to this provision is a discretion on local authorities to

---

[46] Guidance has provided some recent clarification on the scope of personal care. See the Scottish Executive's Guidance Letter on Food Preparation issued in 2004 and Updated Guidance, *Free Personal Care—Assistance with the Preparation of Food*, issued May 2006.

[47] "Evaluation of Free Personal Care", Social Research Findings No.55/2007 (Scottish Executive, 2007).

[48] Scottish Executive News Release, June 14, 2007.

[49] 1968 Act s.5A(4). Services for children are expressly excluded from the definition.

[50] *R. v Kirklees MBC Ex p. Daykin* (1997–98) 1 C.C.L. Rep. 512; *R. v Gloucestershire CC Ex p. Barry* [1997] 2 All E.R. 1 where Lord Clyde stated "What is significant is that s.2(1) is clearly embodied in the whole of the community care regime, distinct only in its particular procedure and the importing of an express duty of performance once the local authority has been satisfied regarding the necessity to make arrangements" at 18b.

[51] "The Range and Availability of Domiciliary Services in Scotland", Social Work Research Findings No.11 (Scottish Office, Home Department, CRU, 1998). The study also noted that Scottish local authorities were more willing to contract with the voluntary rather than the private sector, entering into block and spot contracts respectively. The study suggested that the independent sector was being utilised in more of a specialist manner.

[52] 1968 Act s.10.

make arrangements with voluntary organisations for the provision of assistance in meeting their responsibilities under the Act.[53]

The 2001 Act requires such bodies to register their services; thereafter they will be measured against the national standards of care.

Information needs

7.17 The duty to inform potential clients of the services available was originally introduced by s.1(2) of the Chronically Sick and Disabled Persons Act 1970, which placed a general obligation on local authorities to distribute information on services available from the authority itself or from any other statutory or voluntary body.[54] Local authorities are now compelled by s.5A of the 1968 Act[55] to publish, and review at regular periods thereafter, a community care plan with which to advise client groups on the availability of community care services.[56] Services for children are not to be written into the plan since children's services are excluded from the definition of community care services.[57] A separate duty exists in respect of children under the Children (Scotland) Act 1995. Local authorities should, however, give details of all services that they have a duty to secure under Pt II of the 1968 Act, namely welfare services under s.12, home help and laundry facilities, residential accommodation, respite care, care and aftercare, and the services contained within s.2(1) of the Chronically Sick and Disabled Persons Act 1970. There should also be some reference to facilities provided under the Mental Health (Care and Treatment) (Scotland) Act 2003. While s.5A is not overly specific about what is to be incorporated into the plan it does specify the need for local authorities to consult with health boards, relevant voluntary organisations representing community care client groups, and housing providers. This is reiterated in guidance on community care planning published in 1994, which strongly urges social work departments to produce their plans together with health boards, thereby allowing them to distribute one comprehensive plan and to keep confusion among potential service-users to a minimum.[58] Critically, it implored local authorities to produce plans that were both accessible and concise, and that targeted the appropriate groups and fully informed them of their various rights and options.

Directions produced since the 1990 Act under s.5(1A) specify that the volume and cost of local authority services and those purchased from the voluntary and private sectors should be detailed in the plan.[59] More recent Directions have required that the comparative costs of residential care homes in the public and independent sectors are removed from community care plans when the budget is being set and made public.[60]

Complaints procedure

7.18 Each local authority is bound to implement and publish details of a complaints procedure,[61] though more fundamentally perhaps service-users should be directly provided with details of the complaints procedure in place within their local authority.[62] The procedure should allow a person to make representations concerning the discharge of local authority functions under the

---

[53] 1968 Act s.4.

[54] Dept of Health Circular 12/70, para.5, suggested that those who might benefit by help, and their families, should know what help is available to them and that this is to be secured both by general publicity and by personal explanations.

[55] Inserted by the 1990 Act.

[56] SWSG Circular 11/91 requires new plans to be produced every three years and reviewed on an annual basis. Scottish authorities were detained in their fulfilment of this duty by the reorganisation of local government in 1994.

[57] 1968 Act s.5A(4).

[58] *Community Care Planning*, SWSG Circular 14/94, para.6.

[59] Community Care (Purchasing) Directions 1994.

[60] Community Care Plans (Information) Directions 1997.

[61] Social Work (Representations Procedure) (Scotland) Order 1990 (SI 1990/2519), constituted under s.5B of the 1968 Act.

[62] SWSG Circular 11/91, para.5.10.

1968 Act.[63] For instance if an assessment has not been carried out, or if the outcome is substantially different from the expectations of the service-user, the authority may be at fault. The complaints procedure is intended to rectify anomalies in decision making without involving the courts. The person making the complaint may be represented by somebody else, usually someone with an established interest in the welfare of the individual, for instance a relative, friend or carer. Only those to whom a local authority owes a duty to provide services, and whose need or possible need has been noted by the authority, are allowed to access the complaints procedure.[64]

ASSESSMENT AND CARE MANAGEMENT

The duty to assess

7.19 Assessing need is the starting point of service provision, constituting both a key element in the wider context of community care and a prelude to longer-term care management. However, the statutory provisions that govern its operation are admittedly piecemeal. While s.12(1) of the Social Work (Scotland) Act 1968 engages local authorities in a duty to secure the provision of social work services, it does not actually compel the authority to make an assessment of the need for those services:

> "It shall be the duty of every local authority to promote social welfare by making available advice, guidance and assistance on such scale as may be appropriate for their area, and in that behalf to make arrangements and to provide or secure the provision of such facilities as they may consider suitable and adequate."

Section 2 of the Chronically Sick and Disabled Persons Act 1970 embellishes the more general terms of s.12(1) by requiring local authorities which are "satisfied" that services are necessary to meet needs, to make suitable arrangements in that pursuit.

However, while bringing to the attention of social work departments the potential needs of one particular group of persons in need, the 1970 Act was not very specific regarding the obligation to actually assess that need. Though s.1 did place a duty on local authorities to establish a register of disabled people and to "inform themselves" of the need for arranging social welfare on their behalf, the Act did not in so many words direct councils to undertake assessments. In *R. v Bexley LBC Ex p. B*[65] the court observed that s.2(1) may well give rise to an action for damages since Parliament had provided no statutory remedy for a breach. The reality was that few authorities were observing their obligations under the 1970 Act notwithstanding that a failure to comply with a request for an assessment was unlawful.[66]

The Disabled Persons (Services, Consultation and Representation) Act 1986 makes some provision for needs assessment and allows a disabled person, or representative or private carer to request the local authority to assess the need for any of the services contained in s.2 of the 1970 Act. In other words, they are entitled to request an assessment, which the local authority must subsequently carry out.[67] These provisions were in part designed to remind local autho-

[63] 1968 Act s.5B(1).

[64] 1968 Act s.5B(2).

[65] Unreported July 31, 1995.

[66] Sections 1 and 2 were brought to Scotland by the Chronically Sick and Disabled Persons (Scotland) Act 1970. The initial hesitation to incorporate them into Scots law arose from concerns that the provisions of the 1968 Act already placed a duty on local authorities to make suitable and adequate provision for an umbrella group of persons in need, a definition that expressly included chronically sick and disabled people. The client-group specific duties of the 1970 Act introduced a risk that service provision would become dependent on a statutory status. It was only following a recognition of the imprecise and largely indiscriminate nature of s.12 that ss.1 and 2 were extended to Scotland by virtue of the Chronically Sick and Disabled Persons (Scotland) Act 1972.

[67] 1986 Act s.4.

rities of their obligation to make arrangements to meet needs under the 1970 Act, and in part to provide a statutory impetus for the assessment of those needs.

7.20 However, under these arrangements the duty to carry out an assessment of needs was triggered only by the disabled person himself, or by a carer or representative acting on his behalf. The scope existed for social work departments to rely largely on other people or bodies to be alerted to a social work need. In order to remedy this problem and so as to encourage proactivity across Scottish local authorities, the 1990 Act introduced s.12A of the 1968 Act:

> "(1) Subject to the provisions of this section, where it appears to a local authority that any person for whom they are under a duty or have a power to provide, or to secure the provision of, community care services may be in need of any such services, the authority—
>
> (a) shall make an assessment of the needs of that person for those services; and
> (b) having regard to the results of that assessment, shall then decide whether the needs of that person call for the provision of any such services."

This firmly engages social work departments in a twofold duty to assess need for the wide range of community care services and to decide whether services are necessary to meet the assessed need. Though the provisions do not seem to impel authorities to make arrangements once they are satisfied that services are necessary, recent case law indicates that this is the case.[68]

It is essential to clarify during the assessment that a community care and not an NHS remit exists. There may be a need for advice and assistance alone, or for a further specialist assessment of specific needs. It may be possible to identify that an urgent need exists.[69] Community care services can be provided without an assessment where need is urgent though it should be undertaken as soon as possible thereafter.[70] Both the individual service-user and his carer if there is one should participate in the assessment, which it should be noted is concerned not only with the physical needs of the user, but with his mental and social functioning also.[71]

The provisions of the 1970 and 1986 Acts still carry force. If during a community care assessment a local authority becomes aware that the person appears to be disabled, it is referred to the 1986 Act.[72] This in turn allows the disabled person to insist that an assessment is undertaken of their need for the specific services contained within s.2 of the 1970 Act. It is thereby a feature of s.12A that disabled people are guaranteed an assessment of their disability needs specifically, and of their community care needs more generally. While these are distinct statutory duties they will usually amalgamate to form one comprehensive assessment in practice. It should be noted however that there are two assessment duties incumbent on the local authority in respect of disabled people and,

> "potentially, any community care assessment of a disabled person which does not make it clear that the local authority specifically addressed the possible need for services under section 2 could be open to legal challenge."[73]

7.21 Accordingly, for a person who is chronically sick or disabled, access to a comprehensive assessment of needs is secured through one of three statutory routes. First, a local authority may make an assessment of needs offered in s.2 of the 1970 Act. Secondly it may be compelled to do so by virtue of a request under the 1986 legislation. Thirdly, it may be required to assess community care needs under s.12A of the 1968 Act concurrently with an assessment of disability needs under s.2 of the 1970 Act.

Needs differ in all users of community care. In 1991 the Department of Health issued a Manager's Guide which suggested that need should be equated with the requirements of indi-

---

[68] *MacGregor v South Lanarkshire Council*, 2001 S.L.T. 233.
[69] SWSG Circular 11/91, para.5.2.
[70] 1968 Act ss.12A(5) and (6).
[71] SWSG Circular 11/91, para.5.3.
[72] 1968 Act s.12A(4).
[73] McKay, Annotations in Mays (ed.), *Scottish Social Work Legislation*, E.085.3.

viduals to enable them to achieve, maintain or restore an acceptable level of social independence or quality of life as defined by the particular care agency or authority.[74] "Need" has been found to include psychological as well as physical need,[75] and in considering the provision of respite care the preferences of a mentally disabled patient may well be relevant.[76] In *R. v Haringey LBC Ex p. Norton*[77] the care plan of a multiple sclerosis sufferer was amended further to a reassessment by the local authority so as to meet his personal care needs though not his social, recreational and leisure needs. This had the effect of reducing his care from 24 to five hours a day. The court found that in differentiating between these various needs and rendering some subordinate to others, the local authority had failed to produce a multi-faceted care package in accordance with the legislative requirements. It was subsequently ordered to undertake a reassessment of needs.[78]

An assessment of need for services is not contingent upon those services being currently available from the local authority. This was confirmed by the court in *R. v Royal County Berkshire Ex p. Parke*.[79] The local authority supposed that the duty to assess need was conditional upon it being shown that it had in place existing arrangements to provide services of a kind that, in light of an assessment, the disabled person might need. The court clarified that a duty to assess arises where the local authority has the legal power to provide community care services to an individual and there is no condition that the duty to assess is dependent upon the physical availability of resources.

7.22 Further, the assessment is not reliant upon an individual's means. In its determination, the House of Lords[80] has held that the local authority should disregard the resources of the person during the assessment process:

> "The provision of services under s12 and s13A, was concerned with the needs for any of the services which the local authority were able to provide, not to the question of whether the person was able to pay for them."[81]

The assessment is an opportunity for the local authority to form opinions on the type of care that is required, not simply the type of services. What appears at first to be a demand for home help and laundry facilities may in fact be a more profound need. Local authorities are alerted to the different levels of care that may reveal themselves during an assessment:

> "The aim should be to provide support for the person in their own home, which might include periods of respite care, or the provision of equipment or physical adaptations. A move to more suitable accommodation, possibly in the form of supported accommodation or sheltered housing, together with social support, might be an alternative possibility. Admission to residential care, nursing home care and long-stay hospital care should only be considered where the person's particular dependency needs require the kind of intensive care available in that kind of setting."[82]

Local authorities are urged that service provision should be needs led and not service led.[83] The disparity of need existing across community care client groups as a whole, as well as the vast potential for alternative service provision within different local authorities, is such that needs are best met through an assessment that does not seek to identify the client's suitability for one

---

74 Department of Health, *Care Management and Assessment: Managers Guide* (London: HMSO, 1991).

75 *R. v Avon CC Ex p. M* [1994] 2 F.C.R. 259.

76 *R. v North Yorkshire CC Ex p. Hargreaves* (1997–98) 1 C.C.L. Rep. 104.

77 (1997–98) 1 C.C.L. Rep. 168.

78 In the light of the difficulties that surround community care assessments there are calls to concentrate on the definition of need to facilitate and clarify the process. See M. Preston-Shoot, "Contesting the Contradictions: Needs, Resources and Community Care Decisions" (1996) 18(3) *Journal of Social Welfare and Family Law* 307.

79 (1997) 33 B.L.M.R 71.

80 *Robertson v Fife Council*, 2002 S.L.T. 951.

81 *Robertson v Fife Council*, 2002 S.L.T. 951 at 952–960.

82 SWSG Circular 11/91, para.6.2.

83 SWSG Circular 11/91, para.5.1.

particular service or another. Instead the assessment should seek to identify what the disability, illness or condition demands and the social work authority should subsequently undertake to provide a service which meets that demand. Prior to the introduction of community care a social worker making an assessment may have referred to a menu of services that were available and the eligibility criteria for each.[84] Identifying a need requires the local authority first to establish the difficulties encountered by an individual. Unless the need is accurately detected from the start, the response may be entirely unsuited to the particular needs of the service-user and furthermore a waste of public resources.

Other agencies may need to become involved in an assessment, for instance if housing adaptations are required, or if residential care is thought to be appropriate. Any need for housing or health services that comes to the attention of the social work department in the course of an assessment must to be conveyed to the relevant statutory body.[85]

Joint working

7.23 Guidance stresses the need for collaboration in community care between social work departments, housing authorities, health boards and the voluntary and private sectors. This embellishes the duties placed on local authorities, health boards, NHS trusts and education authorities to co-operate in securing health services and to undertake joint planning and development services for disabled and elderly people.[86]

In an effort to strengthen effective joint working between social work, health and housing agencies, the Joint Future Group ("JFG") was established. After a study of the assessment process the JFG criticised the process as being "bureaucratic, engaged with the individual on too many occasions, and . . . often repeated because of professionals' reluctance to accept the views of others".[87] This reproach led to the commitment of a Single Shared Assessment ("SSA") as recommended in the *Report of the Joint Future Group*.[88] Adopting SSA is to be followed throughout Scotland whereby one professional who is most competent to deal with the case will lead the case along with appropriate involvement from other professionals. To ensure the benefits of joint working it is envisaged that decisions be agreed by all of the professionals involved. It is expected that this new process will offer benefits to the user and agencies. Most importantly this process should avoid duplication of information and assessments, while providing a key contact.[89] To achieve this, the key bodies must establish a local framework which should set out joint working arrangements, procedures and systems for sharing information.[90] To support joint working practice numerous pieces of legislation and guidance have followed. The Community Care and Health (Scotland) Act 2002 and the Community Care (Joint Working Etc.) (Scotland) Regulations 2002 detail the framework for joint resourcing. Guidance builds on the legislation elucidating the payment arrangements between the different agencies including pooling budgets.[91]

---

[84] See Morris, *Community Care: Working with Service Users* (1997), p.33.

[85] SWSG Circular 11/91, para.12.2

[86] National Health Service (Scotland) Act 1978 ss.13 and 13A, inserted by the 1986 Act and more recently the 2002 Act and its subsequent regulations.

[87] Scottish Executive Guidance, *Single Shared Assessment of Community Care Needs*, Circular CCD 8/2001, p.8.

[88] November 2000, Scottish Executive.

[89] Circular CCD 8/2001, p.9.

[90] Circular CCD 8/2001, p.21.

[91] *Implementation of the Provisions on Joint Working in Part 2 of the Community Care and Health (Scotland) Act 2002 and the Community Care (Joint Workings Etc.) Regulations 2002*, Circular CCD 11/2001. In the Scottish Executive's *Review of Care Management in Scotland* it was found that the screening and assessment process varied between local authorities. The authors claim that "the picture across Scotland is a long way from comprehensive use of single shared assessment tools. Only one authority had such a tool for all user groups" (pp.2–3).

Ordinary residence

7.24 In order to determine which local authority is responsible for the provision of services, facilities or accommodation, the test is one of "ordinary residence". In other words, an individual who is ordinarily resident in a given local authority area shall be entitled to assistance by that local authority.[92] Currently, Scottish Office guidance issued in 1996 should be used where the area of ordinary residence is uncertain.[93] As a general note it states that "if there is a dispute about the ordinary residence of a person in need of services it should be debated after the care assessment and any provision of service".[94]

"Ordinary residence" is to be construed according to its ordinary and natural meaning subject to any interpretation that may be applied by the courts in individual circumstances.[95] The construction given by the courts to date indicates some quite varied notions of ordinary residence, including in one instance, voluntary settlement for a settled purpose as part of the regular order of life for the time being.[96] An applicant may have permanent residence outside the United Kingdom, or might fully expect that he will eventually live outside the United Kingdom, and still have ordinary residence therein. Furthermore, a settled purpose might be a specific and limited purpose such as education.[97] A person who has been resident in a place with some degree of continuity and apart from accidental or temporary absences may be deemed ordinarily resident there.[98] In *R. v Waltham Forest LBC Ex p. Vale*[99] the individual concerned was an adult with severe learning disabilities who was totally dependent on his parents. The court deemed that as his position was comparable to that of a small child who is unable to choose where he or she lives, his ordinary residence was the same as that of his parents. In some situations, there is a likelihood that another person or body will act in loco parentis.[100] When undertaking to establish ordinary residence, the local authority must discount certain periods of time, primarily, periods spent in hospital care in another local authority area.[101]

Given the financial implications from the interpretation of ordinary residence, it is understandable why local authorities will contest its application. Thus the Scottish Executive recently produced a consultation document on the current ordinary residence guidance which acknowledged that such disputes are costly and timely.[102] Moreover, with the advent of free personal care, the need for clarity is much needed.[103] On the back of the consultation document, the Adult Support and Protection (Scotland) Act 2007 allows Scottish Ministers to provide legal clarity on the definition.[104]

7.25 Ordinary residence should not be confused with the term "local connection" which binds housing authorities in homelessness issues. If a local connection exists in another area, a person may become the responsibility of the housing authority in that area. However, it will not be possible for a social work authority that is being requested to assess and provide services for a person with no or with unknown ordinary residence, to suggest that the possible existence of a local connection elsewhere means the possible existence of ordinary residence elsewhere also. If

---

92 1968 Act s.86(1).

93 *Ordinary Residence*, SWSG Circular 1/96.

94 SWSG Circular 1/96, para.5.1.

95 See *R. v Barnet LBC Ex p. Shah* [1983] 11 All E.R. 226 at 232j–233g.

96 See *R. v Barnet LBC Ex p. Shah* [1983] 11 All E.R. 226 at 232j–233g.

97 *R. v Barnet LBC Ex p. Shah* [1983] 11 All E.R. 226 at 232j–233g.

98 *Levene v Inland Revenue Commissioners* [1928] 1 A.C. 217.

99 *The Times*, February 25, 1985.

100 *R. v Redbridge LBC Ex p. East Sussex CC* [1993] 1 C.O.D. 256, QBD.

101 1968 Act s.86(3).

102 "Ordinary Residence: Consultation on Proposed Amendment to the Social Work (Scotland) Act 1968: Functions of Local Authorities in Respect of Placed Persons", Scottish Executive Consultation 2005, p.1.

103 "Ordinary Residence", Scottish Executive Consultation 2005, p.1.

104 This section came into force on October 5, 2007.

responsibility is actually transferred to another housing authority, the social work department may only at that stage consider whether ordinary residence is in the same area.[105]

Where a person requires health care, the health authority that holds responsibility for him is the one in which he or she is "usually resident".[106] Again, this is distinct from ordinary residence. Guidance suggests that if there is any doubt as to where a person is usually resident, he is to be treated as usually resident at the address he gives as being where he usually resides. In a limited number of cases, usual residence will be in the area where the person is found to be in need of treatment. It follows therefore that ordinary residence for the purposes of social work care, and usual residence for the purposes of health care, will normally run concurrently.[107]

Managing care

7.26 Guidance issued by the Scottish Office translates care management[108] as a process of relating services to needs. Duties under the community care provisions begin with identifying the group of people who have community care needs, assessing the care needs of the individual, planning and arranging for the delivery of care, monitoring the quality of care provided, and undertaking systematic reviews of needs and the services provided to meet them. Care management is distinct from service provision and is concerned with obtaining for individuals the most suitable and cost-effective services from the statutory, voluntary and private sectors through the execution of the tasks identified above.[109]

A care plan should be comprised following an assessment of needs, outlining any service to be provided or arranged, by whom they are to be provided, and of course, by which means they are to be provided.[110] The plan will usually comprise a variety of services which will combine in meeting the assessed needs. The obligation to follow up a care assessment with a care plan is as onerous as the obligation to carry out an assessment. In *R. v Sutton LBC Ex p. Tucker*[111] the local authority was compelled to provide a care plan for an individual who had been assessed as needing to be removed from hospital and placed in shared residential accommodation in the community. It was found that in failing to devise a plan the council was in breach of its obligations under the 1990 Act to provide services and furthermore was in breach of community care guidance. Similarly, in *R. v Islington LBC Ex p. Rixon*[112] a care plan produced under the community care legislation failed to incorporate a set of overall objectives including the long-term obligations of both service-providers and carers. The plan was found to be defective.

Once an assessment has been carried out and a care plan has been devised it is imperative that service provision for each individual is managed on an ongoing basis. In order that the care plan works to its full potential in meeting the care needs of the user, reviews should be undertaken at regular intervals and reassessments may also be required. Clearly it will be the intention of the local authority to ensure that the objectives identified in the original care plan have been met. Thus further to a reassessment, services should be adjusted to meet any additional needs or to remove facilities that are no longer required. The review should therefore concern all those originally involved in planning services, namely the user, carers, social work departments, housing authorities and providers if a housing need formed or forms part of the overall need, and possibly representatives from the private and voluntary sectors.[113]

7.27 A care package cannot be altered without a reassessment of needs. In *R. v Gloucestershire CC*

---

[105] SWSG Circular 1/96, para.18.

[106] The Functions of Health Boards (Scotland) Order 1991 (SI 1991/570) establishes a process for health boards working out where a person is usually resident.

[107] SWSG Circular 1/96, para.20.

[108] In 2001, the Scottish Executive accepted to change the definition to "intensive care management" as recommended in the Joint Future Group's Report.

[109] SWSG Circular 11/91, paras 4.1–4.5.

[110] SWSG Circular 11/91, para.6.

[111] (1998) 40 B.M.L.R. 137.

[112] [1997] E.L.R. 66.

[113] SWSG Circular 11/91 paras 19.1–19.3.

Ex p. Mahfood[114] the local authority had removed services from 1,000 clients without undertaking or offering to undertake individual reassessments. Its decision to withdraw assistance was deemed unlawful and it was compelled by the court to write to each individual service-user offering reassessments. Only 273 responded and in respect of the remaining three-quarters, the local authority was of the opinion that no further duty existed since an offer for reassessment had been imparted. As a separate action Royal Association for Disability and Rehabilitation ("RADAR") challenged this decision in the High Court[115] which found that an offer to reassess was inadequate. The duty to the service-users was one to actually undertake a reassessment. This did not depend upon a request by the service-user, but upon an appearance of need. Since the initial duty to assess the need for community care services was not triggered by a request or the acceptance of an offer, reassessment must be on the same terms.

Guidance suggests that local authorities appoint care managers with a remit to oversee both care management and service delivery within their area, specifically, to secure the most appropriate services within available resources. It is often more suitable to select an individual from the voluntary sector who has professional knowledge of specialist needs.[116]

Carers

7.28 The shift from institutional to community care has engendered more widespread reliance on the imperative contribution of "community carers"—for instance, people who care for their older relatives, husbands and wives suffering from illness, or their disabled children. In many instances, this is a burden that is assumed progressively over some time and that is not always voluntary. As more people are encouraged to remain within their own homes, someone new must shoulder the responsibilities previously accepted by professional carers in professional settings.

The Scottish Executive issued *Strategy for Carers in Scotland* in November 1999. This document set out a framework to provide better support to carers including proposals for new legislation to allow carers' needs to be assessed directly. Furthermore, an independent Carers Legislation Working Group ("CLWG") was established in January 2000 to focus specifically on the needs of carers. In the *Report of the Carers Legislation Working Group*[117] it was asserted that the role of the carer should be as a key partner in the provision of care, and like any other provider of care they need a range of resources to carry out this role citing information, advice, training skills and respite care as probable services. More importantly the carer should not be asked to contribute to the costs of services for the provision of caring.[118]

It was also suggested by CLWG that carers should have access to independent assessments in all circumstances.[119] Supporting this, the Scottish Executive included the right to independent assessments in the Community Care and Health (Scotland) Act 2002.[120]

Carers' assessment

7.29 The 1990 Act does not contain any specific reference to the need of carers in the community to be assessed although the White Paper *Caring for people* alluded to the cardinal role played by them. In fact, it was to be a "high priority" to provide them with practical support in the light of a certain shift in emphasis from "care in the community" to "care by the community" throughout the 1980s.[121] The growing profile of carers is clearly demonstrated in guidance

---

[114] 94 L.G.R. 593.
[115] *R. v Gloucestershire CC Ex p. RADAR* [1996] C.O.D. 253, QBD.
[116] SWSG Circular 11/91, paras 4.3 and 4.4.
[117] See Scottish Executive website.
[118] *Report of the Carers Legislation Working Group* (2000), Ch.3.
[119] *Report of the Carers Legislation Working Group* (2000), Ch.3.
[120] See paras 7.23–7.24 below on carers' assessment for their new rights.
[121] See DHSS, *Growing older*, Cmnd.8173 (London: HMSO, 1981).

prepared for local authorities on the operation of respite care,[122] while the Carers' National Association exists to support the growing number of carers in Britain.[123] However, this type of informal care should be backed up with services that are appropriate to the needs of both the carer and the individual being cared for.[124]

In 1995 the Carers (Recognition and Services) Act undertook further amendment to the new s.12A of the 1968 Act, which required an assessment of anyone providing a substantial amount of care on a regular basis to the service-user. This in turn has been updated in parts. A carer's right to an assessment has been significantly improved since September 1, 2002 when certain provisions within the 2002 Act commenced. Prior to this period, a carer's right to an assessment under s.12A was dependent on an assessment being requested by a carer over 16 years old and where the cared-for person was having an assessment of their needs. This led to the unjust position that where a cared-for person refused an assessment, the carer was precluded from having their needs assessed. The more recent transition extending carers' rights enables them to access an independent assessment. A carer of adults now has the right to request an assessment at any time of their ability to provide care and the local authority must comply with this request.[125] The carer's assessment must be given due regard in any assessment of the person in need and in any decision apropos provision of community services for that person.[126] Even where no request for an independent assessment has been made, a local authority must consider any substantial amount of care being provided regularly by a carer and seek the carer's views before deciding what services are necessary.[127] The development of carers' rights attempts to ensure that carers are fully involved in planning service provision, and that their abilities to go on caring are ultimately reflected in the final care plan.[128] If they do not foresee their confirmed future involvement, the local authority may have to find alternative means of support for the service-user.

7.30 Carers of disabled people are entitled to an assessment under the Disabled Persons (Services, Consultations and Representation) Act 1986 during an assessment of a disabled person.[129] The new provisions under the 2002 Act are an improvement on those contained in the 1986 Act—applying to all users of community care and being an independent right. Once an assessment of the carer has been carried out under the 1968 Act, the local authority is relieved of its duties under the 1986 Act.

The provisions do not extend to an assessment of paid carers or those who are working for a voluntary organisation,[130] though guidance does indicate that a "carer" may include a person who may be living at a distance from the person for whom they are caring.[131]

To qualify for an assessment the carer should provide a substantial amount of care on a regular basis. This criterion was first introduced in the 1986 Act and has been reproduced in the Carers (Recognition and Services) Act 1995 and 2002 Act. Without any statutory definition it is left to local authorities to interpret this term in relation to individual cases. Policy guidance suggests that local authorities publish the approach taken to interpret "substantial and regular"

---

[122] *Respite Care*, SWSG Circular 10/96.

[123] In 2002 there were an estimated 668,500 people in Scotland providing care for someone within or outwith their own home: Scottish Executive, *Scottish Community Care Statistics 2002*, p.86.

[124] For further reading on all aspects of caring see Bolton (ed.), "Carers Voices: A Report from 1996—A Conference for Informal Carers and Professional Workers in Aberdeen and Aberdeenshire" (1996).

[125] 1968 Act s.12AA, inserted by the 2002 Act s.9.

[126] 1968 Act s.12AA.

[127] 1968 Act s.12A, amended by the 2002 Act s.8, substituting the old provisions that required a request by the carer for an assessment of their ability to provide care.

[128] Final decisions should involve both user and carer so that each is aware of how any services to be provided assist the user, and conceivably how they will assist the carer: SWSG Circular 11/91, paras 5.3 and 6.1.

[129] 1968 Act s.8.

[130] 1968 Act s.12AA, inserted by the 2002 Act.

[131] *Community Care and Health (Scotland) Act 2002. New Statutory Rights for Carers: Guidance*, Scottish Executive Guidance, Circular CCD 2/2003, para.3.5.3.

and consider adopting a consistent approach.[132] In seeking to establish whether someone is providing the requisite level of care to demand an assessment, the authority will wish to look at the type of tasks in which the carer is involved; the amount of time spent with the service-user; the amount of supervision required by the user and whether the carer has made or intends to make a "continuing commitment to the individual concerned".[133]

To enable the carer to continue the role of provider of care, they may receive resources, namely other caring services additional to their support, or support and advice being provided directly.[134] Though the measures introduced by the Carers (Recognition and Services) Act 1995 and the 2002 Act are no doubt welcomed by both service-users and carers, the extent to which they can be fully implemented may be impeded by the constraint of finite local government resources.

Carer information strategies

7.31 To support the right to an independent assessment, local authorities have a duty to inform carers of adults of their assessment obligation.[135] Attendant to this new duty to inform carers is the further development of carer information strategies. In one report it was found that despite carers having a right to a needs assessment, in practice there had been a low take up.[136] It was therefore suggested that to compensate for this there should be a duty on certain agencies to provide information to carers. The 2002 Act introduced for the first time obligations on the NHS to carers. Section 12 of the 2002 Act provides for health boards to submit, at the request of Scottish Ministers, a strategy for disseminating information to carers free of charge. The information must notify carers[137] of the potential right to an independent assessment under the 1968 Act. Scottish Ministers may specify the details of the strategy including submission date, form, content, consultation and timeframes, plus require a review.

Young carers

7.32 Recent statistics estimate that there are approximately 4,900 young carers in Scotland, which strikingly accounts for 3 per cent of the population.[138] Given these significant statistics it is amazing to consider that until recently "young carers" had no corresponding rights to an assessment. To remedy this inadequacy, the 2002 Act recognised the fact that many children are indeed carers of adults and as such afforded child carers new rights to assessments. Child carers providing "substantial and regular" care for an adult in need of community services or to a disabled child, now have a right to request an assessment of their ability to provide care.[139] Any request must be complied with and any results given due regard in the cared-for person's assessment and in any consideration of the provision of services. Local authorities' duty to notify carers applies equally to young carers, ensuring access to an assessment.

> "The primary objective of a young carer's assessment is to safeguard the interests and promote the welfare of the young carer, and to ensure that they are not taking on inappropriate levels or types of caring by ensuring the family have access to alternative support."[140]

---

[132] Circular CCD 2/2003, para.3.5.

[133] *Carers (Recognition and Services) Act 1995 Policy and Practice Guidance*, SWSG Circular 11/96, para.6.

[134] Circular CCD 2/2003, para.8.

[135] 1968 Act s.12AB inserted by the 2002 Act s.9.

[136] Scottish Executive, *Report of the Carers Legislation Working Group* (2000).

[137] Carers in this context are those who care for persons who are patients or are patients who care for other persons: 2002 Act s.12(5).

[138] Scottish Executive, *Community Care Statistics 2002*, p.86.

[139] 1968 Act s.12AA(1), inserted by the 2002 Act s.9 and the Children (Scotland) Act 1995 s.24, substituted by s.11 of the 2002 Act respectively.

[140] Circular CCD 2/2003, para.9.5.1.

It is worth noting that young carers may constitute a "child in need" under the terms of the Children (Scotland) Act 1995 and be embraced by the obligations of the local authority to promote upbringing and welfare.[141]

Community care for disabled children

7.33 The endeavours of the Chronically Sick and Disabled Persons Act 1970 and the Disabled Persons (Services, Consultation and Representation) Act 1986 to meet the needs of disabled people were inclusive of children though the anomalies in the statutory framework were frustrating to younger as well as older segments of the population. The Kilbrandon Report which in 1964 hinted at specialist support for families with disabled children in the community was one of two White Papers to inform the contents and structure of the Social Work (Scotland) Bill. There was some confidence that disabled children would at long last benefit from express legal recognition. The general social work provisions contained in the Social Work (Scotland) Act 1968 were extended to children and their families though how much this impressed upon disabled children in their own right is unclear.

Children (Scotland) Act 1995

7.34 Amendments made to the 1968 Act in 1990 finally distinguished child from adult in the framework of community care, though most fundamentally the Children (Scotland) Act 1995 made a specific commitment to disabled children.[142] In the terms of the White Paper *Scotland's children* which formed the basis of the Act, "services ha[d] continued to concentrate largely on the disability rather than on the child".[143] Until that time, statutory provisions for disabled adults had accommodated the needs of disabled children based principally on the assumption that disability was a stronger bond than childhood itself.[144] A training programme commissioned by the Scottish Office on the Children (Scotland) Act 1995 notes:

> "The provision of services to children with or affected by disability and their families is an area which has largely been neglected by social work as child care workers struggle to manage workloads dominated by child protection issues. The community care legislation has led to some improvement in service and it is to be hoped that the provisions of the Children (Scotland) Act 1995 can build on these so that the needs of these children and young people and their families are addressed in ways which are more comprehensive and responsive to individual circumstances than at present."

Chapter 1 of Pt II of the Children (Scotland) Act 1995 seeks to provide support for children and their families and is underpinned, like the rest of the Act, with Kilbrandon's welfare principle.[145] Local authorities are under a general duty to promote the upbringing and welfare of "children in need" under s.22. This is comparable to the s.12 duty to "persons in need" under the 1968 Act. The term includes children who are disabled, or whose health will be further impaired without adequate service provision.[146] Services that seek to promote the welfare of children in need must therefore be designed in the light of this specific client group and will need to take account of their special needs. More specifically, s.23A binds local authorities in a duty towards children affected by disability, to minimise the effects of the disability which features in their lives, and to provide them with an opportunity to lead lives that are as normal as possible.[147] "Disability"

---

[141] Children (Scotland) Act 1995 s.22.

[142] With the introduction of the Children (Scotland) Act 1995, the general duties under s.12 of the 1968 Act were amended to remove a social work duty towards children.

[143] *Scotland's children: proposals for child care policy and law*, Cm.2286 (Edinburgh: HMSO, 1993), para.4.1.

[144] *Scotland's children*, Cm.2286 (1993), para.4.1.

[145] See Ch.4.

[146] Children (Scotland) Act 1995 s.93(4)(a).

[147] Children (Scotland) Act 1995 s.23(1).

incorporates chronic sickness, disability or mental disorder.[148] Unlike previous legal provisions the Carers (Recognition and Services) Act 1995 extends the duties of local authorities beyond disabled children alone, to children who are affected by the disability of a family member. This is designed to support the position any child living with disability, whether or not the impairment is his own.[149] The general provisions of s.22 of the Carers (Recognition and Services) Act 1995 do not incorporate a duty to make an assessment of needs, merely to provide a range and level of services appropriate to the child's needs. An assessment of a child is triggered only by a request from a parent or guardian.[150] These requirements are in some sense subordinate to the more forceful community care provisions that make up s.12A of the 1968 Act, whereby the duty to assess any adult who appears to have a need creates more impetus for independent social work intervention. The services to which s.22 refers are those contained within Pt II of the Children (Scotland) Act 1995, including the provision of accommodation under ss.25 and 26, the provision of day care under s.27, aftercare under s.28, financial assistance towards education or training under s.30, and a profusion of supplementary assistance.

7.35 It is uncommon for disabled children to be confined to residential establishments except where the most severe of impairments render the parents simply unable to cope.[151] The White Paper for the Carers (Recognition and Services) Act 1995 was quite animated on this issue, stressing that childcare is almost always provided from somewhere within the confines of the family unit. Care for disabled children, it seems, is no exception:

> "The bulk of child care is given through families and not through outside services . . . Many families would prefer services to reinforce their caring capacity and not to offer a substitute for it."[152]

The Carers (Recognition and Services) Act 1995 inserted provisions into Children (Scotland) Act 1995 at s.24 so as not to overlook the imperative role that is played by those caring for disabled children. Section 24 provided that when undertaking an assessment of a child who is presently or foreseeably cared for to a substantial degree and on a regular basis by a carer, that carer may place a request with the local authority for an assessment of his or her capacity to continue as carer. Their assessment was restricted to the circumstances where the disabled child was being assessed. However, this provision has again been amended by the Community Care and Health (Scotland) Act 2002 so that a carer of a disabled child is entitled to an independent assessment at any time.[153] Simultaneously s.24A was inserted into the Carers (Recognition and Services) Act 1995 to oblige local authorities to notify carers of this right. Local authorities must take into account the views of the child, parent, guardian and carer.[154]

7.36 Such rights are only available to carers providing "substantial and regular care". In seeking to interpret the qualification of these terms, commentary on the Children (Scotland) Act 1995 suggests the targeting of the main, or one of the main, carers of the child without whose care the development or welfare of the child would be prejudiced.[155] These provisions are framed in the same light as those that apply to adult service-users and it is their inclusive aim that the local authority will devise a care plan based on the need services, which takes account of the carer's ability to continue caring. Furthermore, anyone providing care for children under a contract of employment or in the capacity of a volunteer for a voluntary organisation is excluded from an

---

[148] Children (Scotland) Act 1995 s.23(2).

[149] Guidance has been produced to advise local authorities on all aspects of the Children (Scotland) Act 1995 including procedures for the assessment of children affected by disabilities: *The Children (Scotland) Act 1995 Regulations and Guidance* (Edinburgh: Stationery Office, 1997).

[150] Children (Scotland) Act 1995 s.23(3).

[151] OPCS, *Surveys of Disability in Great Britain, Report 4* (Office of National Statistics, 1988) revealed that 33,000 disabled children were living in the community and 7,711 in community establishments.

[152] *Scotland's children*, Cm.2286 (1993), para.4.2.

[153] 2002 Act s.11.

[154] Carers (Recognition and Services) Act 1995 s.23(4), inserted by the 2002 Act s.10.

[155] See Norrie, *The Children (Scotland) Act 1995*, 2nd edn.

assessment of this nature. The importance of planning for services is underpinned by the need for families to make informed choices regarding their children and their needs. In this pursuit the local authority is required to publish plans for children's services similar to those that are produced adults, and to review them periodically thereafter.[156] This duty extends to services referred to in Pt II of the Carers (Recognition and Services) Act 1995 and s.5(B) of the 1968 Act thereby incorporating services provided under the Chronically Sick and Disabled Persons Act 1970. In the production of care plans for children, local authorities are required to consult wherever appropriate with bodies providing health services, voluntary organisations and housing bodies in the area.[157] In other words, plans should identify foremost the type of assistance that is actually available and the form in which it is to be received. Again, this largely duplicates the terms of the 1968 Act that relate to adult service-users. Supplementary to the duty to publish plans is a duty to publish information on services provided by the authority and other authorities, and where appropriate those supplied by voluntary organisations which, as always, play an active role in overall service provision.[158]

The Carers (Recognition and Services) Act 1995 as a whole is heavily flavoured with the notion of building and sustaining a fruitful partnership between local authority, parent and child, from which the child will ultimately benefit, a concept that applies to no less an extent in the provisions promoting the welfare of children affected by disability. It is essential as a result that services and facilities are effectively broadcast to those wishing to access them. The *Managers Handbook* impresses upon local authorities the need to stress, in the information they publish about available services, their wish to be proactive, the need for coordinated liaison and the inclusion of family members in that liaison.[159]

COMMUNITY CARE RESOURCES

Charging for services

7.37 Local authorities are under a duty to assess the need which exists for home care services and to make arrangements to provide them.[160] However there is no attending obligation on councils to support these arrangements through their own budgets. Under s.87 of the 1968 Act local authorities may recover from the service-user the cost of services provided under the 1968 Act, sections of the Mental Health (Care and Treatment) (Scotland) Act 2003, and Pt II of the Children (Scotland) Act 1995.[161] These provisions do not apply to care homes. Further a local authority cannot charge for free personal care provided by virtue of s.1 of the 2002 Act.[162]

If a service-user has insufficient means to contribute towards the facilities he is receiving he cannot be compelled to pay.[163] "Means" has been construed as meaning the financial resources of a person: his assets, his sources of income, his liabilities and expenses.[164] However, it will be necessary for the service-user to persuade the authority that his means are not adequate.[165] The

---

[156] Children (Scotland) Act 1995 s.19.

[157] Children (Scotland) Act 1995 s.19(5)(e).

[158] Children (Scotland) Act 1995 s.20.

[159] J. Harris and D. Kelly, *Changing Social Care: A Manual for Managers* (Whiting and Birch Ltd, 1996), p.81.

[160] 1968 Act s.12A and 1970 Act s.2.

[161] Since a local authority is exercising its functions under the 1968 Act when it provides services under the 1970 Act it will also be possible for charges to be made for the provision of s.2(1) services: *R. v Powys CC Ex p. Hambidge* (1997–98) 1 C.C.L. Rep. 182.

[162] 1968 Act s.87(1B), added by the 2002 Act.

[163] 1968 Act s.87(1A).

[164] "If he has a reasonable asset that is part of his means; he has the means to pay ... If he has an asset which he can reasonably be expected to realise and which will (after taking into account any other relevant factor) enable him to pay, his means make it practicable for him to pay": *Avon CC v Hooper* [1997] 1 All E.R. 532 at 537.

[165] "It is for the recipient of the services to discharge this burden of persuasion. He must show that he has insufficient means": *Avon CC v Hooper* [1997] 1 All E.R. 532 at 537; 1968 Act s.87(1A); *Community Care in Scotland. Assessment and Care Management*, SWSG Circular 11/91, para.11.

local authority is not entitled to charge him more than it is reasonably practicable for him to pay. In other words, it is sanctioned to make a "reasonable" charge. The legislation does not seek to qualify this term and it would seem that the final decision would rest heavily upon the circumstances of the individual case. In particular, each local authority will have regard to what has become its own common practice, and equally perhaps to its current budgetary constraints. It is only at this charging stage that an assessment of financial means should be undertaken.[166] In *Avon CC v Hooper*[167] an authority sued the mother of a severely disabled child for the costs which it had incurred maintaining her son. Although he had suffered some degree of brain damage at birth, she had been responsible for his physical and mental impairments in the period since. The court's construction of the English provisions, equivalent to those that apply in Scotland,[168] was that the local authority must have relevant and reasonable grounds for choosing to exercise what is essentially a discretionary power, and may waive that power in the absence of reasonableness. This would seem to be the only bar to enforcing a charge.

It will not be a sufficient or appropriate defence to claim that charges are being made some time after the services were provided. However,

> "if the claim is first made some time after the provision of the services, the local authority must be prepared to justify the reasonableness of making the claim notwithstanding delay."[169]

7.38 Some useful comments were made in *Avon CC v Hooper* regarding the ability of the service-user to meet a delayed payment. The individual in question will be required to demonstrate that his means are insufficient only at the time when the charges are being made, not at the point of service provision some time earlier when he may well have had necessary means to meet the charges. However, he will be entitled to use a defence of reduced means in limited circumstances, namely where the reduction in income came about as a result of the injury or disability with which the services are linked.

Inevitably, community care assessments, including those carried out under the 1970 Act must be provided free of charge, as must free personal care and advice or guidance regarding the availability services. While the legislation is indiscriminate about which categories of persons in need might be more or less liable to charging, the guidance does go as far as to suggest that people who are terminally ill should be exempt, though this will of course depend upon the particular circumstances of the carer.[170]

Independent Living Fund

7.39 Recipients of a disability living allowance who are under threat of entry into residential care may be entitled to receive further financial assistance from the Independent Living (1993) Fund.[171] Assistance is available only further to a local authority community care contribution and accordingly the Fund operates in partnership with local authorities, administering funds to disabled people understood to require some degree of domestic or personal assistance. Once the local authority has provided services or an equivalent cash sum, the 1993 Fund may be required to supplement the applicant up to a maximum of £455 from the 1993 Fund. This fee is calculated on top of the contribution by social services and the applicant. To qualify for an award, an applicant must be aged between 16 and 66. Discrepancies between the income levels of disabled

---

[166] *Robertson v Fife Council*, 2002 S.L.T. 951.

[167] [1997] 1 All E.R. 532.

[168] Health and Social Services and Social Security Adjudications Act 1983 s.1.

[169] *Avon CC v Hooper* [1997] 1 All E.R. 532 at 537d–f.

[170] *Assessment and Care Management*, SWSG Circular 11/91.

[171] The 1993 Fund was introduced to replace the Independent Living Fund which operated prior to the community care arrangements. The Independent Living (Extension) Fund manages all applications processed at the time the ILF was wound up while the 1993 Fund handles all new applications.

and able-bodied people were found to be more prevalent among people below pensionable age.[172]

In a move to target those under the greatest financial pressure the applicant must be in receipt of the highest rate of a disability living allowance, live alone or with people who cannot fully meet their care needs, and be at risk of entering residential care, with savings and capital that total less than £20,750. Assessment is undertaken by the local social work authority and a social worker from the Fund. The aim is to reach a settlement with the applicant. Guidance issued in 1993 details the process involved in making an award.[173]

Local authority resources

7.40 The community care arrangements introduced by the National Health Service and Community Care Act 1990 placed an increasing emphasis on service provision in the home, and in the period since, resources have become a difficult and sensitive issue. Individual service-users are seldom in a position to pay for home care services in full and must rely quite heavily on their local authority to meet their costs.

Both the 1968 and 1970 Acts are silent on the role that resources are to play in local authority decision making. As a starting point however, guidance on community care suggests that resources will be relevant at some stage during the proceedings, probably when services are being agreed upon. Local authorities are advised that in drawing up a care plan, the availability of resources and services for meeting needs will have to be taken into account.[174] Furthermore, in deciding what packages of care should be provided, account should be taken of the costs of service options and budgeting information.[175] A circular published in 1970 stated that "criteria of need are matters for the authorities to determine in light of resources".[176] What appears to be an established principle is reinforced in policy guidance issued on the 1990 Act, and is seemingly entrenched in social work law for the time being:

> "local authorities will also have a responsibility to meet needs within the resources available and this will sometimes involve difficult decisions where it will be necessary to strike a balance between meeting the needs identified within available resources and meeting care preferences of the individual."[177]

A series of decisions emerging from the English courts have since sought to dispel the ambiguity, and in this pursuit have provided firm guidance to the Scottish courts for future challenges to local authority spending. In *R. v Avon CC Ex p. M*[178] the wishes of a service-user to be accommodated in a particular residential care home were upheld by the court notwithstanding the resulting increase in costs incurred by the authority. The applicant's psychological needs were such as to justify provision over and above services which the council felt would meet his basic needs. This did seem to be a positive result for service-users generally. However, indications that this was not to be a decision upon which future considerations would be based emerged shortly after. Recent case law suggests that a lack of resources will be a reliable defence when local government budgets fall short in meeting the demands of service-users. The particular stage at which resources might legitimately be taken into consideration, however, is something that requires a closer look.

7.41 Under the terms of the 1970 Act the local authority is required first to decide whether services are necessary to meet need, and secondly to make the necessary arrangements. Quite

---

[172] *Hansard*, HC Vol.221, col.40 (March 15, 1993).

[173] *Independent Living Arrangements from April 1993. Replacement of the Independent Living Fund*, SWSG Circular 7/93.

[174] SWSG Circular 11/91, para.6.1

[175] SWSG Circular 11/91, para.6.3.

[176] Dept of Health Circular 12/70, para.7.

[177] SWSG Circular 11/91, para.3.25

[178] [1994] 2 F.L.R. 1006.

distinctly, under s.12A of the 1968 Act the local authority is required first of all to assess needs, and secondly to decide whether those needs call for the provision of services. In this latter instance there is no absolute duty that identified needs must be met and it is this omission that has caused judicial adversity and growing concern among service-users, their carers and their representatives.

In *R. v Gloucestershire CC Ex p. Mahfood*[179] home care provision was removed from over 1,000 disabled service-users without a reassessment of their needs. Following a review of the decision, the High Court found that local authorities were entitled to take their resources into account at the stage of assessing a person's need for community care services under the 1990 Act, and when deciding whether it was necessary to make arrangements to meet the assessed needs under s.2 of the 1970 Act. However, once the authority had deemed it necessary to make arrangements to meet the assessed need, it would be under an absolute duty to do so and could not claim that insufficient resources existed to meet what it had confirmed to be a need for services. In other words, in deciding *how* services were to be provided there could be no reference to inadequate funds, though in deciding *whether* services were necessary, resources were relevant.

R. v Islington LBC Ex p. McMillan, was considered alongside *Mahfood*. In this instance, home help services had been removed from the applicant. It was the opinion of the court that the council had properly carried out a balancing exercise, considering the comparative needs of disabled people in its area on the one hand, and available resources on the other hand. If home care assistance was not available while the carer was on leave, an interruption to services would be legitimate. In these particular circumstances the needs of the user were not such that a disruption to service provision would be considered harmful.

The court once more supported this inclination in *R. v Lancashire CC Ex p. Ingham and Whalley*[180] where the user in question required full-time home support so as to avoid an admission to institutional care. Following a reassessment by the local authority domiciliary care was removed and the service-user was allocated a place in a residential care home. The court found that the local authority was fully entitled to take its resources into account both when assessing need and when subsequently deciding whether services were necessary in order to meet that need. Resources were relevant because of the comparative needs of other service-users in the area to whom an equivalent duty was owed. Residential care was clearly a cheaper option than home care support.

Gloucestershire

7.42 In *R. v Gloucestershire CC Ex p. Barry*[181] Barry was a service-user whose cleaning provision had been withdrawn and laundry services reduced on financial grounds. His application for judicial review was part of the multiple action considered earlier. He appealed the decision to the Court of Appeal where it was overturned. Resources were deemed to be neither relevant at the point of assessing need, nor in deciding *whether* services were necessary in order to meet those needs. However, they might be a relevant factor in deciding *how* to meet need.[182]

The House of Lords proceeded to overturn the decision of the Court of Appeal and restore the original order of the High Court, confirming that resources might be a relevant consideration only at the point of deciding *whether* to make arrangements to meet a need and not at

[179] 94 L.G.R. 593, QBD. This was a joint action with *Barry, Grinham, Dartnel and McMillan*. *McMillan* and *Barry* are each considered below.

[180] Unreported July 5, 1995 CO/774/95, QBD.

[181] [1996] 4 All E.R. 421.

[182] For a fuller discussion of the potential implications of the initial Court of Appeal decision see T. Guthrie, "Significance of Resources in Community Care Assessments" (1997) 2(2) S.L.P.Q. 149; B. Schwehr, "The Legal Relevance of Resources—or a Lack of Resources—in Community Care" (1995) 17(2) *Journal of Social Welfare and Family Law* 179 and S. Cragg, "The Court of Appeal gets to the Heart of the Matter" (1996) 236 SCOLAG 121. Also see *R. v Essex CC Ex p. Bucke* [1997] C.O.D. 66, where resources were held to be relevant at the point of deciding how to meet need.

any time thereafter, including decisions as to *how* that need will be met.[183] As a consequence the services that are to be made available under s.2 of the 1970 Act will reflect the resources available to a given authority at a given point in time. Determining whether arrangements are necessary to meet a need, or simply desired, requires the application of criteria that the local authority must formulate and uniformly apply in all subsequent cases requiring an assessment of need.[184]

Specifically, the degree of necessity will be ascertained by matching the severity of the particular condition—the nature and extent of the disability and the manner in which and extent to which quality of life would be improved by the provision of a particular service against the availability of resources. The more limited the resources, the greater the need must be in order to make the resulting expenditure a necessity. Lord Clyde drew a parallel between this process and the daily domestic experience:

> "If my resources are limited I have to need the thing very badly before I am satisfied that it is necessary to purchase it . . . It is not necessary to hold that cost and resources are always an element in determining necessity. It is enough for the purposes of the present case to recognise that they may be a proper consideration. I have not been persuaded that they must always and necessarily be excluded from consideration."[185]

7.43 It was not the majority opinion of the House of Lords, therefore, that Parliament had intended the extensive list of services contained in s.2(1) be provided regardless of the cost involved.[186] It is now entirely possible as a result that in deciding whether arrangements are necessary to meet needs, resources will be a principal determinant. As a consequence, an unmet need may be lawful in light of the criteria developed by local authorities to determine whether services are a necessity. However, in taking this to its logical conclusion, "whereby the necessity is measured by the appropriate criteria, what is necessary to be met will in fact be met and in the strict sense of the words no unmet need will exist".[187] Effectively, real need could be hidden under the guise of predetermined eligibility criteria.[188] The decision essentially creates a Scottish precedent insofar as the provisions of the 1970 Act apply uniformly across Britain.

This ruling would appear to be partially consistent with guidance on both the 1970 and 1990 Acts indicating that resources cannot always be overlooked. However, there is legitimate fear that it is retrogressive to notions of community care,[189] and furthermore that resources may not be a relevant factor to local authorities making decisions outside the ambit of community care,

---

[183] *R. v Gloucestershire CC Ex p. Barry* [1997] 2 All E.R. 1.

[184] However, it is disputed that "operating blanket provision policies in community care services would breach the duty to assess an individual's need for services. It would fetter discretion by failing to consider all the issues relevant to an individual case, thereby failing to consider the possibility that this case may require departure from agreed eligibility criteria": Preston-Shoot, "Contesting the Contradictions: Needs" (1996) 18(3) *Journal of Social Welfare and Family Law* 307, 313.

[185] *Barry* [1997] 2 All E.R. 1, per Lord Clyde at 17a–b.

[186] Though the decision is concerned with an assessment for services under s.2 of the 1970 Act, it is likely that the same principles will apply in a community care assessment under s.12A of the 1968 Act: see Lord Clyde in *Barry* [1997] 2 All E.R. 1 at 18b.

[187] *Barry* [1997] 2 All E.R. 1, per Lord Clyde at 17c.

[188] However, guidance does suggest that "where it is not possible to meet all assessed needs for community care services, information about the nature and extent of the *unmet* needs should be fed into the authority's community care planning process": SWSG Circular 11/91, para.6.5.

[189] "The [*Gloucestershire*] ruling has opened up a series of new questions about community care law and definitions of need within the community. In practice it legitimises tighter eligibility criteria for assessments which could, in turn, impact on the number of carets eligible to ask for an assessment": *In on the Act? Social Services' Experience of the First Year of the Carers Act*, October 1997, p.8, para.1.18.

for instance in relation to childcare and education.[190] Efforts have been made to reverse the decision.[191] In summary the effect of the *Gloucestershire* decision is that while local authorities are bound by a statutory duty of some significance, they are not equally bound to enforce it if they cannot meet the costs of doing so.[192] The decision in *Barry* has been followed in many subsequent cases but arguably equally distinguished.[193] To this end "it is now very difficult to predict in any certainty how any new case will be decided".[194]

MacGregor

7.44 The challenge between needs against resources in relation to s.12 of the 1968 Act was recently settled in the Scottish case, *MacGregor v South Lanarkshire Council*.[195] In this case a 90-year-old man, with poor short-term memory, liability to fall and deafness in both ears was assessed under s.12A as requiring 24-hour nursing care. However, owing to shortage of resources, the man was placed on a waiting list for residential accommodation with an expected delay of seven months; meanwhile no other services were provided to support the assessed need. In his conclusions, Lord Hardie stated:

> "I am of the opinion that once a local authority has determined that the needs of an individual in their area require the provision of particular community services, . . . and that his or her needs cannot be met in any other way, even in the short to medium term, the effect of s12 is to impose a duty on the local authority to provide the necessary assistance to satisfy the individual's needs."[196]

Thus a local authority will be acting ultra vires if it does not take any action to remedy the needs, although the action taken need not provide the optimum care.[197] On the question of resources, the Outer House held that they were only relevant in considering *how* to meet an assessed need but not pertinent to the assessment process under s.12A.

Both *Gloucestershire* and *MacGregor* therefore permit local authorities to look at resources albeit at varying stages—depending on which section a person is being assessed under. However this does not sanction inaction. Both cases demonstrate that it is not lawful to take no action where there is a recognised need.

Waiting lists

7.45 Given the competing struggle of funding needs, the practice of putting people on waiting lists is widely used. In the *MacGregor* case,[198] Lord Hardie acknowledged the legitimacy for waiting

---

[190] Preston-Shoot, "Contesting the Contradictions: Needs" (1996) 18(3) *Journal of Social Welfare and Family Law* 307. In *R. v East Sussex CC Ex p. Tandy* [1998] 2 All E.R. 769 the House of Lords ruled in favour of an applicant whose home tuition had been reduced from five hours to three hours per week by a local education authority in England on the basis that its resources were insufficient to continue meeting the original costs. Resources could only be legitimately taken into account when there was more than one way of providing the mandatory "suitable education".

[191] The Chronically Sick and Disabled Persons (Amendment) Bill sought to preclude allusions to limited resources at any stage in the process of assessment and service provision. The financial constraints of a local authority were to have no significance when assessing either need or the necessity to make arrangements to meet that need. The Bill did not succeed.

[192] See B. Schwehr, "A Study in Fairness in the Field of Community Care Law" (1997) 19(2) *Journal of Social Welfare and Family Law* 159 and T. Guthrie, "The House of Lords and Community Care Assessments" (1997) 2(3) S.L.P.Q. 225.

[193] See S.C. Smith, "Needs and Resources", 1998 S.L.T. 253.

[194] Smith, "Needs and Resources", 1998 S.L.T. 253, 254.

[195] 2001 S.L.T. 233.

[196] 2001 S.L.T. 233 at 236.

[197] 2001 S.L.T. 233 at 237.

[198] 2001 S.L.T. 233.

lists but not where a person is placed on a list and required to wait their turn without the organisation of priority.[199] Further,

> "If the respondents wish to maintain waiting lists to enable them to assess the needs of the community ... it is essential that the respondents undertake regular assessments of the relative needs of the persons on the waiting lists to ensure that they utilise their resources to the best advantage."[200]

Financial assistance

7.46 Local authorities are entitled to some assistance from health boards under the National Health Service (Scotland) Act 1978. Under the terms of s.15 of that Act, the local authority might receive equipment, goods, materials, administrative and professional services, vehicles, plant or apparatus from the health board, or a third party arranged by the Board. The Board is further enabled to undertake maintenance work in buildings or land that are the responsibility of the local authority. Financial support is also available when the health board deems it appropriate, to allow the local authority to perform its functions relating to social work, housing and education.[201]

Direct payments

7.47 Augmenting the provisions contained in s.12(4) of the 1968 Act that authorise emergency cash payments to people in need of social welfare, the Community Care (Direct Payments) Act 1996 inserted new ss.12B and 12C into the 1968 Act to enable direct cash payments to be made by local authorities to individuals who can subsequently procure services themselves. As part of the Scottish Executive's wider ambition to allow individuals to stay at home, these provisions have recently been amended by the 2002 Act. Guidance on the 1968 Act and Regulations have been issued and under the terms of ss.5(1) and 12B of the 1968 Act respectively, local authorities will be required to act in accordance with its policy content.

Under a direct payments scheme the cash recipient effectively assumes responsibility for himself and seeks to make his own arrangements for the acquisition of community care services. Local authorities are now obliged to ask all relevant care groups whether they wish to adopt the scheme.[202]

The authority in question shall determine an appropriate sum though it will obviously need to reflect the individual's contribution. Where gross or net payments have been made to an individual the local authority has the power to recover monies given in excess of need. Conversely an authority may adjust payments to reflect further support to an individual.[203]

Direct payments will be subject to the rules that regulate charging for services with the effect that the assessed amount may be reduced to reflect the user's own contribution to the care package.[204] Once payment has been made the local authority is immediately relieved of its duty to arrange services for the recipient, though only in respect of services to which the payment relates.[205] The local authority can still provide emergency cash to an individual who is receiving direct payments under the separate provisions of s.12 of the 1968 Act.[206] Recipients will be subject to the checks and balances of the local authority, which can request a repayment where

---

[199] There has since been much commentary on the validity of waiting lists. See P. Spiers, "Unlawful Waiting Lists: A Time to Challenge?" (2003) 8(5) E.C.A. 14; "Community Care Assessments: Waiting Lists and Local Authorities' Lack of Resources" (2001) 8(5) W.B. 9 and K. Ashton, "Waiting Lists and Residential Care" (1998) 4(1) E.C.A. 10.

[200] 2001 S.L.T. 233 at 237.

[201] National Health Service (Scotland) Act 1978 s.16A.

[202] 1968 Act s.12B(1), inserted by the 2002 Act s.7.

[203] 1968 Act s.12B(5A) and (5B), inserted by the 2002 Act s.7.

[204] Section 87(1) empowers local authorities to levy charges on the provision of services provided under the 1968 Act.

[205] 1968 Act s.12C.

[206] 1968 Act s.12C.

money is spent inappropriately or not spent at all, or where conditions attached to the payment have been breached.[207]

7.48 The suitability of a user who is receiving direct payments will depend upon their own expectations and wishes. In other words, he must give his consent and be fully satisfied with the arrangements made. Where a beneficiary is incapable of consenting, consent can be executed on their behalf by an individual who has parental responsibilities, is an attorney or a guardian.[208] Further, such individuals may procure services on behalf of the beneficiary.[209]

Initially self-directed support[210] was restricted to disabled people between 18 and 64 years for adult community care services providing they were capable of managing them. In an effort to promote more choice and control in all community care and child services, the Scottish Executive via legislation widened the class of persons eligible to access direct payments. Direct payments are now available to "any person" not excluded by Regulations whose needs require community care services, even where these are child services.[211] Recent guidance provides a useful list of those now eligible.[212]

To widen access to the most suitable services, a new section in the 1968 Act allows payments to be used to pay for services of any local authority.[213] Currently the Regulations are designed so as to prevent direct payments being used to procure services from relatives or people living in the same home as the service-user.[214] However this restriction will be amended when the Adult Support and Protection (Scotland) Act 2007 comes into force. Direct payments can be used to purchase short-term stays in residential care, though cannot be used to purchase more than four weeks' accommodation in a 12-month period.[215] Where periods in residential care are more than four weeks apart, they are not added together if separated by a period of less than four weeks.

RESIDENTIAL CARE

General duty

7.49 With the introduction of community care the emphasis on residential care has shifted. Understandably, it is not heavily endorsed as a community care enhancement. However, intensive care needs often demand an additional dimension of care in a residential setting. This serves in some sense as a compromise between institutional and community living.

The basic right to residential care falls under the general terms of s.12 of the 1968 Act, which requires local authorities to provide "residential and other establishments".

> "[T]he local authority may feel it necessary to make provision, and may in fact make provision under s.12 of the 1968 Act, to have a disabled person accommodated in an 'establishment' in the sense of an institution or other place where he would benefit from supervision and control when he could not without danger or extreme discomfort live in his own home."[216]

---

[207] 1968 Act s.12B(5).

[208] 1968 Act s.12B(1C), inserted by the 2002 Act s.7 and Community Care (Direct Payments) (Scotland) Regulations 2003 (SSI 2003/243) ("2003 Regs") reg.3.

[209] 2003 Regs reg.3(3).

[210] This term is used interchangeably with direct payments.

[211] 1968 Act s.12B(1), as amended by the 2002 Act s.7. The 2003 Regs stipulate who is ineligible for self-directed support.

[212] Scottish Executive, *Self-Directed Support*, Circular CCD 7/2007, pp.96–97.

[213] 1968 Act s.12B(1C), inserted by the 2002 Act s.7.

[214] Specifically, a spouse, cohabitee, parents, children, in-laws, siblings, aunts, uncles or grandparents: 1968 Act s.12B(3) and 2003 Regs reg.4.

[215] 2003 Regs reg. 6.

[216] *Assessor for Edinburgh v Brodie*, 1976 S.L.T. 234 at 238, per Lord Thomson.

A person will be assessed in terms of their need for residential care during a community care assessment.[217] If the social work department feels that needs cannot fully be met at home, relocation in residential accommodation may be deemed appropriate. Provisions written into the National Assistance Act 1948 allow people in need of care and attention to be removed to premises more suited to their needs though in practice this power is rarely exercised.[218] Once residential care has been approved the resident must usually secure financial means with which to fund their care and accommodation. Once an assessment has confirmed that residential or nursing care is required, the individual concerned will be at liberty to choose a home which they feel is the most agreeable.[219] To facilitate this, a topping up arrangement may be made where a person chooses more expensive accommodation. Legislation now clarifies the position that the resident or a third party may pay additional costs towards the accommodation.[220] Guidance on the eligibility criteria provides detail which restricts top-ups from specific resources so that the resident does not prejudice themselves.[221]

7.50 Section 59 of the 1968 Act places a duty on local authorities to provide and maintain residential establishments and embellishes the broader duty found in s.12. Residential care homes may be provided jointly between local authorities or in conjunction with the independent sector. Similar English provisions were examined by the court in *R. v Wandsworth LBC Ex p. Beckwith*.[222] The council in question had sought to transfer three of its four elderly care homes over to the private sector and to close the remaining one. The question placed by the applicant was whether the local authority was under an obligation to provide residential care of its own or whether it was entitled to transfer its responsibilities in whole to the private sector. The court held that a local authority is entitled to discharge its statutory duty to arrange residential accommodation entirely by means of arrangements made with third parties. Furthermore, it was not bound to maintain some accommodation in its own premises for those for whom alternative arrangements had already been made. Lord Hoffmann considered the "mixed economy of care" to which the guidance on community care refers,[223] and understood from such a phrase that a complete shift of provision from the public to the private sector was not outside the powers of local authorities seeking to discharge their community care obligations. In fact, while the Government had not expected that this would be undertaken with immediate effect, this did not construe as a reason for local authorities to retain some residential care provision for themselves.[224] As yet, there has been no equivalent challenge in the Scottish courts though the number of residential care homes managed by the private sector is on the increase.[225]

Local authorities are further required to provide and maintain or make provision of places in residential accommodation with nursing services.[226] Prior to the 1990 Act local authority powers were restricted to providing residential care alone. Removing this constraint and expanding the options with which to keep people out of hospital was central to community care.

Care homes

7.51 It is to be noted at this point that the umbrella term "care homes" covers the two forms of residential accommodation discussed above, namely residential care and nursing homes. Prior

---

[217] 1968 Act s.12A.

[218] National Assistance Act 1948 s.47. Section 48 provides for the protection of that person's property in the event exercise of the powers contained in s.47.

[219] Under the Social Work (Scotland) 1968 Act (Choice of Accommodation) Directions 1993 a person is entitled to choose any home that is available, suitable and affordable.

[220] Community Care (Additional Payments) (Scotland) Regulations 2002 (SSI 2002/265).

[221] *Topping up of Care Home Fees*, Circular CCD 6/2002, p.3.

[222] [1996] 1 All E.R. 129, HL.

[223] *Caring for people: community care in the next decade and beyond*, Cm.849 (1989).

[224] [1996] 1 All E.R. 129 at 132c–g.

[225] In 2005 66 per cent of places in care homes for elderly people were managed by the private sector: see *Care Homes, Scotland September, 2005* (Scottish Executive, 2006).

[226] 1968 Act s.13A.

to the Community Care and Health (Scotland) Act 2002, providing residential care was very distinct from the duty in respect of nursing homes. A residential establishment was defined as one that provides "personal care or support", while a nursing home provided nursing support. The methods of registering and managing the two were different. Local authorities carried out the tasks for residential establishments as opposed to the health board for nursing homes. This distinction has now been abolished under the 2002 Act, which now refers to "care home service", defined as "a service which provides accommodation, together with nursing, personal care or personal support" excluding hospitals, schools and independent health services.[227] Under the 2001 Act care homes are now registered and regulated by the Scottish Care Commission.

The Scottish Commission for the Regulation of Care

7.52 The Regulation of Care (Scotland) Act 2001 established the Scottish Commission for the Regulation of Care (Care Commission) as the new regulator and watchdog of specific care services. The Commission's administration is divided into five regions, with a department residing in each region, plus a headquarters based in Edinburgh.[228] Its remit encompasses a wide range of services for children, adults, and public and private health care.[229] The Act reserves the right for Scottish Ministers to amend the scope of the definition of "care service".[230]

One function of the Care Commission is to regulate care services. Services are to be measured against a set of national standards of care. Subsequently, the same set of standards will be in use across the country, offering consistency to users. These national standards[231] are based on set principles; these are dignity, privacy, choice, safety, realising potential, equality and diversity.

Registration

7.53 Before April 1, 2002, residential establishments providing personal care and support, except those run by the local authority and nursing homes, had to register with the local social work department.[232] This system changed under the Regulation of Care (Scotland) Act 2001 which transferred powers of registration to the Care Commission so that all care homes must now register with the Care Commission. Care home services are defined as a "service which provides accommodation, together with nursing, personal care or personal support, for persons by reason of their vulnerability or need".[233] NHS hospitals and specific schools are exempt from the definition. Any application for registration should therefore be made to the Care Commission.[234] Failure to register a service carries a criminal penalty.

Unlike the previous position where local authorities employed different standards, the 2001 Act undertakes to provide a unified approach via a standard system of registration. The Care Commission is responsible for ensuring by virtue of the registration that all registered care homes meet with the national standards of care. Registered care homes will be issued with a certificate of registration either conditionally or unconditionally.[235]

In pursuit of standards, such conditions may determine the maximum number of persons to be accommodated at one time. Registrations may be refused if a care home is perceived to be unfit by virtue of its premises, facilities, staffing, or run by an unsuitable person by reason of

[227] The 2002 Act refers to the 2001 Act s.2(3) for the definition.
[228] See the Care Commission website at *http://www.carecommission.com.*
[229] For a full definition of these services see the Care Commission website at *http://www.carecommission.com.*
[230] 2001 Act s.3.
[231] To date there are 21 national standards of care; see the Scottish Executive website.
[232] 1968 Act s.61, repealed by the 2001 Act.
[233] 2001 Act s.2(3). A person is "vulnerable or in need" by means of infirmity or age; affected by disability, illness or mental disorder; dependent on alcohol or drugs or of a young age, under s.2(28).
[234] 2001 Act s.7 or under Pt 2 s.33 of the same Act where the applicant is a local authority. The Regulation of Care (Applications and Provision of Advice) (Scotland) Order 2002 (SSI 2002/113) specifies the details to be declared in the application.
[235] 2001 Act s.7.

integrity and good character or otherwise.[236] Section 15 places a duty on the Care Commission to notify applicants of the proposal to refuse registration.

The conditions of registration are subject to modification at any time.[237] A procedure relating to removal or variation of such conditions is set out in ss.14 and 36[238] while appeals to the sheriff against refusal or cancellation of registration are regulated by ss.20 and 39[239] of the 2001 Act.

Inspection and enforcement

7.54 The Care Commission is empowered to examine care homes that are registered, or equally those that it suspects ought to be registered since they provide care home services.[240] To assist this objective, a person authorised by the Commission can conduct interviews to establish the state and management of the facility and the conditions and treatment of the residents. This latter objective may require a medical examination of the resident. Further, documents and records pertaining to the running of the home may be inspected and appropriated. This duty of regulation under s.25 of the 2001 Act ensures mandatory inspections of care homes twice annually, one without prior notification.

To ensure safe and quality services the Care Commission has powers, under the 2001 Act, of enforcement. The enforcement sanctions include improvement notices, cancellation of a registration and condition notices.[241] Where the service is registered under Pt 2 of the Act, the Care Commission must issue a report to Scottish Ministers.[242]

Complaints

7.55 Complaints with regard to services registered under the 2001 Act may be made to the Care Commission by the user, relatives and representatives.[243] Section 6 of the 2001 Act authorises the Care Commission to establish a complaints procedure and further states that the procedure must be kept under review.

This process is detailed in Care Commission Complaints Procedure.[244] The Commission has undertaken to acknowledge all complaints within three working days. Notifications of the proposed investigation, resolution and final decision will be given to the complainant. If the complainant is not satisfied with the final decision they may ask for a review.

Funding

7.56 Charges for residential care are distinct from those made in respect of home care services.[245] In most situations, the local authority and the resident will share the cost between them. The average weekly charge for a place in a residential home depends upon the particular care needs of the individual and the area in which the home is located. Charges can only be made for "hotel costs", i.e. costs after the omission of free personal care and nursing services.[246] Prices vary in homes across Scotland though people with physical disabilities do tend to pay in excess of the

---

[236] Regulation of Care (Requirements as to Care Services) (Scotland) Regulations 2002 (SSI 2002/114).

[237] 2001 Act s.13. The Care Commission can give notice to the body at any time that it intends to impose, vary or remove conditions.

[238] 2001 Act. Section 36 relates to local authorities' applications only.

[239] In relation to local authorities under Pt 2 of the Act.

[240] 2001 Act s.25.

[241] 2001 Act ss.10, 12–13.

[242] 2001 Act s.41.

[243] 2001 Act s.6(1).

[244] See the Care Commission website.

[245] For a comprehensive discussion of the funding process see Circular CCD 6/2004.

[246] See discussion at para.7.13.

average weekly cost for an elderly person. Furthermore, local authority homes by and large carry higher prices than those that are run by either the private or the voluntary sector.[247]

Despite the complex web of recent legislation, funding of places in residential care remains largely regulated by the Social Work (Scotland) Act 1968[248] and the National Assistance Act 1948 ("1948 Act")[249] plus ensuing regulations namely the National Assistance (Assessment of Resources) Regulations 1992 ("1992 Regs").[250] In simple terms, the local authority is required to apply charges for residential care that it has provided to or arranged for permanent residents.[251] This is underpinned by the general principle that those needing residential accommodation should pay for it themselves if they are able to do so.[252] The maximum amount payable is the standard rate, which represents the full cost to the local authority of providing that accommodation.[253] In other words, the resident may be required to meet the full costs of accommodation. The expense that accompanies a stay in residential care has meant that financial responsibility quite often falls exclusively on the resident. However, where he or she is unable to meet the standard rate, the local authority will undertake an assessment of the resident's ability to pay.[254] This financial assessment is often known as the means test. Once the financial assessment is complete, an amount will be agreed upon to reflect the applicant's income and capital.

The means test is a calculation of income, capital and the liability of relatives. Income is estimated on a weekly basis while capital in excess of £20,750[255] will render the resident liable to pay the standard rate in full.[256] Capital below £12,500[257] will not be included in the resident's assessment of ability to pay.[258] Under the present arrangements, where capital falls between these two thresholds, some contribution towards care and accommodation will be required. Relatives of the resident may be liable for some costs towards residential care although it is the Scottish Executive's intention to remove any possibility of liability at the earliest convenience.[259] A liable relative is defined as the spouse or civil partner of the resident in question.[260] Joint resources are to be excluded from the means test although the resident's share of the resource will be calculated.

7.57 There is no stipulated maximum or minimum sum payable: even those on income support will usually be required to make some contribution to community care. The local authority is empowered by s.22(5A) of the 1948 Act to apply charging costs independently of the regulations for the first eight weeks and to begin charging the resident according to the regulations thereafter.

The local authority will not be entitled to include in the resources of the client the sum of his personal requirements. These are set by the National Assistance (Sums for Personal Require-

---

[247] See *Care Homes, Scotland September 2005* (Scottish Executive, 2006), Table 9: Average gross weekly charge March 2003–March 2005.

[248] 1968 Act s.87.

[249] While this is principally an English Act, the provisions that relate to charging for accommodation have been inserted into Pt IV of the 1968 Act, specifically s.87(3).

[250] SI 1992/2977.

[251] 1948 Act s.48. See *Robertson v Fife Council*, 2002 S.L.T. 951 for the stage at which ability to pay should be assessed.

[252] See *R. v Somerset CC Ex p. Harcombe* (1997) 37 B.L.M.R 1 where it was said that the courts should be slow to interfere with funding arrangements when it was clear that careful consideration had been given to all the relevant material circumstances.

[253] 1968 Act s.22(2).

[254] 1968 Act s.22(3).

[255] National Assistance (Assessment of Resources) Amendment (Scotland) Regulations 2007 (SSI 2007/102) ("2007 Regs"). These are amended annually.

[256] 1992 Regs reg.20.

[257] National Assistance (Assessment of Resources) Amendment (Scotland) Regulations 2004 (SSI 2004/103) ("2004 Regs").

[258] Community Care (Disregard of Resources) (Scotland) Order 2002 (SSI 2002/264) art.2(3).

[259] See Circular CCD 6/2004, p.5.

[260] 1948 Act. Payments by a former spouse or civil partner will be calculated as income: 1992 Regs Pt IV.

ments) (Scotland) Regulations 2007 and currently stand at £20.45 per week.[261] This provision is inserted with a view to ensuring that everyone in residential accommodation has at least some income that cannot be exhausted on their care. If special circumstances prevail the local authority may allocate a larger personal allowance than the one set in regulations.[262]

In calculating the amount that an applicant can contribute the local authority may be obliged to disregard specific resources of the resident. By virtue of the Community Care (Disregard of Resources) (Scotland) Order 2002, local authorities must disregard resources contained mainly in Schs 2 and 3 to the 1992 Regs. In some instances the resident's home will be included in the financial assessment and sold to help to pay for costs of residential care.[263] This will of course depend on whether the period in residential care is permanent or temporary. If the resident intends to return home within 52 weeks the home will not constitute an asset.[264] Similarly where the house continues to be occupied by a partner or relative who is aged over 60, a child aged under 16, or an incapacitated relative, the financial assessment will not incorporate the home.[265]

Section 6 of the Community Care and Health (Scotland) Act 2002 provides that an applicant may enter into a deferred payment agreement with the local authority. A deferred payment agreement allows the resident to defer all or certain payments for residential care interest free until expiration and the local authority will meet costs.[266] This agreement will create a standard security in favour of the local authority to the amount reasonably owed. Before an agreement can be made a number of conditions must be met. These conditions are that the financial assessment (excluding the primary residence) found that the applicant has capital at or below £12,500; the applicant does not wish to or is unable to sell their home; a standard security will be agreed to and the security will meet costs.[267]

Where the applicant has not made alternative arrangements to pay for residential care, a charging order may be secured over the resident's property. This order allows a local authority to claim monies owed when the property is sold.[268] It should be noted that unlike the position with the deferred payment agreement, a local authority can do this without consent of the resident.

Disposal of income and capital

7.58 A person shall be treated as in fact possessing *income* that he has disposed of for the purpose of decreasing the amount he may be liable to pay for his accommodation.[269] This is a mandatory requirement in the sense that the local authority will not have the discretion to allow the income disposed of to be discounted from the calculations of the costs of residential care. On the other hand, a person may not be treated as possessing *capital* that he has sought to dispose of for the same reasons. This is referred to as "notional capital". Where a person disposes of assets within six months prior to admission to residential accommodation, knowingly, and with the intention of avoiding charges for that accommodation, the person to whom the assets are transferred will be liable to pay the difference between the actual costs of the care provided, and the amount that the service-user is assessed as being liable to pay, were the disposed-of asset initially retained by him.[270] This provision is one means of redeeming a recoverable sum. In other cases, assets disposed of so as to allow reduced charges for residential accommodation may not be reco-

[261] National Assistance (Sums for Personal Requirements) (Scotland) Regulations 2007 (SSI 2007/103). These figures are increased every April to reflect the rise in inflation.

[262] 1948 Act s.22(4).

[263] A local authority cannot force a sale without a court order.

[264] 1992 Regs reg.2(1).

[265] 1992 Regs Sch.4.

[266] Such agreements terminate by consent of the applicant or 56 days after their death.

[267] Community Care (Deferred Payment of Accommodation Costs) (Scotland) Regulations 2002 (SSI 2002/266). For further information on Deferred Payment Agreements see Scottish Executive Guidance, Circular CCD 7/2002.

[268] Health and Social Services and Social Security Adjudications Act 1983 s.22.

[269] 1992 Regs reg.17.

[270] Health and Social Services and Social Security Adjudications Act 1983 s.21.

verable. In *Yule v South Lanarkshire Council*[271] a resident in a nursing home disposed of her heritage "for love, favour and affection" some 16 months prior to her admission. Since the disposal was outwith the six-month limit, the local authority was not entitled to recover the sum from the third party involved. Notwithstanding that, the council was still entitled to take into account the sum disposed of in calculating the amount that the resident was liable to pay, so long as it was disposed of for the purpose of decreasing the amount for which the resident would be liable, under the terms of the 1992 Regs.[272]

Respite care

7.59 Respite care is a service that targets both users and their carers, and involves an individual either spending a period of time away from the home in a hospital, residential or nursing home, or remaining in the home but receiving care from someone other than the routine carer on a one-off or regular basis. Hospital care is usually limited to circumstances that involve compulsory medical care ancillary to the social care objectives of respite. Day centres are a popular choice for people wishing to join others sharing the same interests.

While this service is not expressly found within the legislative framework it has developed as part of the more general social welfare services under s.12 of the 1968 Act which incorporates residential care generally. The need to make adequate legal provision for respite care was alluded to in the White Paper to the 1990 Act though the 1968 Act has remained essentially the same. Section 2(1) of the Chronically Sick and Disabled Persons Act 1970 refers, in the comprehensive list of welfare services that local authorities are under a duty to arrange, to holidays in holiday homes or otherwise. It is the responsibility of the local social work department to make the appropriate arrangements for respite care though of course it may contract out to the voluntary or private sector.

The duty under s.12A to assess the need for community care services embraces an assessment of the need for respite care and the rules detailed above relating to community care assessments apply in this context. A local authority may respond to a request from a service-user, or may target the recipient on its own initiative. Alternatively, the need for respite care may be brought to its attention through a request for an assessment of the carer's ability to continue caring.

---

[271] 2000 S.L.T. 1249.

[272] For further reading on how one might mitigate liabilities upon transfer of property see W. Neilson, "Residential Care Fees: Protecting the Assets", 2000 S.L.T. 40, 330.

Chapter 8

Social Work and the Criminal Justice System

Introduction

8.01 This Chapter describes the criminal justice process in Scotland, explaining the functions of the police and the Procurator Fiscal in the investigation and prosecution of crime and the key elements of solemn and summary procedure. Given the importance of social work input in criminal justice matters, the emphasis in this Chapter is placed on the sentencing of offenders and their supervision while subject to a community-based penalty or post release from a custodial sentence.[1]

The Role of the Police and Police Powers

Powers of the police

8.02 Police powers are for the most part contained in the Criminal Procedure (Scotland) Act 1995 ("CPSA 1995"). They can be sub-classified into arrest, detention, search and seizure. Additional powers of arrest or detention for various purposes can also be found in specific statutes such as the Road Traffic Act 1988, the Misuse of Drugs Act 1971 and the Terrorism Act 2002.

Arrest, detention and questioning

8.03 Arrests may be made on order of a warrant issued by a justice of the peace, sheriff or a senior judge. Equally, arrests may be made without a warrant. At common law, it is generally accepted that an arrest may be made without a warrant where a constable apprehends someone in the commission of a crime or reasonably suspects someone of committing a crime. The lawfulness of arrest without warrant at common law is generally weighed up in the circumstances. In addition, statute has conferred in many instances the power to arrest without warrant. Arrested persons have the right immediately to have intimation sent to a solicitor and also have the right to a private interview with their solicitor prior to their first appearance in court or their judicial examination.[2]

Sections 13–15 of CPSA 1995 give the police powers of detention and questioning. Section 13 relates to the very early stages of a police enquiry and grants the police certain powers relating to

[1] See Ch.2 for more detailed discussion of the court structure and the sentencing powers of the court.

[2] Criminal Procedure (Scotland) Act 1995 ("CPSA 1995") s.17.

suspects and potential witnesses. It enables a constable who has reasonable grounds for suspecting that a person has committed or is committing an offence at any place to require that person, if found at that place or any place where the constable is entitled to be, to give his name and address and to ask him for an explanation of the circumstances that have given rise to the constable's suspicion.

Anyone else found at the scene that the constable believes has information relating to the suspected offence can also be required to give his name and address. Suspects may also be required to remain with the constable until such time as the address given can be verified or any explanation noted, provided that it appears to him that such checks can be carried out quickly.[3] A constable may exercise reasonable force to detain the person suspected but not any witness.[4] It is an offence to fail, without reasonable excuse, to give the details requested, for which a person may be arrested without a warrant.[5] The Act does not offer any guidance on what amounts to "reasonable suspicion" and courts have demonstrated that they are prepared to give considerable latitude to police officers.[6]

8.04 Section 14 grants the police powers to take persons to and detain them at a police station for the purpose of questioning them prior to charging them with any offence. Where a constable has reasonable grounds for suspecting that a person has committed or is committing an offence punishable by imprisonment, he may detain him for the purposes of carrying out his investigations into the offence and deciding whether criminal proceedings should be instigated against him, and as quickly as is reasonably practicable take him to a police station or other premises.[7] The power to detain is intended to grant the police further time to investigate where there were reasonable grounds to suspect that an offence had been committed but insufficient evidence to proceed to charge a suspect. Detention may last for only six hours or until the subject is arrested, whichever is the earlier, and the suspect must be informed immediately once his detention ends.[8] That person shall not be detained more than once on the same grounds, or on any grounds arising out of the same circumstances. However, it is possible to be detained for a period of less than six hours and released and be subsequently detained for a period which, taken with the earlier detention, does not exceed six hours. At the time of detention the police officer will inform the suspect of the general nature of the offence and the reason for his detention.[9] Records are required to be kept concerning the detention.[10] If a suspect is detained in England and transported to Scotland, there is an allowable four-hour period for the accused to be transported north before the six-hour detention begins.[11] The detained person may, subject to the rules of law relating to the admissibility of evidence, be questioned in relation to the suspected offence and may be searched.[12] The person is under no obligation to answer any question other than to give his name and address and he must be informed of this both on his initial detention and on his arrival at the police station.[13] A constable may use reasonable force in exercising his power to detain and to search a person under s.14.[14]

8.05 A person has the right to have his solicitor and another person reasonably named by him notified of his detention or his arrest without delay. However, the police may delay the notification where it is necessary in the interests of the investigation or the prevention of crime, or

---

[3] CPSA 1995 s.13(2).
[4] CPSA 1995 s.13(4).
[5] CPSA 1995 s.13(6) and (7).
[6] See *Dryburgh v Galt*, 1981 S.C.C.R. 26.
[7] See generally CPSA 1995 s.14. For discussion on "reasonable grounds for suspicion" see, for example, *Wilson and Nolan v Robertson*, 1986 S.C.C.R. 700; *Stark v Brown*, 1997 S.C.C.R. 382; and *Houston v Carnegie*, 2000 S.L.T. 333.
[8] CPSA 1995 s.14(2).
[9] See *Ucak v HM Advocate*, 1998 S.C.C.R. 517 for an instance of the detention of a person unable to speak English.
[10] CPSA 1995 s.14(6).
[11] Criminal Justice and Public Order Act 1994 s.138(6)(a).
[12] CPSA 1995 s.14(7).
[13] CPSA 1995 s.14(9).
[14] CPSA 1995 s.14(8).

the apprehension of offenders.[15] A person arrested on a charge of committing a sexual offence of the type set out in CPSA 1995 s.288C(2) must be told that he is not permitted to conduct his own defence, that it is in his interests to engage the services of a solicitor and that if he does not then the court will do so on his behalf. Failure by the police to comply with the terms of the section does not affect the validity of the arrest of the accused.[16] If the person detained or arrested appears to the police officer to be a child under 16 years of age he is required to notify the person's custodial parent. "Parent" is defined as a parent or guardian, or someone who has actual custody of the child. If the parent is suspected of being involved in the crime the police have the discretion to allow access but in all other cases must grant access to the child by the parent.[17] In *HM Advocate v B*[18] parental access was denied and a confession obtained from the child was subsequently held inadmissible. However, where it is in the interests of the child's welfare or of furthering the investigation, access may be restricted.[19] It is usual for children to be released on an undertaking given by the child or the parent to appear in court at a later date.[20] A child will not be released if he is charged with a homicide offence, or if it is necessary to remove him from association with any criminal or prostitute, or where the police officer believes that the child's liberation may defeat the ends of justice.[21] If the child is not released he will be detained in a place of safety unless a police officer of the rank of inspector or above certifies that (a) it is impracticable to do so; (b) he is of such unruly character that he cannot safely be detained; or (c) by reason of his state of health or of his mental or bodily condition it is inadvisable to detain him.[22] There is power to take a detained or arrested drunken person to a specially designated clinic for treatment of alcohol abuse.[23] The provision is rarely used, owing to absence of designated premises.[24]

Powers of search and gathering evidence

8.06 A person may not be searched to obtain evidence to justify arrest but an arrested suspect may be searched.[25] A police officer must have reasonable grounds for undertaking a search, for instance that the accused is at risk of harming himself.[26] In cases of urgency where evidence might otherwise be lost, the police may without warrant search premises and a person not under arrest.[27] Search and the gathering of evidence may, like arrest, be carried out with a warrant.[28] Many Acts confer the power of search without warrant.[29]

Where a person is arrested, or is detained under s.14, a constable may take fingerprints, palm prints, and such another prints and impressions of any external part of the body, as having regard to the circumstances the constable reasonably considers to be appropriate. All such records of physical data should be destroyed as soon as possible following a decision not to institute criminal proceedings or if no conviction follows a prosecution in respect of a detained person.[30] Such data can be retained, however, where its destruction may result in data from another person being destroyed also resulting in the court being unable to hear evidence it

---

[15] CPSA 1995 s.15(1).
[16] CPSA 1995 s.17A.
[17] CPSA 1995 s.15(4).
[18] 1991 S.C.C.R. 533.
[19] CPSA 1995 s.15(5).
[20] CPSA 1995 s.43(1).
[21] CPSA 1995 s.43(3).
[22] CPSA 1995 s.43(4).
[23] CPSA 1995 s.16.
[24] See Shiels and Bradley, *Criminal Procedure Act 1995*, 5th edn (2006), p.93.
[25] *Jackson v Stevenson*, 1897 2 Adam 255; *Bell v Leadbetter*, 1934 J.C. 74.
[26] *Gellatly v Heywood*, 1997 S.C.C.R. 300.
[27] *HM Advocate v McGuigan*, 1936 J.C. 16.
[28] *Hay v HM Advocate*, 1968 J.C. 40.
[29] See e.g. the Misuse of Drugs Act 1971 s.23 and the Criminal Law (Consolidation) (Scotland) Act 1995 ss.48(1), 49B and 50.
[30] See CPSA 1995 s.18.

would otherwise have had. A constable, on the authority of an officer no lower than the rank of inspector, may take from a person a sample of hair or other material by combing or plucking an external part of the body; a sample of nail or other material from the fingernails or toenails; a sample of blood or other body fluid or tissue or other material from the external part of the body by means of a swab; and again by means of a swab from inside the mouth a sample of saliva or other material. The foregoing procedures are thought to be non-invasive. If the prosecution authorities require evidence that can only be obtained by invasive techniques, such as the securing of blood samples or dental impressions they will require a warrant from the sheriff.[31] The sheriff will take account of the method proposed, the degree of physical invasion, the public interest in the detection of crime and whether there is a need for the procedure at this stage of the proceedings.[32] The police have the power to check prints, samples and impressions against any others held by them in connection with any other offence.[33]

THE PROSECUTION SYSTEM

8.07 The prosecution of crime in Scotland is undertaken by the state in the public interest.[34] Although possible, private prosecutions in Scotland are extremely rare. Only two such prosecutions proceeded in the twentieth century.[35] The person nominally in charge of all public prosecution of crime is the Lord Advocate but most day-to-day prosecutorial functions are carried out on his authority by the Procurator Fiscal.

The Procurator Fiscal, or his or her deputes, conducts cases in the sheriff court and district court and investigates and prepares cases for the High Court. Trials in the High Court are conducted by Crown Counsel, usually advocates or senior prosecutors appointed by the Lord Advocate. In the vast majority of cases, allegations of crime are reported by the public to the police who then trace and interview witnesses, sometimes interview the accused under caution, charge him with an offence and prepare a report which is submitted to the Procurator Fiscal for the area in which the offence took place. Agencies other than the police also report cases to the Procurator Fiscal. Examples of Specialist Reporting Agencies include HM Revenue and Customs, the Health and Safety Executive and the Scottish Environmental Protection Agency, departments of the local authority and the Television Licensing Authority.

8.08 On receipt of a report, the prosecutor has sole responsibility for making a decision about whether or not to prosecute or to take some form of alternative action. The Procurator Fiscal has the power to instruct the police or other reporting agency to make further inquiries if he or she considers that further information is required before a decision can be made about whether or not to take proceedings. The police and other reporting agencies have no prosecutorial role in the Scottish legal system. It is the duty of the Procurator Fiscal to examine the case to see if the allegations against the accused constitute a crime known to the law of Scotland. He needs to be satisfied that the conduct amounts in law to theft, assault, murder or the contravention of a statutory provision that creates a statutory offence.[36] If he is satisfied that it does, then he will examine the case to see if there is any legal impediment to prosecution. For example it may be necessary to take into account any statutory time limits for commencing proceedings. He must also be satisfied that there is sufficient credible and reliable evidence to justify taking proceedings. In effect, the Procurator Fiscal must decide whether there is evidence from at least two

[31] *Hay v HM Advocate*, 1968 S.L.T. 334.

[32] See *Hay v HM Advocate*, 1968 S.L.T. 334; *HM Advocate v Milford*, 1973 S.L.T. 12; *McGlennan v Kelly*, 1989 S.L.T. 832; *Smith v Cardle*, 1993 S.C.C.R. 609; *Hughes v Normand*, 1993 S.L.T. 113.

[33] CPSA 1995 s.20.

[34] See Ch.2 for information on the role of the Law Officers and the Procurator Fiscal.

[35] *J&P Coats Ltd v Brown* (1909) S.C.(J.) 29, 1909 6 (Adam) 19; and *Sweeney v X*, 1982 J.C. 70.

[36] For example the Road Traffic Act 1988 s.3, which creates the offence of driving without due care and attention or without reasonable consideration for other road users, known as "careless driving".

independent sources that the events charged took place and it was the accused who committed them.[37] Once those criteria have been satisfied, the Procurator Fiscal must decide whether the case merits prosecution. Some offences reported by the Procurator Fiscal by the police are very minor or may have taken place some time ago and the Procurator Fiscal has discretion to decide to take no proceedings even though there is sufficient evidence to justify taking proceedings and what is alleged is criminal. The overriding consideration is whether the public interest would be served by proceeding or not. The COPFS Prosecution Code explains that:

> "Assessment of the public interest often includes consideration of competing interests, including the interests of the victim, the accused and the wider community ... The assessment of the public interest involves a careful consideration of all the factors relevant to a particular case."[38]

Factors that the Procurator Fiscal will take into account include[39]:

- the nature and gravity of the offence: the more serious the offence the more likely it is that court proceedings will be taken;
- whether a weapon or weapons were used;
- the impact of the offence on the victim and other witnesses including whether injury has been caused and its severity, or significant financial loss has been sustained;
- the age or other vulnerability of any victim or witness;
- the attitude of the victim, although it is only one of many factors to be taken into consideration and it is unlikely to be a decisive factor on its own in the decision-making process;
- the age, background and circumstances of the accused including his previous criminal record if any;
- the motive for the crime. For example was it sexually or racially motivated; was it spontaneous, planned or part of a course of conduct;
- the age of the offence. If a significant period of time has elapsed since the date of the alleged offence, then it may no longer be proper or possible to take proceedings. However the more serious the offence then the more likely it will be that a prosecution will still be appropriate;
- the effect of prosecution on the accused: in some cases the consequences of prosecution on the accused will be far more serious than the circumstances of the offence would merit;
- the availability of a more appropriate civil remedy; and
- the powers of the court on conviction, such as the power to award compensation, to disqualify from driving or to order a driver to re-sit and pass a test of competence to drive.

Alternatives to prosecution

8.09 Even if there is sufficient evidence to justify proceedings, the prosecutor has the discretion not to proceed where it would not, in his judgment, be in the public interest. Between April 2007 and March 2008 13.6 per cent of the 325,669 cases reported to Procurators Fiscal across Scotland were marked "no proceedings".[40] The most common reasons justifying the decision were that there was insufficient admissible evidence (3.5 per cent of the 13.6 per cent) or that further action would be disproportionate (4.2 per cent). Other, less common reasons included: a civil remedy would be more appropriate; mitigating circumstances; delay by the police, other reporting

---

[37] See Ch.2. paras 2.29–250.
[38] COPFS Prosecution Code (Edinburgh: The Crown Office, 2001), p.6.
[39] COPFS Prosecution Code (2001), pp.6–8.
[40] *http://www.copfs.gov.uk/Publications/2006/09/NoProAll* [Accessed July 1, 2008].

agency or the Procurator Fiscal; time bar; no jurisdiction; not a crime; age of the offence; lack of court resources or staff shortages in the Procurator Fiscal's Office.[41]

Warning letters

8.10 Where the Procurator Fiscal does decide to take proceedings he is not bound to take proceedings in court and has a range of options open to him. Except in cases reported by the Health and Safety Executive, the prosecutor may issue a personal or written warning to the accused. Between April and December 2007 24,505 warning letters were issued.[42] Warnings are more likely to occur in less serious cases where there are clear mitigating circumstances or the accused has no previous convictions. The warning advises that the prosecutor is in receipt of a report of a crime and that a repetition of the alleged conduct would likely result in prosecution.

Conditional offers of fixed penalties

8.11 The prosecutor has the power to offer a conditional offer of a fixed penalty for certain less serious road traffic matters such as speeding, construction and use offences and failure to observe road traffic directions.[43] He may also make a conditional offer of a fixed penalty for any offence for which an alleged offender could competently be tried summarily.[44] This does not include fixed penalty offences as defined by the Road Traffic Offenders Act 1988. The maximum level of fine is £300. In deciding whether to offer a fixed penalty, the Procurator Fiscal will take into account the extent of the accused's previous convictions, the nature of the offence, and the consequences for any victim.[45] Previously whereas the accused was deemed to have declined the offer by doing nothing and was thus liable to prosecution, he is now required to notify the clerk of court within the period specified in the notice that he refuses it. Unless he does so he will be taken to have accepted the offer even though he has made no payment in respect of it.[46] Where no payment is made or the accused ceases payment of instalments, enforcement action may be taken against the accused in respect of any amount outstanding as if it were a fine imposed by the court, provided he has been notified of this fact.[47] If the accused wishes to deny the charge, he must advise the prosecutor of this. He will then face normal criminal court proceedings in which his rights to be presumed innocent until proven guilty and to a fair trial within a reasonable time before an independent tribunal are protected by art.6 of the European Convention on Human Rights and Fundamental Freedoms.

Section 302A of CPSA 1995 permits the Procurator Fiscal to send the accused a notice known as a compensation offer to a maximum of £5,000 setting out the particulars of the alleged offence or offences against him.[48] The accused will have 28 days to pay or to decline the offer. Again, if he does nothing, the accused will be deemed to have accepted the offer. If the accused accepts the offer then he will not be prosecuted for the offence. The Procurator Fiscal may combine a fixed penalty and a compensation offer in respect of the same offence, for example an offence of vandalism.[49]

In terms of s.51 of the Criminal Proceedings etc. (Reform) (Scotland) Act 2007 the Procurator Fiscal will be permitted to send the alleged offender a notice offering him the opportunity of

---

[41] *http://www.copfs.gov.uk/Publications/2006/09/NoProAll* [Accessed July 1, 2008].

[42] *http://www.copfs.gov.uk/About/corporate-info/CaseProcApriJun05* [Accessed July 1, 2008].

[43] Road Traffic Offenders Act 1988 s.75(2); of 234,833 cases reported to the Procurator Fiscal between April and December 2006 10,514 fixed penalties were paid.

[44] CPSA 1995 s.302, as amended; of 306,770 cases reported to the Procurator Fiscal between April and December 2007 18,922 fiscal fines were paid. For comment see P. Duff, "The Fiscal Fine: How Far Can It Be Extended", 1996 S.L.T. 167 and K.A. Meechan, "Extra Judicial Punishment and Procurator Fiscal Fines", 1991 S.L.T. (News) 1.

[45] CPSA 1995 s.302, as amended by the Criminal Proceedings etc. (Reform) (Scotland) Act 2007 s.50(1)(i).

[46] Criminal Proceedings etc. (Reform) (Scotland) Act 2007 s.50(1)(c).

[47] Criminal Proceedings etc. (Reform) (Scotland) Act 2007 s.50(3).

[48] CPSA 1995 s.302A(8).

[49] CPSA 1995 s.302B(1).

performing not fewer than 10 and not more than 50 hours of unpaid work in respect of one or more offences to be completed by a specified date. If the offender accepts the offer and completes the work to the satisfaction of the supervising officer then he will not be prosecuted for the offence. Acceptance of the offer will not be recorded as a conviction. The offender must notify the Procurator Fiscal that he accepts the offer. The Scottish Ministers may by regulations set out the kinds of activity of which the work may consist. This section is not yet in force and is to be piloted with effect from June 2008.

Diversion schemes

8.12 Following a recommendation of the Stewart Committee, social work diversions from prosecution began in early 1982.[50] Those accepted on to a diversion scheme become the voluntary clients of the social work department for a minimum period of six months. Some schemes work on the basis of waived prosecution while others defer a decision to prosecute.[51] Social work diversion has not been incorporated into the full funding arrangements for criminal justice services, therefore it is by no means certain that a diversion scheme will operate in a particular area. Some schemes available locally run by mental health services or organisations such as Sacro might also allow the accused to be offered supervision, support or treatment as an alternative to prosecution. An accused has the option to refuse the offer of diversion and to be prosecuted in court. According to a report from 1989, there was a high incidence of women and elderly persons diverted from prosecution in comparison to other offending groups.[52]

Court proceedings: the preliminary steps

8.13 If court proceedings are merited the Procurator Fiscal must decide whether proceedings should be solemn or summary. In reaching that decision, he will take into account many of the same factors that are relevant to the prosecution decision-making process. A further relevant factor is the sentencing powers of the court in which proceedings are to be taken.[53] For example the accused's criminal record might be such that the summary sentencing powers would not be adequate to deal appropriately with him. In addition there are certain limits on the jurisdiction of the court. Murder, rape and treason can only be prosecuted in the High Court.[54] Certain offences cannot be prosecuted in the district court or JP court. These include robbery, fire-raising, theft by housebreaking, theft or reset where the value of the property stolen is greater than £2,500, or assault resulting in fracture of a limb, or assault to the danger of life or assault by stabbing.[55]

In certain cases such as assault to severe injury, especially if a weapon has been used, or trafficking in controlled drugs, the selection of appropriate court and procedure can be relatively straightforward. In the less obvious cases, the Procurator Fiscal has a degree of discretion to judge whether solemn or summary proceedings are indicated.

Where a prosecutor has stated publicly or advised an accused that he is taking no proceedings, then he is personally barred form reversing that decision. Where a decision has been taken to raise proceedings, the prosecutor must ensure that the decision continues to be appropriate. If new information comes to light or circumstances change, the prosecutor will be required to consider whether the prosecution should continue. Victims and next of kin, but not other bystander witnesses, may request and receive an explanation for the decision not to proceed in a

---

[50] *Keeping offenders out of court: further alternatives to prosecution*, Cmnd.8958 (Edinburgh: HMSO, 1983).

[51] See K. Middleton, "Community Alternatives Reconsidered" (1995) 34(1) *Howard Journal of Criminal Justice* 1.

[52] Stedward and Millar, *Diversion from Prosecution*, Vol.1, *Diversion to Social Work* (Scottish Office, CRU, 1989).

[53] See paras 2.11–2.14 for the sentencing powers of the district court, sheriff court and High Court respectively and paras 8.40–8.66 for the full range of criminal penalties available under Scots law.

[54] CPSA 1995 s.3(6).

[55] CPSA 1995 s.7(8).

case, to discontinue proceedings in a case or a charge, to make substantial charges to a plea or to accept a plea to a reduced charge.[56]

CRIMINAL PROCEDURE

8.14 There are two forms of criminal procedure in Scotland: solemn procedure and summary procedure. Solemn proceedings can be taken in the High court or the sheriff court and are reserved for the more serious criminal matters. Trials under solemn procedure always take place before a jury.[57] Summary proceedings are heard before the sheriff or a justice of the peace in the district or JP court sitting without a jury. This section first explains solemn procedure and then summary procedure. The provisions concerning liberation on bail will be examined in the section on solemn procedure although for most practical purposes they apply equally to summary procedure.

Solemn procedure

8.15 In the vast majority of cases that the law requires or are considered serious enough to be tried before a jury, the accused person will have been arrested by the police as a result of their enquires and will make his first appearance in court from custody not later than the first lawful day after he has been taken into custody. In other cases the prosecutor may receive a report from the police or other reporting agency and initiate proceedings by presenting a petition to a sheriff for a warrant authorising the arrest of the accused and that he be brought before the court for examination. When an accused makes his first appearance in solemn proceedings, he will be served with a copy of the petition which sets out the charge or charges he will face. All solemn proceedings are commenced in the sheriff court, albeit they may subsequently be tried in the High Court of Justiciary.

Judicial examination and committal

8.16 Proceedings on petition take place in private, outwith the presence of the public and the press, any co-accused or their agents. The accused appears before the sheriff accompanied by his legal representative. Also present are the prosecutor, the clerk of court and other court staff, and any police escort. It is almost always the case that the court is informed by the defence agent that the accused makes "no plea or declaration". It is competent for the accused to make or emit a declaration in the presence of the judge but this rarely occurs nowadays.[58] The purpose of a judicial declaration is to allow the accused to make a statement in his own words at the earliest opportunity which might assist his defence.

Under CPSA 1995 s.35, the Crown may, but is not obliged to, seek to judicially examine the accused. The prosecutor usually makes the motion to do so immediately after the accused has made no plea or declaration. The purpose of judicial examination is to have the accused state a defence at an early stage of the proceedings. Where a defence is revealed by the accused the prosecutor is under a duty to investigate it.[59] The accused is not obliged to answer any questions put to him by the prosecutor.[60] However, the failure to answer any question may be commented upon later at any trial by the prosecutor, the judge presiding at the trial or any co-accused, but only where the accused gives evidence or leads evidence from defence witnesses about something

---

[56] *Vital Voices*, Scottish Executive Victims and Witnesses Unit Newsletter, Issue 2 April 2005. *http://www.scotland.gov.uk/Publications/2005/04/19114533/45349* [Accessed July 1, 2008].

[57] There has been one notable exception to this rule; the trial arising from the Lockerbie bombing.

[58] CPSA 1995 s.35(4).

[59] CPSA 1995 s.36(10).

[60] CPSA 1995 s.36(8).

that could have been stated appropriately in answer to the question.[61] In practice, judicial examination is generally reserved for the most serious cases and is not used in every petition case.

Either following judicial examination on first appearance, or immediately after it has been intimated that the accused makes no plea or declaration, the prosecutor will move for what is known as "committal for further examination". The motion is irrespective of whether the accused applies for bail or whether the prosecutor opposes it or not. If bail is refused following committal for further examination, the accused is remanded in custody for up to eight days before making a second appearance in private. The prosecutor may move for judicial examination if it has not already taken place, and then asks that the accused be committed until liberated in due course of law. The accused may renew his application for bail at that stage.

Bail

8.17 The provisions on bail are contained in CPSA 1995 Pt III in ss.22A–33 as amended by the Criminal Proceedings etc. (Reform) (Scotland) Act 2007 ss.1–6.

All crimes and offences, even murder, are bailable.[62] Under CPSA 1995 s.22A, the court must consider the admission of a person appearing from custody to bail on his first appearance on petition or summary complaint, irrespective of whether the accused applies for bail. Where the accused applies for bail, the prosecutor advises the court whether the application is opposed or not and the grounds of opposition to the accused's release.[63]

The prosecutor may oppose an application for bail made in such cases where he or she considers it appropriate to do so. The decision to release the accused on bail or remand him in custody is a matter for the discretion of the court although the attitude of the Crown is very important. However, where the prosecutor does not oppose bail or seek the imposition of additional special conditions, the court may still refuse to admit the accused to bail or add such conditions.[64]

If bail is opposed the Crown serves a custody statement on the accused setting out a brief résumé of the evidence against the accused to show him and his representatives that there are evidential grounds for proceedings being taken. The European Court of Human Rights has held that bail proceedings must be fair and there must be "equality of arms": that is the defence must know what evidence and documents the prosecution holds against the accused before the bail hearing.[65]

8.18 Section 23B states that bail is to be granted except where there is good reason for refusing it having regard to a number of factors set out in s.23C and to the public interest. These factors are that there is "any substantial risk" that the person might if granted bail: abscond or fail to appear at a diet of the court; commit further offences; interfere with witnesses or otherwise obstruct the course of justice, and "any other substantial factor which appears to the court to justify keeping the person in custody".[66] The court must also take into account such factors as the nature and seriousness of the alleged offences; the probable disposal of the case if the person were convicted; whether the accused was subject to a bail or any other court order, such as probation, community service orders, released on licence or on parole, or on deferred sentence at the time of the alleged offence[67]; and the character and antecedents of the accused including the nature of any previous convictions, whether the accused has previously contravened a bail or other court order, or the terms of release on licence or parole and whether the person is serving

[61] CPSA 1995 s.37(8).
[62] CPSA 1995 s.24(1).
[63] *Burn, Petr*, 2000 S.L.T. 538 also reported as *Burn and McQuilken v Procurator Fiscal Glasgow*, 2000 S.L.T. 538.
[64] CPSA 1995 s.23B(5).
[65] *Lamy v Belgium* (1989) E.H.R.R. 529.
[66] CPSA 1995 s.23C(1)(a)–(d).
[67] CPSA 1995 s.23C(2).

or has served a sentence of imprisonment.[68] The court is also required to consider the extent to which the public interest and public safety could be safeguarded by the imposition of bail conditions. Section 23D provides that a person facing solemn proceedings for a sexual, violent or drug trafficking offence who has a previous conviction on indictment for a violent, sexual or drug trafficking offence is to be granted bail only if there are exceptional circumstances justifying it.

8.19 Bail may be granted subject to certain standard conditions set out in CPSA 1995 s.24(5) or such further conditions as the court considers necessary to ensure that the standard conditions are observed and that the accused makes himself available for the purpose of taking part in an identification parade or makes it possible for prints, impressions or samples be taken from him.[69] The standard conditions are that the accused:

- will appear at the appointed time at every diet of the court of which he is given notice[70];
- will not commit an offence while on bail,[71] will not interfere with witnesses[72];
- will not behave in a manner which causes or is likely to cause alarm or distress to a witness[73];
- will make himself available for the purpose of enabling enquiries or a report to be made[74]; or
- if the charge is of a sexual nature, he will not seek to obtain a statement from the complainer other than through his solicitor.[75]

The deposit of a sum of money as a condition of bail is generally prohibited,[76] unless the court is satisfied that the imposition of such a condition is appropriate in the special circumstances of the case.[77] The court must state its reasons for granting or refusing bail.[78]

Sections 24A–24E relate to the remote monitoring of restrictions in movements. In 2005 a two-year pilot scheme to permit electronic monitoring ("EM bail") as an additional bail condition where bail would otherwise have been refused was conducted at sheriff courts in Glasgow, Edinburgh and Stirling and the High Court in Glasgow.[79] The aims of the scheme were to reduce the use of custody for those assessed as eligible for electronically monitored bail who would otherwise have been remanded and to provide additional protection to the public against the possibility of further offending or intimidation of witnesses.[80] It is not yet known whether the scheme will be revived or rolled out across Scotland now that the pilot scheme has ended although initial signs are not encouraging. The study concluded that the scheme appeared to have had a very slight impact on the numbers of accused remanded in custody, and to have not been cost effective.[81]

If it is proved that the offence that the accused was facing was committed while he was on bail, this is an aggravation of the offence charged and will be reflected in the sentence of that offence. It is also a separate criminal offence to fail without reasonable excuse to appear at any diet of which the accused has been given notice while on bail, as it is to breach any of the standard or additional bail conditions, such as approaching or contacting witnesses in the face

---

[68] CPSA 1995 s.23C(3).
[69] CPSA 1995 s.24(4).
[70] CPSA 1995 s.24(5)(a).
[71] CPSA 1995 s.24(5)(b).
[72] CPSA 1995 s.24(5)(c).
[73] CPSA 1995 s.24(5)(ca).
[74] CPSA 1995 s.24(5)(d).
[75] CPSA 1995 s.24(5)(e).
[76] CPSA 1995 s.24(2) and (3)(a).
[77] See *Urquhart, Petr*, 2003 G.W.D. 26–735 where a French citizen was required to lodge a sum of Euros.
[78] CPSA 1995 s.24(2A).
[79] Remote Monitoring Requirements (Prescribed Courts) (Scotland) Regulations 2005 (SSI 2005/141).
[80] Barry et al., "An Evaluation of the Use of Electronic Monitoring as a Condition of Bail in Scotland", Scottish Executive Social Research, Research Findings No.94/2007.
[81] Barry et al., "Electronic Monitoring", Research Findings No.94/2007, p.4.

of a condition not to do so.[82] On conviction on indictment the accused is liable to a fine and imprisonment for a term not exceeding two years.[83] The maximum term of imprisonment for breach of bail conditions in the sheriff court summary cases is 12 months and in solemn five years.[84]

8.20 It is frequently the case that there is insufficient evidence to prosecute an accused for the alleged breach of a bail condition such as a prohibition on contacting or approaching a witness.[85] However, where a constable has reasonable grounds for suspecting that the accused has broken, is breaking or is likely to break any bail condition, he may arrest the accused without warrant.[86] The accused will be brought before the court, wherever practicable not later than the day following his arrest and the court may recall the bail order, release the accused under the original order or may vary the order granting bail to impose any additional conditions it sees fit.[87]

The court has the power to review the bail order and its conditions on the application of the accused or the prosecutor.[88] This usually occurs where there has been a change in the circumstances on which the decision to grant or refuse bail was based. In addition, the accused may appeal against a decision to refuse bail and the prosecutor may appeal the grant of bail in any case.[89] Bail appeals are disposed of before a single judge of the High Court sitting in court or in chambers.[90] Appeals proceed on the basis that the appellant has to satisfy the court that that the judge at first instance was wrong in the exercise of his discretion.

Pre-trial preparation and disclosure

8.21 Once petition proceedings are complete, the Crown prepares what is known as a precognition by interviewing the witnesses, gathering in all the physical evidence such as any weapons, blood or other tissue samples, controlled drugs seized, or documentary evidence. The precognoscer compiles the case and recommends whether further proceedings are indicated and in which court. The case is then submitted to Crown Office for Crown Counsel's instructions on further proceedings. This practice is followed because no solemn proceedings can be initiated without the authorisation and approval of the Lord Advocate or Crown Counsel. All solemn proceedings run in the name of the Lord Advocate, for example *Her Majesty's Advocate v John James Smith*.[91] The part of the indictment that contains the charge or charges that the accused will face is known as the libel. The indictment names the accused, states whether he is on bail or in custody, states the date on and the place at which the alleged crime(s) took place and sets out the manner in which the alleged crime was committed.[92] Annexed to the indictment are a list of the witnesses which the Crown intends to call against the accused, and a list of productions.[93] As the indictment is a public document which is disclosed to the jury who will try the accused, it should not refer to any previous convictions nor should these be referred to in any list of productions annexed to the indictment.[94] If, in the event of conviction, it is intended to ask the court when passing sentence to take into account the previous convictions of the accused, the

---

[82] CPSA 1995 s.27(1).
[83] CPSA 1995 s.27(7).
[84] CPSA 1995 s.27(2)(b)(ii) and (7)(b).
[85] In order to secure a conviction the prosecution must present evidence from at least two independent sources that the accused contravened the condition of bail. The fact that the accused was on bail at the time will be held to be admitted and not requiring of proof, unless challenged by the accused at the commencement of proceedings.
[86] CPSA 1995 s.28(1).
[87] CPSA 1995 s.28(2) and (4).
[88] CPSA 1995 ss.30 and 31.
[89] CPSA 1995 s.32(1) and (2).
[90] CPSA 1995 s.32(4).
[91] CPSA 1995 s.64(1).
[92] The indictment may be in the forms set out in CPSA 1995 Sch.2 or prescribed by Act of Adjournal.
[93] CPSA 1995 s.66(4).
[94] CPSA 1995 s.69(1).

accused must be given prior notice of this by being served with a schedule of previous convictions along with his indictment.[95]

Disclosure

8.22 Traditionally, the defence was not given access to the statements of civilian witnesses. Copies of statements of police officers were made available on request. If the defence wished, it could precognose the prosecution witnesses and so would be issued with a provisional list of Crown witnesses on request in advance of service of the indictment. Since the decisions in the cases of *Sinclair v HM Advocate*[96] and *Holland v HM Advocate*[97] the Crown has undertaken to issue copies of statements given by civilian witnesses to the accused's defence agent on certain terms and conditions. Also statements from police officers along with the previous convictions and details of pending cases for all civilian witnesses are disclosed to the accused's representatives.[98] The policy on disclosure is currently under review.[99] The defence is still entitled to precognosce the Crown witnesses. In the event that a witness refuses to be precognosced, the defence may apply to the court to have a witness cited for precognition on oath before the sheriff.[100]

Procedure where accused desires to plead guilty

8.23 Under CPSA 1995 s.76, where an accused person wishes to plead guilty and have his case disposed of as quickly as possible, there are provisions for him to state his desire to plead guilty by letter. On receipt of the letter the Procurator Fiscal reports the matter to Crown Office for Crown Counsel's instructions, recommending acceptance or rejection of the plea. No witnesses require to be precognosced. If the plea is acceptable then an indictment narrating the charges the accused faces and the court at which he should appear, and when, is served on the accused along with a schedule of previous convictions. No lists of productions or witnesses are required. The accused will appear in open court and plead guilty. He must sign a minute confirming the plea which is countersigned by the judge. The sentencing process then begins. [101] In the event that the accused refuses to plead or tenders a plea of not guilty, the prosecutor deserts the diet for the time being (desertion *pro loco et tempore*). The accused remains committed for trial and the normal trial preparation procedure is re-commenced. If the accused fails to appear at the diet, a warrant will be taken for his arrest.

Time limits in solemn proceedings

8.24 The European Convention on Human Rights art.6(1) provides:

> "(1) In the determination of his civil rights and obligations and of any criminal trial against him, everyone is entitled to a fair trial within a reasonable time by an independent and impartial established by law ... ".

Although this right is now further protected by the Human Rights Act 1998, various safeguards to prevent delay in trials have long been incorporated into Scottish criminal procedure. First, in both High Court and sheriff and jury cases, no accused may be remanded in custody for a total

---

[95] CPSA 1995 s.69(2).

[96] 2005 S.L.T. 563, PC (Sc).

[97] 2005 1 S.C. (PC) 3.

[98] In *Kidd v HM Advocate*, 2005 S.L.T. 375, a conviction for culpable homicide was quashed on the grounds that the failure to disclose the prior inconsistent statements of two witnesses resulted in a miscarriage of justice.

[99] See Scottish Executive , "The Review of the Law and Practice of Disclosure in Criminal Proceedings in Scotland and A Statutory Basis for Disclosure in Criminal Proceedings in Scotland: Proposals for Legislation to Implement the Recommendations of the Coulsfield Report" (Edinburgh: Scottish Government, 2007). *http://www.scotland.gov.uk/Publications* [Accessed July 1, 2008].

[100] CPSA 1995 s.291.

[101] See paras 8.41–8.81 on sentencing.

period of 80 days after full committal unless an indictment is served on him within that time, failing which he shall be entitled to be admitted to bail.[102] Secondly, where the accused is on bail awaiting trial, all solemn trials must be commenced within a period of 12 months from the date of the accused's first appearance on petition.[103] In addition, where the accused is committed for trial in the High Court, an administrative pre-trial calling of the case known as a preliminary hearing must take place within 11 months of first appearance.[104] Perhaps the best known of the safeguards is the so-called "110-day rule" designed to ensure that no person is detained in custody awaiting the commencement of the trial for more than 110 days after full committal. That rule still applies to solemn trials in the sheriff court. There, if the trial does not commence within 110 days of full committal, the accused is entitled to be admitted to bail.[105] Since February 2005 however, in High Court cases the preliminary hearing must begin within 110 days and the trial must commence within 140 days of the date of full committal or else the accused will be entitled to be admitted to bail.[106] In bail cases in the High Court if the preliminary diet or trial does not commence within the 11- or 12-month time limits, then the accused will not face further proceedings on indictment in respect of that offence. The court may on cause shown extend any of the 80-, 110- or 140-day or 11- and 12-month time limits on the application of the prosecution or the defence.[107] In sheriff and jury cases, the accused is entitled to at least 29 clear days' notice from the date of service of the indictment until the commencement of the trial; in High Court cases the accused must have at least 29 clear days' notice between service of the indictment and the commencement of the preliminary hearing.[108] In any solemn case, if an accused fails to appear at a diet of which he has been given notice while on bail, a warrant will be issued for his arrest and the 12-month time limit will be interrupted.

Preliminary hearings and first diets

8.25 Where an accused is to be tried in the High Court, he is served with his indictment and an accompanying notice calling on him to appear and answer to the indictment at a preliminary hearing which usually takes place at the High Court in Edinburgh before a single judge. Not less than two days before the preliminary hearing the prosecutor and the accused's legal representative must communicate with each other in order to prepare a joint written record of the state of preparation of their respective cases and lodge that record with the Clerk of Justiciary.[109] This report will form the basis of much of the judge's pre-trial scrutiny of the preparation of the case. The hearing takes place in public but no witnesses or jurors are present. The purpose of the hearing is to subject such cases to a rigorous system of judicial pre-trial scrutiny designed to ensure that a trial diet is in fact required and that the parties to the case are fully prepared for trial before a trial diet is fixed. At the preliminary hearing, where the case concerns a listed sexual offence or a sexual or violent offence in which a child under the age of 12 is to give evidence the court first ascertains that the accused is legally represented at the preliminary diet and then disposes of any preliminary pleas or preliminary issues of which it has been given notice. This may involve the court in hearing complex legal debate and ruling on the matter. Once these matters have been dealt with, the accused is called upon to plead guilty or not guilty. If he tenders a guilty plea which is acceptable to the Crown, then the Advocate Depute moves for sentence and the sentencing process begins. If the accused pleads not guilty, the court undertakes a thorough examination of the state of preparation of the parties to the

[102] CPSA 1995 s.65(4)(a).
[103] CPSA 1995 s.65(1)(b).
[104] CPSA 1995 s.65(1)(a).
[105] CPSA 1995 s.65(4)(b).
[106] CPSA 1995 s.65(4)(aa)(ii).
[107] CPSA 1995 s.65(5).
[108] CPSA 1995 s.66(6)(a)(ii) and (b).
[109] CPSA 1995 s.72E(2)(a) and (b).

case.[110] If the case involves a sexual offence or is a sexual or violent case where a child aged under 12 years is to give evidence, the court must ascertain whether the accused has secured legal representation to defend him at the trial. It must also establish which of the witnesses included in the list of witnesses are required by the prosecutor or the defence.[111] Both prosecution and defence have a duty to seek to agree uncontroversial evidence and the court must also find out the extent to which they have complied with that duty.[112] If there are any vulnerable witnesses the court should dispose of any child witness notices or vulnerable witness applications that have been set down to be disposed of at the preliminary hearing. Only after these matters have been dealt with to the satisfaction of the court will it fix a trial diet.[113]

Mandatory pre-trial hearings known as first diets have taken place in sheriff and jury proceedings since 1996. First diets in sheriff and jury cases are intended to cover much of the same ground as preliminary hearings in the High Court, but if the accused pleads not guilty the case is continued to the trial diet fixed at the time the indictment is served on the accused.[114]

Solemn procedure trials

8.26 Where the accused has entered a plea of not guilty at the preliminary hearing or first diet, a trial will take place before a Lord Commissioner of Justiciary in the High Court or a sheriff sitting with a jury of 15 persons. The judge or sheriff directs the jury on all legal matters and rules on any questions of law. In addition to this he will impose sentence upon conviction. The jury's role is one of determining the accused's guilt or otherwise.

All solemn criminal trials are recorded either by tape recorder or verbatim by a shorthand writer.[115] At the trial itself the accused will be asked at the outset to confirm his identity. It is a requirement of solemn trials that the accused be present although there is a mechanism for removal of an accused who misconducts himself.[116]

Juries are selected from local residents whose names appear on the electoral register. A substantial number are summoned for jury service but only 15 serve on each jury. They are selected by ballot.[117] There is no legislative procedure for jury vetting in Scotland. It is possible for any party to object to a juror on cause shown.[118] However, it is possible, where all the parties to the trial agree, that a juror may be objected to without any reason being stated.[119] Following selection of the jury, the clerk to the court will read the indictment to the jurors.[120] Jurors will be provided with the indictment and lists of witnesses and productions.[121] Where the accused has lodged a special defence, this will also be read to the jury.[122] The jury swear an oath to try the accused according to the evidence. There are circumstances where the jury might reduce in number from 15. Jurors may fall ill, or for other reasons become unfit to continue to serve as a juror. It is possible for the trial to continue so long as the number of jurors does not fall below 12.[123] Once a jury is sworn in, the judge may make some introductory remarks to the jury and then the prosecution will proceed with its case.

8.27 The prosecution and defence do not make opening speeches. Evidence is always given on oath

---

[110] CPSA 1995 s.72(6)(f)(i).
[111] CPSA 1995 s.72(6)(d).
[112] CPSA 1995 s.72(6)(f)(ii).
[113] CPSA 1995 s.72A(1) and paras 2.29–2.36.
[114] CPSA 1995 s.71.
[115] CPSA 1995 s.93; see *McLaughlan v HM Advocate*, 1996 S.L.T. 304, for an instance of a conviction quashed because proceedings had not been recorded.
[116] CPSA 1995 s.92(1).
[117] CPSA 1995 s.88(2).
[118] CPSA 1995 s.86(2).
[119] CPSA 1995 s.86(1).
[120] CPSA 1995 s.88(5).
[121] CPSA 1995 s.88(5).
[122] CPSA 1995 s.89(1).
[123] CPSA 1995 s.90(1).

or after a solemn affirmation.[124] Trials are open to the public and the press but there may be circumstances where some evidence is taken in private, for example where a child or complainer in a sexual offence is giving evidence. The Crown leads its witnesses in chief. After each has been examined in chief he or she is then cross-examined by the defence. If there are any objections as to the admissibility of evidence or the line of questioning, legal arguments are heard outwith the presence of the jury. In order for the judge to be able to make a decision on such objections it can sometimes be necessary for the court to hold a trial within a trial in which the disputed evidence is heard, outwith the presence of the jury. If it is ruled admissible, then the evidence is led again, this time with the jury in attendance. At the conclusion of the Crown case, the defence may make a submission that the accused has no case to answer in respect of some or all of the charges he faces. If, after hearing legal a submission, the judge is satisfied that the Crown evidence is insufficient in law to justify the accused being convicted of the offence or any other offence of which he could be convicted under the indictment, the judge will acquit the accused on that charge or those charges.[125] If the submission is rejected, then the accused may give evidence and call witnesses. He is not obliged to do so but since 1996 the prosecutor has been entitled, in limited circumstances, to comment upon a failure of an accused to give evidence on his own behalf.[126] If he gives evidence he must do so on oath or under affirmation. The accused and defence witnesses are subject to cross-examination by the prosecution and by any co-accused. At the conclusion of evidence the prosecution and the defence address the jury seeking conviction and acquittal respectively. The defence is always entitled to speak last.[127]

8.28 At the conclusion of the evidence, and after the prosecution and defence have given their closing speeches, the judge directs the jury on the law they should apply in that case. The judge may make reference to certain aspects of the evidence. For example, there may be a certain piece of evidence absolutely vital to the Crown case, and the judge may simply direct the jury that if they do not accept that evidence, they must acquit the accused.[128] The jury's role is to try the accused in accordance with the evidence and determine the accused's guilt or otherwise on that basis.

Following the charge to the jury, the jury will ordinarily retire to consider their verdict.[129] On their return their spokesperson will be asked whether they have reached a verdict and whether the verdict is unanimous or by majority.[130] The jury may find the accused guilty unanimously or by majority, but for a majority verdict to be valid there must be at least eight members of the jury in favour of finding the accused guilty. In circumstances where the number of jurors falls below 15 it is still a requirement that at least eight support any majority verdict.[131] There are three possible verdicts in Scotland: not guilty, guilty and not proven. The practical effect of the not guilty and not proven verdicts is the same. Both are verdicts of acquittal and mean that the accused cannot be tried again for the same matter.[132]

Where the accused has been found guilty the prosecutor will move for sentence and will submit to the judge a schedule of the accused's previous convictions. The defence will offer a plea in mitigation. It is most likely that a social enquiry report will be required before the court can court can proceed to pass sentence and so it is common for the case to be adjourned until a later date for sentencing.[133] Following sentence, or adjournment for sentence, the jury will be discharged.

---

[124] Oaths Act 1978 s.5(1).

[125] CPSA 1995 s.97(1) and (2).

[126] Criminal Justice (Scotland) Act 1995 s.32.

[127] CPSA 1995 s.98.

[128] For discussion of the judge's charge to the jury see A. Stewart, *The Scottish Criminal Courts in Action*, 2nd edn (Edinburgh: LexisNexis Butterworths, 1997), pp.179–182.

[129] See CPSA 1995 s.99 on seclusion of the jury.

[130] CPSA 1995 s.100.

[131] CPSA 1995 s.90(2).

[132] The not proven verdict has been the subject of some criticism: see P. Duff, "The Not Proven Verdict—Jury Mythology and 'Moral Panics'", 1996 Jur. Rev. 1.

[133] See paras 8.33–8.39 below for an explanation of the sentencing process.

Summary criminal procedure

8.29 Discretion as to which court the case is taken in under summary procedure is primarily a matter for the Procurator Fiscal. The severity of the offence and the past record of the accused will often determine whether the case will be brought in the sheriff court or the district or JP courts. Charges in summary procedure proceed by way of a complaint.[134] Attached to the complaint will be a list of the previous convictions of the accused. The complaint will also have guidance on the action the accused may or may not take in response to the citation.

Persons arrested in connection with a criminal offence who are kept in custody must appear in court on the next lawful day. Therefore, those arrested on a Friday evening will not appear in court until Monday morning at the earliest. Police may arrest individuals and release them on an undertaking to appear in court at a certain time on a specified day. Where the accused is in custody or appearing on undertaking, he will be served with the complaint by a police officer. If appearing from custody, the accused will also receive a custody statement setting out a summary of the evidence that may be led in support of the charges against him. In the normal course of events, however, the accused will be served personally or by post with a citation which will be accompanied by the complaint.[135] The Procurator Fiscal now routinely also sends out a summary of evidence with the complaint. This, like the custody statement, is intended to form a basis for early discussion between the prosecution and the defence and the plea to be tendered.

8.30 Whether appearing from custody, or as an undertaking, or in response to citation, the accused will have his case called at a first or pleading diet. If someone who is the subject of an undertaking fails to attend without reasonable excuse, he is guilty of an offence.[136] Where he has been cited to attend the accused may plead guilty or not guilty by letter, appear personally at court on his own behalf or instruct a solicitor or some other person who satisfies the court that they are authorised to act for the accused to appear on his behalf.[137] The citation also informs the accused that if he is charged with a sexual offence then his defence may be conducted only by a lawyer.

At the first or pleading diet, any preliminary objections, either to the competency or to the relevancy of the complaint, must be stated prior to any plea being tendered. The objection may be dealt with at the first diet, but more usually is set down for a further preliminary hearing to resolve the issue at some future date, possibly after the court has heard legal arguments. If there is no preliminary objection or the preliminary objection has been disposed of, it will then be up to the accused or his representative to tender a plea, or to seek to have the first diet continued without plea.[138]

If the accused, or his representative, tenders a plea of guilty, the matter may be disposed of there and then. There are, however, a number of situations when the matter must be continued. For example, in some road traffic cases it may be necessary to adjourn the case until the accused's driving licence is produced in court. In many cases it is not possible for the court to proceed to sentence without first obtaining a report into the accused's background and circumstances (a social enquiry report ("SER")).[139] In addition to this, there may be circumstances where the judge simply wishes an accused who has pled guilty by letter to appear personally for the passing of sentence.[140] Where the case is to be dealt with immediately, the prosecutor provides the court with a note of the accused's previous convictions, if any, and offers a narrative of the events surrounding the offence. The accused or his representative then makes a

---

[134] CPSA 1995 s.138(1).

[135] CPSA 1995 ss.140 and 141.

[136] CPSA 1995 s.22(2). Those appearing on undertaking and those in custody are entitled to legal representation from the duty solicitor. The duty solicitor will be a local practitioner who has agreed to provide service in that court for a given period of time (usually a week). Although clients obtained in this way may remain with the duty solicitor throughout the process many may subsequently revert to other practitioners with whom they may be better acquainted.

[137] CPSA 1995 s.144(2)(a) and (b).

[138] CPSA 1995 s.144(1).

[139] See paras 8.36–8.39.

[140] CPSA 1995 s.144(3)(b).

plea in mitigation. If the accused has responded in writing then the court will consider the terms of the letter having heard from the prosecutor. The court then proceeds to sentence.

8.31 In the event that the accused pleads not guilty, two diets will be fixed; an intermediate diet and a trial diet. If the accused is appearing from custody or on undertaking the question of the accused's release on bail pending the intermediate and trial diets is considered.[141] Where the accused is remanded in custody for a summary trial, the trial must commence not more than 40 days after the bringing of the complaint in court. If the trial is not commenced within that time, the accused will be liberated and proceedings for that offence will be brought to an end.[142]

The intermediate diet, so called because it takes place between the pleading diet and the trial diet, fulfils the same function as the preliminary hearing and first diet in solemn case to ascertain whether the accused is adhering to his plea of not guilty, the state of preparedness for trial of all parties and the extent to which the parties to the trial have complied with their duty to agree uncontroversial evidence.[143] The accused is required to appear unless he is legally represented and the court considers that there are exceptional circumstances justifying non-attendance. Failure to appear may result in the issue of a warrant for the arrest of the accused and the discharge of the trial diet.

In summary criminal trials, the Crown will usually rely upon the witness statements obtained by the police and does not precognosce the witnesses. The rules on disclosure discussed above apply in summary cases. Therefore the statements of prosecution witnesses will be made available to the defence. A list of the prosecution witnesses will also be provided on request. In addition, the Fiscal will be prepared to discuss with the defence solicitor the possibility of agreeing evidence. Witnesses for the defence are cited either by postal citation or by sheriff officer.

8.32 On the day of the trial, there are likely to be a number of trials set down to be dealt with in the court. These will be "called over" and it may be at this stage that an accused decides to plead guilty even though he could have done so at the intermediate diet. If so, the sentencing process will commence. In the event that the accused does not appear, a warrant for his arrest may be issued. There is also the possibility that cases may be adjourned. Following a call-over, in the absence of a change of heart on the part of the accused, the trial will proceed. There are no opening speeches at the trial and the prosecution will lead its evidence first. All witnesses who appear will be required to take an oath or affirmation. As with solemn cases, at the end of the Crown case, the defence may make a submission of "no case to answer".[144] The judge is required to determine whether there is sufficient evidence to convict but he is not at this stage required to rule on the quality of the evidence.[145] If the no-case submission is repelled, the defence may or may not lead evidence on behalf of the accused. There are closing speeches and thereafter the sheriff or the justice of the peace or stipendiary magistrate will reflect upon the evidence, and determine the accused's guilt or innocence. The accused or his representative has the right to speak last.[146] If the accused is found guilty there will be a short plea in mitigation by the defence, and the presiding judge will then proceed to pass sentence or defer for further reports. Prior to the passing of sentence the court will consider any previous convictions of the accused. There are three possible verdicts: guilty, not guilty or not proven.

[141] See paras 8.17–8.20 for bail provisions.
[142] CPSA 1995 s.147.
[143] CPSA 1995 s.148.
[144] CPSA 1995 s.160.
[145] See *Williamson v Wither*, 1981 S.C.C.R. 214.
[146] CPSA 1995 s.161.

SENTENCING OF OFFENDERS

8.33 This section examines the sentencing of adult offenders, that is offenders who are aged 16 or above.[147] The law on sentencing is contained in ss.195–254 of the Criminal Procedure (Scotland) Act 1995 as amended. At present in Scotland there is no formal system of sentencing tariffs or sentencing guidelines. However CPSA 1995 provides a framework of sentencing rules and procedures that courts must observe. Sentencers in Scotland enjoy a very wide discretion in their choice of sentence. The Appeal Court has shown great reluctance to intervene in the undoubted discretion of the court at first instance.[148] As Sheriff Principal Nicholson states, the Scottish Appeal Court has:

> "traditionally adopted an individualised approach to questions of sentence, and has always tended to decide cases on their own facts and circumstances rather than on the basis of any declared principles."[149]

However by virtue of CPSA 1995 ss.118(7) and 189(7), the High Court of Justiciary may pronounce an opinion on the sentence, disposal or order that would be appropriate in any similar case. Section 197 of CPSA 1995 requires any court in passing sentence to have regard to any such opinion as an indicator of the sentence that should be passed. Irrespective of whether guidance is given or not, a court is always restricted by the powers set for that particular court.[150]

The Crown is responsible for presenting all relevant facts or evidence to the court to allow the judge to impose the appropriate sentence, subject to any information in mitigation provided on behalf of the accused. With one exception outlined below, the Crown has no role or interest in the actual sentencing process itself.

8.34 Unlike many other common law jurisdictions, Scotland has been slow to permit the victim any role in the sentencing process. In *HM Advocate v McKenzie*[151] the court held inter alia that sentencing was entirely a matter for the trial judge and that in many cases the victim's views or feelings were "of no significance whatever to the judge's assessment of what was appropriate in the interests of punishment and general deterrence in respect of the offence".[152]

However the Criminal Justice (Scotland) Act 2003 s.14 will, from April 2009, give the victim of certain crimes prosecuted under solemn procedure, principally offences against the person, sexual offences and theft by housebreaking, the opportunity to make a victim statement to the Procurator Fiscal as to the manner in and extent to which the offence has affected or continues to affect the person. A copy of the statement is made available to the accused on the accused pleading or being found guilty and is laid before the court, which must have regard to those aspects of it that it considers relevant to the offence.[153]

Sentencing occurs only after the accused has pled guilty or been found guilty after trial. If the accused has pled guilty, the prosecutor narrates an account of the circumstances of the offence to the court. This is noted by the sheriff or justice of the peace in summary proceedings and is also tape recorded in solemn cases. The offender must also be given the opportunity to address the court in mitigation. This is usually done through his legal representative who may also produce references or letters in support of the plea. Since April 1, 1996, the court has been permitted to take into account the stage in the proceedings for the offence at which the offender

---

[147] The prosecution of children in the adult courts is discussed separately later in this Chapter.

[148] *HM Advocate v Lee*, 1996 S.C.C.R. 205, per Lord Justice General Hope at 212; *HM Advocate v McKay*, 1996 S.L.T. 697.

[149] C.G.B. Nicholson Q.C., *Sentencing: Law and Practice in Scotland*, 2nd edn (Edinburgh: W. Green, 1992).

[150] See paras 2.11–2.14.

[151] 1990 J.C. 62.

[152] 1990 J.C. 62, per Lord Justice General Hope at 70.

[153] "Victims to Get Voice in Court". *http://www.scotland.gov.uk/News/Releases/2008/04/25134303* [Accessed May 9, 2008].

indicated his intention to plead guilty and the circumstances in which that indication was given.[154] This introduced the concept of the discount in sentence for a guilty plea tendered in advance of the trial diet for the first time in Scotland. The court is not obliged to give a discount in sentence where an early guilty plea is tendered.[155] The courts must balance the broad public interest, the nature and circumstances of the offence(s) and the fact of an early guilty plea. However it may still be appropriate having done this to hold that no reduction in sentence should be given.[156] In *Du Plooy v HM Advocate*[157] the High Court gave an opinion which comes within the scope of CPSA 1995 s.118(7) and to which under CPSA 1995 s.197 other courts are obliged to have regard. The court stated that the level of discount was a matter for the discretion of the sentencer and it was not appropriate for it to fix a normal, maximum or minimum discount. The court considered, however, that the discount should not normally exceed a third of the sentence which would otherwise have been imposed had no early guilty plea been tendered. The court also held that where a reduction in sentence was appropriate the court should give a distinct discount and should state in court the extent to which the sentence had been discounted.[158] As a result of an amendment to s.196,[159] the court is now obliged to take into account the stage at which the plea was tendered and the court must state, having taken account of the stage at and the circumstances in which the offender indicated his intention to plead guilty, whether the sentence imposed is different from that which the court would otherwise have imposed, and if it is not, why it is not. Therefore, although the court still retains some discretion not to impose a lesser sentence, the court has to justify the decision to decline to impose a discount.

8.35 Other factors that the court will ordinarily take into account when passing sentence include:

- the time, if any, already spent in custody awaiting trial or sentence[160];
- the offender's previous convictions or lack thereof—in particular their seriousness, frequency and any gaps between them as well as whether they are analogous to the offences being dealt with;
- whether there is any problem such as drug or alcohol abuse, sexual deviancy or anger management issues that could be addressed by an alternative to custody;
- the circumstances of the offender's family background;
- the nature and impact of the offence;
- the attitude of the offender and whether he feels remorse and understands the seriousness of his offending behaviour;
- the risk to the offender or others as assessed in the SER;
- whether the offender's mental state is such that he is fit to be imprisoned or has learning difficulties that may have contributed to the offence or attitude to it.

Social enquiry reports

8.36 As this section will show, social workers make a vital contribution to the sentencing process. A key feature of the social worker's role in the criminal justice system is in the preparation of a pre-sentence report known as a social enquiry report ("SER") into the offender's background circumstances. In practical terms, unless the court intends to discharge the offender absolutely, admonish him or impose a fine, a SER will be needed in almost every case. Ordinarily a social

---

[154] CPSA 1995 s.196.

[155] *Docherty v McGlennan*, 1998 G.W.D. 4–76.

[156] *Gardiner v HM Advocate*, 1999 G.W.D. 16–763.

[157] 2003 S.L.T. 1237.

[158] See F. Leverick, "Making Sense of Sentence Discounting: Du Plooy v H.M. Advocate", 2003 S.L.T. 267; D. Thomson, "Discount of Sentencing Following a Guilty Plea", 2004 S.L.T. 1. For a more detailed critique of the theoretical issues concerning sentence discounts see F. Leverick, "Tensions and Balances, Costs and Rewards: The Sentence Discount in Scotland", 2004 8(3) Edin. L.R. 360.

[159] Criminal Procedure (Amendment) (Scotland) Act 2004 s.20.

[160] CPSA 1995 s.210.

worker is present in court or is at least available in the court building in order to process requests for reports or to supply additional information to the court if requested.

Where a report is ordered, the local authority concerned is statutorily obliged to provide it. The Social Work (Scotland) Act 1968 s.27 states:

> "It shall be a function of every local authority ... to provide a service ... for ... making available to any court such social background reports and other reports relating to persons appearing before the court which the court may require for the disposal of a case."

The provision of SERs is a service for the court, not the offender.[161] There is little by way of statutory guidance on the content of SERs. However, since 1991 a set of National Objectives and Standards for Social Work Services in the Criminal Justice System have set out guidance on the legal framework of, the priorities for and purposes of SERs.

> "Reports provide the courts with the information and advice they need in deciding on the most appropriate way to deal with offenders. They include information and advice about the feasibility of community based disposals, particularly those involving local authority supervision ... In the event of custody, the court requires advice about the possible need for a Supervised Release Order or extended Sentence Supervision on release."[162]

8.37 According to the National Objectives, the main purposes of SERs are: to offer information and advice which can assist the court to decide between the available sentencing options; to assess the offender's risk of re-offending, his attitude to the offence and motivation to change; to ascertain the appropriateness of a community-based disposal involving social work input or the need for supervision on release from custody, and to evaluate the potential risk of harm to others in more serious cases.[163]

The objectives of the report writer in compiling a report are: to engage with the offender and seek to motivate and encourage the offender to encourage the offender to face up to his behaviour and consider its consequences; to negotiate to agree a course of action to address problems and issues relating to offending should the court defer sentence or impose a probation order; to explain the range of uses to which the report can be put and the boundaries of confidentiality.[164]

The issues addressed in SERs include the age of the offender, his family circumstances, financial circumstances, accommodation, employment, education and training, physical and mental health, use of alcohol or drugs, and current emotional problems, information about the current offence, previous offending and the offender's attitude to the offence and previous offending.

8.38 In certain cases, the court *must* obtain pre-sentence reports. In other cases, there is no obligation to do so, but the court might choose to do so anyway. In addition to the SER, where the court is contemplating imposing a community service order, the court will call for the preparation of a community service assessment. When both are asked for, they will often appear in the one report.

The court must call for a pre-sentence SER where it is considering imposing a custodial sentence in any of the following situations:

- where it is dealing with a first offender: CPSA 1995 s.204(2) and (2A);

---

[161] "National Objectives for Social Work Services in the Criminal Justice System: Standards Social Enquiry Reports and Associated Court Services", para.1.91. *http://www.scotland.gov.uk/Publications/2004/12/20474/49336* [Accessed July 2, 2008].

[162] "National Objectives: Standards Social Enquiry Reports and Associated Court Services", para.1.5. *http://www.scotland.gov.uk/Publications/2004/12/20474/49336* [Accessed July 2, 2008].

[163] "National Objectives: Standards Social Enquiry Reports and Associated Court Services", paras 4.1–4.15. *http://www.scotland.gov.uk/Publications/2004/12/20474/49336* [Accessed July 2, 2008].

[164] "National Objectives: Standards Social Enquiry Reports and Associated Court Services", para.1.8. *http://www.scotland.gov.uk/Publications/2004/12/20474/49336* [Accessed July 2, 2008].

- where the offender is under 21 years of age whether or not he is a first offender: CPSA 1995 s.207(3) and (4);
- where the offender is neither a first offender, nor under 21, but has not received a custodial sentence before: CPSA 1995 s.204(2) and (2A);
- where the offender is already under the supervision of the court, i.e. where he is the subject of a, probation order, restriction of liberty order ("RLO"), drug treatment and testing order ("DTTO"), community service order ("CSO"), supervised attendance order ("SAO"), or period of deferred sentence: CPSA 1995 s.203.

If a social inquiry report is not obtained in these situations, the judge cannot imprison the offender.[165]

If a judge is considering imposing any of the following sentences, he must first obtain a report, whatever the circumstances of the case of the offender:

- DTTO: CPSA 1995 s.234B(2);
- RLO: CPSA 1995 s.245A(6);
- CSO: CPSA 1995 s.238(2);
- probation order: CPSA 1995 s.228(1),

or any combination of them, for example a probation order with a CSO.

8.39 Often, an offender with many previous convictions will be remanded in custody until the report is prepared. In such cases, the report must be prepared within 21 days, but in cases where the offender has not been remanded, the period is 28 days or up to eight weeks on cause shown.[166]

If the judge is not considering imposing a custodial sentence, or any of the disposals mentioned in the list above, a report is not needed, and a fine, an admonition or a deferred sentence period can be imposed straightaway. Although the judge need not obtain a report in any other case, often he will opt to do so where there are any areas of concern or difficulties in the offender's background, such as alcoholism, drug abuse, mental illness or sexual deviancy problems.

The requirement that SERs be obtained in so many cases can place a considerable strain on criminal justice social work resources. As a result of the recommendations of the Summary Justice Review Committee, the Criminal Proceedings etc. (Reform) (Scotland) Act 2007 s.24 amends CPSA 1995 s.203 and removes the requirement to obtain a report in respect of an offender who is already under statutory supervision provided the court has access to a report prepared not more than three months before the person was convicted of the offence.[167] In addition, the court will be able to dispense with the requirement to obtain a report in respect of such offenders where, in the light of the likely disposal of the case, for example if a small fine or an admonition were to result, "the report would not be of any material assistance".[168]

Custodial sentences

8.40 Imprisonment is the form of custodial sentence for persons of or over the age of 21.[169] Offenders aged 16 or over but less than 21 years of age are sentenced to detention in a young offender institution.[170] The court may not pass a sentence of imprisonment on any person of 21 or over who has not been previously subject to a custodial sentence, or detention of a young offender in any case "unless the court considers that no other method of dealing with him is appropriate".[171]

---

[165] *Bain v McNaughtan*, 1999 S.L.T. 410; *Auld v Herron*, 1969 J.C. 4.

[166] CPSA 1995 s.201(3), as amended by the Criminal Justice (Scotland) Act 2003 s.21(10).

[167] CPSA 1995 s.203(1A), inserted by the Criminal Proceedings etc. (Reform) (Scotland) Act 2007 s.24, in force from December 10, 2007.

[168] CPSA 1995 s.203(1B).

[169] CPSA 1995 s.207(1).

[170] CPSA 1995 s.207(2).

[171] CPSA 1995 ss.204(2) and 207(3).

If a custodial sentence is imposed in respect of a young offender, the sentencer must state his reasons for doing so, such as the serious nature of the offence, or the extent of the offender's previous criminal record.[172] Before imposing a custodial sentence on a young offender the court must obtain a social enquiry report.[173]

Offenders of and above the age of 21 convicted of murder must be punished by the imposition of a sentence of life imprisonment. Offenders aged less than 18 are ordered to be detained without limit of time and those aged between 18 and 21 are detained in a young offender institution and are liable to be detained for life. At the time of imposing a life sentence, the judge must state the period the offender must serve in prison before being considered for release on licence. This is known as "the punishment part".[174]

Section 205B of CPSA 1995 requires the High Court to impose minimum sentences of seven years' imprisonment or detention in cases where an offender aged at least 18 falls to be sentenced for a third offence for trafficking in Class A drugs, irrespective of the court in which the previous convictions were obtained, unless the court is of the opinion that there are specific circumstances relating to the offender or any of the offences that would make the sentence unjust.

8.41 In keeping with the principle that imprisonment is a sentence of last resort which should be imposed only when there is no appropriate alternative, no one can be imprisoned for less than five days.[175] The Appeal Court has also tried to discourage the imposition of short sentences.[176] The length of any custodial sentence will depend on the gravity of the crime, the accused's previous convictions and his circumstances. The court may take into account any period of time the accused has already spent in custody and backdate the sentence to the date upon which the accused was remanded.[177] It is frequently the case that the offender being sentenced is already serving a custodial sentence or appears on a number of charges, in which case the court must decide whether the sentences should be concurrent or consecutive. As a general rule, where an accused appears on a number of charges, he should be sentenced separately for each charge. Following the decision in *Nicholson v Lees*[178] a number of general propositions are now accepted as offering guidance to judges. The first of these is that the highest custodial sentence that can be imposed is that which may be the maximum imposed for the charge carrying the highest sentence on the complaint or indictment. Where the charges have been separated out for convenience, the court should not impose a sentence which when added together exceeds the maximum that could be imposed in respect of one complaint or indictment. In other circumstances the court should decide whether the sentences should be concurrent or consecutive. If an offender has been sentenced to life imprisonment, any other sentence imposed at the same time or later should be concurrent and not consecutive.[179] Where the offender is serving a sentence and is subsequently sentenced for another matter, it is a matter for the judge's discretion whether it should be consecutive or concurrent.[180] Generally it is not desirable to impose a sentence of imprisonment in conjunction with a non-custodial sentence. Imprisonment cannot be imposed along with a probation order.

---

172 CPSA 1995 s.207(3).

173 CPSA 1995 ss.204(2A)(a) and 207(4).

174 Prisoners and Criminal Proceedings (Scotland) Act 1993 s.2, as amended by the Crime and Punishment (Scotland) Act 1997 ss.16(1) and 62(1), Sch.1 para.14 and Sch.3, and the Convention Rights (Compliance) (Scotland) Act 2001 s.1(3).

175 CPSA 1995 s.206(1).

176 See *MacKenzie v Lockhart*, 1986 S.C.C.R. 663 and *Rowlands v Carnegie*, 1986 G.W.D. 4–64 where sentences of 14 and 30 days respectively were quashed on appeal.

177 CPSA 1995 s.210.

178 1996 S.L.T. 706. See also *Penman v Bott*, 2006 J.C. 183 and J. Chalmers, "Case Comment Penman v Bott", 2006 S.L.T. 108.

179 *McPhee v HM Advocate*, 1990 S.C.C.R. 313.

180 CPSA 1995 s.167(7).

Supervised release orders and extended sentences

8.42 The Crime and Disorder Act 1998 introduced two measures designed to give the public additional, continuing protection from certain offenders convicted on indictment on their release from a period spent in custody: supervised release orders[181] and extended sentences.[182] In cases where an accused has been convicted on indictment of an offence other than a sexual offence and is sentenced to a term of less than four years' imprisonment, the court may, having considered a report about the offender and his circumstances by a relevant officer of a local authority, make a supervised release order, if it considers it necessary to do so to protect the public from serious harm from the offender on his release.[183] The order requires the offender to be under the supervision of a relevant officer of a local authority and to comply with any requirements specified by the court or as the officer may reasonably specify in order to secure the good conduct of the offender or to prevent or lessen the possibility of his committing another offence.[184] Such orders can be for a period not exceeding 12 months after the date of the accused's release.[185]

Where an accused has been convicted on indictment to a period of imprisonment for a sexual or violent offence, if the court intends to impose a period of imprisonment of any determinate length for a sexual offence or a term of four years or more for a violent offence and it considers that the period for which the offender would be subject to licence would not be adequate to protect the public from serious harm from the offender, then it may pass an extended sentence on the offender.[186] An extended sentence is the aggregate of the term of imprisonment and an additional period for which the offender is to be subject to licence.[187] This period may not exceed 10 years for common law sexual offences or violent offences or, for statutory offences, the maximum term of imprisonment provided for in the relevant statute.[188] An extended sentence imposed in the sheriff court may not exceed 10 years, being the aggregate of five years' imprisonment and an extension period of five years.[189] Before imposing an extended sentence the court must obtain both a report into the offender's background and a risk assessment.[190]

Risk assessments and orders for lifelong restriction

8.43 Where the High Court is to impose sentence on a person convicted of an offence other than murder which is a sexual or violent offence or one that endangers life, or is an offence the nature and circumstances of which would indicate that the offender has a propensity to commit an offence that is sexual or violent in nature or endangers life, the court, at its own instance or on the motion of the prosecutor, may, if the risk criteria are met, order that a risk assessment be carried out on the offender.[191] The risk criteria are that the nature of or the circumstances of the commission of the offence of which the convicted person has been found guilty either in themselves or as part of a pattern are such as to demonstrate that there is a likelihood that if at liberty, he will seriously endanger the lives or physical or psychological well-being of members of the public at large.[192] The court may adjourn the case for up to 90 days for a risk assessment to be made on the offender by a person accredited for the purpose by the Risk Management Authority. The offender may be kept in custody or in hospital pending the preparation of the

[181] See generally CPSA 1995 s.207.
[182] See generally CPSA 1995 ss.210A and 210AA.
[183] CPSA 1995 s.209(1) and (2).
[184] CPSA 1995 s.209(3)(a) and (b).
[185] CPSA 1995 s.209(7)(a).
[186] CPSA 1995 s.210A(1)(a) and (b).
[187] CPSA 1995 s.210A(2)(a) and (b).
[188] CPSA 1995 s.210A(3) and (4).
[189] CPSA 1995 s.210(6).
[190] CPSA 1995 s.210A(4).
[191] See generally CPSA 1995 ss.210B–210H.
[192] CPSA 1995 s.210E.

assessment. If the risk criteria are met the court may make an order for lifelong restriction of the offender. The practical effect of making an order is that the offender is sentenced to imprisonment or detention for an indeterminate period.

Fines

8.44 In determining the quantum of the fine, a number of issues are assessed.[193] For example, the accused's past record, the gravity of the offence and the means of the offender are taken into account.[194] It is not competent to impose both a fine and a custodial sentence for the same common law offence. In addition a fine should not be imposed in respect of one charge where the court is deferring sentence on another charge.

As a means of laying down maximum fines for statutory offences, the standard scale was introduced.[195] The standard scale sets out five levels of fine. These are currently level 1: £200, level 2: £500, level 3: £1,000, level 4: £2,500 and level 5: £5,000. In the event that a statute makes no provision for a fine but simply states that the punishment may be imprisonment, the court nevertheless has the power to impose a fine.[196] Where the statutory offence is prosecuted summarily, the maximum fine will normally be stated in the Act as a level on the standard scale.

Ordinarily where the accused has a fine imposed following sentence, he or his representative will ask for time to pay or to be allowed to pay in instalments.[197] Where the accused does not ask for either of these, then the court is within its powers to demand that payment be made immediately. The offender must be allowed at least seven days to pay either the whole fine or the first instalment unless:

- he appears to the court to possess sufficient means to enable him to pay forthwith; or
- he states to the court that he does not wish time to pay; or
- he fails to satisfy the court that he has a fixed abode; or
- the court is satisfied for any other special reason that no time should be allowed.[198]

Where the offender is allowed time to pay or to pay by instalments, the judge may at the same time impose an alternative imprisonment in the event of default of payment, if he considers that having regard to the gravity of the offence, the character of the offender or any other special reason, the offender should be imprisoned with expedience and without further inquiry.[199] It is competent to impose an alternative of imprisonment even where the offence itself is not punishable by imprisonment.[200]

It is possible for an offender to apply to court for further time to pay.[201] The court is required to allow further time unless it is satisfied that the offender's failure to pay has been wilful or that the offender has no reasonable prospects of being able to pay if further time is allowed.[202] A court can also vary instalments of a fine.[203] An offender who has been allowed to pay by instalments can be placed under the supervision of a social worker, either at the time of the imposition of the penalty or at any time thereafter.[204]

8.45 Where the offender has been fined and no alternative has been imposed at the same time, it is not possible to imprison the offender for non-payment unless the offender attends court. If an

---

[193] See generally CPSA 1995 ss.211–224.

[194] CPSA 1995, see also *Paterson v McGlennan*, 1991 J.C. 141; *Reynolds v Hamilton*, 1994 S.C.C.R. 760; *Forsyth v Cardle*, 1994 S.C.C.R. 769.

[195] See CPSA 1995 s.225.

[196] CPSA 1995 s.199(2).

[197] CPSA 1995 s.214(1) and (8).

[198] CPSA 1995 s.214(2).

[199] CPSA 1995 s.214(4); see *Stephen v McKay*, 1998 S.L.T. 280.

[200] See *Kausen v Walkingshaw*, 1990 S.C.C.R. 553.

[201] CPSA 1995 s.214(7).

[202] CPSA 1995 s.215(3).

[203] CPSA 1995 s.214(9).

[204] CPSA 1995 s.217(1), known as fine supervision orders.

offender fails to pay a fine he will be cited to attend a special Fines Enquiry Court, but in circumstances where his whereabouts are unknown, or he fails to appear following citation, a warrant for his arrest may be issued. If a fine supervision order is in place, it is likely that a report from the social worker will be available to the court, and imprisonment cannot be imposed as an alternative unless the court has taken steps to obtain such a report. In respect of offenders under 21, detention cannot be imposed as an alternative unless a fine supervision order has first been attempted, or it is not practical to place the young offender under such supervision.[205] At the Fines Enquiry Court it is likely that having heard the offender, the court may allow further time to pay and perhaps add that imprisonment will be an alternative if there is any future default. It is also possible for a supervised attendance order to be imposed (see below). Where the court does impose an alternative to imprisonment for non-payment and the offender does not pay, the court simply grants a warrant for his arrest and imprisonment or detention. The warrant will specify the period for which the offender must be detained.[206] If the offender is able to pay the full balance of the fine to the arresting officer, the warrant is not enforced. The arresting officer simply then remits the money gathered to the clerk of court who issued the warrant.[207]

Supervised attendance order

8.46 In response to the growing concern about people going to prison for defaulting on payments of a fine the supervised attendance order ("SAO")[208] was introduced in 1990.[209] The SAO is aimed at reducing the number and proportion of offenders who are imprisoned for being in default of a fine, in particular in those imposed in respect of more minor statutory offences that are not punishable by imprisonment in the first instance.

The SAO requires the offender to attend a place of supervision for a stated period, which must be not less than 10 hours. Where the fine does not exceed level 1 of the standard scale, the maximum number of hours is 50. In any other circumstances, the maximum number of hours is 100. On attending the place of supervision, the offender is required to carry out instructions given to him by the supervising officer. A supervised attendance order is available if:

- the offender is over 18 years of age;
- he has failed to pay a fine or a part thereof, and the court would imprison him if it did not make the SAO; and
- the court considers the SAO more appropriate than a custodial sentence.

Where the court receives a report that the offender is in breach of the SAO, or is failing to comply with any of its conditions, it may grant a warrant for the arrest of the offender or cite him to appear before the court. If the breach is proved, the court may revoke the order and impose a custodial sentence or vary the number of hours specified in the order. These alternatives represent a fairly restricted discretion on the part of the court. Imposing a SAO means the original fine has been discharged and accordingly it cannot be reinstated. If the court decides following a breach of a SAO to impose a period of imprisonment, it may exercise this discretion up to the maximum imposed by the particular court. The order is intended to be a low cost order requiring minimum assessment and participation in group activity. Successful completion of the order discharges the fine. Potential attendees are not assessed for suitability pre-sentence but their consent is required.

[205] CPSA 1995 s.217(4).
[206] CPSA 1995 s.224.
[207] CPSA 1995 s.218(3).
[208] See generally CPSA 1995 ss.235 and 237 and Sch.7 paras 1, 3, 4, 5.
[209] Law Reform (Miscellaneous Provisions) (Scotland) Act 1990 s.62.

Supervised attendance orders for 16 and 17-year-olds

8.47 CPSA 1995 also makes separate provision for supervised attendance orders for 16 and 17-year-olds.[210] The court is required to assess whether the 16 or 17-year-old is likely to pay a fine within 28 days, if a fine is the appropriate sentence. In the event that the court does consider that the offender is likely to pay then it should impose the fine and make a supervised attendance order in default of payment of the fine within that period. If the fine is not paid the supervised attendance order comes into effect on a specified date which must be not less than 28 days after the making of the order. There are similar provisions for proportionate reductions in the hours required where part of the fine has been paid.

Where the court considers that the offender is not able to pay within 28 days then it should make a supervised attendance order immediately.

Caution

8.48 Although used relatively rarely, the court may order an offender to find caution, whereby a sum of money is deposited as a guarantee that the offender will be of good behaviour over a certain period of time. The district court has power to order an offender to find caution in a sum not exceeding level 4 on the standard scale and for a period not exceeding six months.[211] The sheriff summary court has the power to order the offender to find caution for a maximum period of 12 months.[212] Caution cannot be paid in instalments. If the offender is of good behaviour throughout the period for which he is required to be, he is entitled to recover the sum paid together with any interest that has accrued.

Compensation orders

8.49 A court may impose a compensation order on an offender.[213] Under CPSA 1995 s.249(1), a compensation order requires a person convicted of an offence to pay compensation for any personal injury, loss or damage caused, directly or indirectly, by the acts that constituted an offence. However a compensation order may not be made where:

- the loss arises from the consequence of the death of any person;
- any injury, loss or damage due to an accident arose out of the presence of a motor vehicle on the road, except where the motor vehicle has been stolen or taken away without authority and is recovered damaged;
- the court gives an absolute discharge; or
- the court defers sentence for some reason.

A compensation order may be a condition of probation.[214] It was observed in *Sullivan v McLeod*[215] that it would rarely be appropriate to impose a compensation order while deferring sentence on another charge, but that each case will turn on its own merits. Compensation orders are often relatively small but nevertheless play an important role in convincing the victim that his loss is addressed in the criminal justice system.

In solemn jurisdiction courts the amount of compensation that may be ordered is unlimited. In the summary courts, the amount that may be imposed has the same maximum as the amount of fine that the court may impose for common law offences. The court must take into consideration the offender's means in determining whether to make a compensation order and the amount of that order. A judge is not entitled to make a compensation order in the absence of

---

[210] See CPSA 1995 s.236.
[211] CPSA 1995 s.7(6)(c).
[212] CPSA 1995 s.5(2)(b).
[213] See generally CPSA 1995 ss.249, 250, 252 and 253.
[214] CPSA 1995 s.229(6).
[215] 1998 S.L.T. 552.

evidence as to the loss or damage being led before the court.[216] It is not thought that corroboration of the amount of loss is required.[217] In assessing the amount of compensation, the conduct of the victim may be taken into account. Any contribution he has made to his own loss will result in the compensation being reduced. If his behaviour is of such culpability that he would not obtain an award from the Criminal Injuries Compensation Authority ("CICA"), then likewise, he should not receive a compensation order.[218] Although the compensation order is designed to be for the benefit of the victim, that person has no power to enforce the compensation order.

Probation

8.50 A probation order[219] requires the offender to be under the supervision of a social worker[220] for a period of no less than six months and no more than three years. It is available for any offence other than murder. Probation requires the offender to work towards an acknowledgement of responsibility for offending behaviour and seeks to reduce the risk of re-offending by combining supervision and control with help, encouragement and challenge.[221] The purpose of a probation order is to place the offender in a situation where they can obtain advice and guidance. Following conviction, the court may adjourn sentencing for the purpose of obtaining a social enquiry report into the circumstances and character of the offender. Such adjournment should be no longer than four weeks or eight on cause shown.[222] Once the social enquiry report has been prepared, it will be sent to the clerk of court who in turn will pass a copy to the offender or his solicitor.[223] Where a judge requires further information about the contents of the report, he may question a social worker in open court in the presence of the accused or ask for a further report to be prepared by the social worker.[224]

Like other orders, when a probation order has been imposed by a judge, he is required to explain in ordinary language the effect and nature of the probation order and also what is likely to happen if the offender fails to comply with the order or commits a further offence. One of the unusual features about probation is that the offender must agree to being placed on probation.

8.51 Probation orders are in a set form. The order will specify the local authority area in which the offender will be living, and will also provide for the offender to be under supervision of a social worker employed by that local authority. All probation orders require the offender to:

- be of good behaviour;
- conform to the directions of his supervising officer; and
- inform the supervising officer at once of any change of residence or place of employment.

The court also has the power to impose individual conditions to be attached to the probation order, for instance, that the offender participate in rehabilitation programmes to address any underlying problems he may have. The court has the power to impose a requirement that the offender live in a particular place for a given period of time but not exceeding 12 months. There is also the opportunity of requiring an offender who is subject to a probation order to undertake a prescribed number of hours of unpaid work. Offenders may be required to pay compensation as a condition of probation. It is also possible that a person who is suffering from a mental

---

[216] *Bruce v Macleod*, 1998 S.L.T. 173.

[217] See C.J. Docherty and G. Maher, "Corroboration and Compensation Orders", 1984 S.L.T. (News) 125.

[218] See *Brown v Normand*, 1988 S.C.C.R. 229.

[219] See generally CPSA 1995 ss.228–233 and Sch.6, and "National Objectives for Social Work Services in the Criminal Justice System: Standards—Probation". *http://www.scotland.gov.uk/publications/2004/12/20472/492902/7/08* [Accessed July 2, 2008].

[220] See G. Moore and C. Wood, "The Power of Positive Sentencing", 1988 S.L.T. 52.

[221] SWSG National Objectives: Standards—Probation, para.7.1.

[222] CPSA 1995 s.201(3)(a) and (b).

[223] CPSA 1995 s.203(3).

[224] See *W v HM Advocate*, 1989 S.C.C.R. 461.

disorder may be required to undergo medical treatment as part of their probation for a period not exceeding 12 months. Since June 2003, it has been possible for a probation order to include a requirement that the probationer comply with such restrictions to his movements as the court sees fit for a period not exceeding 12 months.[225] The probationer is subject to the same remote monitoring provisions as are applied to those on restriction of liberty orders.[226] As the offender must agree to be placed on probation, he must also state his willingness to comply with the requirement.

The probation order represents a conviction and may be referred to in future cases as a previous conviction. In addition to this, a probation order does not prevent an offender having his licence endorsed or being disqualified from driving.[227]

It is possible to have a probation order transferred to another court. This is done by either the probationer or supervising social worker making an application to the appropriate court. Legislation also provides for flexibility in respect of probation orders, and in certain circumstances applications can be made for cancellation or addition of requirements to be attached to the probation order. The court may alter the length of the probation order but may not reduce it or extend it beyond the maximum limit of three years. Moreover, a condition requiring medical treatment for a mental condition can only be added within the first three months of the making of the probation order.

It is open to either the probationer or the social worker to apply to the court to have a probation order discharged. It will only be brought by the social worker where he considers that the probation has achieved its purpose, or in circumstances where the probationer has committed another offence and receives a long-term prison sentence.

8.52 In the not uncommon situation where a probationer fails to adhere to the requirement of a probation order, the social worker may apply to the court for breach proceedings. The social worker submits a report to the court alleging the breach and recommending whether or not proceedings should be taken. The court may either cite the offender to attend, or grant a warrant for his arrest. In other cases, the judge may discuss the case with the social worker before deciding whether to take breach proceedings. If cited or arrested and brought before the court, the offender appears and addresses the alleged failure to comply. If the offender denies he has been in breach of the probation order, evidence will be taken in court to confirm or deny the alleged breach. Breach proceedings are conducted by the Procurator Fiscal. The evidence of only one witness is sufficient to prove a breach of probation conditions.[228] In circumstances where the alleged breach is proved the court may continue the probation order and additionally impose a fine, not exceeding level 3 on the standard scale (except in cases where the breach represents a failure to pay compensation). Alternatively, the court may simply sentence the offender for the original offence which in effect terminates the probation order. As a further alternative, the court may amend the probation order, extending it but not beyond the maximum three years. The court may also, as a variation, impose a community service order in addition to the probation order.

Where the convicted person commits a further offence during the currency of the order, the supervising social worker will report this matter to the court. The probationer will be cited to attend court or have a warrant for his arrest issued. The probation order may be continued or the court may sentence him for the original offence. Ordinarily the further offence will be dealt with in the same court as the one the original probation order was imposed in. In such circumstances, the court may deal with the offender for both the offence and the original offence.

8.53 As a final alternative, the court has the power to impose probation with the condition that the offender submits himself to treatment for any mental conditions. This will require the consent of the probationer. The court must be satisfied that there is evidence from one doctor that the

---

[225] CPSA 1995 s.230A.
[226] CPSA 1995 ss.245A–245J.
[227] Road Traffic Offenders Act 1988 s.46(3).
[228] CPSA 1995 s.232(3).

mental condition of the offender requires and is susceptible to treatment but not so bad as to warrant detention under a hospital order. The probation order must specify whether the treatment is to be as an in-patient or an out-patient in the named hospital, and who will provide the medical treatment. Treatment under the probation order must be for a specific period not exceeding 12 months. There is the power to vary the conditions of treatment, subject to agreement by the probationer and the supervising social worker, without a requirement that the matter return to court. The National Objectives and Standards regulate the frequency of contact between probationer and supervisor, and stipulate the type of offender for whom probation is suitable.

Since February 2006, when making a probation order, the court has been able to provide for a hearing to take place to review the order. The offender must and the officer responsible for his supervision and the prosecutor may attend. The supervising officer must produce a written report on the probationer's progress under the order. Having considered the report the court may amend the order. The effect of making the amendment must be explained to the offender, who must agree to comply with the requirements of the order.[229]

Community service orders

8.54 In any offence, except murder, where the offender is over 16 and the offence is punishable with a custodial sentence, the court has the discretion to impose a community service order[230] as a direct alternative to custody. Such an order cannot be imposed without the court first obtaining a SER.[231] The order requires the offender to perform unpaid work for a specified number of hours which may be not fewer than 80 and not more than 240 in a summary case, or 300 in a solemn procedure case.[232] As the community service order is imposed as an alternative to imprisonment, it must be seen as a community penalty of last resort. It is likely that breach of an order will result in imprisonment.[233] In making a community service order the court must be satisfied that the offender consents; that the community service is available in the area in which the offender resides; and that the court is satisfied following a report from a social worker that the offender is a suitable person for community service and that suitable work is available. Community service assessments are carried out by social enquiry report authors in consultation with community service officers. The court is required to explain in ordinary language the nature and effect of the order and the obligations it places on the offender. In addition, the court is required to warn the offender of the likely consequences were he to breach the order and that the court has the power to review the order. Ordinarily, community service is the only punishment imposed, although there is power for the court to additionally disqualify an offender, make an order for forfeiture, have the offender find caution, or pay a compensation order. A fine cannot be imposed at the same time as a community service order for the same offence. A community service order and a restriction of liberty order cannot be imposed together for the same offence.[234] The order itself will specify the locality in which the offender resides. It will require the local authority to appoint or assign a social worker to supervise the order, and it will state the number of hours that the offender must perform. Community service orders may run concurrently, or consecutively, with other community service orders, or with any period of unpaid work as a condition of probation. The only restriction on this is that the outstanding number of hours' work must not exceed 240 in summary cases or 300 in solemn cases. The offender is always supplied with a copy of the community service order.

---

[229] CPSA 1995 s.229A, as inserted by the Management of Offenders etc. (Scotland) Act 2005 s.12(2).

[230] See generally CPSA 1995 ss.238–241 and "National Objectives for Social Work Services in the Criminal Justice System: Standards—Community Service". *http://www.scotland.gov.uk/Publications* [Accessed July 2, 2008].

[231] *Boyle v McGlennan*, 1999 G.W.D. 28–1337.

[232] CPSA 1995 s.238(1), as amended by the Community Service by Offenders (Hours of Work) (Scotland) Order 1996 (SI 1996/1938).

[233] See, however, Stewart, *The Scottish Criminal Courts in Action*, 2nd edn (1997), p.251.

[234] *Macauley v Houston*, 2006 J.C. 91.

The required work must be completed within 12 months of the date of the order unless that period is extended. The hours of work must not conflict with the offender's religious beliefs, or any time which he would normally work or attend any educational establishment. An offender must produce a medical certificate to explain any absences for sickness reasons. The cost of obtaining a medical report may be refunded to the offender. The certificate will be retained on file until the offender completes the order or breach proceedings are complete.

8.55 In circumstances where there is an alleged breach of the community service order, the supervising social worker will submit a breach report to the appropriate court describing the failure to comply, and recommending whether breach proceedings should be commenced or not. In the event that the court decides to commence such proceedings, the offender will be either cited to attend at court, or a warrant will be granted for his or her arrest. The offender will appear in court and will either admit or deny the failure to comply. In circumstances where there is a denial, evidence must be led by the Procurator Fiscal which will prove a failure or otherwise. The evidence of one witness is sufficient to prove breach of community service. Where the court is satisfied that a breach has taken place, it may impose a fine not exceeding level 3 on the standard scale. It may alternatively revoke the order and deal with the offender for the original offence as if the order had not been made. As a further alternative, it may vary the number of hours provided that the total does not exceed 240 or 300 as may be appropriate. The commission of a further offence while the subject of a community service order does not in itself breach the order. An offender is in breach of the order if he fails to report to the supervising officer or fails to notify him of any change of address or to perform the number of hours of work satisfactorily as the officer instructs.[235]

There is scope within the legislation for either the offender or the supervising social worker to apply to the appropriate court to have the community service order amended, with a view to either extending the period of 12 months during which the hours are to be completed, or varying the number of hours, albeit that no variation beyond the upper and lower limits can be entertained. The court has sole discretion in this matter, and will determine the issue in the interests of justice.

Similarly, the offender or the supervising social worker may make an application for revocation of a community service order. The community service order may be revoked by the court without any further action being taken. Alternatively, it may revoke the order and deal with the offender as if an order had never been made. There are a number of circumstances where revocation may be appropriate: the offender may have become seriously ill, or it has become clear that he is not a suitable person for community service. Another possibility is that the offender has since been sentenced to a long prison sentence and will be unable to undertake the hours of work.

Admonition

8.56 All courts have the power to admonish a convicted person.[236] Admonition is in effect a warning but is a conviction nevertheless. It is therefore only appropriate if the offence is very minor, or there are highly mitigating circumstances. It is often a form of disposal used where the offender has had his sentence deferred for him to be of good behaviour and the offender has complied.

Absolute discharge

8.57 Where it appears to the court to be inexpedient to inflict punishment, it is open to the court to impose an absolute discharge.[237] In summary cases the absolute discharge will occur prior to conviction, whereas in solemn cases the absolute discharge will follow conviction. An absolute

---

[235] CPSA 1995 s.239(1).
[236] CPSA 1995 s.246(1).
[237] CPSA 1995 s.246(2) and (3).

discharge cannot be imposed after conviction in summary cases where the accused has been bound over to be of good behaviour and sentence has been deferred. It is an extremely mild form of sanction.[238] It is possible to have an absolute discharge and have one's licence endorsed or be disqualified from driving. The court cannot, however, additionally impose a compensation order.[239]

Deferred sentence

8.58 The court may defer sentence following a conviction.[240] Sentence may be deferred for any period and on any condition, although in most circumstances sentence is deferred so that the accused can exhibit a period of good behaviour. It is likely that if the accused is of good behaviour during the period of deferral then he can anticipate the court imposing a more lenient sentence such as an admonition. If the accused faces multiple charges it is not appropriate to impose a custodial sentence on one and defer sentence on another.[241] Similarly, again in respect of multiple charges, a fine should not be imposed on one charge and sentence deferred on the other. It is desirable that the sheriff who deferred sentence should hear the recalled case if at all possible. In circumstances where the offender commits a further offence during the period of the deferred sentence, he may be immediately brought before the court.[242] Although there is no statutory requirement to supervise the deferred sentence, social workers are often required to complete a social enquiry report following deferment. Many of those reports contain recommendations for ultimate disposal of the case.

Non-harassment orders

8.59 The non-harassment order ("NHO")[243] was introduced by the Protection from Harassment Act 1997 s.11. The court may impose an order as part of a criminal sentence where a person has been convicted of an offence involving harassment of a person. Harassment involves at least two incidents or a course of conduct prosecuted in the same proceedings.[244] Conduct includes speech and harassment includes causing the victim alarm or distress.[245] The statutory definition of harassment can create practical difficulties for the prosecution. A NHO might appear to be appropriate, but if the prosecutor responds quickly and secures a conviction for a single incident, a NHO will not be available. Equally, it may not be expedient to wait and see if a course of conduct develops after the report of one offence. This is especially so if there is a risk that the gravity of the conduct may escalate. The prosecutor must make the application and the court may grant the order if it is satisfied on a balance of probabilities that it is appropriate to do so in order to protect the victim from further harassment. It is the only criminal penalty that requires such an application by the prosecution before the court can proceed to impose the order. If no such motion is forthcoming, the court may not impose a NHO. NHOs are also available under civil procedure. In the event of conviction for a breach of the order on indictment the penalty is imprisonment for a period not exceeding five years or a fine or both,[246] and on summary complaint the penalty is imprisonment for a period not exceeding six months or a fine not exceeding £5,000 or both.[247]

---

[238] See, e.g. *Galloway v Mackenzie*, 1991 S.C.C.R. 548; *Kheda v Lees*, 1995 S.C.C.R. 63.

[239] CPSA 1995 s.249(2)(a).

[240] CPSA 1995 s.202(1); see A. Smith, "Deferred Sentence in Scotland", 1968 S.L.T. (News) 153; L. Nicholson, "Deferment of Sentence in Scotland", 1993 S.L.T. (News) 1.

[241] See *Lennon v Copland*, 1972 S.L.T. (Notes) 68.

[242] CPSA 1995 s.202(2).

[243] See generally CPSA 1995 s.234A.

[244] CPSA 1995 s.234A(7) and Protection from Harassment Act 1997 s.8. See also *McGlennan v McKinnon*, 1998 S.L.T. 494.

[245] Protection from Harassment Act 1997 s.8(3).

[246] CPSA 1995 s.234A(4)(a).

[247] CPSA 1995 s.234A(4)(b).

Antisocial behaviour orders

8.60 Where an accused person at least 12 years of age is convicted of an offence in the commission of which he engaged in antisocial behaviour and the court is satisfied on a balance of probabilities that the making of an antisocial behaviour order is necessary for the purposes of protecting other persons from antisocial behaviour by the offender, the court may, instead of or in addition to any sentence it could impose, make an antisocial behaviour order in respect of the accused.[248] A person engages in antisocial behaviour if he acts in a manner that causes or is likely to cause alarm or distress or pursues a course of conduct that causes or is likely to cause alarm or distress to at least one other person not of the same household as the offender. Conduct includes speech and a course of conduct must include conduct on at least two occasions. The order prohibits the offender, indefinitely or for a period specified in the order, from doing anything specified in the order. The prohibitions are those necessary for the purpose of protecting other persons from further antisocial behaviour by the offender. Before imposing the order the court must explain in ordinary language the effect of the order, the prohibitions to be included in the order, the entitlement of the offender to appeal against the making of the order and the consequences of failing to comply with it. It is a criminal offence to breach the order. Upon conviction on a summary complaint the offender is liable to imprisonment for a period not exceeding six months, to a fine not exceeding the statutory maximum or both.[249] Upon conviction on indictment the maximum penalty is imprisonment for a term not exceeding five years, a fine or both.[250] If the conduct that brings about the breach proceedings amounts to a separate criminal offence, the prosecution must decide whether to take proceedings for the breach of the order or to prosecute the offender for the separate offence. It is not competent to do both.[251]

Drug treatment and testing order

8.61 Following an amendment to CPSA 1995 by the Crime and Disorder Act 1998 the court may make a drug treatment and testing order[252] when it has been satisfied of three conditions:

(1) that the offender is dependent on, or has a propensity to misuse, drugs;
(2) that his dependency or propensity is such as requires and is susceptible to treatment; and
(3) that he is a suitable person to be subject to such an order.[253]

In seeking to satisfy the final condition, the court is authorised to retrieve samples from the individual concerned, though his consent must first be obtained. Before making the order the court must receive a report from the social work department confirming that the aforesaid conditions have been met. It must therefore be fully alerted to the individual circumstances of the offender before taking any decisions on drug testing and treatment. Whether or not a court may make such an order will depend on whether arrangements exist within the local authority area to give it the necessary effect. In addition, such an order is only available when the offender is aged 16 or above and when he has committed an offence to which an indeterminate sentence is attached. Once more, his consent is central to the making of an order.

The "treatment and testing period" shall be not less than six months and no more than three years in duration. However, the Secretary of State is empowered to alter these two periods thereby increasing or decreasing the period over which the order subsists. In order to regulate

[248] See generally CPSA 1995 s.234AA brought into force on October 28, 2004 by the Antisocial Behaviour etc. (Scotland) Act 2004 (Commencement and Savings) Order 2004 (SSI 2004/420). See also Ch.12.
[249] Antisocial Behaviour etc. (Scotland) Act 2004 s.9(2)(a).
[250] Antisocial Behaviour etc. (Scotland) Act 2004 s.9(2)(b).
[251] Antisocial Behaviour etc. (Scotland) Act 2004 s.9(3).
[252] See, generally CPSA 1995 ss.234B, 234C and 234E–234G.
[253] CPSA 1995 s.234B(3)(c), as inserted by the Crime and Disorder Act 1998 s.89.

the operation of this discretionary power, he may only do so by introducing a statutory instrument which is required to be laid before Parliament.

The purpose of the order is clearly to rehabilitate the offender instead of enforcing a punishment, though the onerous nature of its conditions is expected to serve as some means of formal discipline. The stated aim of the order is the reduction or the elimination of the offender's dependency on, or propensity to misuse, drugs. The treatment may involve residency for some or all of the total period specified by the order in an appropriate institution. On the other hand, the individual may be treated at non-residential premises as an out-patient of that institution. In either case he will be required to allow samples to be taken from his body during the treatment and testing period to ascertain whether or not he is continuing to use drugs. The extent to which the treatment provider is authorised to draw samples is specified in the order made by the court, which must make known the minimum number of samples to be provided each month.

8.62 While the order is in force the offender will be placed under the supervision of a supervising officer with whom he must, as a condition of the order, maintain regular contact in accordance with the particular details of the order itself. The statute details the role to be played by the supervising officer, namely, that he will report on the offender's progress to the appropriate court including the results of all drug tests undertaken, and inform that court if the offender fails to comply with the requirements of the order. It is also the responsibility of the officer in charge of the individual to recognise circumstances which demand that the order should be revoked or varied in any way.

If the supervising officer is satisfied that requirements need to be amended, deleted or inserted, that the order should be entirely revoked, or that it should be increased or decreased in duration within the period authorised by statute, he will need to make an application to the court before which the offender will subsequently have to appear. The court is empowered to amend the order if it is in the interests of justice to do so. If the offender is required to appear in court in these circumstances and fails to do so, the court may issue a warrant for his arrest. As a further means of regulation, each order must arrange for monthly reviews to be undertaken, at which the offender must himself be present. This provides another opportunity for the terms of the order to be varied, though in this instance an amendment cannot be undertaken without the consent of the offender. Once more, a failure to appear at a periodic review of the order may result in the arrest of the offender.

8.63 A failure to comply with the order will amount to an offence punishable by a fine, or may result in the variation or revocation of the order. It is likely in the event of these circumstances that the court will pass another disposal with which the offender is more likely to comply. However the court must first be satisfied that there is evidence of a failure to comply with a condition of the order. In *Tweedie v Higson* the decision of a magistrate to revoke an order and impose a period of custody where he was not satisfied with the rate of the offender's progress under the order was overturned on appeal.[254]

Research carried out into reconviction rates following DTTOs showed that those who completed their orders were less likely to re-offend than those whose orders were revoked. Forty-eight per cent of those who completed their orders had no further convictions in two years. Those who re-offended had a reduced rate of recidivism and the offences committed tended to be less serious.[255] While it cannot be claimed that an offender who completes a DTTO will not offend again, the indications are that this is a disposal that has the potential to have a positive outcome for the offender.

[254] 2002 S.L.T. 443.

[255] G. McIvor, *Reconviction Following Drug Treatment and Testing Orders* (Scottish Executive, 2004).

The restriction of liberty order and electronic tagging

8.64 The restriction of liberty order ("RLO") was introduced by the Crime and Punishment (Scotland) Act 1997.[256] Following a successful pilot scheme operated in sheriff courts in Aberdeen, Peterhead and Hamilton between 1998 and 2000, the scheme has since been extended to other courts in Scotland. Monitoring of those on a RLO is carried out by private contractors.

A RLO can be made in respect of any person aged 16 years or more who is convicted of an offence, where the offence does not carry a sentence fixed by law, such as murder, and the court considers it the most appropriate method of disposal.[257] The aim of a RLO is to impose a curfew on the offender and to restrict his or her movements to such extent as the court thinks fit, which may include the offender being restricted to, or excluded from, a specified place at specified times during each day or week. The offender cannot be restricted to a specific place for more than 12 hours in any one day, and the RLO itself cannot exceed 12 months.

When making the RLO, the court must consider information about the place of restriction and attitudes of people affected by the offender's restriction. The court then has to explain to the offender the effect of the RLO, the consequences if breached, and that the order may be reviewed on application from either the offender or the monitoring company. The offender's consent is needed before the order is made. A copy of the order is sent to the offender and the monitoring company. The period in which the offender has to wear a "tag" will be specified in the order.

It is also possible for both a RLO and a probation order to be made together if the court thinks it is fitting in the circumstances. Factors to be taken into account are the nature of the offence, and the character of the offender. Where both orders are made, the clerk of the court sends a copy of each order to both the person monitoring the electronic tagging and the local authority officer supervising the probationer.

8.65 It is possible for the offender or the person responsible for monitoring the offender's compliance with the order to apply to the court to have the order reviewed. The court, after hearing the offender and the person responsible for monitoring, may in the interests of justice vary the order by amending or deleting any of its requirements, insert new requirements, increase the period for which the order has to run, or revoke the order.

If the court suspects the offender has failed to comply with any requirement of the RLO, it may issue a citation requiring the offender to appear before the court or, if appropriate, the court may issue a warrant for his arrest. If the court is satisfied that the offender has, without reasonable excuse, failed to comply with all the requirements of the RLO, the court may impose a fine, vary or revoke the order. If a fine is imposed, it is deemed to be paid in respect of a conviction or a penalty imposed on a person summarily convicted. Variation of an order is dealt with as above, and if the order is to be revoked, the court may dispose of the offender in the way that would have been competent had the RLO not been made, but must take into consideration the length of time the order has been in operation. If the offender is also subject to a probation order, the probation order will also be discharged.

In cases where both a RLO and a probation order have been made, a breach of a requirement in the probation order may result in any requirement of the probation order being varied by the court,[258] and in addition the court may vary the RLO. Similarly, if the breach relates to a requirement in the RLO, the court, in addition to varying the requirements of the RLO, may vary the requirements in the probation order. If the offender, by act or omission, fails to comply with a requirement in *both* orders the court may vary the requirements of the probation order,

---

[256] See generally CPSA 1995 ss.245A–245I, as inserted by the Crime and Punishment (Scotland) Act 1997 s.5. See also D. Crichton and R. Mays, "Electronic Tagging of Offenders—Scotland Joins in", 1999 (5) S.L.P.Q. 11 and D. Lobley and D. Smith, *Evaluation of Electronically Monitored Restriction of Liberty Orders* (Scottish Executive Central Research Unit, 2000).

[257] A RLO is classed as a sentence for the purposes of this Act: CPSA 1995 s.245A(7).

[258] CPSA 1995 s.232(2)(c).

impose a fine,[259] vary or revoke the RLO, but the offender shall not be liable to be otherwise dealt with in respect of the act or omission. When a RLO is varied or revoked, the person responsible for monitoring the offender's compliance is given a copy of the amended order and is responsible for giving a copy to the offender.

Community reparation orders

8.66 Where an offender convicted of an offence in summary proceedings was at least 12 years old at the time the offence was committed, and committed the offence by engaging to any extent in antisocial behaviour,[260] the court may instead of imposing any other sentence it might have imposed, make a community reparation order in respect of the offender.[261] The court must have been notified by the Scottish Ministers that the local authority responsible for administering the order has made arrangements that would enable an order to be complied with. A community reparation order requires the local authority to appoint a supervising officer for the purposes for determining which prescribed activities the offender should undertake for at least 10 and not more than 100 hours during a period of 12 months beginning with the day on which the order is made. The prescribed activities are intended to enable reparation to be made to a particular person, or groups of persons by a person or persons who have engaged in antisocial behaviour or to reduce the likelihood of persons engaging in antisocial behaviour. It should be noted however that following the conclusion and an evaluation of the pilot schemes, the Scottish Ministers have declined to extend the use of this penalty. Accordingly, at the time of writing, ss.246K–246Q are not in force.

DEALING WITH CHILD OFFENDERS IN THE CRIMINAL JUSTICE SYSTEM

8.67 Most child offenders will be dealt with by the children's hearing system.[262] However, some will require to be dealt with in the court for reasons already set out elsewhere in this book. Those children who are prosecuted may appear in the High Court or sheriff court only. The district court has no jurisdiction to deal with children accused.[263] No child aged under 16 may be prosecuted other than on the instructions of the Lord Advocate. No child under 13 years of age may be prosecuted without the prior express authority of the Lord Advocate.[264] The Lord Advocate has issued guidelines, *Reporting to Procurators Fiscal of Offences Alleged to Have Been Committed by Children*.[265] Children accused of a crime must be kept apart from all other adults accused of crimes, except those with whom they are co-accused.[266] If in custody, the child must be kept separate from ordinary remand prisoners, and if not in custody, the child must be kept in a separate room from other defendants while awaiting a court appearance. A female child must at all times be under the care of a woman.[267]

Unless the child has been removed from the parent's or guardian's custody or care under a court order, the parent or guardian has an obligation to attend any court hearing. The local social work department will be notified of the intention to bring a child before the court and will in the fullness of time prepare a social enquiry report.[268] The press and media generally are

[259] CPSA 1995 s.232(2).
[260] See CPSA 1995 s.234AA(3) and (12).
[261] See generally CPSA 1995 ss.245K–245Q and Curran et al., "'Forced to Make Amends': An Evaluation of the Community Reparation Order Pilots", Scottish Executive Social Research, Research Findings No.95/2007.
[262] See Ch.4, para.4.45.
[263] CPSA 1995 s.42(1).
[264] A.V. Sheehan and D.J. Dickson, *Criminal Procedure*, 2nd edn (Edinburgh: LexisNexis Butterworths, 2003) para.292.
[265] *http://www.crownoffice.gov.uk/Resource/Doc/13547/0000235.pdf* [Accessed July 2, 2008].
[266] See CPSA 1995 s.142 for children charged with summary offences.
[267] CPSA 1995 s.42(10).
[268] CPSA 1995 s.42(7).

restricted in their reporting of a case where a child is involved.[269] They may not disclose his name, address, school or any particulars likely to lead to the child concerned being identified. They may not publish any picture that includes the child. Where the child is simply a witness, the restriction only applies if the courts so directs. The court has the power to lift the restriction at any time where it thinks it is in the public interest to do so.[270] It is an offence to infringe reporting restrictions.[271]

Where a child appears in a summary criminal case the sheriff is required to sit in a different court or building from that in which he would ordinarily conduct criminal business.[272] The numbers attending the court will be strictly controlled and the public will not be admitted.

If the child is remanded awaiting trial or pending conviction he should be committed to the care of the local authority if the court directs, in secure accommodation or a place of safety chosen by the local authority.[273] In circumstances where the child is unruly or depraved and the court is advised that a remand centre is available, the child will be committed there or to prison.[274] Children initially committed to the care of the local authority may, if their behaviour justifies it, have their committal to the local authority revoked and substituted with a committal to a remand centre or prison.[275]

SEXUAL OFFENDERS

8.68 On September 1, 1997 the Government implemented the Sex Offenders Act 1997 designed to register all known sex offenders.[276] The current provisions are contained in the Sexual Offences Act 2003.[277] The information provided to the police is intended to be used for the prevention of crime and the protection of children and vulnerable adults. Section 81 of the Sexual Offences Act 2003 applies to persons formerly subject to the previous notification requirements contained in the Sex Offenders Act 1997.[278] The Sexual Offences Act 2003 requires persons convicted or found not guilty by reason of insanity of one or more of the sexual offences set out in Sch.3 to the Act[279] to notify the police within three days of conviction (the relevant date) of: their date of birth; national insurance number; their name on the relevant date and on the date of notification, or names, if they used more than one at that time; home address and the address at any other premises in the United Kingdom at which they regularly reside or stay; whether they hold any passports and the details contained in them; and any such other information about them or their personal affairs as Scottish Ministers may prescribe in regulations.[280] Any subsequent changes to these details must be notified to the police within three days beginning with the date of the change.[281] Offenders must also make contact with the police on an annual basis during the

---

[269] CPSA 1995 s.47(1), (2) and (3).

[270] The Secretary of State for Scotland can lift reporting restrictions after the trial on similar grounds: see CPSA 1995 s.47(3)(c).

[271] See S.R. Moody, "Publicity in Criminal Cases Involving Children", 1999 Jur. Rev. 1.

[272] CPSA 1995 s.142(1); *Heywood v B*, 1994 S.C.C.R. 554.

[273] CPSA 1995 s.51(1)(a).

[274] CPSA 1995 s.51(1)(b).

[275] CPSA 1995 s.51(3).

[276] The idea of registration is based on American schemes: see Hebenton and Thomas, "Keeping Track?: Observations on Sex Offender Registers in the US", Paper 83, Home Office (1997).

[277] See generally the Sexual Offences Act 2003 ss.80–103.

[278] See *Boyle v HM Advocate*, 2007 S.C.C.R. 286 where the offender who had been subject to the requirements of the Sex Offenders Act 1997 objected unsuccessfully to proceedings being taken against him for failing to comply with the notification requirements on the grounds that the enhanced penalties were not compatible with his rights under ECHR art.7.

[279] See *Nelson v Barbour* [2007] HCJAC 31 for an example of a case where an appeal against the making of a notification requirement succeeded because the offence was not one that came within the ambit of Sch.3.

[280] Sexual Offences Act 2003 s.83.

[281] Sexual Offences Act 2003 s.84.

currency of the notification period.[282] Notification takes place by offenders attending at any one of the prescribed police stations in their local police area and giving an oral notification to any police officer, or other person authorised for the purpose by the officer in charge of the station.[283] Notification is not a punishment in itself and should not be taken account of by a court when considering an appropriate sentence.[284]

Failure to notify the police or the giving of false information are offences punishable on summary conviction with a fine and/or imprisonment for up to six months and on indictment to a term not exceeding five years.[285] Offenders under 18 years of age when convicted will have their notification periods halved.[286] British citizens who commit their offences outside the United Kingdom may nevertheless be dealt with by the Scottish courts.[287]

8.69 The notification periods are set out below.[288]

Description of offender	Notification period
A person sentenced to life imprisonment or to imprisonment for a term of 30 months or more	Indefinite
A person subject to an order for lifelong restriction under CPSA 1995 s.210F(1)	Indefinite
A person admitted to hospital subject to a restriction order	Indefinite
A person sentenced to imprisonment of less than 30 months but more than 6 months	10 years
A person sentenced to imprisonment of less than 6 months	7 years
A person admitted to hospital but no restriction order	7 years
A person within s.80(1)(d) (a person made the subject of a caution in England and Wales)	2 years beginning with that date
A person in whose case a probation order is made	The probation period
A person of any other description	5 years beginning with the relevant date

Where a sentence is adjourned or deferred, the police are still expected to be notified of the conviction even though the registration period will not be known. In practice they will allot the minimum five-year period pending final disposal of the case. Even offenders who are given an absolute discharge will still be the subject of notification requirements. Notification periods start from the "relevant date", which is the date of conviction or finding of insanity or absolute discharge.[289]

Local authorities play an important role in the supervision of sex offenders who have community-based sentences but more than this they will have aftercare responsibilities for up to 12 months, namely to provide guidance and assistance to sex offenders released from prison. There are particular arrangements for local authorities to be notified by prison social work departments of the release of prisoners who have been convicted of offences against children at least four months prior to the offender's release.[290] Because of the various general duties to children

[282] Sexual Offences Act 2003 s.85.
[283] Sexual Offences Act 2003 s.87.
[284] *Re Attorney General's Reference (No.50 of 1997)* [1998] 2 Cr.App.R.(S.) 155.
[285] Sexual Offences Act 2003 s.91.
[286] Sexual Offences Act 2003 s.82(2).
[287] Sexual Offences Act 2003 s.85(4)(d).
[288] Sexual Offences Act 2003 s.82.
[289] Sexual Offences Act 2003 s.82(6).
[290] See "National Objectives for Social Workers in the Criminal Justice System: Standards—Throughcare", Ch.11. *http://www.scotland.gov.uk/Publications* [Accessed July 2, 2008].

(see Ch.4) local authorities are required to make inquiries, protect from risk, assess the need for compulsory measures of supervision and generally promote the welfare of children. In this respect, local authorities are to be regarded as corporate entities whereby all appropriate parts of that authority must investigate the case of a child known to be at risk of exposure to a sex offender.

8.70 While local authorities have a key role in ensuring relevant offenders register with the police, it is the responsibility of the offender to register. The provision of a certificate by the convicting court should leave the offender in no doubts as to the requirement.[291] In fulfilling its role in protecting children, social work departments will from time to time require to know the whereabouts of a sex offender. It was recognised that various protocols established to manage information sharing between criminal justice agencies were not sufficiently comprehensive. *The Concordat: Sharing Information about Sex Offenders* of November 2005 provides for the sharing of information by criminal justice agencies, including criminal justice social work and a number of other public authorities about sex offenders within a nationally agreed framework with the aim of protecting the public. It is the result of the recommendation of the Expert Panel on Sex Offending and the Information Sharing Steering Group ("ISSG") formed by the Solicitor General in 2003 to:

> "Ensure the efficient and effective flow of information between key agencies involved in the management of sex offenders by developing protocols, guidance and strategies."[292]

The Concordat relates to all information irrespective of the form in which it is held concerning sex offenders from the stage at which an offence is first reported to the authorities to the stage at which the offender is being managed in the community following sentence or liberation from custody. Information includes personal and sensitive personal information as defined in the Data Protection Act 1998. Each agency is responsible for assessing whether the information in a particular case can be shared legally.[293] Section 10 of the Management of Offenders (Scotland) Act 2005 also requires police, local authorities and the Scottish Prison Service to establish joint arrangements including sharing of information for assessing and managing the risk posed by sexual and serious violent offenders.

8.71 In assessing risk to children or others, the police may decide to disclose information about a registered sex offender to a third party such as the victim, the victim's family, the offender's new partner, a head teacher or playgroup organiser. Information is limited to that which is necessary and will be disclosed in person by a police officer. Guidance dictates that they should only do so after taking account of the nature and pattern of the offender's previous offending; his compliance with previous sentences or court orders; any predatory behaviour that indicates a likelihood of re-offending; the probability that a further offence will be committed; the likely harm that behaviour may cause; the extent to which potential victims are vulnerable; the potential consequences of disclosure to the offender and his family; and the potential consequences of disclosure for other aspects of law and order. In *R. v Chief Constable of North Wales Ex p. AB*[294] a married couple released from prison following convictions for serious sexual offences against children attempted to settle at a caravan site in North Wales. Following a report compiled by Northumbria Police, the local police were of the opinion that a substantial risk was present since many children were likely to frequent the caravan park during an imminent school holiday. The police asked the couple to move and when they refused the police disclosed information to the park owner who asked the couple to leave. Although they left, an action for judicial review was raised on their behalf. In dismissing the application the court held

---

[291] Sexual Offences Act 2003 s.92.

[292] See Scottish Executive, *The Concordat: Sharing Information About Sex Offenders* (2005), para.4 at *http://www.scotland.gov.uk/Publications/2005/10/27174205/42065* [Accessed July 2, 2008].

[293] *The Concordat: Sharing Information about Sex Offenders*, paras 15 and 16. See also para.11 for the scope of the agreement to share information.

[294] [1999] Q.B. 396, followed by *R (on the application of A) v Chief Constable of C* [2001] 1 W.L.R. 461.

that in reaching the decision to disclose the details of the offences to the park owner, North Wales Police had not acted irrationally, nor was the policy on which this decision was based unlawful. Furthermore, the identity of former sex offenders should only be disclosed to the public when there was a pressing need to do so and once the police had accumulated as much information on the case in hand. Though the applicants should have been given the opportunity to respond to the contents of the report, their representations would have had no bearing on the decision to disclose its details.

Sections 97–103 of the Sexual Offences Act 2003 make provision for the police to apply to the court for a notification order in respect of a person who has been convicted, cautioned or had a relevant finding made against him for a relevant sexual offence committed abroad. The officer can apply for the order if the offender is in or intending to come into his police area. Applications for interim orders can be made.[295]

PRISONS AND SOCIAL WORK

8.72 While there is considerable involvement for the social worker in the criminal justice system leading to the sentencing of offenders, supervision obviously does not end once a disposal has been made. As has been noted elsewhere in this Chapter, there remains a social work role in the supervision of several sentences that entail punishment in the community.[296] In addition to this there is a significant requirement for social work services for those on whom a custodial disposal has been imposed, or who are in custody as an alternative to non-payment of a fine and for those remanded in custody awaiting trial or sentence.

"Throughcare" is the term used to describe the provision of a range of social work and related services to prisoners and their families from the point of remand in custody or sentence, during the period of imprisonment and following release. These services are primarily concerned to assist prisoners to prepare for release, and to help them to resettle in the community, within the law, whether required by statute as part of a licence or because the prisoner seeks such a service. The services are applicable to life prisoners, long-term and short-term prisoners. The requirement for throughcare and aftercare is central to the criminal justice system achieving its aims of protecting the community and reducing re-offending by rehabilitating the offender. In contemporary Scotland, there has been greater emphasis on the supervision of offenders following release, particularly those who are assessed as likely to be a continuing risk to the public after their release, have offended against children or who are sex offenders.[297] Although the principal responsibility for throughcare and aftercare falls upon the local authority, there is voluntary sector provision designed to fill gaps in mainstream provision.[298] Social work provision in prison is a service level agreement between local authorities and the Scottish Prison Service. Prison social workers are provided by the local authority of the area in which the prison is located. There is no statutory basis for the provision of social work services in prison. However, local authorities have a duty under the Social Work (Scotland) Act 1968 s.12 to promote "social welfare" and it is recognised that prisoners should be able to exercise those civil rights not expressly removed by the fact of their imprisonment.[299] Also prison governors need to ensure reasonable assistance so that prisoners can maintain and develop relationships with family and friends and other persons and agencies outwith the prison during the period of imprisonment

---

[295] Sexual Offences Act 2003 s.100.

[296] See generally, "National Objectives for Social Work Services in the Criminal Justice System: Standards—Throughcare". *http://www.scotland.gov.uk/Publications* [Accessed July 2, 2008].

[297] See "National Objectives: Standards—Throughcare", Ch.11. *http://www.scotland.gov.uk/Publications* [Accessed July 2, 2008].

[298] "National Objectives: Standards—General Issues", Ch.8. *http://www.scotland.gov.uk/Publications* [Accessed July 2, 2008].

[299] "National Objectives: Standards—Throughcare", para.28. *http://www.scotland.gov.uk/Publications* [Accessed July 2, 2008].

and in preparation for their release.[300] A close and effective relationship between the Scottish Prison Service and social workers working with prisoners increases the chances of the successful reintegration of an offender into the community following his release and reduces the risk of re-offending.

8.73 The objectives of social work in prisons can be summarised as follows:

- to offer prisoners access to a range and level of social work services similar to those in the community;
- to contribute through advising on, and in some cases, providing, a range of individual and group work programmes to address offending behaviour; and
- to provide appropriate professional support and assistance to help prisoners resettle and reintegrate into society following release.[301]

The National Objectives state that social work services in prisons must:

- be delivered, by fully qualified social workers, as an integral part of local authorities' social work services in the criminal justice system;
- have a particular focus on offending behaviour and seek also to address those problems arising from imprisonment and problems that are likely to confront prisoners on their release;
- help prisoners to maintain, as appropriate, their family and community ties;
- take account of the nature of the prisoner population in the establishment and also take account of the function of the establishment within the prison system; and
- be delivered in a manner that is efficient, fair and consistent without discrimination against race, religion, colour, gender or sexual orientation.[302]

The key roles fulfilled by social workers in the prison system can be stated as:

- assessment of risk and dangerousness to self and others, personal and social need, and re-offending risk in conjunction with other professionals;
- contributing a distinctive social work perspective to the strategic planning of the establishment including programme planning;
- liaison with, and consultancy for, prison staff and managers, including the provision of specific training programmes where required; and
- work with prisoners' families and other social supports to reduce the risk of re-offending on release and to assist reintegration within the community.[303]

Offenders face a multitude of problems on release, not least the problem of finding accommodation. The role of the social worker is to work with the prisoner to develop and achieve a realistic release plan, especially near the time of release. Home circumstance reports will be prepared by community-based social workers for those being considered for release.

8.74 The social work unit in prison will be notified and supplied with the social enquiry report prepared for the case prior to disposal. The court may forward further information such as psychiatric and other reports. Within two days of arrival, the social work unit in the prison must advise the prisoner as to the prison arrangements, a likely timescale for release, the social work help available and generally begin the process of engagement which will allow an assessment of risk at or near the time of release. There are arrangements in place for the local authority to be informed if a prisoner is being considered for release. There are forms for the process of notification and response as well as a procedure for notification of the intention to release. In

---

[300] J. McManus, *Prisons, Prisoners and the Law* (Edinburgh: W. Green, 1995), p.47.

[301] "National Objectives: Standards—Throughcare", paras 37–37.3. *http://www.scotland.gov.uk/Publications* [Accessed July 2, 2008].

[302] "National Objectives: Standards—Throughcare", paras 38.1–38.5. *http://www.scotland.gov.uk/Publications* [Accessed July 2, 2008].

[303] "National Objectives: Standards—Throughcare", paras 39.1–39.4. *http://www.scotland.gov.uk/Publications* [Accessed July 2, 2008].

this way community-based social workers are aware of the imminent release of an offender and can prepare to provide support services and appropriate supervision if that is required.

Local authorities have a statutory duty to provide aftercare services to offenders on their release from prison.[304] The National Standards envisage more than the simple provision of material aid for the released offender. There must be provision of advice, guidance and assistance for persons in the area of the local authority who within 12 months of their release from prison, or another form of detention, request such advice, guidance or assistance.[305] The objectives of this voluntary care are:

- to provide and facilitate a range of services for prisoners and ex-prisoners and where appropriate, their families, to assist them to deal with any problems they may face, particularly following release;
- to assist offenders to reduce risk of their re-offending through the provision of a range of services to meet identified needs;
- to seek to limit and redress the damaging consequences of imprisonment including the dislocation of family and community ties, the loss of personal choice, and the resultant stigma;
- to help prisoners and their families to develop their ability to tackle their own problems;
- to help prisoners and their families, on request, to prepare for release;
- to assist the families of released prisoners to adjust to the changed circumstances arising from the prisoner's return, where such service is needed and requested; and
- to assist ex-prisoners to reintegrate successfully into the community and thus reduce the incidence of crime.

Release from imprisonment

8.75 Offenders sentenced to imprisonment or detention of less than four years are known as short-term prisoners and at present are released unconditionally after serving one-half of their sentences.[306] There is no statutory scheme of supervision of such released offenders though they may apply for voluntary supervision.[307] The only exception concerns sex offenders who are sentenced to more than six months but less than four years in custody who must now be released on licence.[308]

A person sentenced to more than four years' imprisonment is known as a long-term prisoner and must be released on licence once he has served two-thirds of his sentence,[309] unless released earlier, for example on the recommendation of the Parole Board on completion of one-half of his sentence.[310] All prisoners are liable to be returned to custody to serve the unexpired portion of their sentence, in the event that they are convicted of an imprisonable offence committed in the period beginning on the day of their release and ending on the date of expiry of the sentence.[311] In addition, the Scottish Ministers may release on licence certain short-term prisoners serving a sentence of three months or more, or long-term prisoners whose release on having served half of their sentence has been recommended by the Parole Board on completion of at least four weeks or one-quarter of the sentence, whichever is the longer, subject to certain

---

[304] Social Work (Scotland) Act 1968 s.27(1)(b)(ii), as amended.
[305] Social Work (Scotland) Act 1968 s.27(1)(c).
[306] Prisoners and Criminal Proceedings (Scotland) Act 1993 s.1(1).
[307] Social Work (Scotland) Act 1968 s.27(1)(c), as amended by the Law Reform (Miscellaneous Provisions) (Scotland) Act 1990 s.64(4)(a).
[308] Prisoners and Criminal Proceedings (Scotland) Act 1993 s.1AA, inserted by the Management of Offenders (Scotland) Act 2005 s.15.
[309] Prisoners and Criminal Proceedings (Scotland) Act 1993 s.1(2).
[310] Prisoners and Criminal Proceedings (Scotland) Act 1993 s.1(3).
[311] Prisoners and Criminal Proceedings (Scotland) Act 1993 s.16.

conditions.[312] In deciding whether to release the offender Scottish Ministers must have regard to the need for: public protection; the prevention of re-offending, and to secure the successful reintegration of the prisoner into the community. Such prisoners are subject to the standard licence conditions[313] and a curfew condition requiring the prisoner to remain at or stay away from a specified location for not less than nine hours in any one day.[314] Curfew conditions are monitored remotely by the use of an electronic tagging device.

8.76 The Custodial Sentences and Weapons (Scotland) Act 2007 received Royal Assent on April 19, 2007. When, or if, it comes into force, ss.5–53 will reform the law on the release of prisoners. The Act applies to sentences other than life sentences imposed on a person for an offence committed after the Act comes into force. The Act distinguishes between "custody-only sentences" and "custody and community sentences". Custody-only sentences are those less than 15 days in duration. Custody-only prisoners must be released unconditionally on completion of the term of their sentences. Custody and community sentences are those of 15 days or more. When the court imposes such a sentence, it must specify the custody part of the sentence which is an appropriate period to satisfy the requirements for retribution and deterrence, ignoring any period of confinement that may be necessary for the protection of the public. The custody part is usually one-half of the period of the sentence, but if the court is satisfied that it is appropriate to specify a greater proportion, taking into account the seriousness of the offence, whether it was committed when the accused was serving a custodial sentence and any previous convictions it may specify that the custody part can be up to three-quarters of the sentence. For example, if an offender were to be sentenced to a custody and community sentence of six months, the custody part could be between three and four and a half months in duration. Before the expiry of the custodial part, the Scottish Ministers must determine whether the prisoner, if not confined, would be likely to cause serious harm to members of the public. If not, then the prisoner will be released on community licence on the expiry of the custody part. If it is held that he does pose a risk to the public, the case must be referred to the Parole Board. The Parole Board may then direct the Scottish Ministers to release the prisoner and to specify the conditions to be included. The Parole Board may make a determination that if the prisoner were not to be confined, he would be likely to cause serious harm to members of the public. If the Parole Board does make such a determination, the prisoner must be given the reasons for the finding in writing.

THE REHABILITATION OF OFFENDERS

8.77 The principal purpose of the Rehabilitation of Offenders Act 1974 ("1974 Act") is to allow those who have been convicted of offences to put first convictions behind them, and in that way allow them to attempt to re-establish their lives. Central to the re-establishment of citizenship within the community is the ability to secure employment. In this respect and others, the legislation aims to circumvent any discrimination or prejudice that an offender may face in years subsequent to their convictions.

The legislation allows the person who has been convicted of an offence and who has not been convicted of a subsequent offence, within a particular period of time, to treat the conviction as spent.[315] Where the offender is convicted of a second offence of a particular type the rehabilitation period may be extended and it will be considerably longer than the normal periods before the first conviction can be treated as spent. The 1974 Act provisions also apply to children who have committed an offence but have been dealt with by the children's hearing system in Scotland.[316] This will even be so where the disposal of the hearing was to discharge the referral.

A person who has become a rehabilitated person shall be treated by the law as a person who

---

[312] Prisoners and Criminal Proceedings (Scotland) Act 1993 s.3AA.
[313] Prisoners and Criminal Proceedings (Scotland) Act 1993 s.12AA.
[314] Prisoners and Criminal Proceedings (Scotland) Act 1993 s.12AB.
[315] 1974 Act s.1(1).
[316] 1974 Act s.3, as amended by the Children (Scotland) Act 1995 s.105(4) and Sch.4 para.23(2).

has not committed, been charged with, prosecuted for, convicted of, or sentenced for, the offence or offences that were the subject of that conviction.[317] It is thought that the rehabilitated person is not required to disclose his convictions when filling in forms, for instance, when applying for jobs. Nor need he disclose spent convictions in questions at job interviews.[318]

It is important to bear in mind however that an ever-increasing range of occupations such as doctors, solicitors, social workers, teachers, lecturers and those working with children or older people or other potentially vulnerable persons are exempt from the provisions of the legislation and as such convictions must always be disclosed.[319] Moreover, where a person appears in criminal proceedings after the first conviction either as a witness, or as the accused, he is not at liberty to deny the existence of his convictions, or treat them as spent.[320]

8.78 It is also the case that certain offences are excluded from rehabilitation. The following sentences can never be spent: (a) a sentence of imprisonment for life; (b) a sentence of imprisonment or detention for a period exceeding 30 months; (c) a sentence of detention in excess of 30 months passed on a child by the court; and (d) a sentence of detention that has run without limit of time imposed on young offenders who have committed murder.[321] Where an accused has more than one sentence imposed in respect of a conviction and none of the sentences excludes him for rehabilitation, the applicable period for rehabilitation shall be the longer or the longest of those periods of rehabilitation applicable to the offences.[322] The rehabilitation period set down for particular offences whereby they will be considered spent must be halved if the person is under 18 at the time of conviction.[323]

Where a sentence of imprisonment, youth custody or detention for a term exceeding six months but not exceeding 30 months is imposed the rehabilitation period before the conviction is considered spent is 10 years. In respect of sentences of imprisonment, youth custody or detention in a young offender institution for a term not exceeding six months the rehabilitation period is seven years. A fine or other sentence subject to rehabilitation (for example supervised attendance or a compensation order or admonition) has a rehabilitation period for five years. The rehabilitation period for a probation order is five years from the date of conviction. Where the person is under 18 years of age, the rehabilitation period is two and a half years from the date of conviction for a period beginning with the date of conviction and ending when the probation order ceases or ceased to have effect, whichever is the longer.[324] Where an offender is diverted from prosecution there is no conviction, therefore even where the person is applying for a job that is exempt from the 1974 Act, he need not disclose the diversion from prosecution. Under s.9(2) of the 1974 Act it is an offence to disclose details of previous convictions without authorisation.[325] It is not an offence where the disclosure is to: (a) a rehabilitated person; (b) a person reasonably believed to be a rehabilitated person; or (c) another person at the express request of the rehabilitated person or one whom the person disclosing reasonably believed to be such a person.[326] In addition to criminal sanction, a person who maliciously discloses a spent conviction will not be able to defend an action for defamation on the basis that their statement is true.[327]

8.79 It is an offence for anyone who in the course of his official duties has or at any time has had

[317] 1974 Act s.4(1).

[318] See *Property Guards v Taylor and Kershaw* [1982] I.R.L.R. 175.

[319] See Rehabilitation of Offenders Act 1974 (Exclusions and Exceptions) (Scotland) Order 2003 (SSI 2003/231), as amended by the Rehabilitation of Offenders Act 1974 (Exclusions and Exceptions) (Amendment) (Scotland) Order 2006 (SSI 2006/194) and the Rehabilitation of Offenders Act 1974 (Exclusions and Exceptions) (Scotland) Amendment Order 2007 (SSI 2007/75).

[320] 1974 Act s.4(2).

[321] 1974 Act s.5(1), as amended by the Criminal Justice Act 1982 s.78 and Sch.16.

[322] 1974 Act s.6(2).

[323] See 1974 Act s.5, as amended by the Criminal Justice Act 1991 s.68 and Sch.8 para.5.

[324] 1974 Act s.5(4A)(a) and (b), inserted by the Criminal Justice and Public Order Act 1994 s.168(1) and Sch.9 para.11.

[325] 1974 Act s.9(2).

[326] 1974 Act s.9(3).

[327] *Herbage v Pressdram* [1984] 2 All E.R. 769; see also 1974 Act s.8.

custody of or access to any official record or the information contained therein, to knowingly or having reasonable cause to suspect that any specified information he has obtained in the course of his duties is specified information, disclose it otherwise than in the course of his duties.[328] It is also an offence to obtain specified information from official records by means of fraud, dishonesty or bribe. Both of these offences may be particularly pertinent to staff in the social care services.[329] Specified information is defined as information that a named or otherwise identifiable rehabilitated living person has committed, or has been charged with, prosecuted for, or convicted of, any offence that is the subject of a spent conviction.[330] Disclosure in the following circumstances will not constitute an offence:

- disclosure in accordance with statutory duty;
- disclosure to persons or authorities who by virtue of exceptions provided by order of the Secretary of State, have a lawful use for information about spent convictions;
- disclosure to persons or authorities who though not exempted may continue to have a proper use for such information; and
- disclosure for official purposes between officers of the same organisation.

8.80 As previously stated, persons employed in aspects of social work must disclose previous convictions. Schedule 1 to the 1974 Act provides that any employment by a local authority or by any other body in connection with the provision of social services, being employment that is of a kind to enable the holder to have access to any of the following classes of persons in the course of his normal duties, falls within the scope of the considerations above: over the age of 65; suffering from serious illness or mental disorder of any description; addicted to alcohol or drugs; who are blind, dumb or deaf; who are substantially handicapped; who are under the age of 18; and in any employment which is concerned with the administration of, or is normally carried out wholly or partly within the precincts of, female institutions.

Where a judicial authority is satisfied, in the light of any considerations that appear to be relevant, that justice cannot be done in the case in hand except by admitting or requiring evidence related to the person's spent convictions, that judicial authority may admit or require evidence on those convictions.[331] This allows judges in particular proceedings (perhaps actions under the Children (Scotland) Act 1995 for parental rights and responsibilities) to look at the accused's previous record.

---

[328] 1974 Act s.9(2).

[329] See Moore and Whyte, p.358.

[330] 1974 Act s.9(1).

[331] 1974 Act s.7(3); in *Francey v Cunninghame DC*, 1987 S.C.L.R. 6 and *Morton v Dundee DC*, 1992 S.L.T. (Sh Ct) 2, it was held that a licensing committee was a judicial authority.

Chapter 9

HOUSING, BENEFITS AND DEBT

INTRODUCTION

9.01 Housing or financial problems are commonplace, especially among those in social need, regardless of whether they are home owners or tenants, employed or not. An understanding of the law relating to housing, to state benefits and to debt is essential for the social worker. While all three of these areas, in particular that of state benefit, are frequently the subject of legislative change, nonetheless the current legislative framework does provide general rules and principles that are likely to remain. For the provisions relating to specific adaptations required for those who are chronically sick or disabled, reference should be made to Ch.7.

HOUSING IN SCOTLAND

9.02 In Scotland, housing generally falls into three categories:

(1) owner-occupied;
(2) rented from the public sector;
(3) rented from a private landlord (which now includes housing associations).

At the end of 2004 approximately 65 per cent of housing was owner-occupied, around 15 per cent was rented from public sector bodies, around 10 per cent from housing associations and the rest from private landlords.[1] The number of persons in owner-occupation has greatly increased over the past two decades, mostly at the expense of the numbers holding tenancies from local authorities. The proportion of housing association tenancies has also increased during this period, while the proportion of housing rented in the private sector has remained largely steady. The shift from local authority tenancies to owner-occupation is largely due to the introduction of the tenant's right to buy in the public sector, and the ending of local authorities building new rented stock of their own. Inevitably, the availability of good quality local authority housing has declined. Despite this, the local authority remains a key player in public sector housing, as it is the housing authority that has the prime responsibility to perform various statutory duties, including the housing of homeless persons. Some of the other key bodies involved in housing in Scotland, of which the social worker should be aware, include Communities Scotland, housing associations and voluntary organisations.

---

[1] Scottish Government Housing Statistics. *www.scotland.gov.uk/Topics/Statistics/Browse/Housing-Regeneration/TrendTenure* [Accessed July 2, 2008].

Communities Scotland

9.03 Communities Scotland took over most of the functions of Scottish Homes in 2001, except for some residual functions which remained with Scottish Homes. Communities Scotland is directly accountable to the Scottish Ministers, providing them with information and advice on housing issues. For tenants, perhaps the most important function of Scottish Homes is the funding, supervision and control of registered housing associations.

Housing associations

9.04 In Scotland the majority of housing associations are community-based, and as such have formed an important link between community involvement and private investment. Since the Housing (Scotland) Act 1988 ("1988 Act") housing association tenancies are treated as private sector tenancies. The importance of this is that new tenants of housing associations will not benefit from the right to buy provisions. Therefore it is important to establish when a person became a tenant of a housing association. Housing associations are a growing provider of rented accommodation, owing to large-scale transfers of housing stock from local authority control.

Voluntary organisations

9.05 Within the voluntary sector perhaps the most prominent provider of housing information is Shelter. Shelter produces numerous housing titles, runs events and conferences, and commissions and produces housing reports. It is therefore a very useful source of information and advice in respect of the majority of housing queries that are likely to be encountered by the social work profession.

OWNERSHIP, TENANCIES AND RIGHT TO BUY

Owner-occupation

9.06 In Scotland, owner-occupied housing is generally held subject to certain conditions specified in the title deeds. Normally, these conditions are for the benefit of the area, such as the restriction on height of walls or fences, or prohibiting the keeping of certain animals such as bees or ducks. Perhaps more importantly, an owner's freedom of use is limited by the legal obligation that they will respect the rights of their neighbours.[2]

It is important to acknowledge that owner-occupation of housing does not remove problems such as debt or repairs, both of which will be examined later in this Chapter.

Private rented sector

9.07 In the private rented sector the rights and duties of the landlord and tenant are set out in the lease, the contractual agreement between the parties. However even in the private sector the lease will not always be a full measure of the rights of tenants. If the tenant was in occupation before January 1989, it is possible that they could have additional rights as a protected tenant under the Rent Acts. Also, they may have an assured tenancy which gives them additional protection against a landlord seeking to repossess the house.

---

[2] *Fleming v Hislop* (1886) 13R. 304.

Regulated tenancy

9.08 Until January 2, 1989[3] it was possible in the private sector to create a protected, regulated tenancy provided the property being let was a separate dwelling with a rateable value below the prescribed maximum.[4] Regulated tenancies were introduced by the Rent Act 1965 (later incorporated by the Rent (Scotland) Act 1984) and are either a "protected tenancy" where the tenant occupies under a lease, or a "statutory tenancy", where the lease has been validly terminated but the tenant remains in possession since regulated tenancies can only be brought to an end by a court order.[5] In addition to the limitations on the landlord bringing the tenancy to an end a further benefit of a regulated tenancy is that the rent chargeable by the landlord is restricted, through the registration of a fair rent (as opposed to a market rent) for the property, which cannot be exceeded. Both the landlord and the tenant may have the rent reviewed by making an application to the local authority rent officer. Once the rent officer has notified the parties of his decision, either party can appeal the new rent within 28 days to a rent assessment committee.

A regulated tenancy in existence before 1989 may still continue, but no new tenancies can be created except in special circumstances such as a new lease between the same tenant and landlord to prevent landlords circumventing the legislation.[6] Where the tenant of a regulated tenancy dies, then their spouse or the person with whom they lived as husband and wife will be entitled to succeed to the regulated tenancy.[7] If they have no spouse then any person who was a member of the tenant's family and resided with him for a period of two years immediately prior to their death will be entitled to succeed to the property, but only as an assured tenancy; they cannot get a regulated tenancy.

Assured tenancy

9.09 The assured tenancy is designed to afford tenants protection in giving them more security of tenure. However, unlike regulated tenancies, there is no provision for the setting of fair rents. Rent is left for the market to dictate, which tends to produce higher rents. To create an assured tenancy the lease must be of a house let as a separate dwelling to a person or persons for occupation as their only or principal home, provided that the house does not come within the statutory exceptions[8] which include: lets to students by educational institutions or others specified by the Secretary of State; tenancies under shared ownership agreements (where the tenant purchases a percentage of the property and rents the other percentage) within the meaning of the Housing Associations Act 1985; and local authority and other public sector tenancies.

Where an assured tenancy exists the landlord is required to issue the tenant with the terms of the tenancy in writing and to provide a rent book if the rent is to be paid weekly.[9]

Where the assured tenancy is terminated by the landlord issuing a notice to quit, and the tenant remains in possession of the house, a statutory assured tenancy is created. It is not possible for the landlord to repossess the house except by applying to the court.[10] The court must grant the repossession order where any of the grounds set out in Pt 1 of and Sch.5 to the 1988 Act are satisfied, including where the landlord seeks repossession for his own occupation of the premises, or where the landlord has defaulted on his heritable security payments (mortgage), or perhaps more importantly where the tenant is at least three months in arrears with his rent payments.

---

[3] Housing (Scotland) Act 1988 ("1988 Act") s.42.
[4] Rent (Scotland) Act 1984 s.19(1) and (2).
[5] Rent (Scotland) Act 1984 s.11 and Sch.2 Pt II.
[6] 1988 Act s.42(1)(b).
[7] Rent (Scotland) Act 1984 s.3A and Sch.3A para.2(1) and (2), as substituted by the 1988 Act s.46.
[8] 1988 Act s.12 and Sch.4.
[9] 1988 Act s.30.
[10] 1988 Act s.16.

The court may also order repossession on other grounds that relate to the tenant's habits such as persistent delay in rent payment, rent being due, deterioration of the premises or furniture, and the use of the premises for illegal or immoral purposes.[11]

With a statutory assured tenancy the landlord may serve on the tenant a notice proposing a new rent; if the tenant does not agree with it, it may be referred to the rent assessment committee.[12]

Short assured tenancy

9.10 This is a special type of assured tenancy which must be for at least six months in length. The tenancy is a "short" tenancy because unlike the assured tenancy, provided the landlord serves notice in the prescribed form before the tenancy commences, the landlord can end the tenancy by notice. Should the tenant not remove, the landlord will, providing he has followed the correct procedure, be automatically entitled to a court order. The other key difference is that the tenant of a short assured tenancy can apply to the rent assessment committee for a determination of the rent that "the landlord might reasonably be expected to obtain under the short assured tenancy",[13] that is the market rent. The rent assessment committee will only make such a determination if it is of the opinion that the rent paid by the tenant is significantly higher than what the landlord could reasonably expect in relation to other rents in the locality, and where there are a significant number of properties in the area also leased on assured or short assured tenancies.[14]

Tenancies in the public sector

9.11 Until the 1980s tenants in the public sector did not have any special protection and unlike private sector tenants they could not become protected tenants under the Rent Acts. The logic for the distinction between the sectors perhaps reflected the view that the public sector would inevitably treat tenants better than private landlords. However, regulation and extra rights for tenants, including the right to purchase, now apply to the public sector.

Scottish secure tenancy

9.12 The Scottish secure tenancy was introduced by the Housing (Scotland) Act 2001. All secure tenancies under the previous legislation are converted to Scottish secure tenancies.[15] It is important to be able to identify those tenancies that are Scottish secure tenancies. Essentially there are three tests to be met[16]:

(1) the house must be let as a separate dwelling;
(2) the landlord must be a local authority or registered social landlord; and
(3) the tenant must be an individual occupying the house as his or her only or principal home.

Tenants of housing associations are not public sector tenants and cannot become Scottish secure tenants unless they became a secure tenant in the period up to January 2, 1989.[17] Where a housing association tenant has a secure tenancy, they remain a secure tenant provided they continue to rent from the same landlord, even if they change house. This happened in *Milnbank*

[11] 1988 Act Sch.5 Pt 11.
[12] 1988 Act s.24.
[13] 1988 Act s.34(1).
[14] 1988 Act s.34(4).
[15] Housing (Scotland) Act 2001 s.11; Housing (Scotland) Act 2001 (Scottish Secure Tenancy etc.) Order 2002 (SSI 2002/318).
[16] Housing (Scotland) Act 2001 s.11(1).
[17] Housing (Scotland) Act 2001 s.12.

Housing Association Ltd v Murdoch,[18] where the housing association contended that the tenant who had moved house within their stock had lost their secure tenancy. The court decided that the tenant retained the secure tenancy and was entitled to a determination of a fair rent.

Even where a tenant appears to satisfy the three general tests, Sch.1 to the Housing (Scotland) Act 2001 contains certain exclusions. Where the tenancy falls into one of the categories identified there, it will not be a Scottish secure tenancy.

A Scottish secure tenancy may only be terminated in limited circumstances,[19] for example by written agreement of the tenant and landlord, or by four weeks' notice given by the tenant to the landlord. The landlord can also take court proceedings for recovery of possession of the house.[20] To succeed in this, the landlord will have to establish one of the 15 grounds listed in Sch.2 to the Housing (Scotland) Act 2001. The most important of these is the first, that the tenant has failed to pay the rent or has breached any other obligation under the tenancy. In relation to most of the grounds for recovery of possession, an order for recovery of possession will only be made if the court considers that it is reasonable in the circumstances and that the tenant has other suitable accommodation available.[21]

9.13 The procedure for the recovery of possession must be strictly followed. The process is begun by the landlord serving a notice on the tenant in the form prescribed.[22] The purpose of the notice is to make the tenant aware that the landlord is going to start proceedings no earlier than the date specified in the notice, which date must be four weeks later than the date of the notice, but no later than six months from the date of the notice. The notice will identify on which ground the landlord seeks possession.

If the landlord decides to proceed with the repossession of the property he will raise a summary cause action in the sheriff court. The court may decide to adjourn the matter before considering the order on various conditions, such as the payment of rent in instalments by the tenant, the idea being that such an adjournment may allow the tenant the opportunity to rectify his bad conduct, as the case may be.

Right to buy

9.14 The Tenants' Rights, Etc. (Scotland) Act 1980 introduced a specific right to enable a qualifying secure tenant to purchase the dwelling house let to him by islands and district councils as well as other bodies such as Scottish Homes. The rules are now set out in the Housing (Scotland) Act 1987 ("1987 Act"), as amended by the Housing (Scotland) Act 2001.[23]

The tenant must be a public sector secure tenant and must be so at the date of the application to purchase. To be a secure tenant the dwelling must satisfy the conditions described above.[24] In addition, the tenant's landlord must be one of the specified landlords listed in s.61(2) of the 1987 Act, which list has been greatly expanded from that included in the Tenants' Rights, Etc. (Scotland) Act 1980 by the Housing (Scotland) Act 1986.

Even where the landlord is one of the specified landlords they may still be entitled to refuse to sell the house if one of the conditions in s.61(4) applies, which excepts houses such as those provided to tenants with special needs.

9.15 Having established that the tenant is a secure tenant, in order to exercise the right to purchase the tenant must have so been for a period of five years prior to the date of application. In calculating the five-year period account will be taken of time where the property has been occupied by the applicant as the spouse of a secure tenant or as a child/member of a secure

---

[18] 1995 S.L.T. (Sh Ct) 11.
[19] Housing (Scotland) Act 2001 s.12.
[20] Housing (Scotland) Act 2001 s.14.
[21] Housing (Scotland) Act 2001 s.16.
[22] Scottish Secure Tenancies (Proceedings for Possession) Order 2002 (SSI 2002/320).
[23] For fuller discussion, see A. McAllister, *Scottish Law of Leases*, 3rd edn (Tottel, 2002), Ch.6.
[24] See para.9.12.

tenant's family,[25] thereby enabling recently widowed spouses to exercise rights attributed to their late spouse's period of occupation.

The advantage of the right to purchase is that it is linked to a right to a discount. The amount of the discount is based on the time in occupation of the dwelling, with the maximum amount of discount being achieved after 15 years' occupation. If the tenant sells the property within three years of the purchase they must repay a proportion of the discount granted.[26] When selling the property the public sector landlord is entitled to add to the offer of sale "such conditions as are reasonable".[27] For example, it is quite appropriate for the landlord to include obligations to contribute to the maintenance of common parts such as the roof, as well as including other title conditions relating to the amenity of the area such as restrictions on the number of pets, which restrictions are common in tenancy agreements. However, the landlord is specifically prohibited from adding any condition that has the effect of requiring the tenant to pay the landlord expenses[28] or which gives the landlord a right of pre-emption, that is a requirement that if the tenant decides to sell they must first offer the house for sale back to the landlord or a named third party.[29] The principle behind the legislation is to put the tenant in the position of owner in respect of the same property which he rented, and on the same conditions. In *Glasgow DC v Doyle*[30] the tenant was successful in challenging an offer of sale that did not include all the garden ground that he occupied under his tenancy. The council is in general not entitled to redefine boundaries on applications to purchase.

Procedure for purchase

9.16 The process for the purchase of the house is begun by the tenant serving on the landlord an application to purchase, which must be in the prescribed form[31] and will include details of the tenant's period of ownership and any joint purchaser.

Once the application to purchase has been received the landlord has two months either to serve a notice of refusal or to serve on the tenant an "offer to sell". The landlord will refuse the application if the tenant is not a secure tenant, does not have sufficient length of tenancy or where the house forms part of an excluded category such as houses provided for the special needs of persons over pensionable age[32] or houses required for educational purposes.[33] The offer to sell is required to include the important details including the market value of the house, the discount calculated, and the conditions to be attached to the sale.[34]

By this stage, if the tenant wishes to proceed with the purchase he should obtain legal assistance. The tenant will have to pay his own legal fees for the purchase. The tenant has two months to serve a notice of acceptance on the landlord, thereby completing the contract for the purchase,[35] or alternatively the tenant may wish to dispute the terms of the offer and will have to serve a notice for the variation of conditions under s.65 of the 1987 Act or to refer the matter to the Lands Tribunal under s.71(1)(d) alleging that the offer of sale does not conform to the requirements about offer conditions discussed above.[36] Once the applications under s.65 or s.71 have been resolved the tenant will have two months to accept the offer of sale. Once the offer of sale is accepted the contract for purchase is completed.

---

[25] 1987 Act s.61(10).
[26] 1987 Act ss.72–73.
[27] 1987 Act s.64(1).
[28] 1987 Act s.64(3).
[29] 1987 Act s.64(4).
[30] 1993 S.L.T. 604.
[31] 1987 Act s.63(1).
[32] 1987 Act s.69.
[33] 1987 Act s.70.
[34] 1987 Act s.63(2).
[35] 1987 Act s.66.
[36] Requirements of s.63; see para.9.16.

ALLOCATIONS, HOMELESSNESS AND THE DUTY TO HOUSE

Allocation of housing

9.17 In creating housing waiting lists all relevant organisations are "providing services" and are therefore covered by the sex and race discrimination legislation.[37] A person must not be treated less favourably in the allocation of housing by reason of their sex or race. There are also special duties in relation to the housing of chronically sick, disabled or elderly persons, which are explained in Ch.7.[38] Apart from the obligation not to discriminate on these grounds the matter of selection criteria is largely left to the local housing authority, although vetting and restricting access to housing should only be used as a last resort since local housing authorities often are the last hope of housing for some households. Housing should be allocated on an objective and non-discriminatory assessment of housing need.[39]

By virtue of s.21 of the 1987 Act, landlords in the public sector and in housing associations must publish their rules relating to the allocation of housing, comprising:

- priority of allocation of houses;
- transfer of tenants from houses owned by the landlord to houses owned by other bodies; and
- exchange of houses.

The obligation of the authority to make the rules available effectively bars the authority from relying on a ground not specified in the rules. In *Pirie v Aberdeen DC*[40] the authority refused to admit Mr Pirie to the housing list on the ground that his wife, with whom he lived, had been evicted from her previous house for arrears of rent and unsatisfactory conduct. The summary of the rules published by the authority included a ground of unsatisfactory conduct on the part of the applicant, but did not mention unsatisfactory conduct by any other member of the applicant's family. The court decided that in the circumstances, as the ground was not one specified in the summary of rules, the council could not refuse Mr Pirie admittance to the housing list.

9.18 In the event of the authority altering the rules, the alterations must be published within six months. As to the content of the rules, these vary at the discretion of the authority landlord, although some control on the nature of rules applied by local authorities are contained in ss.19 and 20 of the 1987 Act. Section 19(1) provides that any applicant is entitled to admission to the housing list unless under 16 years of age. The authority is also required to give priority to those with large families and those in occupation of housing that does not meet tolerable standards, overcrowded housing or in housing that provides unsatisfactory living conditions.[41]

Furthermore, local authorities are prohibited from imposing on applicants housing conditions that require the applicant to obtain a divorce or judicial separation from their spouse or that the applicant ceases to reside with or in the same house as a specified person.[42]

The obligations to house placed on local authorities do not rest with the creation of a waiting list. Local authorities have a duty to provide accommodation or assistance in obtaining accommodation to persons who are homeless or threatened with homelessness.

Homelessness

9.19 The Housing (Homeless Persons) Act 1977 (now consolidated in Pt II of the 1987 Act) introduced statutory duties on housing authorities to assist those who are homeless or threatened

[37] See the Sex Discrimination Acts 1975 and 1986 and the Race Relations Act 1976.
[38] See para.7.49.
[39] *Housing and Neighbourhood Problems*, SODD Circular 16/98, para.5.7.
[40] 1993 S.L.T. 1155.
[41] 1987 Act s.20(1).
[42] 1987 Act s.20(2)(b).

with homelessness. The issue of homelessness is a target for the Government, which has stated that one of its housing objectives is to "ensure that appropriate housing is available for the roofless and the unintentionally homeless, for community care groups and for any others who are vulnerable and disadvantaged".[43] In order to promote uniformity in housing across the country, the legislation is explained further in the Code of Guidance on Homelessness produced by the Scottish Executive. The Code should in general be followed otherwise the decision may be set aside by the court.[44] However as it is not legislation, authorities may be justified in some occasions from not strictly implementing the Code.[45] In particular, although the Code recommends that housing authorities consult with the social work department in ascertaining the vulnerability of a particular applicant (failure to do so amounting to a failure to take account of material decisions[46]) the housing authority may nonetheless take a different view from that of the social work department.

The duty owed by the housing authority will depend on a number of factors:

- Is the person homeless or potentially homeless?
- Is the person in priority need?
- Are they homeless intentionally?
- Do they have a local connection?

Homeless or potentially homeless

9.20 Homelessness as defined by s.24 of the 1987 Act means more than not having accommodation within Scotland, England or Wales. Even where accommodation is available, the person may still be homeless where the accommodation is not such that the person may occupy it with any member of their family who normally resides with them,[47] where the accommodation is overcrowded[48] or where occupation of the accommodation will probably lead to violence or threats of violence that are likely to be carried out either by someone residing in the property or by someone with whom the person used to reside.[49]

A person is potentially homeless if it is likely that they will become homeless within 28 days. Moreover according to the Code, bed and breakfast or hostel accommodation should be treated as being temporary accommodation only.

Priority need

9.21 Unless an applicant is in priority need, the housing authority need only provide that person with housing advice and assistance. Therefore the definition of priority need is fundamental to housing law. Section 25 of the 1987 Act provides that a person has a priority need for accommodation if he or she is:

(a) a pregnant woman or a person with whom a pregnant woman resides or might reasonably be expected to reside;

(b) a person with whom dependent children reside or might reasonably be expected to reside;

(c) a person who is vulnerable as a result of old age, mental illness, personality disorder, learning disability, physical disability, chronic ill health, having suffered a miscarriage or undergone an abortion, having been discharged from a hospital, prison or the armed forces, or other special reason;

---

[43] Memo. submitted by the Scottish Office to the Select Committee on Scottish Affairs, Minutes of Evidence, para.12.

[44] *R. v Wandsworth LBC Ex p. Hawthorne* [1995] 2 All E.R. 331.

[45] *Mazzaccherini v Argyll and Bute DC*, 1987 S.C.L.R. 475.

[46] *Kelly v Monklands DC*, 1986 S.L.T. 169.

[47] 1987 Act s.24(2).

[48] 1987 Act s.24(3)(d).

[49] 1987 Act s.24(3)(b) and (bb), as amended by the Law Reform (Miscellaneous Provisions) (Scotland) Act 1990 s.65.

(d) a person who is homeless or threatened with homelessness, as a result of an emergency such as flood, fire or any other disaster;
(e) a person with whom a person falling into categories (c) and (d) resides or might reasonably be expected to reside;
(f) a person aged 16 or 17;
(g) a person who is aged 18 to 20 and who is at risk of sexual or financial exploitation or involvement in serious misuse of alcohol, any drug or any volatile substance, or who was looked after by a local authority at the time of ceasing to be school age;
(h) a person at risk of violence or harassment by reason of religion, sexual orientation, race, colour or ethnic or national origins; or
(i) a person who runs the risk of domestic abuse.

The categories above are further explained in the Code of Guidance, which in general encourages authorities to exercise common sense and to adopt a sympathetic approach.[50]

9.22 It will be seen that the scope of this section is considerably broadened by the inclusion under (c), above, of vulnerability due to "other special reason". The Act does not define the meaning of other special reasons and therefore the categories of priority need are not closed: it will always depend on the actual circumstances of the applicant.

A case that demonstrates the use of other special reasons is that of *Wilson v Nithsdale DC*.[51] In this case the applicant was an 18-year-old girl who had left her college course, been unable to return home and who had been sexually assaulted. Unrelated to the assault, a month later she suffered an ectopic pregnancy. She applied for housing but did not mention the assault or any of the consequences of it, and was refused housing. She was referred to a hostel by Women's Aid (which organisation also provided counselling to her) but she was expelled from the hostel due to suspected theft. Again she applied for housing and after inquiries was refused. Nithsdale Council voluntary service advice strongly contradicted this decision, raising the sexual assault and its effects. However, as the girl in a future interview answered "no" when asked if she thought she would be at great risk if not offered accommodation, she was again refused housing. The decision was referred to the court. In reaching the decision that the girl was vulnerable due to special reasons, Lord Prosser explained his view as to how the test for vulnerability should be carried out:

> "The comparison must in my view be with some assumed average or normal or run-of-the-mill homeless person. But if there is a lesser ability to fend for oneself, against that comparison, in a housing context, so that injury or detriment would result when such an ordinary homeless person would be able to cope without harmful effects, then in my opinion vulnerability for special reasons is established for the purposes of the Act, and nothing more special (far less, anything odd or exceptional) is required."[52]

This decision is most useful as it removes the need to establish anything odd or exceptional, and encourages an individually based approach.

Intentionally homeless

9.23 If a person is deemed to be in priority need then the next issue to be considered is whether the homelessness was intentional. The consequences of being homeless intentionally are dramatic since for those in priority need the duty to house is reduced from securing permanent accommodation to providing temporary accommodation. In terms of s.26 of the 1987 Act:

---

[50] Code of Guidance on Homelessness (Scottish Executive, 2004).
[51] 1992 S.L.T. 1131.
[52] 1992 S.L.T. 1131 at 1134A.

"A person becomes homeless intentionally if he deliberately does or fails to do anything in consequence of which he ceases to occupy accommodation which is available for his occupation and which it would have been reasonable for him to continue to occupy."

In determining whether the applicant has deliberately done or failed to do anything the authority must make further inquiries to determine whether the applicant has been made homeless intentionally.[53] In the case of *Speck v Kyle and Carrick DC*[54] the applicant had to leave his accommodation as a result of being dismissed from his employment as area manager with a leisure company, due to his misconduct. The exact misconduct was not specified by the employers. Although the applicant had received warnings relating to stock and staff level deficiencies, and although he had allowed his wife, children and indeed a girlfriend to stay without authorisation, the court held that the authority had not made sufficient investigations to determine whether the applicant had acted deliberately. The authority had to be satisfied that he had deliberately acted in the knowledge that the loss of his job and the accommodation was probable.

Moreover the accommodation has to be available for the occupation of the applicant and this means for the applicant and his family. To be "available" requires the applicant to have a legal right to occupy the accommodation. Further the authority has to consider whether it would have been reasonable for the applicant to have continued to occupy the accommodation. For example, according to the Code of Guidance, if a person has left home because of domestic violence, then they should be treated as not intentionally homeless. Moreover in placing the person the authority should take into account their need to escape the perpetrator of the violence. Equally if a person has been evicted for carrying out antisocial behaviour they should be treated as intentionally homeless.

Local connection

9.24 The local connection test originates in an attempt to prevent some local authorities, such as in the large cities, from having to house those homeless persons that have recently moved there, attracted by the city potential. A person has a local connection with a local authority district if they normally reside there, if they have a family connection such as their parents or siblings or an adult child of theirs residing there or if they are employed there.[55] If the applicant has a local connection to another authority, the local authority can refer the applicant to that authority, unless the applicant or a person who might reasonably be expected to reside with the applicant runs the risk of domestic abuse in the other local authority's area.[56]

Accommodation secured

9.25 Where an applicant is in priority need and is not intentionally homeless the authority must secure accommodation.[57] The accommodation should be permanent. If the authority secures short-term accommodation, it will still need to secure further accommodation when the accommodation initially secured ceases to be available and the person becomes homeless as a consequence. The accommodation secured must be such that it is not overcrowded within the meaning of s.35 of the 1987 Act and not be such that it may endanger the health of the occupants.[58] However, provided both these tests are satisfied, there is no other general test of reasonableness to be applied.[59]

---

[53] 1987 Act s.28(2).
[54] 1994 S.L.T. 1007.
[55] 1987 Act s.27.
[56] 1987 Act s.33.
[57] 1987 Act s.31.
[58] 1987 Act s.32(5).
[59] *Bradley v Motherwell DC*, 1994 S.L.T. 739.

ANTISOCIAL NEIGHBOURS

9.26 Antisocial behaviour ranging from noise and other inconsiderate behaviour to harassment and violence may be seriously detrimental to the quality of life of neighbours. It is a cross-tenure problem, affecting both home owners and tenants. It is recommended that in selling property under the right to buy legislation, public sector landlords should incorporate conditions to combat antisocial behaviour. Tenure is important as it directly affects the remedies available: a tenant's landlord may be able to take action against another problem tenant, but cannot take action against a problem owner-occupier, although the tenant could raise an action of interdict if the disturbance is sufficient in law to amount to a nuisance.[60]

The Protection from Harassment Act 1997 and the Antisocial Behaviour etc. (Scotland) Act 2004 assist housing authorities in dealing with antisocial behaviour in a way that will minimise evictions. One of the key recognitions of housing strategy is the need for housing departments to liaise with social work authorities as well as the police and environmental health. The involvement of social work relates to the various social work duties in respect of social welfare, protection of children and community care—as well as those responsibilities under the criminal justice system such as the supervision of offenders or the support of victims of crime.

It is in the interests of the housing authority to resolve disputes at an early stage. Where a dispute has arisen then depending on its nature various courses of action are possible. Where the dispute is a low level one due to non-communication or misunderstanding, it may be resolved through community mediation.[61] If mediation does not result in agreement then provided that neither party appears at fault the housing authority may effect a management transfer, whereby one family, with their full co-operation, are moved to comparable housing in an area suitable to their needs.

9.27 Where however there is an irresolvable dispute caused by one party then the housing authority should take action against that party, as opposed to persuading the victimised family to move. Where management approaches have failed, the remedies available to the local authority landlord for antisocial behaviour such as noise and disturbance include antisocial behaviour orders under the Antisocial Behaviour etc. (Scotland) Act 2004. These orders are raised in the sheriff court by the local authority or a registered social landlord, not the victims of the antisocial behaviour, so the complainers need not be present. These orders may be sought against any person over the age of 12 who has engaged in antisocial behaviour towards a "relevant person".[62] A relevant person is, where the applicant is a local authority, any person within the area of the authority and, where the applicant is a registered social landlord, any person within property managed by that landlord.[63] The effect of these orders is to prevent the person from doing anything described in the order, thus giving the sheriff some discretion in dealing with the offender.[64] In addition to the antisocial behaviour orders, the Antisocial Behaviour etc. (Scotland) Act 2004 gives the police various powers regarding the dispersal of groups[65] and the closure of premises.[66]

In the event that the antisocial behaviour complained of amounts to the harassment of another, the appropriate recourse would be either to raise the matter with the police as both intimidation and harassment are common law criminal offences or to raise an action under the Protection from Harassment Act 1997. Under this Act a person who is the victim of a course of harassment may seek damages and either interdict including interim interdict or a non-har-

---

[60] For the requirements of nuisance, see e.g. *Watt v Jamieson*, 1954 S.C. 56.

[61] See Mays and Clark, "'It's Good to Talk': Community Mediation in Scotland", 1998 *The Police Journal* 4, and Dignan and Sorsby, *Resolving Neighbour Disputes Through Mediation in Scotland* (SOCRU, 1999).

[62] Antisocial Behaviour etc. (Scotland) Act 2004 s.4(1).

[63] Antisocial Behaviour etc. (Scotland) Act 2004 s.4(13).

[64] Antisocial Behaviour etc. (Scotland) Act 2004 s.19(3).

[65] Antisocial Behaviour etc. (Scotland) Act 2004 s.19.

[66] Antisocial Behaviour etc. (Scotland) Act 2004 s.26.

assment order.[67] A non-harassment order will require the defender to refrain from specified conduct for a specified period, which can be an indeterminate period. Any person who breaches a non-harassment order is guilty of a criminal offence.[68] Racially aggravated harassment has now also been transformed into a criminal offence.[69] Chapter 12 provides a full discussion on antisocial behaviour orders.

HOUSING REPAIRS

9.28 Housing repairs and improvements are of concern to many of those in social need. The methods that are available to deal with problem housing depend on whether the property is rented or owner-occupied.

The rented sector

9.29 In the rented sector, the issue of repair is important in two respects—establishing whether the landlord is liable to have the repair carried out, and determining whether the tenant is entitled to carry out repairs, or improvements, on their own initiative. Dealing first with the landlord's obligations, apart from those specifically provided in the lease, there is at common law an obligation that the property will be fit for the purpose it is let for[70] and this obligation covers all major defects including condensation dampness.[71] In addition, by statute there is implied into all lettings of a house for human habitation, where the rent is less than £300 per week and the lease not more than three years,[72] a condition that the house is at the commencement of the tenancy and will be kept by the landlord during the tenancy in all respects reasonably fit for human habitation.[73] Where the landlord has failed to maintain the house in a reasonably fit state for human habitation the tenant can resort to court action. The court must be satisfied that due to the defect complained of the house was not in all respects reasonably fit for human habitation. In assessing whether the house is reasonably fit for human habitation issues such as disrepair and sanitary defects as well as non-compliance with building regulations are relevant.[74] The landlord has a duty to keep in repair not only the structure and exterior of the house but also the installations such as water and gas supplies.

A further remedy is for the court to serve a nuisance order on the landlord under the Environmental Protection Act 1990—which can be served on either public or private sector landlords. A nuisance order is competent for any person who is an aggrieved person[75] due to the existence of a statutory nuisance under s.79 of the Environmental Protection Act 1990, which includes "any premises in such a state as to be prejudicial to health or a nuisance".[76] The meaning of this provision was tested in *Alison Anderson v Dundee City Council*.[77] In that case the court adopted the view that to be a nuisance the complaint must relate to something substantial and intolerable to the ordinary person; not merely to something that may cause discomfort.

9.30 Alternatively the tenant may pursue a non-court route such as withholding rent (provided

---

[67] Protection from Harassment Act 1997 s.8(5); Mays, Middlemiss and Watson, "Every Breath You Take ... Every Move You Make—Scots Law, the Protection from Harassment Act 1997 and the Problem of Stalking", 1997 Jur. Rev. 331.

[68] Protection from Harassment Act 1997 s.9.

[69] Crime and Disorder Act 1998 Act ss.33 and 96.

[70] *Glebe Sugar Refining Co. v Paterson* (1900) 2 F. 615.

[71] *McArdle v Glasgow DC*, 1989 S.C.L.R. 19.

[72] Landlord's Repairing Obligations (Specified Rent) (Scotland) (No.2) Order 1988 (SI 1988/2155).

[73] Housing (Scotland) Act 2006 ss.13(1)(a) and 14(1). See e.g. *Haggarty v Glasgow Corporation*, 1964 S.L.T. (Notes) 95, brought under the 1987 Act.

[74] Housing (Scotland) Act 2006 s.13(2).

[75] Environmental Protection Act 1990 s.82.

[76] Environmental Protection Act 1990 s.79(1)(a).

[77] 1998 SCOLAG 149.

that is not specifically excluded under the lease) or complaining to the local authority ombudsman.[78] Where the tenant withholds rent, this rent is liable to be paid once the defect has been fixed.

With regard to improvements to the property made by tenants in the public sector, s.28(1) of the Housing (Scotland) Act 2001 provides that "the tenant is not to carry out work, other than interior decoration, in relation to the house without the consent in writing of the landlord, which must not be unreasonably withheld". Therefore tenants do have the power to carry out decoration to suit their taste without the landlord's consent. Where the work is more substantial amounting to repair or improvement, and the consent of the landlord has been given, if the tenant's work has materially added to the value of the house the tenant is entitled to compensation,[79] and more importantly is protected from being charged additional rent in consequence of the improvements they have made.[80]

The owner-occupier sector

9.31 As housing authority the local authority has a duty to ensure that all houses in its area meet a tolerable standard. To meet a tolerable standard houses must satisfy those conditions specified in s.86 of the 1987 Act, which include the conditions that the house be structurally stable, substantially free from rising and penetrating damp, have an adequate supply of piped water, and have satisfactory facilities for the cooking of food within the house. In relation to sub-standard housing the authority has two powers: to force house improvement such as by issuing a repairs notice, and to assist improvement through the provision of housing grants.

Dealing first with the enforced improvement of properties where houses fail to meet this standard, the authority can deal with the houses either individually or, if a large number of houses in a particular area do not meet the standard, as part of a Housing Action Area.[81] The orders that may be made in respect of an individual property comprise closing and demolition orders, improvement orders and repair notices. Closing and demolition orders are used to secure the demolition of a building comprising housing all of which is below tolerable standard, whereas closing is used to prohibit human habitation of housing which forms part of a building in which not all the housing is below tolerable standard.[82] Improvement orders are used where the house fails to meet a tolerable standard and require the owner to bring the property up to tolerable standard within 180 days,[83] whereas repair notices are used where the house is in serious disrepair and require the owner to carry out the repairs specified.[84] The other power of the local authority is to provide grants for improvements and repairs. In general where the work is to provide standard amenities, such as to provide a hot and cold water supply at a fixed bath or shower, to bring the house up to tolerable standard the authority must provide a grant, otherwise the authority has a discretion as to whether to provide these amenities.[85]

STATE BENEFITS

Introduction

9.32 The vast majority of persons in social need have welfare rights. It is essential to ensure that such persons receive the full range of social security benefits to which they are entitled, especially as, for many, social security benefits will be their only source of income. While welfare rights are of

---

[78] Commissioner for Local Administration; for discussion see Ch.2.
[79] Housing (Scotland) Act 2001 s.30.
[80] Housing (Scotland) Act 2001 s.31.
[81] 1987 Act s.89.
[82] 1987 Act ss.114–130.
[83] 1987 Act s.88.
[84] 1987 Act ss.108–112.
[85] 1987 Act Pt XIII.

great importance to social work clients, nonetheless social workers have no formal role in the social security system, and their involvement will often be limited to personal or authority-based decisions as to good practice. It is suggested that the role for the social worker is to ensure that clients apply for and receive all appropriate benefits. In welfare law the receipt of some benefits may entitle the claimant to other assistance, for example where a person is in receipt of income support or income-based jobseeker's allowance their children are entitled to free school meals. Consequently the social worker requires both knowledge of the range of benefits available to different client groups and an appreciation of the need to encourage timely applications for all of such benefits, making use of other professions such as welfare rights officers if employed by the local authority.

General issues

9.33 Benefits are classified in various ways and some of these distinctions are of crucial importance. Where a benefit is classed as a contributory benefit this means that entitlement to that benefit is dependent on the claimant having paid sufficient and appropriate national insurance contributions, whereas a non-contributory benefit is not so dependent. The other most important classification is that of means tested or non-means tested benefits. In order to qualify for a means tested benefit the financial circumstances (income and capital) of the claimant and their family must be such that they fall below a particular threshold figure, while for a non-means tested benefit the financial circumstances of the claimant are largely irrelevant. For the purpose of means tested benefits a family is defined as including both a married or unmarried couple (or a person who is not a member of such a couple) and a member of their household who is a child for which one of them is responsible or a prescribed person for which one of them is responsible.[86] In other words, the income of an unmarried couple is looked at if it appears that the couple live together as if they were husband and wife—such an inference will be drawn from a number of factors such as the relationship of the couple regarding money, the sexual relationship of the couple and whether they have any children together.[87]

As suggested above, the role of the social worker includes ensuring that their client lodges a claim timeously. For all benefits, including payments from the social fund, statutory time limits apply to applications and failure to claim may result in complete disentitlement or at least the loss of some benefit.

9.34 In making a claim the client has a duty to disclose all material facts relevant to the assessment of the benefit. A material fact is one that makes a difference to how much benefit a person should be paid. If a claimant, whether fraudulently or not, misrepresents or fails to disclose a material fact which results in them being overpaid benefit, the Secretary of State may recover the overpayment.[88] It does not matter that the claimant did not intend to act dishonestly; what is important is whether the claimant either misrepresented or failed to disclose a fact that was material to the decision as to their entitlement. Whether a claimant has not done all that could reasonably be expected of them to disclose a material fact that was within their knowledge will depend on the individual circumstances of the claim.[89]

The benefit system operates at a local level with the initial decision on a claim being made by an adjudication officer working within the Benefits Agency.[90] The majority of these decisions can be appealed to a Social Security Appeals Tribunal ("SSAT") or a Disability Appeal Tribunal ("DAT"). From there leave may be granted to further appeal to the Social Security Commissioners, and further leave may permit appeal to the Court of Session. Finally matters may even go to the House of Lords. In applying the legislation official guidance is provided in

[86] Social Security Contributions and Benefits Act 1992 ("1992 Act") s.137.
[87] *Robson v Secretary of State for Social Services* (1982) F.L.R. 232.
[88] Social Security Administration Act 1992 s.71, as amended by the Social Security (Overpayments) Act 1996.
[89] See commentary on s.71: Mesher and Wood, *CPAG's Income Related Benefits: The Legislation* (annually updated).
[90] Except where the benefit in question is administered by another body. For example, tax credits are administered by Her Majesty's Revenue and Customs.

the *Adjudication Officer's Guide* which is published by the Stationery Office. Other guidance can be obtained from the Child Poverty Action Group publications.

Benefits that provide for those on a low income or no income at all apply across the diverse range of client groups of the social worker, and hence knowledge of them is essential for all. Moreover as well as the benefit payments available the social worker needs to be aware of the social fund payments that can be obtained for low income groups in particular circumstances such as for maternity expenses or in an emergency. In addition to the general low income benefits there is range of benefits available to particular client groups, namely persons who are expecting or bringing up children, the disabled and pensioners.

Low income benefits

INCOME SUPPORT

9.35 Income support is the basic benefit for those on either a low income or none at all who are not entitled to jobseeker's allowance. A person in Great Britain is entitled to income support only if they satisfy all of the following.[91]

- They must be over the age of 16 (special rules apply to 16/17-year-olds, so in effect a claimant must be 18 years old or over).
- They must have no income or income does not exceed the applicable amount (the applicable amount relates to the individual or the family unit, whichever is appropriate).
- They must not be engaged in remunerative work and, if a member of a married or unmarried couple, the other member must not be so engaged.
- Except in such circumstances as may be prescribed, they must not be receiving relevant education.
- They fall within a prescribed category of persons, which includes lone parents, persons temporarily looking after another person and persons incapable of work.[92]

The amount of benefit payable will be the result of deducting from the applicable amount of benefit the claimant's income,[93] which is calculated under regs 17 to 22 of the Income Support (General) Regulations 1987. In assessing the applicant's income the income of the applicant's family is taken into account.[94] Any person with capital exceeding £16,000 loses their entitlement to income support.[95] Moreover for every £250 (or part thereof) over £6,000 which an applicant has, they are deemed to receive a weekly income of £1, which will affect the amount of benefit payable to them.[96]

In claiming for income support it is important that the applicant claims all the premiums to which they may be entitled. The following premiums must be considered.[97]

Pensioner premiums—there are three different premiums payable depending generally on the age of the claimant and their partner, namely for persons over 60 but under 75; 75 or over but under 80; and lastly, higher pensioner premium for those over 80 or alternatively for those who, although they are 60 or over but under 80, either satisfy the disability premium test or were in receipt of disability premium within eight weeks of their 60th birthday.

---

[91] 1992 Act s.124(1), as amended by the Jobseekers Act 1995 Sch.2 para.30.

[92] Income Support (General) Regulations 1987 (SI 1987/1967) Sch.1B para.4ZA, added by the Income Support (General) (Jobseeker's Allowance Consequential Amendments) Regulations 1996 (SI 1996/206).

[93] 1992 Act s.124(4).

[94] 1992 Act s.136.

[95] 1992 Act s.134; Income Support (General) Regulations 1987 reg.45, as amended by the Social Security (Miscellaneous Amendments) (No.5) Regulations 2007 (SI 2007/2618) reg.5(9)(b).

[96] Income Support (General) Regulations 1987 reg.53, as amended by the Social Security (Miscellaneous Amendments) Regulations 2005 (SI 2005/2465).

[97] Income Support (General) Regulations 1987 Sch.2 Pt III.

Disability premium—this is applicable to a person under 60 who is in receipt of specified benefits such as attendance allowance or is registered blind or is provided with an invalid carriage or other vehicle under s.5(2) of the National Health Service Act 1977. Severely disabled persons may be entitled to the severe disability premium.

Disabled child premium—this is appropriate where a child of the household for which the claimant is responsible is either receiving disability living allowance (or only not receiving it by virtue of being in hospital) or is registered blind or treated as blind. If the child has capital exceeding £3,000 no premium will be awarded.

Carer premium—this is payable to a person who is in receipt of invalid care allowance or who is treated as receiving it.

Jobseeker's allowance

9.36 This benefit is for unemployed jobseekers who are actively seeking work. Jobseeker's allowance was introduced from October 7, 1996[98] to replace unemployment benefit and income support for those claimants who for benefit purposes require to be actively seeking employment. To qualify for jobseeker's allowance the claimant is required to be available for employment, to enter a jobseeker's agreement, and has to be actively seeking employment.[99] Income support remains available for those who are not required to be available for work such as lone parents, those incapable of work[100]—although a person incapable of work for up to two weeks may, subject to a limit of two such periods in any 12 months, still receive jobseeker's allowance[101]—and those over 60 years of age.

Jobseeker's allowance is composed of two elements: a contribution-based element, based on national insurance contributions, which varies depending on age and can only be claimed for a period of six months, and an income-based element, which is means tested.[102] The method of calculating the components of the benefit is detailed in s.4 of the Jobseekers Act 1995. A person may lose entitlement to jobseeker's allowance if they are voluntarily unemployed or if they fail without good cause to carry out a reasonable jobseeker's direction.[103] Those who receive income-based jobseeker's allowance can claim the same additional premiums as are available to income support claimants, namely family, pensioner, enhanced pensioner, higher pensioner, disability, severe disability, disabled child and carers premiums.

Tax credits

9.37 Two types of tax credit, working tax credit and child tax credit, are normally available.[104] To receive tax credits, you normally have to be aged 16 or over and be normally resident in the United Kingdom.

Child tax credit is payable to those who are responsible for at least one child under 16 or young person in full-time education up to age 19.

Working tax credit is payable to those working at least 16 hours a week. To receive the credit, it is necessary to be responsible for at least one child, or to be disabled, or to be aged 25 or over and work more than 30 hours a week.

The amount of the tax credit received is dependent on income.

A disabled person's tax credit is also available to support those only partially able to work, owing to disability.

---

[98] Jobseekers Act 1995.

[99] Jobseekers Act 1995 ss.1(2)(a), (b), (c) and 6–10; Jobseeker's Allowance Regulations 1996 (SI 1996/207) regs 5–22 and 31–40.

[100] Jobseekers Act 1995 Act Sch.1 para.2.

[101] Jobseeker's Allowance Regulations 1996 reg.55.

[102] Jobseekers Act 1995 ss.2 and 3.

[103] Jobseekers Act 1995 s.19; Jobseeker's Allowance Regulations 1996 regs 69 and 70 as amended by the Social Security Amendment (New Deal) Regulations 1997 (SI 1997/2863).

[104] Tax Credits Act 2002 s.1.

The social fund

9.38 Where those on a low income or no income need to make a large expenditure they may receive a payment from the social fund. The social fund provides two different types of payments:

(1) regulated social fund payments, comprising those payments to which claimants are legally entitled, namely maternity and funeral expenses[105] as well as cold weather payments[106]; and
(2) discretionary social fund payments, being those payments such as community care grants, budgeting loans and crisis loans,[107] which may be made at the discretion of the adjudication officer.

In respect of social fund maternity expenses payments[108] and funeral expenses the general qualifying criteria are whether the claimant is in receipt of qualifying benefits, which include income support and income-based jobseeker's allowance, and the extent of the claimant's capital.[109] The social fund cold weather payments are automatically made to those in receipt of a qualifying benefit[110] (namely income support or income-based jobseeker's allowance where the benefit includes one of the following premiums: pensioner's, disability, higher pensioner, severe disability or disabled child; or the claimant has a child under five years of age) when the average temperature at the weather station for the area in which they reside is either forecast or actually recorded as being under 0ºC for a period of seven consecutive days.[111]

The discretionary payments are far more complicated. Crisis loans and budgeting loans are repayable, although there is no provision for interest to be charged[112]; however, the community care grants will not be repayable.

Budgeting loans are provided to enable claimants to meet special expenses that they cannot meet out of their weekly budget. To qualify the claimant must be receiving income support or income-based jobseeker's allowance and have limited capital.

Crisis loans are made to assist with an immediate short-term need of the claimant or their family, which they could not meet as they have no savings and no alternative means of meeting the need. It does not cover housing costs, holidays, televisions or television licences.

Community care grants are designed to facilitate community care either by helping a person leave an institution or by enabling them to avoid entering an institution. They can also help a family avoid exceptional pressure or stress. To qualify the claimant must be receiving either income support or income-based jobseeker's allowance and have limited capital.

Owing to the discretionary nature of the latter category there is no right of appeal to a SSAT if a claimant is refused or otherwise dissatisfied, although the claimant is entitled to have a review of the decision by a social fund officer within 28 days of the decision.[113] If the claimant is dissatisfied with a review decision, they have the right to request a further review by a social fund inspector.

Housing benefit

9.39 Distinct from the Benefits Agency, the local councils administer housing benefit for those who need help with their rent. Housing benefit does not cover mortgage interest payments, fuel costs

---

[105] 1992 Act s.138(1)(a).
[106] 1992 Act s.138(2).
[107] 1992 Act s.138(1)(b).
[108] See paras 9.41–9.42 on maternity and child benefits.
[109] Social Fund Maternity and Funeral Expenses (General) Regulations 2005 (SI 2005/3061).
[110] Social Fund Cold Weather Payments (General) Regulations 1988 (SI 1988/1724) reg.1A.
[111] Social Fund Cold Weather Payments (General) Regulations 1988 reg.2 and Sch.1, as amended.
[112] 1992 Act s.139(3).
[113] Social Fund (Application for Review) Regulations 1988 (SI 1988/34); *Murray v Social Fund Inspector*, 1996 S.L.T. 38.

and certain other service costs.[114] It is means tested and will not be available to any claimant who, together with their partner, has more than £16,000 in savings. While the level of benefit will vary depending on the circumstances of the claimant, in general those in receipt of income support and income-based jobseeker's allowance may get all their eligible rent paid.

The local councils also administer council tax benefit. Again, the availability of this benefit is determined by means testing; however, persons in receipt of income support or income-based jobseeker's allowance may get all their council tax liability paid. Note that the assessed benefit entitlement is deducted directly from the council tax bill rather than being paid to the claimant.

In addition to council tax benefit, council tax discounts are available to certain disabled persons and their carers.

Extended payment scheme

9.40 Where a person who has been unemployed for more than six months leaves income support or income-based jobseeker's allowance due to an increase in either their own or their partner's earnings, they are likely to experience a gap in their income because of the move from benefits to earnings. This scheme is designed to bridge that gap in income by continuing housing benefit and council tax benefit for a period of four weeks.

Child and maternity benefits

Maternity

9.41 Statutory maternity pay is paid for a maximum of 18 weeks by an employer to qualifying pregnant employees. Where a woman fails to qualify for statutory maternity pay because she is self-employed or because she recently changed or left her job, she may be entitled to maternity allowance. Maternity allowance is a contributory benefit and will depend on the amount of recent employment.[115] An expectant woman who is not entitled to statutory maternity pay or maternity allowance may nonetheless be entitled to incapacity benefit. This is only available for weeks when the mother is not working during the period from six weeks before the baby is due until 14 days after the baby is born.

In addition to the above payments, those in receipt of income support, income-based jobseeker's allowance or working tax credit may be entitled to a social fund maternity expenses payment.[116] This is a one-off, non-repayable benefit that is made to help with the costs of things for a new baby. A claim can be made for this benefit from 11 weeks before the expected week of confinement, until three months after the baby is born. The claim may be by the pregnant woman herself (regardless of age), her spouse or a member of the family of which the pregnant women forms part. It is also available for persons adopting a baby under 12 months of age and in cases of surrogacy, and the claim should be made within three months of the adoption. The amount of the payment is currently £500.

Child benefit

9.42 Child benefit is a non-contributory and non-means tested benefit claimable by almost any person who is responsible for the upbringing of a child under the age of 16, for a child under 19 in full-time, non-advanced education and for a child under 18 registered on a skillseeker programme. The claimant receives a payment for each qualifying child, although the amount paid for the eldest qualifying child is paid at a higher rate.

As well as child benefit, any person who is bringing up a child whose parents are dead, or in circumstances where one parent has died and either the parents were divorced or the other

---

[114] 1992 Act s.130, as amended.

[115] 1992 Act s.35, as amended.

[116] Social Fund Maternity and Funeral (General) Regulations 2005 (SI 2005/3061) regs 5 and 6.

parent is missing or in prison, may also be entitled to guardian's allowance. As with child benefit a payment is made for each child, although the payment for the eldest qualifying child is at a lower rate than that for subsequent children.

The payment of child benefit is important in respect of the home responsibilities protection scheme ("HRP") which is designed to protect the retirement pension of a person who has not paid enough national insurance contributions because of their caring responsibilities at home. Usually HRP is paid to the person who claims child benefit, so it is important to ensure that clients claim child benefit in the name of the person staying at home to provide the care.

Child support maintenance

9.43 The Child Support Agency ("CSA") which was established by the Child Support Act 1991 is responsible for child support maintenance. Child support maintenance is an amount of money that absent parents pay regularly as a contribution to the financial support of their children and is discussed in detail in Ch.3.[117] Where the other parent of the child is living elsewhere in the United Kingdom, the parent bringing up the child may apply to have child support assessed and collected by the CSA. Parents, or their partners, who claim income support, income-based jobseeker's allowance, family credit or disability working allowance, are required to apply for child support maintenance if asked to do so by the CSA.

Benefits for those with disabilities

9.44 In principle the benefit to which a client with a disability is entitled will depend on the extent of their disability, their age and whether the disability was caused by a particular incident such as an industrial injury. For those who require personal care or assistance with mobility the principal benefit is either disability living allowance or disability working allowance for those aged under 65 years and attendance allowance for those aged 65 years or over.

Disability living allowance

9.45 Should a client require help either with personal care or with mobility due to illness or disability then they may be entitled to disability living allowance (as with attendance allowance this may include those blind or deaf).[118] This can be claimed in respect of a child under the age of 16 but over three months, if the child requires more help or looking after than other children of the same age due to disability or illness, or for a child under 16 but over five years who has difficulty in walking or needs extra help in getting around. However this benefit is not payable to those over 65 unless their disability or illness began before their 65th birthday—those over 65 are entitled to attendance allowance discussed below. Provided the person meets the 65-year threshold and has been in need of assistance with personal care or mobility or both for at least three months and is expected to remain in need of such care for at least the next six months, then the amount of benefit payable will depend on the person's care and mobility requirements. Where the claimant is terminally ill (that is, not expected to live six months or more) special rules operate to ensure that they receive the benefit quickly and easily. Disability living allowance is not affected by savings nor is it usually affected by income. However, claimants are not entitled to this allowance if they are in hospital or residential care.

---

[117] See para.3.41.

[118] *Mallinson v Secretary of State for Social Security* [1994] 1 W.L.R. 630, HL; *Cockburn v Chief Adjudication Officer; Secretary of State for Social Security v Halliday; Secretary of State for Social Security v Fairey* [1997] 1 W.L.R. 799.

Attendance allowance

9.46 This non-contributory benefit provides support to those aged 65 or over who need help with personal care because of their illness or disability.[119] The House of Lords has decided that being blind or deaf could amount to a need for attention in connection with bodily functions.[120] Normally the help must have been needed for at least six months, although as with disability living allowance there are special rules to ensure that those who are terminally ill (that is, those not expected to live six months or more) can receive the benefit quickly and easily. This benefit can be claimed even if no one is actually providing the care required, although it cannot be claimed by a person in hospital or residential care.

Benefits for those unable to work

Statutory sick pay

9.47 Statutory sick pay is paid to employed people who are sick for four or more days in a row provided they earn at least £87 gross on average per week. It is currently paid at a rate of £72.55 per week, and payment is made in the same way as wages for a maximum of 28 weeks.

Where a person is employed but incapable of work and cannot get statutory sick pay from their employer, or is self-employed, unemployed or non-employed, they may be entitled to incapacity benefit (see below).

Incapacity benefit

9.48 Incapacity benefit is contribution-based, and as such entitlement depends on whether the claimant has paid sufficient national insurance. Whereas the benefit is paid at a fixed rate for those over pension age, the benefit paid to those under pension age increases after 28 weeks and again after 52 weeks. After 52 weeks the person receives long-term incapacity benefit. If the claimant is also getting the highest level of disability living allowance they will go onto the long-term incapacity benefit after 28 weeks. In the event that incapacity benefit is not available as the claimant has not paid enough national insurance they may be entitled to severe disablement allowance.

Benefits for carers

Carer's allowance

9.49 This may be claimed by those between the ages of 16 and 65 who are spending at least 35 hours a week caring for a severely disabled person who is in receipt of the middle or highest rate of disability living allowance care component, attendance allowance, and in some cases those getting constant attendance allowance under the industrial injuries or war pensions scheme, provided the carer does not earn more than £95 per week after deduction of allowable expenses and is not in full-time education. Note that the benefit must be claimed prior to the carer reaching 65 years of age, but can continue to be received after the carer has reached 65. Where the carer is in receipt of other benefits, these may be increased or decreased by the invalid care allowance.

Benefits for pensioners and widows

9.50 Those over retirement age may be entitled not only to low income or disability benefits but also to a state pension. Currently the pension age for women is 60, whereas for men it is 65.

---

[119] 1992 Act s.64.

[120] *Mallinson v Secretary of State for Social Security* [1994] 1 W.L.R. 630, HL; *Cockburn v Secretary of State for Social Security v Halliday; Secretary of State for Social Security v Fairey* [1997] 1 W.L.R. 799.

However, it is to be made equal by virtue of the Pensions Act 1995, which will come into effect through a staged scheme running for a 10-year period from 2010. Effectively, therefore, the state retirement age for women born on or after April 6, 1955 is now also 65 years of age.

Retirement pension

9.51 The basic retirement pension is paid to those who have reached pension age and have made sufficient national insurance contributions. The pension received by a woman may be based on her own or indeed solely on her late husband's contributions, although in the latter case the amount paid may be less.

Where the claimant is aged over 80 years, if they receive state retirement pension of less than the amount payable on a spouse contribution or indeed no state pension at all, they will receive an over-80 pension, provided they satisfy certain residency conditions. The over-80 pension is paid at a flat rate. A pensioner, whether in receipt of the basic retirement pension or not, may have their pension increased by virtue of either an additional pension or graduated retirement benefit. The additional pension refers to the SERPS scheme, being the earnings-related part of retirement pension. It is based on the level of class 1 national insurance contributions paid by an employee since April 1978. The graduated retirement pension is independent of basic retirement or additional pension and relates entirely to the amount of graduated contributions paid between April 1961 and April 1975.

War pensions

9.52 Where the claimant is unable to work due to injury incurred in military service[121] the claimant may be entitled to a war disablement pension. Additionally a special scheme exists to provide for a war widow's pension.[122] Information and claims should be sought from the War Pensions Agency Distribution Unit.[123]

Widows and widowers

9.53 The benefits available to a widow or widower comprise the tax-free, lump sum benefit, bereavement payment, and either the taxable weekly benefits of widowed parent's allowance or widow's pension. Bereavement payment is a lump sum payment of £2,000 for widows or widowers whose spouses were not entitled to a category A retirement pension when they died, or where the widow or widower is under state pension age at the date of widowhood and the late spouse had paid sufficient national insurance in any one year prior to his or her death.

As for the weekly benefits, widowed parent's allowance is paid to widows with at least one child for whom they are entitled to child benefit.[124] Once entitlement to widowed parent's allowance ends or alternatively where a widow was aged 45 or over when their husband died, she may be entitled to widow's pension. Widow's pension is not available to widowers.

DEBT

Advising on debt

9.54 One of the major problems facing households within Scotland is that of debt. Debt problems are the most common matter referred to the Citizen Advice Bureaux. The reasons for debt problems are various; perhaps the multitude of apparently willing lenders, from shop purchase card

---

[121] Naval, Military and Air Forces, etc. (Disablement & Death) Service Pensions Order 2006 (SI 2006/606).
[122] Grove, "Cruel Trap for War Widows", *The Times*, April 12, 1997, p.33.
[123] *http://www.veterans-uk.info* [Accessed July 1, 2008].
[124] See para.9.42.

companies and credit card companies to bank lenders, to name but a few, and the advertising pressures to own certain commodities, are the major factors in feeding this growing difficulty. In addition, where a person has had previous debt problems, or simply lives in an area where debt repayment is poor, they may well discover that despite the apparent availability of credit, they cannot obtain credit from the traditional sources. For those with no credit rating or those blacklisted, credit may only be available from family, friends or illegal money lenders, often referred to as "loan sharks". Such borrowing should be avoided.

Most debts arise out of contract, for example through purchase of goods from a shop or from a mortgage used to purchase a house. In advising a person with a debt problem, it is necessary to review the following:

- What type of debt contract has the debtor entered?
- Was the person legally able to make the purported contract of debt?
- How much is the debt for?
- What are the date and terms of repayment?
- What can be done when a debtor begins to have difficulties in meeting payments?
- What are the penalties for non-payment?

Nature of the debt

9.55 Basically lending can be divided into two forms. First there is lender credit, where the debtor receives a loan to make a purchase, for example using an overdraft facility on a current account or obtaining a personal loan from a bank. Alternatively, the credit may take the form of vendor credit, that is where the seller provides a credit facility, for example hire purchase. Hire purchase is a mechanism whereby the instalments paid by the debtor are rental payments for an agreed period of hire. At the end of the period of hire the debtor will have an option to purchase the goods from the creditor. Similar to hire purchase is conditional sale: the debtor is to make certain instalments payments, and once the last instalment has been paid, the debtor will become the owner of the goods. The important difference between the two types of credit, lender credit and vendor credit, is that in vendor credit, the debtor does not own the goods on receipt of them: the seller owns the property until all payments due are made; whereas in lender credit, the debtor owns the goods once purchased. Whether the debtor is the owner or the hirer of goods is very important, especially when looking at the recovery of debt.

Capacity to enter a contract of debt

9.56 While the majority of issues are determined from the contract itself, the question as to the ability of the parties to enter into the transaction requires consideration in respect of the following special cases.

Children

9.57 The contractual capacity for children to incur a debt is governed by the Age of Legal Capacity (Scotland) Act 1991.[125] The general position is that persons under the age of 16 cannot enter into any transaction[126] except in the limited circumstances provided for in s.2 of the this Act, which include those contracts that are usual for persons of that age. As incurring a debt would not appear to be usual for a person under 16, in general, any such contracts are likely to be void, making it impossible to sue the child for the unpaid debt. Between the ages of 16 and 18 the young person has full contractual capacity and can be sued for a debt arising out of a transaction,[127] unless the transaction was a prejudicial transaction. A prejudicial transaction may be

---

[125] As amended by the Children (Scotland) Act 1995; see para.3.35.

[126] Age of Legal Capacity (Scotland) Act 1991 s.1(1)(a).

[127] Age of Legal Capacity (Scotland) Act 1991 s.1(1)(b).

set aside by the court before the young person's 21st birthday, and is defined as being a transaction that a reasonable and prudent person would not have made if they had been in the circumstances of the young person. However, a transaction will not be deemed a prejudicial transaction where the young person was acting in the course of their trade, business or profession, where the young person has misrepresented their age, or where the young person has, after attaining 18 years of age, ratified the transaction.[128] Section 4 of the Age of Legal Capacity (Scotland) Act 1991 provides a mechanism for any person seeking to contract with a person over 16 but under 18 years of age to apply to the court to have a transaction ratified.

Mentally incapax

9.58 Once a person has become insane they have no contractual capacity,[129] and any alleged contracts by them are null and void, hence an action of debt will not be enforced. Whether a person is insane and lacks the capacity to understand the contract is a question of fact, the court needing to establish that the party is not able to consent rather than merely being more easy to be persuaded, for example due to intoxication.[130] A curator *bonis* is often appointed to an insane person and the curator has the capacity to contract on behalf of the insane person. However, disputes can still arise especially in relation to purported transactions prior to appointment. In the case *John Loudon & Co. v Elder's Curator Bonis*[131] a wholesale merchant, Elder, ordered goods from Loudon & Co. However, before any of the goods were delivered Elder was certified insane, and therefore Loudon & Co. were advised that the contracts had to be cancelled. Loudon & Co. sued Elder's curator *bonis* for damages but were unsuccessful as Elder was proved to have been insane at the time when the orders were made, and in consequence there could be no liability for breach of contract.

However there is an important exception to this: in terms of s.3 of the Sale of Goods Act 1979, where necessities are sold to a person of unsound mind they must pay a reasonable price for them. Necessities means goods suitable to the condition in life of the person and their actual requirements at the time of sale and delivery. The English case of *Nash v Inman*[132] is a good example of the limitations of the definition of necessities. In this case a Savile Row tailor brought an action for the price of clothing including 11 fancy waistcoats which he had sold to an undergraduate at Cambridge University. The court decided against the tailor, requiring him to prove that the goods were suitable to the student's condition in life, and that the student was not sufficiently supplied with goods of that class at that time.

In the case where an adult is mentally incapable, the Adults with Incapacity (Scotland) Act 2000 provides a mechanism for the appointment of a person to act on behalf of the adult, on either a one-off or a continuing basis.

Amount of debt

9.59 In general, creditors are free to lend whatever amount of money they wish,[133] although normally for larger debts, such as mortgage debts, the creditor will require these to be secured over the debtor's heritable property or other assets. While a contract for a loan need not be in writing to be effective special provisions apply to consumer transactions for the provision of credit or hire for sums less than £15,000. Such agreements are regulated by the Consumer Credit Act 1974 unless they come within s.74 of the Act, which excludes the provision of credit in certain transactions including transactions of under £50 and current account overdrafts. All credit cards, shops' own credit cards and hire purchase agreements are covered by these provisions.

---

[128] Age of Legal Capacity (Scotland) Act 1991 s.3(3).
[129] Stair, *Institutes*, I, x, 3. See paras 6.40–6.42.
[130] *Taylor v Provan* (1864) 2M. 1226.
[131] 1923 S.L.T. 266, OH.
[132] [1908] 2 K.B. 1, CA.
[133] See W. Cowan and H. Ervine, *Consumer Law in Scotland* (Edinburgh: W. Green, 1995), Ch.9, "Buying on Credit".

The significance of the Consumer Credit Act 1974 is that all consumer credit transactions have to follow specified procedures using statutory forms and crucially the debtor must be allowed a cooling-off period where he is entitled to decide not to enter into the agreement. In addition any advertising of these credit facilities must include the APR, annual percentage rate of charge for the credit, as well as most other charges, and should alert the borrower to the risks of non-payment.

However, unless the transaction comes under the Consumer Credit Act 1974 or either the Bankruptcy (Scotland) Act 1985 s.61 (extortionate credit transaction), or the Insolvency Act 1986 s.244, the parties may contract on whatever payment terms they wish. While lenders such as banks have their own self-regulatory codes,[134] with the right to take a complaint to an ombudsman, many other lenders do not.

Date and terms of repayment

9.60 The agreement will specify the date or dates when payment is to be made, the rate of interest to be paid and normally the additional interest applicable in the event of a delay in payment. Indeed even if there is no provision for additional interest on delay in payment, should the creditor be forced to bring the debtor to court to enforce the overdue payment, the creditor will probably seek judicial interest.[135] Not only is it common for the agreement to require additional interest for delays in payment, it is also possible for the agreement to require an early redemption payment in the event that the debtor seeks to pay off the debt early.

Another important issue for a debtor is whether the debt is to be secured on some of their property.[136] Pawnbroking is one such method whereby an item belonging to the debtor is held by the broker until the debtor has repaid the debt and interest. Failure of the debtor to redeem the property entitles the pawnbroker to sell the item. Any profit over the debt and interest should be returned to the debtor.

Another method of attaching property to debts is the granting by the debtor of a standard security over their heritable property, usually the debtor's home, in favour of the creditor. It is now very common for banks and building societies to require the standard security to be for "all sums due" by the debtor, thereby securing not only the lending for the purchase of the house but in addition any other lending made by them to the debtor. Such a clause therefore has serious implications for the self-employed if their business accounts are with the same lender as their mortgage. The standard security ensures that in the event of default by the debtor in making payment, the creditor may serve a notice of default on the debtor, and unless this achieves compliance, the creditor will then move to serving a calling-up notice. Thereafter the creditor would be able to use a number of remedies including the taking of possession of the debtor's home or obtaining the power to sell the property to recover the outstanding debt. Court action is not normally required before the creditor can exercise these remedies, although the debtor (or, in certain circumstances, the debtor's spouse or a person living with the debtor as if a spouse) can apply to the court to have the operation of the standard security suspended for a period.[137] If the property is sold, any surplus on sale is to be repaid to the debtor.

Lastly, security for debt can be obtained over property of the debtor such as life assurance policies through the process of assignation. Effectively the debtor transfers the right to the policy to the lender, in security for a specified debt. On repayment of the debt the creditor will transfer, or "retrocess", the right to the policy back to the debtor.

---

[134] Produced by the British Banking Association.

[135] W.A. Wilson, *The Scottish Law of Debt*, 2nd edn (Edinburgh: W. Green, 1991), para.11.7.

[136] Grier, *Debt* (W. Green, 1998), Ch.7.

[137] Mortgage Rights (Scotland) Act 2001 s.1.

Difficulties in meeting payments

9.61 As soon as a debtor experiences problems in paying all the instalments due by them to their creditors on time, they should seek debt counselling from a registered source.[138] Solicitors and Citizen Advice Bureaux provide debt counselling services and have group licences from the Director General of Fair Trading to perform such work. Effectively, the debt counsellor will attempt to renegotiate with the creditors the debtor's various borrowing agreements in order to reduce the amount of instalment payments, usually by spreading the borrowing over a longer term. The process of replacing one debt arrangement with a new debt arrangement is referred to as novation.[139]

A statutory scheme, the Debt Arrangement Scheme has been introduced by the Debt Arrangement and Attachment (Scotland) Act 2002 to assist those having difficulty in paying their debts. The scheme is administered by the Accountant in Bankruptcy,[140] who is appointed as Debt Arrangement Scheme ("DAS") Administrator. The DAS Administrator appoints money advisers to advise debtors. Following consultation with a money adviser, a debtor can propose a debt payment programme to the DAS Administrator. If the proposal is accepted, and provided that the debtor then complies with the debt payment programme, creditors will not be able to take action to enforce the debt.

Penalties for non-payment

9.62 Where a debtor has failed to make payment, the contract may, as discussed above, provide for additional interest to be paid. Even then, however, if the debt is not paid within a reasonable time the creditor may be compelled to consider what other options are available to them to obtain repayment. Depending on the circumstances the creditor may be able to force payment through the non-court remedies of retention or lien, or may opt to raise court action against the debtor. Alternatively, if the creditor has secured the loan on the debtor's property, such as by taking a standard security in respect of heritable property, the creditor would be entitled to recover their debt through the property secured by seeking repossession and sale of the heritage.

Non-court remedies

9.63 If the debtor has failed to pay for goods under a contract of sale, the seller is entitled to retain the goods pending payment. This is known as a right of lien.[141] In some special areas the law recognises a general right of lien, which arises where the creditor has custody under a contract of goods belonging to the debtor. A general right of lien means a right to withhold a possession under a contract in security for debts that arise from any previous contracts of the same general character between the parties, within the same scope of business. It will normally only arise by either the custom of a trade or profession, such as solicitors, stockbrokers and bankers, or if it is expressly contracted for. The right is a right to withhold only and does not entitle the holder to use or sell the goods, although where retention is not compelling the party to pay the holder could apply to the court for the power to sell.

Court remedies

9.64 In the event of continued non-payment, the creditor may elect to raise court action against the debtor, normally in the sheriff court but occasionally in the Court of Session. The creditor will raise an action for payment, seeking payment of the outstanding debt, interest and the expenses

---

[138] Consumer Credit Act 1974 s.147.

[139] Wilson, *The Scottish Law of Debt* (1991), para.14.1.

[140] Debt Arrangement and Attachment (Scotland) Act 2002 s.8 and Debt Arrangement and Attachment (Scotland) Act 2002 (Transfer of Functions to the Accountant in Bankruptcy) Order 2004 (SSI 2004/448).

[141] Sale of Goods Act 1979 s.41.

of the court action. The appropriate court and procedure will depend on the amount of the principal debt outstanding (that is excluding interest and expenses):

- below £750 — small claims action — sheriff court;
- £750–£1,500 — summary cause — sheriff court;
- over £1,500 — ordinary cause — sheriff court or Court of Session.

These figures are correct at the time of writing. However, the Scottish Government has announced changes with effect from January 1, 2008. The new limits will be £3,000 for small claims, £3,000–£5,000 for summary cause and over £5,000 for ordinary cause.

If a debtor is to be brought to court, they will receive a summons. The majority of debt actions are not defended, and decree in favour of the creditor is normally passed. However, it is important for debtors to seek advice at this stage, since there are options available to them even if they admit the debt. Exactly how the case proceeds depends on the procedure being used. Essentially there are similarities in the three types of court procedure, the major differences relating to the formality of the proceedings. In a court action the successful party will likely be awarded their legal expenses against the unsuccessful party, so if the creditor were to be successful, the debtor would be liable for the creditor's court expenses in addition to the debt.

Small claims

9.65 The small claims action for payment is commenced by a summons, by the creditor completing a form in the style of Form 1 of the Appendix to the Small Claims Rules.[142] The completed summons is prepared together with a service copy summons, and is thereafter signed by the sheriff clerk and served on the debtor. Service is usually by first class recorded delivery post. The debtor/defender will be given 21 days' notice (or 42 days where they are resident outside Europe) to return the response form to the sheriff clerk. In response the debtor may do one of the following:

- Admit the claim and make payment. The claim will then end.
- Admit the claim and apply for a time to pay direction. Time to pay directions were introduced by the Debtors (Scotland) Act 1987 to enable the payment of the debt either by specified instalments or as a lump sum at the end of a specified period. Provided the proposals are acceptable to the creditor, decree will be granted in favour of the creditor with payment being ordered in accordance with the agreed instalments/lump sum payments. However, if the proposals are not acceptable to the creditor then a hearing will take place.
- Admit the claim and intimate an intention to appear to make an oral application for a time to pay direction. Should the debtor fail to attend the preliminary hearing, decree will pass against them.
- Not admit the claim and indicate that they will defend the action. The debtor is then obliged to attend the preliminary hearing, and make representations to the court.
- Make no response. Provided the claim has been properly set out decree will be granted against the debtor.

Where the matter has progressed to a hearing, it will be heard seven days after the return date.[143] In the event of neither the debtor nor the creditor attending court or being represented, the sheriff will normally dismiss the small claim, unless there is sufficient reason for him to do otherwise.[144] For instance, where the creditor has set out a sufficient claim yet the debtor has not lodged defences, the sheriff may grant decree in favour of the creditor.[145] If the debtor attends or

[142] Act of Sederunt (Small Claim Rules) 2002 (SSI 2002/133) ("2002 Small Claim Rules").
[143] 2002 Small Claim Rules r.9.1(3).
[144] 2002 Small Claim Rules r.9.1(8).
[145] 2002 Small Claim Rules r.9.1(7).

is represented but the creditor does not, then provided no defence has been lodged the debtor will normally be absolved.

9.66 The preliminary hearing can be conducted in any manner that the sheriff feels is best suited to identifying the issues at hand. In some courts the sheriff and occasionally the solicitors are encouraged to wear everyday dress to make the proceedings less daunting for the lay persons representing themselves. Provided the matters are sufficiently clear, the sheriff may be able to decide the case without requiring a further hearing.[146]

If a further hearing is required this is referred to as either a full hearing or proof. Both parties are required to attend the hearing or to be represented. The debtor will have the opportunity to make their defences and to make either a written or an oral application for a time to pay direction. Again the sheriff has a discretion as to procedure and the strict rules of evidence are not applied. Either party may give evidence on their own behalf and may lead other evidence. However, should the debtor wish to lead a witness it is their responsibility to ensure that the witness attends the hearing, and to pay the witness's expenses. Once the parties have been heard the sheriff shall if practicable give both his decision and his reasons for it. If he cannot issue a decision at that time, he must do so within 28 days.[147] After 14 days from the making of the decision, an extract decree shall be issued. The extract decree is the final decree, and it is this that the creditor requires in order to commence enforcement action, referred to as diligence, against the debtor.[148]

The decision by the sheriff may include an award of expenses in favour of the successful party, the unsuccessful party having therefore to bear not only their own expenses but also those of the successful party. However, as small claims are designed to be accessible to the lay person, with legal aid not being available, expenses will not be awarded in an action for a claim of less than £200. For claims over £200, the amount of expenses is limited to £75.[149]

Summary cause

9.67 As with small claims actions the summary cause action is begun by the creditor preparing a summons, which normally involves completing the relevant form[150] and attaching to it a statement of claim—the details of the creditor's case. Unlike small claims, in response to a summary cause summons unless the defender has made an offer to the creditor that is acceptable the debtor/defender will need to appear in court either to seek a time to pay direction or to defend the cause.[151] If the debtor has made an acceptable offer the court can simply grant decree accordingly. Otherwise, at the first hearing, the sheriff must grant decree against the defender, dismiss the cause, or fix a proof.

At the proof both parties are entitled to present their own evidence and to lead witnesses. However, as with small claims actions, the party calling a witness is personally liable to ensure attendance of the witness and to pay their travelling expenses. The proof in summary cause actions is more formal, the parties must lead evidence of any facts crucial to their case, and the normal rules of evidence apply.[152]

The sheriff normally will give his or her decision together with reasons at the end of the hearing, although they may reserve judgment, in which instance their decision is to be given within 28 days. Once the decision has been given the issue of expenses will be assessed,[153] and it

---

[146] 2002 Small Claim Rules r.9.3.
[147] 2002 Small Claim Rules r.9.8.
[148] See para.9.69.
[149] Small Claims (Scotland) Order 1988 (SI 1988/1999).
[150] Form 2 is the relevant form for the payment of money: Act of Sederunt (Summary Cause Rules) 2002 (SSI 2002/132) ("2002 Summary Cause Rules") r.4.1(2).
[151] 2002 Summary Cause Rules rr.7.2, 8.1.
[152] See paras 2.27–2.37.
[153] 2002 Summary Cause Rules r.23.3.

is only after this assessment has been carried out by the sheriff clerk that the decree becomes final,[154] enabling the creditor to take further enforcement action, diligence.[155]

Ordinary cause

9.68 The rules for ordinary cause actions vary depending on whether the matter is raised in the Court of Session or in the sheriff court, although there exists a degree of similarity. The marked distinction between ordinary cause and either small claims or summary cause is that ordinary cause actions depend heavily on the written pleadings of the parties. Rather than the proceedings being initiated by a summons on a prescribed pre-printed form, the cause is commenced by an initial writ (sometimes referred to as a petition or summons), prepared by the creditor's legal agents. The formalities of ordinary cause action are such that legal representation should be sought by the debtor on receipt of the initial writ, since if the debtor wishes to defend the action they will need to lodge in court a notice of intention to defend, and enter an appearance. As with the other procedures, failure of the debtor to take action will lead to a decree in absence being pronounced against him. After a period of the parties adjusting their written pleadings, the cause will move to an options hearing, which decides whether a debate, where the parties are arguing on the legal issues of the case only, is to be held, or to a proof, where evidence may be led. As with the other procedures, it is necessary for the creditor to take further action to enforce the court decree in their favour.[156]

RECOVERING DEBTS

Diligence

9.69 The legal procedure by which a creditor enforces a court decree in their favour and recovers the outstanding debt is referred to as diligence in execution of an action. It is also possible for a creditor to seek diligence on the dependence of an action where, having raised a court action against the debtor, the creditor wishes to protect against the debtor absconding, becoming insolvent or otherwise disposing of assets. The forms of diligence on dependence of an action are limited to arrestment and inhibition. The creditor will only be able to use diligence on the dependence if its necessity is justified to the court.[157]

A debtor may, after decree has passed against him and the creditor has begun diligence, apply to the court for a time to pay order,[158] which if granted will suspend further enforcement action for a period specified by the court.

The use of diligence against the person of the debtor, namely civil imprisonment, is generally rare, being limited by statute to the non-payment of fines for contempt of court[159] or for the refusal to payment aliment (maintenance of spouse and children) when in a position to do so.[160] Diligence against the property of the debtor is the most common, and it may usefully be subdivided into diligence against their heritable property (land and buildings and rights relating to land and buildings) and their moveable property (all other property).

---

[154] 2002 Summary Cause Rules r.23.2.
[155] See paras 9.69–9.74 on diligence.
[156] See paras 9.69–9.74 on diligence.
[157] *Karl Construction Ltd v Palisade Properties Plc*, 2002 S.C. 270.
[158] Debtors (Scotland) Act 1987 ss.5–11.
[159] Debtors (Scotland) Act 1880 s.4.
[160] Civil Imprisonment (Scotland) Act 1882 s.4.

Diligence against moveable property

Arrestment

9.70 The main form of diligence against the debtor's moveable property is arrestment. Arrestment applies both to corporeal property (i.e. tangible property) and incorporeal property (i.e. intangible property, such as debts owed to the debtor). Arrestment means the attaching of the debtor's moveable property that is in the custody of a third party, or of money owed to the debtor by a third party, in order to prevent the third party dealing with the property to the prejudice of the creditor. A schedule of arrestment is prepared, which is served on the third party and thereafter, if the third party subsequently deals with the property, for example by returning it to the debtor, the third party will be liable to the creditor for any resulting loss to the creditor.[161] In the event that payment is not made to the creditor, the arrested property or debt can be recovered by the creditor by an action of furthcoming.

Similar in nature to arrestment is the arrestment of earnings introduced under the Debtors (Scotland) Act 1987. This Act created two types of arrestments: earnings arrestments,[162] which relate to ordinary debts and court fines; and current maintenance arrestments,[163] used for enforcing the payment of aliment or periodic allowance on divorce. This entitles the creditor to a direct payment of a statutory prescribed proportion of the debtor's earnings.[164] A debtor may be subject to a maximum of one earnings arrestment and one current maintenance arrestment only, therefore there is a mechanism for the creation of a conjoined arrestment order[165] where more than one creditor is entitled to proceed against the debtor. In such circumstances the payment from the debtor's wages is made to the sheriff clerk for distribution among the creditors.

Attachment

9.71 Attachment is a diligence against corporeal moveable property owned by the debtor and in his custody. In principle, it is available against all of debtor's corporeal moveable property, but there are restrictions on attachment of property kept in a dwelling house. In the case of such property, it will be necessary to seek from the sheriff an "exceptional attachment order".[166] An exceptional attachment order will only be available if the creditor has taken reasonable steps to negotiate settlement of the debt, the creditor has tried other forms of diligence and there is a reasonable prospect of the order recovering enough to cover the expenses, and even then only if the sheriff is satisfied in the circumstances that an exceptional attachment order would be reasonable.[167]

Certain categories of property are excluded from attachment.[168] These are:

- goods reasonably required by the debtor in the practice of his profession, trade or business up to an aggregate value of £1,000;
- any vehicle so required by the debtor not exceeding £1,000 in value;
- a mobile home that is the debtor's only or principal residence; and
- any equipment reasonably required for the maintenance of a garden or yard associated with a dwelling house in which the debtor resides.

In the case of extraordinary attachment, s.45 of the Debt Arrangement and Attachment (Scotland) Act 2002 provides that there are additional items excluded from the diligence. In this case, only "non-essential assets" can be attached. Schedule 2 to that Act contains a list of the

---

[161] *McSkimming v Royal Bank of Scotland*, 1996 S.C.L.R. 547.
[162] Debtors (Scotland) Act 1987 ss.47–50.
[163] Debtors (Scotland) Act 1987 ss.51–56.
[164] Debtors (Scotland) Act 1987 Sch.2.
[165] Debtors (Scotland) Act 1987 ss.60–66.
[166] Debt Arrangement and Attachment (Scotland) Act 2002 s.47.
[167] Debt Arrangement and Attachment (Scotland) Act 2002 s.48(1).
[168] Debt Arrangement and Attachment (Scotland) Act 2002 s.11(1).

items to be considered essential. The list includes such things as medical aids, children's toys and various types of furniture.

The process of attachment involves a sheriff officer visiting the place in which the goods to be attached are kept. Where entrance is denied to the officer, the officer has the power to "open shut and lockfast places for the purposes of executing an attachment".[169] The property to be attached is then to be valued according to likely market value.[170]

In the case of an exceptional attachment order, there are special procedures.[171] First, the officer only has the power of entry if authorised by the sheriff. Secondly, in any event, the officer may not enter a dwelling house to execute an attachment unless he has served notice of it on the debtor at least four days before the intended date. This requirement can be dispensed with if the sheriff, on application by the officer, is satisfied that the requirement of notice is likely to prejudice the execution of the order (for example by inducing the debtor to remove goods from the property). Thirdly, the extraordinary attachment may not proceed in the absence of a person of at least 16 years of age.

The goods are not removed from the property at this point. They are not removed until after the sheriff officer has made a report of the attachment to the sheriff,[172] which the officer is required to do within 14 days of the execution of the attachment.[173] The debtor is not permitted to remove the attached goods.

If the attached goods are not redeemed by the debtor by payment of the debt, they will be sold at auction.

Diligence against heritable property

9.72 Where a debtor owns heritable property there are two types of diligence available.

Inhibition

9.73 The main diligence against an owner of heritable property is inhibition. Inhibition is a personal prohibition that has the effect of preventing the debtor from dealing with any of the heritable property owned by him at the date the inhibition takes effect. Inhibition proceedings are commenced by letters of inhibition or a summons being served on the debtor and a notice is then registered in the Register of Inhibitions and Adjudication. At that point the debtor cannot deal with his property: he may not sell, or grant standard securities, in relation to new loans. Once the debtor has made payment to the creditor, the creditor shall record, at the debtor's expense, a discharge of the inhibition in the Register of Inhibitions and Adjudication. Otherwise, if not discharged, an inhibition prescribes five years after registration.

Adjudication

9.74 The diligence of adjudication is used to attach the debtor's heritable property in payment or security of debt, although this is rarely done. The process is commenced by a summons of adjudication and thereafter a notice of adjudication is registered in the Register of Inhibitions and Adjudications. Once the creditor obtains decree in the court action, and registers this in either the Land Register or Register of Sasines the creditor obtains a right in security over the property, which protects the creditor from the debtor's subsequent insolvency. The creditor cannot sell the property unless 10 years then pass without the debtor redeeming the property by paying off the debt.

In terms of the Bankruptcy and Diligence etc. (Scotland) Act 2007, expected to come into

[169] Debt Arrangement and Attachment (Scotland) Act 2002 s.15(1).
[170] Debt Arrangement and Attachment (Scotland) Act 2002 s.15(2).
[171] Debt Arrangement and Attachment (Scotland) Act 2002 s.49.
[172] Debt Arrangement and Attachment (Scotland) Act 2002 s.19.
[173] Debt Arrangement and Attachment (Scotland) Act 2002 s.17.

force in 2008, adjudication is to be abolished and replaced with a new diligence, land attachment, which will allow the property to be sold by the creditor much more easily.

BANKRUPTCY

9.75 While creditors may use diligence to recover their outstanding debts, no diligence may be begun after a debtor has been adjudged bankrupt, that is sequestrated. Indeed no arrestment, attachment or inhibition carried out within 60 days prior to the date of sequestration will allow that creditor to gain a preference over other creditors, regardless of whether they were aware of the sequestration proceedings. The effect of sequestration is to pass control of the debtor's estate at the date of sequestration to a trustee in sequestration, normally an accountant specialising in insolvency. The duty of the trustee in sequestration is to safeguard the estate of the debtor for the benefit of the creditors, and the trustee is obliged to account annually to the Accountant in Bankruptcy, a public official.

Sequestration proceedings are commenced by a petition to the court from a creditor, an executor of a deceased debtor, a trustee under a trust deed[174] or the debtor himself. After the first order has been made appointing the interim trustee in sequestration, the sheriff clerk will register in the Register of Inhibitions a notice of the sequestration,[175] thereby inhibiting the debtor from dealing with his property. Moreover the interim trustee in sequestration will undertake advertising to invite creditors to intimate their claims against the debtor.[176]

Once the permanent trustee is appointed, he may dispose of the debtor's assets. However, as with attachment, those items protected by the Debt Arrangement and Attachment (Scotland) Act 2002, being items required for the general upkeep of the debtor and his family, cannot be sold by him. In addition, where the debtor has an interest in a home that was occupied as a residence by him with his spouse, or by his spouse or former spouse, or by any child of the family, the property may not normally be sold without the consent of the court.[177]

9.76 Assets acquired after the date of sequestration, *acquirenda*, vest in the trustee, although income received by the debtor after sequestration does not. The trustee may however require the debtor to make a contribution to the debts from his income, provided sufficient remains for the aliment of the debtor and his family, including maintenance for any ex-spouse.

The permanent trustee is only entitled to deal with the assets of the debtor, although the legislation allows the court to reduce gratuitous alienations and unfair preferences. A gratuitous alienation is a transfer for less than market value, and it can be reduced if made within five years before the sequestration if to an associate, or otherwise if made within two years before the sequestration.[178] The term "associate" covers a variety of relationships, such as family relationships[179] and business relationships.[180]

An unfair preference is a transaction entered into by the debtor before the date of sequestration that has the effect of favouring one creditor over the general body of creditors, for example by granting a creditor security for a debt or by paying one creditor rather than others. Such a transaction is reducible if carried out within six months before the date of sequestration.[181]

Once the trustee has ingathered the estate of the debtor he will distribute it among the creditors.[182] Three years after the date of sequestration the debtor will be discharged, except

---

[174] Grier, *Debt* (1998), paras 11.2–11.9.
[175] Bankruptcy (Scotland) Act 1985 s.14.
[176] Bankruptcy (Scotland) Act 1985 s.15(6).
[177] Bankruptcy (Scotland) Act 1985 s.40.
[178] Bankruptcy (Scotland) Act 1985 s.34.
[179] Bankruptcy (Scotland) Act 1985 s.74(2).
[180] Bankruptcy (Scotland) Act 1985 s.74(3).
[181] Bankruptcy (Scotland) Act 1985 s.36(1).
[182] Bankruptcy (Scotland) Act 1985 s.51.

where the trustee has applied to the sheriff to have the discharge deferred.[183] A discharged bankrupt is free to embark on new business adventures, although their financial history will make it difficult to obtain credit.

The Bankruptcy and Diligence etc. (Scotland) Act 2007 makes a number of reforms to the law of sequestration, including the abolition of the role of interim trustee. The Act is expected to come into force in 2008.

[183] Bankruptcy (Scotland) Act 1985 s.54.

Chapter 10

Discrimination and Human Rights

In this Chapter we discuss individual rights and look at how equality and non-discrimination law, together with human rights law, are shaping the social and legal landscape that social work resides within. This Chapter is designed to provide an introduction to this area of the law. It is not exhaustive and, although it pinpoints areas of relevance to a social worker, mainly it demonstrates the importance of having an awareness of these issues. These areas of law are constantly evolving in response to new societal views and realities. It is important as a social worker that you keep abreast of any relevant changes. **10.01**

Equality and Human Rights Commission

Although the concept of equality and non-discrimination lies at the centre of human rights law, until very recently the protection and enforcement of non-discrimination and human rights were separate within Great Britain. While the existing non-discrimination grounds had their own commissions, designed to promote equality and enforce the relevant law, there was no official body charged with the promotion and protection of human rights. This changed with the creation of the Equality and Human Rights Commission ("EHRC") in October 2007. All the pre-existing equality commissions, the Equal Opportunities Commission, Commission for Racial Equality and the Disabilities Rights Commission, were merged into the EHRC and the EHRC was given more responsibility and wider powers than the previous commissions. The EHRC not only brought together the work of the three previous equality commissions, but was given responsibility for the other legal categories of equality: age, sexual orientation and religion or belief, together with human rights. **10.02**

The EHRC was established under Pt 1 of the Equality Act 2006 and although publicly accountable, in relation to its funding, is independent of governmental control. Its mission is to "eliminate discrimination, strengthen good relations between people, and promote and protect human rights".[1] Its remit covers England, Scotland and Wales. Scotland has a separate Commissioner and Committee—the Scotland Commissioner and Scotland Committee, as does Wales. These country Commissioners and Commissions are responsible for the work of the EHRC within that country.

The EHRC's duties are to promote the understanding and the importance of, and encourage good practice in relation to, equality and diversity and human rights; specifically to: promote equality of opportunity and the knowledge and understanding of the legal rights under the equality/non-discrimination Acts and human rights; enforce the equality/non-discrimination **10.03**

[1] The EHRC Mission Statement as stated on its website *http://www.equalityhumanrights.com/en/aboutus/mission/pages/visionmissionandpriorities.aspx* [Accessed October 30, 2007].

Acts; encourage public authorities to comply with their human rights obligations under the Human Rights Act 1998; and work towards the elimination of discrimination.[2]

The EHRC will monitor the effectiveness of equality and human rights law, advise the UK Government as to the law's effectiveness and recommend changes in the law. It can also advise the UK and Scottish Governments about the effect a proposed piece of legislation or a proposed change in the law[3] would have on their equality and human rights obligations. It is envisioned that, like the previous commissions, the EHRC will provide information, advice and assistance in relation to equality and human rights.[4] In particular, it will issue codes of practice, which are admissible as evidence in court.[5] In relation to its enforcement duties, the EHRC may launch an official inquiry or investigate whether a person has committed an unlawful act, in relation to its remit of equality and human rights. If it is satisfied that an unlawful act was committed it can then issue a notice requiring the addressee to prepare an action plan to avoid repetition of the unlawful act. It can also recommend what action should be taken to prevent such repetition.[6]

10.04 The EHRC has the power to apply to the sheriff court for an interdict to prevent an unlawful act taking place[7] or bring a legal action against anyone who publishes or places a discriminatory advertisement or instructs or applies pressure on someone to discriminate. Any such legal action must be initiated within six months of the unlawful act taking place.[8] The EHRC will continue the equalities commissions' work and provide conciliation services for those engaged in a civil action under the non-discrimination/equalities Acts.[9] It may also give legal advice, legal representation, and facilities for the settlement of a dispute or any other assistance to an individual who claims that they have been a victim under the non-discrimination/equalities Acts.[10] However, it will only, realistically, give such help where there is a chance to create legal precedents or to clarify and improve the current law. In relation to the enforcement of human rights, the EHRC only has the power to hold formal inquiries or to take judicial review proceedings to prevent breaches of the Human Rights Act 1998.[11]

THE SOCIAL WORKER AND DISCRIMINATION

10.05 Social work professionals are regularly exhorted to adopt anti-discriminatory practice. As one commentator has argued:

> "social work practice which does not take account of oppression and discrimination cannot be seen as good practice no matter how high [those] standards may be in other respects."[12]

With the advent of the equality duties on public bodies and the anti-discrimination obligations in relation to the provision of facilities, good and services, etc. on all grounds, excepting age, this assertion of good practice has become a legal obligation incumbent on social workers. It is not only in the carrying out of social work duties, however, that anti-discriminatory practice must be adopted: all employers must be non-discriminatory towards those that work for them and in the provision of goods, facilities and services.

Discrimination appears in many guises throughout society. The discussion in this Chapter concentrates on the different types of legally recognised discrimination—direct discrimination, indirect discrimination, harassment and victimisation. It does this in the context of the main six

---

[2] Equality Act 2006 ss.8 and 9.
[3] Equality Act 2006 s.11.
[4] Equality Act 2006 s.13.
[5] Equality Act 2006 s.14.
[6] Equality Act 2006 ss.20 and 21.
[7] Equality Act 2006 s.24.
[8] Equality Act 2006 ss.25 and 26.
[9] Equality Act 2006 s.27.
[10] Equality Act 2006 s.28.
[11] Equality Act 2006 s.30.
[12] See Thomson, *Anti-discriminatory Practice* (1993), pp.10–11.

prohibited grounds of discrimination—sex discrimination; race discrimination; disability discrimination; sexual orientation discrimination; religion or belief discrimination and age discrimination.

The overwhelming majority of anti-discriminatory legislation, in relation to employment, is directly attributable to legislation coming from the European Union. Anti-discrimination law relating to other areas is more appropriately attributed to the UK's human rights obligations. Equality and non-discrimination law has changed dramatically over the past couple of years, with half of the non-discrimination grounds only being legally recognised since 2003.[13] Whereas race and sex non-discrimination laws have been in place now for approximately 30 years, age non-discrimination, as a legally actionable ground, has been in force in the UK only since October 2006.

DIRECT DISCRIMINATION

10.06 Direct discrimination is the most obvious type of discrimination; it is blatant discrimination, where one person is treated less favourably than another because of their sex, race, age, etc. The legal definition of direct discrimination, in relation to sex, is that a person discriminates against a woman directly when he treats her less favourably than he treats a man on the grounds of her sex.[14] The same definition, where the less favourable treatment is linked to the non-discrimination characteristic, is used in relation to all other the non-discrimination grounds. An example of direct discrimination in employment would be if a job advertisement said "accountants needed, only applications from males will be accepted". A decision based on a stereotypical assumption can also give rise to a claim of direct discrimination. This is illustrated by the case of *Skyrail Oceanic v Coleman*,[15] where an assumption that the husband would be the higher earner resulting in the dismissal of the wife, was held be direct discrimination.

The alleged discriminatory treatment must be less favourable, not merely unfavourable.[16] Non-discrimination law is not concerned with ensuring "good" or even fair treatment but rather that people are not treated less favourably in relation to those of a different sex, race etc., in the same position as them. The fact that the treatment is different does not necessarily make it less favourable. The fact that it is less favourable needs to be proved.

In order to prove that discrimination has occurred a comparison must be carried out between the person alleged to be discriminated against and a person in the same or not materially different circumstances except for their sex, race, age, etc. For example, in a race discrimination case, a police officer of Asian descent would use as their comparator a police officer in exactly the same position as them, in rank, etc., but of a different race, such as Caucasian. The question asked is "but for the claimant's race would they have been treated less favourably?".[17] By looking at the treatment of the comparator, this question can be answered. The motive behind the discriminatory act is irrelevant[18]; it is the effect of the act that is decisive. There is no general defence to direct discrimination; unlike indirect discrimination it is not justifiable. There are, however, certain specific exemptions such as genuine occupational requirements, which will be discussed under the relevant grounds of non-discrimination, dealt with below.

---

[13] The Employment Equality (Religion or Belief) Regulations 2003 (SI 2003/1660) and the Employment Equality (Sexual Orientation) Regulations 2003 (SI 2003/1661), both came into force in December 2003. The Employment Equality (Age) Regulations 2006 (SI 2006/1031) came into force in October 2006.

[14] Sex Discrimination Act 1975 ("1975 Act") s.1(1)(a).

[15] [1981] I.C.R. 864, CA.

[16] *Macdonald v Advocate General for Scotland* [2003] UKHL 34.

[17] This "but for" test was developed in the case of *James v Eastleigh BC* [1990] I.R.L.R. 288, HL.

[18] *James v Eastleigh BC* [1990] I.R.L.R. 288 and *Moyhing v Barts & London NHS Trust* [2006] All E.R. (D) 64.

INDIRECT DISCRIMINATION

10.07 In order to prevent people from circumventing the prohibitions against discrimination, anti-discrimination legislation also makes indirect discrimination illegal. The prohibition against indirect discrimination is designed to cover those situations where the discrimination is not quite so obvious. This is where the requirements or criteria on the face of it seem neutral but the effect of them is discriminatory. For example, a requirement that all police officers need to be over 6ft tall would indirectly discriminate against women as, generally, women are shorter than men.

The Sex Discrimination Act 1975 defines indirect discrimination as being where a provision, criterion or practice applies, that would apply equally to a man, that would put women at a particular disadvantage when compared with men and does put that particular woman at that disadvantage, cannot be shown to be a proportional means of achieving a legitimate aim.[19] In order to take an indirect discrimination claim a person would therefore have to point out a specific provision, etc. that applied equally to her and a man, and then choose a pool of people in the same circumstances as her, which she could use to prove the general disadvantage of women. The pool cannot use the protected ground, i.e. sex, as part of its criteria. Then she would have to prove the fact she was actually disadvantaged by such a provision. Taking the above example further, a woman who applied to become a police officer but was rejected for being less than 6ft tall could use statistics to prove that women were on average shorter than men and therefore were disadvantaged in relation to this requirement. Her rejection for the job on those grounds would be used to prove her actual disadvantage. Once she has established a prima facie case of discrimination the burden of proof would shift to the police authority to prove that either she was not in fact discriminated against or, if she was, it was justified. In order to justify the discriminatory requirement the police authority would need to prove that the height requirement was a proportional means of achieving a legitimate aim. For example, they would have to prove that being of a particular height was a necessary condition to be an effective police officer—a practically impossible task.

VICTIMISATION

10.08 Victimisation is where an individual is treated less favourably than another because they have brought proceedings under the anti-discrimination legislation; given evidence in such proceedings; done anything else under or by reference to the anti-discrimination legislation; or alleged that someone has acted in contravention of that anti-discrimination legislation. For example, where Scotland Yard treated a Sikh police officer less favourably in the promotion process because of his previous racial discrimination claims, this has been held to be victimisation.[20] To be able to claim victimisation, an individual does not need to be the person who brought the proceedings; they could simply be a person who gave evidence in such proceedings.

Yet again a comparison must be made between the claimant and a person who has not done any part of the protected act, in order to prove less favourable treatment. This comparator may be real or hypothetical. For example, where a claimant was refused promotion because they had given evidence in a discrimination hearing, the comparator would be someone who was in exactly the same position as the claimant but had not given evidence in a discrimination hearing. The question would then be, would that hypothetical person have been refused that promotion?

---

[19] 1975 Act s.1(2).

[20] *Virdi v Metropolitan Police Service*, as reported in "Race Case Met Officer Wins Victimisation Claim", *Guardian*, October 10, 2007.

HARASSMENT

10.09 Harassment has only very recently been legally accepted as a separate type of discrimination. A person harasses another if on the grounds of sex, race, etc. he engages in unwanted conduct that has the purpose or effect of violating a person's dignity, or creating an intimidating, hostile, degrading, humiliating or offensive environment for that person. The harassment may take any form. It covers situations where a person feels uncomfortable, intimated or bullied in their working environment due to the unwanted conduct of those around them. Although it may well be another employee, or a customer, that creates the harassment conditions, the victim's employer can be vicariously liable.[21]

The harassment definition is focused on the complainant's sex, race, etc.; the characteristics of the harasser are irrelevant. Harassment, more than any other type of discrimination, focuses on the perception of the complainant. Although the courts take an objective view of the behaviour in question, they take the "reasonable" perceptions of the complainant into account in the making of their decision.[22]

EMPLOYMENT DISCRIMINATION

Legal proceedings

10.10 Where an employee, office holder, or a person working under a contract personally to do work, experiences any form of unlawful discrimination in that employment they can lodge a complaint with the employment tribunal. Anyone discriminated against in relation to membership of a trade organisation, vocational training, gaining vocational qualifications or by an employment agency is also able to lodge such a complaint.[23] They must lodge that complaint within three months of the discriminatory act occurring.[24] Once the case starts, the complainant must prove facts from which the tribunal could conclude, in the absence of an adequate explanation that the respondent has committed an act of discrimination or harassment against the complainant.[25] Once the complainant has done that then the burden of proof shifts to the respondent to disprove that any actual unlawful discrimination took place. If the tribunal finds in favour of the complainant they can make a declaration as to the parties' rights and/or order the respondent to pay compensation and/or recommend the respondent to take certain actions to obviate or reduce the effect of the discrimination.[26]

[21] See the Race Relations Act 1976 ("1976 Act") s.32 for an example of where an organisation is liable for a person's actions in the course of employment. In the case of *Equal Opportunities Commission v Secretary of State for Trade and Industry* [2007] I.R.L.R. 327, the High Court held that the Government had incorrectly implemented the Equal Treatment Directive and that the 1975 Act must be amended to ensure that employers are liable, where an employee was subjected to harassment, by knowingly failing to protect that individual from repetitive harassment by a third party.

[22] *R. v Birmingham City Council Ex p. Equal Opportunities Commission* [1989] A.C. 1155.

[23] This is illustrated in the 1975 Act ss.11–15. All of the other relevant employment discrimination legislation has a similar provision.

[24] This is illustrated in the 1975 Act s.76(1). All of the other relevant employment discrimination legislation has a similar provision.

[25] This is illustrated in the 1975 Act s.63A(1). All of the other relevant employment discrimination legislation has a similar provision.

[26] This is illustrated in the 1975 Act s.65. All of the other relevant employment discrimination legislation has a similar provision.

Sex discrimination in employment

10.11 In social work services women comprise a majority of the workforce.[27] Not unlike the situation in other occupations, there is often disparity between those who have supervisory, managerial or leading policy roles and those who form the majority of the workers.[28] The large workforce also comprises a substantial block of part-time workers (most of whom are female). While it is recognised that among professional social workers there are moves towards uniform qualifications and greater emphasis on enhancing professional status, it is a fact that large numbers of the social workforce are not social workers but operate in some other care capacity. It is in these groups that one is most likely to find occupational segregation. The nature of the workforce and the nature of the work make sex discrimination a very real issue for social work employees both in their own workplace environment and in furthering the aspirations of many of the clients they seek to serve as they too confront discrimination in their workplaces and elsewhere in society.

The law on sex discrimination is found principally in the Sex Discrimination Act 1975, as amended ("1975 Act"). The 1975 Act prohibits direct discrimination,[29] indirect discrimination,[30] victimisation[31] and harassment,[32] on the ground of the claimant's sex. Although the 1975 Act frames discrimination in terms of a women being discriminated against on the grounds of her sex, it identically protects men from being discriminated against on the grounds of their sex.[33] The 1975 Act also prohibits direct discrimination on the grounds of gender reassignment and indirect discrimination in relation to the arrangements made for absence from work or vocational training to undergo or recover from gender reassignment. Section 2A states that a person is discriminating against another person if he treats that person less favourably than he treats or would treat another person on the grounds that that person intends to undergo, is undergoing or has undergone gender reassignment. It should also be noted that the 1975 Act protects married people, or those in civil partnerships, from being directly or indirectly being discriminated because of their marital status.[34] The same protection is not given to unmarried persons. This therefore means that a policy favouring married people would not be discriminatory under the 1975 Act. Discrimination on the ground of pregnancy or maternity leave is also prohibited under the 1975 Act.[35]

10.12 Part II of the 1975 Act prohibits unlawful discrimination in employment if the person works wholly or partly in Great Britain.[36] This protection covers not just an employee but anyone contracted personally to execute any work or labour, including apprentices. The legal protections in the 1975 Act are therefore designed to cover the self-employed, as well as employees, as long as their contracts specify that they are personally to undertake the work in question. If, for instance, a person is personally contracted by a residential home to be a care assistant then they would fall within the protection of the 1975 Act.

The 1975 Act spells out exactly what situations are covered within employment. While only the EHRC has the power to bring an action against an employer who places a discriminatory employment advert,[37] the law does not simply regulate adverts. The 1975 Act makes it unlawful to discriminate in respect of the arrangements made to determine who should be offered employment.[38] It is therefore unlawful discrimination to put in place procedures or adopt

[27] See Pahl, "Men and Women in Social Services", in S. Balloch et al, *Working in the Social Services* (London: National Institute for Social Work, 1995), p.147.

[28] Pahl, "Men and Women in Social Services" in Balloch et al. *Working in the Social Services* (1995), p.147.

[29] 1975 Act s.1(1)(a).

[30] 1975 Act s.1(1)(b).

[31] 1975 Act s.4.

[32] 1975 Act s.4A.

[33] 1975 Act s.2.

[34] 1975 Act s.3.

[35] 1975 Act s.3A.

[36] 1975 Act s.10.

[37] 1975 Act s.38.

[38] 1975 Act s.6(1)(a).

policies and attitudes that show an intention to discriminate, even after the placing of a non-discriminatory advert.[39] For instance, the nature of questions asked at the interview can show that the employer's intention or arrangements are discriminatory.[40] Questions as to a candidate's intention to have children and how that might impact on their work could be an example of this. Many employers also may use application forms that ask a number of questions regarding the person's sex, marital status and children. Such questions are not in themselves discriminatory; it is how an employer acts on such information that shows whether there is discrimination.

The second basis on which there may be unlawful discrimination in the employment field is where the employer offers to a person terms of employment that are different from those offered to another employee of the opposite sex in the same circumstances of employment.[41] The employer may have a lawful reason for this, and if he can show that there is a genuine material difference between the two applicants that had nothing to do with their sex, it will not be unlawful to offer terms that are different. Where women are offered terms that are deemed to be chivalrous, for example starting late or finishing early, men must be likewise offered the same terms of employment.

10.13 A third variation of unlawful discrimination in employment is by refusing or deliberately omitting to offer employment to someone because of that person's sex.[42] It can be unlawful discrimination not to appoint someone to a post because the employer believes it is work undertaken properly by someone of the opposite sex, even in situations where no one is appointed to the post.[43] It is unlawful discrimination for an employee not to be offered opportunities of promotion, transfer or training, or access to any other benefits, facilities or services, or for an employer to refuse or deliberately omit to afford an employee access to them.[44] Moreover, it is unlawful discrimination for an employer to dismiss a person or subject him or her to any other detriment on the grounds of sex.[45] It is no defence on the part of the employer to argue that the dismissal took place because of pressure from other employees.[46] Nor is it lawful for an employer to discriminate by requiring employees of a certain sex to do unusual or inconvenient work and not require members of the opposite sex to do the same, even in situations where they pay additional monies to those undertaking such work.[47] There is also a "catch-all" category that makes it unlawful to discriminate against a woman by subjecting her to any other detriment. The question to ask here is whether the treatment is "of such a kind that the reasonable worker would or might take the view that in all the circumstances it was to his detriment".[48] It is not necessary to show any actual physical or economic consequences, it can simply be enough that a person's standing with their colleagues is reduced.[49] It is also unlawful for an employer to subject any person, whom he employs or who has applied to be employed by him, to harassment.[50]

10.14 The 1975 Act permits discrimination in certain circumstances. First, it is lawful to discriminate in order to give effect to statutory provisions to protect women.[51] For example it is permissible to discriminate against pregnant women in order to protect them against health risks that are specific to them alone. Moreover, discrimination is permitted by an employee where it is

---

[39] See *Brennan v Dewhurst Ltd* [1984] I.C.R. 52, where the manager made it clear he intended to employ a man in the post of butchery assistant.

[40] See *Saunders v Richmond upon Thames LBC* [1977] I.R.L.R. 362.

[41] 1975 Act s.6(1)(b).

[42] 1975 Act s.6(1)(c).

[43] See *Roadburg v Lothian RC* [1976] I.R.L.R. 283.

[44] 1975 Act s.6(2)(a).

[45] 1975 Act s.6(2)(b).

[46] See *Munro v Allied Suppliers* Unreported 1977 I.R.L.R..

[47] *Jeremiah v Ministry of Defence* [1979] I.R.L.R. 436.

[48] *Shamoon v Chief Constable of the Royal Ulster Constabulary* [2003] I.C.R. 337, at para.35.

[49] *Shamoon v Chief Constable of the Royal Ulster Constabulary* [2003] I.C.R. 337, at para.35.

[50] 1975 Act s.6(2A).

[51] 1975 Act s.51.

a genuine occupational requirement that a person of a particular sex is required.[52] There is a genuine occupational requirement where:

(1) the nature of the job calls for authentic male or female characteristics, perhaps in the field of acting or dramatic arts;
(2) the job needs to be held by a person of a particular sex in order to preserve decency or privacy because:
  (a) it is likely to involve physical contact with a person in circumstances where that person might reasonably object to it being carried out by a person of the opposite sex;
  (b) persons of one sex might reasonably object to the presence of the opposite sex because of their state of undress or the using of sanitary facilities;
(3) the job is likely to involve the holder doing his work, or living, in a private home and needs to be held by a person of one sex because objection might reasonably be taken to allowing a person of the other sex:
  (a) such a degree of physical or social contact with a person living in the home; or
  (b) the knowledge of intimate details of such person's life which would be allowed to, or available to, the holder of the job;
(4) the employee is required to live in premises provided by the employer, and those that are available are not equipped with separate sleeping accommodation and sanitary facilities and it is not reasonable to expect the employer to equip these premises or provide those facilities;
(5) the job has to be done by a person in a hospital, prison or a staff professional for people who need special care, supervision or attention;
(6) the holder's job provides personal services promoting welfare or education that can be most effectively provided by one sex;
(7) the job is likely to involve performance of duties outside the United Kingdom in a country whose laws or customs are such that duties could not be effectively performed by someone of the opposite sex; or
(8) the job is one of two held by a married couple.

In social services there are a number of situations that may give rise to genuine occupational requirement. The situations detailed in (2), (4), (5) and (6), above, seem particularly relevant. It is not uncommon for social care and social service jobs to be advertised that will only be filled by persons of a particular sex. If the reasons for this sex discrimination would fall within any of the foregoing provisions, then the discrimination is lawful and no legal claim of discrimination can be made.

Racial discrimination in employment law

10.15 The Race Relations Act 1976, as amended ("1976 Act") contains provisions very similar to the Sex Discrimination Act 1975. It seeks to prevent discrimination on racial grounds that are related to colour, race, nationality or ethnic or national origins. The word "ethnic" is to be given a broader meaning than race. The factors to be considered are: a long shared history of which the group is conscious as distinguishing it from other groups; a cultural tradition including social customs and manners; a common geographical origin or descent from common ancestors; a common language; a common literature; a common religion different from that of neighbouring groups; and being a minority or being an oppressed or a dominant group in a large community.[53] Religion is not in itself considered a racial ground and is now dealt with under

[52] 1975 Act s.7.
[53] *Mandla v Dowell Lee* [1982] 3 All E.R. 1108.

separate legislation, as discussed below. For the purposes of racial grounds, Scotland and England are to be considered places of national origin and, accordingly, to discriminate against persons from one nation or the other is unlawful discrimination.[54]

Like the Sex Discrimination Act 1975, the 1976 Act provides for direct and indirect discrimination,[55] victimisation[56] and harassment.[57] It is direct racial discrimination to treat one person less favourably on racial grounds than another.[58] The discrimination need not necessarily be related to the racial characteristics of the particular person; the discrimination could be experienced by someone not following instructions to discriminate against another because of their race[59] or by someone because of their association with someone of a different race, etc. Different treatment is not necessarily discrimination, providing it is not due to race, although the employer may have some problems in satisfying the court or tribunal of this.[60] Segregating a person from other persons on racial grounds is to be considered as treating that person less favourably than another.[61] As in every other area of discrimination, the motive behind the different treatment is irrelevant; all that matters is whether actual discrimination or disadvantage occurred.[62]

Although the definition of indirect discrimination mentioned in the above paragraph is applicable in relation to racial discrimination, it is only applicable to certain grounds, i.e. race, ethic or national origin. The definition of indirect discrimination in respect of colour or nationality is different; the old definition remains applicable.[63] The old definition is that a person discriminates when he applies a requirement or condition that would apply equally to persons not of the same racial group but that (1) is such that the proportion of persons from the same racial group who are able to comply with it is considerably smaller than the proportion of persons not of the same racial group who can comply with it; and (2) cannot be shown to be justifiable irrespective of the colour or nationality of the person to whom it applies and it is to the detriment of that person in that they cannot comply with the requirement or condition.[64] This definition covers fewer situations than the newer definition and is more difficult to prove. For example, if a job specification states that good command of the English language and UK experience is preferred, while this could be seen to fall within the parameters of new indirect discrimination definition, it would not come within the remit of the old definition.[65]

10.16 It is unlawful to discriminate on racial grounds in respect of employment. In particular, it is unlawful to discriminate on racial grounds in the arrangements for determining who shall be offered employment; the terms that are offered; or by refusing or deliberately omitting to offer employment.[66] Following employment, it is unlawful to discriminate against an employee in the terms of employment that are given to that employee; in the way in which the employee is afforded opportunities of promotion, transfer and training, or access to benefits, facilities or services; or in dismissing the employee or subjecting them to any other detriment.[67]

Employers must not only be careful about their attitude and actings towards their employees; they must also be mindful that they are vicariously liable for anything done by their employees in the course of their employment. This liability arises whether or not it was done with the

---

[54] *Northern Joint Police Board v Power* [1997] I.R.L.R. 610, EAT.
[55] 1976 Act s.1.
[56] 1976 Act s.2.
[57] 1976 Act s.3A.
[58] 1975 Act s.1(1)(a); see *Glasgow City Council v Zafar*, 1998 S.C. (H.L.) 27.
[59] *Showboat Entertainment Centre Ltd v Owens* [1985] All E.R. 836, EAT.
[60] *Barclays Bank Plc v Kapur* [1989] I.R.L.R. 387; *Weathersfield Ltd v Sargent* [1998] I.R.L.R. 14.
[61] *Pel Ltd v Modgill* [1980] I.R.L.R. 142.
[62] *R. v Commission for Racial Equality Ex p. Westminster City Council* [1985] I.C.R. 827.
[63] 1976 Act s.1(1).
[64] 1976 Act s.1(1).
[65] *Perera v Civil Service Commission (No.2)* [1983] I.C.R. 428.
[66] 1976 Act s.4(1).
[67] 1976 Act s.4(2).

employer's knowledge or approval.[68] The only defence that an employer has to being held vicariously liable is that they took all reasonably practicable steps to prevent the employee acting discriminatorily.

Again, in similar fashion to the 1975 Act, the 1976 Act lays down certain genuine occupational qualifications, in relation to nationality and colour, where it is permissible to engage what would otherwise be considered discriminatory practices. There may be a genuine occupational qualification that:

(1) the job involves participation in dramatic performance or entertainment, and for reasons of authenticity the person requires to belong to a particular racial group;
(2) the job involves participation as an artist or photographic model and again a person of a particular racial group is required for reasons of authenticity;
(3) the job involves working in a place where food and drink are provided and consumed by members of the public in a particular setting for which a personal or partnership group is required for reasons of authenticity;
(4) the holder of the job provides persons of a racial group with personal services promoting their welfare, and those services or most of them should be provided by persons of that racial group.[69]

Obviously para.(4) may well be relevant in the field of social services. However, an employer seeking to discriminate in the employment field should be careful. In *Tottenham Green Under-Fives Centre v Marshall*[70] the phrase "promoting welfare" was held to have a wide meaning. Notwithstanding this, in *Lambeth LBC v Commission for Racial Equality*[71] the local authority was held to be discriminatory in seeking to engage only Afro-Caribbean and Asian community members for jobs in the housing benefits department. It appears the word "genuine" is instructive in this matter. If it can be shown that there is a real need for the person to be of a particular racial grouping or origin then it is likely that condition will escape sanction. This stance appears to reflect the new legal reality in relation to the categories of race, ethnic or national origins, where there is now only one general occupational qualification. This general occupational qualification states that where "being of a particular race or of particular ethnic or national origins is a genuine and determining occupational requirement" and that requirement has been proportionately applied then the discrimination will not be unlawful.[72] This general exception will cover the situations outlined above but will go further and cover any other applicable circumstances.

Disability discrimination in employment law

10.17 It was not until mid-1990 that attempts were made by the Government to outlaw discrimination against disabled persons. These attempts culminated in the Disability Discrimination Act 1995, as amended ("DDA 1995"). There are now several Codes of Practice, covering different parts of the Act, which help to flesh out the meaning of the various legal provisions of DDA 1995.[73] Codes of Practice are not legally binding but can be submitted as evidence and used as guidance in tribunal proceedings. DDA 1995 has similar provisions to the 1975 and 1976 Acts. It is however the most legally unique of all the discrimination categories. Not only does DDA 1995 contain different types of discrimination from those in other categories, as outlined below, it also allows for and promotes positive discrimination in favour of disabled persons. DDA 1995

---

[68] For example see the 1975 Act s.41 and 1976 Act s.32.
[69] 1976 Act s.5.
[70] [1989] I.R.L.R. 147.
[71] [1990] I.R.L.R. 231.
[72] 1976 Act s.4A.
[73] The Disability Code of Practice "Code of Practice on employment and occupation" was produced by the Disability Rights Commission, now part of the EHRC, and came into force in October 2004.

only protects disabled people from discrimination; non-disabled people placed at a disadvantage, in relation to a disabled person, are not protected by DDA 1995.

A person has a disability, for the purposes of DDA 1995, if he has a physical or mental impairment that has a substantial and long-term adverse effect on his ability to carry out normal day-to-day activities.[74] While in the past mental impairment needed to be "clinically well-recognised", there is no such restriction now. It is immaterial how the impairment was caused; it is the effect that is important. The question is whether there is impairment. Therefore, although addictions are excluded from DDA 1995,[75] any impairments arising out of them, e.g. liver failure, will be covered under the Act.[76] Certain specific impairments such as depression, dyslexia, asthma, chronic fatigue syndrome, etc. are mentioned in the Guidance[77] as coming within the definition of disability. A person diagnosed with cancer, HIV, multiple sclerosis or as being blind/partially blind is automatically deemed by DDA 1995 to be disabled from the point of diagnosis.[78]

In relation to whether the adverse effect of the impairment is substantial, the extra time taken to do a task and the actual effects of the impairment, looked at accumulatively, should be taken into account. Where the impairment is under treatment or correction the "but for" test should be applied to see if "but for" such treatment the impairment would fall within the disability definition. If it would, then that person is classed as disabled.[79] For the purpose of deciding whether a person has or had disability, the long-term effect of an impairment is seen to be one that has lasted at least 12 months.[80] The provisions of DDA 1995 in respect of employment and services are to extend to those who have in the past had a disability but now no longer have it.[81] The intention behind these provisions is to prevent discrimination against those who have for example a history of past mental illness, etc.

10.18 It is unlawful for an employer to discriminate against a disabled person: (a) in the arrangements that he makes for the purposes of determining to whom he should offer employment; (b) in the terms in which he offers that person employment; or (c) by refusing to offer or deliberately not offering him employment.[82] It is also unlawful for an employer to discriminate against a disabled person in his employment: (a) in terms of the employment that he affords him; (b) in the opportunity he affords him for promotion, a transfer, training or receiving any benefits; (c) in refusing to afford him, or deliberately not affording him, any such opportunity; or (d) by dismissing him, or subjecting him to any other detriment.[83] It is also unlawful for a person to publish or cause to be published a job advertisement that indicates that an application from a disabled person is unwelcome.[84] The EHRC (as opposed to an individual complainant), however, is the only "person" able to take legal action in respect of this.[85]

DDA 1995 recognises five types of discrimination: direct discrimination; disability-related discrimination; failure to make reasonable adjustments; victimisation; and harassment. A person directly discriminates against a disabled person if, on the ground of the disabled person's disability, he treats the disabled person less favourably than he treats or would treat a person not having that particular disability whose relevant circumstances, including his abilities, are the same as, or not materially different from, those of the disabled person.[86] An example of direct

---

[74] DDA 1995 s.1(1); see also DDA 1995 Sch.1 para.4.
[75] Disability Discrimination (Meaning of Disability) Regulations 1996 (SI 1996/1455) reg.3.
[76] *Power v Panasonic UK Ltd* [2003] I.R.L.R. 151, EAT.
[77] "Guidance on Matters to be Taken into Account in Determining Questions Relating to the Definition of Disability", issued by the Secretary of State under DDA 1995 s.3 with effect from May 2006 (by SI 2006/1005), para.A6.
[78] Guidance under DDA 1995, para.A10.
[79] DDA 1995 Sch.1 para.6.
[80] DDA 1995 Sch.2 para.5.
[81] DDA 1995 s.2.
[82] DDA 1995 s.4(1)(a), (b) and (c).
[83] DDA 1995 s.4.
[84] See DDA 1995 s.16B for the exact wording.
[85] DDA 1995 s.16B(5).
[86] DDA 1995 s.3A(5).

disability discrimination would be where an employer did not shortlist a disabled games teacher for the sports coach role because it assumed that she would not be able to teach by example. In this scenario, the employer made no attempt to see if its assumptions were true in the individual circumstances or ascertain how important teaching by example was to the sports coach role. In not shortlisting the disabled sports teacher, the employer has treated the disabled games teacher less favourably than a person not having that disability. Direct disability discrimination cannot be justified[87] so in this example the employer would be liable for discrimination under DDA 1995.

A person also discriminates against a disabled person if (a) for a reason related to the disabled person's disability he treats him less favourably than he treats or would treat others for whom that reason does not or would not apply; and (b) he cannot show that the treatment in question is justified.[88] In order for such treatment to be justified the reason must be both material to the circumstances of the particular case and substantial.[89] Disability-related discrimination is the only type of disability discrimination that can be justified. This ground of discrimination is similar to direct discrimination; it differs, however, in that the reason for the less favourable treatment relates to the disability but is not the disability itself. The trick is to look at the reason for the treatment and compare the disabled person's treatment with someone to whom the reason does not apply. The Disability Code of Practice gives a helpful example of disability-related discrimination in para.4.30. A disabled woman is refused an administrative job because she cannot type. She cannot type because she has arthritis. A non-disabled person who was unable to type would also have been turned down. The disability-related reason for the less favourable treatment is the woman's inability to type, and the correct comparator is a person to whom that reason does not apply—that is, someone who can type. Such a person would not have been refused the job. Nevertheless, the disabled woman has been treated less favourably for a disability-related reason and this will be unlawful unless it can be justified. This treatment is not direct discrimination because the comparator for direct discrimination is a person who does not have arthritis, but who is also unable to type.

10.19 The most unusual and unique type of disability discrimination is however the duty to make reasonable adjustments. A person discriminates against a disabled person if he fails to comply with a duty to make reasonable adjustments imposed on him in relation to the disabled person. DDA 1995 s.4A states that where (a) a provision, criterion or practice applied by or on behalf of an employer; or (b) any physical feature of premises occupied by the employer, places the disabled person concerned at a substantial disadvantage in comparison with persons who are not disabled, it is the duty of the employer to take such steps as it is reasonable, in all the circumstances of the case, for him to have to take in order to prevent the provision, criterion or practice, or feature, having that effect. Examples of the steps an employer may have to take include making adjustments to premises; allocating some of the disabled person's duties to another person; transferring him to fill an existing vacancy; altering his working hours; assigning him to a different place of work; allowing him to be absent during working hours for rehabilitation, assessment or treatment; giving him, or arranging for him to be given, training; acquiring or modifying equipment; modifying instructions or reference manuals; modifying procedures for testing or assessment; providing a reader or interpreter; and providing supervision or any other support.[90] An employer should therefore carry out an assessment of what steps may be required to ensure that a disabled person is not placed at a substantial disadvantage.

In deciding what adjustments are reasonable for an employer to carry out the courts may take into account the extent to which the adjustments would prevent the effect in question; the extent to which it is practical for the employer make such adjustments, i.e. the financial and other costs

---

[87] DDA 1995 s.3A(4).
[88] DDA 1995 s.3A(1)(a).
[89] DDA 1995 s.3A(3).
[90] DDA 1995 s.18B(2).

that would be incurred by the employer in taking the steps; how it might disrupt any of his activities; the extent of the employer's financial and other resources and the availability to the employer of financial or other assistance with respect to taking the steps; the nature of his undertakings and size of his undertaking; and where the step would be taken in relation to a private household the extent to which it would disrupt the household or any person residing there.[91] The employer only has a duty to make reasonable adjustments if he knew or should have reasonably known that the person was disabled.[92]

A disabled person is protected from harassment for any reason that relates to their disability[93] and victimisation.[94] It should be noted that like sex discrimination, and unlike the other discrimination categories, the definition, as set out in DDA 1995, only relates to discrimination done in relation to the claimant's disability. There is no prohibition against discrimination that is due to a person associating with a disabled person or because a person is perceived to be disabled, for example. This position is currently under legal challenge and, after a referral to the European Court of Justice, the judicial interpretation of disability discrimination may be changed to include associative discrimination.[95]

Discrimination on the grounds of religion or belief in employment law

10.20 Since December 2003 it has been unlawful under the Employment Equality (Religion or Belief) Regulations 2003,[96] as amended ("Religious Equality Regs") to directly or indirectly discriminate, victimise or harass a person on the basis of religion and belief in the field of employment and vocational training. As the definition of direct discrimination and harassment in the Religious Equality Regs refers to discrimination or harassment "on grounds of religion or belief",[97] associative discrimination or discrimination due to a person's perceived religion or belief is also prohibited under these regulations. The Religious Equality Regs apply, as in other employment anti-discrimination legislation, to the recruitment process, terms and conditions of employment, promotion, transfer, training, dismissal or any other benefit.[98] The protection given by the Religious Equality Regs covers any religion, religious or philosophical belief or the lack of such religion or beliefs.[99] The scope of the Religious Equality Regs therefore stretches past conventional religions, covers atheists, and has the potential to cover non-religious views within the category of "philosophical belief".

There are two limited exceptions where it is permissible for an employer to discriminate on the ground of religion or belief. The first is where, having regard to the nature of the employment or the context in which it is carried out, being of a particular religion or belief is a genuine and determining occupational requirement and it is proportionate to apply that requirement in the particular case.[100] This exception would cover ministers of a church, for instance. The second exception relates to where an employer has an ethos based on religion or belief and, having regard to that ethos and to the nature of the employment or the context in which it is carried out, being of a particular religion or belief is a genuine occupational requirement for the job and it is proportionate to apply that requirement in the particular case. This could cover the religion of a teacher in a religious school, for instance.

---

[91] DDA 1995 s.18B(1).

[92] DDA 1995 s.4A(3).

[93] DDA 1995 s.3B.

[94] DDA 1995 s.55.

[95] The Employment Appeal Tribunal determined in *Attridge Law v Coleman* [2007] 2 C.M.L.R. 24 that a reference should be made to the European Court of Justice ("ECJ") on whether Council Directive 2000/78 included associative discrimination. If the ECJ did believe that the Directive included associative discrimination then DDA 1995 would be interpreted by the courts accordingly.

[96] SI 2003/1660.

[97] Religious Equality Regs regs 3(1)(a) and 5(1).

[98] Religious Equality Regs reg.6.

[99] Religious Equality Regs reg.2(1).

[100] Religious Equality Regs reg.7(2).

Discrimination on the grounds of sexual orientation in employment law

10.21 The Employment Equality (Sexual Orientation) Regulations 2003,[101] as amended ("Sexual Orientation Regs") came into force in December 2003, at the same time as the Religious Equality Regs. The Sexual Orientation Regs make it unlawful to discriminate against someone on the grounds of sexual orientation. It does not matter if someone is sexually orientated towards someone of the same or opposite sex or both sexes,[102] they are protected from discrimination. The types of discrimination and stages of discrimination are the same as outlined in relation to discrimination on the grounds of religion or belief. Similarly, associative discrimination or discrimination due to a person's perceived religion or belief is also prohibited under the Sexual Orientation Regs in relation to direct discrimination and harassment.

Although indirect discrimination can be justified by the showing that there is a legitimate aim behind the discriminatory practice, etc. and that the practice was proportionate to that aim,[103] an employer is only allowed to directly discriminate where a genuine occupational requirement is proved to apply. There are only two limited genuine occupational requirements[104] allowed in the Sexual Orientation Regs. Regulation 7 states that, having regard to the nature of the employment being of a particular sexual orientation is a genuine and determining occupational requirement and it is proportionate to apply that requirement then the discrimination will not be unlawful. Regulation 7 also allows discrimination where the employment is for the purpose of religion. This means that discrimination is allowed in order to comply with certain religious beliefs or avoid a situation where another's beliefs conflict with a person's sexual orientation.

Age discrimination in employment law

10.22 Age discrimination is the most recent addition to British discrimination law. The Employment Equality (Age) Regulations 2006,[105] as amended ("Age Regs") came into force in October 2006. The Age Regs apply to persons of any age—young or old. The types of discrimination and stages of discrimination are the same as outlined in relation to discrimination on the grounds of religion or belief. In relation to direct discrimination, the discrimination can be on the grounds of that person's actual or apparent age.[106] With regard to the indirect discrimination definition, discrimination is dealt with in relation to "age group".[107] This is defined as being a group of persons defined by reference to age, whether by reference to a particular age or a range of ages.[108]

If a person's age is greater than or within six months of the employer's normal retirement age or, if the employer does not have a normal retirement age, the age of 65, then they are not protected from discrimination, within the Age Regs, in relation to the arrangements that employer makes for the purpose of determining to whom he should offer employment or in the decision of whether to employ that person.[109] This therefore means that an employer can reject a person for being too old for employment if they are older than 65 years old or older than the company retirement age.

There is the usual general genuine occupational requirement for the discrimination not to be unlawful: where, having regard to the nature of the employment, possessing a characteristic related to age is a genuine and determining occupational requirement and it is proportionate to apply that requirement.[110] The Age Regs include a great many exceptions additional to those

---

[101] SI 2003/1661.
[102] Sexual Orientation Regs reg.2(1).
[103] Sexual Orientation Regs reg.3(1)(b)(iii).
[104] Sexual Orientation Regs reg.24.
[105] SI 2006/1031.
[106] Age Regs reg.3(1) and (3)(a).
[107] Age Regs reg.3(1)(b).
[108] Age Regs reg.3(3)(a).
[109] Age Regs reg.7(4).
[110] Age Regs reg.8.

stated in other employment anti-discrimination legislation. Apart from the usual exception for national security, they also allow for dismissal on the grounds of retirement once the person is 65 years old or over,[111] although the employer has a duty to properly consider an employee's request to work beyond retirement age. The Age Regs also allow for a difference in wages due to age, as set out in the National Minimum Wage Act 1998[112] and specifically allow employers to discriminate in relation the length of service given by an employee. However, after five years' service, the way in which the employer uses the length of service criterion must fulfil a business need, i.e. encourage loyalty.[113]

DISCRIMINATION IN OTHER FIELDS

10.23 Owing to the influence of not only European Union legislation but also the UK's international, regional and domestic human rights obligations, there has been a growth in equality and anti-discrimination obligations outside the field of employment. Anti-discrimination legislation now makes discrimination in education and the provision of goods, services, facilities and premises, on the basis of sex, race, disability, sexual orientation, and religion or belief, unlawful. At present, age anti-discrimination legislation only covers the field of employment and vocational training and discrimination in the provision of further and higher education.[114] Although the anti-discrimination provisions contained in the 1975 Act, 1976 Act and the Equality Act 2006 are broadly similar, the provisions held within DDA 1995 are different. Disability discrimination will therefore be dealt with separately under this section.

Discrimination in education

10.24 The 1975 and 1976 Acts prohibit direct and indirect sex and race discrimination or victimisation, by providers of all full- or part-time education, in the application process, the terms on which education is offered and the way in which education is given, i.e. in access to benefits, facilities or services.[115] This therefore means that state, independent and special schools, colleges and universities cannot discriminate on the basis of sex or racial grounds. There is also a general duty on education authorities, public funding bodies and the training and development agency for schools not to discriminate in their duties. This duty has been to some extent superseded by the gender equality duty placed on all public bodies as discussed below in para.10.47. The duty not to discriminate also covers financial assistance given to students.[116]

The 1976 Act makes harassment, in the provision of education, unlawful. In relation to sex, the prohibition of harassment only extends to further and higher education. State, independent and special schools cannot discriminate on the grounds of religion or belief[117]; however, harassment is not expressly prohibited. Part 3 of the Equalities Act 2006 empowers the Minister to extend the statutory protection given in relation to religion and belief, to sexual orientation. This "empowerment" includes reference to a definition for harassment. It is therefore expected that when a statutory instrument is drafted to make discrimination in the provision of education by schools, on the grounds of sexual orientation, unlawful it will include a prohibition against harassment.[118] At that time it is envisioned that the Religious Equality Regs will expressly include a prohibition against harassment. In any case, the courts have recognised that harass-

---

[111] Age Regs reg.30.
[112] Age Regs reg.31.
[113] Age Regs reg.32.
[114] Age Regs reg.23.
[115] 1975 Act s.22; 1976 Act s.17.
[116] *R. (on the application of Bidar) v Ealing LBC* (C209/03) [2005] Q.B. 812, ECJ.
[117] Equality Act 2006 s.49.
[118] At this point it would be usual to amend the Equality Act 2006 to prohibit harassment on the grounds of religion or belief.

ment is a form of direct or indirect discrimination[119] so, even without a specific harassment prohibition, harassment is unlawful. There are exceptions to the Religious Equality Regs for single sex schools and "faith schools" to accept only pupils of a certain sex or religion.

As can be seen from the above, the specific anti-discrimination protection given varies depending on the ground of discrimination. Where the coverage of specific anti-discrimination legislation falls short, there may be other remedies in human rights law. For instance, the first Protocol to the European Convention on Human Rights 1950 provides for a right of education. This right, combined with the general anti-discrimination article, art.14 of the Convention, means that the provision of education, among other things, must be not be discriminatory on the basis of sex, race, colour, language, religion, etc.[120] The European Court of Human Rights has determined that sexual orientation comes within art.14 of the European Convention on Human Rights.[121] To that extent discrimination on the ground of sexual orientation is prohibited within the provision of public functions.

Discrimination in the provision of goods, services and facilities

10.25 The 1975 Act, 1976 Act and the Equality Act 2006 make it unlawful for any person concerned with the provision (for payment or not) of goods, facilities or services to the public or a section of the public to discriminate, on the basis of sex, race, or religion and belief, against a person who seeks to obtain or use those goods, facilities or services by refusing or deliberately omitting to provide her with any of them, or with them in like quality, in the like manner and on the like terms as are normal in relation to other members of the public.[122] For example, a hotel cannot refuse a room to an Asian person, while giving a room to an African person.

Harassment is currently only expressly prohibited on racial grounds,[123] although, as stated above, such treatment is already unlawful as part of the existing discrimination law. It should be noted that the discrimination is only unlawful in relation to the public provision of goods, etc., so services provided by private clubs are therefore not covered. This means, for example, that clubs can have rules that prevent women or Christians from joining or, if joined, from certain services. Where a club has more than 25 members it cannot, however, discriminate in the granting of membership, on racial grounds.[124]

Public authorities, while carrying out functions of a public nature, or any private company, in carrying out public functions, are expressly prohibited, under the 1975 and 1976 Acts and the Equality Act 2006, from doing a discriminatory act or subjecting a person to harassment.[125] This means that where social work duties are contracted out by the local authority or other public bodies, the organisations that carry out such duties have a statutory duty to do so in a non-discriminatory manner. This means that all processes and practices should be non-discriminatory and the work be carried out in a non-discriminatory manner.

10.26 There are however some exceptions that are pertinent for social workers. In relation to race discrimination only, the prohibition against discrimination in the provision of goods, services, etc. does not apply where a person takes a person into their home and treats them as if they were a part of their family.[126] This means therefore that where a carer wishing to adopt or foster a child, for instance, wants a child of their own racial group, this is allowed under the 1976 Act. Discrimination is also allowable under s.35 of the 1975 Act where services or facilities are restricted to one sex because:

---

119 *Smith v Gardner Merchant* [1999] I.C.R. 134, CA.

120 M. Connolly, *Discrimination Law* (London: Sweet & Maxwell, 2006), p.278.

121 *Salgueiro Da Silva Mouta v Portugal* (33290/96) [2001] 1 F.C.R. 653, judgment given on December 21, 1999.

122 1975 Act s.29; 1976 Act s.20; Equality Act 2006 s.46.

123 1976 Act s.20(3).

124 1976 Act s.25.

125 1975 Act s.21A; 1976 Act s.19; Equality Act 2006 s.52.

126 1976 Act s.23(2).

(1) the place is, or is part of, a hospital, resettlement unit or other establishment for persons requiring special care, supervision or attention; or
(2) the place is (permanently or for the time being) occupied or used for the purposes of an organised religion, and the facilities or services are restricted to men so as to comply with the doctrines of that religion or avoid offending the religious susceptibilities of a significant number of its followers; or
(3) the facilities or services are provided for, or are likely to be used by, two or more persons at the same time; and
    (a) the facilities or services are such, or those persons are such, that male users are likely to suffer serious embarrassment at the presence of a woman; or
    (b) the facilities or services are such that a user is likely to be in a state of undress and a male user might reasonably object to the presence of a female user.

Additionally a person who provides facilities or services restricted to men does not unlawfully discriminate if the services or facilities are such that physical contact between the user and any other person is likely, and that other person might reasonably object if the user were a woman. For example, where there is only one bed left in a double occupancy room within a care home, it would be permissible to only offer that bed to a person of the same sex as the other occupant of that room.

In relation to non-profit organizations, where conferring benefits on persons of one sex only is a main object or purpose of that body then they can restrict their membership or provision of services, etc. to simply that sex. For example, this means that it is lawful for an organisation to be set up to help female victims of domestic violence and only allow women to reside in their care homes.

Disability discrimination outside employment

10.27 Part III of DDA 1995 covers discrimination outside the field of employment and vocational training. In particular, it covers the provision of any goods, services or facilities, the disposal or letting of premises, public authority services, education and public transport. Section 19 makes it unlawful for a provider of services to discriminate against a disabled person by refusing to provide to the disabled person any services, goods or facilities that he provides, or is prepared to provide, to members of the public; in the standard of service which he provides to the disabled person or the manner in which he provides it to him; or in the terms on which he provides a service to the disabled person. It also makes the failure to make a reasonable adjustment unlawful, where the effect of that failure makes it impossible or unreasonably difficult for the disabled person to make use of any such service.[127]

It should be noted that this duty not to discriminate is only in relation to goods, services or facilities provided to the public so it will not cover the design and manufacture of goods unless they are sold direct to the public.[128] Private clubs with more than 25 members similarly cannot discriminate against a disabled person.[129] It is also unlawful for a public authority, or a person carrying out functions of a public nature, to discriminate against a disabled person in the carrying out of its functions.[130] This means that any social services have to be carried out in a way that does not discriminate against a disabled person.

DDA 1995 only disallows two types of discrimination: disability-related discrimination and the duty to make reasonable adjustments in relation to areas outside employment and vocational training. Direct discrimination is included within the broader category of disability-related discrimination. As disability-related discrimination has the ability to be justified, this

---

[127] DDA 1995 s.19.
[128] Connolly, *Discrimination Law* (2006), p.333.
[129] DDA 1995 s.21F.
[130] DDA 1995 s.21B.

means that direct discrimination may therefore be justifiable outside the field of employment.[131] The duty to make reasonable adjustments includes not just adjustments to physical features, such as the widening of doors to allow wheelchair access, but also the removal of practice, policy or procedure that makes it unreasonably difficult or impossible for the disabled person to use that service. In *Ross v Ryanair*[132] the court held that the fact that the departure gate was a long way from the check-in desk made it unreasonably difficult for disabled fliers to use this service. What Ryanair should have done was provide some sort of transportation for disabled persons to enable them to use this airport.

The duty to make reasonable adjustments means that service providers should assess the needs of disabled persons in relation to the provision of their services and make any adjustments necessary to facilitate their use of the service to the same standard that a person without that disability enjoys it. This is a continuing duty. A provider of services does not have to take any steps that would fundamentally alter the nature of the service in question or the nature of his trade, profession or business or where the costs would go over a set maximum amount.[133] Where an auxiliary aid or service would enable or facilitate the disabled person's use of a service, then the provider of that service should provide it, e.g. an audio tape with information on it.

10.28 There are two general justifications for discrimination in relation to the provision of services, one in relation to health and safety and the other if the person has insufficient capacity to enter into a contract.[134] In relation to public authority functions there are some additional justifications. The usual acceptable justification of achieving a legitimate aim in a proportionate manner is applicable. Further, where the discrimination against a disabled person is necessary for the rights and freedoms of others or where the authority would incur substantial additional costs in providing services to a disabled person, discrimination will also be allowed. This reflects an appreciation of the tight resource allocation restraints a public authority is under. These justifications also cover the situation where, for example, two disabled persons, mentally incapable of looking after a child, wish to adopt. In this situation the adoption agency can refuse their adoption application.

A person cannot discriminate in the actual offering of premises to a person, in the terms offered, the access to benefits or facilities in relation to those premises or in eviction or any other detriment[135] or in withholding consent for assignment or subletting of a tenancy to a disabled person.[136] The duty to make reasonable adjustments only applies to the letting of premises.[137] This duty does not apply where the premises are, or have been, the only or principal home of the person letting those premises if those premises have not been let by a letting agency.[138] If any auxiliary aid or service is required to facilitate the use of the premises this should also be reasonably provided, on request.

Some discrimination, in relation to housing, is capable of being justified. Aside from the justifications relating to general health and safety and incapacity to contract, discrimination may be allowable where the accommodation of the disabled person's needs would prevent or unreasonably restrict the enjoyment of that property and its amenities by others living in that property. For example a tenant with mobility issues could be asked not to park her mobility vehicle in the hall outside the entrance to her flat if it prevented other tenants from being able to properly access their flats.

The specific mention of transport within DDA 1995 is unique among the anti-discrimination Acts. The provision of transport and provision of services on transport is expressly excluded

---

[131] Connolly, *Discrimination Law* (2006), p.334.
[132] [2005] 1 W.L.R. 2447.
[133] DDA 1995 s.21(6) and (7).
[134] DDA 1995 s.21(4)(a) and (b).
[135] DDA 1995 s.22.
[136] DDA 1995 s.22.
[137] DDA 1995 s.24D.
[138] DDA 1995 s.24B.

from the anti-discrimination provisions discussed above[139] and given special treatment within DDA 1995 Pt V. This part of the Act allows the Government to set access standards for taxis, trains and other public service transport, such as buses, trams, etc. These standards are designed to ensure that disabled persons can get on to and off the vehicles in safety and without unreasonable difficulty (and, in the case of disabled persons in wheelchairs, to do so while remaining in their wheelchairs) and to be carried in such vehicles in safety and in reasonable comfort.[140] The Government has produced regulations dealing with such access standards. These standards relate to things like doors, door controls, wheelchair space, etc.

10.29 In relation to education, it is not just discrimination in relation to the provision of educational services that is unlawful; there is also a duty placed on each local education authority to prepare and implement an accessibility strategy for disabled persons within schools. This strategy should improve disabled pupils' access to the curriculum, the school's physical environment to enable greater access to education and related services and the communication of information to disabled pupils. It is unlawful for education providers to treat a disabled person less favourably, for a reason related to their disability or to fail to make reasonable adjustments[141] in relation to admissions, teaching and learning and other services that are provided wholly or mainly for students,[142] including school trips, sports, leisure facilities, meals, etc. or by exclusion from an education institution or course. The same duties lie on providers of further and higher education[143] and, to the extent applicable, in relation to the conferment of qualifications.[144] Education providers must provide auxiliary aids and services as part of their legal duty to make reasonable adjustments, as well as adjustments to their premises where there are physical features that are placing disabled persons at a substantial disadvantage. In order for such a duty to fall on educational providers they should know that the pupil was disabled.[145] Discrimination can be justified if the reason is material to the particular case and substantial[146] or where it involves a permitted form of selection for schools, such as academic ability. In determining whether discrimination is justified the courts will look at what is reasonable. Harassment is also unlawful in relation to the provision of further and higher education and the gaining of a qualification.[147]

Discrimination in the provision of housing and premises

10.30 It is unlawful to discriminate on the basis of sex, race, and religion or belief[148] in the actual offering of premises to a person, in the terms offered, the access to benefits or facilities in relation to those premises or in eviction or any other detriment.[149] The 1975 and 1976 Acts and the Equality Act 2006 expressly extend this duty, making it unlawful to withhold consent for assignment or subletting of a tenancy on the basis of sex, race, religion or belief.[150] This means, for instance, that a landlord cannot refuse to let his flat out to a person of the Muslim faith.

Until specific protection is created by the Minister, ss.8 and 14 of the Human Rights Act 1998 can be used to protect against discrimination on the ground of sexual orientation in the disposal of premises. There is a statutory exception in all the relevant anti-discrimination Acts that

---

139 DDA 1995 s.21ZA.
140 DDA 1995 ss.32, 40, 46.
141 DDA 1995 s.28B.
142 DDA 1995 s.28A.
143 DDA 1995 s.28R.
144 DDA 1995 s.31AA.
145 DDA 1995 ss.28B(4) and 28S(3).
146 DDA 1995 ss.28B(7) and 28S(5).
147 DDA 1995 s.31AC.
148 The minister is empowered under Pt 3 of the Equality Act 2006 to extend these provisions to sexual orientation.
149 1975 Act s.30; 1976 Act s.21; Equality Act 2006 s.47.
150 1975 Act s.31; 1976 Act s.24; Equality Act 2006 s.47(3).

allows an owner to discriminate in the letting of part of that property, where he or a close relative, occupies the dwelling in question and rents out to up to six persons.[151]

Public body equality duty

10.31 Now, not only is it unlawful for public bodies to discriminate in the exercise of their functions, they also have a positive duty, in the exercise of their function, to eliminate unlawful discrimination and harassment, and promote equality of opportunity between those of a different sex,[152] race[153] and for disabled persons.[154] The 1976 Act additionally exhorts public authorities to promote good relations between persons of different racial groups,[155] while DDA 1995 places the most duties on public bodies. In addition to those duties stated above, it also states that public bodies must have due regard to the need to take steps to take account of disabled persons' disabilities, even where that involves treating disabled persons more favourably than other persons; promote positive attitudes towards disabled persons; and, encourage the participation of disabled persons in public life.

It should be noted that public bodies include any person who has functions of a public nature so universities, health authorities, councils, prisons, etc. are all included, as are any contracted-out public services. Therefore, where social work services are the legal duty of a public body, regardless of who carries them out in practice, those services have to be planned and implemented in line with the public body equality duties.

It is unusual for legislation to impose positive duties. The positive duties laid on public bodies, especially in relation to disabled persons, are wide reaching and underline the acceptance of the fact that a more proactive approach needs to be taken to ensure equality in today's society. Inequality and discrimination are still rife in our society, as demonstrated by research published by the Equal Opportunities Commission, before its dissolution. The Gender Equality Index stated that, working on current trends, it would take 195 years for Westminster Parliament to have an equal amount of male and female MPs and the rape conviction rates of 5 per cent would never improve unless action was stepped up.[156]

10.32 The public body equality duties are designed to make equality central to the way public bodies work. It is hoped that this will then create better informed and thoughtful decision making that more clearly understands the variety of needs within society and therefore creates targeted and more effective policies and an efficient allocation of resources. It is a way of building equality into key decision-making processes. Instead of placing the responsibility for social change on individuals bringing private legal actions, the equality duties place a duty on public authorities to prove that they treat those of a different sex and race and disabled persons equally. This means that public policies, procedures and practices should take into account the different needs of men and women, different races and disabled persons. For instance, the local or central authority could build on effective strategies developed to prevent domestic violence and help the victims; translate vital information documents into different languages to assist minorities in the local authority area; or give disabled persons given a higher profile role in politics.

Taking the gender equality duty as an example, in order to properly fulfil their duty public bodies should research to see how their actions differently affect men and women, consult with employees, service-users, trade unions and other stakeholders, assess the different impact of their policies and practices on men and women, identify priorities and create objectives, draft

---

[151] 1975 Act s.32; 1976 Act s.22. The Equality Act 2006 s.48(1) has a slightly different definition, which makes little real difference.

[152] 1975 Act s.76A.

[153] 1976 Act s.71A.

[154] DDA 1995 s.49A.

[155] 1976 Act s.71A.

[156] "Gender Equality Index, July 2007", commissioned by the Equal Opportunity Commission. *http://www.gender-agenda.co.uk/downloads/GenderEqualityIndex.pdf* [Accessed October 24, 2007].

and implement an action plan to achieve these objectives, publish a gender equality scheme and review progress every three years.[157]

The EHRC enforces the public body equality duties. If after it has carried out an assessment, the Commission thinks that a public body has failed to comply with its equality duty then it can issue a notice requiring that body to comply with its duty. If it fails to comply with the notice then the EHRC can ask the courts for an order requiring that body to comply.[158] If, therefore, a person feels that a public body is not fulfilling its statutory equality duty, then they would take the matter to the EHRC for assessment.

HUMAN RIGHTS AND THE SOCIAL WORKER

10.33 The UK has been legally obliged by the European Convention on Human Rights (Convention) to ensure the effective promotion and protection of human rights within the United Kingdom, for the past 50 years. It was, however, only with the advent of the Human Rights Act 1998 ("1998 Act") that the Convention was brought into British domestic law. Until the coming into force of the 1998 Act, people could not simply take a legal action on the basis of a breach of the Convention in a British court. The 1998 Act changed this. Section 7 of the 1998 Act created new civil law rights that are directly enforceable, by those affected, against public authorities. This means that where someone feels that they have had their human rights violated by a public authority, they can take them to court.

Only the state owes human rights obligations to those within its jurisdiction. Therefore, the only person that the 1998 Act makes liable for a human rights violation is a public authority. The 1998 Act allows a "victim" to take a human rights claim against a public authority, or rely on a Convention right in any legal proceedings where their Convention rights have been violated.[159] This means that a person cannot take another private individual or company, etc. to court stating that they have violated their human rights. It is therefore important to know exactly what a public authority is under the 1998 Act. A public authority, as defined in s.6(3) of the 1998 Act, is a court or tribunal and any person who is exercising functions of a public nature. This does not include the Legislator. The 1998 Act, unfortunately, does not define what "functions of a public nature" are. This has therefore has been left for the courts to decide. Statutory bodies such as the Department of Health, inspectorates, NHS trusts and primary care trusts, hospitals, local authorities, local authority run care homes are all examples of public authorities.[160] The difficulty however comes in relation to determining when private providers of certain "contracted-out" public services are deemed to be public authorities and therefore are liable under the 1998 Act.

10.34 Functions of a public nature have been stated to include:

> "the exercise of the regulatory or coercive powers of the state. Thus, were a public authority to have power to delegate the task of regulating care homes to a private body, that regulation would be a function of a public nature. Again, it is common ground that privately run prisons perform functions of a public nature. In a similar category are private psychiatric hospitals when exercising their powers of compulsory detention under the Mental Health Act 1983: see *R (A) v Partnerships in Care Ltd* [2002] 1 WLR 2610, 2619."[161]

---

[157] "What is the Gender Equality Duty?" Leaflet published by the Equal Opportunities Commission. *http://www.equalityhumanrights.com/en/publicationsandresources/Gender/Pages/Generaladviceandinformation.aspx* [Accessed October 27, 2007].

[158] Equality Act 2006 s.32.

[159] 1998 Act s.8. A "victim" is someone who has actually suffered the consequences of the alleged breach, or there is a risk that they will be directly affected by the alleged breach in the future: *Dudgeon v UK* (7525/76) (1981) 3 E.H.R.R. 40, judgment given on October 22, 1981.

[160] *Eighteenth Report of the Joint Committee on Human Rights*, Annex: "Human Rights laws and standards in healthcare", para.8.

[161] *YL v Birmingham City Council* [2007] UKHL 27, at para.63.

While a private provider of mental health care has been found to be exercising functions of a public nature,[162] care homes operated by private companies have, however, not been deemed to be public authorities, even where residents are placed there and mostly funded by the local authority.[163] The House of Lords, in *YL v Birmingham City Council*, gave some guidance as to how to determine a function of a public nature.[164] It felt that it was relevant to consider whether the state had taken responsibility for seeing the task performed, what the public interest was in having that task undertaken, the extent to which the function was publicly funded and whether the function involved the use of any statutory coercive powers, e.g. detention under the Mental Health Act 1983.[165] This last point was seen as crucial. The majority of the Law Lords felt, in this case, that there was a distinction between the local authority's statutory duty to arrange the care and accommodation and the actual provision of such care. They determined that the actual provision of such care was not an inherently governmental function and therefore the private care home in providing such care was not performing "functions of a public nature". If the actual provision of care had been an inherent governmental function, such as the provision of certain social care services, then it is highly probable that the provider of such services would have been liable, in relation to those services, under the 1998 Act.

10.35 It should be noted that even where government bodies have contracted out certain duties they still have an obligation to ensure that people's Convention rights are effectively protected in relation to those duties.[166] This means that the private body carrying out functions of a public nature and the contracting-out public authority can both be liable for the breach of Convention rights. Where a private operator has "breached" a Convention right, the responsibility and liability for the breach still also lie on the government. This was demonstrated in *R (D & K) v Secretary of State for the Home Department*,[167] where the court awarded damages against the Secretary of State on the grounds that the real responsibility for the art.8 breach in respect of a detention centre, run by a private operator, lay with him. This means that where a governmental body contracts out any part of its statutory obligations it should bear its human rights obligations in mind and incorporate such responsibilities and liability into that contract. The courts are still reluctant to place liability for a breach of a Convention right on private actors, regardless of what functions they may undertake. This attitude may change in the future, however, as the Legislator and Executive are currently pushing for more expansive interpretation of "functions of a public nature".[168]

The 1998 Act places a duty on the courts to decide the cases before them in a way that is compatible with Convention rights, unless they are prevented from doing so by an Act of Parliament.[169] They are helped in this duty by a further obligation to interpret legislation in conformity with the Convention[170] and the European Court of Human Rights decisions.[171] This, therefore, means that where a person claims that one, or more, of their human rights under the 1998 Act has been breached by a public body, the courts will look to see whether this is true, taking the case law of the European Court of Human Rights into consideration. If the public

---

[162] *R. (on the application of A) v Partnerships in Care Ltd* [2002] 1 W.L.R. 2610.

[163] *YL v Birmingham City Council* [2007] UKHL 27.

[164] Although this guidance was given by Baroness Hale of Richmond and Lord Bingham in their dissenting judgments it was accepted to a large extent in the other Law Lords' judgments.

[165] *YL v Birmingham City Council* [2007] UKHL 27, at paras 65–71.

[166] *YL v Birmingham City Council* [2007] UKHL 27, at para.44.

[167] [2006] EWHC 980.

[168] The Secretary of State for Constitutional Affairs was an interested party, alongside the Claimant in *R (Johnston and Others) v Havering London Borough Council* [2007] EWCA Civ 26, trying to argue that the private care home was exercising functions of a public nature. For further discussion on this see the Parliamentary Joint Committee on Human Rights, Ninth Report of Session 2006–07, *The Meaning of Public Authority under the Human Rights Act*, HL Paper 77/HC 410, Ch.2. *http://www.publications.parliament.uk/pa/jt200607/jtselect/jtrights/77/77.pdf* [Accessed November 22, 2006].

[169] 1998 Act s.6.

[170] 1998 Act s.3.

[171] 1998 Act s.2(1).

body defends its action by claiming that it is acting under an Act of Parliament, the courts will take that Act into account. In their consideration, however, they will try to interpret that legislation in such a way as to make it compliant with the Convention. If they are unable to do so and the legislation is incompatible with Convention rights, the courts can issue a Declaration of Incompatibility.[172]

A Declaration of Incompatibility does not affect the validity or continued use of the legislation but merely acts as a prompt for Parliament to make legislative changes to ensure compatibility with the Convention. Only the Court of Session or the House of Lords, in Scotland, may issue a Declaration of Incompatibility. If the courts feel that the public body is not forced to violate the human right in order to comply with a piece of legislation then, where the breach is ongoing or not happened yet, they can issue an interim interdict to prevent such a breach. If the breach has already occurred and has caused damage, then an order for financial compensation can be given.

The Scottish Parliament does not have the power to legislate in a way incompatible with the Convention. Section 29(1) of the Scotland Act 1998 states that an Act of the Scottish Parliament is not law where it is incompatible with any of the Convention rights. All Bills are scrutinised before and on their introduction to the Scottish Parliament to ensure compatibility with the Convention.[173] Section 57(2) of the Scotland Act 1998 also disallows the Scottish Executive from making any subordinate legislation, or doing any act incompatible with the Convention rights.

10.36 The human rights protected under the 1998 Act ("Convention rights") are: the right to life[174]; prohibition against torture or inhuman or degrading treatment[175]; prohibition of slavery and forced labour[176]; right to liberty and security of person[177]; right to a fair trial[178]; no punishment without law[179]; right to respect for private and family life[180]; freedom of thought conscience and belief[181]; freedom of expression[182]; freedom of assembly and association[183]; right to marry[184]; prohibition of discrimination[185]; right to property[186]; right to education[187]; right to free elections[188]; abolition of the death penalty.[189] It should be noted that there is no freestanding equality and non-discrimination provision in the Convention. Although Protocol 12 to the Convention does set out a general prohibition against discrimination by public bodies, in art.1, the UK has not yet ratified this Protocol. In the UK, therefore, the prohibition of discrimination can only be invoked in relation to another human right within the Convention.

Although some human rights are absolute rights, which can not be limited, some human rights have been drafted in such a way that certain, specified, limitations are allowed. This enables a balancing process to occur where the human right in question is weighed alongside other interests. Only where an article has a limitation clause can the state lawfully interfere with that human right and then only with the legitimate aim of safeguarding one, or more, of those interests listed in that limitation clause. Usually those interests are, as found within art.8, the rights and freedoms of others; the protection of health and morals; public safety; and national

---

[172] 1998 Act s.4.
[173] Scotland Act 1998 ss.31(1) and 19.
[174] 1998 Act Sch.1 Pt I; Convention art.2.
[175] 1998 Act Sch.1 Pt I; Convention art.3.
[176] 1998 Act Sch.1 Pt I; Convention art.4.
[177] 1998 Act Sch.1 Pt I; Convention art.5.
[178] 1998 Act Sch.1 Pt I; Convention art.6.
[179] 1998 Act Sch.1 Pt I; Convention art.7.
[180] 1998 Act Sch.1 Pt I; Convention art.8.
[181] 1998 Act Sch.1 Pt I; Convention art.9.
[182] 1998 Act Sch.1 Pt I; Convention art.10.
[183] 1998 Act Sch.1 Pt I; Convention art.11.
[184] 1998 Act Sch.1 Pt I; Convention art.12.
[185] 1998 Act Sch.1 Pt I; Convention art.14.
[186] 1998 Act Sch.1 Pt II; First Protocol to the Convention art.1.
[187] 1998 Act Sch.1 Pt II; First Protocol to the Convention art.2.
[188] 1998 Act Sch.1 Pt II; First Protocol to the Convention art.3.
[189] 1998 Act Sch.1 Pt III; Thirteenth Protocol to the Convention art.1.

security. The state's interference, to protect such interests, must be in accordance with, or prescribed by, law. This means that the interference must be allowed by law and that part of the domestic law should be accessible and precise. The interference must also be "necessary in a democratic society". This has been interpreted by the European Court of Human Rights ("ECtHR") to mean that the interference must go no further than necessary to protect the relevant interest[190] and there must be some proportionality between the impact the interference has on the human right and the legitimate aim the interference is pursuing. Where the state interference in an individual's human right intrudes upon the private, intimate, life of that individual, the leeway the state is given is less and more justification is required to legitimise such interference.[191]

10.37 In general the Convention rights have been interpreted as negative rights. This means that states must merely refrain from certain actions, e.g. not torture their citizens. Some positive obligations have, however, been developed by the ECtHR under certain of the Convention rights, e.g. the right to life and the prohibition against torture. These positive obligations mean that the state must actually take certain steps to ensure the right in question. For example, a state has positive obligations under many articles of the Convention to take steps to prevent violations of an individual's human rights by other private individuals. These include taking general steps, such as enacting laws to punish and deter such violations: as in *X and Y v The Netherlands* (8978/80),[192] where Dutch law did not afford an effective remedy to a mentally disabled girl who had been raped by a relative of the directress of the care home where she lived. They also include making effective use of the steps which the law provides: as in *Z v United Kingdom* (29392/95),[193] where a local social services authority did not use its powers to protect children whom they knew to be at risk of serious abuse and neglect.[194]

As the area of human rights law is huge, we can only briefly touch on some of the relevant aspects of the law in relation to social work. In particular we will look in more detail at the right to life[195]; prohibition against torture or inhuman or degrading treatment[196]; right to liberty and security of person[197]; and the right to respect for private and family life.[198] Many public bodies already have dedicated human rights training and resources for their staff[199] and you should use these resources, where available, to increase and maintain your knowledge in this area.

Article 2—the right to life

10.38 The right to life is one of the most fundamental Convention rights; without your life you do not need human rights. The rest of the Convention rights, to varying extents, simply impact on the quality of life you have. Article 2 protects the right to life; it does not protect the converse of that, the right to die,[200] nor does it prohibit abortion. In art.2 of the Convention, the right to life is phrased as: "Everyone's right to life shall be protected by law. No one shall be deprived of his life intentionally . . . ". The only exceptions to this are where the death penalty is provided for in law, which it is not within the UK, and where the loss of life resulted "from the use of force, which is no more than absolutely necessary" in the defence of a person from unlawful violence,

---

[190] D. Hoffman and J. Rowe, *Human Rights in the UK: An Introduction to the Human Rights Act 1998*, 2nd edn (Harlow: Pearson Longman, 2006), p.105.

[191] *Dudgeon v UK* (7525/76) (1981) 3 E.H.R.R. 40, judgment given on October 22, 1981.

[192] (1986) 8 E.H.R.R. 235, judgment given on March 26, 1985.

[193] [2001] 2 F.L.R. 612, judgment given on May 10, 2001.

[194] *YL v Birmingham City Council* [2007] UKHL 27, at para.57.

[195] 1998 Act Sch.1 Pt I; Convention art.2.

[196] 1998 Act Sch.1 Pt I; Convention art.3.

[197] 1998 Act Sch.1 Pt I; Convention art.5.

[198] 1998 Act Sch.1 Pt I; Convention art.8.

[199] For example, the NHSLA provide a free Human Rights Act information service to the NHS. It is, at present, freely available to members of the public. It includes a database of relevant human rights cases and fact sheets at *http://www.nhsla.com/HumanRights/* [Accessed November 6, 2007].

[200] *Pretty v UK* (2346/02) [2002] 2 F.L.R. 45, judgment given on April 29, 2002.

or to effect a lawful arrest or to prevent the escape of a lawfully detailed person or in lawful action taken for the purpose of quelling a riot or insurrection.

In order to make the right to life effective the European Court of Human Rights has imposed procedural obligations on a state to have criminal laws in place to prevent killings, undertake effective investigations into a killing sufficient to identify and bring the culprit to court and provide effective remedies for the killing.[201] It has also imposed a duty on the state to safeguard those people within its jurisdiction.[202] This duty includes taking operational measures to protect a life at risk from criminal acts of another,[203] such as removing a child from their family where the authorities knew, or ought to have known, at that time of an immediate risk to the life of that child from a member of their immediate family.[204] The ECtHR has stressed, however, that such positive obligations are not to be interpreted in a way as to impose an impossible or disproportionate burden on the state. It recognises that there is a range of policy decisions relating to the use of state resources, which states have to assess on the basis of their aims and priorities. It does however place an obligation upon states to take account of democratic values and the Convention rights when developing future aims and in the allocation of resources. As a subset of this overarching positive obligation, the state also has a growing responsibility to minimise or reduce any serious risks to health, particularly when the state is in some way responsible for those risks, e.g. through exposure to nuclear radiation, etc.[205]

10.39 The state has more responsibility for those directly within its care than otherwise. Where a person is in the custody of the state, whether in prison, remand centre, psychiatric hospital or care home, etc., certain safeguards have to be in place to protect that person's life and, if they die, a proper investigation or inquest carried out. The ECtHR has accepted that a state may be legally responsible for negligent health professionals or negligent co-ordination of work but not where that state had taken all reasonable steps to ensure a high level of professional standards. Where appropriate mechanisms and procedures are in place, a state will therefore not be held liable. States do, however, have a duty to investigate and establish the cause of death of those within its care, allocate blame and apportion liability to the relevant individuals.

Edwards v United Kingdom (46477/99)[206] is an example of where the state was held liable for a death in custody. In this case, Edwards, a mentally ill person, was arrested and remanded in custody. He was killed by his cellmate, who also had a mental illness, known about, but not picked up in the screening. His cellmate had a history of violence and had previously seriously assaulted a cellmate. Although the police, Crown Prosecution Service and the magistrates all knew the cellmate's history, the prison had not been made aware of the cellmate's criminal, medical or violent history. The prison similarly did not pick up on Edwards' vulnerability due to his mental illness. The ECtHR held that the failure of the agencies involved in this case (medical profession, police, prosecution and court) to pass information about the cellmate on to the prison authorities and the inadequate nature of the screening process on the cellmate's arrival in prison breached the state's obligation to protect the life of Edwards.[207] Public authorities must take reasonable measures to protect those within their custody from self-harm, either by force feeding or placing them on suicide watch.[208] Therefore as social workers you must always ensure that there are policies and procedures in place to ensure the protection of those within your care not just in relation to their life but also in relation to the quality of their care, as seen below.

[201] *Kalac v Turkey* (20704/9) (1999) 27 E.H.R.R. 552, judgment given on July 1, 1997; *Gulec v Turkey* (21593/93) (1999) 28 E.H.R.R. 121, judgment given on July 27, 1998; *Isayeva v Russia* (57950/00) (2005) 41 E.H.R.R. 39, judgment given on February 24, 2005.

[202] *Pretty v UK* (2346/02) [2002] 2 F.L.R. 45, judgment given on April 29, 2002; *LCB v UK* (23413/94) (1999) 27 E.H.R.R. 212, judgment given on June 9, 1998.

[203] *Osman v UK* (23452/94) [1999] 1 F.L.R. 193, judgment given on June 9, 1998.

[204] This test arose out of the *Osman* case.

[205] *LCB v UK* (23413/94) (1999) 27 E.H.R.R. 212, judgment given on June 9, 1998; *Guerra v Italy* (14967/89) (1998) 26 E.H.R.R. 357, judgment given on February 19, 1998.

[206] (2002) 35 E.H.R.R. 19, judgment given on March 14, 2002.

[207] *Edwards v UK* (46477/99) (2002) 35 E.H.R.R. 19, judgment given on March 14, 2002, at para.66.

[208] R. Reed and J. Murdock, *A Guide to Human Rights Law in Scotland* (Edinburgh: Butterworths, 2001), p.163.

Additionally, most importantly, you should follow such policies and procedures and abide by the values that underpin them when carrying out your duties.

Article 3—prohibition against torture

10.40 The duty under art.3 is concise and succinct: "No one shall be subject to torture or to inhuman or degrading treatment or punishment." There are no limitations to this article; it is an absolute right. The Convention prohibits in absolute terms torture or inhuman or degrading treatment regardless of the victim's conduct.[209] A state has a duty to protect those within its jurisdiction from any foreseeable risk of such treatment occurring, i.e. preventing private individuals from violating this human right by operation of an effective criminal legal system. In particular, however, once a person is in the custody or power of a state then they should be safe from physical and mental ill-treatment; if this duty is breached, the state is liable. Ignorance of illegal actions is not an acceptable excuse—public authorities are strictly liable for the conduct of their subordinates.[210]

Article 3 has three distinct categories of prohibited treatment: torture; inhuman treatment; and degrading treatment. The definitions of these categories were set out by the European Court of Human Rights in *Ireland v United Kingdom* (5310/71),[211] and have been followed and developed in subsequent cases. The ill-treatment categories cascade down with torture, the most serious category, at the top of the scale. Torture is seen as an aggravated form of inhuman or degrading treatment or punishment. Torture was defined, in the *Ireland* case, as "deliberate inhuman treatment causing very serious and cruel suffering".[212] The distinction between it and the other categories was found to derive principally from a difference in the intensity of the suffering inflicted.[213] Normally torture will be associated with the purpose of obtaining information or inflicting punishment. Torture may be a one-off event or an accumulation of inhumane and degrading treatment.[214] Suffering can be physical, mental or both.

10.41 Inhuman treatment was similarly defined, in the *Ireland* case, as being treatment that causes intense physical and mental suffering.[215] Usually inhuman and degrading treatment is simply grouped together as one combined category of ill-treatment. Ill-treatment must attain a minimum level of severity if it is to fall within the scope of art.3. The assessment of this minimum is relative: it depends on all the circumstances of the case, such as the duration of the treatment, its physical and/or mental effects and, in some cases, the sex, age and state of health of the victim.[216] Degrading treatment has been described by the ECtHR as treatment that arouses feelings of fear, anguish and inferiority capable of humiliating or debasing the victim and possibly breaking their physical or moral resistance or driving the victim to act against his will or conscience.[217] In considering whether a punishment or treatment is "degrading" within the meaning of art.3, the court will take into consideration whether its object was to humiliate and debase the person concerned and whether, as far as the consequences are concerned, it adversely affected his or her personality in a manner incompatible with art.3. There does not however need to be a specific intention to humiliate or debase the person in question for the treatment to be held to be degrading. For instance, lack of appropriate medical care may amount to treatment contrary to art.3.[218]

When looking at whether the treatment or punishment concerned is incompatible with art.3 you should take into consideration the "victim's" vulnerability and their inability to complain

---

[209] *Chahal v UK* (22414/93) (1997) 23 E.H.R.R. 413, judgment given on March 14, 2002.
[210] *Ireland v UK* (5310/71) (1979–80) 2 E.H.R.R. 25, judgment given on January 18, 1978, at para.159.
[211] (1979–80) 2 E.H.R.R. 25, judgment given on January 18, 1978.
[212] *Ireland v UK* (5310/71) (1979–80) 2 E.H.R.R. 25, judgment given on January 18, 1978, at para.167.
[213] *Ireland v UK* (5310/71) (1979–80) 2 E.H.R.R. 25, judgment given on January 18, 1978, at para.167.
[214] *Aydin v Turkey* (23178/94) (1998) 25 E.H.R.R. 251, judgment given on September 25, 1997.
[215] *Ireland v UK* (5310/71) (1979–80) 2 E.H.R.R. 25, judgment given on January 18, 1978, at para.167.
[216] *Tekin v Turkey* (22496/93) (2001) 31 E.H.R.R. 4, judgment given on June 9, 1998.
[217] *Keenan v UK* (27229/95) (2001) 33 E.H.R.R. 38, judgment given on April 3, 2001, at para.110.
[218] *İlhan v Turkey* (22277/93) (2002) 34 E.H.R.R. 36, judgment given on June 27, 2000.

coherently, or at all, about how they are being affected by any particular treatment.[219] In your work as a social worker you therefore need to take into consideration a person's vulnerability and ability to express their true feelings when agreeing on a course of action or drawing up a care plan. In *Keenan v United Kingdom* (27229/95)[220] the ECtHR held that the lack of effective monitoring of a mentally ill prisoner, including the dearth of properly kept records, and the lack of informed psychiatric input into his assessment and treatment disclosed significant defects in the medical care provided. It held that those factors, together with the imposition of serious disciplinary punishment, constituted inhuman and degrading treatment and punishment. In *Price v United Kingdom* (43185/98, 43186/98)[221] the ECtHR found that where a severally disabled person in detention risked developing bedsores, was unable to go to the toilet or keep clean except with great difficulty and was dangerously cold, this was degrading treatment and therefore violated art.3. The living conditions experienced by persons within the power of public authorities can therefore violate art.3. This needs to be taken into consideration in relation to the provision of social care services, as does the fact that cost and inconvenience are not relevant to an art.3 consideration.[222] Adherence to art.3 requires that a basic minimum level of care must be provided. Article 3 is an absolute duty; lack of funds is not an allowable justification for violating this duty.

10.42 Article 3, like art.2, contains positive duties such as the duty to investigate and punish alleged violations, as discussed above in para.10.57. States are required to take measures designed to ensure that individuals within their jurisdiction are not subjected to torture or inhuman or degrading treatment, including ill-treatment administered by private individuals.[223] This "prevention" duty includes taking operational measures to protect a person from the ill-treatment of another, using the *Osman* test. In *Z v United Kingdom* (29392/95)[224] the ECtHR supported the assertion that these operational measures "should provide effective protection, in particular, of children and other vulnerable persons and include reasonable steps to prevent ill-treatment of which the authorities had or ought to have had knowledge".[225] In this case, the neglect and abuse suffered by the four children reached the threshold of inhuman and degrading treatment. This treatment was brought to the local authority's attention. It was under a statutory duty to protect the children and had a range of powers available to it, including the removal of the children from their home. The children were, however, only taken into emergency care four and a half years after their condition was first brought to the local authority's attention. The court found that the failure of the system to protect those children from serious, long-term neglect and abuse was a violation of art.3.

In the similar case of *E v United Kingdom* (33218/96)[226] the ECtHR held that, where the live-in partner of a mother with children had been found guilty of sexual offences and he was continuing to have close contact with the children, social services should have been aware that the children remained at potential risk. Social services failed to take steps that would have enabled them to discover the exact extent of the problem and, potentially, to prevent further abuse taking place. The court found that the lack of investigation, communication and co-operation by the relevant authorities had a significant influence on the course of events and that proper and effective management of their responsibilities might avoided, or at least minimised, the damage suffered. The court therefore held that there was a breach of art.3 in this case.[227] It should be noted that the human rights system does take account of and acknowledges the difficult and sensitive decisions facing social services and the important countervailing principle

---

[219] *Keenan v UK* (27229/95) (2001) 33 E.H.R.R. 38, judgment given on April 3, 2001, at para.111.
[220] (2001) 33 E.H.R.R. 38, judgment given on April 3, 2001.
[221] (2002) 35 E.H.R.R. CD316, judgment given on July 29, 2003.
[222] *Napier v Scottish Ministers* [2002] U.K.H.R.R. 308.
[223] *A v UK* (25599/94) [1996] 3 F.C.R. 569, judgment given on September 23, 1998.
[224] [2001] 2 F.L.R. 612, judgment given on May 10, 2001.
[225] *Z v UK* (29392/95) [2001] 2 F.L.R. 612, judgment given on May 10, 2001, at para.70.
[226] [2003] 1 F.L.R. 348, ECHR, judgment given on November 26, 2002.
[227] *E v UK* (33218/96) [2003] 1 F.L.R. 348, ECHR, judgment given on November 26, 2002, at para.100.

of respecting and preserving family life; it simply operates to enforce certain minimum conditions and the creation and operation of effective protection systems. While, however, public authorities owe a duty of care to those vulnerable people that they have a duty to protect, they do not owe a duty to other associated people, such as parents, in relation to their investigation of allegations of abuse.[228]

The treatment of a protesting patient under the Mental Health Act 1983 is a potential invasion of his rights under arts 3 and 8.[229] The giving of medical treatment without consent where it is medically necessary and in the best interests of the individual does not, however, normally breach art.3.[230] The correct test for determining if treatment should be given to a detained mental patient, against their will, is whether it has "convincingly been shown that the treatment is a medical necessity".[231] Inadequate health care in relation to those in detention can be a violation of art.3[232] depending on the particular circumstances of each case. The denial of state support to people lacking other means of subsistence or shelter has been consistently held in British domestic law to be a violation of art.3.[233]

Article 5—right to liberty

10.43 The right to liberty and security of person, held within art.5 of the Convention, is a qualified right. A person can be deprived of his liberty, in accordance with a procedure set out in law, where he has been:

(1) lawfully detained after conviction by a competent court; or
(2) lawfully arrested or detained for non-compliance with the lawful order of a court or in order to secure the fulfilment of any obligation prescribed by law; or
(3) lawfully arrested or detained for the purpose of bringing him before the competent legal authority on reasonable suspicion of having committed an offence or when it is reasonably considered necessary[234] to prevent his committing an offence or fleeing after having done so; or
(4) where the person is a minor, detained by lawful order for the purpose of educational supervision or his lawful detention for the purpose of bringing him before the competent legal authority; or
(5) lawfully detained to prevent the spreading of infectious diseases, of persons of unsound mind, alcoholics or drug addicts or vagrants; and
(6) lawfully arrested or detained to prevent his effecting an unauthorised entry into the country or of a person against whom action is being taken with a view to deportation or extradition.

---

[228] *D v East Berkshire Community NHS Trust* [2005] UKHL 23.

[229] *R (on the application of Wilkinson) v (1) Responsible Medical Officer Broadmoor Hospital, (2) The Mental Health Act Commission Second Opinion Appointed Doctor & Secretary of State for Health (interested party)* [2001] EWCA Civ 1545.

[230] *Herczegfalvy v Austria* (10533/83) (1993) 15 E.H.R.R. 437, judgment given on September 24, 1992. The ECtHR stated in this case that "as a general rule, a measure which is a therapeutic necessity cannot be regarded as inhuman or degrading. The Court must nevertheless satisfy itself that the medical necessity has been convincingly shown to exist", at para.82.

[231] *R (on the application of N) v M* [2002] EWCA Civ 1789.

[232] *McGlinchey v UK* (50390/99) (2003) 37 E.H.R.R. 41, judgment given on April 29, 2003.

[233] *R. (on the application of Limbuela) v Secretary of State for the Home Department* [2005] UKHL 66 as discussed in J. Wadnam et al, *Blackstone's Guide to The Human Rights Act 1998*, 4th edn (Oxford: Oxford University Press, 2007), p.126.

[234] Reasonable suspicion has been interpreted by the ECtHR to presuppose "the existence of facts or information that would satisfy an objective observer that the person concerned may have committed the offence. What may be regarded as 'reasonable' will however depend upon all the circumstances": *Fox, Campbell and Hartley v UK* (12244/86, 12245/86, 12383/86) (1991) 13 E.H.R.R. 157, judgment given on August 30, 1990, para.32.

This list of limitations is an exhaustive one; if the deprivation of liberty does not fall within the six limitations stated above then it is a breach of art.5.[235]

Article 5 also sets out certain procedural safeguards that apply to all criminal cases. Every person who is arrested shall be informed promptly, in a language that he understands, of the reasons for his arrest and of any charge against him.[236] Everyone arrested or detained in accordance with the provisions of para.1(c) of art.5 shall be brought promptly before a judge or other officer authorised by law to exercise judicial power and shall be entitled to trial within a reasonable time or to release pending trial. Release may be conditioned by guarantees to appear for trial.[237] Every person who is deprived of his liberty by arrest or detention shall be entitled to take proceedings by which the lawfulness of his detention shall be decided speedily by a court and his release ordered if the detention is not lawful.[238] Everyone who has been the victim of arrest or detention in contravention of the provisions of this article shall have an enforceable right to compensation.[239]

10.44 Article 5, as a whole, requires an overall consideration of the necessity and proportionality of the arrest and/or length of detention.[240] It is designed to provide protection against arbitrary interference of either a substantive or procedural nature by a public authority.[241] Article 15 of the Convention allows a state to derogate from certain of its obligations under the Convention in a time of war or public emergency. The current UK Government has made use of this section to derogate from its art.5 obligations on the basis that there is a terrorist treat to the UK constituting a public emergency.[242] In particular, the derogation is to cover the exercise of the extended power to detain contained in the Anti-terrorism, Crime and Security Acts.

The first question to ask, in relation to art.5, is whether there has been a deprivation of liberty. The ECtHR has made it clear that deprivation of liberty may take numerous forms other than classic detention in prison or strict arrest.[243] Although deprivation of liberty is different from simply restricting someone's freedom of movement, restriction of movement can be held to be a deprivation of liberty; it depends on degree and intensity of the restrictions. In assessing whether art.5 has been breached, account should be taken of a whole range of factors such as the nature, duration, effects and manner of execution or implementation of the penalty or measure in question on the actual person detained.[244] Control orders have, for instance, been seen as a deprivation of liberty by the House of Lords.[245]

The second question to ask is whether the detention has been made in compliance with law. The law in question must be sufficiently clear and precise to allow an individual to reasonably foresee that the deprivation of liberty would be the consequence of his actions.[246] Additionally, the deprivation of liberty must be proportionate, made in good faith and comply with art.5 of the Convention. Proportionality is measured by comparing the means and aim of the detention with the consequences that the interference would have on that person's art.5 right. Once the lawful reason for the detention has passed, the person should no longer be detained.[247] A person

---

[235] *Ciulla v Italy* (1991) 13 E.H.R.R. 346 (11152/84), judgment given February 22, 1989.

[236] Convention art.5(2).

[237] Convention art.5(3).

[238] Convention art.5(4).

[239] Convention art.5(5).

[240] Hoffman and Rowe, *Human Rights in the UK* (2006), p.159.

[241] Reed and Murdock, *A Guide to Human Rights Law in Scotland* (2001), p.203.

[242] Human Rights Act 1998 (Designated Derogation) Order 2001 (SI 2001/3644).

[243] *Guzzardi v Italy* (7367/76) (1981) 3 E.H.R.R. 333, judgment given on November 6, 1980, at para.95.

[244] *Engel v the Netherlands* (5100/71, 5101/71, 5102/71), judgment given on June 8, 1976, at para.59; *Guzzardi v Italy* (7367/76) (1981) 3 E.H.R.R. 333, judgment given on November 6, 1980, at paras 92, 94.

[245] *Secretary of State for the Home Department v JJ* [2007] UKHL 45.

[246] *Steel v UK* (68416/01) [2005] E.M.L.R. 15, judgment given on February 15, 2005.

[247] *Weeks v UK* (9787/82) (1988) 10 E.H.R.R. 293, judgment given on March 2, 1987; *Stafford v UK* (46295/99) (2002) 35 E.H.R.R. 32, judgment given on May 28, 2002.

whose conviction has been quashed on appeal has, however, been legally detained until that point.[248]

10.45 In relation to a minor being detained under art.5(1)(d), the concept of "educational supervision" must not be equated rigidly with notions of classroom teaching. The concept is wider than simply traditional education; it can cover many aspects of a local authority's exercise of parental rights for the benefit and protection of the child involved.[249] While a minor can be held lawfully in a detention centre under this section, the centre must either apply some sort of educational regime or merely be a precursor to such a regime.[250]

Article 5(1)(e) deals with the most important category in relation to social work, the lawful detention of those of unsound mind, alcoholics, drug addicts and vagrants, etc. Most of the case law in this area relates to the detention of those of unsound mind. The ECtHR allows states a great deal of leeway in deciding the definition of "unsound mind". At the same time it disallows the detention of a person simply because his views or behaviour deviate from the norms prevailing in a particular society.[251] In *Winterwerp v Netherlands* (6301/73), the ECtHR set out certain minimum conditions that must be fulfilled in relation to determining whether a person can be lawfully be detailed due to an "unsound mind":

> "In the Court's opinion, except in emergency cases, the individual concerned should not be deprived of his liberty unless he has been reliably shown to be of 'unsound mind'. The very nature of what has to be established before the competent national authority—that is, a true mental disorder—calls for objective medical expertise. Further, the mental disorder must be of a kind or degree warranting compulsory confinement. What is more, the validity of continued confinement depends upon the persistence of such a disorder."[252]

10.46 In principle the detention of a person of unsound mind will only be lawful if that person is detained in a hospital, clinic or other appropriate institution.[253] This is to emphasise the fact that persons of unsound mind should be in therapeutic detention regimes.[254] The mental condition does not have to be treatable to be justified under art.5; the detention can be for the purposes of control and supervision to avoid danger to the individual concerned or others.[255] Article 5 is concerned mostly with ensuring that the loss of liberty is carefully scrutinised. It is crucial that there are effective mental health detention procedures in place and that they are adhered to, to ensure that a person is not unlawfully detained. However, the courts are cognisant that there must be room for mental health specialists to manoeuvre in order that they can act in the best interests of the patient and the public.[256] In *Johnston v United Kingdom*, the ECtHR stated that:

> "a responsible authority is entitled to exercise a similar measure of discretion in deciding whether in the light of all the relevant circumstances and the interests at stake it would in fact be appropriate to order the immediate and absolute discharge of a person who is no longer suffering from the mental disorder which led to his confinement. That authority should be able to retain some measure of supervision over the progress of the person once he is released into the community and to that end make his discharge subject to conditions. It cannot be excluded either that the imposition of a particular condition may in certain circumstances justify a deferral of discharge from detention, having regard to the nature of the condition and to the reasons for imposing it. It is, however, of paramount importance that appropriate safeguards are in place so as to ensure that any deferral of discharge is

---

[248] *Benham v UK* (19380/92) (1996) 22 E.H.R.R. 293, judgment given on June 10, 1996.
[249] *Koniarska v UK* (33670/96) (2000) 30 E.H.R.R. CD139, judgment given on October 12, 2000.
[250] *Bouamar v Belgium* (9106/80) (1989) 11 E.H.R.R. 1, judgment given on February 29, 1988, at para.50.
[251] *Winterwerp v Netherlands* (6301/73) (1979–80) 2 E.H.R.R. 387, judgment given on October 24, 1979.
[252] *Winterwerp v Netherlands* (6301/73) (1979–80) 2 E.H.R.R. 387, at para.39.
[253] *Winterwerp v Netherlands* (6301/73) (1979–80) 2 E.H.R.R. 387.
[254] This can be adduced from the ECtHR's judgment in *Ashingdane v UK* (8225/78) (1985) 7 E.H.R.R. 528, judgment given on May 18, 1985.
[255] *Reid v UK* (50272/99) (2003) 37 E.H.R.R. 9, judgment given on February 20, 2003.
[256] *Johnston v UK* (119/1996/738/937), judgment given on October 24, 1997.

consonant with the purpose of Article 5 § 1 and with the aim of the restriction in sub-paragraph (e) and, in particular, that discharge is not unreasonably delayed."[257]

10.47 Article 5 not only sets out the categories in which detention is legal, it also lays down certain procedural guarantees that need to be adhered to in relation to depriving someone of their liberty. Although art.5(2) states that anyone arrested is entitled to be promptly advised of the reasons for their arrest, this right has been interpreted in such a way as to ensure that all detainees, under art.5(1), should be informed of the reasons for their detention at the first available opportunity.[258] This wider application of art.5(2) is part of the art.5(4) right whereby every person detained is entitled to take proceedings by which the lawfulness of his detention shall be speedily decided by a court and his release ordered, if the detention is unlawful. A court, for the purposes of this article, is given a wider interpretation than simply the usual meaning of the word. Whether a decision-making body qualifies as a court is primarily a question of whether it is impartial and independent, provides appropriate judicial procedures and procedural guarantees and has the authority to order the release of the detainee. The specific procedures required vary in relation to the type of detention in question.

Article 5(4) places a duty on states to review detention. The question the courts have to answer is, looking at the reason for the detention, is the reason sufficient in law to justify the detention?[259] This review duty does not just exist at the start of the detention but may also involve a periodic review structure, particularly to inquire whether the reason for a person's detention still exists, e.g. if a person is still of unsound mind. In relation to mental health, art.5(4) does require periodic reviews[260] although the ECtHR has given little guidance on how often those reviews should be. Generally, the review system must be flexible enough to ensure that a person's individual circumstances can be taken into consideration.

Article 8—right to personal autonomy

10.48 Article 8 is, to a certain extent, a "catch all" human right that enables individuals to have the space free from state interference, to live, develop, express themselves and enter into relationships with others. It is the right to personal autonomy and protects the quality of life of an individual.[261] Under art.8: "Everyone has the right to respect for his private and family life, his home and his correspondence." Article 8(2) however specifies certain express limitations to that right. The state has to refrain from interfering with an individual's rights, except where such interference is in accordance with the law and is necessary in a democratic society in the interests of national security, public safety, the economic well-being of the country, for the prevention of disorder or crime, for the protection of health or morals, or for the the protection of the rights and freedoms of others. While the art.8 right has been interpreted widely—from the prohibition of publication of wedding photos in the certain media[262] to the non-criminalisation of same sex relationships[263]—the limitations to it are to be strictly construed.

A state does not simply have a duty of non-interference; it also has a positive right to act to protect the private lives of those under its jurisdiction. "In determining whether or not a positive obligation exists, regard must be had to the fair balance that has to be struck between the general interest of the community and the interests of the individual."[264] This balance between the individual's right to autonomy and privacy and the community's interests is one that lies at the very heart of art.8 and, indeed, the entire Convention.

The right to respect of private life covers the physical and moral integrity of an individual. It

---

[257] *Johnson v UK* (119/1996/738/937), judgment given on October 24, 1997, at para.63.
[258] *X v UK* (7215/75) (1981) 3 E.H.R.R. 63, judgment given on November 5, 1981, at para.66.
[259] Hoffman and Rowe, *Human Rights in the UK* (2006), p.172.
[260] *Megyeri v Germany* (13770/88) (1993) 15 E.H.R.R. 584, judgment given on May 12, 1992, at para.22.
[261] *Pretty v UK* (2346/02) [2002] 2 F.L.R. 45, judgment given on April 29, 2002.
[262] *Douglas v Hello! Ltd* [2007] UKHL 21.
[263] *Dudgeon v UK* (7525/76) (1981) 3 E.H.R.R. 40, judgment given on October 22, 1981.
[264] *Cossey v UK* (10843/84) [1991] 2 F.L.R. 492, judgment given on September 27, 1990, at para.37.

is primarily intended to ensure the development, without outside interference, of the personality of each person in his relations with other people and the outside world.[265] This includes a person's sex life,[266] sexual identity[267] and mental health.[268] In relation to interferences with "a most intimate part of an individual's private life", such as a person's sex life, "particularly serious reasons" must exist before those interferences can satisfy the requirements of art.8(2) of the Convention.[269]

10.49 A "vulnerable person" or person under the power or care of a public authority has an art.8 right to be treated with dignity and respect and have the opportunity to develop their own personality and social relations with others. This means that they should have access to essential economic and social activities and to an appropriate range of recreational and cultural activities.[270] The courts, however, accept that public authorities are under resource constraints and therefore need to undertake a prioritisation of resources exercise.[271] While art.8 may be relevant to complaints about the adequacy of public funding for health services, or the delay in providing such health care, it does not guarantee a right to free medical care.[272] The courts will merely look and see if the state has struck a fair balance between the needs of the individual and the community, taking the weight of each interest into account. The courts do not, however, feel that it is appropriate for decisions regarding financial resources to be taken by the judiciary, and usually decline to substitute their own view for that of the public authority.[273]

The paucity of financial resources does not affect the duty of public authorities to take into account art.8 and its concepts of personal autonomy and dignity, both in relation to their decision making and to ensure their actions are appropriate and proportionate. This can be illustrated by the case of *R. (on the application of Madden) v Bury MBC*,[274] where the court held that the council should have entered into a meaningful consultation with the elderly residents of its care homes following a decision to close those homes.

10.50 The right to respect for family life is very important in relation to child custody cases, marriage and divorce. Article 8 imposes a duty on the state to take into account how a family may be affected by its decisions. A "family" encompasses those who are married and/or living together and/or parents to a child, regardless of whether the parent's relationship is ongoing or not[275] or whether the child is living with one or other of the parents or living in care.[276] The courts will take account of de facto family ties and include near relatives, e.g. grandparents, within the definition of "family", where they are seen as an integral part of that family unit.[277] This part of art.8 usually operates to protect the right of the family to live together and, for instance, not allow separation through deportation[278] or be consulted in relation to a public authority decision that will affect the future of that family.[279] Article 8 also operates to allow a "non-custody" divorced parent access to and contact time with their children. The state must

---

[265] *Botta v Italy* (21439/93) (1998) 26 E.H.R.R. 241, judgment given on February 24, 1998; *Bensaid v UK* (44599/98) (2001) 33 E.H.R.R. 10, judgment given on February 6, 2001.

[266] *Lustig-Prean and Beckett v UK* (31417/96, 32377/96) (2000) 29 E.H.R.R. 548, judgment given on September 27, 1999.

[267] *Christine Goodwin v UK* (28957/95) [2002] I.R.L.R. 664, judgment given on July 11, 2002.

[268] *Bensaid v UK* (44599/98) (2001) 33 E.H.R.R. 10, judgment given on February 6, 2001.

[269] *Bensaid v UK* (2001) 33 E.H.R.R. 10, para.82.

[270] Justice Munby, *Human Rights and Social Welfare Law: The Impact of Article 8* (Social Care Institute for Excellence, 2006).

[271] *R. (on the application of F) v Oxfordshire Mental Healthcare NHS Trust* [2001] EWHC Admin 535.

[272] *Valentina Pentiacova v Moldova* (14462/03) (2005) 40 E.H.R.R. SE23, judgment given on January 4, 2005.

[273] For an example of this, see *R. (on the application of F) v Oxfordshire Mental Healthcare NHS Trust* [2001] EWHC Admin 535.

[274] [2002] EWHC 1882 (Admin).

[275] *Keenan v UK* (27229/95) (2001) 33 E.H.R.R. 38, judgment given on April 3, 2001.

[276] *Olsson v Sweden (No.1)* (10465/83) (1989) 11 E.H.R.R. 259, judgment given on March 24, 1988.

[277] *Marckx v Belgium* (6833/74) (1979–80) 2 E.H.R.R. 330, judgment given on June 13, 1979.

[278] *Nasri v France* (19465/92) (1996) 21 E.H.R.R. 458, judgment given on July 13, 1995.

[279] *TP and KM v UK* (28945/95) [2001] 2 F.L.R. 549, judgment given on May 10, 2001.

have very weighty reasons, which fall within art.8(2), to deny a parent contact with their children.

The decision to take a child into care, and any decisions made while they are in care, must be taken considering the best interests of the child; it is not enough that the child simply would be better off in care.[280] The best interests of the child are of paramount importance and override their parents' art.8 rights, when necessary. Although the state is allowed some discretion in relation to its decisions in this area, the ECtHR is consistent in requiring a state, where the child is not to be adopted, to regard the care decision as temporary and ensure that procedures are in place to allow parents and child easy and regular access to each other.[281]

The parents retain their parental and access rights under art.8 and it is only when it is in the best interests of the child for access not to be permitted, that these parental rights can be overridden. The ECtHR has stated that while art.8 contains no explicit procedural requirements, the decision-making process involved in measures of interference must be fair and afford due respect to the interests safeguarded by art.8.[282] It gave further guidance as to what this procedural duty entails in *W v United Kingdom*:

> "There are three factors which have a bearing on the practicalities of the matter. Firstly, there will clearly be instances where the participation of the natural parents in the decision-making process either will not be possible or will not be meaningful—as, for example, where they cannot be traced or are under a physical or mental disability or where an emergency arises. Secondly, decisions in this area, whilst frequently taken in the light of case reviews or case conferences, may equally well evolve from a continuous process of monitoring on the part of the local authority's officials. Thirdly, regular contacts between the social workers responsible and the parents often provide an appropriate channel for the communication of the latter's views to the authority ... [W]hat has to be determined is whether, having regard to the particular circumstances of the case and notably the serious nature of the decisions to be taken, the parents have been involved in the decision-making process, seen as a whole, to a degree sufficient to provide them with the requisite protection of their interests. If they have not, there will have been a failure to respect their family life and the interference resulting from the decision will not be capable of being regarded as 'necessary' within the meaning of Article 8."[283]

10.51 This means that where social workers' decisions have an impact on family life, the family members should be consulted and involved in the decision-making process to the fullest extent practically possible.

The "home" category of art.8 has been given a broad interpretation by the courts; it is not limited to a place in which a person is living at that time, as long as you have sufficient "continuing links", i.e. intend to return and think of it as home.[284] It can cover personal business premises.[285] For a property to qualify as a home an individual need not actually own the property in question but just have strong ties to it.[286] A property will not qualify, however, by reason merely of a person's right to a home or housing. Where, however, local authorities have a duty to provide housing, they cannot discriminate in their allocation policies or procedures, under art.14 of the Convention.

Social workers should be aware that respect for "home" stretches to encompass a particular residence where the person has become settled. In *R. v North and East Devon HA Ex p. Coughlan*,[287] the court found that the health board had breached a paraplegic patient's art.8

[280] *Johansen v Norway* (17383/90) (1997) 23 E.H.R.R. 33, judgment given on August 7, 1996.
[281] *Johansen v Norway* (17383/90) (1997) 23 E.H.R.R. 33, judgment given on August 7, 1996.
[282] *TP and KM v UK* (28945/95) [2001] 2 F.L.R. 549, judgment given on May 10, 2001, at para.72.
[283] *W v United Kingdom* (9749/82) (1988) 10 E.H.R.R. 29, judgment given July 8, 1987, at para.64.
[284] *Gillow v UK* (9063/80) (1989) 11 E.H.R.R. 335, judgment given on November 24, 1986.
[285] *Niemietz v Germany* (13710/88) (1993) 16 E.H.R.R. 97, judgment given on December 16, 1992.
[286] *Mentes v Turkey* (23186/94) (1998) 26 E.H.R.R. 595, judgment given on November 28, 1997.
[287] [2000] All E.R. 850.

right by moving her after she had become accustomed to living where she was and they had been promised her that she could stay there permanently. This case means that great care has to be taken when moving a person in local authority accommodation. Whether a person is in local authority housing or a care home, any decision to move them must take account of their art.8 rights; consultation is therefore advised as a minimum.

The "correspondence" element of art.8 is the right to uninterrupted and uncensored communication with others; this therefore normally prevents the tapping of a person's phone, a surveillance operation or opening of mail, monitoring of emails, etc. by the state. Considerations of national security can obviously act here as a limiting factor but the interference must be "in accordance with law". The domestic law allowing such monitoring must fulfil the tests of accessibility and foreseeability and clearly set out the scope and explain how the power is to be exercised.[288] The law must be particularly precise and the surveillance properly managed and conducted in line with the law.[289]

The issue of interference with correspondence is clearly engaged in relation to the opening of prisoners' mail. While the ECtHR has held that the opening and reading of a prisoner's mail by the prison authorities breached art.8,[290] it all depends on the interests being balanced and how proportionate the intrusion is. In *R. (on the application of Szuluk) v Governor of Full Sutton Prison*,[291] for example, the Court of Appeal held that it was lawful and proportionate for a prison medical officer to read a prisoner's correspondence with his doctor.

10.52 The storage and use of information relating to a person's private life by a public authority, without express consent, is an interference with a person's art.8 "privacy" right and must therefore be justified, by reference to art.8(2), by the state. The ECtHR finds that the protection of personal data is of fundamental importance to a person's privacy under art.8 and is necessary to preserve their confidence in the public authority.[292] In fact only an overriding requirement in the public interest can justify such a breach of confidentiality.[293] The 1998 Act requires a balance to be struck between the public and private interests of maintaining confidentiality, in relation to medical and other information, and the public and private interests in permitting disclosure in certain circumstances.[294] Where records have been disclosed the relevance and sufficiency of the reasons behind that disclosure will be rigorously scrutinised. Even where disclosure is justified, in order to protect a person's art.8 rights, it can be limited and conditions placed on the disclosure.[295] It is also vital that there are procedures and safeguards in place to protect the disclosure process from abuse.[296] Where there is a genuine need to disclose confidential information across departments and public authorities, the courts will take that into account, as well as the fact that the information retains its confidential nature, in its art.8 determination.[297]

Where a person seeks the disclosure of information held on them by a public body, it has been held by the ECtHR in *Gaskin v United Kingdom*[298] that the public body should take into account the right of an individual to "information necessary to properly know and understand their childhood", etc. before coming to a disclosure decision. In other words, under art.8, a public body must assess the various competing interests before coming to any decision in relation to disclosure of information and records.

---

[288] *Lambert v France* (23618/94) (2000) 30 E.H.R.R. 346, judgment given on August 24, 1998.
[289] *Kopp v Switzerland* (23224/94) (1999) 27 E.H.R.R. 91, judgment given on March 25, 1998.
[290] *Campbell v UK* (13590/88) (1993) 15 E.H.R.R. 137, judgment given on March 25, 1992.
[291] [2004] EWHC Civ 1426.
[292] *Z v Finland* (22009/93) (1998) 25 E.H.R.R. 371, judgment given on February 25, 1997.
[293] *Z v Finland* (22009/93) (1998) 25 E.H.R.R. 371, judgment given on February 25, 1997.
[294] *R. (on the application of S) v Plymouth City Council* [2002] EWCA Civ 388.
[295] *R. (A Child) v W Primary Health Care Trust* [2004] EWHC 2085 (Fam).
[296] *Z v Finland* (22009/93) (1998) 25 E.H.R.R. 371, judgment reached on February 25, 1997.
[297] *MS v Sweden* (20837/92) (1999) 28 E.H.R.R. 313, judgment given on August 27, 1997.
[298] [1990] 1 F.L.R. 167.

CONFIDENTIALITY

10.53 Information is central to the effective operation of any public authority and social work is no exception. What is significant about social work is that a great deal of the information that is required is of a personal and confidential nature. There is therefore a need for the development of policies, strategies and procedures that will ensure that information is managed effectively and all legal responsibilities are complied with.[299] This may be important for legal and organisational reasons, but also it is integral to the retention of client confidence in both the social worker and the practice of social work.

Scots law recognises a breach of confidence as a delict, i.e. a legally actionable breach of a duty of care. The law relating to a breach of confidentiality is designed to provide a remedy against someone deriving a benefit from disclosing information that was given to him in confidence. A duty of confidence arises when a person discloses information to another in circumstances where it is reasonable to expect that the information will be held in confidence. It is breached by the disclosure of such information. The disclosure of the information need not be in bad faith, but may be done negligently. There is no absolute right to confidentiality: as shown above, often disclosure will be in the public interest. Where this is the case, the disclosing party will have an absolute defence.[300] Thus, for example, the police may disclose information about sex offenders.

Public interest disclosure will cover the prevention, detection or exposure of a crime or seriously antisocial conduct; preventing the public being misled by some public statement or action of the individual concerned; or informing the public about matters directly affecting the discharge of any public function of the individual concerned or for the protection of public health and safety.[301] However, the court will act to restrict a claim of public interest where the interests of justice so require. In *Parks v Tayside RC*[302] a foster mother who claimed she had contracted hepatitis B from a child placed in her care sought social work records relating to the child and his birth mother. The court took the view that the public interest in seeing that justice was done would far outweigh any public interest in confidentiality. In *R. v Higgins*[303] it was held that a local authority could refuse to disclose files containing information about a boy's special educational needs under public interest immunity.[304]

10.54 Where a party is able to establish a duty of confidence and a breach of it, the remedies are interdict, which restrains the unauthorised disclosure (if it has not already taken place), or damages (where it has and there is a loss or injury to the person whose information it is).

Social work departments take confidentiality very seriously. A Code of Guidance, *Confidentiality of Social Work Records*, issued under s.5 of the Social Work (Scotland) Act 1968, was produced by the Social Work Services Group in 1989 and still is applicable to local authorities, as amended, but not voluntary or private organisations.[305] Parts of the Code match the principles enshrined within the later Data Protection Act 1998. The Code must be read together with the Data Protection Act, as fully explained below. The Code identifies some applicable general principles:

- All information should be regarded as confidential. There should be clear guidelines on

---

[299] "The Social Services Information Agenda", National Institute for Social Work Briefing No.17, July 1996. *http://www.nisw.org.uk/polb/fulltext/niswb17.httr*.

[300] F. Gurry, *Breach of Confidence* (Oxford: Clarendon Press, 1984), pp.325–352; see also Scottish Law Commision, *Breach of confidence* (No. 90), Cmnd.9385 (1984).

[301] See also *Breach of confidence*, Cmnd.9385 (1984).

[302] 1989 S.L.T. 345.

[303] [1996] 1 F.L.R. 137.

[304] See also *Re C (Disclosure)* [1997] 2 W.L.R. 322; *Oxfordshire CC v L and F* [1997] 1 F.L.R. 235; *Re M (A Minor: Disclosure)* [1998] 1 F.L.R. 734; *Re R (Disclosure)* [1998] 1 F.L.R. 433; *Re W (Disclosure: Adoption Details)* [1998] 2 F.L.R. 625; *Re M (Disclosure)* [1998] 2 F.L.R. 1028; *Re L (Care: Confidentiality)* [1999] 1 F.L.R. 165.

[305] *Confidentiality of Social Work Records*, SWSG Circular 1/89.

the circumstances in which relevant personal information may be shared both within social work departments and with other agencies.

- Information supplied by donors for one purpose should not be used for another purpose; the purpose, or purposes, for which the information may be used should be established with the donor at the outset.
- Information supplied by donors should not be disclosed without the donor's consent in other than exceptional circumstances. Social work departments should give an undertaking to donors to this effect, and explain where exceptional circumstances may apply. The timing and manner of any disclosure is a matter of professional judgment, taking into account statutory requirement and whatever relevant guidance may be available.[306]

10.55 Personal information should normally be available only to staff in social work directly involved with the service-user and to a limited range of others who may need personal information to carry out their duties, including: social work finance staff for assessment purposes; legal advisers; other agencies, particularly if providing services on behalf of the authority or working in partnership with them; senior staff in their supervisory or management roles; social work students, their fieldwork teachers and tutors while undertaking direct work with service-users; researchers engaged in evaluative studies and other investigations relative to service provision; informal carers working with a social work department on a voluntary basis; members of a committee of inquiry, the local government ombudsman, or officers of the Secretary of State.

Exceptionally disclosure may be required by law or in the public interest, thereby overriding a person's right to have information kept confidential. Professional legal advice should be sought in each case and information disclosed should be the minimum necessary to meet the requirements of the situation. Where statute or the courts demand disclosure local authorities are not required to obtain consent, but should notify the donor, where practicable. Examples of where disclosure would be required include the preparation of social enquiry reports, children's hearing requirements, the provision of information to appointees such as curators *ad litem* or reporting officers, etc. Co-operation with the police may also require disclosure where such disclosure is needed to prevent, detect or prosecute serious crime. There is no definition of what constitutes a serious crime and accordingly advice should be sought from senior colleagues on the issue of disclosure; the police have the power to seek a court order compelling disclosure. Where there is a risk to personal and public health medical advice should be sought as to the necessity and manner of disclosure. Disclosure through the media should not take place, without consent, unless the welfare or other interests of the subject may be served by making personal information publicly available or by advertisement.[307]

Local authorities are expected to have clear policies and procedures on the issue of disclosure. It is expected that those policies will specifically deal with children and young persons. Sensitive information should not be disclosed without the consent of the child or, where that child is, for reasons of age, lack of maturity or mental capacity, incapable of giving informed consent, the child's parent or guardian or other person with parental rights and responsibilities.[308] Where a person is incapable of managing their own affairs because of mental illness or handicap, the consent to the disclosure of the curator *bonis*, nearest relative, or other person acting as a legal representative of the subject, should be sought when considering a request for disclosure of information.[309]

---

[306] SWSG Circular 1/89, para.10.

[307] See Moore and Woods, *Social Work and the Criminal Law in Scotland*, 3rd edn (1998), pp. 364–365; see also SWSG Circular 1/89, para.13.

[308] SWSG Circular 1/89, para.18.

[309] SWSG Circular 1/89, para.19.

DATA PROTECTION LAW

10.56 The Data Protection Act 1998 ("DPA 1998") protects individuals in relation to the processing of personal data and regulates the free movement of such data. DPA 1998 contains a number of data protection principles and created a Data Protection Commissioner, who has considerable investigation and enforcement powers. It is up to individuals to enforce their rights under DPA 1998, but the Commissioner can assist them. Individuals enforce their rights by direct application to the courts. DPA 1998 covers computerised records and manual records held in relevant filing systems.

Data protection principles

10.57 Part I of Sch.1 to DPA 1998 contains the data protection principles. These are:

(1) Personal data shall be processed fairly and lawfully. In relation to whether the personal data have been processed fairly the method by which they were obtained shall be considered; this means that the data subject should know the purpose behind the processing of the information and the person giving the information should be authorised to supply such data.[310] This principle accords with principle 3 of the Code of Guidance.
(2) Personal data shall be obtained only for one or more specified and lawful purposes, and shall not be further processed in any manner incompatible with that purpose or those purposes. This principle accords with principle 2 of the Code of Guidance.
(3) Personal data shall be adequate, relevant and not excessive in relation to the purpose or purposes for which they are processed. This means that only the minimum necessary information needed should be kept.
(4) Personal data shall be accurate and, where necessary, kept up to date. There is a duty on the data controller to keep their register entry up to date.[311] Where the information is out of date, there is a defence that the data controller did everything reasonably possible to keep the records up to date.[312]
(5) Personal data processed for any purpose or purposes shall not be kept for longer than is necessary for that purpose or purposes. Organisations should have policies and procedures designed to determine and ensure that when the purpose for which the information was gained is no longer relevant, those records are destroyed.
(6) Personal data shall be processed in accordance with the rights of data subjects under DPA 1998.
(7) Appropriate technical and organisational measures shall be taken against unauthorised or unlawful processing of personal data and against accidental loss or destruction of, or damage to, personal data.
(8) Personal data shall not be transferred to a country or territory outside the European Economic Area unless that country or territory ensures an adequate level of protection for the rights and freedoms of data subjects in relation to the processing of personal data.

Rights of data subjects and others

10.58 A person is legally entitled to be given information by any data controller, where his personal data are being processed by, or on behalf of, that data controller. This means that where personal data are being held on a person then, once they put in a proper written request and

---

[310] DPA 1998 Sch.2.
[311] DPA 1998 s.20.
[312] DPA 1998 s.20.

paid any required fee, they should be told what personal information is being kept, why it is being kept, to whom the information may be disclosed, and who the source of that information was.[313]

The controller can refuse to comply with the request where information relating to another individual will be disclosed unless that other individual has consented to the disclosure, or it is reasonable in all the circumstances to comply with the request without the consent of that other individual. There is an obligation on the data controller to provide an accompanying explanation of terms if the data are unintelligible.[314] The data controller is not required to supply or respond to repeated requests unless there is a reasonable interval between them.[315]

Section 10 of DPA 1998 allows a person, at any time by notice in writing to a data controller, to require the data controller to stop, or not to begin, processing any of their personal data because such processing will, or is causing, substantial damage or distress to him or to another, and the damage or distress is, or would be, unwarranted. The data subject cannot object where he has already consented to the processing or where processing is necessary for contractual purposes or to fulfil a legal obligation or the vital interests of the data subject.

10.59 In addition to the right to seek a court order compelling compliance, an individual who suffers damage due to a breach of DPA 1998 by a data controller can seek compensation from the data controller.[316] They can also apply to the court for an order to rectify, block, erase or destroy those data and any other personal data that contain an expression of opinion which appears to the court to be based on the inaccurate data.[317] The court may also order that the data controller notify third parties to whom the data have been disclosed of the rectification, blocking, erasure or destruction.[318] Any court actions in relation to DPA 1998 can be initiated in the sheriff court or the Court of Session.[319] A child of sufficient age (12 years old or over) and maturity can exercise his rights under DPA 1998.[320]

Not surprisingly, considerable amounts of data are exempt from the provisions of DPA 1998. Data required for the purpose of safeguarding national security are exempt.[321] Likewise data processed for:

- the prevention or detection of crime;
- the apprehension or prosecution of offenders; or
- the assessment or collection of any tax or duty or any imposition of a similar nature,

are exempt from the subject information provisions and non-disclosure provisions.[322]

Section 30(3) gives the Secretary of State the power to exempt or modify DPA 1998 obligations in relation to personal data processed by government departments or local authorities or by voluntary organisations or other such if processed in the course of, or for the purposes of, carrying out social work in relation to the data subject or other individuals. This will only be done if it is perceived that the application of DPA 1998 obligations would be likely to prejudice the carrying out of social work. The Data Protection (Subject Access Modification) (Social Work) Order[323] fleshes out s.30. It provides that where personal data have been processed fairly and lawfully then social workers are exempt from DPA 1998 subject information obligations, to the extent that the application of those provisions would be likely to prejudice the carrying out of social work because serious harm to the physical or mental health or condition of the data

---

[313] DPA 1998 s.7.
[314] DPA 1998 s.8(2).
[315] DPA 1998 s.8(3).
[316] DPA 1998 s.13(1).
[317] DPA 1998 s.14(1).
[318] DPA 1998 s.14(3).
[319] DPA 1998 s.15(1).
[320] DPA 1998 s.66.
[321] DPA 1998 s.28.
[322] DPA 1998 s.29.
[323] SI 2000/415.

subject or any other person would be likely to be caused.[324] Where social workers have obtained personal data only for one or more specified and lawful purposes, and have processed those data in any manner compatible with that purpose, then they are exempt from DPA 1998 subject information obligations.[325]

[324] Data Protection (Subject Access Modification) (Social Work) Order art.5(1).
[325] Data Protection (Subject Access Modification) (Social Work) Order art.4.

Chapter 11

Immigration and Asylum

Introduction

11.01 Immigration and asylum are political and emotive issues, which are inevitably linked to the questions of expenditure, law and cultural perspectives. Immigration relating to asylum issues is becoming one of the biggest, and largely unexplored, challenges that social work has faced for some time. In fact, law and government policy have a direct impact and implication in social work and social welfare practice of Scotland. For example access to local social services is redefined by immigration and asylum policy. Health care, housing and educational needs of these groups of persons will be examined in the following sections of this Chapter. The question of cost of immigration and asylum is commonly presented in negative terms devoid of any consideration in terms of benefits such as the payment of taxation, contribution to labour and the increase in diversity. Asylum is regularly depicted as damaging to the national interest and the media plays an important role in perpetrating a negative picture of refugees and immigrants as illegals, criminals, terrorists and bogus. This pathological image of immigrants and asylum seekers provides a dystopia of immigration and refugee law and ignores the reality behind past and present movement of people as a part of human history presenting a narrow view of a nation.

Restrictions to immigration, as a whole, without any consideration of the needs of the nation and the realities of individuals' circumstances normally proceed in response to unawareness and discrimination. This approach takes no notice of the economic and social contribution of "outsiders" to the country: filling shortages in the labour market rather than competing directly with native-born labour, enabling a faster rate of economic growth and helping to increase cultural prosperity.[1] As migration moves to the top of the UK political agenda, the treatment of asylum seekers and immigrants is seriously questioned. The realism of this scenario is that of a sombre effect on the social cohesion of the country.[2]

11.02 Asylum focuses on a rather more humanitarian character. The rationale behind it is the provision of protection for certain individuals who fulfil the required criteria of refugee status, in need of individual security and safety. The arrival of asylum seekers and refugees has brought a new challenge for those working with community services. The integration of these new arrivals

---

[1] For a discussion of the economic contribution of immigration see D. Coyle, "The Economic Case for Immigration" (2005) 25(1) *Economic Affairs* 53. In her article, Coyle's application of economic analysis to this important question suggests that the benefits of immigration often exceed the costs. Also Home Office research suggested that in 2002 immigrants paid £2.5bn more in taxes than they took in benefits. "Analysis: Who Gains from Immigration?" *BBC News*, June 17, 2002. *http://news.bbc.co.uk* [Accessed November 6, 2007].

[2] For a discussion of the UK asylum system see Independent Asylum Commission, *Fit for the Purpose Yet? A Nationwide Review of the UK Asylum System* (Independent Asylum Commission in association with the Citizen Organising Foundation, 2008).

plays an important role in rebuilding refugees' lives as well as for society as a whole. One must bear in mind that asylum seekers are ordinary people facing extraordinary circumstances. The asylum process entails not only the adoption of a body of international and domestic norms, but also the implementation of the services buttressing the legal regime so as to facilitate the adequate delivery of protection. In order to improve the quality and effectiveness of protection available within a country a study of the availability of the resources for processing applications for protection, reception facilities and lawful residence needs to be considered.

The foundations of social work are based on a mixture of humanitarian principles and government policies. These provide the motivation for incorporating immigration as a legitimate social work issue. Social workers are therefore expected to work with these client groups with the necessary professionalism and values.[3] This Chapter considers the general framework of asylum and welfare policy in relation to asylum seekers and refugees. The aim is to provide a cultural and legal framework for social workers and general practitioners enabling them to expand their knowledge base in relation to asylum questions. The author is aware of the lack of literature that defines the legal framework and policy of asylum in Scotland and hopes that this Chapter helps to illuminate the understanding and work of those involved in this area by giving guidance and pointing in the direction of where to find further information.

11.03 This Chapter therefore focuses on the basic principles of law and policy formulation in relation to refugees, as derived from international law. It is important to consider the international legal context in order to understand where the UK framework emerged from. The content of this Chapter is neither prescriptive nor exhaustive; it offers a starting point for those involved in this area. This is an ever-changing and growing area for governmental policy, the European Union and international law. The Chapter begins with a historical perspective of immigration and clarifies the concepts of immigrant and refugee. Subsequently, the relationship between human rights and refugee law is explored. The substantive contents of the legal definition of "refugee" and the protection status provided by the Convention Relating to the Status of Refugees 1951 ("Refugee Convention") and the text of the Protocol Relating to the Status of Refugees 1967 ("1967 Protocol") are identified. The Chapter also explains the common European framework for asylum, highlighting the shortcomings of the Refugee Convention. Finally, the standards of treatment that should be afforded to refugees are examined. These standards, for example the right to undertake paid work, access to education and health services, are essential to and simultaneously challenging for a model of national welfare system which is both empowering and humanitarian.

HISTORICAL PERSPECTIVE

11.04 Immigration control serves as a mechanism for controlling groups of people entering a country. The history of immigration control can be traced back to the United States Government's establishment of Ellis Island as the Federal Immigration Center for New York in 1890. In European history immigration control is rather a new but increasingly restrictive phenomenon.[4] At the beginning of the 1900s laws were enacted to control Jews' entrance into Eastern Europe. During the period following the First and Second World Wars, which generated unprecedented death tolls and labour shortages, immigration became crucial for European countries. However, this movement of foreign workers soon led European states to impose restrictions on immigration.

Recent state practice on immigration control demonstrates that the industrialised world is highly concerned with immigration and asylum. The United Nations High Commissioner for Refugees ("UNHCR") has expressed recently that:

---

[3] The five basic values of social work are human dignity and worth, social justice, service to humanity integrity and competence: British Association of Social Workers, "The Code of Ethics for Social Work" (BASW, 2003). *http://www.basw.co.uk/* [Accessed April 18, 2008].

[4] T. Hayter, *Open Borders: The Case against Immigration Controls* (London: Pluto Press, 2000).

> "UK immigration controls, much like many other states particularly in Europe, provide very limited legal channels for a refugee to enter in order to apply for recognition of their refugee status. As a result, most refugees seeking to enter the UK are forced to do so 'illegally', either using forged travel documents, or avoiding immigration controls altogether."[5]

11.05 Despite the fact that refugees and asylum seekers account for a relatively small proportion of the global movement of people, the negative aspects of a massive influx of immigrants and asylum seekers have dominated the news headlines. Intolerance and public confusion fuelled by security concerns have prompted industrialised countries to put in place a series of stringent measures which serve as deterrents to immigration and asylum. In reality, extra-visa requirements, carrier sanctions, airline liaison officers and the e-borders programme dressed up in the clothes of national security and "migration management" provide very limited legal channels for a refugee to enter in order to seek asylum, and as such may push them to do so illegally. Table 1 shows figures that dismiss the belief that the main countries of asylum are in the industrialised West.

As a first consideration, it is important to distinguish between immigrants, who are people coming to a country in order to establish a life and reside permanently, and refugees, who are people in need of international protection because of persecution. Note that the distinction between an economic migrant and a refugee is sometimes imprecise. For instance a person's story that appears, in first instance, to be ground on primarily an economic motive may, as a matter of fact, also absorb a political element that entails persecution.[6]

Table 1. Major refugee arrivals during 2005 (10 largest movements)

Country of origin	Main countries of asylum	Total
Togo	Benin/Ghana	39,100
Sudan	Chad/Uganda	34,500
Democratic Republic of Congo	Uganda/Rwanda/Burundi	15,600
Somalia	Yemen	13,600
Central African Republic	Chad	11,500
Iraq	Syria	10,500
Burundi	Rwanda/Tanzania/Uganda	6,100
Bhutan	Nepal	1,500
Rwanda	Uganda	1,500
Russian Federation	Azerbaijan	500

Source: *Refugees by Numbers* (Geneva: UNHCR, 2006). *http://www.unhcr.org/basics/BASICS/3b028097c.html* [Accessed January 16, 2008].

The United Kingdom policy

11.06 Migration is an intrinsic element of the history of the United Kingdom, in particular that related to the British Empire.[7] However, this geographical movement of people becomes oddly restricted when it relates to immigration. The Aliens Act 1905 restricted Jewish refugees fleeing pogroms in Eastern Europe. The Aliens Restriction Act 1914 gave the Home Secretary the power to regulate the entry, stay and deportation of aliens during the First World War. In the

---

[5] United Nations High Commissioner for Refugees ("UNHCR"), "Submission to: The Conservative Party National and International Security Policy Group" (London: UNHCR, March 2007). *http://www.unhcr.org.uk/info/briefings/SecPol RevGrpMar07.html* [Accessed April 24, 2008].

[6] The concept of persecution is discussed in paras 11.14 and 11.15.

[7] For a discussion of the history of immigration control in the UK, see D. Hayes and B. Humphries (eds), *Social Work Immigration and Asylum* (London: Jessica Kingsley Publishers, 2004).

1960s for example, the Commonwealth Immigrants Act 1962 took automatic rights of entry to Commonwealth citizens by setting up work vouchers. In 1968 the Commonwealth Immigrants Act 1968 removed British passports from Ugandan Asians, fleeing persecution from Amin's policies of "Africanisation".[8]

This restrictive pattern is a trend that has continued and is reflected in, for example, the Commonwealth Immigrants Act 1962, the Immigration Act 1971 and the British Nationality Act 1981 which introduced "patrial" and "non-patrial" categories of people and abolished the principle of *jus solis*.[9] The situation was even further tightened by the feeble idea of prevention of terrorism via restricting refugees' entrance to the country (see for example UK Terrorism Acts 2000 and 2006). However, up until the 1980s more people emigrated from the UK than immigrated to it.[10] The issues of migration and refugees are highly political and emotive and are inevitably linked to the question of cost.

Whereas previously humanitarian aims had been key drivers, post 1979 the discourse of welfare changed to a totally business-oriented model where the making of a profit, rather than assisting people, was the sole driver of the social enterprise. Social workers have therefore adopted a more mundane and technical approach towards their "clients" over the past 29 years. It is widely acknowledged that organisational changes affect work in state organisations.[11] Those involved in social work with people subject to immigration controls cannot easily escape such an environment.

The reality is that the UK is a diverse, multicultural society. In 2001, 8.3 per cent (4.9 million) of the total population were born overseas.[12] In 2005, applications for asylum in the UK fell by 24 per cent compared to 2004. As can be seen from Figure 1, the number of cases awaiting an initial decision at the end of the year was 5,500, the lowest level for a decade. Forty-one per cent of all applications in 2005 were from African nationals and 22 per cent were from nationals of the Middle East, all of which have a particular colonial history with this country. The UK experienced more than double the fall in applications compared with the rest of the EU25.[13]

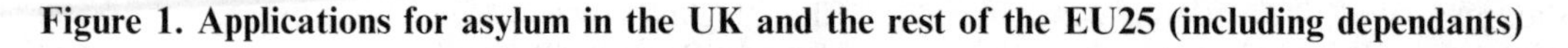

Figure 1. Applications for asylum in the UK and the rest of the EU25 (including dependants)

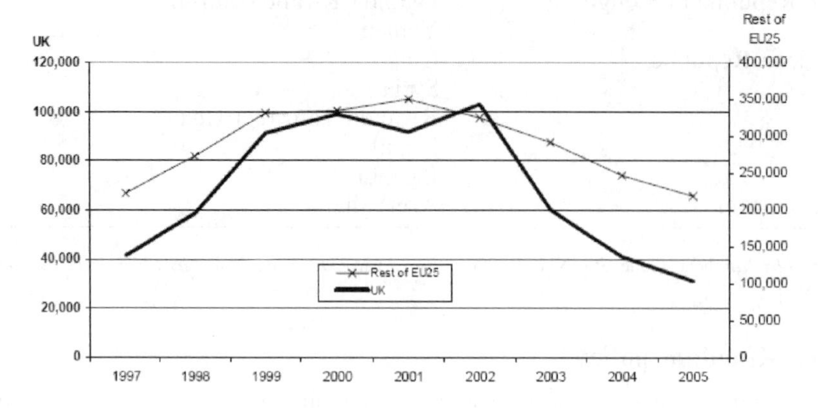

Source: *Home Office Statistical Bulletin* (2006)

[8] D. Hayes, "History and Context: The Impact of Immigration Control on Welfare Delivery", in Hayes and Humphries (eds), *Social Work Immigration and Asylum* (2004).

[9] Hayes, "History and Context", in Hayes and Humphries (eds), *Social Work Immigration and Asylum* (2004), p.14.

[10] House of Commons, *A Century of Change: Trends in UK statistics since 1900*, Research Paper 99/111 (1999). *http://www.parliament.uk/* [Accessed December 16, 2007].

[11] For a discussion of the ways organisational changes affect work in state organisations see C. Jones, "Voices from the Front Line: State Social Workers and New Labour" (2001) 31(4) *British Journal of Social Work* 547.

[12] "National Statistics Online" (NSO, 2005). *http://www.statistics.gov.uk* [Accessed October 15, 2007].

[13] K. Bennet, T. Heath and R. Jeffries, *Home Office Statistical Bulletin 14/07: Asylum Statistics United Kingdom 2006*, 2nd edn (London: Home Office, 2007), p.3.

ASYLUM V REFUGEES

Asylum

11.07 The definition of "asylum" has various interpretations within the context of refugee law. Asylum is rather a modern concept imposed by governments, particularly in Europe, to refer to the fashion in which different legal and administration systems manage potential entrants to a country granting them a particular status.[14]

Asylum or the term "territorial asylum" is granted by a state to an individual within its borders. This notion has been complementary to the Latin American state practice "diplomatic asylum", which operates under similar criteria, but it is granted by a state to individuals outside its territory, particularly in its diplomatic missions, in its consulates, on board its ships in the territorial waters of another state, on board its aircraft and in its military installations in foreign territory.[15]

The legal basis for asylum can be found in art.14(1) of the Universal Declaration of Human Rights ("UDHR"): "Everyone has the right to seek and to enjoy in other countries asylum from persecution." International law has not however provided for the reciprocal right to enter and reside in a country different from the individual's own. Therefore the capacity for allowing an individual to enter the territory of a country remains with the host country. This exercise of sovereignty is accompanied by the obligation of *non-refouler* (not to expel or return) a refugee in any manner whatsoever to the frontiers of territories where their life or freedom would be threatened on account of their race, religion, nationality, membership of a particular social group or political opinion.[16] However, this benefit may not be claimed by a refugee if there are reasonable grounds for regarding them a danger to the national security or the community of the country of refuge.[17] The principle of *non-refoulement* is widely accepted as a fundamental principle in international law.[18]

Refugees

11.08 The term "refugee", on the other hand, can be applied generally to individuals in flight. Evidence suggests that individuals take flight owing to a diverse range of circumstances: persecution, oppression, economic distress or environmental disasters. Nevertheless, in terms of international law the concept of refugee has a verifiable content and concrete meaning. In consequence, an individual who seeks to escape intolerable conditions such as poverty may be excluded from international protection under refugee law.

The Refugee Convention, which is the primary source of refugee law, declares a person to be a refugee if they fulfil the relevant criteria set out in the definition.[19] The Refugee Convention also provides for the occasions where a refugee who meets the statutory definition is not afforded international protection.[20]

---

[14] G. Clayton, *Textbook on Immigration and Asylum Law*, 2nd edn (Oxford: Oxford University Press, 2006), p.387.

[15] See *Colombian-Peruvian Asylum Case*, 1950 I.C.J.

[16] See also the obligation of *non-refoulement* under art.3 of the European Convention on Human Rights 1950; art.7 of the International Covenant on Civil and Political Rights 1966; and art.3 of the UN Convention against Torture 1984.

[17] Refugee Convention art.33.

[18] For a discussion of the nature of *non-refoulement* see UNHCR, "The Principle of *Non-Refoulement* as a Norm of Customary International Law: Response to the Questions Posed to UNHCR by the Federal Constitutional Court of the Federal Republic of Germany in Cases 2 BvR 1938/93, 2 BvR 1953/93, 2 BvR 1954/93" (UNHCR, 1994). *http://www.unhcr.org/publ/RSDLEGAL/437b6db64.html* [Accessed April 21, 2008].

[19] *UNHCR Handbook on Procedures and Criteria for Determining Refugee Status*, 2nd edn (Geneva: UNHCR HCR/IP/4/Eng/REV, 1992), para.28.

[20] Refugee Convention art.1(d), (e) and (f).

Figure 2. Applications for asylum in the UK

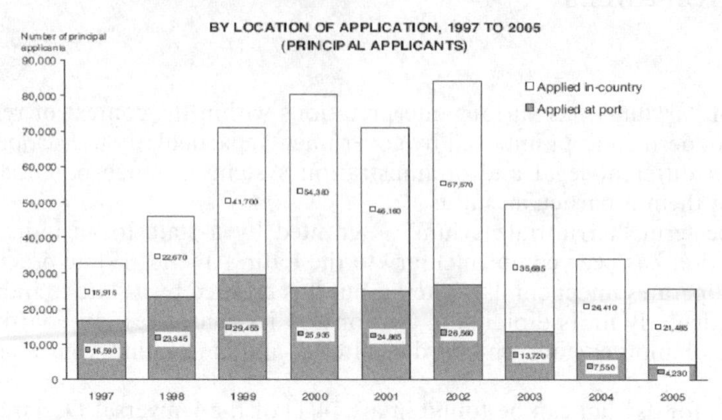

Source: *Home Office Statistical Bulletin* (2006)

It should be noted that refugee status and asylum are not one and the same thing. While asylum can be granted to anyone, refugee status is accorded under the terms of the Refugee Convention. Finally, it is worth mentioning that new definitions of a refugee have been put forward to address perceived gaps in the narrow legal protection afforded to refugees today.[21]

UNITED NATIONS REFUGEE AGENCY

11.09 The origin of the current legal framework for the protection of refugees has its origins in the International Refugee Organisation ("IRO") established in 1946. The IRO was the forerunner of the Office of the United Nations High Commissioner for Refugees ("UNHCR") established on December 14, 1950 by the UN General Assembly to provide international protection and seek a permanent solution, by assisting governments, to the problems of refugees.

The agency is mandated to lead and co-ordinate international action to protect refugees and resolve refugee problems worldwide. For this purpose the UNHCR works with the Scottish Government in a variety of asylum projects. The UNHCR seeks also durable solutions by facilitating the voluntary repatriation of refugees and their reintegration into their country of origin, or alternatively by assisting their integration into their countries of asylum or their resettlement in third countries.[22] The UNHCR mandate extends to persons other than those who fall within the Refugee Convention definition.[23] For example, internally displaced persons were brought within the general mandate of the UNHCR in 2006. The High Commissioner for Refugees is elected by the General Assembly and her work is described in the Statute of the UNHCR as being "of an entirely non-political character" as well as "humanitarian and social".

---

[21] See, for instance, Organisation of African Union Convention, the Cartagena Declaration 1994 and the Bangkok Principles 2001. These instruments will be discussed below.

[22] For example, in 2007 40 African refugees were resettled in the Scottish town of Motherwell.

[23] The Statute of the Office of the United Nations High Commissioner for Refugees para.9 states: "the High Commissioner shall engage in such additional activities, including repatriation and resettlement, as the General Assembly may determine, within the limits of the resources placed at his disposal."

THE LEGAL FRAMEWORK

The Refugee Convention

11.10 The Refugee Convention is the most important instrument on which the UNHCR's work is based.[24] The Refugee Convention contains a general description of the term "refugee". This definition is critical to recognition of refugee status and the determination of who is entitled to UNHCR protection. As mentioned previously, the mandate of the UNHCR also includes other persons who are without, or unable to avail themselves of, the protection of their state of origin. The Refugee Convention is clearly influenced by the existing human rights instruments of that point in time, according refugees a broader range of rights such as the freedom to practise religion, access to the courts and public education as well as social assistance.

However, the Refugee Convention also indicates the obligations of refugees towards host countries, the people undeserving of refugee protection and cessation of refugee protection. The Refugee Convention lays out also the conditions under which a refugee ceases to be a refugee: (a) by reason of voluntary acts of the individual; and (b) by reason of a change of circumstances.[25] Furthermore, it gives authority to the UNHCR to supervise the Refugee Convention's application. For the understanding of this subject continual reference and analysis of this instrument will be made. The United Kingdom of Great Britain and Northern Ireland is a contracting party of the Refugee Convention and 1967 Protocol.[26]

The interaction with domestic legal systems

11.11 Despite the fact that the Refugee Convention (in conjunction with the 1967 Protocol), is the most important international instrument in the determination of refugee status, its reception into domestic law depends on a state's approach to international law. However, it cannot be ignored that a number of norms contained in these two instruments reflect international customary law,[27] which implies a direct binding effect on any state. The right to asylum is incorporated as a fundamental right in the constitutional arrangement of some countries[28]; other countries have incorporated this right into their legal system by way of secondary legislation[29]; however, others, such as the UK, are silent on this right.

Other sources of international refugee law

11.12 Additional sources of international refugee law are found in the interpretative guides to the decisions of the UNHCR's Executive Committee,[30] and in the body of customary international law.

DEFINING ASYLUM SEEKERS AND REFUGEES

11.13 An asylum seeker is a person who has submitted an application for protection under the Refugee Convention and is waiting for that asylum claim to be decided by the Home Office.

[24] In 1951, the application of the Refugee Convention was limited to persons who acquired refugee status as a consequence of events occurring before January 1, 1951. In 1967 the Protocol Relating to the Status of Refugees (1967 Protocol) specifically removed this temporal limitation.

[25] Refugee Convention art.1C(1)–(6) clarifies the circumstances in which refugee status will be withdrawn.

[26] The UK ratified the Refugee Convention in 1954 and the 1967 Protocol in 1968.

[27] For example, art.3 (non-discrimination) or art.33 (prohibition of *refoulement*) of the Refugee Convention.

[28] See for instance, art.16 of the German Constitution and art.36 of the Colombian Constitution.

[29] For example France, Denmark and Bolivia.

[30] Commonly known as ExCom, these are delivered by the Executive Committee of the High Commissioner for Refugees. This body was established, in 1958, pursuant to para.4 of UNHCR's Statute by the Economic and Social Council ("ECOSOC").

"Refugee", on the other hand, is a term of art. The general definition of who is a refugee emanates from art.1A(2) of the Refugee Convention. Accordingly, a refugee is an individual who:

> "owing to well-founded fear of being persecuted for reasons of race, religion, nationality, membership of a particular social group or political opinion, is outside the country of his nationality and is unable, or owing to such fear, is unwilling to avail himself of the protection of that country; or who, not having a nationality and being outside the country of his former habitual residence as a result of such events, is unable or, owing to such fear, is unwilling to return to it."

This simple form of words presents a number of difficulties. In other words, the person must:

(1) be outside their country of nationality;
(2) be unable or unwilling to avail themselves of the protection of that country, or to return there, as a consequence of (3);
(3) have a well-founded fear of persecution; and
(4) attribute this persecution to reasons of religion, race, nationality, membership of a particular social group or political opinion.

11.14 Numbers (1) and (2) are self-explanatory. Number (3) encapsulates one of the most intricate components of the definition: the well-founded fear of persecution, which in turn has to be couched in terms of religion, race, nationality, membership of a particular social group or political opinion. "Well-founded fear" involves two elements: fear and well-founded. Fear is a subjective and often personal element. On the other hand, well-founded is an objective element that derives from a specific and real situation. Both of these elements must be demonstrated to exist in order for a person to qualify for refugee status. Finally, a definition of persecution is lacking in the Refugee Convention. However, a reading of arts 31 and 33 of the Refugee Convention leads one to presuppose that a threat to life or freedom on account of race, religion, nationality, political opinion or membership of a particular social group amounts to persecution.[31]

Persecution may also stem from sections of the population as opposed to state activities.[32] In this vein, the European Union Qualification Directive[33] also affords protection to refugees when persecution is perpetrated by non-state actors. It is possible, therefore, to argue that a serious and systematic violation of civil and political rights will amount to persecution.

Grounds of persecution

11.15 The substantive grounds of persecution contained in the Refugee Convention are:

(1) race;
(2) religion;
(3) nationality;
(4) membership of a particular social group;
(5) political opinion.

It is necessary to remember that the grounds are not exclusive and they may overlap; in addition the five grounds are developed on the premise of non-discrimination.

---

[31] The UN Convention against Torture 1984 art.1 defines persecution in broader terms. This definition restricts persecution to acts arising from public officials (or private individuals acting in an official capacity).

[32] For a discussion of non-state actors see *UNHCR Handbook* (1992), para.65.

[33] Council Directive 2004/83/EC of 29 April 2004.

Exclusion clauses

11.16 A refugee can be excluded from such status at domestic level, regardless of the existence of criteria contained in art.1A of the Refugee Convention, if they are assisted by an UN agency other than the UNHCR. Thus, they are not considered to be in need of protection.[34] In this sense, art.1F of the Refugee Convention lays out the types of crimes that exclude the perpetrators from the benefits of international protection. The author of such a crime is considered "undeserving of refugee protection". The interpretation and application of art.1F is restrictive. The list is divided into three categories:

(1) crimes against peace, crimes against humanity, and war crimes;
(2) serious non-political crimes;
(3) acts contrary to the purposes and principles of the United Nations.

The materialisation of any of these three circumstances will result in the exclusion from refugee status in the terms of the Refugee Convention.

ASYLUM LEGISLATION IN THE UK

11.17 Legislation and government policies around asylum are complex and consistently changing. In addition to the legislation outlined in para.11.03, this includes three rather recent Acts dealing with asylum, immigration and nationality (2002, 2004 and 2006), these are highlighted below. As of March 5, 2007, the Home Office has put all new applications for asylum into the New Asylum Model ("NAM"). In addition, immigration, human rights and European legislation also affect asylum policy. Understanding and accommodating the new challenges is a key property for all those working with this area.

Legislation	Description
Asylum and Immigration Appeals Act 1993	Introduced appeal rights for asylum seekers, finger-printing of applicants and detention of asylum seekers.
Asylum and Immigration Act 1996	Restricted benefits and employment to applicants.
Human Rights Act 1998	Incorporated the European Convention on Human Rights into UK law (art.3).
Immigration and Asylum Act 1999	Home Office set up the National Asylum Support Service ("NASS") created to administer support to asylum seekers, which included subsistence vouchers and the option of accommodation. Asylum seekers removed from mainstream welfare system.
Nationality, Immigration and Asylum Act 2002	NASS support conditional on asylum claim being submitted "as soon as reasonably practicable" and on applicant's co-operation with authorities. Asylum seekers not allowed to work or undertake vocational training.
Asylum and Immigration (Treatment of Claimants, etc.) Act 2004	Sanctioned asylum seekers who enter UK with no travel documents "without reasonable excuse". Restricted appeal system and legal aid.

[34] Refugee Convention art.1D–F.

Immigration, Asylum and Nationality Act 2006	Introduced a new right of appeal for people who are no longer recognised as refugees but who are permitted to stay in the UK on some other basis. Limited the right of appeal against refusal of entry clearance (as a dependent, a visitor or a student) and contained several provisions on deprivation of British citizenship.

Problems with the current definition of refugees

11.18 An overview of art.1 of the Refugee Convention (which defines, among other things, who is a refugee) demonstrates that the instrument was created in order to address a particular situation: the post-war refugee crisis. Today the Refugee Convention therefore applies in a limited number of circumstances. In consequence, people seeking asylum due to the devastating consequences of current humanitarian crises such as natural disasters, economic hardships and internal armed conflicts would not be able to qualify as statutory refugees.

Armed conflicts generate large numbers of refugees. If we have a look at the countries that produced the largest number of refugees and asylum seekers in 2003 at the top of the list are those experiencing long-standing conflicts: Palestine, Afghanistan, Sudan and Myanmar. Simultaneously Sudan, Congo-Kinshasa, Colombia, Uganda and Angola headed the list for the largest number of internally displaced persons.[35]

"Whereas old wars are thought to distinguish between combatants and noncombatants, new wars are understood to blur this distinction. In fact, combatants are thought to prefer to target civilians."[36]

Kaldor notes that there has been a,

> "dramatic increase in the ratio of civilian to military casualties. At the beginning of the twentieth century, 85–90 percent of victims in war were military. In World War II, approximately half of all war deaths were civilian. By the late 1990s, the proportions of a hundred years ago have been almost exactly reversed, so that nowadays approximately 80 percent of all casualties in wars are civilian."[37]

11.19 Generalised violence involves not only a systematic infringement of the basic human rights of individuals but also a continuous disruption of food production together with deterioration of the social services and basic structures of the nation such as economy, education and healthcare systems. The reasons for flight are numerous. However, the protection under the auspices of the Refugee Convention is limited. In addition the Refugee Convention does not apply in mass-influx situations. In order to deal with these situations, a number of countries are giving exceptional protection to these "refugees".

The picture is grim and all these circumstances should be acknowledged by those who provide a wide range of services to asylum seekers and refugees in Scotland, and the UK, recognising the unique social purpose of public service organisations.

---

[35] US Committee for Refugees and Immigrants, "World Refugee Survey 2004" (2004). *http://www.refugees.org/article.aspx?id=1156* [Accessed October 5, 2007].

[36] E. Melander, M. Öberg, and J. Hall, "The 'New Wars' Debate Revisited: An Empirical Evaluation of the Atrociousness of 'New Wars'", Uppsala Peace Research Papers No.9 (Department of Peace and Conflict Research, Uppsala University, Sweden). *http://www.pcr.uu.se/publications/UPRP_pdf/UPRP_No_9.pdf* [Accessed May 3, 2008].

[37] M. Kaldor, *New and Old Wars: Organized Violence in a Global Era* (Cambridge: Polity Press, 2002), p.100.

INTERNATIONAL REFUGEE LAW AND HUMAN RIGHTS LAW

11.20 The relationship between international refugee law and human rights is a long-lasting one. Human rights law has, from its initiation, been connected to the development of refugee law. Similarly, human rights issues have been used to ground a form of practice that is central to social work, community development and broader human services.[38] This argument extends the application of human rights beyond the realm of theoretical analysis into the professional practice and social action. The basic human rights are prescribed by the International Bill of Rights.[39] Despite the fact that the responsibility of respecting, promoting and ensuring human rights rest primarily with states, all individuals have a duty towards the realisation of these rights. Within international law, this protection extends to every individual under their jurisdiction, including asylum seekers, refugees and those afforded subsidiary protection status.[40]

Derogations

11.21 Human rights are the foundation of dignity, autonomy and justice in a civilised society. Human rights are inalienable. The recognition of human rights should always be accompanied by the capacity of people to enforce them. However, in times of public emergency, states can derogate from their obligations under international law, provided that such measures do not involve discrimination on any ground.[41] Nevertheless, no derogation is permitted in relation to "core" rights within the International Covenant on Civil and Political Rights ("ICCPR").[42] In the current state of affairs, the "war on terror" has considerably changed the conditions of international protection.[43] In this line of ideas, governments and their agencies should fully realise the human implications of denial of humanitarian protection.

The European human rights system in UK law (Human Rights Act 1998)

11.22 The European human rights system is governed by the European Convention on Human Rights 1950 ("Human Rights Convention"). The Human Rights Convention aims to achieve greater unity between Member States, among other things, by "the maintenance and further realisation of human rights and fundamental freedoms". The Human Rights Convention has been supplemented by 14 Protocols.[44] This body of work inspired by the Universal Declaration of Human Rights ("UDHR") focuses on civil and political rights such as the right to life, the right to freedom from torture, the right to liberty, the right to marry and the right to freedom of speech and association. The Human Rights Convention does not explicitly contain social and economic rights. However, the protection of social and economic interests such as the environment and social security can also be enforced through another civil or political rights.

---

[38] J. Ife, *Human Rights and Social Work: Towards Rights-Based Practice* (Cambridge: Cambridge University Press, 2001).

[39] The International Bill of Rights is formed by the Universal Declaration of Human Rights ("UDHR"), the International Covenant on Civil and Political Rights ("ICCPR") and the International Covenant on Economic, Social and Cultural Rights ("ICESCR").

[40] UNHCR Executive Committee No.82 (1997) reminds states of "the obligation to treat asylum-seekers and refugees in accordance with applicable human rights and refugee law standards as set out in relevant international instruments".

[41] For example: solely on the ground of race, colour, sex, language, religion or social origin.

[42] See for example arts 6, 7, 8(1) and 8(2) of the ICCPR.

[43] For a discussion of non-derogable rights see Inter-American Court of Human Rights Advisory Opinion on Habeas Corpus in Emergency Situation, January 30, 1987.

[44] Protocols are international agreements that follow or develop further an international convention on a particular subject. For example in respect of the Human Rights Convention, the right to education: Protocol 1; or the abolition of the death penalty: Protocol 6; or the right of appeal in criminal matters: Protocol 7.

The United Kingdom and the European Convention on Human Rights

11.23 The Human Rights Convention was incorporated into domestic law via the UK Human Rights Act 1998 ("1998 Act") which entered into force on October 2, 2000. The 1998 Act lays out the 13 Convention rights and Protocols that the UK has ratified to date. The purpose of the 1998 Act is to give further effect to the rights and freedoms guaranteed under the Human Rights Convention. In *R. v DPP Ex p. Kebilene*[45] the House of Lords refused to enforce the principle of legitimate expectation in relation to Convention rights before October 2, 2000. The 1998 Act s.3 sets out the principle of interpretation:

"So far as it is possible to do so, primary legislation and subordinate legislation must be read and given effect in a way which is compatible with the Convention rights."

In relation to the Human Rights Convention the 1998 Act includes:

- the right to life (art.2);
- prohibition of torture (art.3);
- prohibition of slavery and enforced labour (art.4);
- the right to liberty (art.5);
- the right to a fair trial (art.6);
- no punishment without law (art.7);
- the right to respect for private and family life (art.8);
- freedom of thought, conscience and religion (art.9);
- freedom of expression (art.10);
- freedom of assembly and association (art.11);
- the right to marry (art.12);
- the right to an effective remedy (art.13);
- prohibition of discrimination (art.14).

The Human Rights Convention and the 1998 Act are in line with the amending treaties of the European Union ("EU") which strengthen the area of fundamental rights.[46] In other words, human rights law forms an integral part of European Community ("EC") law. In consequence, the Common European Asylum System should be consistent with the EU and EC principles relating to the protection of human dignity[47] as well as with the provisions of the Human Rights Convention.

11.24 Interestingly, the Human Rights Convention is exceedingly relevant in asylum matters. The scope of protection under art.3 of the Human Rights Convention, for example, is higher than that of art.33 of the Refugee Convention.[48] In *Chahal v United Kingdom*[49] the European Court of Human Rights ("ECtHR") held that, as the prohibition in art.3 is absolute, the threat to *Chahal* as an individual was such that his conduct in the United Kingdom could not be a material consideration. According to the ECtHR:

> "Article 3 enshrines one of the most fundamental values of democratic society ... The Court is well aware of the immense difficulties faced by States in protecting their Communities from terrorist violence. However, even in these circumstances, the Convention

---

45 [1999] 3 W.L.R. 972.

46 The Treaty of Amsterdam proclaims that the Union declares itself to be established on the principles of "liberty, democracy, respect for human rights and fundamental freedoms, and the rule of law", principles that are common to the Member States.

47 e.g. the European Convention on Extradition (December 13, 1957); the European Convention on Repatriation of Minors (May 28, 1970); the European Convention for the Prevention of Torture and Inhuman or Degrading Treatment or Punishment (November 26, 1987) and the European Social Charter (May 3, 1996).

48 Human Rights Convention art.3: "No one shall be subjected to torture or to inhuman or degrading treatment or punishment."

49 (1996) 23 E.H.R.R. 413.

> prohibits in absolute terms torture or inhuman or degrading treatment or punishment, irrespective of the victim's conduct."[50]

Article 3 of the Human Rights Convention provides an absolute guarantee of protection to everyone from torture, inhumane or degrading treatment or punishment, including those facing the real and immediate risk of ill-treatment. Within art.33 of the Refugee Convention,[51] on the other hand, the protection is restricted to "refugees" and may be read as "only" perpetrated by a state agent. In *HLR v France*[52] the ECtHR faced the issue of non-state actors as agents of persecution. The ECtHR asserted that:

> "Owing to the absolute character of the right guaranteed, the Court does not rule out the possibility that Article 3 of the Convention may also apply where the danger emanates from persons or groups of persons who are not public officials. However, it must be shown that the risk is real and that the authorities of the receiving State are not able to obviate the risk by providing appropriate protection."[53]

Finally, it is worth briefly considering the "extraterritorial" effect of the Human Rights Convention. In *Soering v United Kingdom*,[54] the ECtHR was of the opinion that the applicant's extradition to the US (non-state party) would expose him to inhumane or degrading treatment or punishment, a violation of art.3 of the Human Rights Convention.

THE EUROPEAN UNION AND ASYLUM POLICY

11.25 As mentioned before, the EU Member States' asylum framework and policies are to a great extent influenced by their joint membership of the EU.[55] The result is the creation of the Common European Asylum System.

The Common European Asylum System

11.26 The Common European Asylum System is based on the principle of integration or harmonisation. The key legal sources are set up by Council Directive 2003/9/EC (which sets out the minimum standards for the reception of asylum seekers), Council Regulation (EC) No.343/2003 (establishes the criteria and mechanisms for determining the Member State responsible for examining an asylum application), Council Directive 2004/83/EC (provides the minimum standards for the qualification and status of third-country nationals or stateless persons as refugees or as persons who otherwise need international protection) and Council Directive 2005/85/EC (lays down the minimum standards on the procedures for making decisions on asylum claims). These instruments provide the foundation of the EU asylum system and set the minimum criteria for the Member States to comply with when implementing asylum legislation. In making a common policy, the EU is progressively pursuing one of the fundamental objectives of this regional institution, which is to offer its citizens an area of freedom, security and justice without internal borders.

---

[50] (1996) 23 E.H.R.R. 413.

[51] The Refugee Convention art.33 sets out: "(1) No Contracting State shall expel or return ("refouler") a refugee in any manner whatsoever to the frontiers of territories where his life or freedom would be threatened on account of his race, religion, nationality, membership of a particular social group or political opinion. (2) The benefit of the present provision may not, however, be claimed by a refugee whom there are reasonable grounds for regarding as a danger to the security of the country in which he is, or who, having been convicted by a final judgement of a particularly serious crime, constitutes a danger to the community of that country."

[52] (1998) 26 E.H.R.R. 29.

[53] (1998) 26 E.H.R.R. 29.

[54] (1989) 11 E.H.R.R. 439.

[55] In 1997 all affairs related to free movement of persons, controls on external borders, asylum, immigration and safeguarding of the rights of third-country nationals, and judicial co-operation in civil matters were "centralised" by the Treaty of Amsterdam.

STANDARDS OF TREATMENT FOR ASYLUM SEEKERS AND REFUGEES

11.27 The importance of discussing the international legal context is that the obligations of the UK in relation to the standards of treatment for refugees emanate from the Refugee Convention and other international human rights instruments applicable in this jurisdiction.[56] The standards have direct, yet not critically discussed, implications in social work practice and welfare provisions. For this reason, the following sections of this Chapter focus on the standards of treatment laid down in different instruments for asylum seekers, that is, people who have submitted an application for asylum under the Refugee Convention and the statutory standards of treatment for refugees. International minimum standards for reception and treatment are expected to be implemented domestically. However, their realisation rests on the economic, political and social capacity of national states and although there may be diverse approaches to dealing with asylum seekers and refugees, between countries or regions, international refugee and human rights standards should be respected.

Social work challenges

11.28 There is a diversity of reasons that may avert host states from providing basic rights to asylum seekers during the refugee status determinations procedure. A fundamental dilemma is the economic burden placed on the host state, especially when set against competing national priorities. In conjunction with financial matters, the security concern has become an important element of resistance since the events of 9/11 in the USA, the July 7 bombing in London and the June 30 Glasgow airport attack in 2007. The exclusive focus that is given to these issues diverts attention from the positive aspects of immigration and the failures of the asylum system as such.

In a global perspective, the UK receives less than 0.5 per cent of the world's refugee population. In Scotland the population is ageing and has dipped below 5 million. This is a major area of concern for the Scottish Executive and Scottish business. Indeed, the promotion of specific measures within Scottish policy such as Scottish Executive's Fresh Talent Initiative aims to redress demographic trends. Immigration is key to the economic and social prosperity of the nation.[57]

A key aspect for social work is the role that an efficient asylum system can play in reducing the length of time of the refugee status determination process without jeopardising the rights of the asylum seekers. The importance of reducing the length of time in the asylum process is to reduce the time that asylum seekers need to be supported by the National Asylum Support Service ("NASS") and minimise the amount of publicly funded labour available in the social work services. This is an area that requires further academic research and one that could provide a way of addressing the current financial and social concerns. Social workers are not excluded from the current climate surrounding asylum issues. Frontline staff should be prepared to overcome the many real and fictional challenges of working with asylum seekers and refugees. The appropriate professional training and work experience will help them to offer the services required by these clients. Therefore this section aims to provide a ready source of information on standards of treatment.

The standards

11.29 The Refugee Convention sets out a number of obligations of states in relation to refugees and asylum seekers. The most significant provisions of the Refugee Convention, which were created in order to guarantee international protection for people in need, are the principle of *non-*

---

[56] For example the Human Rights Convention and the 1998 Act.

[57] See *http://www.asylumscotland.org.uk/* [Accessed May 23, 2008].

refoulement (not to expel or return)[58] and the prohibition of punishment for illegal entry.[59] These two provisions are directly applicable to refugees before a formal recognition of their refugee status in national law.

The Refugee Convention omits explicit provisions for the treatment of asylum seekers. Therefore, the importance of international human rights for the establishment of an adequate framework for the standards of treatment of asylum seekers (and refugees) is paramount.[60] The International Bill of Rights, which consists of the Universal Declaration of Human Rights 1948, the International Covenant on Civil and Political Rights 1966 and the International Covenant on Economic, Social and Cultural Rights 1966, contains human rights provisions applicable to all individuals regardless of their status.[61] In reality, the most basic rights to which asylum seekers and refugees are entitled only require the host state to refrain from certain violations. Any differential treatment between asylum seekers with regard to the minimum core rights can however be justified by reference to reasonable legal grounds. The Executive Committee of the High Commissioner's Programme has on several occasions drawn attention to the obligations of states to "treat asylum-seekers and refugees in accordance with applicable human rights and refugee law standards as set out in relevant international instruments".[62]

It is also important to mention that states face considerable economic difficulties in complying with minimum standards for reception and treatment of asylum seekers and refugees. Therefore, states have the obligation to develop innovative approaches to support the social and vocational integration of asylum seekers and refugees. This is an area of potential conflict given its impact on rights. As always, some questions may emerge in this context: should refugees enjoy the same rights as citizens of the host state or should they only receive comparable treatment? And are their needs different from any regular citizen who is in search of a safe and secure life?

Standards for asylum seekers

11.30 Asylum seekers will face numerous challenges upon their arrival in Scotland, these are both social and economic in nature. However, there are a few that affect directly the provision and organisation of social care services, namely welfare, health, probation and childcare including education.

Minimum basic human standards

11.31 The Executive Committee of the High Commissioner's Programme identified, in situations of large influx, pending arrangements for a durable solution, 16 "minimum basic human standards" that asylum seekers should enjoy, including[63]:

- freedom of movement;
- recognition as people before the law enjoying free access to the judicial system;
- the right to receive all necessary assistance and be provided with the basic necessities of life and treatment in accordance with the Universal Declaration of Human Rights;
- the respect for family reunification; and
- adequate provision for the protection of minors and unaccompanied children.

---

[58] Refugee Convention art.33.

[59] Refugee Convention art.31.

[60] The UN Convention on the Elimination of all Forms of Discrimination against Women 1979 is applicable in the context of the reception of asylum seekers. The UN Convention on the Rights of the Child 1989 provides key guidance for the creation and execution of reception policies in this area, particularly the "best interest" principle. At regional level for example EU Council Directive 2003/9/EC lays down minimum standards for the reception of asylum seekers.

[61] See for example art.25(1) of the Universal Declaration on Human Rights; art.11(1) of the International Covenant on Economic, Social and Cultural Rights; arts 14, 16, 17, 18 and 27 of the International Covenant on Civil and Political Rights; ICESCR General Comment 4 of 1991.

[62] UNHCR, ExCom No.82 (XLVIII) 1997.

[63] UNHCR, ExCom Conclusions No.22 (XXXII) 1981.

Detention, financial and medical assistance will be discussed in turn.

Detention

11.32 The general rule is that asylum seekers should not be detained. The detention of asylum seekers should only take place in exceptional instances.[64] These exceptions are expressly laid down in the UNHCR *Guidelines on Applicable Criteria and Standards relating to the Detention of Asylum Seekers.*[65] Should an asylum seeker be detained, their detention has to meet the general national guarantees and principles of international human rights law.[66]

The use of prisons should be avoided. In the case that separate detention facilities are not already in use, asylum seekers should be accommodated separately from convicted criminals or prisoners on remand.[67]

In addition the detention should not prejudice the asylum process. The UNHCR should have access to detained asylum seekers so that they can be informed as to their rights. Special provision should be made for stateless persons, women and minors, for example accommodation in residential homes or foster care placements. Child asylum seekers should have access to education.

Financial assistance and medical assistance

11.33 Financial resources are fundamental to the maintenance of an adequate standard of living and to facilitate a smooth integration in the host country or re-integration into the country of origin. Housing, food and clothing as well as healthcare protection and community development are some of the basic needs of asylum seekers. States may provide this support either via their social welfare system or through income generation schemes. The way of providing these basic necessities is entirely up to the host country. As seen above asylum seekers are not allowed to work[68] in the UK; accordingly they should be provided with all the welfare support.[69] It is particularly important to make available to children, women and elderly people the social services required to meet their specific needs.

The UN Committee on Economic, Social and Cultural Rights in relation to the highest attainable standard of health, specifies that:

> " ... States are under the obligation to respect the right to health by, inter alia, refraining from denying or limiting equal access for all persons, including prisoners or detainees, minorities, asylum seekers and illegal immigrants, to preventive, curative and palliative health services; abstaining from enforcing discriminatory practices as a State policy; and abstaining from imposing discriminatory practices relating to women's health status and needs. Furthermore, obligations to respect include a State's obligation to refrain from prohibiting or impeding traditional preventive care, healing practices and medicines, from marketing unsafe drugs and from applying coercive medical treatments, unless on an exceptional basis for the treatment of mental illness or the prevention and control of communicable diseases. Such exceptional cases should be subject to specific and restrictive conditions, respecting best practices and applicable international standards, including the

---

[64] *Revised Guidelines on Applicable Criteria and Standards relating to the Detention of Asylum Seekers* (Geneva: UNHCR, 1999), Guideline 3.

[65] The detention centre should not be a regular prison and asylum seekers should be segregated from common criminals.

[66] Among others the individual's right to be informed of the reasons for their detention in a language and in terms which they understand, the right to habeas corpus and access to legal assistance.

[67] Above, fn.64, Guideline 10.

[68] Nationality, Immigration and Asylum Act 2002.

[69] See, e.g. *Handbook for Planning and Implementing Development Assistance for Refugees (DAR) Programmes*, (Geneva: UNHCR Refworld, 2005). *http://www.unhcr.org*.

> Principles for the Protection of Persons with Mental Illness and the Improvement of Mental Health Care."[70]

In reality, reception centres may represent an acceptable solution, for a limited period. However, reception centres or other types of communal accommodation should meet certain minimum standards, including access to health care; particular consideration should be given to those asylum seekers in need of immediate mental health treatment because of torture or severe trauma.

In practice, detention issues, the financial constraints of asylum seekers and the likelihood of physical or mental health harm resulting from the refugee's experiences of persecution remind us of the importance of providing competent care to patients and clients seeking asylum in Scotland.

Standards for refugees

11.34 Subsequent to discussing some of the minimum standards of treatment for asylum seekers such as detention, financial assistance and health care, it is worth noting that an asylum seeker's essential needs will be greater once they have been recognised as a refugee and granted residence in the host country.

In order to fully integrate within society refugees should be able to enjoy a wider range of human rights and not only the minimum standards provided upon arrival. Essential needs go beyond minimum standards: they cover a wider variety of standards, which reach beyond life-saving protection and basic aid.

As a general rule human rights instruments provide the framework for the realisation of human needs. However, in practice enjoyment of the benefit of such instruments depends on the relationship between the individual and the state.[71] In *stricto sensu*[72] refugees are not citizens of the host country, so they do not enjoy the complete national protection of that state. This point is important and grades in a different approach to this refugee problem.[73] The Refugee Convention provides the norms relating to standards of treatment of refugees. In view of the increasing importance of asylum issues it is important to enunciate the provisions for minimum standards for the treatment of refugees. In 2006 the UNHCR included an Introductory Note to the Refugee Convention, which related to standards of treatment of refugees:

> "The Convention consolidates previous international instruments relating to refugees and provides the most comprehensive codification of the rights of refugees yet attempted on the international level. It lays down basic minimum standards for the treatment of refugees, without prejudice to the granting by States of more favourable treatment. [...]"

Thus a better protection or standard of treatment offered by a state party should not be undermined by the provisions of the Refugee Convention.[74]

Categories of treatment

11.35 A contracting state shall accord to refugees the same treatment as is accorded to aliens generally, except where the Refugee Convention contains more favourable provisions.[75] The

---

[70] See General Comment No.14 of the Committee on Economic, Social and Cultural Rights. Twenty-second session, Geneva, 25 April–12 May 2000 (E/C.12/2000/4) No.34.

[71] A state may restrict its human rights obligations by making reservations to articles of an international instrument (Convention) at the time of signature, ratification or accession.

[72] *Stricto sensu* or in the stricter sense.

[73] UNHCR has codified a number of these standards, reflecting its concern with the issue. See, for instance, ExCom Conclusion No.22 (1981) on the protection of asylum seekers in situations of large-scale influx.

[74] See Council Directive 2001/55/EC of July 20, 2001 on minimum standards for giving temporary protection in the event of a mass influx of displaced persons, which applies to all EU Member States except Denmark and Ireland.

[75] Refugee Convention art.7.

Refugee Convention is based on the fundamental principles of non-discrimination and international protection. In relation to particular provisions, the standard of treatment falls within one of three categories:

(1) National treatment. Refugees are to be accorded the same treatment as nationals in many respects. For example, non-discrimination, freedom of religion and the religious education of their children, the protection of intellectual property, access to the courts, legal assistance, rationing, elementary education, public relief, labour legislation and social security and fiscal charges.
(2) Most-favoured-nation treatment. This is to be understood as the most favourable treatment accorded to nationals of a foreign country. For example, in respect of the right to association and wage-earning employment.
(3) Aliens' treatment. The minimum standard that refugees should receive is that accorded to aliens. For example, with regard to housing.

Non-derogable rights

11.36 The Refugee Convention permits reservations by the contracting parties to the provisions. However, there are a number of rights that cannot be suspended such as:

- the definition of the term "refugee": art.1;
- non-discrimination: art.3;
- freedom to practise their religion: art.4;
- free access to the courts of law: art.16; and
- the prohibition of expulsion or return (*refoulement*): art.33.

The Refugee Convention standards

Non-discrimination (art.3)

11.37 This is a fundamental provision that enlightens most international human rights instruments. The Refugee Convention is founded on the principle of non-discrimination as to race, religion or country of origin. No derogation is possible in regard to this article.

Religion (art.4)

11.38 The contracting states, within the territories, should treat refugees at least as favourably as state nationals with regard to the freedom to practise their religion and the religious education of their children. No derogation is possible in regard to this article.

Moveable and immoveable property (art.13)

11.39 The general rule is that the personal status of a refugee is governed by the law of the country of his domicile or, if he has no domicile, by the law of the country of his residence. As regards the acquisition and lease of moveable and immoveable property and other rights pertaining to it, contracting states shall treat refugees as favourably as possible and, in any event, not less favourably than they treat aliens generally in similar circumstances.

Artistic rights and industrial property (art.14)

11.40 As regards to the protection of industrial property, artistic and scientific works, contracting states shall offer a standard of treatment equal to that they accord their own nationals.

Right of association (art.15)

11.41 In relation to the right to association, a contracting state shall accord to refugees lawfully staying in their territory the most favourable treatment accorded to nationals of a foreign country.

Access to courts (art.16)

11.42 In respect of access to the courts, including legal assistance and exemption from the requirement to give security for costs in court proceedings, a refugee should receive the same treatment as nationals of the host state. No derogation is possible in regard to this article.

Wage-earning employment (art.17)

11.43 A refugee lawfully staying in a contracting state shall be offered the most favourable treatment accorded to nationals of a foreign country in the same circumstances in relation to wage-earning employment. In the view of Canada (Reservation to arts 23 and 24), "lawfully staying" refers only to a refugee admitted for permanent residence.

Self-employment (art.18)

11.44 The standard of treatment imposed by the Refugee Convention in relation to the right to engage on their own account in agriculture, industry, handicrafts and commerce and to establish commercial and industrial companies is not to be less favourable than that accorded to aliens generally in the same circumstances. A contracting state shall endeavour to secure the same standard for refugees who are desirous of practising a liberal profession (art.19) and as regard housing (art.21).

Rationing (art.20)

11.45 Refugees shall be accorded the same treatment as nationals, where a rationing system exists.

Public education (art.22)

11.46 A contracting state shall accord to refugees the same treatment they accord to nationals with regard to elementary education. In relation to education other than elementary education, and in particular as regards study, the recognition of foreign school certificates, diplomas and degrees, the remission of fees and charges and the award of scholarships, refugees should be treated no less favourably than aliens generally in the same circumstances.

Public relief (art.23)

11.47 The standard of treatment with respect to public relief and assistance for refugees lawfully staying in a contracting state are the same as accorded to their nationals.

Labour legislation and social security (art.24)

11.48 A contracting state shall accord to refugees lawfully staying in its territory the same treatment as accorded to its nationals with regard to labour legislation and social security.

Freedom of movement (art.26)

11.49 Refugees lawfully staying in a contracting state are to be accorded the right to choose their place of residence and to move freely within its territory. The standard is subject to any regulations applicable to aliens generally in the same circumstances.

Identity papers (art.27)

11.50 Refugees who do not possess a valid travel document should be provided with identity papers. Note that there is no link to lawful residence in this provision.

Fiscal charges (art.29)

11.51 Refugees shall not be subject to duties, charges or taxes of any description whatsoever other or higher than those that are or may be levied on their nationals in similar situations.

Refugees unlawfully in the country of refuge (art.31)

11.52 An area of considerable controversy in a nation is the status of foreigners who have entered the country illegally. Article 31 determines the standard of treatment to be accorded to refugees who, coming directly from a territory where their life or freedom was threatened in the sense of art.1, are present in a contracting party's territory without authorisation, provided that they present themselves without delay to the authorities and show good cause for their illegal entry or presence. The article sets out the obligation on a contracting state not to impose penalties on account of their illegal entry or presence. However, it is possible for a contracting state to impose necessary restrictions on movement, provided such restrictions are essential and limited to the national security considerations.

Expulsion (art.32)

11.53 A contracting state shall not expel a refugee lawfully in their territory except on grounds of national security or public order. The expulsion of a refugee shall be only in pursuance of a decision reached in accordance with due process of law, except where there are compelling reasons of national security.

Prohibition of expulsion or return (*refoulement*) (art.33)

11.54 A contracting state shall not expel or return a refugee in any manner whatsoever to the frontiers of territories where his life or freedom would be threatened on account of his race, religion, nationality, membership of a particular social group or political opinion. This article contains a general rule of international law. However, this benefit may not be claimed by a refugee whom there are reasonable grounds for regarding as a danger to the security of the host country, or who, having been convicted by a final judgment of a particularly serious crime, constitutes a danger to the community of that country.

VULNERABLE GROUPS

11.55 Regional and UN treaty-monitoring bodies complement minimum standards of treatment and provide for petition procedures at both individual and state levels. Despite the fact that the right to family unity is not formally mentioned by the Refugee Convention,[76] this principle is worth considering. Family unity provides refugees with security to settle and integrate easily into a host country. The UN Convention on the Rights of the Child 1989, for example, considers family reunification as an essential right of a child who is seeking refugee status.[77] Children have a need for special care and assistance because of their vulnerability, dependency and developmental age. Female refugees and asylum seekers experience particular problems that are very

---

[76] Recommendation B of the Final Act of the 1951 UN Conference of Plenipotentiaries on the Status of Refugees and Stateless Persons recommends governments to take the necessary measures for the protection of the refugee's family.

[77] The UN Convention on the Rights of the Child 1989 art.22.

much related to gender issues.[78] Safety, sexual exploitation and discrimination are three specific issues of concern in relation to women refugees.[79]

In refugee situations, women, children and elderly persons are frequently overlooked. The result is that these individuals are put in a precarious position. Service providers should focus on the circumstances of deprivation and exclusion of women, children and other vulnerable people subject to high risk of exploitation and abuse. One of the aims of an efficient refugee system is ensuring that the basic needs of these most vulnerable refugees are met. Such needs include, for example:

- educational needs;
- medical needs;
- psychological needs;
- religious needs;
- cultural needs;
- recreational needs.

Durable solutions and the end of the refugee plight

11.56 International protection is a substitute for national protection. The fundamental question after discussing the refugee definition and the standards of treatment is: what about the future of these patients and clients? In fact, refugee policy is equally concerned with seeking durable solutions to the problem of people being forced to flee from their homes and cross an international border. Refugees very often find themselves in protracted refugee situations, dependent upon aid and charity and marginalised from the majority of society. The pursuit of durable solutions, which provide adequate standards of treatment for refugees, is central to resolving refugee crisis. The UNHCR promotes three forms of durable solutions for refugees[80]: voluntary repatriation, local integration[81] and resettlement.

Local integration is of great importance for this Chapter since it is the durable solution that requires the major effort and support from the host government and the local communities. The process involves three interconnected components:

(1) A legal process that grants the refugee a wider range of rights and entitlements by the host state. The standard here corresponds to same privileges enjoyed by citizens. This process leads to permanent residence and eventually the acquisition of citizenship.
(2) An economic process that facilitates the refugee to engage in wage-earning employment, thus becoming able to contribute to the economic life of the host state and less dependent on aid and assistance.
(3) Social, cultural and political processes that enables refugees to live alongside the host population without fear of discrimination and in a participatory way.

REFUGEE SERVICES IN SCOTLAND

11.57 The complexity of refugee issues requires the participation of a number of additional services provided by specialised agencies. In Scotland the following agencies play an important role in supporting the work of those involved with asylum seekers and refugees[82]:

---

[78] (a) A woman may experience gender punishment for non-gender behaviour, for example rape for political activity; or (b) a woman may experience a non-gender punishment for gender behaviour, for example 100 lashes for wearing make-up and non-conformity with social norms; or (c) a woman may experience specific treatment because of her gender, for example female genital mutilation, bride burning and forced marriage.

[79] *UNHCR Policy on Refugee Women*, UN doc. A/AC.96/754 (Geneva: UNHCR, 1990).

[80] UNHCR "Framework for Durable Solutions for Refugees and Persons of Concern" (May 2003) available at *http://www.unhcr.org* [Accessed October 28, 2007].

[81] Refugee Convention art.34 recommends that states facilitate the naturalisation of refugees.

[82] For more sources see *http://www.scottishrefugeecouncil.org.uk/* [Accessed October 28, 2007].

- COSLA Refugee and Asylum Seekers Consortium
  COSLA Strategic Migration Partnership
  Suite 203, 69 Buchanan Street
  Glasgow G1 3HL
  Website: *http://www.asylumscotland.org.uk*

- NHS Health Scotland
  National Resource Centre for Ethnic Minority Health
  Clifton House, Clifton Place
  Glasgow G3 7LS
  Website: *http://www.nrcemh.nhsscotland.com*

- Scottish Refugee Council
  Glasgow Head Office
  5 Cadogan Square (170 Blythswood Court)
  Glasgow G2 7PH
  Website: *http://www.scottishrefugeecouncil.org.uk*

- British Red Cross
  UK Office
  44 Moorfields
  London EC2Y 9AL
  Website: *http://www.redcross.org.uk*

- Scottish Executive
  Website: *http://www.scotland.gov.uk*

CONCLUSION

11.58 Asylum and immigration has grown to be a prominent subject in the UK, and particularly within social work activities. The amount of services, costs and help that asylum seekers and refugees need, as a response to the commitments acquired by the nation via international obligations and standards, is considerable. However, there is a tendency to focus on and build negative images of these human beings, which are a long way from the truth. What we should not forget is that they are people with particular needs who have often risked their lives to come to a safe country in order to rebuild their lives. As such they deserve the protection and assistance that would enable them later to make a positive contribution to the economy and society of the host country.

This Chapter started by setting out the background and historical perspective to immigration and asylum issues. International law, to a large extent, relating to refugees and asylum seekers defines the responsibilities at the national level. The Refugee Convention and the national framework in turn set out the rules and guidelines within which social workers must work with asylum seekers and refugees. It is hoped that this Chapter has provided a good understanding of the legal background (both national and international) for those working with asylum seekers and refugees in the UK.

In common with many of the instruments discussed in this Chapter, the social work profession is underpinned by principles of social justice and human rights. Refugee law is also there to alleviate the plight of those in need of international protection.

11.59 International protection emerges as a subsidiary to national protection. The primary responsibility for the respect, protection and fulfilment of human rights and freedoms rests within the state of origin. Nevertheless, in certain events international protection is required, thus it is the responsibility of the international community to improve burden sharing for hosting large numbers of refugees and better the standards of treatment of refugees. The realisation of refugees' rights depends largely on the relationship between public perceptions and asylum policies. The mission of social workers involved in this area is to make more accessible public services to asylum seekers and refugees and provide a better service to them. The exclusion of refugees and asylum seekers from the basic welfare services that are available to citizens would not only be inhumane and discriminatory, but would threaten fundamental social concepts such as integration and statehood.

Chapter 12

Antisocial Behaviour

Introduction

12.01 Antisocial behaviour, ranging from noise and other inconsiderate behaviour at one extreme to harassment and violence at the other may be seriously detrimental to the quality of life of communities. It can affect both home owners and tenants. Antisocial behaviour orders ("ASBOs") were introduced in Scotland under ss.19–21 of the Crime and Disorder Act 1998 and first came into effect in July 1999. The Antisocial Behaviour etc. (Scotland) Act 2004 ("2004 Act"), which repeals the provisions in the 1998 Act, is a more wide-ranging piece of legislation than its predecessor.[1] It came about as a result of a consultation paper entitled *Putting Our Communities First: A Strategy for Tackling Anti-Social Behaviour*.[2] It reflects measures introduced in England and Wales under the Anti-social Behaviour Act 2003. As well as extending the provisions on ASBOs, the 2004 Act introduces a range of new measures designed to tackle what are believed to be the problems associated with antisocial behaviour. With the aim of achieving a consistent approach to combating antisocial behaviour across Scotland, the Scottish Executive has issued extensive guidance to local authorities, police and registered social landlords on how the legislation should be used.[3]

In addition to the measures in the 2004 Act, acceptable behaviour contracts ("ABCs") are intended as a pre-emptive first step to have a person involved in antisocial behaviour to recognise the effect of the behaviour on others and refrain from such conduct in future.[4] Acceptable behaviour contracts are non-statutory written agreements between the local authority, the police, school or housing association and an individual who is or has been involved in antisocial behaviour. They are voluntary measures but failure to comply with the terms of the contract may result in statutory measures being taken.[5] They can be used in respect of adults and children.

The main provisions of the 2004 Act will be considered in this Chapter with particular attention being paid to those measures of the greatest relevance to social workers. These include the making ASBOs applicable to children aged between 12 and 15, the creation of police powers

[1] See generally the Antisocial Behaviour etc. (Scotland) Act 2004 ("2004 Act") and T. Guthrie, *Antisocial Behaviour Legislation* (Edinburgh: W. Green, 2005).

[2] Scottish Executive (2003).

[3] Available at *http://www.antisocialbehaviourscotland.com* [Accessed July 1, 2008].

[4] Scottish Executive, "'Sticks and Carrots'. Guidance on: Acceptable Behaviour Contracts" (Edinburgh: Scottish Executive, 2005), para.9. *http://www.antisocialbehaviourscotland.com/asb/files/Acceptable%20Behaviour%20Contracts%20Guidance.pdf* [Accessed July 1, 2008].

[5] Scottish Executive, "'Sticks and Carrots' Guidance" (2005), para.18. *http://www.antisocialbehaviourscotland.com/asb/files/Acceptable%20Behaviour%20Contracts%20Guidance.pdf* [Accessed July 1, 2008].

to disperse groups and to close buildings, provisions to tackle noise nuisance, measures concerning housing and the introduction of parenting orders.

ANTISOCIAL BEHAVIOUR STRATEGIES

12.02 Part 1 of the 2004 Act requires local authorities and chief constables to work together to prepare and publish a strategy for dealing with antisocial behaviour in their areas.[6] The strategy must:

- assess the extent and types of antisocial behaviour in the authority's area[7];
- set out the arrangements made for consultation with individuals and community bodies in the areas in which antisocial behaviour does or is likely to occur about how to deal with it[8];
- state the range and availability of services designed to deal with antisocial behaviour, its consequences and prevention[9];
- set out the range and availability of mediation and other services for victims of and witnesses to antisocial behaviour[10]; and
- make provision for the co-ordination of the discharge of the respective functions of the local authority and chief constable, the exchange of information between them and other parties with an interest in dealing with antisocial behaviour.[11]

Strategies must be kept under review and may be revised.[12] Any revised strategy must be published and must follow consultation with the Principal Reporter, registered social landlords in the authority's area, and such community bodies and individuals as the local authority sees fit.[13] The local authority should seek to include in the consultation persons who have been adversely affected by antisocial behaviour.[14] In preparing the strategy, local authorities and chief constables are required to have regard to guidance issued by Scottish Ministers.[15] In preparing guidance, Scottish Ministers must themselves consult those persons they see fit.[16] Scottish Ministers also have the power to require any person holding information relating to antisocial behaviour to supply that information to the local authority or the chief constable for the purpose of drawing up an antisocial behaviour strategy.[17]

Local authorities are required periodically to publish reports on how the strategy has been implemented and the results of that implementation. Scottish Ministers may by regulations provide for the form, content and frequency of publication of such reports.[18]

Scottish Ministers may make regulations to secure the participation of registered social landlords in the preparation review or revision of antisocial behaviour strategies.[19]

---

[6] See generally the 2004 Act Pt 1.
[7] 2004 Act s.1(1)(a) and (b).
[8] 2004 Act s.1(1)(c).
[9] 2004 Act s.1(1)(d).
[10] 2004 Act s.1(1)(e).
[11] 2004 Act s.1(1)(f).
[12] 2004 Act s.1(4).
[13] 2004 Act s.1(5) and (6).
[14] 2004 Act s.1(7).
[15] 2004 Act s.1(8), see Scottish Executive, "Guidance on Antisocial Behaviour Strategies". *http://www.antisocialbehaviourscotland.com/asb/files/Guidance%20on%20Antisocial%20Behaviour%20Strategies.pdf* [Accessed July 1, 2008].
[16] 2004 Act s.1(9).
[17] 2004 Act s.1(10).
[18] 2004 Act s.2.
[19] 2004 Act s.3.

ANTISOCIAL BEHAVIOUR ORDERS

12.03 Part 2 of the 2004 Act relates to antisocial behaviour orders. The Explanatory Note to the 2004 Act describes antisocial behaviour orders as "preventative orders to protect people affected by antisocial behaviour from further acts or conduct that would cause them alarm or distress".[20] They are civil orders intended to address conduct that might escalate to a level where criminal proceedings would be appropriate and patterns of behaviour that "cumulatively cause considerable alarm or distress to the community".[21]

Section 4 permits a local authority or a registered social landlord ("a relevant authority") to apply to the sheriff court for an antisocial behaviour order in respect of the person specified in the application ("a specified person"). Registered social landlords include housing associations, many of which have taken over the provision of housing in the rented social sector from local authorities. Applications are made to the sheriff within whose sheriffdom the specified person is alleged to have engaged in antisocial behaviour.[22] Local authorities and registered social landlords are required to have regard to any guidance given by the Scottish Ministers about the discharge of their functions under Pt 2 of the 2004 Act.[23]

The sheriff may make an antisocial behaviour order if satisfied that:

- the specified person is at least 12 years of age;
- the specified person has engaged in antisocial behaviour towards a person within the area of the local authority ("a relevant person");
- an antisocial behaviour is necessary for the purposes of protecting the relevant person from further antisocial behaviour by the specified person.

Where the application is made by a local authority, a "relevant person" is any person within the boundaries of the local authority even though the person need not be ordinarily resident there. Where the applicant is a registered social landlord, a relevant person will be someone residing in property provided or managed by them, or someone in or likely to be in, the vicinity of such property.[24]

12.04 Antisocial behaviour is defined in s.143 of the 2004 Act, which states that a person, A, engages in antisocial behaviour if he/she:

- acts in a manner that causes or is likely to cause alarm or distress; or
- pursues a course of conduct that causes or is likely to cause alarm or distress

to at least one person who is not of the same household as A.

Conduct includes speech and a course of conduct must involve conduct on at least two occasions. The definition is widely drawn and makes no reference to the cause of the behaviour or the intentions of the specified person. It is possible for a relevant authority to make an application in respect a single instance of the behaviour where there is evidence that it has caused or was likely to have caused alarm, or where the conduct amounts to a course of conduct. In deciding whether to impose an order, the sheriff must disregard any conduct or act of the specified person that the person shows was reasonable in the circumstances.[25] In theory those with no or limited control over their actions such as those with autistic spectrum disorders, learning difficulties or serious mental illness could be made the subject of an ASBO.[26] However,

---

[20] 2004 Act Explanatory Note Pt 2.

[21] Scottish Executive, "Guidance on Antisocial Behaviour Orders" (2004), para.15. *http://www.scotland.gov.uk/library5/social/asbsg.pdf* [Accessed July 1, 2008].

[22] 2004 Act s.4(10).

[23] 2004 Act s.16. See "Guidance on Antisocial Behaviour Orders" (2004). *http://www.scotland.gov.uk/library5/social/asbsg.pdf* [Accessed July 1, 2008].

[24] 2004 Act s.4(13).

[25] 2004 Act s.4(3).

[26] See Guthrie, *Antisocial Behaviour Legislation* (2005), p.113, and Scottish Executive, "Guidance on Antisocial Behaviour Orders" (2004), para.28. *http://www.scotland.gov.uk/library5/social/asbsg.pdf* [Accessed July 1, 2008].

the court may hesitate to impose an order the nature of which the specified person has little prospect of understanding or complying with.

Where the specified person is a child, the sheriff must require the Principal Reporter to arrange a children's hearing for the purpose of obtaining its advice as to whether an order is necessary and the sheriff must have regard to that advice. The application of s.4 to children aged between 12 and 15 was a controversial extension to the terms of the 2004 Act as it appears to demonstrate a move towards the punishment of a child from the traditional welfare model.[27] The reason for the change was stated to be the necessity of dealing "with a small number of persistently difficult young people for whom the hearing system has not proved effective in changing behaviour".[28] However, it appears that very few ASBOs have in fact been made in respect of young people.[29] Instead, acceptable behaviour contracts appear to be used as an alternative method of addressing antisocial behaviour in children.[30]

12.05 An antisocial behaviour order is couched in negative terms and prohibits the specified person from carrying out any of the actions specified in the order. The order may be for an indefinite or a specified period.[31] The prohibitions that may be imposed are those that are necessary to protect relevant persons from any further antisocial behaviour by the specified person.[32] The prohibited actions may be, but need not be, criminal in themselves. An example of a non-criminal restriction is a prohibition on entering certain areas, such as shopping malls. If an ASBO is made on the application of the local authority, the order may also impose such prohibitions as are necessary for the purpose of protecting other persons known as affected persons from further antisocial behaviour by the specified person.[33] The 2004 Act makes no provision for any support to be given to, or for there to be any intervention to assist, the specified person to address the underlying problem behaviour.

Although applications for ASBOs are civil proceedings, the House of Lords in the English case of *R. (on the application of McCann) v Manchester Crown Court* decided that the standard of proof for establishing whether an order is appropriate is proof beyond reasonable doubt.[34] In *Aberdeen City Council v Fergus*, however, in a case concerning the imposition of an interim order, the court held that the sheriff had been correct not to apply the criminal standard of proof. The decision whether to make an interim order or not, having decided that the conditions set out in s.7(2) had been satisfied, was an exercise of judgment or evaluation.[35] The rules of civil evidence will be applied.[36] The sheriff must be satisfied that there is evidence that establishes the circumstances justifying the imposition of an ASBO. If so, the sheriff must then exercise his or her discretion and decide whether the making of the order is necessary in order to prevent a relevant person from antisocial behaviour in future.[37]

12.06 Before making an application for an order a relevant authority must consult the relevant consultees. Local authorities are required to consult the chief constable of the police force area for the area that includes the area of the authority, the chief constable of each police force area for an area where there is an affected person, consult each local authority in whose area there is

---

[27] Guthrie, *Antisocial Behaviour Legislation* (2005), p.7; T. Bateman, "Ignoring Necessity: The Court's Decision to Impose an ASBO on a Child" (2007) 19(3) C.F.L.Q. 304.

[28] Per Margaret Curran, Minister for Communities, Official Report, June 17, 2004, col.9169.

[29] As at March 30, 2008, only 14 such orders had been made since October 2004: "ASB Use of the Measure Statistics to End-March 2008". *http://www.antisocialbehaviourscotland.com/asb/files/Use%20of%20the%20Measures%20-Statistics%20-%203rd%20anniversary%20stats%20-%20up%20to%20end%20March%202008%20(2).pdf* [Accessed July 1, 2008].

[30] C. Towns, "ASBO, the Young Misfit" (2006) 51(11) J.L.S.S. 52.

[31] 2004 Act s.4(5).

[32] 2004 Act s.4(6).

[33] 2004 Act s.4(7).

[34] [2003] 1 A.C. 787.

[35] 2006 Hous. L.R. 90; 2006 G.W.D. 36–727; T. Guthrie, "Legislative Comment Antisocial Behaviour", 2005 S.L.T. 145.

[36] Guthrie, "Legislative Comment Antisocial Behaviour", 2005 S.L.T. 145.

[37] Guthrie, "Legislative Comment Antisocial Behaviour", 2005 S.L.T. 145, 146.

an affected person and, if the specified person is aged between 12 and 15, the Principal Reporter.[38] Authorities are also encouraged to consult other organisations involved in addressing and preventing antisocial behaviour.[39] Before making an application for an order or interim order in respect of persons aged 16 or over, registered social landlords must consult the chief constable of the police force for the area in which the specified person lives or appears to live and notify the local authority for the area in which he or she is or appears to be resident [Accessed July 1, 2008].[40] Where the specified person is a child, a registered social landlord shall consult the local authority within whose area the specified person appears to reside about the proposed application. Where the specified person is not a child, it must notify the local authority of the proposed application.[41]

Where an order is made in respect of a child the sheriff has the power to require the Principal Reporter to refer the case to a children's hearing.[42] In addition to making the ASBO, the sheriff may make a parenting order in respect of a parent of the child provided that the sheriff is satisfied that the making of the order is necessary in the interests of preventing the child from engaging in further antisocial behaviour and court has been notified by the Scottish Ministers that the local authority area has the services in place to enable the order to be complied with.[43]

Before making an order and where the specified person is present in court, the sheriff shall explain to the specified person in ordinary language, the effect of the order, the powers the sheriff has to vary or revoke the order and the entitlement of the specified person to appeal against the making of the order.[44]

The relevant authority or the person subject to the order may apply to the court to have the order varied or revoked. Again there is a requirement for relevant authorities to consult before such orders may be applied for. Where the person subject to the order is under the age of 16, the views of the Principal Reporter must be sought and taken into account.[45] A copy of an ASBO or interim order that is made, varied or revoked must be served on the person subject to the order either in person or sent to him or her by registered post or recorded delivery. It must also be given to the relevant authority that applied for the order.[46]

12.07 Interim antisocial behaviour orders were introduced by the Criminal Justice (Scotland) Act 2003 and are now covered by s.7 of the 2004 Act. Where an application is made for an ASBO, it can include a request for an interim order. Applications for interim orders can only be considered where an application is made under s.4 and notice of the application for an ASBO and an interim order has been intimated on the specified person. The sheriff may make an interim order if he is satisfied that the conditions in s.4(2)(a) and (b) are met and the making of an interim order is necessary for the purpose set out in s.4(2)(c). If the specified person is a child, the sheriff must have regard to a written statement of views expressed by the Principal Reporter.[47] The applicant must establish a prima facie case that there has been antisocial behaviour and that an interim order is necessary to protect against future conduct. Whether or not that condition has been met is a matter for the exercise of the sheriff's discretion.[48] In *Glasgow Housing Association v O'Donnell*, a case decided under the Crime and Disorder Act

[38] Scottish Executive, "Guidance on Antisocial Behaviour Orders" (2004), para.72. *http://www.scotland.gov.uk/library5/social/asbsg.pdf* [Accessed July 1, 2008].
[39] "Guidance on Antisocial Behaviour Orders" (2004), para.74. *http://www.scotland.gov.uk/library5/social/asbsg.pdf* [Accessed July 1, 2008].
[40] "Guidance on Antisocial Behaviour Orders" (2004), para.75. *http://www.scotland.gov.uk/library5/social/asbsg.pdf* [Accessed July 1, 2008].
[41] 2004 Act s.4(11).
[42] 2004 Act s.12.
[43] 2004 Act s.13.
[44] 2004 Act s.4(8).
[45] 2004 Act s.5.
[46] 2004 Act s.8.
[47] 2004 Act s.7(3).
[48] *Glasgow Housing Association v Sharkey*, 2005 S.L.T. (Sh Ct) 59.

1998, the court decided that as there had been no occurrence of the behaviour complained of in the application for two months, an interim order was not necessary.[49] In *Edinburgh City Council v Gibson*, where an interdict on similar grounds was already in force, an application for an interim order was refused where there was some evidence of improvement in the specified person's behaviour.[50]

Although ASBOs and interim orders are civil orders that may prohibit non-criminal conduct, breach of an ASBO or an interim order is a criminal offence. A person who is subject to an order and without reasonable excuse does anything prohibited by the order is guilty of an offence and is liable on summary conviction to imprisonment for a period of not more than six months or a fine not exceeding the statutory maximum or both. On conviction on indictment a person is liable to imprisonment for a term not exceeding five years or a fine or both.[51] Where the conduct complained of could also constitute a criminal offence, referred to in the 2004 Act as a separate offence (for example, if the conduct amounts to breach of the peace or vandalism) and a person is charged with the separate offence, he or she will not be liable to be prosecuted for the breach of the order.[52] When sentencing a person convicted of a separate offence, provided that the existence of the order is libelled in the complaint or indictment, the court shall have regard to the fact that the person was subject to an ASBO or interim order, the number of orders or interim orders and any previous convictions for breaching orders.[53] Children under the age of 16 who are found to have breached an ASBO or interim order cannot be sentenced to a period of detention.[54] Section 11 of the 2004 Act grants a constable the power to arrest without warrant a person he reasonably believes is committing or has committed an offence under s.9.

12.08 In pursuit of the principles of good communications and information sharing established in Pt 1 of the 2004 Act, where a registered social landlord receives a copy of an ASBO or interim order as made or varied, or receives notice of the revocation of an order or recall of an interim order, it shall give a copy to the relevant local authorities.[55] This enables local authorities to keep a record of ASBOs and interim orders, as they are required to do by s.15 of the 2004 Act. The record must include the person in respect of whom the order was made, the prohibitions imposed by the order, the duration of the order, any variations to it and the date of revocation or recall if applicable. On request, the local authority must share information contained in the record to the Scottish Ministers, the Principal Reporter, any other local authority, a chief constable or a registered social landlord.[56]

Research carried out for the Scottish government shows that between April 1999 and the end of March 2006, 1,200 applications had been made for ASBOs and 842 orders had been granted.[57] In 2005–06, there had been allegations of breaches in 49 per cent of the ASBOs granted.[58] As a result, the Scottish Government has announced a review of national antisocial behaviour strategy but it is maintained that there are no plans to repeal the 2004 Act.[59]

---

[49] 2004 Hous. L.R 78; 2004 G.W.D. 29–604 and Guthrie, "Legislative Comment Antisocial Behaviour", 2005 S.L.T. 145, 147.

[50] 2006 S.L.T. (Sh Ct) 49; 2006 Hous. L.R. 37; 2006 G.W.D. 12–219.

[51] 2004 Act s.9(1) and (2).

[52] 2004 Act s.9(3). See also *Gordon and Conway v Griffiths*, 2008 J.C. 87.

[53] 2004 Act s.9(4) and (5).

[54] 2004 Act s.10.

[55] 2004 Act s.14.

[56] 2004 Act s.15.

[57] DTZ and Heriot-Watt University, "Use of Antisocial Behaviour Orders in Scotland" (2007), paras 2.4 and 2.10. *http://www.scotland.gov.uk/Resource/Doc/198276/0053019.pdf* [Accessed July 1, 2008].

[58] DTZ and Heriot-Watt University, "Use of Antisocial Behaviour Orders in Scotland" (2007), Table 5.3, p.62. *http://www.scotland.gov.uk/Resource/Doc/198276/0053019.pdf* [Accessed July 1, 2008].

[59] Scottish Executive, "Review of the National Antisocial Behaviour Strategy" (2007). *http://www.antisocialbehaviourscotland.com/asb/files/Scottish%20Government%20Review%20of%20the%20National%20Antisocial.pdf* [Accessed July 1, 2008].

DISPERSAL OF GROUPS

12.09 Part 3 of the 2004 Act introduces powers permitting the dispersal of groups.[60] Section 19 provides that where a senior police officer of the rank of superintendent or above has reasonable grounds for believing that any members of the public have been alarmed or distressed as a result of the presence or behaviour of groups of two or more persons in public places in any locality in the officer's police area, known as the relevant locality, and that antisocial behaviour is a significant, persistent and serious problem in the relevant locality, the officer may authorise the use of powers of dispersal contained in s.21 of the 2004 Act. Public place is defined widely to include private premises to which the public have access whether on payment or not as well as the common parts of buildings, roads and doorways and places to which the group has gained access unlawfully.[61] Before authorisation can be given, the local authority must be consulted. Authorisation must be in writing and must specify the locality, the grounds justifying the authorisation and when the powers are exercisable. The period of authorisation cannot exceed three months. Before the powers may be exercised, the senior officer must ensure that an authorisation notice is published in a newspaper and displayed in a conspicuous place or places within the locality. Such notices must contain details of the terms of the authorisation.[62] Section 20 also permits the withdrawal of any authorisation.

Section 21 of the 2004 Act sets out the powers exercisable under an authorisation. Where a constable has reasonable grounds for believing that the presence or behaviour of a group of two or more persons in any public place in the locality is causing or is likely to cause alarm or distress to any members of the public, the constable may give a direction:

- requiring the group to disperse;
- requiring any of the group who do not live within the locality to leave the locality or any part of it; and
- prohibiting the return of those who do not live in the locality to the locality or any part of it within 24 hours.

The constable may require compliance with the direction immediately or in such a way as he may specify.[63] Directions may be given orally to any one person in the group or to two or more persons together and may be withdrawn or varied by the constable who gave it.[64]

12.10 It is an offence punishable on summary conviction by a fine not exceeding level 4 on the standard scale or imprisonment for a term not exceeding three months knowingly to contravene a direction given to a person under s.21 without reasonable excuse.[65] A constable may arrest without warrant a person that he or she reasonably suspects has committed or is committing an offence under s.22(2).[66] The powers of dispersal do not extend to picketing action or authorised procession.[67] Even if only one person in a group is misbehaving, if an authorisation has been granted, the powers of dispersal may be exercised.[68]

The effectiveness and practicability of this part of the 2004 Act is open to question. The provisions of Pt 3 met with considerable opposition during the passage of the Bill. Chief among

---

[60] See Scottish Executive, "Guidance on Dispersal of Groups" (2004). *http://www.antisocialbehaviourscotland.com/asb/files/Guidance%20on%20Dispersal%20of%20Groups.pdf* [Accessed July 1, 2008]. A total of 18 dispersal notices were served between October 1, 2004 and March 31, 2008: "ASB Use of the Measure Statistics to End-March 2008". *http://www. antisocialbehaviourscotland.com/asb/files/Use%20of%20the%20Measures%20Statistics%20-%203rd%20anniversary %20stats%20-%20up%20to%20end%20March%202008%20(2).pdf* [Accessed July 1, 2008].

[61] 2004 Act s.25.

[62] 2004 Act s.20.

[63] 2004 Act s.21(4).

[64] 2004 Act s.22(1).

[65] 2004 Act s.22(2).

[66] 2004 Act s.22(3).

[67] 2004 Act s.21(5).

[68] 2004 Act s.25(2).

the objections to the provisions were that the police already had adequate powers to move on persons under the pre-existing law, for example under the law relating to breach of the peace. However, it is suggested that the greatest difficulty with Pt 3 is that unless the police exercise their powers with care, there is a danger that they may simply move a problem from one locality to another within their own or another police force area. Also, as a direction may not exceed a period of 24 hours at a time, there is the possibility that the police may be required to exercise their powers in respect of the same persons on a number of occasions in the same locality before it can be established whether the exercise of the powers is having the desired effect. As authorisations have a maximum duration of three months unless they are renewed, it is by no means certain that the problem of groups congregating and acting in an antisocial manner may not recur in the same locality, if the underlying issues have not been addressed. The Guidance acknowledges this and notes that the powers should be used as part of a range of measures designed to tackle antisocial behaviour.[69]

CLOSURE OF PREMISES

12.11 A senior police officer of the rank or superintendent or above may authorise the service of a closure notice prohibiting access to premises by anyone who is not habitually resident in or the owner of the premises.[70] The power to authorise a closure notice may be exercised only when the senior officer has reasonable grounds for believing that a person has engaged in antisocial behaviour at any time in the three months immediately preceding and the use of the premises is associated with the occurrence of "relevant harm", defined as significant and persistent disorder or significant, persistent and serious nuisance to members of the public.[71] Both requirements must be satisfied before a notice may be authorised. As with other parts of the 2004 Act there must first be consultation with the local authority. In addition, reasonable steps must be taken to ascertain the identity of any person who lives on, has control of or has responsibility for or an interest in the premises.

A closure notice must be served by a constable by fixing at least one copy of the notice to at least one prominent place on the premises, each normal means of access to the premises and any outbuildings that are used as part of the premises. A copy must also be served on any person named in the notice.

12.12 Thereafter, and usually no later than the first court day after the day on which the notice is served, the senior officer applies to the sheriff for a closure order. The application must specify the premises in respect of which the order is sought, the grounds on which it is made and be accompanied by such supporting evidence as to enable the sheriff to decide whether to grant or refuse the application.[72]

A closure order results in all or any part of the premises being closed completely for a period of not more than three months.[73] The order may include such provisions as the court considers appropriate to control access to other parts of the building in which the premise are situated. For example, where a closure order is in respect of one flat in a tenement building, there will most probably still be other residents who will need to gain access to their homes. The sheriff

---

[69] "Guidance on Dispersal of Groups". *http://www.antisocialbehaviourscotland.com/asb/546.201.211.html* [Accessed July 1, 2008]. Guthrie, *Antisocial Behaviour Legislation* (2005), p.25.

[70] See generally the 2004 Act Pt 4 and Scottish Executive, "Guidance on Closure of Premises" (2004). *http://www.scotland.gov.uk/Resource/Doc/26350/0025273.pdf* [Accessed May 5, 2008]. A total of 42 closure orders have been made between October 1, 2004 and March 31, 2008: "ASB Use of the Measure Statistics to End-September 2007". *http://www.antisocialbehaviourscotland.com/asb/files/Use%20of%20the%20Measures%20Statistics%20-%203rd%20anniversary%20stats %20-%20up%20to%20end%20March%202008%20(2).pdf* [Accessed July 1, 2008].

[71] 2004 Act ss.26 and 40.

[72] 2004 Act s.28.

[73] 2004 Act s.29.

may extend the period of closure for a period of six months or less on the application of a senior police officer.[74]

The sheriff may make a closure order if he or she is satisfied that:

(1) a person has engaged in antisocial behaviour on the premises;
(2) the use of the premises is associated with antisocial behaviour;
(3) the making of the order is necessary to prevent the occurrence of relevant harm for the period specified in the order.[75]

The sheriff has the discretion to decide whether to make the order even if the three conditions are met.[76]

In deciding whether to make a closure order, the sheriff must take into account the ability of a person who lives in the premises to find alternative accommodation and the extent of any vulnerability of any person who is not responsible for the antisocial behaviour.[77] Ordinarily, the sheriff should make his or her determination not later than on the second day after the day on which the application is made, but the sheriff may postpone the determination for not more than 14 days to enable the occupier of the premises specified in the closure notice, any person who has control or responsibility for those premises or any other person with an interest in the premises to show why a closure order should not be made.[78] Where the sheriff does postpone determination of the application, the sheriff may order that the notice is to remain in effect until the determination is made.[79] In *Commissioner of Police of the Metropolis v Hooper*,[80] it was held that an order can be made only if the evidence suggests that interference with a person's rights under arts 6 and 8 of the European Convention on Human Rights can be justified.

12.13 In *McIlravie v Wallace*,[81] the first reported case in Scotland to consider the terms of Pt 4, the neighbours of W, an 18-year-old single man, who included a 98-year-old veteran of two world wars who had lived in his home for 40 years and a woman with severe learning difficulties, had suffered from the effects of W's antisocial behaviour for a period of two years. The conduct complained of included the holding of many parties that went on until the early hours of the morning, the playing of loud music, shouting, the banging of doors and the comings and goings of many people at all hours of the day and night. Repeated complaints had been received by Fife Council, representatives of which had witnessed the behaviour for themselves. The only period of respite was a period of five months when W was absent from the premises. The court heard of the unsuccessful attempts by a number of bodies to address the matter. W had been informed that homeless accommodation would be made available to him and that he would be able to apply for a new tenancy. Although the sheriff noted that the test of necessity for the order was high, on the facts of the case before him he was satisfied that the order was necessary in that the behaviour was "of significant duration" and "of significant burden to neighbours" and efforts to resolve the matter to no avail. The sheriff highlighted the importance of describing precisely and unambiguously the extent of the premises in respect of which closure is sought and suggested that a plan of the property could be annexed to the application. This is because the person in respect of whom the order is made must be given fair notice of the area covered by the closure. The order reserved to the council access to the premises for the purpose of repair and maintenance and to W in order for him to remove his personal belongings.[82]

12.14 In *Application by the Superintendent of Fife Constabulary*[83] the premises were used for drug

---

[74] 2004 Act s.32.
[75] 2004 Act s.30(2).
[76] Guthrie, *Antisocial Behaviour Legislation* (2005), p.34.
[77] 2004 Act s.30(3).
[78] 2004 Act s.30(4), (5) and (6).
[79] 2004 Act s.30(7).
[80] [2005] EWHC 340.
[81] 2005 S.L.T. (Sh Ct) 2; also known as *Re Superintendent of Fife Constabulary's Application.*
[82] 2004 Act s.34.
[83] 2007 WL 41190484.

dealing. Arrangements were to be made to assist the respondent to obtain and take her methadone prescription during the time that any order was in force. It was reiterated that an order must be necessary to prevent relevant harm; it must be more than desirable. It was also held that the onus of proof is on the applicant but that the standard of proof was to the civil standard of the balance of probabilities. Concern had been expressed in the case that much of the supporting evidence was anonymous and hearsay. As these are civil proceedings hearsay evidence is admissible. The court held that evidence has been presented explaining the reasons for the statements being anonymous and so proper weight could be attached to the content of these statements.

There is a right of appeal to the sheriff principal against the making or extension of or refusal to make or extend a closure order.[84]

If a person remains or enters premises in contravention of a closure notice or a closure order without reasonable excuse, or if a person obstructs a person acting to secure closed premises, he or she shall be guilty of an offence. On summary conviction a person guilty of an offence is liable to a fine not exceeding level 4 of the standard scale or to imprisonment or detention for a period not exceeding three months. Where a person has, within a period of two years, been convicted of an analogous offence the maximum penalty is increased to a fine not exceeding the statutory maximum or to imprisonment for a period not exceeding nine months or both.[85] A constable may arrest without warrant a person he reasonably believes is committing or has committed an offence under s.37(1) or (2).

NOISE NUISANCE

12.15 The provisions in the 2004 Act are designed to complement existing legislation to combat noise pollution.[86] Before the local authority can make use of the provisions of Pt 5 of the 2004 Act, it must make a resolution that ss.43–47 of the 2004 Act, known as the "noise control provisions" apply to the area of a local authority.[87] Section 41 sets out the procedures for so resolving and the steps that the authority must take to publicise the terms of the resolution. The resolution must state the date from which and the times and the days on which the provisions will apply to the area. The local authority must arrange for a notice to be published in a local newspaper in its area on consecutive weeks, with the second notice appearing at least one month before the commencement date. It must also send intimation to Scottish Ministers and each adjoining local authority. The notice must state that the resolution has been passed, the commencement date and the nature and the periods set out in the resolution. Resolutions may be revoked or varied. Such changes must also be notified and publicised.[88] For the purposes of this part of the 2004 Act noise nuisance is established by a noise exceeding a set limit, which varies according to the time of day rather than by demonstrating the existence of nuisance or that there are a reasonable grounds for alarm or annoyance.[89]

Where a complaint is received that excessive noise is coming from relevant property during a period to which the resolution applies, the local authority must ensure that the matter is investigated by an officer of the authority. If the authority is satisfied that any such noise would or might exceed the permitted level, the officer may serve a warning notice to the effect that any

---

[84] 2004 Act s.36.

[85] 2004 Act s.37.

[86] See generally the 2004 Act Pt 5 and Scottish Executive, "Guidance on Noise Nuisance" (2004). *http://www.scotland.gov.uk/Resource/Doc/26350/0025278.pdf* [Accessed July 1, 2008]. There were 7,312 noise nuisance warnings and 496 noise nuisance fixed penalty notices issued between October 1, 2004 and March 31, 2008: "ASB Use of the Measure Statistics to End-September 2007". *http://www.antisocialbehaviourscotland.com/asb/files/Use%20of%20the%20Measures%20Statistics%20-%203rd%20anniversary%20stats%20-%20up%20to%20end%20March%202008%20(2).pdf*. [Accessed July 1, 2008]

[87] 2004 Act s.41.

[88] 2004 Act s.42.

[89] Guthrie, *Antisocial Behaviour Legislation* (2005), p.40.

person responsible for the noise may be guilty of an offence. There is no need to prove that the noise actually caused a nuisance. The notice may be served by delivering it to any person at or near the premises who appears to the officer to be responsible for the noise or leaving it at the property if it is not reasonably practicable to identify the person responsible for the noise.[90] The warning notice comes into effect no sooner than 10 minutes after it has been served and comes to an end when the noise control period comes to an end or when the permitted noise level changes.

12.16 If a person who has been served with a notice is responsible for a noise that emitted from the property during the time specified in the notice and that noise exceeds the permitted level, he or she will be guilty of an offence. The maximum penalty on summary conviction is a fine not exceeding level 3 on the standard scale. A defence is available if the person can show that there was a reasonable excuse for the noise continuing. If the person can raise a prima facie case for the existence of the defence, the prosecution must prove beyond reasonable doubt that there was no reasonable excuse.[91] Section 46 permits a police officer or an authorised officer of the local authority to issue a fixed penalty notice offering the person the opportunity to pay a fixed penalty. Payment of a fixed penalty of £100 within 28 days of issue discharges liability to prosecution.

Where a warning notice has been served in respect of noise, and a local authority officer has reason to believe that at any time in the period specified in the notice noise exceeding the permitted level has emitted from the property, the local authority may seize any equipment used to make the noise. If entry to the premises to seize the equipment is refused, a warrant may be sought from the sheriff.[92] Wilful obstruction of a person exercising his or her powers under s.47 is an offence punishable on summary complaint by a fine not exceeding level 3 on the standard scale.[93]

Scottish Ministers may by regulations prescribe the maximum level of noise that may be emitted from relevant property. Different levels may be prescribed for different periods in the week, areas, times of year or other circumstances.[94]

THE ENVIRONMENT

12.17 Part 6 of the 2004 Act is concerned with controlled waste and litter and is unlikely to be of any practical concern to social workers.[95] Sections 56 and 57 amend the Environmental Protection Act 1990. Section 57 introduces new powers to officers of the local authority, constables or authorised officers of a waste regulation authority who may issue fixed penalty notices for contraventions of s.33(1)(a) and (c) of the Environmental Protection Act 1990. The offences address the deposit, treatment, keeping or disposal of controlled waste. Section 58 permits a local authority to serve a graffiti removal notice on a person who owns, leases, occupies, controls, operates or maintains a "relevant surface" that has been defaced by graffiti where it appears to that authority that the defacement is detrimental to the amenity of the locality or racially or sexually offensive.[96] The notice requires the person on whom it is served to remove, clear or take such action to remedy the defacement described in the notice within 28 days of service of the notice.

---

[90] 2004 Act s.44.
[91] 2004 Act s.45.
[92] 2004 Act s.47.
[93] 2004 Act s.47(7).
[94] 2004 Act s.48.
[95] See generally the 2004 Act Pt 6 and Scottish Executive, "Guidance on Graffiti Removal" (2004). *http://www.scotland.gov.uk/Publications/2004/10/20149/45694* [Accessed July 1, 2008].
[96] See the 2004 Act s.60 for the terms of a graffiti removal notice and the provisions for service.

HOUSING: ANTISOCIAL BEHAVIOUR NOTICES

12.18 Part 7 of the 2004 Act is intended to address problems of antisocial behaviour in the private rented sector.[97] The local authority may serve a notice on a private sector landlord requiring the landlord to take the steps set out in the notice for the reduction of the antisocial behaviour described in the notice by persons occupying or visiting the property owned by the landlord.[98] The steps required of the landlord can include recovery of possession, if that is necessary in order to prevent or halt the behaviour by the occupier or visitor.[99] The notice specifies the consequences of failure to comply before expiry of the period set out in the notice and must inform the landlord of the right to request a review. If the local authority is aware of the identity of an agent or factor who acts on behalf of the landlord then the authority shall also serve a copy of the notice on that person.[100] In addition to houses and flats, the provisions apply to hostel and bed and breakfast type accommodation.[101]

Where a landlord fails to comply with the terms of the order the local authority has two possible remedies. First, the local authority may apply to the sheriff for an order suspending the payment of rent or any other charges due to the landlord. The sheriff must be satisfied that it would be reasonable to expect the landlord to take the action set out in the notice. The making of an order does not affect the validity of the lease.[102] Either party may appeal the decision to make or refuse to make an order to the sheriff principal.[103] The sheriff may revoke or suspend an order made under s.71 on the application of either party on the grounds that the landlord has complied with the terms of the notice, or that it would otherwise be unreasonable for the order to continue in place.[104]

12.19 The local authority may also apply to the sheriff for a management control order in respect of the house to which the notice relates. Before making an order, the sheriff must be satisfied that the landlord has not taken the action specified in the notice, that having regard to the circumstances it would be reasonable for the landlord to take that action and in order to deal with the antisocial behaviour it is necessary to make the order. A management control order transfers to the local authority the landlord's rights and obligations under the lease for a period up to 12 months.[105] Either party may apply for the revocation of a management control order.[106] Section 78 permits Scottish Ministers to prescribe which expenses incurred by a local authority may be recovered from a landlord where the landlord fails to comply with the notice and the local authority has taken steps to deal with the antisocial behaviour.

A landlord who fails to take the action specified in a notice that has been properly served on him, shall be guilty of an offence punishable on conviction on summary complaint to a fine not exceeding level 5 on the standard scale. The landlord has a defence if he can show that there was a reasonable excuse for the failure to act.[107]

Registration of landlords

12.20 Each local authority must maintain a register of properties occupied under a lease.[108] The register must be open to public inspection. The owner of any house that is occupied by anyone

[97] See generally the 2004 Act Pt 7.
[98] 2004 Act s.68.
[99] Guthrie, "Legislative Comment Antisocial Behaviour", 2005 S.L.T. 145.
[100] 2004 Act s.68(4).
[101] 2004 Act s.81.
[102] 2004 Act s.71.
[103] 2004 Act s.72.
[104] 2004 Act s.73.
[105] 2004 Act s.74.
[106] 2004 Act s.76.
[107] 2004 Act s.79.
[108] See generally the 2004 Act Pt 8.

who is not a member of the owner's family must apply to be entered in the register. Buildings being used for care homes, school care accommodation, independent healthcare services and secure accommodation are exempt, as are holiday homes and houses used by religious orders.[109] The local authority, registered social landlords and Scottish Homes are also exempt.[110] Registration will be permitted only if the person seeking registration is a fit and proper person to act as a landlord under the lease.

PARENTING ORDERS

12.21 A three-year-long national pilot of parenting orders commenced in April 2005. Section 102 gives the court the power to make a parenting order in respect of the parent of a child.[111] For the purposes of Pt 9, parent means any individual who is a relevant person as defined in s.93(2)(b) of the Children (Scotland) Act 1995. This includes persons with parental responsibilities and rights and those without such responsibilities who have de facto charge and control of the child. The local authority or the Principal Reporter may apply for an order to the sheriff of the sheriffdom where the parent ordinarily resides. The court may make the order if it is satisfied that the child has engaged in antisocial behaviour, or that the child has engaged in criminal conduct and that the making of the order is desirable in the interests of preventing the child from engaging in such behaviour, or that the making of the order is desirable in the interests of improving the welfare of the child. The sheriff also has the power to make a parenting order where he or she is making an antisocial behaviour order in respect of a child. In most cases the parties involved will already be known to the local authority and the Principal Reporter.

Parenting orders must not exceed 12 months in duration. They require the person specified in the order to attend such counselling or guidance sessions as may be directed by a supervising officer appointed by the local authority during the currency of the order for a period not exceeding three months.

The requirement to attend the parenting programme need not be included if the parent has been subject to a previous order in respect of the same child.[112] A parenting order requires the parent to perform certain actions that are intended to reduce the rate of offending or antisocial behaviour in the child and could require the parent to exercise control over the behaviour of their child so as to ensure that he or she attends school, avoids disruptive contacts or is adequately supervised.[113] Conflict with religious beliefs or the needs of education or work should be avoided where practicable.[114] A copy of the order must be served on the parent.[115]

The court may revoke a parenting order on the application of the local authority or a parent.[116] Where the local authority is the applicant, it must first consult with the Principal Reporter.

12.22 Before making, varying or revoking an order, the court must, having regard where practicable to the age and maturity of the child, give the child an opportunity to indicate whether he or she wishes to express views and if so to express them, give the parent the opportunity to be heard and ascertain the circumstances of the family and the likely effect of the parenting order.[117] A child who is at least 12 years of age is presumed to be of sufficient age and maturity to form a

---

[109] 2004 Act s.83(6) and (7).

[110] 2004 Act s.83(8).

[111] See generally the 2004 Act Pt 9 and Scottish Executive, "Guidance on Parenting Orders" (2005). *http://www.antisocialbehaviourscotland.com/asb/files/parenting_order_guidance.pdf* [Accessed July 1, 2008].

[112] 2004 Act s.103.

[113] Scottish Executive, "Guidance on Parenting Orders" (2005), paras 41 and 42. *http://www.antisocialbehaviourscotland.com/asb/files/parenting_order_guidance.pdf* [Accessed July 1, 2008].

[114] 2004 Act s.110.

[115] 2004 Act s.104.

[116] 2004 Act s.105.

[117] 2004 Act s.108(1).

view.[118] Where the parent is present in court, before making varying or revoking a parenting order, the court must explain in ordinary language the effect of an order and its terms and the consequences of failure to comply with it.[119]

Section 109 sets out the factors of which the court must take account before an order can be made, varied or revoked. Paramount consideration should be given to the welfare of the child. In addition, consideration should be given to the views of the child expressed in pursuance of s.108 and the information gathered about the family circumstances of the parent. Account should also be taken of any voluntary steps taken by the parent to address the behaviour although the making of an order is not precluded by the taking of such voluntary steps. However the Guidance does indicate that a parenting order should usually only be made where "a parent has been offered support on a voluntary basis and has refused to engage with that support and where their behaviour is having a negative impact on their child".[120]

Failure to comply without reasonable excuse with any requirement specified in the order or any direction in the order is a criminal offence punishable on summary conviction by a fine not exceeding level 3 on the standard scale.[121] The Guidance suggests that efforts should be made to secure compliance with the order before taking steps to raise proceedings for failure to comply.[122]

FURTHER CRIMINAL MEASURES

12.23 Part 10 of the 2004 Act introduces various additional criminal measures, some of which are discussed elsewhere in this book. Section 118 inserts a new s.234AA into the Criminal Procedure (Scotland) Act 1995 and introduces the criminal antisocial behaviour order in respect of a person convicted of an offence involving antisocial behaviour.[123]

Section 120 introduces the community reparation order as a criminal penalty. However, following a pilot study into their use in three areas in Scotland, Scottish Ministers have decided not to implement the measure.[124]

Section 121 extends the application of restriction of liberty orders to children. The court may not impose such an order without first obtaining a report from the local authority and also being satisfied as to the services provided for his or her support and rehabilitation while the order is in force.[125]

Section 122 creates the offence of selling a spray paint device to a person under the age of 16. On summary conviction a person guilty of an offence is liable to a fine not exceeding level 3 on the standard scale. It is a defence for the accused person to show that he or she took all reasonable precautions and exercised all due diligence to avoid commission of the offence. It remains to be seen how effective this measure will be as it limits the sale of spray paint devices only. Other markers, such as ordinary paint and permanent markers will still be available to under-16s. Retailers who sell spray paint devices must display in a prominent place a statement that "it is illegal to sell a spray paint device to anyone under the age of 16". Failure to do so is an offence punishable on summary complaint by a fine not exceeding level 2 on the standard scale.[126]

---

[118] 2004 Act s.108(6).

[119] 2004 Act s.108(2), (3) and (4).

[120] Scottish Executive, "Guidance on Parenting Orders" (2005), para.10. *http://www.antisocialbehaviourscotland.com/asb/files/parenting_order_guidance.pdf* [Accessed July 1, 2008].

[121] 2004 Act s.107.

[122] Scottish Executive, "Guidance on Parenting Orders" (2005), paras 81–84. *http://www.antisocialbehaviourscotland.com/asb/files/parenting_order_guidance.pdf* [Accessed July 1, 2008].

[123] See Ch.8, para.8.74.

[124] See Ch.8, para.8.81.

[125] See paras 12.26–12.27.

[126] 2004 Act s.123.

Seizure of vehicles warnings and vehicles seizures

12.24 Scottish Ministers have the power under s.127 to make regulations as to the removal and retention of motor vehicles seized under s.126 of the 2004 Act.[127] Where such regulations are in force, a constable in uniform who has reasonable grounds to believe that a motor vehicle is being or has been used in a manner that amounts to an offence of careless driving or a contravention of the prohibition of off road driving under ss.3 or 34 of the Road Traffic Act 1988 and is causing or is likely to cause alarm, distress or annoyance to members of the public, may:

- order the person who is driving the vehicle to stop;
- seize or remove the vehicle; and
- enter premises, other than a private dwelling house, where he has reasonable grounds for believing the vehicle to be.[128]

The officer may use reasonable force, if necessary, to exercise any of the powers under s.126(3). However the officer must not seize the vehicle unless the constable has warned the person using the vehicle that if the use continues the constable will seize the vehicle, or it appears that after the warning the use has continued. A warning need not be given if it would be impracticable to do so or a warning has already been given in respect of a different vehicle.[129] Between October 2004 and March 2008 a total of 4,870 seizure of vehicles warnings were given and 520 vehicles seizures were made. The vast majority of warnings were given in Grampian and Lothian and Borders and the most seizures took place in Grampian.[130]

A person who fails to comply with an order to stop under s.126(3)(a) commits a criminal offence and will be liable on summary conviction to a fine not exceeding level 3 on the standard scale.

FIXED PENALTIES

12.25 Part 11 of the 2004 Act confers powers on police officers to serve fixed penalty notices in respect of a range of offences that might be described as antisocial.[131] Following a successful 12-month pilot project conducted by Tayside Police s.128 came into force across Scotland on March 10, 2008 as part of the Scottish Government's wider programme of summary justice reform.[132]

A police officer who has reason to believe that a person aged 16 or over has committed a fixed penalty offence in a prescribed area may give a fixed penalty notice in respect of the offence. Scottish Ministers may fix the level of penalty payable, but it may not exceed level 2 on the standard scale. At present the penalty is £40.[133] Payment of a fixed penalty discharges a person from any liability to be convicted of the offence to which the notice relates.[134] Section 128 sets out a list of fairly minor, statutory and common law offences in respect of which fixed penalty notices can be issued.[135] If a fixed penalty notice is issued the recipient is deemed to have accepted it unless he or she asks to be tried for the alleged offence. The person must ask to be

---

[127] See the Police (Retention and Disposal of Motor Vehicles) (Scotland) Regulations (SSI 2005/80), which came into force on March 17, 2005.

[128] 2004 Act s.126.

[129] 2004 Act s.126(5).

[130] "ASB Use of the Measure Statistics to End-March 2008". *http://www.antisocialbehaviourscotland.com/asb/ files/Use%20of%20the%20Measures%20Statistics%20-%203rd%20anniversary%20stats%20-%20up%20to%20end%20March%202008%20(2).pdf* [Accessed July 1, 2008].

[131] See the 2004 Act Pt 11.

[132] See the Antisocial Behaviour (Fixed Penalty Offence) (Prescribed Area) (Scotland) Regulations 2007 (SSI 2007/15).

[133] Antisocial Behaviour (Amount of Fixed Penalty) (Scotland) Order 2005 (SSI 2005/110).

[134] 2004 Act s.129.

[135] These are: the Licensing (Scotland) Act 1976 ss.78 and 79; the Civic Government (Scotland) Act 1982 ss.47, 50(1) and (2), 54(1); the Criminal Law (Consolidation) (Scotland) Act 1995 s.52(1); the Local Government (Scotland) Act 1973 ss.201 and 203; breach of the peace and malicious mischief.

tried in the manner set out in the fixed penalty notice before the expiry of a period of 28 days beginning with the date on which the notice is given.[136] If the person does not pay the penalty and does not request a hearing he or she is liable to pay £60, being a sum one and a half times the penalty, to the clerk of the district court or a JP court. The penalty can then be recovered in the same way as a district court fine.

A fixed penalty notice may be revoked by the constable if he or she is satisfied that the offence to which the notice related was not committed and the notice ought not to have been issued to the person named as the person to whom it was issued. If the notice is revoked, any amount paid as part of the penalty must be returned to the person who paid it.[137]

CHILDREN'S HEARINGS

12.26 Part 12 of the 2004 Act makes amendments to supervision requirements under the Children (Scotland) Act 2005.[138] Section 135 gives the children's hearing the power to impose a movement restriction condition on a child as an alternative to requiring the child to reside in secure accommodation. Before doing so one or both of two conditions must be met. These are that the child having previously absconded from secure accommodation is likely to abscond and if he does so it is likely that his physical or mental welfare will be at risk and that the child is likely to injure himself or some other person. A movement restriction condition operates in the same way as a restriction of liberty order.

Section 135 sets out a process whereby the duties imposed on a local authority under a supervision requirement are clearly set out and can be enforced in the event of non-compliance.

Section 137 amended the Children (Scotland) Act 1995 to give additional powers to the Reporter and to children's hearings where a child has been excluded from school and the local authority appears to be failing to comply with its duty to provide education for such children. The matter can now be reported to Scottish Ministers who have the power to compel local authorities to discharge their educational duties.

12.27 It remains to be seen whether, or the extent to which, these measures will address the problems associated with antisocial behaviour in Scotland. Although some research has been conducted into the use of antisocial behaviour orders, the other measures are as yet untested.[139] A significant obstacle to the success of the measures can be said to be the refusal or failure of the person in respect of whom the measures are sought to address the underlying causes of the behaviour or to refrain from the conduct complained of. Dispersal notices and directions and closure orders might be criticised for simply displacing the problem to another area and causing significant and persistent disorder or nuisance to different members of the public. However, it is suggested that the greatest shortcoming of the legislation is that it creates a number of new criminal offences to punish those who fail to comply with orders where the conduct prohibited in the various orders does not necessarily involve behaviour that is criminal per se.

---

[136] 2004 Act s.131(2), (3) and (4).

[137] 2004 Act s.133.

[138] See the 2004 Act Pt 12.

[139] See the DTZ and Heriot-Watt University, "Use of Antisocial Behaviour Orders in Scotland" (2007). *http://www.scotland.gov.uk/Resource/Doc/198276/0053019.pdf* [Accessed July 1, 2008].

INDEX